Dexter Smith

Cyclopedia of Boston and Vicinity

Dexter Smith

Cyclopedia of Boston and Vicinity

ISBN/EAN: 9783337224172

Printed in Europe, USA, Canada, Australia, Japan

Cover: Foto ©ninafisch / pixelio.de

More available books at **www.hansebooks.com**

AMERICAN HOUSE,
BOSTON.

Centrally and Conveniently Located for Either Business or Pleasure.

American Plan, $3.00 per day and upwards } According to size and location
Rooms only, $1.00   "   "   "   "   } of Rooms.

HENRY B. RICE & CO.   HANOVER STREET,
PROPRIETORS.   *Near Washington St.*

UNITED STATES HOTEL, BOSTON.

Pleasure Parties, Ladies, and Families,

Visiting or passing through Boston, may secure ROOMS, WITH OR WITHOUT MEALS, and will find every attention at the **United States**, the nearest first-class Hotel to all the great Retail Stores; having Waiting and Toilet Rooms, Ladies' Package Room, and every convenience.

2000 Horse Cars Pass Three Sides of The Hotel,

Connecting with every Railway and Steamboat, and all Places of Amusement and Interest in the City, Suburb, or Seashore, giving facilities for Conventions, Clergymen and Teachers' Meetings, Excursion, Pleasure, and Theatre parties,

WHOLLY UNEQUALLED BY ANY HOTEL IN BOSTON.

☞ Passengers to and from all **Southern** or **Western Points**, by either **Boat** or **Rail**, save all **Carriage Fares**.

REGULAR TRANSIENT CHARGES WILL BE FOR   } According to Size, Location, and
Rooms only . . . . . . $1.00 and upwards.   } Convenience, and
Single Meals 75   } whether occupied by one or more
For Full Day's Board . . . . 2.50   } persons.

For Special Rates, full particulars will be given, with maps, circulars, etc., on application to **TILLY HAYNES**, United States Hotel, BOSTON.

ARMSTRONG TRANSFER CO.

"THE OBJECT OF THIS COMPANY" is to offer the public a well-arranged "BAGGAGE EXPRESS SYSTEM."
"THE PRINCIPAL FEATURES" of this department will be the checking of baggage at residences and hotels to any Railroad or Steamboat in the city, and of defining a proper delivery and handling of baggage.
"BAGGAGE CALLED FOR" and delivered in any part of the City.
"AT ALL PRIVATE RESIDENCES" baggage will be delivered in any part of the house desired, without extra charge.
"SPECIAL RATES" made with parties leaving town for the Summer season, who may have large lots of baggage for transfer to and from Railroad Stations and Steamboat Landings.

OFFICES:

Revere House,
211 Washington Street,
Adams House,
Old Colony R. R. Station,
Eastern R. R. Station,
105 Arch Street,
Boston & Albany R. R. Station,
N. Y. & N. E. R. R. Station,
Boston & Maine, R. R. Station,
Boston & Lowell R. R. Station,
129 Eliot Street.

TELEPHONE CALL 1832.
GENERAL OFFICES, 111 ARCH STREET.

GEO. W. ARMSTRONG, President.

EDWARD A. TAFT, General Manager.   FRED S. LEONARD, Superintendent.

THE BOSTON CAB COMPANY,

TELEPHONE NO. 1746.

General Offices, 42 SUMMER STREET.

BRANCH OFFICES:

105 Arch Street,   129 Eliot Street.

Boston & Providence R. R. Station,

and at all Armstrong Transfer Co.'s Offices at Railroad Stations.

The Company are prepared to furnish at any time the most elegant line of vehicles to be found in this city, consisting of coaches, landaus, broughams, extension broughams, victorias and coupes.

The drivers are uniformly dressed in dark green coachman coats and silk hats, with white rubber coats and hat covers for rainy weather.

For shopping, calling, driving, and for theatre and party work, the service of this company is unequalled.

Rates: 25 cents from any station to any other station, for each passenger without baggage. No charge will be made for hand luggage.

FRED. S. LEONARD,   EDW. A. TAFT,
Superintendent.   President.

THE
SHORE LINE TRAINS

Leave BOSTON for NEW YORK

AT

10 A.M., 1.00 and 11.00 P.M.

Leave New York for Boston

AT

8 A.M., 1.00 and 11.00 P.M.

SUNDAYS

From Boston and New York

AT 11.00 P.M.

A. A. FOLSOM,

Sup't Boston & Providence Railroad

MISS JEANNETTE VAN BUREN

Of Hotel Glendon, BOSTON, MASS., takes pleasure in calling attention to the following testimonial:—

My dear Nellie,

These lines will fully authorize you to teach the fundamental principles of my Italian method of singing. I am glad to be able to add, that besides acknowledging your aptness for this task, I consider you to be exceptionally conscientious, persevering and painstaking.

What you have learnt, is right, and what you will teach, you will teach right well.

Wishing you the success you deserve, I remain, Dear Nellie,

yours faithfully,
Erminia M. Rudersdorff

During the Summer months, until October 1st, address care OLIVER DITSON & Co.

ENTIRELY NEW AND ORIGINAL.

Indispensable to every Lady and Gentleman.

BASSETT'S ELITE MUCILAGE.

Richly PERFUMED with the Extracts of Rare Flowers

WILL NEVER MOULD OR SOUR; WILL NOT DRY UP LIKE ORDINARY GUMS; WILL STICK STRONGER AND BETTER THAN ANY MUCILAGE EVER PRODUCED.

25 CENTS A BOTTLE.

For Sale by all the Leading Stationers.

Joseph T. Brown & Co., Boston,

SOLE PROPRIETORS.

The Boston School of Oratory

FOUNDED IN 1873
WILL COMMENCE ITS 14th YEAR

October 7th, 1887.

Students received for a two years' or a one year's course.
   The Delsarte System of Expression.
      Complete Course of Vocal Training.
         Thorough Instruction.
            The Newest Thought and the Best Methods.
               Rooms large, well ventilated, and thoroughly heated.

ADDRESS,
  No. 7 BEACON STREET, BOSTON.
    MOSES TRUE BROWN, PRINCIPAL.

Tremont School of Music,

550 Tremont St., cor. Waltham, Boston, Mass.

Private Lessons, $10, $12, $15, $20, and $22 per Term.

SIXTY-FIVE INSTRUCTORS.

Vocal Music, Piano, Organ, Violin, Viola, Violoncello, Contra Basso, Guitar, Harp, Zither, Flute, Piccolo, Cornet, Bassoon, Saxophone, Clarinet, Oboe, Tympani, Drum, French Horn, Tuba ; Harmony, Theory, and Counterpoint ; Elocution ; English Branches, English Literature, Bookkeeping; Latin, Greek, French, German, Italian, and Spanish Languages; Art Embroidery; Charcoal and Crayon Drawing, Oil Painting, Water Color and Decorative Painting on Silk, Satin, China, Tiles, etc.

    Languages taught by native teachers ; Italian method in vocal music and the Delsarte System of dramatic gesture in elocution. Particular attention paid to beginners, as well as advanced scholars, by able teachers in all departments. ALL LESSONS GIVEN PRIVATELY. CONCERTS, RECITALS, AND LECTURES given throughout the school year Instruction given at pupils' residences if desired; also, evening lessons.

    THE PROSPECTUS mailed free to any address on application to

                Miss FANNY E. BRUCE,
                            PRINCIPAL.

*Very truly yours,
Charles Bickford,
Elocutionist.*

Elocution, Oratory, ─────✠
✠─────── and Dramatic Art.

⊲BICKFORD'S ⊛ SCHOOL⊳

Special attention given to Reading, as an elegant Art for Home and Society, as well as thorough instruction in Voice Cultivation, Expression, Gesture and Action, for public reading, Platform and Pulpit Oratory, and public and private Dramatic Representations.

Prof. Chas. Bickford, Principal,

Miss Elsie Russell, Assistant.

18 BOYLSTON ST., (B.Y.M.C. Union Building,) BOSTON, MASS.

ADAMS HOUSE.

EUROPEAN PLAN.

Washington Street, Boston.

GEO. G. HALL, Proprietor.

Near all the leading Dry Goods Stores and Theatres.

Clark's Hotel,

577 & 579 Washington St., Boston.

——— FOR GENTLEMEN ONLY ———

EUROPEAN PLAN!

Rooms, $1 per day and upwards. All the latest Modern Improvements.

PALMER, BACHELDER & CO.

Diamonds and Rich Jewelry,
   Paris Marble Mantel Clocks,
      Geneva Music Boxes,
         Opera and Field Glasses,
Choice Articles in Pottery,
   Engagement Rings,
     Queen Chains,
       Watches and Wedding Silver,

=AT=

146 TREMONT STREET.

PALMER, BACHELDER & CO.

CHAS. M. CASHIN,
News and Theatre Ticket Agent,
YOUNG'S HOTEL, BOSTON.

Tickets secured six days in advance for all places of Amusement.

 Orders received by Mail, Telephone or Telegraph will meet with prompt attention.

 Orders received in advance for Symphony, Rehearsal and Concert Tickets for the coming season.

Opera Glasses of the best quality for sale and to let.

Prompt attention paid to delivering of Boston and New York Daily Papers at Places of Business.

TELEPHONE NO. 1010.

Private School for Boys,

165 TREMONT STREET, BOSTON.

Preparation for College, Institute of Technology and Business.

THOROUGH INSTRUCTION GIVEN IN ELEMENTARY ENGLISH STUDIES.

LEROY Z. COLLINS.

Mr. HALE'S SCHOOL

18 BOYLSTON PLACE, BOSTON,

PREPARES FOR { MASSACHUSETTS INSTITUTE OF TECHNOLOGY
AND
HARVARD COLLEGE — WITHOUT GREEK.

The same preparation for the Institute final and the Harvard preliminary examination. An additional year required for the Harvard final. Address, ALBERT HALE.

MADAME E. GARRETTE

Will receive pupils in her celebrated and unique method for placing, developing, and cultivating the voice, its essential point being an entire absence of conscious physical effort, the most delicate voices can by no possibility be strained, and voices badly worn can positively be restored.

Madame "Garrette's Method" has received the highest encomiums from the following distinguished artists and teachers:

MADAME ADELINA PATTI,
  MADAME MARCHESI,
    MADAME GIULIA VALDA,
MADAME NEVADA,
  SIGNOR LAMPERTI,
    HERR MAURICE STRACKOSH,
and many eminent Boston Artists.

Pupils thoroughly prepared for Italian and English Opera, Oratorio, and Concerts.

Further particulars can be obtained by addressing,

MADAME E. GARRETTE,
CARE OF OLIVER DITSON & CO., Washington Street, Boston.

MRS. FLORA E. BARRY'S
School of Vocal Instruction
124 CHANDLER ST., BOSTON.

Special attention given to Pupils preparing for the Stage, either in Concert, Oratoria or Opera; Classic Songs and Ballad music in English, French, German or Italian.

TERMS: For twenty lessons of one hour each - $80.00.
    " " " three-quarters of an hour, 60.00.
    " " " half an hour, 45.00.
One half invariably in advance. No reduction for absence.

MISS ABBY H. JOHNSON'S
HOME AND DAY SCHOOL FOR YOUNG LADIES
18 NEWBURY STREET, BOSTON.

The Next School Year will open September 28, 1887.
MISS ABBY H. JOHNSON.   MISS MARY E. BLAIR.

TEACHERS FOR 1886-87.

Miss MARIA E. CARTER, Botany.   Miss ELIZABETH M. CHADBOURNE,
　　　　　　　　　　　　　　　　Natural Sciences, and Drawing and Painting in Water Colors.
Mlle. LEONTINE NOURY, French,   Miss FRANCES H. MANNY, French & German.
Miss JENNIE E. IRESON, Elocution,   Fraulin BERTHA VON SECKENDORFF, Ger.
Mr. GEORGE W. DUDLEY, Vocal Music.   Miss GERTRUDE BELDEN, Latin & Gymnastics.

LECTURERS

Rev. J. T. DURYEA, D. D., Mental and Moral Science.
　　　　　　　　　　　Miss LUCY LARCOM, English Literature.
And others.

MRS. S. H. HAYES,
Home and Day School,
68 CHESTER SQ., BOSTON.

16th Year Opens October 4th, 1887.

The Private School for Boys

At No. 5 Charles Street, for many years conducted by Miss M. A. Mathews, will re-open on Tuesday, October 4, 1887, under the management of Miss H. M. Greenwood.

Applications may be made at the School before June 11, or may be sent during the summer months to Post-Office Box 1202, Boston.

REFERENCES.

Mrs. Louis Agassiz, 16 Quincy St., Cambridge. Francis E. Bacon, Esq., 66 State St., Boston.
Professor Geo. A. Bartlett, 27 Beck Hall, Cam. Professor F. Bocher, 12 Ho'yoke Place, Cam.
Arthur Gilman, Esq., 5 Waterhouse St., Cam. John P. Hopkinson, Esq., 20 Boylston Pl., Boston.
　　　　Professor John Williams White, Concord Avenue, Cambridge.

PREPARATORY SCHOOL FOR GIRLS,
76 Marlborough Street.

Miss S. Alice Brown and Miss Amelia L. Owen
Will open October 3, a CLASSICAL and SCIENTIFIC SCHOOL for girls twelve years old and over.
　　Students prepared for SMITH, VASSAR, WELLESLEY, HARVARD and MASS. INSTITUTE of TECHNOLOGY. Special students received for advanced work and for Laboratory practice. For further particulars address

MISS BROWN,
76 Marlborough Street, Boston.

MISS H. E. GILMAN'S
Home and Day School
FOR YOUNG LADIES AND MISSES,

No. 44 Rutland Square, Boston.

1886-1887.

LANGUAGES!

BERLITZ SCHOOL of LANGUAGES, 154 Tremont Street, Boston, and all other large cities. Recognized as the best for learning to SPEAK, Read and Write Foreign Languages.

MRS. JENNIE L. MILLER,
Teacher of Mental Tone Method of Singing,
ADDRESS CARE OF

OLIVER DITSON & CO.

During the Summer Months.

WALKER'S PRIVATE DANCING ACADEMY.
24 DWIGHT STREET, BOSTON.

THIS popular establishment opens the first Friday in October, at 7.30 P.M. for young Ladies and Gentlemen. The first Saturday in October, at 3 P.M. for Misses and Masters.
Particular attention paid to the cultivation of deportment, and pupils taught to dance as people in polite society do to-day. Faithful, patient and experienced teachers spare no pains to satisfy patrons and pupils. Mr. Walker was admitted to the New York Society of Professors of Dancing, in March, 1879; the only Boston teacher in the Association.
For further particulars please call or write to
Yours faithfully,

RUSS B. WALKER.

ART SCHOOL.

81 Boylston Street,

SECOND DOOR FROM WILLIAMS & EVERETT'S.

Massachusetts, Boston, 69 Chester Square.

GANNETT INSTITUTE FOR YOUNG LADIES.

Family and Day Pupils. Full corps of teachers and lecturers. Preparatory, Intermediate, Collegiate and Special Courses.

The thirty-fourth year will begin Wednesday, Sept. 28, 1887. For catalogue and circular, apply to Rev. GEO. GANNETT, A.M., Principal.

MISS RACHEL NOAH,

Late of Boston Theatre,

Elocution and Dramatic Action,

ADDRESS,

HOTEL CREIGHTON, or BOSTON THEATRE.

Boston School of Languages,

44 BOYLSTON ST., PELHAM STUDIOS,

JULES A. HOBIGAND, A.M. - - - Principal.

French, German, Spanish and Italian
TAUGHT BY NATIVE TEACHERS.

Natural Method. Day and Evening Classes.

Students fitted in the most thorough manner for any college or professional school.

Special course for youth of both sexes in the modern languages and English branches.

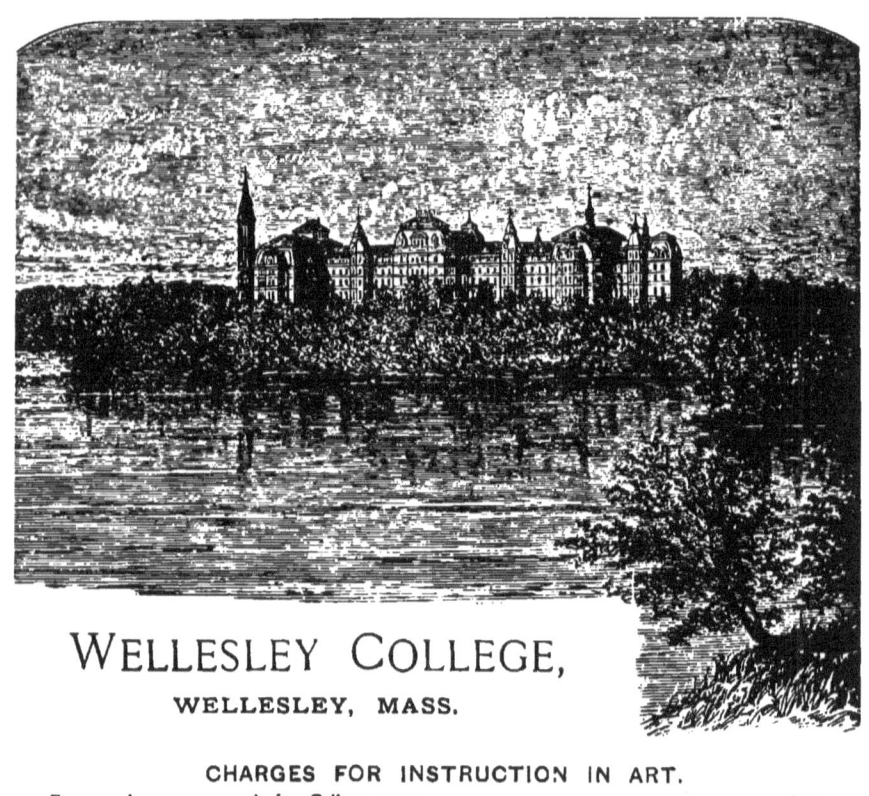

WELLESLEY COLLEGE,
WELLESLEY, MASS.

CHARGES FOR INSTRUCTION IN ART.

For one lesson per week for College year	$36.00
For two lessons per week for College year	66.00
For three lessons per week for College year	90.00

(The lessons are to be two and one-half hours in length.)

CHARGES FOR MUSIC LESSONS.

For private instruction, for the College year, on Piano, Organ, Violin, or in Vocal Music, two lessons per week	100.00
One lesson per week	50.00

(Lessons forty-five minutes each.)

For the same instruction, for the College year — two half-hour lessons per week,	75.00
Harmony, class of two, each student,	40.00
class of three, each student,	30.00
class of four, each student,	25.00
Ensemble playing, class of three, each student,	35.00
Interpretation and Analysis, class of three, each student,	25.00
Sight-Singing. (Lessons forty-five minutes, weekly,)	15.00
All Students pay for the use of Piano or Reed Organ, one period daily, for the year,	10.00
For two periods daily,	20.00
For three periods daily,	30.00
For use of the Pipe Organ, one period daily, for the year,	15.00
For two periods daily,	30.00

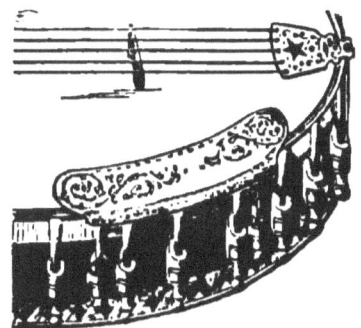

FAIRBANKS & COLE,
Correct Instruments and Instruction.
Boston.

A. C. Fairbanks,   W. A. Cole,
121 Court St.   178 Tremont St.

Turkish, Russian, Roman, Electric and Sulphur
BATHS
17 BEACON STREET, · BOSTON.

The best known remedy for Colds and Rheumatism, Recommended by business and professional men. Every lady who prizes good health and a beautiful complexion should not fail to take these Baths. The attendants are persons of long experience, and there is no place, in the country where so thorough and satisfactory a bath is given.

Boston Storage Warehouse.
WEST CHESTER PARK, NEAR HUNTINGTON AVENUE.

A Brick Building, erected by a Corporation, for the safe-keeping and storage of Paintings, Statuary, Pianos, Mirrors, Household Furniture, Carriages, Trunks, Packages and limited kinds of Merchandise.

The Warehouse is divided each fifty feet into sections by brick walls, with fireproof doors shut at night. Above the basement the building is subdivided into separate rooms of different dimensions with locked door. No lights or matches permitted, and the warehouse closed at sunset. Automatic Fire Alarm, Watch Clocks and other precautions provided for the protection of property. Two Steam Elevators for the conveyance of patrons and goods to the several stories.

For Rates, apply at Warehouse.

F. W. LINCOLN, GENERAL MANAGER.

TELEPHONE No. 4268.

Back Bay and Huntington Avenue Horse-Cars pass the Warehouse.

259 BOYLSTON STREET.

This private school offers unusual advantages for boys and girls, from the **kindergarten** age to those preparing for **business,** the **Institute of Technology,** or **college.**

Minute care is given to the **health** and the **individual needs** of each pupil.

Special students are admitted to all regular classes.

Especial attention is invited to the arrangements for **young children.**

Visitors are always welcome.

ESTABLISHED IN 1828.

GEORGE L. OSGOOD,

SCHOOL OF OLD ITALIAN

ART OF SINGING,

149 A TREMONT STREET,

BOSTON.

— OF —

Boston and Vicinity.

"*These hills where once the Indian dwelt,
These plains o'er which the red deer ran,
These shores where oft our fathers knelt,
And wild doves built, unscared by man;
I love them all, for they to me
Are as some pleasant memory.*"

BY

DEXTER SMITH.

BOSTON:
CASHIN & SMITH,
PUBLISHERS.

Copyright, 1887, by CASHIN & SMITH. All rights reserved.

BERKELEY SCHOOL,

Y. M. C. A. Building, cor. Boylston & Berkeley Sts.

FOR BOYS AND GIRLS.

PRIMARY GRAMMAR,
and HIGH SCHOOL GRADES.

Special Courses for Special Students.

Prepares for College, Institute of Technology, and Business. Separate study room for girls. Daily gymnastic training.

Circulars sent on application.

References: Ex-Gov. Rice, Ex-Gov. Gaston, Judge J. W. McKim, Dr. A. P. Peabody, &c.

CHARLES R. ADAMS,

159 TREMONT ST., BOSTON.

VOCAL CULTURE,

IN ALL ITS BRANCHES.

Pupils wishing to prepare for the Operatic Stage will have the advantage of a stage and scenery for dramatic practice with Mr. Adams.

PREFACE TO SECOND EDITION.

In presenting the CYCLOPEDIA for another year it would certainly seem ungrateful on the part of the Publishers and Author were they to omit to express their obligations to all who have so heartily aided in the circulation of the first edition of this book.

To the Press of the country especially are the warmest thanks due for the prompt and hearty manner in which they received, endorsed and gave the CYCLOPEDIA OF BOSTON the benefit of their editorial influence. Such a unanimous verdict has had the effect of creating a wide, steady and constantly increasing demand for the book, as it could not fail to do, with so powerful a lever in its interest.

In order that our readers may have some idea of the kind words said of this work we excerpt a very few lines as examples of the criticisms it has received:

Harper's Weekly, (New York), says: "DEXTER SMITH'S CYCLOPEDIA OF BOSTON is a quaint and useful companion to travellers in the Hub."

The *Boston Gazette* considers it "the most complete guide to Boston that has yet appeared. It would be difficult to suggest any essential point that has been overlooked in the compilation of this work, which fills, with great thoroughness, a void that has long been felt. It is at once a guide, a handbook and a blue book."

The *Boston Beacon* says "it contains a vast amount of curious and interesting information, particularly in regard to education, music and amusements in Boston and vicinity. The article, 'Exhibition of Battle-Flags,' is a good example of the editor's industry and good sense."

The *Boston Times* considers it "a unique compilation and one of value."

The *Boston Traveller* says "it is a handsome book, of the utmost value both to the tourist and to the citizen. The book is simply invaluable."

The *Boston Home Journal* thinks "it is a monument of industry, careful research and judicious compilation. The more it is examined the more fully it will be appreciated."

The *Salem Gazette* considers it "the very best Guide Book of Boston ever issued."

Hundreds of other notices of the same tenor might be quoted if necessary.

This edition of the CYCLOPEDIA is provided with a more copious Index than the former, thereby rendering the vast amount of information more readily accessible to those who may wish to consult its pages.

The Publishers will be grateful for any suggestions as to future editions, it being their design to constantly improve the work with each succeeding year.

Communications intended for the Author may be addressed to

DEXTER SMITH, 303 Marlborough Street,

Or CHAS. M. CASHIN, Young's Hotel, Boston.

Sheffield Tooth Crowns
— OR —
Artificial Teeth Without Plates,

Restoring the Expression of the Mouth, giving no annoyance in articulating, and perfectly replacing the Natural Teeth for Mastication.

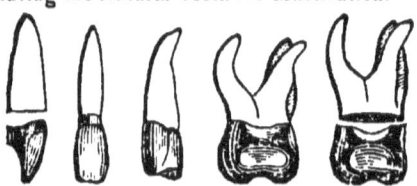

Cut shows the Crown ready to be cemented to the root, the gold band going under the free margin of the gum, excluding all moisture and preventing decay of the root. Special attention given to the treatment of ulcerated teeth. General dentistry at moderate prices. Send or call for references and illustrated pamphlet.

Dr. W. A. LYON,
157 Boylston Street, Boston.

BOSTON CITY GOVERNMENT.

HUGH O'BRIEN, MAYOR. Salary, $10,000. Office, City Hall.

Board of Aldermen. Aldermanic Districts, established 1884.
John H. Sullivan, District 1, Wards 1 and 2 (East Boston).
P. J. Donovan, District 2, Wards 3, 4, and 5 (Charlestown).
John A. McLaughlin, District 3, Wards 6, 7, and 8.
Tilly Haynes, District 4, Wards 9 and 10.
Charles W. Smith, District 5, Wards 11 and 16.
William P. Carroll, District 6, Wards 12 and 13.
Charles M. Bromwich, District 7, Wards 14 and 15 (South Boston).
Charles H. Allen, District 8, Wards 17 and 18.
P. James Maguire, District 9, Wards 19 and 22 (Roxbury).
Nathan G. Smith, District 10, Wards 20 and 21 (Roxbury).
John H. Lee, District 11, Wards 23 and 25 (Brighton and West Roxbury).
Samuel J. Capen, District 12, Ward 24 (Dorchester).

Common Council.
PRESIDENT, DAVID F. BARRY.

Ward 1.—John A. Webster, Henry Carstensen, Frank R. Morrison.
Ward 2.—William A. Foss, Thomas O. McEnaney, Jeremiah F. Coleman.
Ward 3.—William H. Murphy, Peter J. Gallagher, John F. Sundberg.
Ward 4.—George N. Fisher, jr., Patrick Coyle, Edwin F. Dunn.
Ward 5.—Samuel J. Cochran, Edward F. Reilly, Maurice J. McKenna.
Ward 6.—William J. Mahoney, John J. Murphy, Augustus L. Perry.
Ward 7.—John Gallagher, William B. F. Whall, Roger Haggerty.
Ward 8.—Edward J. Harrington, Thos. F. Kelley, John J. Kennedy.
Ward 9.—William Power Wilson, Andrew B. Lattimore, Frank Morison.
Ward 10.—Jacob Fottler, Nathaniel W. Ladd, Edward Sullivan.
Ward 11.—Andreas Blume, William R. Richards, George P. Sanger, jr.
Ward 12.—William H. Whitmore, Cornelius F. Desmond, Thomas F. Tracy.
Ward 13.—Joseph B. Gomez, Edward J. Leary, John J. Teevens.
Ward 14.—Albert F. Lauten, Edward J. Powers, Frank J. Tuttle.
Ward 15.—William S. McNary, Michael J. Carroll, Thomas F. Nunan.
Ward 16.—David F. Barry, Thomas J. Keliher, John W. Hayes.
Ward 17.—Robert H. Bowman, John W. O'Mealey, S. Edward Shaw.
Ward 18.—Henry Frost, Augustus G. Perkins, Frank B. Thayer.
Ward 19.—Barth. J. Connolly, Thomas H. Duggan, James H. Sullivan.
Ward 20.—James F. Davern, John Murphy, Charles H. Dolan.
Ward 21.—Henry S. Dewey, Cassius Clay Powers, John H. Norton.
Ward 22.—John C. Short, Richard Sullivan.
Ward 23.—Lewis L. P. Atwood, Sidney L. Burr, George R. Fowler.
Ward 24.—Robert W. Light, Louis M. Clark, Edmund F. Snow.
Ward 25.—John T. Chamberlain.

Clerks and Messengers.
City Clerk, Jas. H. O'Neil. Salary, $1,000; and for Assistant Clerks, $11,100.
Asst. City Clerk, John T. Priest. Salary, $2,500.
Clerk Common Council, Joseph O'Kane, Salary, $2,000.
Clerk of Committees, James L. Hillard. Salary, $3,500.
Asst. Clerk of Committees, John P. Brawley. Salary, $2,500.
Messenger to City Council, Alvah H. Peters. Salary, $2,500.
Asst. Messenger, Foster M. Spurr. Salary, $1,500. *Second Asst.*, Charles E. Silloway. Salary, $1,200. *Third Asst.*, Harry H. Osborn. Salary, $1,000.

Assessors' Department.
Assessors—Thos. Hills, *Chairman*. Salary, $3,500. Benj. Cushing, *Secretary*. Salary, $3,200. Joshua S. Duncklee, John J. Murphy, John M. Maguire. Salary, $3,000 each. Denis H. Morrissey, *Clerk*, Office, City Hall, first floor.

First Assistant Assessors, $7 per day.

Benj. F. Palmer.	E. Mertain Hatch.
John H. Duane.	Dennis F. Brennan.
Fred'k H. Temple.	John J. Gartland.
Dennis G. Quirk.	Samuel Hichborn.
Geo. S. Pendergast.	John H. Giblin.
Jas. T. Gallagher.	James Fagan.
Chas. B. Hunting.	Wm. W. Lord.
Patrick F. Sullivan.	Edw. W. Dolan.
John Pattison.	John H. Griggs.
Edw. B. Dailey.	John C. Cook.
William A. Wheeler.	Andrew J. Browne.
Horace Smith.	Robert Culbert.
Geo. A. Comins.	James B. Shea.
William H. Hart.	Charles E. Temple.
Wm. H. Cundy.	R. Hutchinson.
James Carney.	John Pierce.
J. S. Macdonald.	Henry Pierce.
Eugene J. O'Connor.	Geo. W. Warren.

Second Assistant Assessors, $5 per day.

Chas. W. Odiorne.	John A. Collins.
Jas. P. McEneany.	Daniel F. Maguire.
John Bryant.	Chris. A. Scheele.
Chas. W. Pearson.	William Gordon.
Peter F. Hagerty.	Geo. A. King.
Dennis Bonner.	Jonas Hagar.
Hugh F. Sheran.	T. F. Shaughnessy.

John A. Barry.
John W. Martin.
Chas. O. Burrill.
John Robertson.
Martin Dowling.
John R. Briggs.
Stephen Murphy.
J. D. Mulchinock.
Daniel M. Driscoll.
Dennis J. Casey.
Hubert Pope.
John J. Nawn.
Henry H. Page.
Henry L. Carter.
James P. Fox.
Isaac W. Clarke.
John McDonald.
John H. Cronin.
John J. Dailey.
Geo. E. Hall.
Coolidge Barnard.
Edward Scates.

Registrar's Department.
City Registrar, Nicholas A. Apollonio. Salary, $2,550. Clerks, Jas. W. Allen, F. D. Rideout, John M. Ludden. Office, City Hall.

The City Registrar keeps the records of the Births, Deaths and Marriages, and grants Certificates of all Intentions of Marriage.

Financial Departments.
City and County Treasurer, Alfred T. Turner. Salary, $6,000; and $21,000 for permanent clerks.
Cashier, Benj. S. Turner. *Teller,* Ellison B. Cushing. *Paymasters,* Wm. T. Gibbons, Chas. G Gibson, John D. Carty, Thos. Fay, Jr., Chas. J. Vaughn, Reuben Peterson. *Book-keeper,* George B. Ager. *Bond and Interest Clerk,* Z. T. Cushman. *County and Trustee Clerk,* J. E. Hunt. *Draft Clerk,* W. I. Pelletier. *Clerk and Messenger,* T. J. O'Daly. *County Paymaster,* Edmund A. Macdonald.
City and County Collector, James W. Ricker. Salary, $5,000; and $12,200 for permanent clerks.
Cashier, Francis R. Stoddard; *Chief Clerk,* Charles E. Tucker; *Asst. Clerk,* E. B. Blasland; *Department Clerks,* Christopher A. Connor. Chas. R. Brown; *Clerk of Deeds, Real Estate, etc.,* Geo. L. Hutchins; *Book-keeper,* Geo. D. Underwood; *Clerk,* Edward A. Morrissey.
Deputy Collectors, Leavitt B. Palmer, Romanzo N. Wiswall, Sylvester H. Hebard, Abraham G. Wyman, Edwin B. Spinney, William H. McIntosh, Charles A. Barry, Elbridge G. Wallis, Isaac W. Derby, Denis A. Sullivan, George W. Conant, J. Edward Priest, Chas. H. Orr, William H. Badlam, James G. Davis, John A. Devlin. [Appointed by Collector. Salary $1,700 each.]
City Auditor, James H. Dodge, Salary, $5,000; and not exceeding $17,700 for clerk hire.

The first day of each month is pay day. Bills presented to the several departments on or before the 15th of one month are ready for payment at this office on the first of the next month, if properly approved.

Sinking Fund Commission.
Newton Talbot, *Chairman,* Jas. H. Dodge, *Secretary.* Alfred T. Turner, *Treasurer.* Stanton Blake, Mahlon D. Spaulding, Henry C. Weston, A. D. Weld, Jr., Joseph H. Gray.

Boston Water Board. Office, City Hall.
Water Commissioners. — Horace T. Rockwell, till 1889, *Chairman;* Thomas F. Doherty, till 1887, William B. Smart, till 1888.
Clerk of the Water Board. — Walter E. Swan. Salary, $2,000.
City Engineer. — William Jackson, $6,000 and use of horse and vehicle.

Cochituate Water Works.
Water Registrar. — William F. Davis. Salary, $3,600; office, City Hall.
Superintendent Eastern Division. — Ezekiel R. Jones, 221 Federal Street. Salary, $3,000. *Superintendent Western Division.* — Desmond Fitz Gerald; office at Chestnut Hill Reservoir. Salary, $3,000.
Superintendent of Meter Division. — George S. Follansbee, 221 Federal Street. Salary, $2,000.
Superintendent of Inspection and Waste Division. — Basement City Hall, D. B. Cashman. Salary, $2,500.

Mystic Water Works.
Office, City Hall Building, Charlestown. Hours, 9 to 5.
Chief Clerk. — Joseph H. Caldwell. Salary, $2,500.
Superintendent. — J. Henry Brown. Salary, $2,000.
Engineer. — Bernard Born. Salary, $1,200.

Public Schools. School Committee.

Term expires January, 1890.
Wm. H. Grainger.
Nahum Chapin.
James S. Murphy.
Geo. R. Swasey.
Jas. A. McDonald.
Chas. T. Gallagher.
John C. Crowley.
Richard Walsh.

Term expires January, 1888.
Francis A. Walker.
John W. Porter.
John G. Blake.
Russell D. Elliott.
Samuel Eliot.
Gerald Griffin.
Joseph D. Fallon.
A. Gaston Roeth.

Term expires January, 1889.
Timothy J. Dacey.
Wm. C. Williamson.
Edwin H. Darling.
George B. Hyde.
Raphael Lasker.
William A. Dunn.
Henry Canning.
Boardman Hall.

Superintendent of Public Schools. Edwin P Seaver. Office, School Committee Rooms, Mason Street. Office hours from 1 to 2 p. m. Saturdays 12 to 1 o'clock. Salary, $4,200.
Secretary, Phineas Bates. Salary, $2,880. *Auditing Clerk,* Wm. J. Porter. Salary, $2,880. Office, School Committee Rooms, Mason Street. Rooms open from 9 a. m. to 5 p. m.; Saturdays, close at 2 p.m.
Supervisors, Samuel W. Mason, Louisa T. Hopkins, G. H. Conley; Ellis Peterson, Robert C. Metcalf, John Kneeland. Salary, $3,780.

OLD BOSTON.

A French Reason for Boston's Crooked Streets. When M. de Chastellux was in Boston a gentleman remarked to him: "Marquis, you find a crooked city in Boston?" "Ah! ver good, ver good," replied the Chevalier; "it show de liberte!"

America's First Pianoforte Manufactory. In the year 1800, Benjamin Crehore made the first pianoforte constructed in this country, in Milton, a suburb of Boston. He associated in business with himself Lewis Babcock, who afterward established a pianoforte manufactory on Washington Street, near Castle Street. Babcock's brother and a friend comprised the new firm of Babcock, Appleton & Babcock. They were not successful. John Mackay succeeded them, removing the manufactory to Cambridge Street. Jonas Chickering — who has been styled "the father of pianofortemaking" — disposed of his first pianoforte in Boston, April 15, 1823.

An Early Temperance Movement. October 25, 1630, Governor Winthrop wrote in his diary as follows: "The Governor, upon consideration of the inconveniences which had grown in England by drinking one to another, restrained it at his own table, and wished others to do the like, so as it grew, by little and little, into disuse."

An English gentleman visiting Boston was asked what impressed him as the most remarkable thing about Boston. His reply was, "The women!"

Ann Pollard was the first woman to set foot in Boston. She lived to be 105 years of age.

An Old Handbill. In the possession of the Massachusetts Historical Society (whose rooms are at 30 Tremont street) is a handbill of which the following is a copy:

To the Freemen of this and the Neighboring Towns:
Gentlemen:
You are desired to meet at Liberty Tree* this day, at Twelve o'clock at noon: then and there to hear the persons to whom the Tea shipped by the East India Company is consigned make a public resignation of their office as Consignees, upon Oath; and also swear that they will re-ship any Teas that may be consigned to them by said Company, by the first vessel sailing for London. O. C., *Secretary.*
BOSTON, Nov. 3, 1773.
☞ Show us the man that dare take down this.
(*The Liberty Tree stood at the corner of Washington and Essex Streets).

An Old Placard. The following is a copy of a placard issued in Boston upon the arrival of the tea, the destruction of which led to such important results in the history of the American Republic:

FRIENDS! BRETHREN! COUNTRYMEN!
That worst of plagues, the detested TEA, shipped for this port by the East India Company, is now arrived in this harbour. The hour of destruction, or manly opposition to the machinations of tyranny, stares you in the face. Every friend to his country, to himself and posterity, is now called upon to meet at Faneuil Hall at nine o'clock THIS DAY (at which time the bells will ring) to make a united and successful resistance to this last, worst, and most destructive measure of administration.
Boston, Nov. 29, 1773.

An Old-Time Celebration. In 1759, when the news of the fall of Quebec was received in Boston, a great bonfire was kindled on Copp's Hill. Fifty or more barrels of tar, several cords of wood and other combustibles were burned. Fort Hill was also the scene of an illumination, the province paying for them, as well as for thirty gallons of rum for the people.

Appearance of Boston in 1687. A Frenchman — a native of Languedoc — wrote of Boston in 1687 as follows: "We arrived at Boston after having fallen in with a number of very pretty Islands that lie in front of Boston, most of them cultivated and inhabited by Peasants, which form a very fine View. The Town is built on the Slope of a little Hill, and is as large as La Rochelle. The Town and the Land outside are not more than three Miles in Circuit, for it is almost an Island; it would only be necessary to cut through a Width of three hundred Paces, all Sand, which, in less than twice twenty-four Hours would make Boston an Island, washed on all Sides by the Sea. The Town is almost wholly built of wooden Houses; but, since there have been some ravages by Fire, building of wood is no longer allowed, so that at this present writing very handsome Houses of Brick are going up."

Art in the Olden Time. In 1787 it was written: "Art and Sciences seem to have made a Greater Progress here in Boston than in any other part of America. The Arts are undeniably Much Forwarder in Massachusetts-Bay than in either Pennsylvania or New York. The Public Buildings of Boston are more elegant, and there is a More General Turn for Music, Painting and the Belles-lettres." What was true of Boston in 1787 also applies to the great city of to-day.

Artistic Works of 1716.
In the Boston *News-Letter* of Aug. 27, 1716, was the following advertisement:
This is to give notice, that at the House of Mr. George Brownell, late School Master, in Hanover Street, Boston, are all sorts of Millinary Works done; making up Dresses and flowering of Muslin, making of furbelow'd Scarfs, and Quilting and Cutting of Gentlewomen's Hair in the newest Fashion, and also young Gentlewomen and Children taught all sorts of fine works, as Feather-work, Filigre and Painting on Glass, Embroidering a new way, Turkey-work for Handkerchiefs, two ways, fine new-Fashion Purses, flourishing and plain Work, and Dancing cheaper than was ever taught in Boston. Brocaded work for Handkerchiefs and short Aprons upon Muslin; Artificial Flowers work'd with a needle.

A Poem by Rev. Mather Byles in the *New England Journal*, published in Boston in 1727 (Boston's fourth newspaper), on Governor Burnet's arrival, contained the following lines:
"Welcome, Great Man, to our desiring eyes!
Thou Earth! proclaim it; and resound, ye Skies!
Voice answering Voice, in joyful Concert meet,
The Hills all echo, and the Rocks repeat;
And Thou, O BOSTON, Mistress of the Towns,
Whom the pleased Bay with am'rous arms surrounds,
Let thy warm Transports blaze in num'rous Fires,
And beaming Glories glitter on thy Spires;
Let Rockets, streaming, up the Ether glare,
And flaming Serpents hiss along the Air!"

A Typical Boston Mansion of Provincial Days.
Fennimore Cooper, the novelist, thus described the famous Frankland House, on Garden Court Street. Bostonians held this house in high esteem: "The house was of bricks, and of an exterior altogether more pretending than most of those in the lower parts of the town. It was heavily ornamented in wood, according to the taste of a somewhat earlier day, and presented a front of seven windows in its two upper stories, those at the extremes being much narrower than the others. The lower floor had the same arrangement, with the exception of the principal door. The walls were divided into compartments by raised panel-work beautifully painted with imaginary landscapes and ruins. The glittering varnished surfaces of these pictures were burdened with armorial bearings, which were intended to illustrate the alliances of the family. Beneath the surbase were smaller divisions of panels, painted with various architectural devices; and above it rose, between the compartments, fluted pilasters of wood, with gilded capitals. A heavy wooden and highly ornamental cornice stretched above the whole. The floor, which shone equally with the furniture, was tesselated with small alternate squares of red cedar and pine, and in the centre were the 'salient lions' of Lechmere. On either side of the ponderous and labored mantel were arched compartments, denoting use. The sliding panels displayed a buffet groaning with massive plate." Cooper's description of the house is historically accurate.

Banishment of Roger Williams.
On Oct. 13, 1635, Roger Williams, for "heresy," was banished.

Bargains in Real Estate.
In the year 1830, Lucius M. Sargent bought at public auction three acres, three quarters and eight rods (165,526 feet) lying between Tremont Street and Shawmut Avenue, for two hundred and sixty-nine dollars and eighty cents. The same property would now sell for at least one million dollars.

Beacon on Centry Hill.
The law for the placing of the beacon which gave the Hill its name is to be found in the following resolution of the Court of Assistants, March 4, 1634: "It is ordered that there shall be forthwith a Beacon sett on the Centry (Sentry) Hill, at Boston, to give notice to the Country of any Danger, and that there shall be a Ward of one person kept there from the first of April to the last of September; and that upon the Discovery of any Danger the Beacon shall be fired, an allarum given, as also Messengers presently sent by that Towne where the Danger is discovered to all other Townes within this jurisdiccon." The beacon consisted of a tall pole, with an iron pot filled with tar at its top. The shaft was about sixty feet high, and at its top about two hundred feet above high tide of the sea. On the sides of the pole were placed treenails, upon which one could climb to light the fire in the kettle of tar at its top as a signal of danger. (A good illustration of this beacon may be seen on the cover of the paper edition of this book). The beacon was blown down, November, 1789, and was replaced by a monument, the panels of which are still to be seen on the walls of Doric Hall, State House, Beacon Street, (head of Park Street, near the Common.) (See *Historical Tablets*).

Benjamin Franklin's Birthplace,
on Milk Street, is thus described:
"Its front upon the street was rudely

clapboarded, and the sides, and rear were protected from the inclemencies of a New England climate by large, rough shingles. In height the house was about three stories; in front, the second story and attic projected somewhat into the street, over the principal story on the ground floor. On the lower floor of the main house there was one room only. This, which probably served the Franklins as a parlor and sitting-room, and, also, for the family eating-room, was about twenty feet square, and had two windows on the street; and it had also one on the passage way, so as to give the inmates a good view of Washington Street. In the centre of the southerly side of the room was one of those noted large fire-places, situated in a most capacious chimney; on the left of this was a spacious closet. On the ground floor, connected with the sitting-room through the entry, was the kitchen. The second story originally contained but one chamber, and in this the windows, door, fire-place, and closet were similar in number and position to those in the parlor beneath it. The attic was also, originally, one unplastered room, and had a window in front, on the street, and two common attic windows, one on each side of the roof, near the back part of it." Josiah Franklin, Benjamin's father, was a silk dyer. He came to Boston from Banbury, England, in 1684. Benjamin was buried in Philadelphia, why it does not appear, as he wrote from France, in 1784, " I long much to see again my native place, and *to lay my bones there.*" In his will he wrote: "I was born in Boston and owe my first instructions in literature to the free grammar schools established there. I have therefore considered these schools in my will."

Benjamin Waterhouse, who introduced vaccination into America, in 1800, is thus described by Oliver Wendell Holmes: "A brisk, dapper old gentlemen, with hair tied in a ribbon behind, and, I think, powdered, marching smartly about with his gold-headed cane, with a look of questioning sagacity, and an utterance of oracular gravity. The good people of Cambridge listened to his learned talk when they were well, and sent for one of the other two doctors when they were sick."

Boston Common was not a gift from any one. It was purchased outright. Says Edwin L. Bynner, in the Memorial History of Boston: "Our title to the Common is easily traced; it originally formed part of the possessions of William Blackstone (Blaxton), the first white settler, whose ownership was acknowledged and confirmed by an entry in the Town Records as early as 1633, by which it was agreed that William Blackstone shall have fifty acres set out for him, near his house in Boston, to enjoy forever. The next year, 1684, Blackstone sold the whole parcel of land to the town, except only six acres immediately joining his house. The land thus coming into the possession of the town as public property was directly committed (Dec. 18, 1634, to the care of Winthrop and others to divide, and to leave 'such portions in common for ye use of newe comers, and ye further benefit of ye towne, as in theire best discretions they shall think fitt;' and six years later we find its alienation or appropriation to other purposes guarded against by an order passed March, 1640, to the following effect: 'Also agreed upon that henceforth there shall be no land granted eyther for houseplott or garden to any person out of ye open ground or common field which is left betweene ye Centry Hill and Mr. Colbron's end; except 3 or 4 Lotts to make up ye street from bro. Robt. Walker's to ye Round Marsh.'"

Bostonians In 1788. Brissot de Warville wrote in that year: "They (the Bostonians) unite simplicity of morals with that French politeness and delicacy of manners which render virtue more amiable. The young women here enjoy the liberty they do in England, — that they did in Geneva when morals were there, and the Republic existed; and they do not abuse it."

Boston in a Sad Plight. Thomas Dudley, Deputy Governor to Winthrop, wrote to the Countess of Lincoln, — mother of Lady Arabella Johnson, — under date of March 28, 1631, as follows: "We found the Colony in a sad and unexpected condition, above eighty of them being dead the winter before, and many of those alive weak and sick; all the corn and bread amongst them all hardly sufficient to feed them a fortnight."

Boston in 1699. Edward Ward, of London, visited Boston in that year, and this is the picture he drew of the old town and its people: "Boston, whose name is taken from a town in Lincolnshire, England, is the metropolis of all New England. The houses in some parts join as in London. The buildings, like their women, being neat and handsome; and their streets, like the hearts of the male inhabitants, are paved with pebble. In the chief or high street there are stately edifices, some of which have cost the owners two or three thousand pounds the raising; which, I think, plainly proves two old adages true, viz: That 'a fool and his money are soon parted,' and 'Set a beggar on horseback and he 'll ride to the devil,' for the fathers of these men were tinkers and peddlers."

Boston in 1719. According to Daniel Neale, who described Boston in 1719: "The Bay of Boston is spacious enough to contain in a manner the Navy of England. The masts of ships here, and at proper seasons of the year make a kind of Forest of Trees. At the bottom of the Bay is a noble pier, 2000 feet long, with a row of Warehouses on the North side, for the use of Merchants. Ships of the greatest burthen may unlade without the help of boats or lighters. From the head of the pier you go up the chief street of the Towne, at the upper end of which is the Towne House or Exchange, a fine piece of building, containing, besides the walk for the Merchants, the Council Chamber, the House of Commons, and another spacious room for the sessions of the Courts of Justice."

Boston Massacre. The first actual conflict between the residents of Boston and the British troops occurred in King (State) Street, March 5, 1770. The troops were called "lobsters," in derision by street-urchins, on account of their scarlet coats. "He's the soldier who knocked me down!" shouted a boy, pointing to a sentinel who had just before hit the lad with the butt-end of his musket. This was at the corner of Exchange Lane and King Street. Some one in the crowd cried—"Knock the lobster down!" Others shouted—"Kill him!" The sentinel quickly loaded his gun, and retreated up the steps of the Custom House, which then stood on that corner. "He's going to fire!" exclaimed a voice. Henry Knox, who was passing, said to the soldier—"If you dare to fire you shall die for it!" "Well," replied the sentinel, "if they touch me, I'll shoot them!" The crowd began to throw snowballs and other things at him, when he levelled his musket at them and shouted for assistance. A sergeant, with seven men, came to his relief. Capt. Thomas Preston, of the Twenty-Ninth, joined his men, making ten. There were about sixty people in the front of the Custom House. "You cowardly scoundrels," shouted some one, "put down your guns and we're ready for you!" Clubs were soon brought to bear against the soldiers, who had provoked the mob by pressing them back with their bayonets. Seven of the soldiers fired, killing Crispus Attucks, Samuel Gray and James Caldwell, and fatally wounding Samuel Maverick and Patrick Carr. Six others were wounded seriously.

Boston's Early English Proclivities. It is not to be wondered at that Londoners have ever felt very much at home in Boston. The architecture of London was almost perfectly reproduced in Boston. The fashions of the clothes worn by ladies and gentlemen in Boston, were copied from the London mode. Even in the speech of the people the similarity obtained among the descendants of the early settlers. Benjamin Franklin remarked this feature of the Bostonians particularly, after residing in Philadelphia. Alluding to the English tone of his Boston visitors, he said: "I enjoy the company and conversation of its (Boston's) inhabitants, when any of them are so good as to visit me; for, besides their general good sense, which I value, the Boston manner, turn of phrase, and even tone of voice and accent in pronunciation, all please and seem to refresh and revive me." It is superfluous to add that the Boston of to-day sustains all of its former English tone, the city taking its fashions in social customs, dress, etc., from London.

Boston's Early Names. Boston's Indian name was Shawmutt, signifying "living fountains" in their dialect. It was afterwards called Trimountaine, owing to the fact that its principal hill had three distinct peaks. (This hill was once called Centry (Sentry) Hill, afterwards Beacon Hill.) Boston received its present name, Sept. 7, 1630, being called after Boston, England.

Boston's Elegance in 1766. John Adams' Diary contains the following: "Dined at Mr. Nick Boylston's—an elegant dinner indeed. Went over the house to view the furniture, which alone cost a thousand pounds sterling. A seat it is for a nobleman, a prince. The Turkey carpets, the painted hangings, the marble tables, the rich beds with crimson damask curtains and counterpanes, the beautiful chimney clock, the spacious garden, are the most magnificent of anything I have ever seen."

Boston Harbor Blockaded. On May 10, 1774, British Men-of-War effectually blockaded Boston Harbor.

Boston in 1687. A writer in that year said: "As for wild beasts in Boston, we have here plenty of bears, wolves in great number, and plenty of rattlesnakes."

Boston's First Performance of Shakespeare's "Macbeth" was announced as "A Dialogue on the Horrid Crime of Murder."

Boston's Famous Teapot. Oliver Wendell Holmes has written:

"Fast spread the tempest's darkening pall;
The mighty realms were troubled;
The storm broke loose, but first of all
The Boston teapot bubbled.

The lurid morning shall reveal
A fire no king can smother,
When British flint and Boston steel
Have clashed against each other!"

Boston's First Dancing School was opened in 1735, and under cover. It was announced as a "School for reading, writing, cyphering, dancing, and the use of the needle." About this time an application for an exhibition of tight-rope dancing was refused, as it might "tend to promote idleness in the Town."

Boston Stone. In the early days of the Town the houses, inns and shops were not numbered, but at certain points were placed curious emblematic stones, signs, etc., to point the way, or to mark the position of various buildings. Thus, what is so widely known as the Boston Stone, which may to-day be seen imbedded in the outer wall of a building on Marshall st., Creek sq., near Hanover st., was used as a symbol by a painter, who, in 1701, opened a little shop on this spot, having removed here from London. The Stone—or Stones, for there are two, the lower one having been used as a paint-mill, and the upper spherical one as a grinder—was brought here from England. The Stone is placed in the wall quite near the ground. Upon it is the inscription: ' Boston Stone, 1737." The historic old landmark is considered to be of the greatest interest by antiquarians and other sight-seers, some of whom are almost constantly to be found in the vicinity. (Near the Boston Stone is the Painter's Arms, a description of which is given as indicated in the Index of this work.)

Boston's Three-Peaked Beacon Centry Hill. Wood, the voyager, in 1633, spoke of "three little hills on top of a high mountain." This description referred to Centry or Sentry Hill, now known as Beacon Hill; the other hills were afterwards known as Copp's and Fort Hills.

Boston Tea-party. The story of the famous Boston Tea-Party is thus graphically told by Rev. Edward G. Porter: "In the summer of 1773 the news of the tea tax aroused a universal spirit of resistance. It was known to be an insidious measure, skilfully contrived to collect a duty without apparent cost to the purchaser, the tribute being nominally paid by the East India Company in London. But it was only another test case, involving a recognition of the supremacy of Parliament, and every one understood it. Samuel Adams was busy with his fellow-patriots making arrangements for the proper reception of the 'detested tea.' The consignees were cautioned in advance by the 'Liberty Tree ' committee. The clubs and newspapers were of one mind on the subject. Numerous town meetings were held, first in Faneuil Hall and then in the Old South, at which it was unanimously determined, upon Adams's motion, that the tea should be sent back and that no duty should be paid upon it. It was a difficult matter to convince the authorities that this vote of the town was imperative. Everything was done by the leaders in the way of warning, personal visitation and reasonable delays, to facilitate the execution of the people's order, but official obstructions prevented up to the very last day before the ships would be subject to confiscation. That was the memorable Thursday, the sixteenth of December, 1773—*that day of days in Boston history*— when the largest town meeting that was ever held, numbering, it is said, seven thousand men, filled the Old South and all its approaches. The deliberations of the morning were adjourned to three o'clock to allow time for Rotch, the owner of the ' Dartmouth,' who had been refused a clearance at the Custom House, to obtain the necessary sailing-permit of the Governor, then at his country-seat in Milton. The afternoon session was prolonged for hours waiting for the merchant's return. Addresses were made by Adams, Young, Quincy and others, and the vote was taken again, and without a dissenting voice, that the tea should in no case be landed. ' Who knows,' said Rowe, ' how tea will mingle with salt water?' a remark which elicited loud applause. We cannot but respect the patience of such a gathering, and the restraining influence exercised by the leaders at this critical juncture. Night is drawing on. The speeches have all been made, and now there are long intervals of silence. Only a few faces can be distinguished in the dim candle-light. In the pulpit sits Samuel Adams, the moderator, whose presence there is enough to control any assembly on any occasion. Some in that company—perhaps not many—are in the well-kept secret which is likely soon to astonish the town. Others not far away—a dauntless band—are holding themselves in readiness for the signal. And yet all is quiet, profoundly quiet. At last, about six o'clock, Rotch appeared and reported that the Governor had refused the pass. Then the moderator rose and said, ' This meeting can do nothing more to save the country.' Scarcely had the words fallen from his lips, when a war-whoop was heard at the door, and a band of men, disguised as Indians, swept by on their way to Griffin's wharf (now Liverpool wharf), followed by the crowd. The teaships were boarded and placed under guard, while the ' braves' in the light of the moon removed the hatches, hoisted the chests upon deck, and emptied all their contents into the sea. There was no resistance, no noise, no exultation. When the work was done, they all retired quietly to their homes, and by ten o'clock that night a Sabbath stillness prevailed throughout the town."

Boston Witchcraft. In 1648, June 13, Margaret Jones was tried, convicted and hanged (from a branch of the Great Elm on Boston Common) for witchcraft. In 1656, Ann Hibbins met a similar fate. Other victims were executed for the same "crime" in Boston, (near'y fifty years before the outbreak of the witchcraft delusion in Danvers, then known as Salem Village, in 1692). Governor Endicott pronounced the sentence of death on Dame Hibbins, who was denied even Christian burial.

Boston Women in 1781. The celebrated Abbe Robin—who accompanied Count de Rochambeau and his six thousand French troops who came to assist in the War for American Independence, as chaplain —— wrote as follows from Boston in June, 1781: "Piety is not the only motive that brings the American ladies in crowds to the various places of worship. The church is the grand theatre where they attend to display their extravagance and finery. There they come, dressed off in the finest silks, and overshadowed with a profusion of the most superb plumes. The hair of the head is raised and supported upon cushions to an extravagant height. The ladies are large, well proportioned; their features generally regular, and their complexions fair without ruddiness. They have less cheerfulness and ease of behaviour than the ladies of France, but more of greatness and dignity. I have even imagined that I have seen something in them that answers to the ideas of beauty we gain from those master-pieces of the artists of antiquity, which are yet extant in our days. The stature of the men is tall, and their carriage erect, but their make is rather slim, and their colour inclining to pale. They are not so curious in their dress as the women, but everything upon them is neat and proper." (Boston then contained about 30,000 inhabitants).

Branding. On September 14, 1784, Thomas Joyce was branded with the letter B for burglary.

Brighton was originally called "Little Cambridge."

British Troops in Boston. There were 13,800 British soldiers in Boston, March 17, 1775.

Bunker Hill, Charlestown District. Oliver Wendell Holmes, in "Grandmother's Story" writes thus:

"I had heard the musket's rattle of the April running battle;
Lord Percy's hunted soldiers, I can see their red coats still;
But a deadly chill comes o'er me as the day looms up before me,
When a thousand men lay bleeding on the slopes of Bunker's Hill."

Bunker Hill Monument was completed June 17, 1843.

Burgoyne, when informed that Boston was surrounded by provincials, (June, 1775,) ejaculated, "What? Ten thousand peasants keep five thousand King's troops shut up! Let us get in, and we'll soon find elbow-room!" The General was nick-named "Elbow-room Burgoyne" after that.

Cambridge was originally called "Newe-towne."

Boston became a city May 1, 1822.

Carlyle, with historical inaccuracy, wrote as follows: "Rev. John Cotton is a man still held in some remembrance among our New England friends. He had been minister of Boston in Lincolnshire; carried the name across the ocean with him; fixed it upon a new small home he had found there, which has become a large one since,—the big busy capital of Massachusetts, — *Boston*, so called. John Cotton, his mark, very curiously stamped on the face of this planet; likely to continue for some time." The fact is that Boston was named three years *before* the arrival of Rev. John Cotton.

Caucus. The term *Caucus* was first used about 1724, in connection with political meetings. They were originally called "*Calkers*' meetings," being principally organized by calkers or ship-building mechanics.

Charlestown's Famous Engine. The Massachusetts Spy, of April 8, 1773, in alluding to a fire in Boston speaks of the aid rendered by "the engine from Charlestown, esteemed the best in America."

Charter. On March 4, 1628 (9, O. S.), Charles I., of England, granted Letters-Patent to Sir Henry Rosewell and others as a body corporate "by the name of the Governor and Company of the Massachusetts Bay in New England." In the State Archives, in Boston, is preserved the original document, upon which is the following indorsement: "A perpetuity granted to Sir Henry Rosewell and others of parts of Newe England in America. (Signed) Wolseley." The paper bears the autograph signature of Wolseley.

Christ Church, Salem st. From the belfrey of this church, built in 1723, lanterns were hung out on the night before the Concord and Lexington battles. (See *Historical Tablets*.) A poem by Edwin B. Russell commemorates this event:

"And here the patriot hung his light
Which shone through all that anxious night,
To eager eyes of Paul Revere;
There, in the dark churchyard below,
The dead Past 'wakened not to know
How changed the world, that night of fear."

Churches in Early Days. Of the established churches of the Massachusetts Colony the first was at Salem; the second at Charlestown; the third in Boston; the fourth at Dorchester; the fifth at Roxbury.

Colonial Architecture. In 1637 Samuel Symonds wrote to John Winthrop, Jr., describing a house he was to build at Ipswich: "I would have wood chimnyes at each end, the frames of the chimnyes to be stronger than ordinary, to beare good heavy load of clay for security against fire. You may let the chimnyes be all the breadth of the howse, if you think good; the 2 lower dores to be in the middle of the howse, one opposite to the other. Be sure that all the dorewales in every place be soo high that any man may goe vpright vnder. It makes noe great matter though there be noe particion vpon the first flore; if there be, make one biger than the other. I would have the howse strong in timber, though plaine and well brased."

Continental Money. At a meeting of Boston merchants at Faneuil Hall, June 16, 1779, it was "Resolved, That all those who shall hereafter dare refuse Continental money, or require hard money for rents or any article whatever, shall not remain among us, but be transported to our enemies as unworthy or dangerous members of society."

Cows not Allowed on Boston Common. In 1830 it was forbidden to pasture cows on the Common.

Cradock House. The old Cradock House, built in Medford, in 1639, is still standing.

Creek Square and vicinity is an extremely interesting locality for historians to visit. (See *Boston Stone*, *Painter's Arms*, *Old North End*, and *Old Houses*).

Dark Day. On May 19, 1780, occurred the noted "dark day" in Boston. A lady residing near Common Street in great alarm sent her servant to Rev. Mather Byles to ask him the cause of the unnatural state of things. "Tell your mistress," said Byles, "that I am as much in the dark as she is!"

David Crockett. In May, 1834, "Col. Davy Crockett" created a great sensation in Boston.

Decay of the Indians. Charles Sprague, the famous Boston poet, wrote of the Indians, in 1830:

"Alas! for them,—their day is o'er,
Their fires are out from shore to shore;
No more for them the wild deer bounds,
The plough is on their hunting-grounds;
The pale man's axe rings through their woods,
The pale man's sail skims o'er their floods,
Their pleasant springs are dry."

George Edward Ellis, in the Memorial History of Boston, says: "There were places in this state where feeble remnants of partially-civilized natives remained a little longer than at Natick. But the longer they survived the more forlorn was the spectacle they presented, as poor pensioners and vagabonds, the virility of their native nobleness in the wild woods crushed in abject abasement before the white man, their veins mixed with African rather than with English blood."

Devonshire Street was called Pudding Lane in provincial days.

Dickens. Charles Dickens first visited America, landing at Boston, in 1842. He was tendered a reception at Papanti's Hall, Feb. 1.

Drunkenness. In 1690 the penalty for drunkenness was a public whipping, or a fine of one crown.

Dwelling-Houses in 1654. Boston in 1654 had about 150 dwelling-houses.

Early Encouragement of Art in Boston. The Academy of Arts and Sciences was founded May 4, 1780.

Early History of Roman Catholicism in Boston. Writes The Very Reverend William Byrne—Vicar-General of the Diocese) in The Memorial History of Boston: "One hundred years ago (about 1780) there were about one hundred Catholics in Boston. These were for the most part either French, Irish or Spanish. . . . They had then no church organization, no church, no regular place of worship, and only the occasional ministrations of transient priests. . . . These missionaries were succeeded by the Rev. John Thayer, a native of Boston, a convert to the Catholic faith, who had been a Congregational minister. During this gentleman's travels in Europe in 1781-83, he learned and accepted the doctrines of the Roman Catholic Church.

. . . After being ordained priest he returned to America, and visited Dr. Carroll, of Baltimore, the Superior of the missions in the United States. Dr. Carroll assigned him to the Boston mission. On his arrival in Boston, Jan. 4, 1790, he found the Catholics using as a place of religious assembly and worship, a small chapel on School Street. This chapel had been previously occupied by a small Huguenot congregation, but was the property of Mr. Perkins, from whom Father Thayer obtained, in 1790, a lease for a few years. This may be said to be the first regularly organized church society of Roman Catholics in Boston."

Early Literature. Boston achieved its literary pre-eminence—which it still holds—early in the history of the country. In 1719, Daniel Neal, the well-known writer, in describing Boston, wrote: "The Exchange is surrounded with Booksellers' Shops, which have a good trade. There are five printing-presses in Boston, which are generally full of work, by which it appears that humanity and the knowledge of letters flourish more here than in all the other English plantations put together, for in the city of New York there is but one Bookseller's Shop, and in Virginia, Maryland and Carolina none at all."

Early Settlers. In July, 1630, a fleet of ten ships (including the "Arbella") from Yarmouth, England, arrived in Boston Harbor, bearing a band of men, self-reliant, resolute and determined, who were to establish a home for the oppressed of all the nations of the earth. This company included John Winthrop, John Wilson, Isaac Johnson, Thomas Dudley, and other equally heroic, sturdy men.

Eavesdropping in 1699. Salutary lessons were often taught eavesdroppers and busybodies in early days. Edward Ward wrote home to England, as follows: "A good cudgel, applied in the dark, is an excellent medicine for a malignant spirit. I knew it experienced at Boston, with a very good success upon an old rigged precisian, one of their select, who used to be more than ordinarily vigilant in discovering even little irregularities in the neighborhood. I happened, one night, to be pretty merry with a friend, opposite the zealot's dwelling, who got out of his bed in his waistcoat and drawers, to listen at our window. My friend, having oft been served so, had left unbolted his cellar trap-door, as a pitfall for Mister Busic-Body, who, stepping upon it, sunk down with an outcry like that of a distressed mariner in a sinking pinnace. My friend, having planted a cudgel ready, ran down stairs, crying, 'Thieves!' and belabored old troublesome very severely before he would know him. He crying out, 'I am your neighbor!'—'You lie, you rogue!' says my friend, 'my neighbors are honest men. You are some thief, come to rob my house!' By this time I went down with a candle, my friend seemingly wonderfully surprised to see 'twas his neighbor, and one of the select, too, put on a counterfeit countenance, and heartily begged his pardon. Away trooped the old fox, grumbling and shrugging his shoulders, and he afterwards became the most moderate man in authority in the whole Towne of Boston."

Education in Colonial Days. A law passed Nov. 11, 1647, read as follows: "To the end that Learning may not be buried in the graves of our Forefathers, it is ordered in all the Puritan Colonies that every Township, after the Lord hath increased them to the number of fifty households, shall appoint one to teach all children to write and read; and when any Town shall increase to the number of one hundred families, they shall set up a Grammar School, the master thereof to be able to instruct youth so far as they may be fitted for the University; provided that if any Town neglect the performance hereof, above one year, that every such Town shall pay five pounds to the next School, till they shall perform the order."

Effects of Early Rising. President Quincy of Harvard College, and John Quincy Adams, who were "addicted to the vice of intemperate early rising," one day complimented Judge Joseph Story by attending one of his lectures at Harvard University Law School, and had hardly become seated before they both fell asleep. Judge Story, pointing to them, said to the amused students: "Gentlemen, you see before you a melancholy example of the evil effects of early rising." Shouts of laughter awoke the worthy slumberers.

Experiences of Early Settlers. Captain Roger Clap—one of a company coming from Plymouth, England—arriving at Hull, Boston Harbor, (after a ten-weeks' tempestuous voyage), May 30, 1630, and who settled in Dorchester, wrote: "When we came to Nantasket, Captain Squeb, who was Captain of that great Ship of Four Hundred Tons, would not bring us into Charles River, as he was bound to do; but put us ashore, and our goods, on Nantasket Point, and left us to shift for ourselves in a forlorn Place in this Wilderness. But, as it pleased God, we got a Boat of some old Planters, and laded her with Goods; and some able men, well armed, went in her unto Charlestown: where we found some Wigwams and one House, and in the House there was a man which had a boiled Bass, but no Bread that we see: but we did eat of his Bass, and then went up Charles

River, until the River grew narrow and shallow, and there we landed our Goods, with Labour and Toil, the Bank being steep. And, Night coming on, we were informed that there were hard by us Three Hundred Indians. One English man that could speak the Indian language (an old Planter) went to them, and advised them not to come near us in the Night, and they came not. In the Morning some of the Indians came and stood at a distance off, looking at us, but came not near us: but, when they had been awhile in view, some of them came and held out a great Bass (fish) towards us; so we sent a man with a Bisket (biscuit) and changed the Cake for the Fish. Afterwards they supplied us with Bass, exchanging a Bass for a Bisket-Cake, and were very friendly unto us. Alas! had they come upon us, how soon might they have destroyed us! I think we were then not above Ten in number."

Faneuil Hall as a Theatre. During the possession of Faneuil Hall by the British, in 1775-6, it was used as a theatre by the troops. In September, 1775, "Zara" was performed, General Burgoyne having written the prologue and epilogue. On January 8, 1776, a performance was in progress, one of the actors at the moment caricaturing George Washington — when a sergeant rushed upon the stage, shouting: "The Yankees are attacking the works on Bunker Hill!" The audience believed this to be a part of the play, until an aide-de-camp hastily gave the order — "Officers to their posts!" and the play was over.

First Almanac. The first almanac was published by John Foster, in 1678.

First Bank. The establishment of the first bank (Massachusetts) was on March 18, 1784.

First Battles of the Revolutionary War. The beginning of the War of the Revolutionary War was at Lexington and Concord near Boston, the battles at those towns having been fought April 19, 1775.

First Board of Trade. A Board of Trade was first organized in Boston, April 28, 1854.

First Burying-Ground. The first interments in King's Chapel Burying-ground were on June 5, 1630.

First Directory. The first Boston Directory was issued in 1781.

First Military Company. The first company of military organized in the United States was the present Ancient and Honorable Artillery Company, of Boston, June 1, 1638.

First Police in Boston. The organization of Boston's first regular police force took place June 20, 1822.

First Printing-Press. America's first printing-press was set up in Cambridge, near Boston, in 1638, and one was established in Boston, by John Foster, in 1676.

First Railway in the United States. Gridley Bryant's railway, known as the Granite Railroad, was in operation Oct. 7, 1826, when a train of cars first passed over the whole length of the road. Horses furnished the motive power. Bryant also devised the switch, the portable derrick, the turn-table and moveable truck. The Granite Railroad was four miles long and cost $50,000. It was in use for forty years. It was located in Quincy, near Boston. It afterwards became the property of the Old Colony Railroad Company, a modern railway was laid on the right of way, and opened Oct. 9, 1871, forty-five years after the original opening of the Granite Railway in 1826.

Freemen's Oath. The following is a copy of the freeman's oath of colonial times in Boston:

I, A. B., being by God's providence an inhabitant and freeman within the jurisdiction of this Commonwealth, do freely acknowledge myself to be subject to the Government thereof, and, therefore, do hereby swear by the great and dreadful name of the Everlasting God that I will be true and faithful to the same, and will accordingly yield assistance and support thereunto, with my person and estate, as in equity I am bound; and I will also truly endeavor to maintain and preserve all the liberties and privileges thereof, submitting myself to the wholesome laws and orders made and established by the same. And further, that I will not plot nor practice any evil against it, nor consent to any that shall so do; but will truly discover and reveal the same to lawful authority, now here established for the speedy preventing thereof. Moreover, I do solemnly bind myself in the sight of God, that when I shall be called to give my voice touching any such matter of this State, wherein freemen are to deal, I will give my vote and suffrage as I judge, in mine own conscience, may best conduce and tend to the public weal of the body, without respect of persons or favor of any man. So help me God, in the Lord Jesus Christ.

Gas. Gas-light was seen in Boston earlier than in any other place in the United States, Nov. 26, 1815; the first meeting of a Gas Company being held July 14, 1826; and the first street gas-lamp was lighted—in Dock Square—Jan. 1, 1829.

General Gage and the Boston Boys. There have been poems written, stories told, and pictures painted of an event said to have had its occurrence in the early days of the Revolution, when the Boston Boys complained to General Gage that their coasting-place on Boston Common had been broken up by the British soldiers. We find the following account of the incident in Higginson's Young Folks' History: "In Boston the troops made themselves still more unpopular. There was soon a quarrel between them and the boys, for the soldiers used to beat down the snowhills that the boys had heaped up on the Common. After appealing in vain to the captain, the boys finally went to Governor Gage and complained. 'What!' he said, 'have your fathers been teaching you rebellion, and sent you here to exhibit it?'—'Nobody sent us, sir,' said one of the boys. 'We have never injured nor insulted your troops; but they have trodden down our snowhills, and broken the ice on our skating-ground. We complained, and they called us young rebels, and told us to help ourselves if we could. We told the captains of this, and they laughed at us. Yesterday our works were destroyed for the third time, and we will bear it no longer.' The Governor, with surprise, said to one of his officers, 'The very children here draw in a love of Liberty with the air they breathe. You may go, my brave boys, and be assured, if my troops trouble you again they shall be punished.' "

Gentlemen's Dress in 1795. A New York merchant visiting Boston in 1795 wrote home that "the broad aisle of Brattle Street Church was lined by gentlemen in wigs, with cocked hats, and scarlet coats." Ruffles of lace, silk stockings, and polished shoes, with buckles, were also portions of the costume.

Going from Boston to Roxbury was a perilous journey in 1713. In January of that year, "one Bacon, of Roxbury, going home in his slade (sled or sleigh) with three horses, was bewilder'd in the dark, himself found dead with the cold, next morning, one of the horses drowned in the Marsh, the other two not yet heard of."

Griffin's Wharf. Near the foot of Pearl Street. Now known as Liverpool Wharf. This was the scene of the famous "Boston Tea-Party." (See *Boston Tea-Party*). In the spring of 1773 the East India Company obtained an Act of Parliament authorizing the Company to export Teas to America without paying the ordinary duty in England. Ships were dispatched to America with the Tea, on every pound of which a tax of threepence had been imposed. The following graphic account of the result is condensed from an article in the Memorial History of Boston: " When this news became known all America was in a flame. The people had taken their stand upon a principle, and not until that was recognized would they withdraw their opposition."

Hair-Dressing in 1800. Monsieur Alexandre Lavigne, from Paris, established a hair-dressing shop in Boston, and announced that he would arrange ladies' hair " in the Greek, Flora or Virginia fashions," while the hair of the gentlemen would be cut "*a la* Brutus*,*" or " *a la* Titus," as desired.

Harvard Theatre. A theatre was opened in Cambridge, called the Harvard Theatre, April 28, 1830. (See *Eventful Playbills*).

Harvard University in 1781. The distinguished Abbé Robin, of France, wrote from Boston as follows, in 1781: "The Europeans have long been convinced of the natural and moral dangers to be apprehended in acquiring education in large towns. The Bostonians have advanced farther; they have prevented these dangers. Their University is at Cambridge, seven miles from Boston on the banks of Charles River, in a beautiful and healthy situation. There are four Colleges, all of brick, and of a regular form. The English troops made use of them as barracks in 1775, and forced the professors and students to turn out. The Library contains more than 5,000 volumes; and they have an excellent printing-house, well furnished, that was originally intended for a College for the native Indians. To give you an idea of the merit of the professors, it will be sufficient to say that they correspond with the *literati* of Europe, and that Mr. Sewall in particular, Professor of the Oriental languages, is one of those to whom the Author of genius and ability has been lavish of those gifts; their pupils often act tragedies, the subject of which is generally taken from their national events, such as the Battle of Bunker's Hill, the Burning of Charlestown, and the Fall of British Tyranny." (The statement made by this writer that Cambridge is seven miles from Boston arose from the fact that in those days communication between the two places was by way of Boston Neck. The distance by present methods is about three miles).

Headquarters of Louis Philippe. Louis Philippe stayed in the Hancock House, in Corn Court,out of Dock Square,while making his residence in Boston during the French Reign of Terror.

Historical Swords. Thackeray's celebrated story of "The Virginians" opens as follows: "On the library wall of one of the most famous writers of America (William Hickling Prescott) there hang two swords which his relations wore in the great War of Independence. The one sword was gallant'y drawn in the service of the King (by Captain Linzee, commander of the Sloop-of-War "Falcon," which cannonaded the works on Breed's (Bunker) Hill; the other was the weapon of a brave and honored republican soldier." (The latter was Colonel William Prescott, who threw up the works on Bunker Hill, June 16, 1775. Both of these swords are now to be seen on the walls of the Massachusetts Historical Society's Rooms, 30 Tremont st.

Home of General Joseph Warren. The residence of General Joseph Warren who fell at Bunker Hill —was upon a site on Hanover Street, now covered by the American House.

Home of Samuel Adams. The residence of this patriot in 1769 was in Brattle Square.

Home of Anne Hutchinson. The residence of Anne Hutchinson stood on the corner of Washington and School streets where is now the Old Corner Bookstore. This remarkable woman, who, said Coddington, "had broken no law of God nor of man," was brutally banished by Governor Winthrop, in 1636. What was her offence? She had simply dared to comment upon the sermons delivered by the minister of that day. It is a marvel that she escaped being hanged from a branch of the Great Elm on the Common.

How Changes Go On. A writer in the Boston *Transcript* of April 12, 1886, says: "The gradual changes that go on from day to day and year to year are not always appreciated by those who live in them, but they become startling to one who has been away and returns after a lapse of time to a familiar place. When I was a youngster, forty or more years ago, I walked every morning from Roxbury over the Neck to State Street, and was well acquainted with the houses and places of business in the whole distance. Within a few days I have again carefully looked over the whole route. I find *only three* parties continuing business between the Norfolk House and State Street, who are now located where they were in 1846. These are H. K. Taylor, 236 Washington Street; Joseph T. Brown, Washington Street, corner of Bedford Street, and Little, Brown & Co., near State Street. Less than forty years—only thirty years, or a single generation—changes almost entirely the names and occupations of a business locality."

Increase Mather, preaching on the great Fire in Boston in 1711 said: "Has not God's holy day been profaned in New England? Has it not been so in Boston this last summer? Have not burdens been carried through the streets on the Sabbath Day? Nay, have not bakers, carpenters, and other tradesmen been employed in servile works on the Sabbath Day? When I saw this, my heart said, 'Will not the Lord for this kindle a fire in Boston?'"

Indian Questions. John Eliot,—the famous missionary to the Indians about Boston, in 1631, gave the following as among the questions asked him by the Indians: "Whether ye Devil or man was made first? Whether there might not be something,—if only a little,—gained by praying to ye Devil? Why does not God, who has full power, kill ye Devil that makes all men so bad? If God made hell in one of ye six days, why did he make it before Adam had sinned? If all ye world be burned up, where shall hell be then? Are all ye Indians, who have died, now in hell, while only we are in ye way of getting to Heaven? Why does not God give all men good hearts, that they may be good? Whither do dying little children go, seeing that they have not sinned?"

Indian Scalps. An old Proclamation,—to be seen in a showcase at Bates Hall, (Public Library, Boylston Street), offering a bounty for Indian prisoners and scalps, possesses great interest to antiquarians. It was issued by the Governor of the Province of Massachusetts Bay, in Boston, May 27, 1696, and offers "Fifty Pounds per Head for every Indian Man, and Twenty-five Pounds per Head for any Indian Woman, or Child (male or female, under the age of fourteen years), taken or brought in prisoner; the Scalps of all Indians Slain to be produced and delivered to the Commissioners for War, etc."

John Hancock's Vanity. Hancock was as vain as a peacock. He was sarcastically called "King Hancock." A writer said, March 11, 1778, "John Hancock, of Boston, appears in public with all the pageantry and state of an Oriental prince. He rides in an elegant chariot, attended by four servants dressed in superb livery, mounted on fine horses richly caparisoned, and escorted by *fifty* horsemen with drawn sabres, one half of whom precede, and the other follow, his carriage."

Julien, the famous French caterer, opened a "Restorator" in Boston in 1793. (Who has not eaten the Julienne soup, made from the receipt original with him?) According to an advertisement of his in the *American Apollo*, of July 26, 1793, he was "established in Leverett's Lane, opposite the Quaker's Meeting-House, where any person can call for as much or as little refreshment as he pleases, and pay for no more than he consumes. Excellent wines and cordials, good soups and broths, pastry in all its delicious variety, a la mode beef, bacon, poultry, and generally all other refreshing viands will be kept in due preparation." This was probably the first eating-house to be established on the a la carte plan in this city or country.

King's Chapel.

Tremont st., cor. of School st. The old King's Chapel— on the site of the present one—was built in 1688, and was a small, unpretentious building, of wood. Its steeple was surmounted by a large rooster, under which was a conspicuous crown. The steeple was a very high one. The church had no pews for several years; but, in 1693, some English naval officers belonging to Sir Francis Wheeler's fleet, then in the harbor, contributed £56, and the pews were built. The expensive communion service was given by King James II. (for whom the chapel was named) and Queen Mary of England. The carpet, cushions, Bible, prayer-book, surplices, etc., were gifts from Queen Mary (of Modena). The Chapel was rebuilt to more than double its original size, in 1710. The first organ ever used in America stood in the western gallery. The walls were hung with the escutcheons of the King and of the Vice-Regal Governors. "It was a strange sight among the bare churches of New England." The present stone Chapel was erected in 1749. On the evacuation of Boston by the British, March 17, 1776, Dr. Cauer, the rector, fled with them, taking the plate, records, etc., a portion of which were afterwards recovered from his heirs. George Washington attended an oratorio given here, Oct. 27, 1789. The old Latin schoolhouse having been demolished to make room for the extension of the stone Chapel, Joseph Green, a noted writer of that period (who lived on School Street, near the Cromwell's Head Inn), wrote, in 1748, as follows:

"A fig for your learning! I tell you the Town
To make the Church larger must pull the School down!
'Unhappily spoken!' exclaims Master Birch,
'Then Learning, it seems, stops the growth of the Church!'"

Kissing in Boston in Provincial Times.

According to Edward Ward, who came from London to Boston in 1699, "If you Kiss a woman in public, though offered as a courteous salutation, if any information is given to the Select members, both shall be whipped or fined. But the good-humored lasses, to make you amends, will Kiss the Kinder in a corner! A captain of a ship, who had been on a long voyage, happened to meet his wife and Kissed her in the street, for which he was fined ten shillings, and forced to pay the money. Another inhabitant of the town was fined ten shillings for Kissing his own wife in his garden, and, obstinately refusing to pay the money, endured twenty lashes. And at his rate one of the delightfulest customs in the world will in time be quite thrown out of fashion, to the old-folk satisfaction, but to the young one's lamentation, who love it as well in New England as we do in the Old."

Lafayette's Headquarters.

The celebrated old Ticknor House, on the corner of Beacon and Park Streets,— built in 1804, by Thomas Amory—was occupied by Lafayette during his sojourn in Boston in 1824. (George Ticknor, the famous historian of Spanish literature, lived and died in this renowned building, which is still standing in an excellent state of preservation). It is recorded that when on Harvard University Commencement Day, Mayor Quincy called for Lafayette at this house, a large crowd gathered about the carriage. "Have you ever been in Europe, Mr. Quincy?" asked Lafayette. "No," replied the Mayor. "Then," rejoined Lafayette, "you can have no idea of the character of a crowd in Europe. I declare, in comparison, the people of Boston seem to me like a population selected from the whole human race." Charles Sprague, the eminent poet, wrote the following inscription for an arch placed on Washington Street, just above Dover Street, under which Lafayette passed when received by the city:

"The fathers in glory shall sleep
That gathered with thee to the fight;
But the sons will eternally keep
The tablet of gratitude bright:
We bow not the neck; we bend not the knee;
But our hearts, Lafayette, we surrender to thee!"

Law Against Wearing Lace.

In 1636, the General Court, sitting in Boston, issued the following order: "The Court, taking into consideration the great, superfluous, and unnecessary expenses occasioned by reason of some new and immodest fashions, as also the ordinary wearing of silver, gold and silk laces, girdles, hat-bands, &c., hath therefore ordered that no person, either man or women, shall hereafter make or buy any apparel, either woolen, silk or linen, with any lace on it, silver, gold, silk or thread, under the penalty of forfeiture of such clothes."

Law Prohibiting the Use of Tobacco.
In 1638, it was "ordered that no person shall take tobacco publicly, nor privately in his own house, under the penalty of two shillings and six pence."

Lions and Bears.
According to William Wood, who wrote in 1634 concerning the animals in Boston and vicinity, the following were here:

"The kingly Lion and the strong-arm'd Beare,
The large-lim'd Mooses, with the tripping Deare,
Quill-darting Porcupines and Rackcoones be
Castell'd in the hollow of an aged tree."

Lord Percy's Head quarters.
At the corner of Essex and Columbia Streets Lord Percy's headquarters were established during the British occupation of Boston in 1775-6. The building was demolished in April, 1886.

Margaret Jones
was noted as the first witch executed in Massachusetts. She was hanged in Boston, June 15, 1648, forty-four years before the Danvers (Salem Village) witchcraft. John Hale wrote of Margaret Jones as follows: "She was suspected, part'y because that, after some angry words passing between her and her neighbors, some mischief befell such neighbors in their creatures (cattle or the like); part'y because some things supposed to be bewitch'd, or have a charm upon them, being burned, she came to the fire and seemed concerned. The day of her execution I went, In company of some neighbors who took great pains to bring her to confession and repentance; but she constantly professed herself innocent of that crime. Then one prayed her to consider if God did not bring this punishment upon her for some other crime; and asked if she had not been guilty of stealing many years ago. She answered, she had stolen something, but it was long since, and she had repented of it, and there was grace enough in Christ to pardon that long ago; but as for witchcraft she was wholly free from it,—and so she said unto her death."

Marriage in Boston in 1687.
Wrote a French visitor in that year: "The English who inhabit these countries are, as elsewhere, good and bad, but one sees more of the latter than the former, and they do not lead good lives. There are in Boston those who practice no formality of marriage except in joining hands."

Mary Chilton.
In King's Chapel Burying-ground (on Tremont Street, near S hool Street) was buried Mary Chilton, who was the first woman to come ashore at Plymouth. She afterwards became the wife of John Winslow, and died in 1679. The following lines are from a poem by George Bancroft Griffith:

" Fair beams that kiss the sparkling Bay
Rest warmest o'er her tranquil sleep.
Sweet exile! love enticed away
The first on Plymouth Rock to leap!
* * * * * *
O ye who 'round King's Chapel stray,
Forget the turmoil of the street;
Though loftier names are 'round her, lay
A wreath of flowers at Mary's feet!"

Music in the Public Schools.
The Hawes School, South Boston, has the honor of having been the first school in the city into which the study of music was introduced—Lowell Mason being the teacher—in 1838.

New England's Crisis,
a poem by Benjamin Tompson, "ye renowned poet of Boston," in 1682, contrasts the degeneracy of that period with the good old days when—

"Men had better stomachs at religion
Than I to capon, turkeycock or pigeon,
When honest sisters met to pray, not prate
About their own and not their neighbor's state."

Odd, Old Advertisement.
The following is a copy of an advertisement which appeared in the Boston *Columbian Centinel*, April 13, 1802:

A CURIOUS MACHINE has lately been advertised, which will *churn, scrape potatoes, rock a cradle* and *darn stockings.'* However curious and useful this may appear, there is *another machine* (old invention which not only performs *all* these things, but even *more—it enables us to obtain them'* This last machine is in the form of a lottery-wheel; and if any dispute its superiority over the *new* invention, let them purchase a *ticket* and try the experiment!

Oldest Charitable Society.
The oldest mutual relief organization in Boston, and probably in the country, is the "Scots' Charitable Society," which was founded in 1657. In the language of their own records, "Some Gentlemen Merchants and others of the Scots' Nation residing in Boston, New England, from a compassionate concern & affection to their indigent Countrymen in these parts, voluntarily formed themselves into a Charitable Society, Anno Domini, 1657." In referring to this Society, Edward Everett said: "It would be doing injustice to a Society of this description, though it may bear a foreign name, to regard it as an institution of foreigners." Since then there have been formed in

Boston Societies designed for the relief of the English, German, French, Italian, Irish, Belgian, Portuguese, Swiss, Scandinavian and Hebrew residents.

Old-Fogyism in Boston. The following, an editorial in the *Courier* of June 27, 1827, reads oddly enough to-day: "Alcibiades, or some other great man of antiquity, it is said, cut off his dog's tail that *quidnuncs* might not become extinct from want of excitement. Some such notion, we doubt not, moved one or two of our natural and experimental philosophers to get up the project of a railroad from Boston to Albany, — a project which every one knows, who knows the simplest rule in arithmetic, to be impracticable, but at an expense little less than the market value of the whole territory of Massachusetts; and which, if practicable, every person of common-sense knows would be as useless as a railroad from Boston to the moon." This is a specimen of the conservative spirit that has hindered progress in Boston for scores of years.

Old Inns. In the early days of the town of Boston the Inns — or Taverns — were built like those of England, and named in a similar manner. After the Declaration of Independence, however, the feeling of hatred toward the mother country was so intense that in common with many other English fashions, this form of nomenclature was abandoned. The same spirit was exhibited in changing the names of the streets, and Royal Alley became Blackstone Street, Queen Street became Court Street, King Street became State Street. Of late years, a reaction has set in, and streets and hotels are being named after the English. Witness our Royal, Victoria, Brunswick, Bristol, Berkeley and other hotels, and our Arlington, Clarendon, Dartmouth, Exeter, Gloucester, Hereford, Marlborough, Newbury and other streets. The following were some of the famous Inns of olden times: "The Green Dragon," the most noted of them all, in Union Street; the "Red Lyon Inn," on the corner of North and Richmond Streets, kept by Nicholas Upsall, a Quaker; "Black Horse Inn," on what is now Prince Street; the "Ship Tavern," or "Noah's Ark," corner of North and Clark Streets; "The Golden Candlestick;" "The Key;" "The Star Tavern;" "The Elephant Tavern;" "The Blue Anchor," "The Bunch of Grapes," etc. On old Newbury Street (now Washington Street, near West Street) "The White Horse," "The Lion" and "The Lamb Tavern." (The "Lamb Tavern" was the original of the present Adams House). There is still open in Williams Court, leading from Court Square to Washington Street, an old alehouse called "The Bell-in-Hand."

Old Names of Streets. It is interesting to trace the changes that have taken place in the street-nomenclature of Boston. What was called Adams Square in 1880 was named Dock Square in 1710, and Around the Towne Dock in 1673; Boylston Street in 1808 was Frog Lane in 1699; Devonshire Street, in 1786, was Pudding Lane in 1709 and afterwards Black Jack Alley; Exchange Street in 1816 was formerly Royal Exchange Lane; High Street, since 1798, was Cow Lane in 1707; Hollis Street, since 1732, was Broad Alley in 1721; Kilby Street, since 1769, was Mackerel Lane in 1708; Leverett Street, named 1793, was Green Lane previously; North Street, 1853, was Ann Street, Ship Street, Fish Street, etc., in portions; Park Street, 1803, was Centry (Sentry) in 1783; Williams Court was Peck's Arch; Portland Street, 1807, was Cold Lane in 1707; Prince Street, in 1793, was Black Horse Lane in 1690; Province Street, in 1834, was Governor's Alley in 1730; Salem Street was Back Street; State Street, in 1781, was King Street in 1707; Summer Street, 1703, was Seven Star Lane; Temple Place, 1830, was Turnagain Alley in 1708; Tileston Street, 1820, was Love Lane in 1700; Walnut Street, 1730, was Coventry in 1733; Washington Street, 1788, bore several names; the part of it from Dock Square to School Street was called Cornhil l—from School to Winter Street it was known as Marlborough—from Winter to Essex it was Neweberry (or Newbury)—and above Essex Street it was Orange Street. These names were all consolidated into Washington Street about 1823. Winter Street, in 1708, had been called B'ott's Lane, etc. (Boston not only had Spring, Summer and Winter Streets nearly a century ago, but it also had its Milk and Water Streets).

Old South End. In 1816 the South End of Boston was in the vicinity of Hanover Street, near its present junction with Washington Street. How the old fogies of those days would have stared at one who should have expressed the opinion that in less than a hundred years the South End would be miles away, and the extreme North End take its place. Boston still possesses its old fogies.

Old Time Bill-of-Fare. Captain Roger Clap, from Plymouth, England, who settled in Dorchester, in May, 1630, wrote to his children in England as follows: "It is not accounted a strange thing to drink Water, and to eat Samp, or Homine, without Butter or Milk. Indeed it would be a strange thing to see a piece of Roast Beef, Mutton or Veal; though it was not long before there was roast Goat. Once I had a Peck of Corn for a little Puppy-Dog. Frost-fish, Muscles and Clams are a relief to many."

Old-Time Boston Dudes. In
April, 1800, a writer in the *Centinel* describes "the Frenchified American beau" in Boston streets, with shaggy hair, spotted linen neckerchief, and a green coat. "His hat is about the size of Aunt Tabby's snuff-box, and is stuck upon the very crown of his head. In his hand he commonly carries a stick of wood, which seems to weary him very much, especially in summer."

Old-Time Conservatism.
When the idea of constructing the Old Colony Railway was first advanced, there was a public meeting held in Quincy to protest against it. One speaker stated that the opening of such a communication with Boston would affect the price of oats, and destroy the business of a stage proprietor who carried six or eight passengers to and from the city every day. Dorchester was equally opposed to the construction of the road, and the people there desired to have the tracks laid only in the outskirts of the town.

Old-Time Picture of Boston.
Count de Rochambeau was sent from France in 1780 with six thousand men to assist the United States in the War for Independence. He was accompanied by the Abbe Robin, chaplain, and a famous writer of that day, who wrote home in June, 1781, as follows: "Wind and weather brought us safe into the harbour of Boston. We discovered through the woods, on the side toward the West, a magnificent prospect of houses, built on a curved line, and extending afterwards in a semi-circle above haf a league. This was Boston. These edifices, which were lofty and regular, with spires and cupolas intermixt at proper distances, did not seem to us a modern settlement so much as an ancient city, enjoying all the embellishments and population that never fail to attend on Commerce and the Arts."

Old-Time Punishments. In
addition to the stocks and the pillory, Colonial laws required criminals to wear in public and in private, letters designating the nature of their offences. Thus drunkards wore a capital letter D; heretics the letter H; adulterers the letter A, etc., sewed upon the breasts or sleeves of their outer clothes. Hawthorne, in his "Scarlet Letter," takes one of those punished by this law for a heroine, laying the scene of his story in Boston. A dramatization of this tale was produced at the Boston Theatre, a few years since, with Jean Davenport Lander in the leading role of Hester Prynne. Hester Prynne was buried in King's Chapel Burying-ground, near the corner of Tremont and School sts.

Opening of a Railway. The
Boston *Advertiser* of May 12, 1834, contained the following advertisement:

BOSTON AND WORCESTER RAILROAD. The Passenger Cars will run daily from the Depot, near Washington Street, to Newton, at 6 and 10 o'clock, A. M., and at 3½ o'clock, P. M., and Returning, leave Newton at 7, and a quarter past 11, A. M., and a quarter before 5, P. M. Tickets for the passage, either way, may be had at the Ticket Office, No. 617 Washington st., Price 37½ cents each, and for the return passage, of the Master of the Cars, Newton.

Compare this advertisement with the time-table of trains now running between Boston and Newton.

Opening of Boston Railways.
Boston and Worcester, to Newton, May 16, 1834; to Worcester, July 4, 1835. Boston and Providence, June 11, 1835. Boston and Lowell, June 27, 1835.

Opening of the Public Garden.
The beautiful Public Garden of Boston—said to be the finest example of public flower-gardening in the country—was enclosed in May, 1863, when it first became one of the pleasure grounds of Boston.

Painter's Arms. A painter, who
came from England in 1701, opened a little shop on what is now known as Marshall Street, on the corner of Hanover Street, and, as was the custom in those days, placed in the front of his house his coat-of-arms, carved in wood. This carving is to-day to be seen in a well-preserved condition, embedded in the front wall of the building standing on this corner, Hanover and Marshall sts., and attracts the attention of antiquarians from all parts of the country. It is in close proximity to another noted land-mark, the Boston Stone—described under its proper head in this Cyclopedia—and they constitute two of the most famous historical features of even the historic old North End of Boston, which abounds in the most interesting points of interest to those who take a just pride in the early important events of our nation's progress.

Panda Pirates. The notorious
"Panda" pirates, twelve in number, were tried in October, 1834; five of them were hanged, June 9, 1835, and a sixth met the same fate, September 12, 1835.

Parade of the Ancient and Honorable Artillery, October 6, 1701.
Samuel Sewall, commander of this renowned Company (organized in 1638 and still flourishing), gave the following account of a training-day: "Very pleasant fair wether; artillery trains in

the afternoon (Sewall in command); march with the company to the Elm. Go to prayer, march down and shoot at a mark. By far the most missed, as I did for the first. Were much contented with the exercise. Led them to the trees agen; perform'd some facings and doublings. Drew them together, propounded the question about the colours; 'twas voted very freely and fully. I informed the Company I was told the Company's halberds, etc., were borrowed; I understood the leading staff was so, and therefore ask'd their acceptance of a Half-Pike, which they very kindly did. They would needs give me a volley, in token of their Respect, on this occasion. The Pike will, I suppose, stand me in fourty shillings, being headed and shod with silver. Were treated, by the Ensign, in a fair chamber." This report is from Sewall's Diary.

Patriotic Women of Old Boston.
In 1768, three hundred married women of Boston signed an agreement not to drink tea until the revenue act should be repealed. The young maidens followed, agreeing to the following: "We, the daughters of those patriots who have appeared . . . for the public interest . . . do now with pleasure engage with them in denying ourselves the drinking of foreign tea."

Paul Revere's Home.
Paul Revere's house stood on Charter Street, near the foot of Hanover Street, where Revere Place is now. It was a three-story brick house, painted light yellow, with the end to the street, the door opening upon a small green space. It was destroyed about the year 1847, giving way to the tide of "improvement" which has engulfed so many of Boston's historic old landmarks, and bids fair to continue to pursue its irresistible course.

Pen-Picture of Boston in 1654.
Edward Johnson wrote and sent to London for publication the following description of Boston in 1654: "The Center Towne and Metropolis of this Wilderness is Boston. The chief Edifice of this City-like Towne is crowded on the Sea-bankes, and wharfed out with great industry and cost; the buildings beautiful and large, some fairly set forth with Brick, Tile, Stone and Slate, and orderly placed with comly streets, whose continuall inlargement presages some sumptuous City. The wonder of this moderne age is that a few years Should bring forth such great matters by so meane a handfull. But now behold the admirable acts of Christ; at this, His people's landing, the hideous Thickets at this place were such that Wolfes and Beares nurst up their young, from the eyes of all beholders, in those very places where the streets are now full of Girles and Boys, sporting up and down, with a continued concourse of People."

Peter Faneuil,
who gave Faneuil Hall to the town of Boston, was fond of good living. In March, 1742, he wrote to one of his correspondents in London: "Send me, by the very first opportunity for this place, five pipes of your very best Madeira wine, of an amber colour, of the same sort which you sent to our good friend DeLancey, of New York. As this wine is for the use of my house, I hope you will be careful that I have the best." In another letter, he wrote: "Send me the latest, best book of the several sorts of cookery, which pray let be of the largest character, for the benefit of the maid's reading."

Picture of the Boston of a Hundred Years Ago.
From an address delivered by Rev. Dr. George E. Ellis, we take the following description of old Boston: "The homes of many of the merchant princes and high magistrates were relatively more palatial than are any in the city to-day. They stood conspicuous and large, surrounded by generous spaces, with lawns and trees, with fruit and vegetable gardens, and fields for pasture, and coach and cattle barns. There were fine equipages, with black coachmen and footmen. There were still wide unfenced spaces, and declivities and thickets, where the barberry-bush, the flag and the mullein-stalk grew undisturbed. There were many quaint old nooks and corners, taverns and inns, coffee-houses—the drinking-vessels in which were not especially adapted to that beverage—shops designated by emblems and symbols, loitering places for news and gossip, resorts of white boys and negroes for play or roguery, and some dark holes on wharf or lane. . . . There were some two thousand buildings, four being of stone, of which King's Chapel alone remains. Between Beacon and the foot of Park Street stood the Workhouse, the Poorhouse and the Bridewell,—all facing the Common. On the site of the present Park Street Church stood the Granary: opposite, a large manufactory-building used by the British for a hospital. The Jail occupied the site of the present Court-House. King and Queen Streets—now State and Court Streets—were the most compactly covered, and lined with taverns, dwellings, marts and offices of exchange. The House provided by the Province for the British Governor was opposite the Old South, standing far back, stately, commodious, with lawn and trees to Washington Street. The old State House, with a dignity which it has not now, held the Halls of the Council and the Representatives, with Royal portraits and adornings. How little is there here now which the patriots and citizens of the old days, if they came back, would recognize!"

Pirates in Provincial Times.
William Fly was hanged at Nix's Mate,

Boston Harbor, for piracy, and his body left upon the gibbet, his bones hanging and rattling in the air for a long time, as a warning to pirates. This was in May, 1726, yet the superstitious believe that the ghost of William Fly still haunts Nix's Mate.

Plays in Boston in 1714.

A letter written by Judge Samuel Sewall, March 3, 1714, contains the following: "There is a Rumor, as if some designed to have a Play acted in the Council chamber next Monday, which much surprises me, and as much as in me lies, I do forbid it. The Romans were very fond of their Plays; but I never heard they were so far set upon them as to turn their Senat House into a Play House. It cannot be a Honor to the Queen to have the Laws of Honesty and Sobriety broken in upon. Let not Christian Boston goe beyond Heathen Rome in the practice of Shamefull Vanities."

Plea for More Manufacturers.

The Boston *Gazette*, in the Spring of 1788, said: "Until we manufacture more it is absurd to celebrate the Fourth of July as the birthday of our Independence. We are still a dependent people; and what is worse, after the blood and treasure we have expended, we are actually taxed by Great Britain."

Popular Old Comic Songs.

In 1820 one of the most popular comic songs, sung in Boston (at the theatre, and at Harvard College (before the students in the college yard, by actors from Boston, was "Judy O'Callaghan;" which had the following refrain:

"Only say
That you love Barney O'Flanaghan;
Don't say nay,
Charming Judy O'Callaghan!"

Proclamation by Washington.

The following is a copy of a highly interesting old document:

By His Excellency
GEORGE WASHINGTON, ESQ.:

Captain-General and Commander-in-Chief of the Forces of the Thirteen United Colonies.

WHEREAS the Ministerial Army have abandoned the Town of Boston; and the Forces of the United Colonies, under my command, are in possession of the same;
I have therefore thought it necessary for the Preservation of Peace, Good Order and Discipline, to publish the following Orders, that no person offending therein may plead Ignorance as an Excuse for their Misconduct.

All Officers and Soldiers are hereby ordered to live in the strictest Peace and Amity with the Inhabitants; and no Inhabitant or other Person employed in his lawful business in the Town is to be molested in his Person or Property, on any pretence whatever.—If any Officer or Soldier shall presume to strike, imprison or otherwise ill-treat any of the Inhabitants, they may depend on being punished with the utmost severity—and if any Officer or Soldier shall receive any insult from any of the inhabitants, he is to seek Redress in a Legal Way, and no other.

* * * * * *

All Officers of the Continental Army are enjoined to assist the Civil Magistrates in the execution of their Duty, and to promote Peace and Good Order.—They are to prevent as much as possible, the Soldiers from frequenting Tippling-Houses.

* * * * * *

Given under my Hand at Head-Quarters in Cambridge, this Twenty-fifth Day of March, 1776

GEORGE WASHINGTON.

Protest Against Sabbatarian Laws.

In 1802 the following appeared in the *Centinel*:

"In Superstition's days, 'tis said
Hens laid two eggs on *Monday*,
Because a hen would lose her head
That laid an egg on Sunday.

Now our wise rulers and the law
Say none shall wash on Sunday;
So Boston folks must dirty go;
And wash them twice on Monday."

This was written in consequence of the law forbidding bathing on Sunday at the foot of the Common.

Punishment of Women in 1648.

In this year of our Lord in Boston, a Mrs. Oliver was publicly whipped for "reproaching the magistrates," and had a cleft stick put on her tongue for half an hour for "reproaching the elders."

Punishment for Profanity.

In June, 1631, Philip Ratcliff had his ears cut off for using profanity.

Quakers in Roxbury.

May 28, 1661, Judah Browne and Peter Pierson, Quakers, were tied to a cart's tail and whipped through the town with 10 stripes after receiving 20 stripes at Boston.

Quakers were hanged and buried on Boston Common, near the Great Elm, in 1660. Governor Endicott was bitterly opposed to religious freedom for others, although he insisted upon having it for himself. That spirit of intolerance exists to-day among certain people, but it has happily almost died out. Longfellow, in his "John Endicott," puts the following words into the Governor's mouth, but they do not agree with the extreme measures advocated by that bigoted functionary for exterminating the Quakers:

"Four already have been slain;
And others banished upon pain of death,
But they come back again to meet their doom,
Bringing the linen for their winding-sheets.
We must not go too far. In truth I shrink
From shedding of more blood. The people murmur
At our severity."

Hawthorne based his "Gentle Boy"—one of his "Twice-told Tales" on the persecution of the Quakers in Boston.

Quarrel at the Town Pump.

An Englishman, Edward Ward, in 1699, wrote home to London: "I was mightily pleased, one morning, with a contention between two boys at a pump in Boston, about who should draw water first. One jostled the other from the handle, and he would fill his bucket first, because his master said prayers and sung psalms twice a day in his family, and the other's master did not. To which the witty knave made this reply: 'Our house stands back in a court. If my master had a room next the street, as your master has, he'd pray twice to your master's once, that he would; and therefore I'll fill my pail first, marry will I!' and did accordingly." The old Town Pump, here referred to, stood in the middle of Washington Street, a few yards north of Court Street towards Cornhill.

Railway Speed in 1834.

We read in the Boston *Advertiser* of April 8, 1834, that the engine of the trial train run the day before between Boston and Newton "travelled with ease at the rate of twenty miles an hour."

Regulating the Height of Dogs.

July 1, 1728, dogs were so numerous in Boston that a law was passed forbidding any person to keep a dog "above ten inches in height."

Roxbury in 1634.

In a work called "New Englands Prospect," by William Wood,—"printed at London, at the Three Golden Lyons in Corne-hill, neere the Royall Exchange, 1634,"—Roxberry is described as "a faire and handsome countrey-towne, the inhabitants of it being all very rich. It is well-woodded and watered, having a cleare and fresh Brooke running through the Towne."

Sabbath-Breaking.

In "ye olden tyme" any form of Sabbath-breaking was looked after very carefully. Sunday began at sunset on Saturday. Shopkeepers were not allowed to keep open on Saturday evening. Witness the following copy of a proclamation issued by the town authorities:

BOSTON, June 9, 1746.

By order of His Majesty's Justices of the Peace in the town of Boston: Whereas there appears a growing negligence of duly observing and keeping the Lord's Day, the Justices in the town of Boston have agreed to Walk and observe the Behaviour of the People of said Town of Boston on said Day; and they judge it proper to give this Public Notice thereof; and all persons profaning the Lords' Day by *walking, standing in the streets*, or any other way Breaking the Laws made for the due observation of the Lord's Day, may expect the execution of the Law upon them for all disorders of this kind.

Samuel Adams.

The people of the United States can never sufficiently revere the memory of Samuel Adams. He was born in Boston, Sept. 16, 1722; graduated at Harvard College 1740; took his Master's Degree 1743; proposed a Union of the Colonies in Opposition to the Parliament of Great Britain, 1764; declared for Independence, 1768; demanded the removal of the British Troops from Boston, 1770; opposed the Landing of the Tea, 1773; signed the Declaration of Independence, 1776; died, in Boston, Oct. 2, 1803, in his 82d year; committed to the Checkley Tomb, Granary Burying-Ground. Adams has justly been termed "The Father of the American Revolution." Among the other titles bestowed upon him have been "The American Cato," "The Chief Incendiary," "Tribune of the People," "Cromwell of New England," "The Last of the Puritans," etc. Adams was born in Purchase Street. When fourteen years of age, he was admitted to Harvard, with the intention of becoming a minister, stimulated as he had been, by the preaching of Edwards and Whitefield. His father, becoming unsuccessful in business, placed him in a mercantile position. He then began to take strong interest in public affairs. In 1765 Adams was sent to the Legislature, and annually after that for ten years. He was a leader, with pen and voice. Governor Hutchinson termed him "Master of the Puppets." Governor Barnard said of Adams: "Every dip of his pen stings like a horned snake." Governor Gage offered to confer upon him such benefits as would be satisfactory, if he would withdraw his opposition to the administration, and, by changing his course, make his peace with King Henry VIII. Adams answered, "Sir, I trust I have long since made my peace with the King of Kings!" Witnessing the Battle of Lexington he said to Hancock: "What a glorious morning for America!" Neither Washington nor Jefferson were in favor of cutting loose from the mother country at this time; but Adams considered that the 19th of April had done away with British rule in the Colonies. Samuel Adams was "the organizer of the American Revolution."

Saturday Night Law.
In October, 1679, the General Court ordered that "there be a ward from sunset on Saturday night, until nine of the clock or after, consisting of one of the selectmen or constables of Boston who shall walk between the fortifications and the town's end, and, upon no pretence whatsoever, suffer any cart to pass out of the town after sunset; nor any footman or horseman without such good account of the necessity of his business as may be to their satisfaction."

Settlers of 1630.
In the New England's Memorial (1669) mention is made of several of the early English settlers of Boston 1630 as follows: "That blessed Servant of Christ, Mr. Isaac Johnson; that Reverend and Worthy man, Mr. John Wilson, eminent for Love and Zeal; and that famous Patern of Piety and Justice, Mr. John Winthrop, with divers other precious Sons of Sion, which might be compared to the most fine gold."

Servants in Boston in Olden Time.
In 1687, a French gentleman, sojourning in Boston, wrote home as follows: "You can bring with you hired Help in any vocation whatever; there is an absolute need of them to till the Land. *You may also own Negroes and Negresses*; there is not a House in Boston, however small may be its means, that has not one or two. You employ Savages to work your Fields in Consideration of One Shilling and a Half (thirty-seven cents a Day and Board. Negroes cost (*to own*) from twenty to forty Pistoles (the Pistole was then valued about ten francs, making the negroes worth from forty to eighty dollars apiece) according as they are skilful and robust. There is no Danger that they will leave you, nor hired Help likewise, for the Moment one is missing from the Towne you have only to notify the Savages (Indians) who, provided you promise them something, and describe the Runaway, he is right soon found. Labour is very dear. A man cannot be got to work for less than twenty-four Pence (fifty cents) a Day and found."

Shopkeeper Beaux in 1800.
The shopkeeper beau of nearly a hundred years ago is thus described in the *Centinel*, of Boston, of April 23, 1800: "He will spring at one leap over a counter four feet high to pick up a lady-customer's handkerchief; he makes the most handsome bow, says the most civil things, and talks surprisingly fast and sensibly about the odor of a roll of pomatum, or the vulgarity of wearing our own hairs."

Siege of Boston.
Washington began his siege of Boston March 4, 1776, taking possession of the city March 17.

Slave-Owners in Old Roxberry.
In 1739, Roxbury Boston Highlands, had numerous owners of negro slaves. In that year, some of the principal slave-owners—Thomas Baker, Nathaniel Brewer, Ebenezer Dorr, John Holbrook, Edward Ruggles, James Jarvis, Noah Perin, Jr., John Williams, Ebenezer Weld, Jonathan Seaver and Joseph Williams—sent a petition to the Town to have negro slaves "abroad in the night at unseasonable hours" punished. The Revolution brought around the abolition of slavery in Boston.

Slavery.
In 1781 it was declared that slavery no longer existed in Boston or Massachusetts.

Spinning Maidens.
One summer afternoon, in 1743, members of a society formed to encourage industry and frugality, celebrated their fourth anniversary by making a public demonstration, about three hundred young female spinsters, decently dressed, appeared on the Common at their spinning wheels. The wheels were placed regularly in three rows, and a young woman was seated at each wheel. The weavers also appeared, cleanly dressed, in garments of their own weaving. One of them worked at a loom on a stage carried on men's shoulders, attended with music. There was a large number of spectators.

Spring Lane
(running from 278 Washington Street to 101 Devonshire Street) abounds in historical associations of the deepest interest. "It recalls," says Drake, "the ancient Spring-gate, the natural fountain at which Winthrop and Johnson stooped to quench their thirst, and from which, no doubt, Madam Winthrop and Anne Hutchinson filled their flagons for domestic use. The gentlemen may have paused here for friendly chat if the rigor of the Governor's opposition to the Schismatic Anne did not forbid. The handmaid of Elder Thomas Oliver Winthrop's next neighbor, on the opposite corner of the Spring-gate fetched her pitcher—like another Rebecca—from this well; and grim Richard Brackett, the jailer, may have laid down his halberd to quaff a morning draught."

Swearing.
The penalty for swearing in 1639 was a fine of one crown, or to have a hole bored through the tongue with a hot iron.

Talleyrand visited Boston in July and August, 1794. According to William Sullivan he was of middle stature, with light hair, sallow complexion and blue eyes; his body large and protruberant in front, his lower limbs small and his feet deformed.

Tax-Assessors were first appointed, by the Court, Aug. 9, 1632.

Tea was first used in Boston in 1635.

Theatrical Riot. The Edmund Kean riot, at the old Boston Theatre, occurred in 1825.

The King's Missive. In 1657, a Quaker, Samuel Shattock, was publicly whipped for expostulating against the gagging of another Quaker. Shattock was banished, subsequently. He went to London, secured a royal order from the King to have all Quakers arrested in Boston sent to England for punishment, and returned here to inform Governor Endicott of the order of the King. All Quakers were released from jail. However, Quakers were after that whipped at the cart's tail through the streets of Boston. The Quaker poet, Whittier, has in his poem, "The King's Missive," graphically described the proceedings. We select the following stanzas from that poem:

"One brave voice rose above the din;
Upsall—gray with his length of days—
Cried, from the door of his Red Lion inn,
'Men of Boston! Give God the praise!
No more shall innocent blood call down
The bolts of wrath on your guilty town;
The freedom of worship dear to you
Is dear to all, and to all is due.

"'I see the vision of days to come,
When your beautiful City of the Bay
Shall be Christian liberty's chosen home,
And none shall his neighbor's rights gainsay;
The varying notes of worship shall blend
And as one great prayer to God ascend;
And hands of mutual charity raise
Walls of salvation and gates of praise!'

So passed the Quakers through Boston town,
Whose painful ministers sighed to see
The walls of their sheep-fold falling down,
And wolves of heresy prowling free.
But the years went on, and brought no wrong;
With milder counsels the State grew strong,
As outward Letter and inward Light
Kept the balance of truth aright."

Tom and Jerry was the name of a famous old drink in Boston and New England, having been in vogue as early as 1825. A member of a temperance society in 1830 was disciplined for drinking, and the excuse was that the intoxicated man had not been drinking anything, but had "eaten some Tom and Jerry with a spoon."

Unique Old Advertisement.
In 1805 the following was published in a paper issued in a suburb of Boston. It well illustrates the variety of goods kept in an old-time country store. (The Arch was over the bridge at the line dividing Dorchester and Milton).

EXTRA.

To be sold at the store opposite the Arch over Milton Bridge, the following articles viz:

Salt Pork and Powder, Shot & Flints
Cheese, Sugar, Rum & Peppermints
Tobacco, Raisins, Flour & Spice
Flax, Cotton, Wool and sometimes Rice
Old Holland Gin and Gingerbread
Brandy & Wine, all sorts of Thread
Segars I keep, sometimes one bunch,
Materials all for making Punch.
Biscuit and Butter, Eggs & Fishes
Molasses, Beer and Earthen Dishes
Books on such subjects as you'll find
A proper food to feast the mind.
Hard Soap & Candles, Tea & Snuff,
Tobacco pipes perhaps enough;
Shells, Chocolate & Stetson's Hoes
As good as can be (I suppose)
Straw Hats, Oak Baskets, Oxen Muzzles
A thing which many people puzzles
Knives, Forks, Spoons, Plates, Mugs,
Pitchers, Platters
A Gun with Shot wild geese bespatters
Spades, Shovels, Whetstones, Scythes & Rakes
As good as any person makes
Shirts, Frocks, Shoes, Mittens, also Hose
And many other kinds of Clothes
Shears, Scissors, Awls, Wire, Bonnet Paper
Old Violin and Cat Gut Scraper
Tubs, Buckets, Pails and Pudding Pans
Bandanna Handkerchiefs & Fans
Shagbarks and Almonds, Wooden Boxes
Steel Traps (not stout enough for Foxes
But excellent for holding Rats
When they elude the Paws of Cats)
I've more than Forty kinds of Drugs
Some good for Worms and some for Bugs
Lee's, Anderson's & Dexter Pills
Which cure at least a hundred Ills
Astringents, Laxatives, Emetics
Cathartics, Cordials, Diuretics,
Narcotics, Stimulants & Pungents
With half a dozen kinds of Unguents
Perfumes most grateful to the Nose
When mixed with Snuff or dropd on clothes
One Medicine more (not much in fame)
Prevention is its real name
An ounce of which (an author says)
Outweighs a Ton of Remedies
I've many things I shall not mention
To sell them cheap is my intention
Lay out a dollar when you come
And you shall have a glass of Rum

N. B. Since man to man is so unjust
'Tis hard to say whom I can trust
I've trusted many to my sorrow
Pay me to-day. I'll trust to-morrow
Dorchester, June 1, 1805.

Vanity in Boston in 1740.
The celebrated Whitefield had occasion to rebuke the vanity manifested by Boston mothers in 1740. He wrote: "Jewels, patches, and gay apparel are commonly worn by the female sex. I observe little boys and girls commonly dressed up in the pride of life; and the infants that were brought to baptism were wrapped in such finery that one would think that they were brought thither to be initiated into, rather than to renounce, the pomps and vanities of this wicked world. Boston, however, is remarkable for the external observation of the Sabbath."

Voting
was performed in old times by the voice, also by the raising of hands. Grains of corn were afterwards used for "yes" and beans for "no." Then came written ballots. Printed ballots were first used in 1839.

Washington's Fun at Cambridge.
According to Samuel Longfellow in his "Life of Henry Wadsworth Longfellow," Craigie House, Washington's Headquarters in Cambridge, the "Father of his Country" occasionally unbent from his characteristic dignity. The author says: "Among the traditions of the house are two stories of 'Washington's laughter.' In the first an old woman had one day been arrested in the American lines as a spy and brought before General Putnam. He thought the matter important enough to be referred to the commander-in-chief, and took the woman to headquarters. Arrived at the gate she refused to go in. Whereupon Putnam seized her, and lifting her on his back, bore her up the pathway to the door. This, Washington, looking from his window, beheld, and laughed heartily at the spectacle of 'Old Put' and his burden. At another time, the second story runs, several of the generals were at the Vassall House when word was brought that the British were making a demonstration from Boston. The officers rushed for their accoutrements, and General Greene's voice was heard calling to the barber, 'My wig! where is my wig?' 'Behind the looking-glass, general,' said Lee; and the mirror revealed that Greene's wig was already on his head. Again Washington joined in the general laugh."

Washington's Library.
A large portion of the Library once belonging to George Washington now forms a small part of the Boston Athenaeum Library, 10 B Beacon Street.

Washington,
while visiting Boston, in 1789, wrote in his diary as follows, regarding the cotton-duck manufactory: "They have twenty-eight looms at work, and fourteen girls spinning with both hands the flax being fastened to the waist. Each spinner can turn out fourteen pounds of thread per day, when they stick to it. They are the daughters of decayed families; none others are admitted."

Water.
The great celebration of the introduction of Cochituate water into Boston occurred Oct. 25, 1848.

What a Stray Pig in the Streets of Boston Brought About.
Says Winthrop: "There fell out a great business upon a very small occasion. In 1636 there was a strange sow in Boston." Several claimants for the sow caused considerable controversy, and led to the celebrated dispute between the magistrates and the deputies concerning "The Negative Voice" and finally resulted in dividing the Legislature of Massachusetts into two coordinate branches—Magistrates and Deputies—or, Senators and Representatives.

What John Josselyn Thought in 1675.
According to John Josselyn, gent., who came to Boston from London, in 1675,—publishing on his return to England at the Green Dragon, St. Paul's Churchyard, an account of his impressions:— "Many of the houses in Boston stand upon piles, close together, on each side of the street, as in London, and furnished with many fair shops. Their streets are many and large, paved with pebble-stone, and the South side adorned with gardens and orchards. The Towne is rich and very populous, much frequented by strangers; on the South there is a small but pleasant Common, where the gallants, a little before Sunset, walk with their marmalet-madams, as we do in Moorfields, till the nine a clock Bell rings them Home to their respective habitations, when presently the Constables walk their rounds to see good orders kept, and to take up lawless people."

Winthrop and the Indians.
The settlers of Boston, owing to the fact that the peninsula was so easily guarded, had but little to fear from the Indians, who were generally friendly, and desired to "trade" with the English. In March, 1631, the powerful Chicatal of came with his sannops and squaws, from Neponset, and presented Governor Winthrop with a hogshead of corn. The Governor gave the party a dinner. In April, the Indian chief returned and wanted to trade with the Governor for an English suit of clothes. But Winthrop reminded him

that it was undignified for sagamores to swap, and gave orders to his own tailor, and had the great Indian Chief put into a brand new suit of clothes of the latest London fashion from head to foot. Chicatabot was therefore the first Indian "dude" on record.

Women's Rights in 1777.

Mrs. John Adams wrote, July 31, 1777, of affairs in Boston: "There is a great scarcity of sugar and coffee—articles which the females are very loath to give up, especially whilst they consider the scarcity occasioned by the merchants having secreted a large quantity. . . . It was rumored that an eminent, wealthy, stingy merchant (who is a bachelor) had a hogshead of coffee in his store, which he refused to sell the committee under six shillings per pound. A number of females—some say a hundred—assembled with a cart and trunks, marched down to the warehouse and demanded the keys, which he refused to deliver. Upon which one of them seized him by the neck and tossed him into the cart. Upon his finding no quarter he delivered the keys, when they tipped up the cart and discharged him; then opened the warehouse, hoisted out the coffee themselves, put it into the trunks, and drove off. A large concourse of men stood amazed, silent spectators of the whole transaction!"

HISTORICAL TABLETS.

Tablets. From among the many tablets to be found in public and private places, in streets and squares, and within and without buildings, we have selected a number as being of extreme interest to the thousands of American and foreign tourists who visit the New England Metropolis.

A Tablet on the front of the Old South Meeting-House has an inscription as follows:

OLD SOUTH.
CHURCH GATHERED, 1669.
FIRST HOUSE BUILT, 1670.
This House Erected, 1729.
DESECRATED BY BRITISH TROOPS, 1775-6.

In the portico of the (new) Old South Church, 267 Boylston Street, corner of Dartmouth Street, is a Tablet bearing the following inscription:

1669.
OLD SOUTH CHURCH,
Preserved and Blessed
of God for More Than
TWO HUNDRED YEARS
WHILE WORSHIPPING ON
ITS ORIGINAL SITE
CORNER OF
WASHINGTON AND MILK STREETS
Whence it was
Removed to this Building
In 1875
AMIDST CONSTANT PROOFS OF HIS
Guidance and Loving Favour.
Qui transtulit sustinet.

At the same place is a Tablet, fastened upon which are three gravestones, two of them originally set up in the Old South Meeting-House Burying-Ground, at the corner of Washington and Milk Streets. These stones are of quaintly carved Welsh slate, bearing the following inscriptions:

HERE LYETH BURIED
E
Y BODY OF
JOSHUA SCOTTOW
AGED 83 YEARS
D   E
DEC JANUARY Y
20   169$\frac{7}{8}$

ANN QUINSEY
AGED 13 YEARS
D   RE
DEC SEP Y 3
1676

HERE LYETH
E
Y BODY OF
R
JOHN ALDEN SENIO
AGED 75 YEARS
DECEASED MARCH
170$\frac{1}{2}$

On the building numbered 17 Milk Street, may be seen a Tablet bearing the following inscription:

BIRTHPLACE OF FRANKLIN.

Upon the iron fence enclosing the dwellings numbered 29 and 30, on Beacon st., opposite the Common, and near the State House, may be read the following:

HERE STOOD THE RESIDENCE OF
JOHN HANCOCK;
A PROMINENT AND PATRIOTIC
MERCHANT OF BOSTON;
THE FIRST SIGNER OF THE
DECLARATION OF AMERICAN INDEPENDENCE;
FIRST GOVERNOR OF MASSACHUSETTS
UNDER THE STATE CONSTITUTION.
ERECTED 1737.   REMOVED 1863.

A Tablet placed on the fence around the spot where the Old Elm formerly stood, on the Common, is inscribed as follows:

THE OLD ELM.
THIS TREE HAS BEEN STANDING
HERE FOR AN UNKNOWN PERIOD.
IT IS BELIEVED TO HAVE EXISTED
BEFORE THE SETTLEMENT OF BOSTON;
BEING FULLY GROWN IN 1722;
EXHIBITED MARKS OF OLD AGE
IN 1792; AND WAS NEARLY DESTROYED BY A STORM IN 1832.
PROTECTED BY AN IRON ENCLOSURE IN 1854.
J. V. C. SMYTH, MAYOR.

To the foregoing another Tablet has been added, which reads thus:

THE OLD ELM
DESTROYED BY A GALE,
FEB. 15TH, 1876.
THIS ELM PLANTED
1876.

The inscription on the far-famed Boston Stone, Marshall Street, near Hanover, is as follows:

BOSTON STONE, 1737.

(See article on *Boston Stone*).

Early in the present century duels were fought on Castle Island, Boston Harbor, where Fort Independence now stands. A memorial stone there records that

NEAR THIS SPOT, ON THE
25TH DECR., 1817,
FELL LIEUT. ROBERT F. MASSIE,
AGED 21.
HERE HONOUR COMES, A PILGRIM GRAY
TO DECK THE TURF THAT WRAPS HIS CLAY.

Upon the front wall of Christ Church, Salem Street, a tablet was placed, Oct. 17th, 1878, having an inscription as follows:

THE SIGNAL LANTERNS
OF PAUL REVERE
DISPLAYED IN THE STEEPLE
OF THIS CHURCH,
APRIL 18, 1775,
WARNED THE COUNTRY
OF THE MARCH OF THE
BRITISH TROOPS
TO LEXINGTON AND CONCORD.

At the corner of Washington and Essex Streets is a building known as Liberty Tree block. On this spot stood, in 1776, a very large and wide-spreading elm tree, beneath the branches of which the Sons of Liberty were organized. This elm thus came to be known as the Liberty Tree. (During the Siege of Boston the British soldiers cut down the tree). On the front of the Liberty Tree Block is a large Tablet bearing a design of the memorable Liberty Tree.

On the corner of Tremont and Court Streets there stood until 1883—when it was demolished to make room for the present great building on that site—an old structure formerly known as the mansion-house where Washington lived while in Boston in 1789. A Tablet on the old building bore this inscription:

OCCUPIED BY WASHINGTON,
OCTOBER, 1789.

No Tablet has yet been placed on the new building.

In Cambridge, a short distance from Harvard square, stands a large elm tree, upon which is a Tablet inscribed as follows:

UNDER THIS TREE
WASHINGTON
FIRST TOOK COMMAND
OF THE
AMERICAN ARMY,
JULY 3, 1775.

There is a Tablet on Summer Street, marking Daniel Webster's Home.

The following is a copy of an inscription on tablet placed in Doric Hall, State House, (Beacon st., head of Park st.):

THE LEGISLATURE
OF
MASSACHUSETTS
CONSECRATE
THE NAMES OF
MAJOR JOHN BUTTRICK
AND
CAPTAIN ISAAC DAVIS,
WHOSE VALOUR AND EXAMPLE
EXCITED THEIR FELLOW-CITIZENS
TO A
SUCCESSFUL RESISTANCE
OF A SUPERIOR NUMBER
OF
BRITISH TROOPS,
AT
CONCORD BRIDGE,
THE 19TH OF APRIL,
1775;
WHICH WAS
THE BEGINNING
OF A
CONTEST IN ARMS
THAT ENDED IN
AMERICAN INDEPENDENCE.

In 1791 there was erected on Centry (Beacon) Hill a monument to replace the wooden beacon (a cut of which may be seen on the right-hand side of the cover of this work) which was blown down, Nov. 26, 1789. In the panels of the monument were inscriptions designed to commemorate leading events of the American Revolution. These panels are now to be seen on the walls of the corridor opening on the right from Doric Hall, State House, Beacon St., having been placed there Feb. 21, 1861. The inscriptions on the south and east side panels are as follows:

TO - COMMEMORATE
THAT - TRAIN - OF - EVENTS
WHICH - LED
TO - THE - AMERICAN - REVOLUTION
AND - FINALLY - SECURED
LIBERTY - AND - INDEPENDENCE
TO - THE - UNITED - STATES
THIS - COLUMN - IS - ERECTED
BY - THE -|VOLUNTARY - CONTRIBUTIONS
OF - THE - CITIZENS
OF - BOSTON.
MDCCXC.

AMERICANS
WHILE - FROM - THIS - EMINENCE
SCENES - OF - LUXURIANT - FERTILITY
OF - FLOURISHING - COMMERCE
& - THE - ABODES - OF - SOCIAL - HAPPINESS
MEET - YOUR - VIEW
FORGET - NOT - THOSE
WHO - BY - THEIR - EXERTIONS
HAVE - SECURED - TO - YOU
THESE - BLESSINGS.

The third panel commemorates the passage of the Stamp Act, 1765; repeal of same, 1766; establishment of Board of Customs, 1767; British Troops fired on the inhabitants of Boston, March 5, 1770; Tea Act passed, 1773; Tea destroyed in Boston Harbor, Dec. 16, 1773; Port of Boston shut and guarded, June 1, 1774; Provincial Congress at Concord, Oct. 11, 1774; Battle of Lexington, April 19, 1775; Battle of Bunker Hill, June 17, 1775; Washington took command of the American Army, at Cambridge, July 3, 1775; Boston evacuated by the British, March 17, 1776; Independence declared, July 4, 1776. Hancock, President.

The monument from which these panels were taken was removed Oct. 9, 1894. The gilt eagle surmounting the monument is placed above the speaker's chair in the House of Representatives, State House.

At the State House there are fac-similes of the Memorial Stones of the Washington Family in the parish church of Brington, near Althorp, Northamptonshire, England, the burial-place of the Spencers. These Stones were presented by the Right Honorable Earl Spencer to Honorable Charles Sumner, and by him given to the State of Massachusetts, Feb. 22, 1861. These Memorial Stones are of Lawrence Washington (father of John Washington, who was great-grandfather of George Washington) and of Robert (uncle to John Washington).

The famous Parting Stone (dividing stone) stands at the corner of Washington and Centre Streets in the Roxbury District. It was erected by Paul Dudley, and bears on its front the following:

THE PARTING STONE.
1774.
P. DUDLEY.

On its Northerly side:

CAMBRIDGE.
WATERTOWN.

Southerly side:

DEDHAM.
RHODE ISLAND.

On the Common by the Brewer Fountain, near Park Street, are two tablets placed near two young trees, inscribed respectively as follows:

PLANTED
BY THE
GOVERNOR
ARBOR DAY, 1886.

PLANTED
BY THE
MAYOR,
ARBOR DAY, 1886.

EVENTFUL PLAYBILLS.

A Chronologically-Arranged series of copies of playbills of the opening of old theatres in Boston, as well as present ones; bills of the performances at the first or last appearances of celebrated actors; and other old, rare or curious bills, are here collected as interesting to all lovers of the Drama.

Copy of an Old Bill. (This Boston Theatre was opened on the corner of Federal and Franklin Streets, Feb. 3, 1794).

BOSTON THEATRE.
Federal Street.

On Wednesday Evening, Sept. 28th, 1796, will be presented the Tragedy of
ROMEO & JULIET.

Romeo.................................Mr. Chalmers
Friar Lawrence.....................Mr. Jones
Capulet..............................Mr. Kenny
Montague..........................Mr. Rowson
Tybalt................................Mr. Fawcett
Benvolio...........................Mr. McKenzie
Paris................................Mr. Downie
Friar John.........................Mr. Clarke
Prince.............................Mr. Beete
Balthazar.........................Mr. Ratcliffe
Peter..............................Mr. Villiers
Apothecary......................Mr. Hamilton
Mercutio..........................Mr. Marshall
Lady Capulet....................Mrs. Rowson
Nurse..............................Mrs. Baker
Juliet..............................Mrs. Marshall
  In Act 2d, A Grand Masquerade. Act 4th, a Funeral Procession and Solemn Dirge.

After which will be performed the farce of the

APPRENTICE.

Dick, with the Original Epilogue........
..................................Mr. Chalmers
Wingate..........................Mr Kenny
Watchman........................Mr. Clarke
Simon.........By a Young Gentlemen
(Being his first appearance on any stage.)
Charlotte........................Mrs. Rowson

N. B. The Doors, till Monday, October 3d, will be opened at half-past Five o'clock, and the Curtain rise precisely at half-past Six — from the 3d of October the Doors will be opened at Five and Performances begin at Six o'clock. Tickets and places to be had every morning (Sunday excepted) at 10 o'clock, at the office of the Theatre. The entry to the Pit is through the Box passage front door.

What would the theatre-goers of the Boston of to-day say to having the curtain rise at six o'clock? About this period there were two theatres in Boston, the other, the Hay-market, having been opened on Tremont Street, corner of Boylston Street, Dec. 26, 1796. (See copy of *Opening Bill of Haymarket Theatre.*) A great rivalry existed between these establishments until the Boston Theatre was destroyed by fire, Feb. 2, 1798. It was rebuilt and reopened Oct. 29, 1798.

Opening of the Hay-Market Theatre. This Theatre stood on the corner of Tremont and Boylston Streets. The following is a copy of the opening bill: We have followed the printing *literally*.

HAY-MARKET THEATRE.
BOSTON.

On Monday Evening, December 26, 1796, will be presented
the favorite Comedy of
THE BELLE'S STRATAGEM.
(Preceding the piece an occasional Address, written and to be spoken by Mr. Powell.

Doricourt, Mr. S. Powell.
Sir George Touchwood .....Mr. Marriott
  (His first appearance in Boston).
Flutter, Mr. Powell.
Saville........................Mr. Dickinson
  (His first appearance on any stage).
Courtall, Mr. Taylor.
Villers............by a Young American
Gibson..........................Mr. Cunnington
Hardy..........................Mr. Simpson
  (From the Theatre-Royal, Bath.
   His first appearance in America).
  In Act 4. A Masquerade Scene, in which will be introduced
  A Pastoral Ballet Dance,
  Composed by Mons. Francisqui.
A Pas de Six, by Messieurs Dubois, Renaud, Rogers, Severns, Mesdames Pick and Sevens and Mrs. Gowen. A Pas de Deux, by Mons. Francisqui and Madame Val. A Pas Seul, by Mons Lege. A Pas Seul, by Mons. Francisqui. To conclude with a Dance by Mons. Lege, Mons. Francisqui and Madame Val.
  To which will be added a Grand, Historical and Tragi-Heroic Pantomine, called

MIRZOR AND LINDOR.

Interspersed with Dances, Fights, &c., under the direction of Mons. Francisqui.
Mondor, Gov. of an island in America....
..................................Mons. Val
Lindor, a French Colonel in Garrison in the island, Friend of Mondor, and secretly in love with Mirza............
................................M. Francisqui

Commander of a Spanish Privateer in love with Mirza, but not beloved by her, and likewise friend of Mondor... ....Mons. Lege
Valet de Chamber........ Mr. Cunnington
Mirza's mother, with a song....Mrs Pick
Mirza, daughter of the Governor. Mme. Val

In Act 3, the Entering and Marching of the Savages. Lindor orders a Military Evolution with the Savages, to remind the Governor of the Manner the Europeans and the Savages formerly went to War. In addition to the Above, a new Federal Overture, prepared by Mr. Van Hagen.

First and second row of Boxes 6s.; third row, 3s. 9d.; Pit, 2s.; Gallery, 1s. 6d. To begin precisely at Six o'clock.

VIVAT RESPUBLICA.

The Hay-Market Theatre was taken down in 1803.

Charlotte Cushman's Debut.

The greatest actress America has ever produced, Charlotte Cushman, made her first appearance, on any stage, in Boston nearly sixty years ago, the actual date having been Thursday, March 25, 1830. Our readers may desire to preserve a copy of the program distributed on that memorable occasion, and it is therefore presented here. Her name did not appear on the bill. She was modestly announced as "a young lady," as will be seen by reference to numbers 2, 6 and 14 on the program. She was then in her fourteenth year:

SOCIAL CONCERT.

A Vocal and Instrumental Concert

Will be given by a number of Amateurs to their friends on Thursday evening, March 25, 1830,
At the Hall, No. 1 Franklin avenue, Boston. Mr. Farmer will preside at the pianoforte.

Part I.

Overture, pianoforte, Mr. Farmer, "Caliph of Bagdad."
Song, by a young lady, "Take this Rose." Pianoforte accompaniment.
Solo, Mr. Coupa. Guitar.
Chorus, "Hunter's Chorus."
Duet, Mr. Pray and Mr. Chase. Flutes.
Song, by a young lady, "Oh, merry row the bonny bark." Pianoforte accompaniment,
Song, Mr. Coupa, "The Soldier's Adieu." Guitar accompaniment. Translation From the French.

Part II.

Pianoforte, Mr. Farmer. Variations..... ....G. Farmer
Glee, "A little farm well tilled." By Messrs. Steadman, Barry and Chase.
Rondo, Messrs. White and Coupa. Violin and guitar.
Trio, "Sweet Home"...........Kuffner

Solo, flute, Mr. Pray, "O Dolce Concer to," with variations. Pianoforte accompaniment.
Glee, "See our bark," Messrs. Steadman, Barry and Chase.
Song, by a young lady, "Farewell, My Love"......................G. Farmer
To commence at seven o'clock precisely.
A. S. CHASE...................Manager

Miss Cushman originally had no idea of going upon the dramatic stage. She had a beautiful, rich contralto voice, and was ambitious for a lyric career. Her voice partially failing her, however, she adopted the dramatic profession, with results known to the whole artistic world. Only one of those appearing at this concert is now living, "Mr. Pray" being our well-known fellow citizen, ex-Alderman John F. Pray, formerly a boot and shoe dealer on Washington Street.

Old Harvard Theatre Playbill. (Cambridge). The following copy of an old playbill possesses interest:

HARVARD THEATRE.

THE Proprietors have the pleasure to announce to the Public that this Establishment will be opened for the ensuing season under the management of the well-known abilities of Mr. Seth Sweetser. This evening,
April 28th, 1830,
will be presented *for the first time*, the new Prize Tragedy, called
SAMPSON;
or, the Fox-Hunter!
To conclude with a comic recitation, comic songs and a Farce. Box tickets, 81; pit, third tier, 50 cents; side gallery, 37½ cents; gallery, 25 cents. Printed at University Press.

Opening Program of the New Boston Museum, Nov. 2, 1846. The Boston Museum was originally located on Tremont Street, corner of Bromfield Street, (near where Horticultural Hall now stands) opening June 14, 1841. It was removed to its present site and reopened Nov. 2, 1846, with the following bill:

THE THREE CLERKS.

After which, song, by Miss Bernard. Her first appearance in the United States; Followed by the vaudeville, "Did you ever send your Wife to Brighton?" Ball-Room Fancy Dance, by Miss Adelaide Phillipps; to conclude with the Farce of
THE SECRET.

Edwin Booth's First Appearance on any Stage. Edwin Booth, America's great tragedian, now a resident of Boston, made his first appearance on any stage at the Boston Museum, on Monday evening, Sept. 10, 1849. The following is a copy of the cast of the tragedy in which he appeared:

RICHARD III,
Or, The Battle of Bosworth Field.
(By William Shakspere.)

DUKE OF GLOSTER, afterwards King.... ....MR. BOOTH
Tressel,(his first appearance on any stage) ....*Edwin T. Booth*
King Henry 6th ....Mr. Whitman
Duke of Buckingham........J. A. Smith
Duke of Norfolk................Bassett
Prince of Wales........Miss A. Phillipps
Duke of York... ....Miss Arvila
Earl of Richmond......Mr. W. H. Smith
Lord Stanley........... ....Curtis
Earl of Oxford....................Toohey
Sir William Catesby............. Muzzy
Sir Richard Ratcliffe..............Aiken
Lieutenant of Tower...........Williams
Lord Mayor.......................Warren
Sir Walter Blunt.................Howe
Tyrrell...........................Deering
Queen Elizabeth..........Miss L. Gann
Lady Anne.............. .....Mrs. Thoman
Duchess of York... ....Miss Judah
Ladies..... Miss Rees, Mrs. H. Mestayer, Misses Simpson, Thompson, Vincent, Mason, Whiting, Christie.

The Mr. Booth, who played Richard III., was Junius Brutus Booth, Sr., the father of Edwin, whose middle name is Thomas), Mr. Frank Whitman died from softening of the brain some years since; Mr. J. Alfred Smith is now at the Forrest Home, near Philadelphia; Miss Adelaide Phillipps (who played the Prince of Wales) died in Boston 1882, after fulfilling a grand operatic career; the Warren of the cast is the eminent William Warren, the greatest and most versatile comedian America has ever produced. He is now living in retirement in Boston, having made his farewell appearance on any stage at the Boston Museum, in 1881. Mr. W. H. Smith is dead, as are also Miss Louisa Gann, Mr. W. H. Curtis and Mrs. Judah. Mrs. J. R. Vincent was not then a member of the Boston Museum Company. The bill on this occasion also included the farce, "Slasher and Crasher"; Mr. Warren as *Slasher*; Mr. Thoman as *Crasher*; Mr. Curtis as Blowhard; Mr. J. A. Smith as Brown; Mrs. Judah as Dinah; Miss Adelaide Phillipps as Rosa. Among the manager's announcements were the following: Seventh Season Boston Museum; Exhibition-room open at 6½ o'clk; performance commencing at 7½ o'clk; admission to museum and entertainment, 25 cents; chi'dren under 12 years of age, 12 1-2 cents; a limited number of seats may be secured during the day at 50 cents each. Stage manager, W. H. Smith; musical director, T. Comer. Hobbs & Prescott's Washington Street line of Omnibusses leave the Museum every evening at the close of the performance. Fare 12 1-2 cents. Also, coaches for Roxbury.

An Old Minstrel Bill. The 104th performance of Ordway's Æolian Vocalists was given at Harmony Hall (corner of Washington and Summer sts., over Jones, Ball & Poor's), April 5, 1854 (John P. Ordway, manager and director), with the following

PROGRAMME.
PART I — As Citizens.
1. Blow On....Ball, Ordway, White and Howe.
2. Bark before the Gale.....Ball, White and Howe.
3. White Squall....Geo. Warren White
4. The Spirit of Love...Stephen B. Ball
Descriptive Piece—(Comic).
Miss Jemima Twist, or the Old Maid of 45, in Character........Marshall S. Pike.
Solo—Pianoforte........John P. Ordway

Intermission of Five Minutes,
For Change of Costume.

PART II—As Northern Darkies.
1. Introductory Overture....Full Band
2. Dinah's Wedding Day (from Leonora) ....Company
3. Sweet Nellie Brown........S. B. Ball
4. Way Down in Cairo.....G. W. White
5. What shall dis Darky Do.... ....Jerry Bryant
6. Grand Post-Horn Quick Step....... ....Full Band

PART THIRD.
Gems from Massaniello, Bohemian Girl, Sonnambula and Lucia di Lammermoor.
Cornet-a-Piston Solo........P. S. Gilmore

PART IV--As Southern Darkies.
1. Overture..................Full Band
2. Phantom Chorus (Sonnambula)..... ....Company
3. Dandy Broadway Swell...F. B. Howe
4. Clem Brown.............M. S. Pike
5. Nelly Bly...............G. W. White
6. Bone Solo............Jerry Bryant
7. Accordeon Solo........C. A. Bryant
8. Banjo Solo............Jerry Bryant
9. Banjo Duet-Dutch-White and Bryant
10. Lucinda Snow (Dance....M. S. Pike
11. Breakdown Hornpipe..Jerry Bryant

Of this Company J. P. Ordway, Jerry Bryant, S. B. Ball and G. W. White are dead. The latter died March, 1886, near Boston. P. S. Gilmore is now the famous band-master, to whom Boston has never ceased to be grateful for his efforts in improving band music here, as well as for his enterprise in organizing the two famous Jubilees. Ordways Æolians opened later in the old Province House building, Washington Street (1852), and were succeeded by Morris Brothers, Pell and Huntley's Minstrels.

Opening of the New National Theatre. This theatre was located upon the corner of Portland and Traverse Streets, and replaced what was known as the old National Theatre, which was opened Aug. 15, 1836, and destroyed by fire April 22, 1852. (Previous to the old National there stood on the same site the Warren Theatre — named in honor of General Joseph Warren — opened July 3, 1832, by William Pelby). The *new* National Theatre was opened on Monday evening, November 1, 1852, by Joseph Leonard. The program comprised George Colman the Younger's

THE HEIR AT LAW.

Dr. Pangloss............Douglas Stewart
(His first appearance in America).
Daniel Dowlas............Wm. H. Curtis
Dick.......................Mr. Prior
Kenrick..................S. D. Johnson
Lady Duberly..........Mrs. Archbold
Cicely..................Mrs. W. H. Smith
(Other characters by the company) and the Farce of

JOHN DOBBS,

the latter being played by Cornelia Jefferson, Bertha Lewis, Douglas Stewart, W. H. Curtis, S. D. Johnson and V. Hays. Previous to the performance of the comedy, W. M. Leman read an original address written by W. O. Eaton. (The "Douglas Stewart" of the bill was the *nom de theatre* of Edward A. Sothern, who, on this occasion made his first appearance in America, and who later became famous as the impersonator of *Lord Dundreary*. His performance of Dr. Pangloss was a disappointment). John Holloway was musical director; S. Lake, ballet-master. Prices were as follows: Dress circle and parquette, 50 cents; second or family circle, 25 cents; third circle or gallery, 25 cents; private boxes, single ticket $1. Doors were opened at 6.30, the curtain rising at 7 o'clock. Canton Street, Dover Street, Cambridge, Roxbury, Charlestown and South Boston omnibusses were run at the close of the performance, and a train for old Cambridge left at 11.15 every evening except Saturday.

Opening of the Present Boston Theatre. On Monday evening, September 11, 1854, the magnificent Boston Theatre was first opened to the public, under the management of Thomas Barry. It is in most respects to-day what it was then, the finest theatre on this continent. There may be some few others that nearly approach it in size of auditorium, but as respects grandeur, breadth and depth of stage, height of proscenium, acoustic effects, and general resources, as well as roomy corridors and anterooms, no other dramatic establishment in the country rivals it. This is the testimony of all the great foreign stars who make tours in America. On the occasion of its opening the following bill was presented, after National airs and Rossini's overture to William Tell had been performed by Thomas Comer's orchestra, and a prize address had been delivered by John Gilbert (written by T. W. Parsons):

THE RIVALS.

By Richard Brinsley Sheridan.
Sir Anthony Absolute......John Gilbert
Captain Absolute.....George Pauncefort
(From Theatre Royal, Dublin, 1st app. in America).
Sir Lucius O'Trigger......Thomas Comer
Falkland..................H. F. Daly
Acres......................John Wood
(From Theatre Royal, Manchester, 1st app. in America).
David..................Moses W. Fiske
Fag...................N. T. Davenport
Coachman..................S. D. Johnson
Lydia Languish....Julia Bennett Barrow
(From Theatre Royal, London).
Julia....................Mrs. W. H. Smith
Mrs. Malaprop........Mrs John Gilbert
Lucy..................Mrs. M. W. Fiske

LOAN OF A LOVER.

Captain Amersfort............W. Cowell
Peter Spyk..................John Wood
Swyzel....................G. W. Johnson
Delve.....................Mr. Holmes
Gertrude................Mrs. John Wood
Ernestine............Miss Emma Taylor

Other members of the company were Miss Adelaide Biddles (now Mrs. Chas. Calvert), Miss Clara Biddles (Mrs. Thomas Barry), Mrs. Hudson Kirby, James Bennett, J. B. Howe, T. E. Morris, N. C. Forrester and John H. Selwyn. The architects were Jonathan Preston, E. C. and J. E. Cabot. The theatre was built by a stock company, including many prominent citizens. Mr. Barry continued as manager for five years. In 1860-1 Bernard Ullman became manager, and gave the theatre the name of the Academy of Music. (*See Boston Theatre in Histories of the Theatres*).

First Night of the Continental Theatre. Messrs. Morris Brothers, Pell & Trowbridge, managers of the Minstrel Hall on Washington Street, opposite the head of Milk Street (in the old Province House), where they had been successful for about ten years in providing entertainments, became ambitious to become managers of the legitimate drama, and built on Washington Street, corner of Harvard Street, the Continental Theatre. (The site was previously occupied by the Apollo Garden, and the Continental Clothing House now stands on the spot.) The theatre opened Monday evening, Jan. 1, 1866, with the following bill:

MONEY!

Alfred Evelyn	R. S. Meldrum
Sir John Vesey	Wm. J. LeMoyne
Lord Glossmore	T. M. Hunter
Sir Frederick Blount	W. H. Otis Stout
	J. W. Delano
Graves	Frank Hardenburgh
Capt. Dudley Smooth	
	James Dickson (Wyman)
Sharp	J. E. Adams
Old Member	George F. Ketchum
Clara Douglas	Mrs. D. R. Allen
Lady Franklin	Mrs. J. H. Rogers
Georgina	Miss Susan Floc

THE ROUGH DIAMOND.

Margery	Mrs. James Dickson (Wyman)
Lady Plato	Mrs. T. M. Hunter
Marian	Miss Seabrook
Sir William Evergreen	D. R. Allen
Lord Plato	J. W. Delano
Capt. Blenheim	J. E. Adams
Cousin Joe	Frank Hardenburgh
John	L. Kelly

Napier Lothian was the musical director, his orchestra including Frederick Ford, A. Suck, Henry C. Brown, R. Goering, A. Hamann and C. Higgins. J. L. Saphore was stage manager, Orin C. Richards, scenic artist, and L. A. Zwisler, treasurer. The theatre was closed in 1872, and soon after converted to business uses. The causes attributed as potent in the want of success of this theatre were numerous, the chief reasons entertained by many being that it was "too far up town;" others thought it was erected in so short a period of time—three months and a half—that it could not be strongly constructed. We are inclined to believe that poor management was the principal cause of its failure.

Opening Night of Selwyn's Theatre.

Selwyn's Theatre, which stood on the site of the present Globe Theatre, was opened on Monday evening, Oct. 28, 1867, when the following bill was performed:

The performance will be inaugurated by an Overture, with Chorus, composed expressly for the occasion by Mr. CHARLES KOPPITZ on the following Ode written by DEXTER SMITH, entitled:

OUR MOTTO.

We cu'l the minds' immortal gems
Which sparkle o'er each land and age
And, crowned with Art's enchanting hues,
We set them on our magic stage;
Within our charmed mirror gaze
And judge if the reflection's true;
As we shall well perform our part
We hope for cheering smiles from you.

National airs by Mr. Charles Koppitz's Orchestra (composed of George Loesch, Henry Suck, R. Eltz, Theo. Verron, Chas. Verron, H. Kebehahn, F. Schlimper, A. L. DeRibas, M. Arbuckle, Joseph Wrba, P. Kalkmann, Paul Eltz, L. Murphy, W. Regestein, W. Saul, H. Simpson). After which, for the first time in Boston, a new Comedy from the French of Victorien Sardou's "La Famille Benoiton," entitled

THE FAST FAMILY.

Monsieur Didier	Frederic Robinson
Monsieur Benoiton	G. H. Griffiths
M. Le Vicomte de Champrose	H. F. Daly
Prudent Formichel	Stuart Robson
Monsieur Formichel	H. Pearson
Francois	H. S. Murdoch
Polydore Benoiton	Mary Cary
Fanfan Benoiton	Ella Chapman
Clotilde	Mrs. F. S. Chanfrau
Blanche	Caroline Carson
Rose	Louise Anderson
Adolphine	Mrs. G. H. Griffiths
Josephine	Miss F. Skerrett

Other members of the company included Kitty Blanchard, now Mrs. McKee Rankin, Mrs. M. Wilkins, Amalie Harris, G. K. Fortescue, Harry Josephs, Geo. F. Ketchum and Chas. H. Steadman. (The death of Harry Murdoch of the foregoing cast occurred at the burning of Brooklyn Theatre, Dec. 6, 1876, 300 lives having been lost). Selwyn's Theatre was built by Messrs. Arthur Cheney and Dexter H. Follett. The name was changed to that of the Globe Theatre, Sept. 12, 1870, Charles Fechter assuming the management. It was burned May 30, 1873. Rebuilt, and the present Globe Theatre reopened Dec. 3, 1874. D. W. Waller, Manager. Leased and opened by John Stetson, Sept. 3, 1877.

Edwin Forrest's Last Appearance on any Stage.

On Tuesday evening, April 2, 1872, the great tragedian, Edwin Forrest, played for the last time on any stage at the Globe Theatre, in this city. The following is a copy of the bill on that occasion:

RICHELIEU.

Cardinal Richelieu	Edwin Forrest
Chevalier de Mauprat	W. E. Sheridan
Baradas	H. F. McManus
Gaston, Duc D'Orleans	W. C. Pope
Sieur de Beringhen	Colin Stuart
Joseph	F. F. Mackay
Huguet	J. W. Jennings
Francis	Willie Seymour
Governor of Bastile	E. B. Holmes
Clermont	J. H. Howland
Captain of Guard	E. Stuart
Goaler	G. Sherman
1st Secretary	H. Meredith
2d Secretary	D. S. Harkins
3d Secretary	W. F. Owen
Page	Miss Lizzie Hunt
Julie de Mortimer	Mrs. Thomas Barry
Marian de Lorme	Mrs. T. M. Hunter

(The support of Mr. Forrest during this engagement, which was cut short by the illness of the star, was made up from the stock company regularly engaged at the Globe Theatre for the season of 1871-2. In addition to the artists mentioned in this cast, the company included Miss Josephine Orton (Mrs. B. E. Woolf), Miss Amalie Harris, Miss Adelaide Hind, Miss Ada Gilman, Miss Amy Ames, George C. Boniface, John T. Raymond, J. B. Fuller, E. B. Holmes, James G Peakes (now in opera), and Wm. R. Floyd who was manager, Arthur Cheney being proprietor. Charles Koppitz was musical director. Martin Drake was ticket-agent). It was Mr. Forrest's intention to play *Virginius*, in Sheridan Knowles' tragedy of that name, on Wednesday evening; but on the morning of that day a severe cold which he had taken developed into pneumonia, and his physician forbade him to play. On Nov. 30, of the same year, Mr. Forrest gave a reading at Tremont Temple in this city, which was his last public appearance in any capacity. He died, in Philadelphia, Dec. 12, 1872. During his later years he suffered greatly from the gout.

Charlotte Cushman's Farewell.
The last appearance on any stage of Charlotte Cushman — the greatest actress America has ever produced — took place at the Globe Theatre on the evening of Saturday, May 15, 1875. The following was the bill on that important occasion:

MACBETH.
Duncan..................J. C. Dwnn
Malcolm..................Lin Harris
Donaldbain..............Miss Wilkes
Macbeth.................D. W. Waller
Banquo..................C. F. Fyffe
Macduff.................G. B. Waldron
Lenox...................R. B. Darcie
Rosse...................Stuart Clarke
Fleance................Miss Portia Albee
Siward..................S. Howard
Seyton..................J. P. Denel
Wounded Officer.........J. Sands
1st Apparition.........Miss Lizzie Queen
2d Apparition.........Miss Addie Vankenish
3d Apparition...........Miss Pelby
1st Officer............George Connor
2d Officer..............John Taylor
1st Murderer............J. Pitman
2d Murderer............T. E. Francis
Physician..............Charles Pierson
1st Witch...............E. Coleman
2d Witch...............Miss Annie Hayes
3d Witch...............J. H. Connor
Lady Macbeth..Miss Charlotte Cushman
Gentlewoman.............Miss Athena

At the close of the performance of the tragedy Miss Cushman was presented with a Testimonial by a number of her friends; the presentation address being delivered by Mr. Curtis Guild. Mr. Arthur Cheney was the proprietor and manager of the theatre; Mr. D. Waller, stage manager. The executive staff comprised Mr. James Mulligan, treasurer;

Mr. B. F. Lowell, business agent; Mr. F. F. Ford, musical director; Messrs. Geo. Heister, George W. Dayton and Joseph Schell, scenic artists; Mr. John D. Lundy, machinist; Mr. John G. Williams, appointments; Mr. George Sevey, gas engineer; Mr. Martin Drake, ticket agent.

Pinafore's First American Performance.
Gilbert and Sullivan's operetta, "Pinafore," originally produced at the Savoy Theatre, London, was first brought out in America at the Boston Museum, Monday evening, Nov. 25, 1878, where it had a run of 66 performances before it was played before any other American public. The original American distribution of characters was as follows:

PINAFORE.
Sir Joseph Porter, K. C. B...............
.........................George. W. Wilson
Captain Corcoran.........James H. Jones
Ralph Rackstraw...........Rose Temple
Dick Deadeye.............Benj. R. Graham
Bill Bobstay............Joseph S. Haworth
Bob Beckett.............William Morris
Tom Tucker..............Little Gertrude
Tom Bowline.............W. Melbourne
Josephine...........Miss Marie Wainwright
Little Buttercup......Miss Lizzie Harold
Hebe..................Miss Sadie Martinot
Musical director, John J. Braham, (now of the Bijou Theatre). Miss Rose Temple was Mrs. James H. Jones: Miss Marie Wainwright is now Mrs. Louis James; Miss Lizzie Harold is now Mrs. William J. Comley; "Little Gertrude" is Miss Calef. Previous to Mr. R. M. Field's decision to bring out this operetta, several other managers had declined to take the venture, considering the work "too English" to ever become successful in this country. How well their judgment has been verified is illustrated by the record of its performances in America. Since Mr. Field took the initiative step in introducing this class of operas to our public, not only "Pinafore," but "Patience," "Iolanthe" and "The Mikado", have had long and prosperous seasons here, "Iolanthe" reaching a run of 150 performances at the Bijou Theatre, and "The Mikado" making a record of 161 consecutive representations at the Hollis Street Theatre.

Opening Bill of the Park Theatre.
The Park Theatre was opened to the public for the first time on the evening of Monday, April 14, 1879, with the following program:
LA CIGALE.
La Cigale..................Lotta
Marignan...............J. J. Sullivan
Michu....................F. Bennett
Count de Hoppe..........W. H. Wallis
Edgar............Clement D. Bainbridge
Carcassonne............Edward Marble

Bi Bi	H. B. Bradley
Filoche	Frederick Percy
Donald	P. A. Anderson
Turlot	J. P. Cooke
Legs	Master Cooke
Servant	Mr. Parker
Countess de Latour	Mrs. Charles Poole
Adele	Agnes Proctor
No. 6	Miss Cameron
No. 7	Miss Doyle

The executive staff of the Theatre was as follows: Henry E. Abbey, lessee and manager; W. W. Tillottson, business manager; Francis G. Harding, treasurer; E. R. Byram, advertising agent; Edward N. Catlin, musical director; W. R. Holmes, chief usher; J. F. Villa, doorkeeper; J. S. Schell, scenic artist; J. D. Lundy, master machinist; J. H. Marshall, property maker; Thomas Hughes, gas engineer. Mr. John B. Schoeffel became a partner of Mr. Abbey in the management of this Theatre, March 8, 1880. Messrs. Abbey & Schoeffel are the present managers. Miss Lotta is the owner of the Theatre.

The First Night Bill of the Windsor Theatre.

Under the name of The Novelty Theatre, the present Windsor Theatre was opened to the public on Monday evening, Dec. 15, 1879. The following is a copy of the opening bill:

HOME.

Alfred Dorrison	Sir Randal Roberts
Capt. Montralfe	J. W. Lanergan
Mr. Dorrison	J. H. Howland
Bertie Thompson	W. C. Cowper
Mrs. Pinchbeck	Miss Emmie Wilmot
Dora Thornbough	Miss Lillie Ashby
Lucy Dorrison	Miss Amy Ames

Mr. F. H. Butler was the manager. Mr. John H. Woods was musical director; Mr. M. M. Whelan, business agent; Mr. Wm. Ackerman, treasurer; Mr. David Richards, scenic artist; Messrs. Curtis & Weld, costumers. In his announcement Manager Butler said: "Boston is rapidly extending its territorial limits, and the march of business is constantly 'up town;' in reality the Novelty Theatre is the central theatre of Boston, and the management intend to make it a convenience to the public as well as an agreeable resort for their patrons in South Boston and Boston Highlands, who, by the various horse-car lines, can easily reach the theatre door and at the conclusion of the performance take the same cars direct for their homes." The Windsor has been almost constantly open regularly every season since that time. Manager Butler did not long continue its manager. Mr. Charles H. Thayer was at one time its manager, and his control of the house was signalized by an extremely creditable production of "Billee Taylor." The scenery was especially realistic and beautiful.

William Warren's Fiftieth Anniversary.

The celebration of the 50th anniversary of the adoption of the profession of the stage by William Warren—the greatest and most versatile comedian America has ever produced—occurred at the Boston Museum on Saturday afternoon and evening, Oct. 28, 1882. "The Heir-at-Law" was given in the afternoon and "The School for Scandal" in the evening, cast to the full strength of the company engaged for the 42d regular season of this theatre. We give the cast—as a matter of record—of the

SCHOOL FOR SCANDAL.

Sir Peter Teazle	William Warren
Charles Surface	Charles Barron
Joseph Surface	George R. Parks
Sir Oliver Surface	Alfred Hudson
Sir Benjamin Backbite	J. B. Mason
Crabtree	George W. Wilson
Moses	William Seymour
Careless (with song)	Geo. C. Boniface, jr.
Rowley	James Barrows
Trip	James Nolan
Snake	Fred. P. Ham
Sir Harry Bumper	J. S. Maffitt, jr.
Sir Toby	J. R. Pitman
Sir William	Charles A. Warde
Servants {	George H. Cohill
	A. R. Whytal
Lady Teazle	Miss Annie Clarke
Mrs. Candour	Mrs. J. R. Vincent
Maria	Miss Norah Bartlett
Lady Sneerwell	Miss Kate Ryan
Lady Jane Modish	Miss Miriam O'Leary
Lady Betty Curricle	
	Miss Gertie Blanchard
Lady Dundizzy	Miss Mary Sears
Lady Frizzle	Miss Mary Russell

Mr. R. M. Field, manager; Mr. William Seymour, stage manager; Mr. J. R. Pitman, prompter; Mr. George Purdy, musical director; Messrs. C. B. Whittemore and B. R. Ambrose, box-office attaches. William Warren's first appearance in Boston was made at the Howard Athenæum, Oct. 5, 1846, as *Sir Lucius O'Trigger* in "The Rivals," his first appearance at the Boston Museum, Aug. 23, 1847, as *Billy Lackaday* in "Sweethearts and Wives," and as *Gregory Grizzle* in "My Young Wife and Old Umbrella." With the exception of one season, when he made a tour of the country under the direction of Manager Henry C. Jarrett, Mr. Warren has been a member of the regular Museum company. In commemorating his 50th anniversary of his going upon the stage, *his 35th season at the Boston Museum* was also celebrated on this occasion. At the end of the regular season of 1882-3, Mr. Warren appeared for the last time upon any stage, —reassuming his famous impersonation of *Eccles* in "Caste." Mr. Warren has played 577 different characters at the Boston Museum, which is believed to be a larger number than has been performed by any other American actor.

Bijou Theatre Opening. (1882).

Washington Street. The present theatre known as the Bijou succeeded on the same site the Gaiety Theatre (See *Gaiety Theatre*), which was opened in the Melodeon Building (See *Melodeon*), which was built on the site of the Eagle Theatre (See *Eagle Theatre*). The Bijou Theatre was constructed for the Boston Bijou Theatre Company, Thomas N. Hastings, President; Edward N. Hastings, treasurer; George H. Tyler, general manager. The opening of the theatre occurred on Monday evening, Dec. 11, 1882, with the following bill:

The entertainment will commence with the National airs, Bijou Orchestra. Opening address, written expressly for the occasion, by Wm. T. W. Ball, delivered by Geo. W. Blish. To be followed with the great Comic Opera, by Gilbert and Sullivan, under the management of Ed. E. Rice, and by special permission of R. D'Oyly Carte. Chas. Harris, stage manager, from the London theatres, wil superintend the first presentation in this city of

IOLANTHE;
Or, the Peer and the Peri.

The Lord Chancellor.Mr. Henry E. Dixey
Strephon................Sig. Brocolini
The Earl of Tolloller.Mr.W. H. Fessenden
The Earl of Mt. Ararat Mr. Edw. Temple
Private Willis........Mr. G. Kammerlee
The Train Bearer.....Mr. James H. Finn
Iolanthe................Miss Clara Poole
Phyllis............Miss Janet Edmondson
The Fairy Queen....Miss Mary A. Sanger
Celia................Miss Annie Calloway
Lelia................Miss Hattie Delaro
Fleta................Miss Sylvia Gerrish

On this occasion the Edison Incandescent Light was for the first time employed to illuminate a theatre auditorium in Boston. "Iolanthe," first given in this city on the opening of this theatre, was performed for 150 consecutive times, and was succeeded by "Pounce & Co.," (comic opera, libretto and score by B. E. Woolf) and given for 50 consecutive representations, these two operas filling out the first regular season of this theatre.

Opening of the Hollis-Street Theatre.

The opening of the beautiful Hollis-Street Theatre, built mostly within the walls of the old Hollis Street Church (which had been abandoned by the congregation worshipping there, for the same reason that the Old South, Brattle Street, Baldwin Place, and other churches had been deserted, namely, that the members of their congregations had left their former residences near those places of worship, owing to the steady encroachment of business). The Hollis Street Theatre was opened on the evening of Monday, November, 9, 1885. After the reading of a dedicatory ode by its author, Nathaniel Childs, the following bill was presented:

THE MIKADO.
Mikado of Japan.......Arthur Wilkinson
Nanki-Poo................S. Cadwallader
Ko-Ko....................John Howson
Poo-Bah..................Sig. Brocolini
Pish-Tush.................George Olmi
Yum-Yum........ .... Miss Laura Clement
Pitti-Sing............. Miss Hattie Delaro
Peep-Bo.........Miss Perle Dudley
Katisha..................Miss Rosa Cooke

The operetta, played in Boston for the first time on this occasion, was given 161 consecutive performances. The cast was changed in some of its characters several times. Miss Louise Montague replaced Miss Clement as *Yum-Yum* for a few nights, and was succeeded by Miss Ida Mülle. Mr. Howson had several successors, Richard Mansfield being the principal. Miss Cooke relinquished Katisha, and Mrs. Flora E. Barry assumed the part. Messrs. Cadwallader, Brocolini and Olmi played throughout the run. John J. Braham was the musical director; John A. Thompson, scenic artist; William Dixon, stage-manager; Frank G. Harding, treasurer; Edward C. Bellows, ticket agent. Isaac B. Rich, proprietor and manager; Charles J. Rich, assistant manager. The "Mikado" was succeeded by "Nanon," March 29, 1886.

Joint Appearance of Booth and Salvini.

On the evening of May 10, 1886, the Boston Theatre was crowded to repletion to witness Edwin Booth and Tommaso Salvini as *Iago* and *Othello*, respectively, in Shakspeare's tragedy. The cast was as follows:

OTHELLO.
Othello.............Sig. Tommaso Salvini
Iago....................Mr. Edwin Booth
Emilia..................Mrs. D. P Bowers
Desdemona...... Miss Marie Wainwright
Brabantio............ Mr. C. W. Couldock
The Doge of Venice......Mr. Barton Hill
Cassio............ Mr. Alexander Salvini
Montano.................Mr. John A. Lane
Roderigo.........Mr. George W. Wilson
Lodovico.................Mr. James Willis
Gratiano................Mr. Alfred Hearn
Paulo................Mr. E. E. Delamater
A Herald................Mr. Stuart Clarke
A Messenger............ Mr. Royal Roche

The same bill was repeated May 12,-15; and 14, "Hamlet" was given, with Mr. Booth as *Hamlet* and Sig Salvini as the *Ghost*, Mrs. Bowers as *Gertrude*, Miss Wainwright as *Ophelia* and Miss Rachel Noah as the *Player Queen*. These performances were under the management of Mr. Charles H. Thayer, and were brilliantly successful.

BOSTON DATA.

Some of the important events in the history of Boston are here recorded in a convenient form for reference:

Ante-Colonial Period.
1614..Captain John Smith explored Boston Harbor.
1621..Miles Standish visited the peninsula
1625..Wm. Blaxton arrived from England, and was the first white man to settle.

Colonial Period.
1628. John Endicott first Governor of the Colony.
1630........................ Boston founded
1630..John Winthrop arrived, bringing the first Charter.
1630 .... Sir Richard Saltonstall came
1630.. ....First General Court
1631.. Clams and acorns the principal food
1631................. ......John Eliot came
1633...................John Cotton arrived
1634.................... First free school
1634..........Wearing gold-lace forbidden
1634..Boston Common bought of Wm. Blaxton.
1635..........Rev. Richard Mather arrived
1635............Boston Latin School founded
1635..................Sir Henry Vane came
1636........Anne Hutchinson controversy
1636....................Strangers watched
1636....................Vane made governor
1637.....First lawyer came from England
1638...............Harvard University founded
1638..Ancient and Honorable Artillery Company formed.
1638............Harvard had nine students
1638............ East Boston Ferry opened
1639..................First pillory set up
1639............Rev. Increase Mather born
1639.................Stocks first used
1639 .... First post-office
1639... ....Bay Psalm-book printed
1643 ....Union of N. E. Colonies
1643 ....Indian sachems surrendered
1644 ....General Court divided
1646 ....Eliot preached to Indians
1647..................Selectmen chosen
1648....................Shoemakers licensed
1649................Gov. Winthrop died
1652..............Water introduced
1652... ....First reservoir
1652.............Natick an Indian town
1656......... .... .College for Indians
1657....Scots' Charitable Society founded
1654..............First Town House
1659..Quakers hanged on Boston Common
1663.................Indian Bible printed
1675.................King Philip's War
1675................Long hair forbidden
1677 .... First dry dock
1677.............. Sagamore Philip slain
1686..First bank in Boston; the first in the United States.
1692..Sir William Phipps arrived, with second charter.

Provincial Period.
1700..............Queen Anne proclaimed
1706.............Benjamin Franklin born
1711..... Mails to New York once a week
1711............Indian scalps exhibited
1714................. George I. proclaimed
1722................First map published
1728.........Duels fought on the Common
1743........................Peter Faneuil died
1748..............Old State House built
1756.............Boston Common enclosed
1760.............. George III. proclaimed
1762................Paddock elms set out
1770....................Boston Massacre
1773...............Boston Tea Party
1775.......... Battle of Bunker Hill
1775....................Siege of Boston
1776.........Washington entered Boston
1776 ....British evacuation of the city

Declaration of Independence.
1783......Peace with England proclaimed
1784.......Thomas Jefferson visited the city
1789..... Washington last visited Boston
1791....Mass. Historical Society founded
1793..............John Hancock died
1795.............State House dedicated
1800.............Navy Yard established
1800..Vaccination introduced in Boston; first time in America.
1804............Boston Athenæum found'd
1804.............South Boston annexed
1804.....Beacon Hill monument removed
1805........Exportation of ice begun
1807............Columbian Museum opened
1810............Boylston market opened
1812............Daily Advertiser published
1815............Gaslight first exhibited
1816........James Monroe visited Boston
1820.............Milldam constructed
1822.............Boston became a city
1822......Police department organized
1826........Eye and Ear Infirmary opened
1826........ .Quincy Market established
1826 ....United States Hotel opened
1827........Franklin Monument unveiled
1828...Am. (Boston) Peace Society organized.
1828........Washington Statue unveiled
1828........Harvard Monument erected
1829........First gas-light, Dock Square
1829.......Horticultural Society founded
1829 ....Temple Club organized
1829................Tremont House built
1830.................East Boston settled
1830..........Daily Transcript established
1831......Mount Auburn Cemetery opened
1831..............Daily Post established
1833.....Andrew Jackson visited Boston
1834................Farm School founded
1834.............Ice exported to Calcutta
1834..........Davy Crockett visited Boston
1835.............American House opened
1837.....Charitable Irish Society founded
1838..............Nathaniel Bowditch died
1838..... Boston Weekly Pilot established
1839..............Lowell Institute founded

1839—1881

1839............First express established
1840....First Liverpool steamship service
1840................Envelopes first used
1842..................Dickens first came
1843...Fitchburg Railway opened (to Waltham).
1843....Bunker Hill Monument dedicated
1843......President Tyler visited Boston
1843..............Gen. Winfield Scott came
1843...............J. B. Gough's first lecture
1845...........Howard Athenæum opened
1845...........Morse invented telegraph
1845........Historic-Genealogical Society founded.
1845...........Old Colony Railway opened
1845..............Suffolk Club organized
1845...............Young's Hotel opened
1845...........Daily Traveller established
1846..Ether administered as an anæsthetic for the first time anywhere, at Massachusetts General Hospital.
1846..................First telegraph line
1846...............Daily Herald established
1847...............Custom House erected
1847........President Polk visited Boston
1847................Revere House opened
1848........Warren Museum established
1848.........Cochituate water introduced
1849.........Beacon Hill reservoir built
1849.....................Parkman murder
1850................John W. Webster hanged
1851...............Minot's Ledge destroyed
1852...............Kossuth visited Boston
1852................Fire alarm established
1852..............Daniel Webster's funeral
1852........Boston Music Hall dedicated
1852..............Somerset Club organized
1853..............Caledonian Club founded
1854................Public Library opened
1854..................Boston Theatre built
1854..................Anthony Burns riot
1854............Boston Art Club founded
1855...............Parker House opened
1856............Franklin Statue erected
1856.................Horse-cars first ran
1857..Am. Society of Hibernians founded
1857........Atlantic Monthly established
1857............Back Bay filling-in began
1857..........Washingtonian Home opened
1859...............Public Garden laid out
1859............Webster Statue dedicated
1860...............Boston College founded
1860......Prince of Wales visited Boston
1861..........Great Civil War excitement
1862...................Drafting begun
1863.............Hancock House removed
1863....................Draft riot
1863...................Union Club formed
1864...............City Hospital opened
1864..........Gold brings 1.94 premium
1864............Horticultural Hall built
1865..............Edward Everett died
1865..............Carney Hospital opened
1865................City Hall dedicated
1865.........North End Mission founded
1865.............Garroting excitement
1865.......Murder of the Joyce children
1865........Horace Mann statue unveiled
1865.....Gen. Grant's first visit to Boston
1865..Return of the Massachusetts troops
1866.......Brighton Soldiers' Monument
1866................First ocean cable laid
1867....................Roxbury annexed
1867......Boston Conservatory opened
1867..Dorchester Soliders' Monument raised.
1867......New Masonic Temple dedicated
1867.........N. E. Conservatory founded
1867...........John Albion Andrew died
1867.............Everett statue unveiled
1867................Dickens' last visit
1868.......Brewer Fountain presented
1868............Ether Monument erected
1869..President Grant visited Boston; he came again in the following years: 1871, 1872, 1873, 1875.
1869...................Dorchester annexed
1869......Boston University incorporated
1869..Equestrian statue of Washington set up.
1870.........Prince Arthur visited Boston
1870................Boffin's Bower opened
1870.......Museum of Fine Arts founded
1871..........Duke Alexis visited Boston
1871...........Andrew Statue unveiled.
1871................Apollo Club organized
1871..West Roxbury Soldiers' Monument raised.
1871............Scollay Building removed
1871.....Boston Base Ball Club formed
1871....Revere accident, 32 persons killed
1872...Charlestown Soldiers' Monument unveiled.
1872..............Abijah Ellis murdered
1872.........................Great fire
1872............Charles Lane murdered
1873..........Normal Art School founded
1873.................Brighton annexed
1873...........Boylston Club organized
1873..............West Roxbury annexed
1873.........Brighton Abattoir opened
1873..............Charlestown annexed
1873......Public Library opened Sundays
1873.........Normal Art School founded
1874.............Cecilia Club organized
1874..........New Globe Theatre built
1874............Paddock Elms removed
1874..............Hotel Brunswick opened
1875..........LaGrange Street explosion
1875............Glover Statue unveiled
1875.............Mabel Young murdered
1876..........Thomas W. Piper hanged
1876......Homœopathic Hospital opened
1876.............Old Elm blown down
1877..Army and Navy Monument dedicated.
1877..........Moody and Sankey meetings
1877..First telephone used in America; from Boston to Salem.
1878.........Sunday Budget established
1878................Forest Garden opened
1878.............Sumner Statue unveiled
1879.......Associated Charities organized
1879.............Joseph F. Frye murdered
1879................Park Theatre opened
1879......Dudley Street Opera House built
1879.............Quincy Statue unveiled
1879.........Emancipation Group placed
1880.........New Tremont Temple opened
1880..First electric light (Scollay Square)
1880................Adams Statue erected
1880.............St. Botolph Club founded
1880.............Winthrop Statue unveiled
1881..............Prescott Statue erected

1882..Armstrong Transfer System adopted
1882..............Bijou Theatre opened
1883..............New Adams House built
1883..............Charles W. Slack died
1885..............Soldiers' Home carnival
1885..............Horse-car fares five cents
1885..............Alfred P. Peck died
1885..............Postage reduced to two cents
1885..............Street-car tickets abolished
1886..............Garrison Statue unveiled

AMUSEMENT DATA.

The Stage! Where Fancy sits, creative queen,
And waves her sceptre o'er life's mimic scene;
Where young-eyed Wonder comes to feast his sight
And quaff instruction while he drinks delight;
The Stage! That threads each labyrinth of the soul,
Wakes laughter's peal and bids the teardrop roll;
That shoots at folly — mocks proud Fashion's slave,
Uncloaks the hypocrite and brands the knave.
CHARLES SPRAGUE.

1686..Cotton Mather spoke on stage plays
1745..............Plays performed in private
1750..............Law prohibiting all plays
1750..............Actors to be fined five pounds
1750..Penalty for leasing halls for theatres
1776..Burgoyne's "Blockade of Boston" played by British soldiers at Faneuil Hall.
1778..............................First circus
1784....Laws against theatres re-enacted
1786..Stoughton Musical Society formed
1789..Washington heard oratorio selections at King's Chapel.
1792..Royal Tylers "The Contrast" played
1792..New Exhibition Hall (or Board Alley Theatre) opened.
1792..First American play,"The Contrast"
1792..Otway's "Venice preserved" first given.
1792..Shakspeare's "Hamlet" first given
1792....."Romeo and Juliet" first given
1792..........Theatrical managers arrested
1794..First Boston Theatre (first regular theatre) opened.
1796..Haymarket Theatre (second regular theatre) opened.
1796..Elizabeth Kemble Whitlock appeared.
1796.....Boston had two regular theatres
1798..........First Boston Theatre burned
1798..Boston Theatre rebuilt and reopened
1803..........Haymarket Theatre demolished
1804....Edition of Shakespeare published
1809..........John Howard Payne appeared
1810..John Gibbs Gilbert born, on Richmond (now Parmenter) Street.
1811...George Frederick Cooke appeared
1815..Handel and Haydn Society founded
1816..............Edwin L. Davenport born

1816..Charlotte Cushman born, on Richmond (now Parmenter) Street.
1818....James W. Wallack first appeared
1818..............Oratorio first given here
1818............." Messiah " first given here
1821..........Edmund Kean first appeared
1822..Opening of Junius Brutus Booth
1822..........Henry J. Finn first appeared
1823..City Theatre (Washington Gardens) opened.
1825..........................Edmund Kean riot
1826..........Wm. C. Macready appeared
1827..Old Tremont Theatre opened, (on site of Tremont Temple).
1827......Boston debut of Edwin Forrest
1827..........James H. Hackett appeared
1828..........John Gibbs Gilbert appeared
1830..........Charles John Kean came
1830..............Debut here of Master Burke
1832..Warren (Joseph) Theatre built (afterwards called the "National";
1833..............Arrival of Thomas Barry
1833......Boston debut of Fanny Kemble
1833......Tyrone Power appeared here
1833..Boston debut of Charles Kemble
1833........." Mount of Olives " first given
1834........J. Sheridan Knowles came
1835............." The Odeon " dedicated
1835..Charlotte Cushman's first appearance on the dramatic stage.
1836..James E. Murdoch's Boston debut
1836..........................Lion Theatre opened
1837..............Ellen Tree-Kean appeared
1837..Harvard Musical Associat'n formed
1837..........................John Vandenhoff came
1838......Fanny Ellsler first danced here
1838..Debut here of Jean Davenport Lander.
1839............E. L. Davenport appeared
1840......Boston debut of Wm. Creswick
1840..............Vaudeville Saloon opened
1840..............J. B. Buckstone came
1841..............Boston Museum opened
1841..........Olympic Saloon established
1842............George Vanderhoff appeared
1842..........................Eagle Theatre opened
1843..W. H. Smith joined Museum Company.
1843....Adelaide Phillipps first appeared
1843......Boston debut of John Brougham
1844..G.G.Spear joined Museum Company
1844..............................Ole Bull appeared
1844.." The Drunkard " had 100 performances at Boston Museum.
1845..........Anna Cora Mowatt appeared
1845..........Howard Athenæum opened
1846..........Julia Dean first played here

1846....."Aladdin," 91 times, at Museum
1846..Boston debut of William Warren at the Howard Athenæum.
1847..J. A. Smith joined Museum Comp'y
1847........J. R. Anderson appeared first
1847...William Warren's first appearance at the Boston Museum.
1847........First Italian opera given here
1849..Edwin Booth's first appearance on any stage, at the Boston Museum.
1849....Mendelssohn Quintet Club formed
1849......Barney Williams' Boston debut
1850..........Jenny Lind's first concerts
1852..........."Silver Spoon" first played
1852............G. V. Brooke first appeared
1852............Boston Music Hall built
1852..Mrs. J. R. Vincent joined Museum Company.
1852..E. A. Sothern's first appearance in America, at the National Theatre.
1852.."Uncle Tom's Cabin," 107 performances, at Boston Museum.
1852..Feb. 5, Jenny Lind, of Stockholm, Sweden, was married to Otto Goldschmidt, of Hamburg, Germany, Louisburg Square, Boston.
1853.........Joseph Jefferson first appeared
1853...Boston debut of Eliza Logan Wood
1853......Maggie Mitchell's Boston debut
1854....Agnes Robertson Boucicault came
1854..........Dion Boucicault appeared
1855..Rachel's Boston debut, at the Boston Theatre.
1855................F. B. Conway appeared
1856..The Marsh Family of Children came
1856.........Beethoven Statue unveiled
1857.........Charles James Mathews came
1857..Jas. Nolan joined Museum Comp'y
1858..Lawrence P. Barrett first appeared (as a member of the Boston Museum Company).
1860..Josephine Orton joined Museum Company.
1860..........John McCullough first came
1860..Mr. and Mrs. Henri Drayton appeared.
1860......................Patti in opera
1860..Kate Reignolds joined Museum Company.
1861..Annie Clarke joined Museum Company.
1861.......Charles Dillon's Boston debut
1861.......Kittie Blanchard first appeared
1863..W. A. Mestayer made his first appearance on any stage at the Boston Museum.
1863..John Wilkes Booth's last appearance here, at Boston Museum.
1864.."Rosedale" played 101 times at Museum.
1864.........R. M. Field became manager
1864......."Robert le Diable" given here
1866......Adelaide Ristori first appeared
1866.........Parepa-Rosa first heard here
1866..........Continental Theatre opened
1866.."Black Crook" at Continental Theatre.
1866–67....."Black Crook" ran 133 times
1867.."Caste" produced at Boston Museum.
1868...............Fanny Janauschek came
1869..Charles Barron joined Museum

1869.................Jenny Van Zandt came
1869................Alide Topp heard first
1869................First Gilmore Jubilee
1870......Isabel Glyn Dallas appeared
1870......Petersilea Academy established
1870.................Rose Hersee appeared
1870.........Boston debut of Anna Mehlig
1870..Run of "She Stoops to Conquer" at Boston Museum, 35 performances
1870....Boston debut of Charles Fechter
1870.........Tom Karl first appeared here
1871..Christine Nilsson's first appearance in opera in America, at the Boston Theatre.
1871......Bach's "Passion Musik" given
1871..Saturday night performances first given regularly at Boston Museum
1872.....Gilmore's World's Peace Jubilee
1872.....Arabella Goddard appeared
1872............Rubinstein first came here
1873...........Tomasso Salvini first came
1873................Di Murska heard here
1873.................Pauline Lucca came
1873..............Beethoven Quintet formed
1873....Lillian Adelaide Neilson appeared
1875..Hans von Bulow appeared here, his debut in America.
1876..George W. Wilson joined Museum Company.
1876..........Death of Charlotte Cushman
1876............Tietjens first heard here
1877................Clara Morris first came
1877..Superb production of Sardou's "The Exiles" at Boston Theatre by Eugene Tompkins.
1877............Mary Anderson appeared
1878...."Pinafore" at Museum, 194 times
1878................Gaiety Theatre opened
1878.............Modjeska first appeared
1878.."Pinafore" first given in the United States at the Boston Museum.
1878.."Cosette" produced at Boston Theatre.
1879..Boston Ideal Opera Company first appeared as an organization at Boston Theatre, in "Pinafore."
1879.."Drink" produced at Boston Theatre.
1879..Novelty (now Windsor) Theatre opened.
1879............Union Opera House opened
1879..J. B. Mason joined Museum Company.
1879..William Seymour joined Museum Company.
1879.."Andre Fortier" produced at Boston Theatre.
1879.........Rafael Joseffy appeared
1880................Sarah Bernhardt came
1880.."Voyagers in Southern Seas" produced at Boston Theatre.
1880....Halleck's Alhambra (S.B.) opened
1880.........Ocean Garden (S. B.) opened
1881..Boston Symphony Orchestra formed
1881.."Michael Strogoff" produced at Boston Theatre.
1882.."The World" produced at Boston Theatre.
1882............Adelaide Phillipps died
1882.."Youth" produced at Boston Theatre.

1883............William Warren retired
1883..."Jalma" produced at Boston Theatre.
1883............Great Organ removed
1883..Henry Irving first appeared here. His receipts, at the Boston Theatre, on one of his weeks there, exceeded $24,000, the largest sum he received anywhere in the United States during any week.
1884..."The Silver King" produced at Boston Theatre.

1885............Judic appeared here
1885............Marianne Brandt appeared
1885............H. K. Oliver died
1885............"Mikado" first given here
1885-86.."Mikado" had 161 performances
1886............Lilli Lehmann's debut
1886............"Lakme" first heard here
1886............Booth-Salvini joint appearance
1886..Eugene Tompkins assumed the sole management of the Boston Theatre.

"AFTER LIFE'S FITFUL FEVER."

And what were life—life's work all done
The hopes, loves, joys that cling to clay?
All—all departed,one by one,
And yet life's load borne on for aye!
Decay! decay! 'tis stamped on all.
All bloom—in flower and flesh—shall fade,
Ye whisp'ring trees, when we shall fall
Be our long sleep beneath your shade!
          JOHN PIERPONT.

"Sometimes in thought, we sit apart,
And ask ourselves the *How* and *When*
Will come to us that only hour
That cometh surely to all men.

When all along the eastern hills
Comes silently the flush of dawn,
And earth lies bathed in cooling dews,
And birds are welcoming the morn?

Or when the noon with her bold eye
To silence awes the feathered choir,
And in the fulness of her prime
The morning's tender charms expire?

Or when the sunset paints the sky
In glowing clouds of pearl and gold,
And day glides noiselessly from sight,
And evening's balm the earth enfold?

Or will the cry—"*Behold, He comes!*"
Sound through the stillness of the night,
When all the earth lies hushed in sleep,
And stars look down with chastened light?

Perhaps the dear old earth enwrapped
In winter's fleecy garb may lie,
And winds may blow, and storms may rage,
And snows obscure the sullen sky.

Will that day find us wandering?
Or in the dear home of our birth,
Amid the old familiar scenes
Will our eyes see the last of earth?

Will strange eyes meet our darkening sight?
Or faces loved with life-long love,
That smile through tears to strengthen us,
And give us hope to meet above?

Vain questions all! We may not know
That time or place, but calmly rest,
Assured by this one simple thought,
Our Father's time and way are best!"

Strangers here often ask: "Where was Longfellow buried?" "Was Wendell Phillips laid in Mount Auburn?" "And where were Emerson, Hawthorne, Everett, Sumner, and other eminent persons buried?" We have endeavored to answer all these inquiries here, and to give as complete and as accurate a list of the noted persons interred in the cemeteries of Boston and vicinity as possible. Visitors to this city from remote sections of the United States and from Europe visit the grave of Longfellow and place flowers upon it as a tribute to the memory of the most illustrious American poet, and especially on Memorial Day, May 30, are the resting-places of the dead in the various cemeteries covered with beautiful floral designs.

Henry Wadsworth Longfellow............Mount Auburn
Wendell Phillips..................Milton
Charles Sumner..........Mount Auburn
Ralph Waldo Emerson............Concord
Edward Everett............Mount Auburn
Daniel Webster............Marshfield
Louis Agassiz............Mount Auburn
Nathaniel Hawthorne............Concord
Charlotte Cushman........Mount Auburn
John Harvard..................Charlestown
Nathaniel P. Willis........Mount Auburn
Erminia Rudersdorff......Mount Auburn
Francis Antony Matignon..St. Augustine
H. D. Thoreau..................Concord
Adelaide Phillipps............Marshfield
John Albion Andrew............Hingham
Junius Brutus Booth, jr.......Manchester
Nathaniel Bowditch........Mount Auburn
Fanny Parnell............Mount Auburn
Rufus Choate............Mount Auburn
George Peabody..................Peabody
Mary Devlin Booth........Mount Auburn
Jared Sparks............Mount Auburn
John Murray............Mount Auburn
Epes Sargent............Mount Auburn
Thomas Dowse............Mount Auburn
Sarah Payson Willis......Mount Auburn
Abbott Lawrence........Mount Auburn

William Ellery Channing.Mount Auburn
Amos Lawrence...........Mount Auburn
Jonas Chickering..........Mount Auburn
James T. Fields............Mount Auburn
John Gorham Palfrey.....Mount Auburn
Henry F. Durant..........Mount Auburn
Josiah Quincy..............Mount Auburn
Paran Stevens..............Mount Auburn
Hosea Ballou...............Mount Auburn
Alvin Adams...............Mount Auburn
Gaspard Spurzheim........Mount Auburn
Owen Marlowe..............Forest Hills
Joseph Warren..............Forest Hills
Thomas J. O'Flaherty......St. Augustine
John Eliot.........................Roxbury
Admiral Winslow............Forest Hills
Richard Mather................Dorchester
Mary Chilton. 1679..........King's Chapel
Crispus Attucks...................Granary
John Winthrop............King's Chapel
Lady Andros...............King's Chapel
John Cotton................King's Chapel
Peter Faneuil......................Granary
Samuel Sewall....................Granary
Paul Revere.......................Granary
Robert Treat Paine...............Granary
Josiah (father of Ben.) Franklin.Granary
John Hancock....................Granary
M. Julien..........................Common
Gilbert Stuart....................Common
Increase Mather...............Copp's Hill
Cotton Mather................Copp's Hill
Samuel Mather................Copp's Hill
Paul Dudley......................Roxbury
Thomas Beecher.............Charlestown
William Stoughton............Dorchester

In Copp's Hill Burying Ground, Charter Street, is the Mather tomb, upon which is the following inscription:

THE REVEREND DOCTORS
INCREASE, COTTON,
AND SAMUEL MATHER
WERE INTERRED IN THIS VAULT.
'TIS THE TOMB OF OUR FATHERS.
MATHER CROCKER'S.
I. Died Aug. 27, 1723. Æ 84.
C. Died Feb. 13, 1727. Æ 65.
S. Died June 27. 1785. Æ 79.

A stone at Copp's Hill, erected to the memory of Ammy Hunt, 1767, has engraved upon it:

A SISTER OF SARAH LUCAS LYETH HERE
WHOM I DID LOVE MOST DEAR;
AND NOW HER SOUL HATH TOOK ITS
FLIGHT
AND BID HER SPITEFUL FOES GOOD
NIGHT.

In the old Dorchester Burying-Ground, Dorchester District, is a stone over the grave of General Humphrey Atherton, 1661, having upon it the following words:

TWO TROYPS
OF HORS WITH HIME
HERE CAME,
SVCH WORTH HIS LOVE
DID CRAVE,
TEN COMPANYES OF FOOT,
ALSO MOVRNING,
MARCHT TO HIS GRAVE.
LET ALL THAT READ
BE SVRE TO KEEP
THE FAITH AS HE HATH DONE,
WITH CHRIST HE LIVS
NOW CROWNED, HIS NAME
WAS HVMPHREY ATHERTON.

COLLEGES AND SCHOOLS.

Abandoning the methods ordinarily employed by writers on educational institutions, we have endeavored to state the exact truth concerning the schools herein named—and we believe we have included every one in Boston—not for the purpose of advertising any, but for the express benefit of the readers of this work. During an experience of many years in an editorial capacity, we have received thousands of letters from young men and women in various sections of the United States, Canada, Cuba, Mexico and other countries, making enquiries as to the various branches of study pursued, the character of the school, the educational standard maintained, the rates of tuition, and other questions, to which we have replied to the best of our knowledge. Finding the task of replying separately and in detail becoming somewhat burdensome, and increasing as the years go on, trespassing largely upon our time, we have decided to put our replies in print, and have therefore arranged the matter to form the principal feature of this work. We have been accumulating it for several months, and, like all other works of this kind when once undertaken it has grown upon our hands to a surprising extent. We have not had space to go into an extended history of any school, owing to the great number of them, but have concisely placed together such facts as will enable intending pupils to form an accurate idea of the expense of pursuing any course of study in the leading scholastic city in America. It is but just to say here that in no instance has any mention of any school herein been made for money, or under any other influence, the matter having been prepared entirely without the knowledge of the directors of the schools named.

Abatable disagreeable or inconvenient surroundings are so frequently to be found environing students, in many cities and towns, that it is not surprising that greater progress is not made by pupils. Not only were the locations of the most of the colleges and schools of Boston and vicinity selected with a view of obtaining as quiet and pleasant natural surroundings as it is possible to find in the great and bustling metropolis of New England, but the directors of such renowned educational institutions as Harvard University — the oldest, largest, most richly endowed and most distinguished college on the continent — Boston College, Boston University, Tufts College, New England Conservatory of Music — the largest music school in the world — Institute of Technology, Harvard Law School, Harvard Medical School, Wellesley College, Chauncy Hall School, Lasell Seminary, Boston Conservatory of Music, Normal Art School, Petersilea Academy, Boston School of Languages, Tremont School of Music, College Lafayette, Mendelssohn Musical Institute, Berkeley School, Gannett Seminary, Cowles Art School, School of Sculpture, Lowell School of Design, School of Modlling, School of Expression, Allen's Stenographic Institute, Abercrombie Oratorio School, Adams Operatic School, Boston College of Music, Boston School of Oratory, Lawrence Scientific School, Harvard School of Music, School of all Sciences, Free Weaving School, Free Pattern-Making School, Boston School of Elocution, Sauveur School of Languages, Delsarte School of Oratory and Dramatic Art, Monroe Conservatory of Oratory, Harvard Annex, School of Industrial Science, School of Mechanic Arts, School of Architecture, College of Liberal Arts, Notre Dame Academy, Naval Training School, Boston Cooking School, Hintz Art School, Training Schools for Nurses, College of Pharmacy, Berlitz School of Languages, Bijou Dramatic School, Bligh School of Elocution, Hayden's Guitar School, Sawyer's Commercial College, Perkins Institute, Comer's Commercial College, Bussey Institute of Agriculture and Horticulture, College of Physicians and Surgeons, Boston Commercial College, Bryant & Stratton College, Burdett Business College, Boston Dental College, Columbus School of Languages, Harvard Dental School, Harvard School of Veterinary Medicine, Metaphysical College, Boston Divinity School, Munich Art School, Titcombe Art School, Normal Writing School, De la Motte Musical School, Horace Mann School, School of Manual Training, School of Theology, Harvard Divinity School, School for the Blind, and others, most fully realize the enormous collateral advantages to be derived from the privileges of the Boston Public Library, containing 475,000 volumes, (the largest free reference library of foreign and American books in this country,) and other fine free libraries; the great Museum of Fine Arts, open on Saturdays and Sundays free to all; the famous Boston Natural Society's Rooms, free to visitors on Wednesday and Saturday afternoons; the noted Agassiz free Museum of Comparative Zoology; the great free Botanical Garden; the Peabody (free) Museum of Archæology; the Barnum free Museum of Natural History (Tufts College); the Warren Museum of Natural History; the collections of the Massachusetts Historical Society, the Historic-Genealogical Society; the Bostonian (Old State House)

Society, and the Old South collection; Exhibitions of Paintings, Flowers, Fruit, etc.; Symphony Concerts and instructive musical performances, at low prices; lectures, *free*, and at moderate rates of admission; *free* reading-rooms in great numbers and variety; gymnasiums, etc., etc. In fact, this city offers such unrivalled and remarkable *free* auxiliaries to the student pursuing almost any branch of education, it is not surprising that thousands of young persons, from all sections of the country, are thronging to obtain an academic, musical, or art education in Boston, the literary, musical and art centre of the United States, the second commercial city of the country; and having within a radius of less than twenty-five miles a population of *more than a million of people.*

Abbott Academy. (1829). Andover. Established for the education of girls. Languages—French and German; music, painting, elocution, zoology, geology, botany, etc., are among the branches taught. Terms, per year, for board and instruction,—excepting music, drawing and painting—$300. Andover is twenty miles from Boston.

Abercrombie Boston Oratorio School. (1885). 181 Tremont st. Boston is the home of Oratorio in the United States, its Handel and Haydn Society having long occupied the foremost position among the Choral Societies of America. It ranks well with similar organizations in England. Recognizing Boston's pre-eminence in this department of musical art, Charles Abercrombie, who has for some years occupied the position of tenor at Her Majesty's Chapel Royal, St. James Palace, London, and a pupil of the most eminent masters of London, came here at the opening of the musical season of 1885-6 and established an Oratorio School, the only institution of the kind anywhere, which is attracting pupils from every section of the United States and Canada. His success has been so phenomenal that he has decided to remain permanently in Boston. His method combines the best features of the systems of his famous teachers.

Academy for Teaching Band Music. (1871). 281 Columbus av. Under the direction of J. B. Claus, the distinguished Band Master. Terms: 20 one-hour lessons, in classes of four pupils, $15.

Adams Academy. Quincy. For preparing boys for Harvard University. Tuition *free* to those residing in Quincy.

Adams Operatic School. (1885). 159 Tremont st. Upon his retirement from active professional duties upon the operatic stage, Charles R. Adams, the greatest dramatic tenor America has yet produced, decided to establish himself in Boston as a teacher of singing. He soon became known as one of the foremost vocal teachers of the world, and pupils from all parts of the United States came to obtain instruction from him. Many who had contemplated going to Europe for a course of study changed their plans and came to Boston instead, thereby saving money, to say nothing of the time, the discomforts of ocean voyages, foreign travel, etc. Finding a great desire among his pupils for operatic instruction, he established in the autumn of 1885 an operatic school. He had constructed a stage, with scenery, properties, and all the appointments of a regular theatre, on a small scale to be sure, but amply sufficient to enable his pupils to appear in scenes from operas, in costume, and before audiences invited to witness their performances, some of which would do credit to artists of recognized ability. Boston now has an Operatic School in which any city might well take pride.

Agricultural Schools. (See *Bussey Institute, Farm School and Boston University College of Agriculture*).

Allen's Stenographic Institute. 15 State st. Among the noted institutions for imparting *practical, useful* knowledge in Boston, Allen's Stenographic Institute must be mentioned among the foremost. Its reputation is not merely local; it extends to the most distant sections of the United States and the Canadas, from all of which come pupils to prepare themselves for active and profitable duties in life. A knowledge of stenography is one of the most valuable acquisitions that can possibly be learned by one in any position in life; it is equally important to the student, the professional gentleman and the business man. Allen's Stenographic Institute is the oldest, largest, and most noted Shorthand School in New England. By the method taught here the student learns *each principle*, both mentally and mechanically, applies it in general literature, and is enabled to read it before taking the next step, and therefore where there is an inclination, and time for practice, with even the most ordinary ability, there is no possibility of a failure to make the art practicable; that is, to report an average speaker verbatim; because, with the first lesson, the student will be enabled to write with from one-seventh to one-twentieth as many strokes as would be required in longhand writing, and, consequently, when as well learned, the shorthand should be written nearly *seven times as fast.* Whenever a person can write more rapidly than by longhand, and read it, it will be in that proportion more valuable than longhand, in taking notes of lectures in school or elsewhere; in writing letters from dictation, or in other cases where time in writing is to be saved. The value of a complete system is incalculable. Terms of Tuition: For each single lesson, $3; for instruction for one school month, $20; for the usual course of three months (sixty lessons), $45; six months' instruction, for those desiring to become expert, $75; instruction on type-writers, per month, $5; instruction by mail, $15 for twenty lessons. G. G Allen is the Principal of the school.

American Academy of Arts and Sciences. (1780), 10 B Beacon st. Formed for the object of promoting the knowledge of the Natural History of America and its antiquities, as well as the encouragement of agricultural, art, astronomical, commercial, geographical, manufacturing, mathematical, medical, meteorological, philosophical and other studies, discoveries and observations, by means of lectures, libraries, etc.

Andover Theological Seminary. (1807). Andover. Instruction; undergraduate course, Junior year, Exegesis, (Hebrew Scriptures); Greek Scriptures; Science and Christianity, (Instruments of Science,—Processes, Products, Distinctions, Validations; Biblical History; Systematic Theology; Elocution. Middle year: Systematic Theology; Biblical Theology; Biblical History; Exegesis; Christianity and Science; Elocution. Senior year: Sacred Rhetoric; Pastoral Theology; Church History; Exegesis; Christianity and Science; Elocution. Open to all denominations. Annual expenses; term bills, $10; fuel and lights, $10; board, $136.50. Total for one year, $156.50. Andover is twenty miles from Boston.

Annex. (See *Harvard Annex*).

Arboriculture School. (See *Bussey Institute School*).

Architectural School. (See *School of Architecture*).

Art Schools. (See *Bartlett School of Modelling, Boston School of Sculpture, Cowles Art School, Fine Art Museum Classes, Hintz Art School, Juglaris Art School, Munich Art School, Nolen Art School, Normal Art School, Petersilea Academy, Springer Art School, Stone Art School, Titcomb's Art Academy*, and other Art Schools described in this department).

Bartlett School of Modelling, 334 Federal st. Tuition, $25 per month. Truman H. Bartlett, Director.

Berkeley School. 174 Boylston st., cor. Berkeley st. James B. Taylor (literature, history, and elocution), Edwin De Meritte (Latin and Greek), Walter C. Hagar (mathematics), and ten other instructors in various branches. For boys and girls. This school is rapidly attaining an enviable reputation for its thoroughness, the ability of its Faculty, and the practical character of its instruction. Its chief departments are the literary, classical, mathematical, scientific; and that of modern languages. For graduation, however, a pupil is not required to complete the studies of more than three departments or their equivalents. The literary department is exceedingly thorough. Special students in literature are taken. Declamations and compositions are required of every regular pupil every four weeks, thus allowing time for careful preparation and correction in each of these two important exercises. Short drills are given in vocal gymnastics, and opportunities afforded for rehearsing declamations. The classical department is famed for its elevated standard. The mathematical department aims at imparting not only accuracy and quickness of calculation, but also originality of thought and logical reasoning. The departments of natural sciences, modern languages, physical culture, etc., are also superintended by some of the ablest teachers in the country. Terms, from $140 to $180; with French or German, $20 extra. School opens its departments in September. (Take any Back-Bay horse-car, Vendôme or Clarendon-st. line, West End, Huntington av., or Dartmouth-st. lines.)

Berlitz School of Languages. (1878). 154 Tremont st. Languages taught largely by object-teaching. Tuition for French or German, in small classes, one lesson a week each person, 13 weeks, $6; 39 weeks, $16.50; 5 lessons a week, 13 weeks, $18; 39 weeks, $50. Private lessons, 12 lessons, $15. Lectures *free* to all students.

Bickford School of Elocution, 48 Boylston st. Charles Bickford, Director. This most centrally and pleasantly located school is in the building of the Boston Young Men's Christian Union. Mr. Bickford has for years been recognized as one of America's leading elocutionists, and he is equally successful in imparting the principles of his method to his pupils. The value of a graceful, easy, cultivated manner of delivery is one that cannot be overestimated by any young man, even if one has no idea of following the profession of the pulpit, the stage, the platform or the bar. The subject of Expression is just now foremost in the educational institutions of Boston, and this agitation cannot fail to benefit the Bickford School of Elocution, as its methods are based upon *natural* principles, supplemented by artistic finish. There are to-day many of the graduates of this celebrated school, filling positions in various sections of the country, and winning approval for their *perfect* system of elocution. Those intending to adopt the profession of the Drama cannot do better than to learn the principles of tho art of expression, gesture, etc., at this school, for the groundwork will then be so thoroughly accomplished that future work will be easy and more satisfactory than as if, as in some cases, there is more to *unlearn* than to learn, after a faulty beginning. Terms: Elocution class, $10; dramatic, $10; Shakspeare class, $5; ladies' afternoon class, $15; private instruction, 20 lessons, $50; single lesson, $3 to $5.

Bicycle Schools. (See *Columbia Bicycle School*, *Murray Bicycle School*, and *Stall Bicycle School*.)

Bijou Dramatic School. (1885). 540 Washington st. (opposite Bijou and Boston Theatres). Pupils prepared for the dramatic stage. Pupils are formed into companies, rehearsed in legitimate tragedies, dramas, comedies, etc., with full and complete stage business and effects, thus giving them experience in the art. Competent pupils are guaranteed positions. Edith Stanmore, Principal. No class lessons. Single lessons, $3; ten, $25; twenty, $40. Hours for lessons, 10 A. M. to 9 P. M.

Bird School of Art. 492 E 4th st., South Boston.

Blind, School For. (See *Perkins Institute*.)

Blish School of Elocution. Tremont Temple, 78 Tremont st. George W. Blish, Director. Prof. Blish is well known as an elocutionist. Instruction is here given to those desirous of studying for the stage, the platform, the pulpit, or the bar. Dramatic expression, gesture and stage business practically taught. Pupils' matinees are given, thus enabling students to become familiar with audiences and to acquire repose, before going before the general public.

Boston College. (1860). 761 Harrison av. Established by the Fathers of the Society of Jesus, who now conduct it. It was incorporated by the State of Massachusetts May 25, 1863. The College confers such degrees as are usually given by colleges in the Commonwealth, with the exception of medical degrees. It is intended for day scholars only. The high standard of education at this great college is universally conceded. It has English and classical courses. The Faculty numbers twenty-one professors, with Rev. Edward V. Boursaud as president. Terms: $30 per session, of five months, a fee of $10 for diploma, and $5 for laboratory expenses during the Philosophy year. Sessions begin on the 1st Monday in September and on the 1st Monday in February. (Take Norfolk House horse-cars.)

Boston Commercial College. 639 Washington st. Principal, W. H. Moriarty. One of the well-known business schools of the city. Branches taught: Penmanship, Arithmetic, Book-keeping.

Boston Conservatory of Music. (1867). 154 Tremont st. Julius Eichberg, director. This is one of the great music schools of the country, and of the world, and is renowned for its thoroughness. It is especially famed as a violin school. Upwards of 25,000 pupils, representing every section of the continent, have already gone forth from this celebrated school of music. The class system prevails, with not more than four pupils in a class. Lessons are one hour in duration. Prices of tuition: For one term of 20 lessons, in class of four, $20; beginners in instrumental music, $15. Private instruction if desired. Board secured for $5 per week, upwards. Diplomas conferred. Terms begin in April, September, November, and February. (See *Eichberg's Violin School*).

Boston Cooking School. (1882). 174 Tremont st. Principal, Mrs. David A. Lincoln. Fees, 12 lessons, $12, including materials. Second course, 12 lessons, $15. Third course, fancy cooking, 12 lessons, $15. Nurses' course, 6 lessons, $5. Students furnish themselves with napkin, tea-spoon, note-book and pencil. Mrs. Sarah E. Hooper, president.

Boston Correspondence School of New Testament Greek. 38 Bromfield st.

Boston Dental College. (1868). 485 Tremont st. President, Isaac J. Wetherbee, D.D.S.; Clerk, Edmund G. Flint, D.D.S.; period of instruction, three years. Students have access to the great hospitals of the city, and to the dissecting-room and library of the college. The Boston Public Library, which contains one of the largest and best collections of medical and dental books in the world, is open free to all students. Fees of the Boston Dental College: For matriculation, $5; for one year, $100; for demonstrator's ticket, $5. No fee for diploma. Board procured for students at rates from $4 upward. Year begins in September. Dean, J. A. Follett, M.D., 219 Shawmut av. (Take any Tremont-st. horse-car line.)

Boston Divinity School. 176 Tremont st. Rev. L. R. Eastman, Senior Principal.

Boston Evening Free Schools (1868). For any person over 12 years of age. Sessions are held every evening (except Saturday and Sunday) from 7 to 9 P. M., from September to March, at the following places: Eliot School, North Bennet st.; Anderson Street School; Wells School, Blossom st., cor. McLean; Quincy School, Tyler st.; Franklin School, Ringgold st.; Comins School, Tremont st., cor. Terrace, Roxbury District; Dearborn School, Dearborn pl., Roxbury District; Bigelow School, Fourth st., cor. E, South Boston; Lincoln School, Broadway, near K st., South Boston; Lyman School, Paris st., cor. Decatur; Warren School, Pearl st., cor. Sumner, Charlestown District.

Boston Evening Free Schools in Drawing. (See *Free Drawing Schools*.)

Boston Evening High School. (1869). (*Free*). Montgomery st. Sessions every week-day evening except Saturday, from September to March, (except legal holidays).

Boston Grammar Schools. (See *Free Grammar Schools*).

Boston High School for Boys. (1821). Montgomery st. English Branches. Head Master, Francis A. Waterhouse.

Boston High School for Girls. (1852). West Newton st. Head master, John Tetlow.

Boston Latin School for Boys. (1635). Warren av. Head Master, Moses Merrill. The oldest educational institution in the United States, Harvard College being the next in age.

Boston Latin School for Girls. (1878). West Newton st. Head Master, John Tetlow. Master, William Gallagher.

Boston Normal School. For Girls. (1854). Dartmouth st. Head Master, Larkin Dunton.

Boston Riding Academy. 1209 Washington st., so. of Windsor Theatre. Fred. R. Graves, Manager, John McMeown, General Asst. Course of lessons in riding, §10.

Boston Riding School. East Dedham st., cor. Albany st. H. L. de Bussigny, Proprietor. This noted Academy for Instruction in Riding occupies the entire square, bounded by East Dedham, Albany, Plympton, and Thorn sts., and covers nearly half an acre of ground. The ring and stable are on the ground. The ring is one hundred and fifty feet long, and sixty feet wide, and is said to be the largest in the country. Class instruction. Lesson hours: Ladies, 10 to 12; and 2 to 3. Gentlemen, 9 to 10 and 4.30 to 6.30. Hours reserved for children on Saturdays. Terms: Single lessons, $2. Ten lessons, $15. Horses boarded, $7 per week. Footmen in livery in constant attendance. (Washington st. horse-cars pass East Dedham st. A coach leaves corner of Beacon and Dartmouth sts. at regular intervals, for patrons of this School.)

Boston School of Acting. 178 Tremont st. Director, J. A. Bleecker. One of the most successful dramatic schools in the United States. Pupils are taught *practically* by taking part in companies formed for the actual production of plays before audiences. Terms: $40, for single course of 20 lessons; one year's course (7 months), $200.

Boston School of Elocution. (1874). 18 Boylston st. The Fobes method of elocution is here taught, as follows: First, a series of gymnastics, to give strength and elasticity to the muscles used in speaking, to expand the chest, and to get a correct position of body, so that speaking may be without effort and yet powerful. Second, a system of vocal exercise, for daily practice, to train the voice in tone, quality, movement, pitch, inflection, force, stress, articulation and right manner of breathing. Third, the application of the vocal exercises to the reading of short extracts, showing the effect when thus applied. Fourth, reading of selections from various authors, with criticisms, showing the difference between the seven styles: conversational, narrative, descriptive, didactic, public address, declamatory, and emotional or dramatic. Walter K. Fobes, Principal; Clara S. Barnes, Assistant. Terms: ten hour lessons (private) from Mr. Fobes, $30; from other teachers, $15.

Boston School of Expression. (1884). Freeman pl., 15 Beacon st. There is probably no school of elocution or dramatic training so much discussed today in every section of the United States —as well as in the capitals of Europe—as the Boston School of Expression. New York and London papers have devoted columns to it; teachers everywhere are seeking for information regarding it, and pupils are coming to it from every quarter of the globe. Judging from actual results, this school has obviously struck upon most novel and sensible methods of teaching elocution and oratory. Its plan is extremely scientific and elaborate, but there is no difficulty in comprehending its natural principles. Merely mechanical elocutionary training, such as has been imparted in an ordinary, old-fashioned manner, throughout the country, for so many years, is not sufficient for the intellectual and progressive Faculty of this school, who rather endeavor to educate the artistic instincts, and to combine all the powers of thought, emotion and will. Their motto is: "It is the *soul* that must speak!" In developing the voice they use the methods of the old Italian masters in the training of the singing voice. The *whole body* is educated as the instrument of expression, thus securing ease, precision and harmony. Pantomimic gymnastics form a portion of the course. Orators without mannerisms are produced. Pupils come from 24 different States and countries, among them being teachers, clergymen, lawyers, singers, and students who will follow an artistic career. Pupils have thus far applied in larger numbers than can well be accommodated, in order to avail themselves of the remarkable benefits of this new system. It has been the endeavor to allow no student of ability to leave the school for lack of money. There is unbounded enthusiasm among the pupils of this great school, which is creating so much interest all over the world in educational circles just now. Tuition: Each year, 7 hours per week, $100; electives, each hour, once a week, for the year, $15; for half year, $10. S. S. Curry, Ph. D., 10 Beacon st., is the Principal.

Boston School of Languages.

(1879). Pelham Studios. 44 Boylston st. Jules A. Hobigand, A. M., Principal. For the past six years this excellent school has been noted as one of the leading institutions of its kind in the United States. Its reputation is well deserved, as it is based upon genuine merit. The standard of the school is a lofty one; its system is thorough, and the methods employed are such as will at once commend themselves to the practical student, who is generally desirous of attaining the knowledge of a language as quickly as is compatible with a thorough command of it. The languages taught here are French, German, Spanish and Italian. The instruction is imparted by *native teachers*, by natural methods. In addition to the modern languages, the English branches are taught. Students are prepared for any College or professional school in the country, in the most thorough manner. There are special courses for the youth of both sexes. The wide reputation of the Principal of this school is an assurance of the completeness characterizing every department of the institution. He is careful to see that the ability of every pupil is developed in the most natural manner, and is constantly exercising a most beneficial supervision over the school. He is assisted by a faculty of teachers of skill and experience, the results of whose instruction are most gratifying to the pupil who is really in earnest to accomplish all that is possible in obtaining a linguistic education, or one of preparation for a university. This school is admirably located near the corner of Tremont and Boylston sts., and but a few steps from the great Public Library.

Boston School of Oratory.

(1873). 7 Beacon st. and 1 Somerset st. This great school has a world-wide fame, and deservedly so, for its high standard of education, its thoroughness in every department, its Faculty of Instruction, (comprising some of the most eminent professors and teachers in the United States), its success in teaching the great art of Expression, combined with its large number of accomplished graduates, place it in the foremost ranks of the educational institutions of America. The fact that at the head of its Faculty is Professor Moses True Brown, the distinguished teacher of the Synthetic Philosophy of Expression, and recognized by the collegiate circles of the world as a master of his art, is of itself sufficient to attract pupils from every section of the continent. Professor Brown is assisted by Miss Maida Cragin, Teacher of Voice Culture and the Delsarte System of Gesture; Miss Clara T. Power, Teacher of Elementary Elocution and Calisthenics; Professor Hamlin Garland, Teacher of English Literature; Professor Amos E. Dolbear, Lecturer on the Acoustics of the Voice, and other noted teachers. Not only has this school won vast reputation throughout the United States, but it has also awakened interest in Europe for its *systematic* instruction in the speech arts. Its claims to leadership in schools of its class are based upon its twelve years in the successful service of the science and art of expression. Its avowed objects are: to substitute simple, natural modes of expression for the faulty delivery which so universally prevails in the reading-circle, the college, the public school, the pulpit, on the platform and stage; to establish a system of teaching founded on *exact knowledge and experience;* to impart such a thorough knowledge of the structure of the instrument of the human voice as may lead to intelligent methods of training this wonderful organ. The course of instruction embraces every branch of Expression in all of its applications: Physical Training, Respiration, Vocal Culture, Articulation, Orthœpy, the Laws of Inflection and Emphasis, Dramatic Reading and Recitation, Gesture, etc. Tuition, $100 per year. (See *Summer School of Oratory*.)

Boston School of Sculpture.

394 Federal st. Truman H. Bartlett, Director. This School of Sculpture and Modelling is noted throughout the country as being a labor of love on the part of its projector rather than an arrangement for making money. Mr. Bartlett is

an enthusiast in the art of which he is so prominent an exponent, his fame being national as well as local, and he enters into his work with such ardor as to infuse the same spirit into his pupils. Day and evening students are received. Perhaps the thoroughly unselfish manner in which this important school is conducted cannot be better illustrated than by quoting an extract from a reply sent to a stranger to Mr. Bartlett who wrote to inquire the terms of instruction at the school. He answered: "Terms depend on how much the student can pay. Some pay nothing; others, $25 per month."

Boston School of Takigraphy. (Shorthand). 274 Columbus av. Mrs. M. A. Chandler.

Boston School of Telegraphy. 120 Tremont st.

Boston Shorthand Bureau. 186 Washington st. Branches taught: shorthand, type-writing. Tuition: course of 15 hourly lessons, $10; single lessons, 75 cents; amanuensis course (type-writing and dictation), 10 lessons, $5. Beale & Lovejoy, managers.

Boston Training School for Nurses. (1873). Massachusetts General Hospital, Blossom st., foot of McLean st. Two years' course: pay, $10 per month, first year; $14, second year. Most desirable ages for pupils, 25 to 35 years.

Boys' Institute of Industry. (1884). 375 Harrison av. Classes in carpentry, every day, from 4 to 6 o'clock, P. M.

Boston University. (1869). 12 Somerset st. Original corporators: Isaac Rich, Lee Claflin, Jacob Sleeper. The Boston University comprises the College of Liberal Arts (12 Somerset st.), The College of Music (27 East Newton st., Franklin sq.), The College of Agriculture (Amherst), The School of Theology (36 Bromfield st.), The School of Law (10 Ashburton pl.), The School of Medicine (East Concord st.), The School of All Sciences (12 Somerset st.). President of the University Council, William F. Warren, S.T.D., LL.D., 12 Somerset st. Terms, College of Liberal Arts: tuition, $100; incidental expenses, $10; room, $36 to $90; board, 36 weeks, $108 to $180; text-books, stationery, etc., $20 to $25. College Year Commencement in June. Dean, William E. Huntington, Ph.D., 12 Somerset st.

Boston University College of Agriculture. (1867). Amherst. The regular course of study at the Boston University College of Agriculture occupies four years, and those who satisfactorily complete it receive from the College the degree of Bachelor of Science; the diplomas being signed by the Governor of Massachusetts, who is President of the Corporation. The regular course includes every branch of ordinary farming and gardening, and is both theoretical and practical. Each topic is thoroughly discussed in the lecture room, and again in the plant-house or field, where every student is obliged to work for six hours each week. Students are allowed to perform additional work, all labor being paid for at the rate of twelve and a half cents per hour. Expenses: Tuition, $26 per term; room-rent, $5 to $10 per term; board, $2.50 to $3.50 per week. Annual expenses, including books, $200 to $350. There are nearly one hundred *free* scholarships. Any person desiring admission to the College of Agriculture can apply for one of these Scholarships to the Senator of his district. (Amherst is 20 miles from Palmer. Palmer is on the Boston and Albany Railway, 84 miles from Boston.)

Bradford Academy. (1804). Bradford. A Seminary for young ladies, well known and of excellent repute. The pupils represent every part of the country. Miss Annie E. Johnson is the Principal. Having been founded in 1803, and incorporated in 1804, it is the oldest seminary for young ladies in the United States. Branches taught: English branches, ancient and modern languages, music, drawing, painting, etc. Tuition, including English branches, Latin and French, Greek or German, and vocal music in classes, for the year, $60; with board, etc., $350. Bradford is about thirty miles from Boston, on the Western division of the Boston and Maine Railway.

Brighton High School. Academy Hill, Brighton District. Master, Benjamin Wormelle.

Bryant-Stratton Commercial School. (1870). 608 Washington st. Principal, H. E. Hibbard. Penmanship, book-keeping, banking, etc. Rates of tuition, $40 for term of 10 weeks. No class system. Visiting hours, 9 to 10 A. M. and 1 to 2 P. M. School year begins on first Monday in September.

Burdett Business College. 167 Tremont st. Principals and proprietors, C. A. and F. H. Burdett. Business courses: Book-keeping,—double and single entry—arithmetic, penmanship, commercial law and correspondence, grammar and spelling; practical instruction in brokerage, agencies, etc. Terms: business course, 12 weeks, $30; per month, $12; penmanship, 20 lessons, $10; (teacher's course), $100; ornamental penmanship, per hour, $5. Evening sessions, business studies, $15; entire session, $25; business writing, $10 and $15.

Business School. (1828). 259 Boylston st. Chauncy Hall School has a department for preparing pupils for practical business life. Arithmetic, book-keeping, spelling, composition, penmanship, etc., are taught. Terms: $140.

Bureau. (See *Boston Shorthand Bureau.*)

Business Colleges and Schools. (See *Allen's Stenographic Institute, Berkeley School, Boston Commercial College, Boston School of Takigraphy, Boston School of Telegraphy, Boston Shorthand Bureau, Bryant-Stratton Commercial School, Burdett Business College, Chauncy Hall School, Comer Commercial College, French's Business College, Hafey Writing Academy, New England Telegraph, Normal Writing School, Reckers-Bradford School; Sawyer's Commercial College.*)

Bussey Institute School of Agriculture and Horticulture. (1870). Jamaica Plain District. A department of Harvard University. The great estate contains 360 acres, 137 of which are taken for the uses of the arboretum. (See *Arnold Arboretum.*) The grounds are naturally exceedingly beautiful, comprising upland, woodland, hills and meadows, among which are rippling brooks, the scene being one of the most charming to be found anywhere, especially within the precincts of a great commercial city. It has all the attractions of a rural landscape, combined with such artistic features as have been tastefully added. Very few of the inhabitants of the crowded city know what a sylvan spot can be reached in a ride of a few minutes' duration; but when the charms of this region are fully realized, as they will be when the park of 164 acres (120 acres of the arboretum and 44 acres adjoining) is made free to the public. The Bussey School was established here through the princely liberality of the late Benjamin Bussey, who bequeathed the valuable estate for the purpose of founding a school of agriculture, together with funds to be applied toward the same purpose. The school was opened in 1870, suitable buildings having been erected and roadways laid out. The school now has several eminent instructors, practical education being given to numerous students. Recitations, lectures, experiments, etc., conducted here are reported widely, and the Institute is assuming a foremost position among the great educational institutions of the land. The scientific study of agriculture and horticulture is one that may well interest the youth of this country, and the Bussey Institute, by its facilities for experimental investigation, its means, and the thorough methods of its Faculty, must continue to attract students from every section of the continent. Those who do not intend taking degrees are permitted to join the school at any time without examination, and take up any branch they please. Candidates for the degree of Bachelor of Agricultural (or Horticultural) science, if not fitted, are required to pass one year at the Lawrence Scientific School (Cambridge). Fees, academic year, $150; half year, $75; any single course, $40 a year.

Camilla Urso, Violin Lessons. This famous artiste receives pupils at certain times of the season when she is not away from Boston giving concerts. 451 Washington st.

Carpentry Schools. (See *Boys' Institute, Hemenway School, Manual Training School, North Bennet Street Industrial School, School of Mechanic Arts, Institute of Technology, South End Industrial School*).

Catholic Academies. (See *Boston College, Sacred Heart Academy, Notre Dame Academy* (Berkeley st.)., *Notre Dame Academy* (Roxbury District).

Catholic Theological Seminaries. (See *Boston College; St. John's Ecclesiastical Seminary*).

Chauncy Hall School. (1828). 259 Boylston st. Founded by Gideon F. Thayer. Now conducted by Ladd (Wm. H.) and Daniell (M. Grant), assisted by thirty teachers. Branches taught: Languages, book-keeping, elocution, declamation, penmanship, singing, drawing, chemistry, physics, botany, mineralogy, zoology, and military drill. For boys and girls. For *more than half a century* this School has been celebrated throughout America for its high standard, its thorough and effective methods, and, also, for its watchful care over the *bodily health* of its pupils. This School makes a specialty of taking healthy, bright children, particularly boys, who wish to make more rapid progress than the arrangements of public schools allow; backward boys or girls, who are assisted by extra teachers; delicate children, who cannot study out of school; those who have unusual talent for music, painting, or modern languages, and other children who are so susceptible to changes of heat or cold, and need to study in an even, well-ventilated temperature. Chauncy Hall School is delightfully located, fronting Copley sq.; fresh air and sunshine contribute greatly to the other great advantages of its situation. These collateral benefits should be regarded by every parent and guardian who desires to see the young pupil possess "a sound mind in a healthy body." It is certainly a model private school in every particular.

This School makes a specialty of preparing boys for business, professional schools, etc., in addition to fitting pupils for the Institute of Technology, and for Harvard University, both of which great colleges contain graduates of Chauncy Hall School. Tuition: English course, $125; High School department, $175; Grammar School department, $150; one language, $25; Classical course, $200, including the branches required for admission to Harvard. (Cars of the Vendome (Back Bay) line pass the door).

Chinese School. Mount Vernon Church, Ashburton pl. 2.30 and 7.30 P.M. on Sundays.

City Training School for Nurses. At the City Hospital, Harrison av., opp. Worcester sq. 2 years' course. Pay: $10 per month, first year; $14 second. Ages preferred, 24 to 35 years.

Classes for Women. Members of the Women's Educational and Industrial Union, (1877, 74 Boylston st. fee, $1 per year), have classes in book-keeping, stenography, language, gymnastics, embroidery, millinery, music, drawing, etc.

Classes in Pipe-Organ Playing. (1871), 281 Columbus av. Thorough courses of study. The average student is within a reasonable period of time qualified to undertake the direction of a choir, and to fulfil the other duties required of a church organist. (No class lessons are given on the great Pipe Organ. Terms: 20 half-hour lessons, $30; 20 one-hour lessons, $50.

Classes in Military Drill. (1828), 259 Boylston st. At Chauncy Hall School boys are taught the drill of a United States soldier as far as it can go at school, according to Upton's Tactics. When changes are made in army drill, corresponding changes are made in the school drill. (See *Chauncy Hall School*).

Classical School. 174 Boylston st., cor. Berkeley st. Edwin De Méritte, Director. Pupils prepared for Harvard University. Candidates for final examinations at the College allowed to choose their maxima from the four groups named by the University. Special Students, either classical language, $30 half-year. (See *Berkeley School*).

College Lafayette. 181 Tremont st. This school has become one of the great educational institutions of Boston and New England, chiefly from the ease and facility with which its pupils acquire the modern languages. The system in use here is a practical one, and appeals to the *common-sense* of the student, and the best test of its efficiency is in the successful *results* obtained. The Faculty comprise *native* and graduate teachers. The languages taught are French, German, Italian and Spanish. The grammar of each language, its literature and conversation carried on in it, in conjunction with translations from and into any language, are especial features of the excellent system of MM. Alba-Raymond and Genoud, whose reputation is a sufficient guaranty of thoroughness in every department of the College. The school is in an excellent location, overlooking the Common, and is easily accessible from all sections of the city and suburbs, as well as from all the railway stations, by means of a large number of horse railway lines which pass the door. It is also within a few steps of the great central Public Library, among the volumes of which are many standard works in the languages taught at the College Lafayette. Lessons are given privately and in classes. There are day and evening sessions. Pupils can arrange to have instruction given at their residences, an accommodation which finds ready appreciation. One can begin studies at any time. Terms of tuition, 65 lessons, $18. Lectures in French are given every Saturday, at 10.45 A. M., *free* to all pupils.

College of Agriculture, Boston University. (1867). Amherst. The Boston University College of Agriculture is one of the leading schools of the kind in the world. It is located in the beautiful Connecticut valley, on a farm of 400 acres. The buildings are on a most extensive scale. Agriculture is taught *practically* as well as theoretically. Each candidate for admission to this college must pass a satisfactory examination in English grammar, arithmetic, geography, algebra, and the history of the United States. The course of study is for a period of four years. Among the branches pursued are botany, horticulture, agriculture, chemistry, geology, veterinary science, zoölogy, mathematics, physics, civil engineering, military science, with drill exercises, languages (English, French and German), science (mental, moral and social). The degree of Bachelor of Science is awarded to graduates. Instruction includes lectures, practical exercises, experiments, etc. The annual expenses for tuition, including text-books, average from $250 to $350.

College of Letters. Tufts College, College Hill, Medford. Elmer H. Capen, D.D., President. (See *Tufts College*).

College of Liberal Arts. (1873). 12 Somerset st. (For males and females). The aim of this noted college is to furnish that liberal education which is the true preparation for the study of a learned profession, or for a life devoted to letters, education, or public affairs. It accordingly provides thorough and systematic instruction in all those branches of literature, philosophy and science, known as the Liberal Arts. The degrees of Bachelor of Arts and Bachelor of Philosophy are conferred at this college. Expenses: the only annual fees required from regular students in the College of Liberal Arts are: tuition, $100; incidentals, $10.

College of Music, Boston University. (1872). 27 East Newton st., Franklin sq. This college of music forms one of the great group of colleges comprising the Boston University (12 Somerset st.). *It is the only institution of its grade and kind in America.* This college of music is designed for students of the average proficiency of *graduates* of the best American conservatories of music. The advantages accruing to it from its location in Boston, and from its close association with Boston University, are very great. Here persons devoting themselves to this profession are enabled to complete a liberal education before beginning their special musical training. The best years for acquiring scholastic culture are also the best years for cultivating the voice, the ear and the hand. A generous intellectual and æsthetic culture is needed by every professional musician, and it is best acquired in connection with his special studies. The applicant for taking the piano-forte course at this college will be tested as to familiarity with Cramer's studies (Bülow), books 1 and 2; or Clementi's Gradus ad Parnassum (Tausig edition); Bach's Three-part Inventions; Moscheles, op. 70; Mayer, op. 119, book 1; Bach's French and English Suites; Kullak's Octaves, op. 49; Beethoven's Sonatas, etc. Candidates for the organ course will be examined in Rink's Organ School; Lemmens, Bach, Mendelssohn, and others. Tuition in voice, piano-forte or organ courses, including composition and lectures, §200 per year. The opportunities for culture outside of the college in Boston are too numerous to recapitulate. The Boston Public Library and the library of the college furnish a collection of *ten thousand volumes* relating to music, access to which is *free.*

College of Pharmacy. (Massachusetts). (1823). 1151 Washington st. The first apothecary shop in Boston of which history gives any account was that of William Davis, which was opened in 1646 on Washington st., a few steps north of the head of State st. The town pump was set up near his shop, in 1650. Mr. Davis had a residence on State st., near Kilby st. He was captain of the Ancient and Honorable Artillery Company--the oldest military organization in the country, having been formed in 1638, and is still an active company—from 1664 to 1672. The earliest movement for the improvement of pharmacy by legal means was made by the Massachusetts Medical Society, Nov. 8, 1786, when the Legislature was petitioned to prevent the sale of poor and adulterated drugs. The Massachusetts College of Pharmacy was formally instituted in January, 1823. Early in this century apothecaries feeling a need of increased scientific knowledge were accustomed to resort to the Harvard Medical College. Courses of lectures were delivered before the members of the College of Pharmacy about 1858. In 1867 efforts were made to form a class of drug-store clerks of Boston. Twenty young men joined the class. The results were so successful that the College resolved to establish a permanent practical School of Pharmacy. The institution has steadily grown, and the students now represent a number of cities and towns outside of Boston, who are attracted by the high standard of scientific knowledge imparted. The College has one of the largest pharmaceutical libraries in the United States, in addition to complete files of foreign journals devoted to this subject. The regular course of instruction occupies six months, from October to March of every year. (Elective courses in microscopical and systematic Botany are offered to classes of twelve or more.) Fees: Preliminary examination for matriculation, $4 ($2 to students employed by members); examination for graduation, $10; each of the Professors' courses, $15; all special courses, $15. The College occupies a building on Washington st., just above Dover st. Horse-cars from all parts of the city and railway stations pass frequently.

College of Physicians and Surgeons. 34 Essex st. (See *Medical College for Women and Men*).

Collins' Private School for Boys. Tremont st. Director, Leroy Z. Collins. No school for boys and young men in the United States enjoys a higher reputation than this, and in no institution of a similar class is there a higher standard of education nor a more thorough system employed. Instruction in elementary English studies is here imparted in the most through manner; French and German is taught by the most accomplished *native* teachers; while the departments devoted to preparing students for Harvard (and other universities), the Massachusetts Institute of Technology (and other scientific schools), as well as for business life, are carefully and systematically organized, and carried out with a view to the pupil's successfully passing any examination. Terms: $200 a year.

Columbia Bicycle School. The Columbia Bicycle and Tricycle Riding

School is located at 597 Washington st. Open from 7.30 A. M. to 6 P. M. daily, except Sundays. Terms: one lesson, with attendant, half hour, 50 cents; without attendant, 25 cents; one lesson, without attendant, one hour, 50 cents; Season tickets, good for one lesson a day, for thirty days, $5. Students of all branches will find that a morning or evening run on a bicycle or tricycle on the fine roads in the beautiful suburbs of Boston, will give renewed vigor to their intellectual faculties.

Columbus School of Languages and Sciences.
Knickerbocker Building. 178 and 179 Tremont st. Director, C. Veneziani, Ph. D. (Heidelberg). This school has taken its place among the leading educational institutions in the land. Its objects are to impart instruction in ancient and modern languages—their respective literatures, romance, philology — and in the sciences; and to prepare students for Harvard University, Massachusetts Institute of Technology, and all other Colleges and Scientific Schools. Languages are taught by a practical, scientific and philological method, with especial reference to the individual capabilities and requirements of each pupil. In the sciences, some departments of the Columbus School actually include the whole curriculum of the leading Universities. The departments are arranged as follows: I. Modern Languages — French, German, Italian and Spanish. II. Ancient Languages - Latin and Greek. III. Romance, Philology. IV. Literature of all of these Languages. V. Sciences, mathematics, chemistry, natural philosophy and descriptive astronomy. VI. Preparatory department, for fitting students for Colleges and Scientific Schools. Professor Veneziani's experience as Doctor of Philosophy of the great Boston University is a sufficient guarantee as to his ability in preparing students for college courses.

Comer Commercial College.
(1840). 666 Washington st. Principal, Chas. E. Comer. Branches taught: Penmanship, arithmetic, book-keeping, banking, etc. Tickets for tuition, good for one year, are sold as follows: 30 tickets, of two hours each, $12; 60 tickets, of five hours each, equal to 10 weeks of 6 days each, $35. (Take any Washington st. horse-car.)

Commercial Colleges and Schools.
(See *Allen's Stenographic Institute, Berkeley School, Boston Commercial College, Boston School of Telegraphy, Boston School of Telegraphy, Boston Shorthand Bureau, Bryant-Stratton Commercial School, Burdett Business College, Chauncy Hall School, Comer Commercial College, French's Business College, Hafey Writing Academy, New England Telegraph, Normal Writing School, Reekers-Bradford School, Sawyer's Commercial College.*

Concord School of Philosophy.
(1878). Concord. Throughout the length and breadth of the land has the Concord School of Philosophy made its influence felt, and the beautifully located and historic old town attracts quite a number of the great thinkers and educators of the country every summer. It is only 19 miles from Boston, is easily reached by two great railway lines, the Boston and Lowell, and Fitchburg, and those who attend the sessions of the school can keep their lodgings in the city if they do not care to remain in Concord over night. The idea of the establishment of this school occurred to its principal founder, the distinguished A. Bronson Alcott, as early as 1842, and, some English friends co-operating with him, he began the formation of a library of philosophic works in that year. The opening of the school, however, was delayed until the year 1879. It received warm encouragement from Ralph Waldo Emerson, Benjamin Pierce (of Harvard University), Ednah D. Cheney, William T. Harris, Thomas Wentworth Higginson, Cyrus A. Bartol, Francis B. Sanborn, David A. Wasson and Thomas Davidson, all of whom delivered lectures before the school during the first session (1879), the attendance largely exceeding the expectations of the Faculty. Julia Ward Howe, George Parsons Lathrop, and other well-known men and women have contributed lectures. The sessions were originally held in Mr. Alcott's study, Orchard House, but during the second year of the School the Hill-Side Chapel was built, and all meetings are now held there. The permanent and active members of the Faculty are Messrs. Alcott, Harris, Emery and Sanborn. Regarding purposes of the School, we quote from Mr. Sanborn's sketch of the institution, as follows: "The variety of subjects considered during the six summers that the school has existed shows that its scope is not a narrow one; and the wide diversity of opinion among those who have spoken from its platform may serve as a guarantee that no limitation of sect or philosophical Shibboleth has been enforced. The aim of the Faculty has been to bring together a few of those persons, who, in America, have pursued, or desire to pursue, the paths of speculative philosophy; to encourage these students and professors to communicate with each other on what they have learned or meditated; and to illustrate, by a constant reference to poetry and the higher literature, those ideas which philosophy presents." Eighth session of the school, July 14, 1886, the lectures and conversations of the first week being on Dante and his Divine Comedy; the second on Plato and his Influence in Philosophy. Terms, $5 for the season; single tickets, 50 cents.

Conducting, School of. (1867). Franklin sq. Carl Zerrahn, Director. Pupils are here taught the *practical* use of the baton.

Conservatories of Music. (See *Boston Conservatory of Music, Boston University College of Music, Harvard School of Music, Mendelssohn Musical Institute, New England Conservatory of Music, Parisian Academy of Music, Perkins Musical Institute, Petersilea Academy of Music, Tremont School of Music*).

Conservatory Course of Study in Public School Music. Franklin sq. H. E. Holt, Director. Classes are formed for the object of enabling pupils to sing any music at sight, especial attention being given to the matter of preparing pupils for church situations.

Conservatory School of Languages. (1867). 27 East Newton st., Franklin sq. The German, French and Italian languages are taught here by an especially effective system. Lessons are given in classes or privately.

Conservatory Tuning School. (1867). Franklin sq. Principal, F. W. Hale. Superintendent of tuning, at factory, E. W. Davis. Ladies as well as gentlemen are taught to master the tuning of piano-fortes, pipes and reed organs.

Cowles Art School. (1873). New Studio Building. 145 Dartmouth st. This celebrated Art School is established in a commodious, finely-located building, especially designed for it. The studios are of good size, well lighted and ventilated, and furnished with every convenience. The success of this school has thus far been simply phenomenal in the history of similar institutions in this or any other country. Taking the famous Académie Julian, of Paris, as a model, the Cowles School seeks to give art students such advantages as are particularly and peculiarly valuable, and in addition to the design of giving a continuous and thorough training in art, the school has a purpose to meet, in a wholesome way, the needs of a considerable number of earnest students who are not able to attend for long periods at a time, or who have been obliged to gain their instruction in an irregular and unequal manner, and require the making up of deficiencies in special lines of study, or of those who need some instruction to better fit them for special work, *as a means of livelihood*. The *practical* features of the arrangements of the school are as worthy of commendation as are its artistic phases. One mission of this school — according to the prospectus — is "to aid in diffusing some correct knowledge of art among those who study it as a recreation, and who, without the privilege, which the school gives, of consulting their convenience as to the time of attendance, or without having its opportunities *suited to their means*, would never receive that education — even if limited — of their natural taste, which tends to elevate the general appreciation of good Art. An arrangement is made by which students who are compelled to attend irregularly may do so." The school is under the management of Frank M. Cowles, one of the most thorough, conscientious and able conservators of art in the United States, to whose friendly encouragement many a successful artist is willing to bear grateful testimony. We can ourselves vouch for the almost marvellous progress of several pupils under his direction, having witnessed their gradual, but constant improvement, and listened to their praise of his painstaking kindness. The Faculty of this great school, which is recognized not only throughout America, but in Europe as well, as a model one, includes Dennis Miller Bunker (drawing and painting the figure and head, from the flat, cast and life, artistic anatomy and composition), Abbott F. Graves (painting flowers and still life), Mercy A. Bailey (drawing, painting, water colors and perspective), Frederick M. Turnbull, M. D. (lectures and demonstrations of artistic anatomy); J. Harvey Young, Edgar Parker and Henry Hitchings (visitors), Frank M. Cowles (manager). Tuition: for regular course, 2 lessons from one teacher, use of studio, models, all day, for 5 days in each week, 1st month, $15. Reductions are made to continuous students. For season, 35 weeks, $100 for new student. Special students, 5 lessons, $8; 9 lessons, $14. Saturday classes, 1 lesson, $2; per month, $6. Evening classes, $8 per month. (Take Dartmouth st., Back Bay or Columbus av. cars).

Cyr School of French Language. Richwood House, 258 Tremont st. M. Narcisse Cyr is the Director, his name being a sufficient guarantee of the excellence and thoroughness of the school, which has attained more than a national reputation. Its pupils represent every section of the country.

Dana Hall School. Wellesley. This is a school established for the purpose of preparing pupils to enter Wellesley College. Greek, Latin, music and art are taught in courses arranged with special reference to corresponding courses at the College.

De la Motte Private Music School. 36 Commonwealth av. Distinguished throughout the country for the brilliancy, ease and finish with which its pupils interpret the works of the masters, under the instruction of Mlle. Gabrielle de la Motte.

DeLestrade-Burkart School of French and German Languages.
179 Tremont st. A method original with this school is in successful operation here. The Principals consider the method of translation generally used, as ineffective; while in their opinion the so-called natural method causes too great a strain upon the nervous system. In order that one may get an idea of their method, the Principals will give a *free* lesson to any one desiring it. Tuition, (private): 12 lessons, $15; three persons, each, $8.75.

Delsarte School of Oratory and Dramatic Art.
(1881). 147 Tremont st. Here is taught the System of Expression formulated by M. François Delsarte, of whom Edwin Forrest said, "No other teacher ever succeeded in basing the Art of Acting on *a positive science.* This Delsarte philosophy, has, in *fifteen minutes,* given me a deeper insight into the philosophy of my own art, than I had myself learned in *fifty years* of study." This school is under the direction of Mrs. J. S. Heald, an eminent instructor in Dramatic Art. The large number of graduates and advanced pupils of other methods who have studied (and are at present studying) the Delsarte System at this school, testify to the importance of the system. The course of instruction is true, thorough, and practical in every branch, and no more pupils are admitted than can receive *personal* instruction from the Principal, whose long and successful experience as a teacher in this city is her highest testimonial. Ladies and gentlemen are prepared for the stage or the platform. Vocalists are taught dramatic action, gesture, and expression. Amateurs are coached. Defective utterance is cured. Classes are limited to five pupils, and are held day and evening, in Vocal Culture, Elementary Elocution, Platform Oratory, Dramatic Art, Gesture, etc. There are, also, special classes on Saturdays, for non-resident teachers and school children. Also, classes in Shakespeare and classical poetry. Private instruction is given when desired. Tuition: Classes, 20 lessons, $10; private, $40. The Booth Dramatic Club, connected with this school, affords students opportunities for practical experience on the stage. (See *Booth Dramatic Club*).

Dental School of Harvard University.
(1868). North Grove st., Boston. The course of study for the first of the three years is the same as that of the first year of the Harvard Medical School Course, lessons during that time being given by the instructors of the Medical School, the dental pupils joining the medical pupils. After the first year the students attend the Dental school. Students are given practice in operations of dentistry. Instructors and Demonstrators are in attendance every day of the academic year in the Infirmary, a department of the Massachusetts General Hospital. Students have access to the various hospitals of the city, as well as to the dissecting-room, museum and library of the Harvard Medical School. Degree of Doctor of Dental Medicine conferred. Tuition: $200, first year; $150, second; $50 any year following. Graduates of other recognized dental schools are admitted to the courses of operative and mechanical dentistry, paying $50 for each course.

Dental Schools.
(See *Boston Dental School, Dental School of Harvard University.*)

Divinity School.
Tufts College, College Hill, Medford. Elmer H. Capen, D. D., President. (See *Tufts College.*)

Dramatic Schools.
(See *Bickford School of Elocution, Bijou Dramatic School, Boston School of Expression, Boston School of Oratory, Delsarte School of Oratory and Dramatic Art, Lothian Dramatic Lessons, Monroe Conservatory of Oratory, Rachel Noah's Lessons in Dramatic Action*).

Draper-Hall Riding School.
83-97 West Dedham st. One of the largest and best conducted Riding Academies in America. Terms: Single lessons, one hour, $2; twenty lessons, $25; Road lessons, $5. Lessons for ladies, 9 to 12, 2 to 4. Gentlemen, 7 to 9, 4 to 6. Exercise rides for both sexes, 12 to 2. Evenings, 7 to 9. Music on Tuesday and Saturday evenings, from 7.30 to 9. Horses boarded for $6 per week. Horses trained to saddle. Telephone to principal Hotels and business houses. (Take Washington st. or Tremont st. horse-cars).

Dress-Making School.
(1880). Young Women's Christian Association. Gray st., near Berkeley st. Day classes, $10 for the course; evening classes,—for working girls,—$2 for the course.

Edith Abell's Vocal Lessons.
Miss Edith Abell occupies a foremost rank among American vocal teachers. She fits pupils for the concert, opera and oratorio stage. Music Hall Building.

Eichberg's Violin School.
(1867). 154 Tremont st. Julius Eichberg, Director. This is considered to be the best Violin School in America. Mr. Eichberg was in his youth a pupil of the greatest artists in Europe, and has become renowned as a soloist and as an orchestral conductor. It is doubtful if Europe can afford such thorough instruction on the

Violin as can be had here. Tuition: one term of 20 lessons (in class of 4), $20. Beginners, first term, $15. Some of the most distinguished violin *virtuosi*, including such artists as Edouard Remenyi, have accorded high praise to this school. Mr. Remenyi, in a letter to Mr. Eichberg, says: "I need not tell you that there is nothing like your Violin School in America; honestly there is scarcely anything better in Europe. *If a man wants to learn to play the violin, he certainly can learn it at your school.* My dear Eichberg, let me congratulate you on your success, and thank you as only one can to whom the violin in particular—and music in general—is so dear." Wilhelmj, Ole Bull and others have warmly commended the system of instruction here. (See *Boston Conservatory of Music*).

Evening Classes in Dressmaking. Industrial Department of Young Women's Christian Association. Gray st., near Berkeley. $2 for the course.

Farm School. Thompson's Island, Boston Harbor. Free school for poor but not vicious boys. Not a reform school, but a charitable educational institution. Boys are taught agriculture, English branches, music, etc.

Fast French Classes. 174 Boylston st., cor. Berkeley st. At the Berkeley School, classes in French, composed of beginners who wish to make rapid progress, have been formed. Terms, $25, half year.

Flora E. Barry's School of Vocal Instruction, and for Preparing Artists for the Lyric Stage. 124 Chandler st. Mrs. Barry has more than a local reputation as an artiste and teacher. She has filled engagements with some of the most celebrated Opera Companies in the country most successfully, receiving the highest praise of critics and public—among them the Hess Grand English Opera Company, the Mahn English Opera Company, etc.—and her recent artistic performances at the Hollis Street Theatre are fresh in the minds of all who witnessed them. Mrs. Barry has for some years been one of the brightest ornaments of our local lyric stage, not only in opera, but in concert and oratorio as well, being equally successful as an exponent of the classical or lighter schools. Even so critical an authority as John S. Dwight, the severest musical critic in America, has given her the highest praise, as will be seen by the following extract from his *Journal*: "It was pleasant to hear again the warm, rich tones of Flora E. Barry, who sang her beautiful selections in her usual refined artistic style, and with true musical feeling. She loses nothing of the purple bloom or tenderness of her voice. A more sympathetic, purely musical contralto we do not know; such a voice certifies to a fine musical nature." Mrs. Barry has the rare faculty of imparting her perfect method, as many of her pupils bear witness. Boston is indeed fortunate in possessing so eminent a teacher. She makes an especial feature of preparing students for concert, oratorio and operatic stage. Terms: 20 half-hour lessons, $45; 20 one-hour lessons, $80.

Free Carpentry Schools. Free schools in Carpentry have been established at the Boys' Institute, 375 Harrison av., Hemenway School, Tennyson st., Manual Training School, Warren av., North Bennet Street Industrial School.

Free Carpet-Making School. (1872). 191 Boylston st. One of the schools of the Massachusetts Institute of Technology, known as the Lowell (John) School of Design. The work-rooms are located on Garrison st.—between Huntington av. and St. Botolph st.—on the Back Bay. (See *Lowell Free School of Design*).

Free Classes in Domestic Service. (1866). Y. W. C. A. Gray st. Tuition and board free to girls of 15 years and upwards, who take a three months' course in house service.

Free Classes in Engineering. 191 Boylston st. Lowell Institute, evenings.

Free Classes in History. 191 Boylston st. Lowell Institute, evenings.

Free Evening Drawing Schools. (1871). Pupils must be over 15 years of age. Location of schools: For Mechanical Drawing, Starr King School, Tennyson st.; Stevenson Building, Central sq., E. B.; City Hall, City sq., Charlestown District; Municipal Court Building, Roxbury District. Free-hand Drawing, Latin School, Warren av., and at all the other schools named, except the Starr King School. Open on Monday, Wednesday and Friday, from 7.30 to 9.30 P. M. Instruments loaned to the needy.

Free Evening Elementary Schools. (1868). For any person over 12 years old. Location of Schools: (City proper) Eliot Schoolhouse, North Bennet st.; Anderson-Street Schoolhouse; Wells School-house, Blossom st., cor. McLean st.; Quincy School-house, Tyler st., Franklin School-house, Ringgold st., (South Boston), Bigelow School-house, 4th st., cor. E st.; Lincoln School-house, Broadway, near K st.; (East Boston), Lyman School-house, Paris st., cor. Decatur st.; (Charlestown District), Warren

School-house, Pearl st., cor. Summer st.; (Roxbury District), Comins School-house, Tremont st., cor. Terrace st.; Dearborn School-house, Dearborn pl. Branches: Reading, Writing, Arithmetic, etc. Regular attendance is required. Sessions, 7 to 9 P. M.

Free Evening High School.
(1869). Montgomery st. Sessions, 7.30 to 9.30 P. M. Every week-day evening except Saturday and legal holidays, from the last Monday in September, to the first Friday in March, except the week preceding the first Monday in January. Regular and punctual attendance is required from all who enter as pupils.

Free Classes in History.
(See Old North Free Classes).

Free Classes in Mending.
(1881). 13 Burroughs pl., Hollis st. Free instruction to women.

Free Classes in Telegraphy.
Girls' Industrial Club, 27 Chambers st. Evenings.

Free Cooking Classes.
(1881). 13 Burroughs pl., Hollis st. Lessons given to girls and women. Free evening classes.

Free Courses of Instruction.
191 Boylston st. Open to persons of either sex over 18 years of age. Given in the evening, by the Lowell Institute, at the Institute of Technology. Branches: mathematics, mechanics, physics, drawing, chemistry, geology, natural history, biology, English, French, German, history, navigation, nautical astronomy, architecture and engineering.

Free Education in Nautical Astronomy.
191 Boylston st. Lowell Institute. Evenings.

Free Evening Drawing Classes for Newsboys and Bootblacks.
(1879). 16 Howard st. Open from 7 to 10 P. M. A school of drawing, etc., for all newsboys and bootblacks who exhibit a taste for the fine arts.

Free Grammar and Primary Schools.
The Public Schools of Boston have long held a foremost position among the Educational Institutions of the country. The excellence of the methods employed, the high standard, and the thoroughness of the system have commanded the admiration of all who have examined them. Since the year 1634, when the first free school was opened, the growth of the plan has been gradual, progressive and far-reaching, until to-day

Boston has the most perfect Public School system in the country. The locations of the Free Public Schools are as follows: Adams (1856), Belmont sq., E. Boston; Agassiz (1849), Burroughs st., Jamaica Plain District; Allston (1848), Cambridge st., Allston District; Andrew (1873), Dorchester st., Washington Village; Bennett (1847), Chestnut Hill av., Brighton District; Bigelow (1849), South Boston; Bowdoin (1821), Myrtle st; Brimmer (1844), Common st.; Bunker Hill, Charlestown District; Chapman, (1849), E. Boston; Charles Sumner, (1862), Roslindale District; Comins, 132 Tremont st.; Dearborn, Dearborn pl.; Dillaway, Kenilworth st.; Dorchester-Everett, Dorchester Dist.; Dudley, Dudley st.; Dwight, (1844), 115 W. Springfield st.; Eliot, (1713, No. Bennet st.; Emerson, (1865, E. Boston; Everett, 1860, 232 Northampton st.; Franklin (1865), Ringold st.; Frothingham, Charlestown Dist.; Gaston (1873), South Boston; George Putnam, Roxbury Dist.; Gibson, Dorchester Dist.; Hancock (1822), Parmenter st.; Harris, Dorchester Dist.; Harvard (1636), Charlestown Dist.; Hillside (1858), Jamaica Plain Dist.; Hyde (1885), Hammond st.; Lawrence (1844), South Boston; Lewis, Dale st.; Lincoln (1859), 648 Broadway, S. B.; Lowell (1874), 310 Centre st.; Lyman (1837), E. B.; Mather, Dorchester Dist.; Minot, Neponset Dist.; Mount Vernon (1862), W. Roxbury Dist.; Norcross, (1858), S. B.; Phillips (1844), Phillips st.; Prescott, Charlestown Dist.; Prince, (1880), Exeter st.; Quincy (1847), Tyler st.; Rice (1867), Dartmouth st.; Sherwin (1870), Madison sq.; Shurtleff (1869), S. B.; Stoughton 1856, Dorchester Dist.; Tileston, Mattapan Dist.; Warren (1840), Charlestown Dist.; Wells, 1833, Blossom st.; Winthrop (1886), 246 Tremont st.; School for Deaf Mutes, Warrenton st.

Free Hand Drawing School.
(See School of Mechanic Arts.)

Free High Schools.
For boys of 13 and girls of 14, graduates from grammar schools. There are eight of these High schools, two in the city proper, and one each in the Charlestown, East Boston, Roxbury, Dorchester and Brighton Districts.

Free Industrial Training School.
(1835). Young Women's Christian Association. Gray st., near Berkeley st. Tuition, with board, free to girls between 16 and 20 years of age, who take a three months' course in house service.

Free Instruction in Architecture.
11 Boylston st. Lowell Institute. Evenings.

Free Instruction in Bookkeeping.
Girls' Industrial Club. 27 Chambers st.

Free Instruction in Mathematics. 191 Boylston st. Evenings.

Free Kindergartens. (1879). Among the grand philanthropic institutions of Boston are the Free Kindergartens, established and supported by Mrs. Quincy A. Shaw. Wishing to test the advisability of opening Kindergartens among the poorer classes of the community as a preparation for the public schools, and as a part of the great public school system—this noble, public-spirited lady founded, at her own expense, the most perfect organization of Kindergartens in the country. So successful was the plan, that it has since been continued and enlarged by her. Children from the age of three-and-a-half to six years are received, from 9 to 12 M., from September to July. The Kindergartens are located as follows: Sharp Schoolhouse, Anderson st.; Wells Schoolhouse, Blossom st.; Baldwin Schoolhouse, Chardon ct.; 64 No. Margin st.; Cushman Schoolhouse, Parmenter st.; 39 No. Bennet st.; Porimort Schoolhouse, Suelling pl.; Guild Schoolhouse, East st.; Ward Building, Hudson st.; Warren Chapel, 10 Warrenton st.; Howe Schoolhouse, Fifth st., S. B.; 933 Albany st.; 147 Ruggles st.; Cottage pl.; Tremont st. Any further information concerning these Schools will be given by Miss Laliah B. Pingree, 302 Marlborough st., between 1 and 2 P. M.

Free Latin School. (1635). Warren av. The oldest school in the United States, even ante-dating Harvard University (founded in 1638, three years later). The Public Latin School for Boys occupies the largest and finest building used by any public school in the land, located on Warren av., Dartmouth and Montgomery sts. Among the famous pupils of this School have been Benjamin Franklin, John Hancock, Samuel Adams, Charles Sumner, Ralph Waldo Emerson, and others. It is a school in which Boston takes the greatest pride.

Free Latin School for Girls. (1878). West Newton st. Prepares girls over 11 years old for the higher branches, or for a collegiate course.

Free Lessons in Chemistry. 191 Boylston st. Lowell Institute. Evenings.

Free Lessons in Drawing. 191 Boylston st. Lowell Institute.

Free Lessons in Engineering. 191 Boylston st.

Free Lessons in Geology. 191 Boylston st. Lowell Institute. Evenings.

Free Lessons in Modern Languages. 191 Boylston st. Lowell Institute.

Free Lessons in Navigation. 191 Boylston st. Lowell Institute. Evenings.

Free Lessons in Oil-Cloth Pattern Making. (See *Lowell School of Design.*)

Free Lessons in Penmanship. Girls' Industrial Club. 27 Chambers st.

Free Lessons in Printing. 39 North Bennet st.

Free Lessons in Shoemaking. 39 North Bennet st.

Free Lowell School of Design. (For males and Females). (1872). The (John) Lowell School of Practical Design was established for the purpose of promoting Industrial Art in the United States. The expenses of this school are borne by the John Lowell Institute Fund, and *Tuition is free to all pupils, male or female.* The school occupies rooms, for drawing and weaving, in the Lowell Institute Building, on Garrison st., Boston. The weaving room affords students an opportunity of working their designs into actual fabrics of commercial sizes, and of every variety of material and of texture. The room is supplied with two fancy chain-looms for dress goods, three fancy chain-looms for fancy woollen cassimeres, one gingham loom and one jacquard loom. The school is constantly provided with samples of all the novelties in textile fabrics from Paris, such as brocaded silks, ribbons, alpacas, armures and fancy woollen goods. Students are taught the art of making patterns for prints, ginghams, delaines, silks, laces, paper-hangings, carpets, oil-cloths, etc. The course is of three years' duration, and embraces: 1. Technical manipulations; 2. Copying and variations of designs; 3. Original designs or composition of patterns; 4. The making of working drawings, and finishing of designs. Instruction is given personally to each student over his (or her) work. The class is under the personal direction of Charles Kastner, assisted in the weaving department by Joseph Caldwell, and in the designing department by Delphina Weston. All correspondence relating to the John Lowell Free School of Practical Design, should be addressed to the Secretary of the Massachusetts Institute of Technology, 191 Boylston st., Boston.

Free Modelling Schools. Free classes in modelling are open to those who have taken the first year's course in mechanical and free-hand drawing, at the Latin School, Warren av., and at the other free evening drawing schools. (See *Free Evening Drawing Schools*.)

Free Normal Art School. (1873). 145 Washington st. Established and maintained by the State. This great school is designed as a training school for teachers of industrial art. It aims to provide for high skill in technical drawing, and for Industrial Art culture. Candidates of both sexes must be sixteen years of age, or over; must bring a certificate of moral character; must be able to pass an examination in the common English branches, and in free-hand drawing of ornament from copy. The school offers a four years' course of training in the mechanical and artistic branches, and their practical application to industry. The discipline of the school is made as simple as possible. Pupils are expected to govern themselves. Faculty: George H. Bartlett, Principal (free-hand light and shade drawing; W.F. Brackett architecture and perspective; A. K. Cross, geometry and instrumental drawing; Charles M. Carter drawing in the public schools; Miss A. M. Davis free-hand drawing, Albert H. Munsell sculpture and advanced perspective; Miss D. L. Hoyt painting in water colors; Miss M. A. Bailey painting in oil; Miss M. T. Jones (curator). More than four hundred pupils have already passed the examination and completed the certificate works in the several classes, and received certificates or diploma. Tuition is free to students residing within the St. b., who intend to teach drawing in the Public Schools. Tuition to those coming from other States, $30 per term. Special students, $2 per term. (Take any cars going south on Washington st. to Deacon House, No. 1645).

Free Normal School for Girls. (18... Dartmouth st., cor. Appleton st. Girls over 18 years of age are here trained for teachers. Sessions, 9 to 2, except on Saturday.

Free Pattern Making School. (1872). 101 Boylston st. Free instruction is here given to males and females in the art of making patterns for prints, ginghams, delaines, silks, laces, paper-hangings, oil-cloths, etc. See *Lowell Free School of Designs*.

Free Sewing Classes. (1881). 13 Burroughs pl., Hollis st. Free Sewing class for girls on Saturdays, at 2.

Free Roxbury Latin School. 1645. Kearsarge av., near Warren st., Roxbury District.

Free School for the Deaf. Horace Mann School, Warrenton st. Small fee required from non-residents of Boston.

Free School in Millinery. Girls' Industrial Club, 27 Chambers st. Evenings.

Free School of Biology. 191 Boylston st. Lowell Institute. Evenings.

Free School of Cooking. North Bennet Street Industrial School, Ruggles Street Church for girls; South End Industrial School, 45 Bartlett st., Roxbury; Trinity House, 13 Burroughs pl.

Free School of Dressmaking. First Church, Marlborough st., Saturday, at 2.30 P. M.; Girls' Industrial Club, 27 Chambers st.; South End Industrial School, 45 Bartlett st., Roxbury District.

Free School of Laundry Work. 39 North Bennet st.

Free School of Loom-Work. Garrison st. (See *Free Lowell School of Designs*.

Free School of Manual Training. 1884. Basement of Latin School, Warren av. For boys of grammar schools, over 14. Carpentry taught.

Free School of Natural History. 141 Boylston st., Lowell Institute, evenings.

Free Sewing Schools for Children. Ruggles-Street Church, Roxbury, Thursday afternoons; First Church, Marlborough st., Saturday, at 2.30 P. M.; 54 Meridian st., East Boston, Saturday afternoons; New South Church, Shawmut av., Parmenter-Street Chapel, 10 to 12 on Saturdays; Church of the Good Shepherd, Cortes st., Saturdays, 10.30 to 12; Girls' Industrial Club, 27 Chambers st., evenings; St. Paul's Church, 134 Tremont st., Saturday mornings, Trinity Chapel, Boylston st., cor. Clarendon, Saturdays, 10 A. M.; Children's Mission, 277 Tremont st., Saturday, 2.30 P. M.; 48 Charity Building, Chardon st., Saturday, 1 P. M.; North End Mission, 201 North st., Saturday, 10 to 12; 13 Burroughs pl., Saturdays, at 2 P. M.

Free Sewing School for Women. 201 North st., Fridays, 2 to 4.

Free Singing Classes. (1881). 13 Burroughs pl., Hollis st. Free lessons in singing; evenings.

Free Vacation Schools. Established for the purpose of providing occupation for school-children, in July and August, when the Public Schools are closed, and for keeping them from the bad influences of the streets. Educational and industrial training.

Free Weaving School. (1872). 191 Boylston st. Free instruction in practical weaving is given to males and females, by able teachers. Pupils are fully taught to work their designs into real fabrics. (See *Lowell Free School of Design*).

French's Business College. (1848). 174 Boylston st., cor. Berkeley st. Charles French, A. M., Principal. One of the oldest Commercial Schools in the United States. Branches taught: Business arithmetic, penmanship, English grammar, spelling, book-keeping, business papers, correspondence, banking, exchange, commercial law, French, German, Spanish, history, etc. Terms: $35 for three months' course.

Gannett Institute for Young Ladies. (1854). 69 Chester sq. The courses of study comprise three regular departments—Preparatory, Intermediate and Senior—four years being allotted to the studies of the last department, the branches including algebra, natural philosophy, chemistry, history of England, English analysis, mythology, French or Latin, exercises in composition, physiology by lectures, geometry, trigonometry, rhetoric, modern and mediæval history, American literature, astronomy, art, Shakespeare, mental philosophy, moral philosophy, evidences of Christianity, ancient history, Homer, Wordsworth, classical literature, etc. A partial course may be taken, or a selection of studies is permitted. There are also French, German and Latin courses, with an additional course for post-graduates. Music, drawing and painting are taught as extras. Tuition: day pupils, senior department, $200 per annum; intermediate, $150; preparatory, $125; pupils under 12, $100; under 10, $80; family pupils, board and tuition, $500 for the scholastic year. The high educational and moral standing of the Gannett Institute has given it a national reputation, as will be seen by perusing the list of names of the pupils and the various sections of the country they represent. The Institute now occupies three large buildings, in a pleasant, healthful and quiet location.

Garrett Music Lessons. There is no vocal teacher in America who has a more thorough and perfect system of voice training than Mme. Wm. Garrett. Foreign teachers express themselves as being delighted with the method of pupils coming from Mme. Garrett. (200 Columbus av).

Gilder School of Pianoforte Playing. John Francis Gilder, the recognized exponent of the brilliant School of Pianoforte Playing, illustrated by Gottschalk, receives a few special pupils when not on concert tours. 451 Washington st.

Hafey Writing Academy. 125 Tremont st. Established by Madame Hafey, for the teaching of English Angular Penmanship, so much in vogue among the ladies of Boston and vicinity.

Harvard Annex. (*College for Women*). (1879). Cambridge. The Society for the Collegiate Instruction of Women by Professors and other instructors of Harvard University, has established in Greenough House, Garden st., overlooking Cambridge Common, America's Great College for Women. It is placed far beyond all other existing schools for the gentler sex, not only on account of the extremely high standard adopted by its Board of Management, but also by reason of its unique advantage in having instruction given by eminent Professors of the foremost University on the continent, in addition to many instructors of the same institution, comprising a Faculty of nearly fifty of the leading educators of the land. The President of the Society for the Collegiate Instruction of Women, under whose auspices the Harvard Annex has been steadily prosperous, is Mrs. Louis Agassiz. Arthur Gilman is Secretary (5 Waterhouse st., Cambridge); the Treasurer being Miss Lillian Horsford (27 Craigie st., Cambridge). The Executive Committee include Miss Alice M. Longfellow, James B. Greenough, and Joseph B. Warner. Members of the Corporation are Charles Eliot Norton and Henry L. Higginson. The courses of study include Hebrew; Sanskrit and Comparative Philology; Greek; Latin; English; German; French; Italian; Philosophy; Political Economy; History; Fine Arts; Music; Mathematics; Physics; Astronomy; Chemistry; Natural History. Candidates should make formal application for admission to the Secretary, who will furnish blanks for the purpose. Special students who wish to pursue only higher studies, will not be required to pass the regular examinations, provided they satisfy the instructors of their ability to pursue these special studies with advantage. The courses of study given here are similar to those offered at Harvard University, thereby fully realizing, at last, *the equal education of the sexes*. Any student, at the end of her period of study, is entitled to a certificate, stating the studies in which she has passed satisfactory examinations. Any one passing with distinction such examinations as are required for Honors in Harvard University, shall receive a certificate to that effect. One pursuing a four years' course of study, such as would be accepted for the degree of Bachelor of Arts in Harvard University, will be entitled to a certificate to that effect. The Sargent Private Gymnasium is open for the use of the young women, *free of charge*. Fees: The fee for a full year's instruction is $200; for a single course—or two half courses—$75. The Board of Management will see that the students secure suitable lodgings, and will assist them with advice and other friendly offices. A list of approved lodging places is in the hands of the Secretary.

Harvard Divinity School. (1815). Cambridge. Graduates of any College are admitted without examination. Full course, three years. Instruction is given in theology, ecclesiastical history, New Testament criticism and interpretation, Hebrew and Biblical literature. Tuition: $50 a year.

Harvard Medical School. (1782). Boylston st. Boston. This is the leading School of Medicine in the United States. Its *one hundred and third* annual catalogue has been issued. Instruction is given by lectures, recitations, clinical teaching and practical exercises. The degree of Doctor of Medicine is conferred, upon the completion of three years of study. A new building has recently been erected, at a cost of more than a quarter of a million of dollars. Among the Professors are Oliver Wendell Holmes, Henry J. Bigelow, J. Collins Warren and more than fifty other eminent Instructors. Fees and expenses: For matriculation, $5; for one year, $200; for a half year alone, $120; for graduation, $30. Board: a list of boarding-houses in the vicinity of the College, with rates from $5 to $10 per week, is furnished by the janitor of the College Building. The Boylston Medical Prizes, open to competition, are awarded annually.

Harvard School of Comparative Zoology. (1859). Established principally through the efforts of the late Louis Agassiz, who was its Director while he lived. Here the Harvard University courses on geology, entomology, etc., are given. The Museum contains the Natural History Collections of the University. Special students are received by the instructors and assistants in their respective departments in the Museum.

Harvard University. Cambridge. (1638). This is the oldest, largest and most famous college in the United States. It was founded only eight years after the settlement of Boston. The University comprises the following departments: Harvard College; The Divinity School; The Law School; The Lawrence Scientific School; The Medical School; The Dental School; The Museum of Comparative Zoölogy; The Bussey Institute; The Arnold Arboretum; The Botanic Garden; The Observatory; The Library and The Peabody Museum of American Archæology and Ethnology. Of these departments, The Medical School, The Dental School, The Bussey Institute and the Arnold Arboretum are in Boston, the seat of the University being in Cambridge, however. In order to give an idea of the vast wealth of this renowned University it may be stated that the invested funds of the College Corporation aggregate about five millions of dollars. The Faculty numbers 160, about one-third of them being Professors. There are nearly 1,500 students at present. Deserving students are assisted pecuniarily by various scholarships, (free and otherwise), loan funds, etc. Harvard University has *nearly fifty buildings*, (stone or brick), in Cambridge and Boston, in use for college purposes: among them being Massachusetts Hall built in 1720, Harvard Hall (1766), Holden Chapel (1744), Hollis Hall (1763), Stoughton Hall (1806), Holworthy Hall (1812), University Hall (1815), Gore Hall (1841), Boylston Hall (1858), Appleton Chapel (1858), Museum of Comparative Zoology (1860), Gray Hall (1863), Thayer Hall (1870), Holyoke Hall (1871), Mathews Hall (1872), Weld Hall (1872), Memorial Hall (1874), Peabody Museum 1877, Sever Hall (1880), Hemenway Gymnasium (1880). (See various departments under respective heads).

Harvard University. Cambridge. Cost of a year in the College. It will be seen from the following table of expense, that the sum of $484 is as low as can be estimated for the necessary expenses—including clothing and laundry—of a year at this great University. Rigid economy will be required in order to do this, but no saving that will be in the least detrimental to the health of the student.

	Least	Economical	Medical Students	Very Hard
Tuition	$150	$150	$150	$150
Books and Stationery	28	35	45	61
Clothing	79	120	150	300
Room	22	30	100	175
Furniture (annual average)	10	15	25	50
Board	133	152	52	304
Fuel and light	11	15	30	45
Washing	15	20	40	50
Societies and subscription to sports (annual average)			35	50
Servant				25
Sundries	45	65	85	150
Total	$484	$592	$812	$1360

Harvard University Examinations. Cambridge. Out-of-town examinations are held June 1, 2 and 3, at the following places (in addition to the examination in Cambridge, in Sever Hall, on the days named): Adams Academy, Quincy; Phillips Academy, Andover; Phillips Exeter Academy, Exeter, N. H.; Young Men's Christian Association Rooms, New York, N. Y.; Academy of Natural Sciences Hall, Philadelphia, Pa.; Law School Rooms, Cincinnati, Ohio; Chicago Athenæum Rooms, Chicago, Ill.; Central High School Building, St. Louis, Mo.; Boys' High School Rooms, San Francisco. At these places the *first* examination only is held; the second examination taking place in Cambridge *only*, Sept. 29, 30 and Oct 1. A fee of five dollars is paid in advance by every candidate who is examined at any place other than Cambridge. The whole fee of a candidate who proposes to divide his examination between two years is payable in the year when he begins his examination. The fee should be sent by check, postal order or registered letter to Allen Danforth, Bursar, Harvard University, Cambridge, Massachusetts, at the same time that the candidate sends his name to the Secretary, so that each may be received on or before June 18th.

Harvard University. Order of examinations. *First Day:* 8 A. M., Applicants meet officer in charge; 9 to 10, Cæsar and Virgil; 10 to 11, Latin Translation at sight and Composition; 11.30 to 12.30, Xenophon at sight; 12.30 to 1.30, Sentences to be translated into Greek. (The foregoing are prescribed). 3 to 4, Cicero; 4 to 5, Virgil and Ovid; 5 to 6 Latin Composition. (Elective I). *Second Day:* 8 to 9.30 A. M., Algebra; 9.30 to 10, Arithmetic, (Prescribed); 10 to 11, Translation of Herodotus at sight; (Elective II). 11.30 to 12.30, Ancient History and Geography; 10.30 to 2, English; 3 to 4, Plane Geometry, (Prescribed); 4 to 5, Greek Prose Composition; 5 to 6, Homer, Iliad; (Elective II). *Third Day:* 8 to 9, A. M., French or German; 9 to 10, Physics (Prescribed); 10.30 to 12, Trigonometry; 12 to 1.30, Solid Geometry; (Elective III.) 3 to 4.30, Physics; 4.30 to 6, Chemistry *or* Botany. (Elective IV.)

Harvard University School of Music. It is superfluous to state that no School of Music in the world has a more exalted standard than that maintained at the Harvard University Musical Department. Under the direction of John Knowles Paine, who is universally recognized as America's foremost native composer, this institution takes rank with the renowned Music Schools of Berlin, Leipsic, Stuttgard, Paris, London and other cities of the Old World. Indeed, since its establishment, numbers of students have attended this school instead of going abroad to study. The courses are in general as follows: For the first course some proficiency in pianoforte or organ playing is required; the third course requires a knowledge of musical notation; the advanced courses are the second, fifth and sixth. *Course* 1: The fundamental principles of the theory of music are embodied in the study of Harmony, which treats of the different chords in their natural relations and combinations. Richter's Harmony is used as the basis of the instruction, with illustrations and explanations in the class-room. The work will consist chiefly of written exercises on figured basses, which will be played over and corrected in the class-room. Before the close of the year well-known chorals and national airs will be harmonized. *Course* 2: Counterpoint applies the principles of harmony to the melodious treatment of the several voice parts in combination. The art of musical composition begins properly with this course, and is therefore indispensable to the thorough student. Richter's Counterpoint is used in teaching this course. The work consists principally of written exercises on given themes, in the following order: chorals and other melodies harmonized, using passing notes; the different orders in counterpoint in two, three and four voices; double counterpoint in the octave; free imitative counterpoint in two, three and four voices. The simple forms of free composition, organ preludes, songs and part songs, will be composed by the students in this course. *Course* 3: The History of Music, comprehending the whole field of Musical Art. The gradual development of music from ancient to modern times is traced, giving the history of Gregorian church music; the origin and development of the modern scales and counterpoint; the choral music of the Flemish and Italian masters of the 15th and 16th centuries; history of the opera, cantata, oratorio; instrumental music, with the development of the present classical forms of composition as represented by the great masters; musical instruments, ancient and modern, etc., etc. Vocal and instrumental illustrations are performed in the class-room. Instruction is given in this course in the form of lectures, the following books being recommended for reference: Von Dommer's Musik Geschichte, Ritter's History of Music (2 volumes), Bonavia Hunt's Concise History of Music; Grove's Dictionary of Music. (A full list of works on this subject will be supplied by Professor Paine.) *Course* 5 is the most advanced course in strict composition, naturally succeeding courses 1 and 2. Richter's Canon and Fugue is the text-book. The time is mainly occupied in composition of original and given themes, consisting of choral variations, various kinds of canons, and two, three and four-part fugues. *Course* 6: A knowledge of Musical Form (or thematic construction) is essential to the thorough understanding and appreciation of the works of the great composers, as embodied in their immortal Symphonies, Overtures, String Quartets, Sonatas, etc. Lectures will also be given in this course. Pauer's Musical Forms is used as a text-book. The principal instrumental works of Haydn, Mozart, Beethoven, Schumann, Mendelssohn, and others are analyzed. Each work is played upon the pianoforte by Professor Paine, in the class-room. This course requires inventive talent and ability to compose in the following forms of free instrumental music: Prelude, Etude, Song without words, Nocturne, March, Polonaise, Minuet, Scherzo, Rondo, and finally the *complete Pianoforte Sonata*. The last two courses have an important bearing on final honors. Tuition: fee for each full course, one year, for special students, $15. Cost of books used: Richter's Harmony, $1.63; Richter's Counterpoint, $1.63; Von Dommer's Musik Geschichte, $4.40. Ritter's History of Music (2 vols.), $2.50; Richter's Canon and Fugue, $1.63; Pauer's Musical Forms, 75 cts. (The School is in Cambridge, at the University, half an hour's ride by street cars from Bowdoin Square, or from Park Square. (See *Harvard University*).

Hayden's Guitar Lessons.
146 A Tremont st. Winslow L. Hayden has for many years been recognized as one of the most eminent teachers of the guitar in the United States, and it is generally conceded that he has no superior. Fully comprehending the resources of that fashionable and charming instrument, and having completely mastered them, he has no difficulty in imparting his knowledge to his pupils. Either as a solo instrument or as furnishing a sweet and beautiful accompaniment to singing, the guitar is becoming more popular every year. Mr. Hayden has especially arranged a large number of standard songs for the guitar, a catalogue of which he will freely send to any application by mail or otherwise. In these days when nearly every young lady learns to play the pianoforte, it should be borne in mind that the guitar lends variety and beauty to music of the drawing-room. It is rapidly taking its proper place among the favorite musical instruments of the home. Mr. Hayden receives pupils from all sections of the United States and Canada, all of whom will cheerfully testify to his ability, patience and successful results. Terms, at office, hour lessons, 12 lessons (one lesson per week) $15; 20 lessons (two a week), $25; at pupil's residence, 12 lessons, $24; 20 lessons, $40.

Hemenway Free Industrial School for Girls. (1884).
Starr King School-house, Tennyson st. Girls from 9 to 18 years of age are taught cooking and other useful branches.

Hintz Private School of Art, Languages and English Literature. (1885).
248 Newbury st. Instruction in this School is based upon the principles underlying methods employed in the best German schools, as well as the latest practical and natural methods of the Boston Normal School. The courses of study include the English branches, penmanship, German and French languages, botany, zoology, geography, music, illustrative drawing, sketching at sight, modelling in clay, principles of perspective, applied design, color, original illustration, pastel, water-color, crayon and charcoal sketching from objects, pen-and-ink sketching, etc. Terms of tuition: $150 per year, for beginners; $200 per year for advanced pupils. Lessons in Art, $20 for ten lessons.

Holt Singing Classes.
Sleeper Hall, 27 East Newton st. Under the auspices of the New England Conservatory of Music. Instructor, H. E. Holt. Tuesday evenings, at 7. Tickets for course, $2.

Horace Mann School for the Deaf. (1869).
Warrenton st. Articulation taught. Industrial training.

Institute Society of Arts. (1861).
Devoted to Education in the practical Sciences. Associate membership, $5; annual assessment, $5. This is a department of the Massachusetts Institute of Technology, 191 Boylston st.

Juglaris Art School.
161 Tremont st. Tommaso Juglaris, Director. This is one of the best and most flourishing Art Schools in the United States, as it would naturally become with so able and renowned a Principal. The Juglaris Art School is conducted upon the plan of the leading Art Schools of Paris, to which there are none superior. All branches of Art are taught, but *figure drawing*, oil and water-color painting, nude and costume model, composition, artistic anatomy and decorative art are the special features of instruction. Other courses of study include perspective, still-life and landscape, while such *practical* branches as those pursued with a view to becoming illustrators for books, magazines and papers (either in pen-and-ink or colors), are most successfully taught. Terms: day-school, per month, $20; 3 months, $55; 8 months, $125; evening-school, per month, $10. School year, from October 1 to May 31. The location, opposite the Common, is pleasant, and is easily to be reached from all sections of the city, and suburbs, various lines of street-cars passing the door. (Its rooms are in the building with *Sawyer's* renowned *Commercial College*). (See *Summer School of Art*).

Kindergartens. (See *Free Kindergartens*).

Kindergarten. Hotel Cluny, Boylston st. Mrs. A. K. Brown.

Kindergarten. Normal Class, 29 Hanson st.

Kindergartens. Northfield st., near Tremont st. Mrs. Ella L. Sparks.

Kindergarten for the Blind. Roxbury District, near Jamaica Pond. Six acres of land have been purchased here in a healthful, beautiful and accessible location—the Hyde estate—and would be an excellent site for the Perkins Institute, South Boston, in case it should be desirable to remove it. The special kindergarten, or preparatory infant school for sightless boys and girls under nine years of age, is being established here.

Lasell Seminary. (1851). Auburndale. Seminary for young women. Principal, Charles C. Bragdon, A. M. Terms, including board, use of furnished room, light, heat, washing and tuition for the school year, $400; for day pupils, $90. This is one of the largest and most noted seminaries for young women in the United States. Terms begin September 17, January 7, April 8. Commencement June 16. (Auburndale is 9 miles from Boston State House. Boston & Albany Railroad).

Lawrence Scientific School. (1847). Cambridge. A department of the great Harvard University. Named in honor of Abbott Lawrence, who gave $50,000 toward the establishment of the school, and increased his donation subsequently by a large amount. There are four courses of instruction, each covering a period of four years. There is a course in civil and topographical engineering; one in chemistry; one in natural history; and one in mathematics, physics and astronomy. Examinations in English, French or German, arithmetic, algebra, geometry, four books of Cæsar, four of Virgil, the Latin grammar, plain and analytic trigonometry, elementary descriptive chemistry, elementary physics and modern geography, must successfully be passed for admission, if degrees are desired. Special students, however, (not candidates for degrees), are admitted *without examination*, to take up such studies as they desire. Degrees of Civil Engineer and Bachelor of Science are conferred. Persons preparing to teach are afforded special facilities. Tuition: $150 a year.

Lothian Dramatic Lessons. Napier Lothian, of the Boston Theatre, has had success in training young ladies and gentlemen for the dramatic stage. His long experience in connection with dramatic and musical matters, in Boston, renders his instruction valuable. Tuition, $3 per lesson.

Massachusetts College of Pharmacy. (1823). 1151 Washington st. President, Henry Canning, 109 Green st. Terms for tuition: Preliminary examination for matriculation, $4; examination for graduation, $10; each of the professors' courses, $15. All special courses, $15. Term begins last Monday in September. Students can consult the library of the college, which is probably the largest and best pharmaceutical library in the United States, as well as the great Public Library, which has a vast collection of medical literature.

Massachusetts Institute of Technology. (1861). 191 Boylston st. This Institute comprises The School of Industrial Science, The School of Mechanic Arts, The John Lowell School of Practical Design, The Society of Arts, etc. This vast conservatory of arts and sciences is doing a grand practical work in educating young men and women, who come from all sections of the country, in the useful branches, whereby they may have the means of earning an independent livelihood. In these great schools are taught mathematics, mechanics, geology, mineralogy, physiology, chemistry, physics, civil-engineering, architecture, languages, literature, history, drawing, designing, weaving, pattern-making, carpentry, mechanical engineering, applied mechanics, mining, metallurgy, political economy, biology, wood-turning, foundry-work, forging, vise-work, machine-tool work, etc. The expense of attending The School of Industrial Science (males), tuition, is $200 per year; School of Mechanic Arts, males, $150 per year; John Lowell School of Practical Design (males and females), drawing, designing, weaving, etc., *the tuition is free*. There are also *free* evening courses of instruction for both sexes in mathematics, mechanics, physics, drawing, chemistry, geology, natural history, biology, navigation, nautical astronomy, architecture, engineering, history, English, French, and German. Francis A. Walker, president. The faculty comprises 70 professors and teachers. The school year begins in September. (Take any Back Bay, Huntington av., or Dartmouth-st. horse-car).

Massachusetts Metaphysical College. 571 Columbus av. Rev. Mary B. G. Eddy.

Massachusetts School for the Feeble-minded. (1848). 723 East Eighth st., South Boston. Mental and industrial training.

Massachusetts School of the Blind. (1829). Perkins Institute, 383 E. Broadway, South Boston. Central office, 37 Avon st. Pupils are educated and trained in trades and professions. This is an educational Institute, and not an Asylum, as many suppose. Course of Tuition, 5 to 7 years. Cost of Instruction, board included, $300 per year. Blind pupils only received, aged between 9 and 19 years.

McLean Training School for Nurses. (1886). Washington st., Somerville Postal District, Boston. Two years' course. One month's probation. Pay: $14 per month, first year; $16, second year. Pupils received between 21 and 35 years of age. Diplomas given.

Medical School for Women and Men. (Boston College of Physicians and Surgeons). 34 Essex st. This School has been regularly chartered, having obtained rights from the Legislature of Massachusetts to give instruction and confer diplomas. Its founders present the following as their reasons for the establishment of this new college: 1. To afford *women* as well as men an opportunity to obtain a complete and thorough medical education, in a medical school in Massachusetts, well equipped with competent instructors, and supplied with all conveniences for practical instruction in every department of such education, and with suitable lecture, laboratory, and dissecting rooms and apparatus. 2. To afford this education to both *women* and men for *a moderate price*—one considerably *less* than that required for graduation by some of the old and well-established schools in this State; and this result to accomplish, without placing the standard of instruction below that of the older colleges, but ever maintaining such standard, and the requirements for graduation and its degrees equal, at least, to the *best* medical college in the country. It is hardly necessary to add that this college is becoming firmly established, as a great educational institution founded on such a broad and laudable basis would naturally be, as its objects and plans strongly appeal to the fair-minded and public-spirited men and women of Boston, Massachusetts and the United States, in fact, for its influence is growing to be national rather than to be locally circumscribed. Complying with the act of incorporation, an educational board was appointed, consisting of members of the Massachusetts Medical Society, the halls were opened for courses of study (similar to those pursued in other colleges), examinations, lectures, etc., and diplomas have been conferred upon the graduates.

Mendelssohn Musical Institute. 5 Columbus sq. E. B. Oliver, Principal.

Military Schools. (See *Chauncy Hall School, College of Agriculture, English High Schools*).

Monroe Conservatory of Oratory. 36 Bromfield st. The first School of Oratory in this country embracing a systematic and comprehensive course of study based upon the absolute principles of the philosophy of expression was established by Professor Lewis B. Monroe, and was successfully continued until his death, which occurred in 1879. In the year following, C. W. Emerson, M.D., Professor of Philosophy of Expression, Æsthetics, Physiology and Hygiene of the Voice and Oratorical and Dramatic Action, opened the present school. Prof. Emerson, a graduate of the Monroe school, and subsequently a member of the Faculty, called about him nearly all of the members of the Faculty formerly associated with Prof. Monroe, and, concurring in the belief that the new school should take the name of the Monroe Conservatory of Oratory, as suggested by Mrs. Monroe, it was accordingly given that title. The design of the school is to teach Oratory as an Art, resting upon absolute laws of nature, explained and illustrated by exact rules of science, and to give a thorough and systematic training in all the principles upon which this art is based. It qualifies students to become professors and teachers of elocution and oratory in the colleges and schools of the land; to supply the ever-increasing demand for teachers who have studied not merely to become brilliant readers, but to be masters of the great system of laws underlying the art of expression. Its curriculum comprises voice culture, the focus of right placing of tones; Bell's method or visible speech; analysis; rendering; declamation; reading of poetry; humorous reading and recitation; delivery of sermons; Bible and hymn reading; philosophy of expression; dramatic reading and recitation; gesture; dramatic action; art criticism; English literature; lectures, etc. The school year is divided into three terms of equal length. The full course, entitling the student to a diploma of graduation, occupies two years, from October till May. Tuition: for first term of attendance, $45; second term, $38; third term, $30; on Saturday only for school year, $35; two days per week, school year, $50; course of private lessons, $50. English literature to members, per term, $8.

Munich Art School. 19 Temple place.

Murray Bicycle School. (1885). 100 Sudbury st. Bicycling and Tricycling taught. Terms: 50 cents a lesson. Joseph S. Murray is the Principal.

Music Schools. (See *Abercrombie Oratorio School, Adams Opera School, Boston Conservatory of Music, Harvard School of Music, Hayden's Guitar School, Mendlessohn Musical Institute, New England Conservatory of Music, Rudersdorff School, Tremont School of Music, Boston College of Music, Eichberg's Violin School, Parisian Academy of Music, Petersilea Academy of Music, Perkins Musical Institute.*)

Naval Cooking School. April 21, 1885. A naval Cooking-School was established on the United States Receiving Ship, Wabash, at the Navy Yard, junction of Wapping and Water sts., Charlestown District.

Naval Training School. Water st., junction Wapping st., Charlestown District. At the United States Navy Yard there is a Boys' Training School for Naval Seamen. Applicants for enlistment must be 14 to 18 years of age, in good health, of good character, must be able to read and write, must desire to become sailors, and must have the consent of parents or guardians. Applicants must be accompanied by a parent or guardian, and must apply to the Commanding Officer of the United States Steamer, "Wabash," Navy Yard, Charlestown District. Branches taught: Practical Seamanship; Elements of an English Education, etc. Pay, $9.50 per month, and board; increased to $10.50 and $11.50, according to good behavior and proficiency. Outfit furnished, and charged to the boy's account.

New England Conservatory of Music. (1867). The largest music school in the world. Located in Franklin sq. About 40,000 pupils have already taken lessons at this school. The building is of immense size, being 230 feet on Newton st., 210 feet on James st., and 7 stories high, having accommodations for 550 lady boarding-students. About 2,200 students are constantly in attendance, representing 55 states, territories, provinces, and foreign countries. There are nearly 100 instructors. The class system prevails, although private lessons are given. Terms: for a year's instruction, etc.: Tuition, voice and piano, each per term, first grade, $10; second grade, $15: four terms, $100 for both; rent of pianoforte per term, $7.50; four terms, $30; board and room for forty weeks, at $5.00 to $7.50, $200 to $300; washing, $12; sheet music, $10; making a total expense for one year of $385 to $600. Hon. Rufus S. Frost is president; Eben Tourjee, mus. doc., director. The Faculty includes some of the most eminent professors in the world. At the head of the vocal department are Signor August Rotoli (the famous Italian teacher who came here from Rome, where he occupied one of the highest positions in that land of song) and John O'Neill; the instrumental teachers include such artists of world-wide fame as Otto Bendix, Carl Faelton, Leandro Campanari, Timothie d'Adamowski, Alfred De Seve and many others. (Take any Washington-st. horsecar going to South End, or any Tremont-st. car that goes through Dover st.).

New England Conservatory Violin School. (1867). 27 East Newton st., Franklin sq. Faculty; Leandro Campanari, Timothie Adamowski, Alfred De Seve, Benjamin Cutter, Hermann Hartmann. Tuition, in classes of 4, first grade, $6 for one and $10 for two lessons per week; second grade, $15; third, fourth, fifth and sixth grades, $20 per term, two lessons per week. Private lessons if desired. Advanced students have frequent opportunities of playing at recitals and public concerts of the Conservatory, and when sufficiently advanced can join the Conservatory orchestra.

New England Hospital Training School for Nurses. (1862). Codman av, 2933 Washington st., Roxbury District. 18 months' course. Pupils 21 to 30 years of age preferred. Pay $1 per week for first six months; $2 for second; $3 for last six months. Practical experience given.

New England Industrial School for Deaf Mutes. (1876). Beverly. Instruction in sign and oral methods. Industrial training.

New England Telegraph Institute and Company. (Incorporated under the laws of Massachusetts). 266 Washington st., cor. Water st. One of the most *useful* branches of instruction as well as business, is that of Telegraphy. A practical knowledge of it is almost sure to secure a business opening, good operators being always in demand. During the year 1885 there were more than one hundred millions of telegraphic messages sent. Many newspapers and business men now have *private* wires, and require special operators. There are now over 75,000 operators employed, the number having been 24,000 in 1877. Salaries range from $40 to $125 per month. The demand for operators is generally larger than the supply. The business, besides being profitable, is reliable, light, pleasant, steady, easily learned, fascinating and educating. In order to learn telegraphy easily and quickly one should be a fair penman, have a good ear, and in three months' time one can progress sufficiently to take charge of a *minor* office. At the New England Institute students are given regular circuit practice on all their wires, transmission of messages, etc., and are also taught the setting up of instruments, batteries, etc. Terms: 3 months, $25; evening, per term, three months, $15.

There are no extra expenses, all necessary stationery being furnished. Railway tickets obtained for suburban pupils at one-half the usual rates. The Manager of the New England Institute and Telegraph Company is Mr. Chas. H. Gilmore, Jr., formerly Superintendent of Telegraph for the Old Colony Railway Company, and late Superintendent of Telegraph for the Boston and Lowell Railway Company, and having had experience since 1860, and a practical knowledge of electricity in all of its branches, he is eminently fitted to teach young persons, of both sexes, a practical knowledge of a profitable business.

Noble's (G. W. C.) Classical School for Boys and Young Men. (1866), 174 Tremont st., opp. the Common. This school has established a reputation far beyond the City and State for its high rank. It offers a thorough preparation of boys and young men for admission to Harvard University, (as the college where the standard of scholarship actually required for passing the prescribed examinations is the highest ; and also furnishes, by means of some substitutions in place of certain studies of the special classical course, an equally suitable preparation for the Institute of Technology. Especial pains are taken, throughout the entire course, to make the preparation for the study of mathematics—which fills so important a place in the course of our best colleges—*no less thorough* than the instruction in the classics. Due attention is given to the other English branches which are properly pursued at this stage of a boy's education. French and German are regular studies of the school. The school year is of forty weeks. Tuition, $200 per annum. We take from Mr. Noble's circular the following, as the course of study of the First Class: Latin; Cicero against Cataline, and Archais.—Cicero at sight.—Enid and Ovid at sight.—Composition; Greek; (Homer's Iliad, I-III.—Herodotus. — Composition. — Greek at sight; Geometry; (Wentworth's Plane and Solid Geometry). German; (Sheldon's Elementary German Grammar.—Reading at sight).

Normal Art Lessons. Courses of ten black-board lessons in illustrative drawing, to teachers, including D. Lessons on the method of handling the crayon for quick, effective results; 2. on the application of drawing in teaching geography, zoology, botany, and other subjects; (3), on light and shade; 4, on composition — natural specimens and other objects being furnished for study — are given at the Normal School, cor. of Appleton and Dartmouth sts., by W. Bertha Hintz, on Monday afternoons. Terms, for the course, $10. (See *Hintz School of Art*).

Normal Writing Institute. 1870, 26 Essex st. Devoted exclusively to the teaching of penmanship. Terms: Writing, 30 lessons, $7; 60, $12; 90, $15. Flourishing, 20 lessons, $7; plain and ornamental lettering, etc., 3 months, $30. Instruction is given individually. H. C. Kendall is the president of the institute.

North Bennet Street Free Industrial School. 1880), 39 North Bennet st. Industrial department of the public school system. Classes, 9 to 6. Branches: Carpentry; shoemaking; printing; laundry; sewing; cooking; housekeeping, etc. Recreation and reading rooms. Free classes during the day for children of the public schools; in the evening special free classes for older girls and women.

Notre Dame Academy. (1854). 283 Washington st., Roxbury District. Boarding and Day School. No institution of an educational nature in the United States has a higher reputation for thoroughness and discipline. This renowned school was established under the auspices of Right Reverend Bishop Fitzpatrick. The large building is delightfully situated, as it is surrounded by six acres of grounds, being at once healthful and secluded, affording the very best conditions for progress in studies. Numbers of young ladies avail themselves of the privileges of the day school, while others are home pupils, being furnished with board as well. The courses taught include the English branches, languages, etc. Tuition, including board, $200 per annum.

Notre Dame Academy. Berkeley st., near cor. Boylston. The novitiate of the sisterhood attached to the Academy of Notre Dame in the Roxbury District. Terms, per half session of five months: Tuition, $25; music, $24; painting and drawing, $20; dinner at the Academy, if desired, $20. Reached by both lines of Back Bay horse-cars,—Vendome and Clarendon st., by West End, Dartmouth st., or Huntington av. lines).

Old North Free Classes in History. 1887, Parmenter st. Chapel. For young and old. Wednesday evenings, in winter, at 7.30. Free tickets at Old South Meeting House, Washington st., cor. Milk st.

Organ School. 154 Tremont st. The Boston Conservatory Organ School is far-famed for the thoroughness and excellence of its instruction. Julius Eichberg, Director. The uniform degree of success attending the system of instruction employed in all the departments of the renowned Boston Conservatory is exemplified in the organ department. (See *Boston Conservatory of Music*).

Organ Schools. (See *Boston Conservatory of Music; Boston University College of Music; Harvard School of Music; Mendelssohn Musical Institute; New England Conservatory of Music; Perkins Musical Institute; Petersilea Academy of Music; Truette Organ School, Tremont Temple; Ward's (Julius E.) Music Rooms*).

Parisian Academy of Music. (1885). Hotel Boylston, corner of Tremont and Boylston sts. The Directors of this celebrated music school—Prof. Albert Pégou and Mme. Pégou—are from the Paris Conservatoire, the former having held various prominent positions in Paris as President and Conductor of the Schools' Philharmonic Society; violin leader of the Haydn Quartet; baritone soloist of the Boïeldieu Choral Society, etc., while the latter also evidenced a great degree of versatility, having been piano-soloist of Sivori's and Erard's Concerts, and of Pasdeloup's Symphonic Concerts; assistant professor of the Bourgault-Ducoudray Choral Society, etc. The courses of instruction at the Parisian Academy of Music are as follows: Vocal music—French, Italian, and English singing, solfeggio. Instrumental music—pianoforte, violin, organ, harmony and composition. There are also courses for the study of oratorio and opera (soli and chorus); chamber music, (strings, pianoforte and strings, two pianofortes—four and eight hands—organ); study of opera dramatic action. Tuition can be given in *English, French, Italian or Spanish*, by which pupils are enabled to perfect themselves in language as well as in music. This is an *unique* feature in musical instruction, and one that has found great favor with many students. Another specialty which has largely commended itself to pupils, is to be found in the *musicales* given frequently, when *musical analysis*, explanation of the artistic touch, use of the pedals, etc., are given in the most interesting manner. In fact, the study of vocal or instrumental music at the Parisian Academy is not a dry, laborious process, but a fresh, vigorous, *enjoyable* series of exercises. There is a refined musical atmosphere pervading the entire system of study here that inspires and stimulates the most apathetic pupil. Now that this Academy is becoming more generally known, through the success of its pupils, young persons are coming to avail themselves of its benefits from all sections of the United States and Canada. We do not know of any other music school in this country that is conducted on the system of the famous Paris Conservatoire, and by Professors from that institution. Tuition: Elementary classes, per quarter, $15; superior classes, per month, $8; courses, per month, $4; private lessons, singing, 10 half-hour lessons, $22.50; pianoforte, $22.50. (The Academy is most centrally and pleasantly located, all Tremont st., Back Bay and Railway station street-cars passing near the Hotel Boylston).

Perkins Institution and Massachusetts School for the Blind. (1829). 553 East Broadway, South Boston. The early organizers and promoters of this School, (the fame of which has extended throughout Europe, it having been the first institution in the world to establish courses of systematic instruction for the blind) were Dr. Sam'l G. Howe and Dr. John D. Fisher, the latter of whom suggested the founding of such a school. Among the liberal donors of the school have been Col. Thomas W. Perkins and others. The most noted pupil of this Institute is Laura Bridgman, *blind, deaf and dumb*, whose instruction by Dr. Howe is a living witness of his triumph as an instructor. Her case is celebrated as the most marvellous result of the system of this school, in every quarter of the globe. Several institutions in Europe have already been founded upon the model so successfully established here. Among the branches taught are music—for which it is famous —(see *Perkins Musical Institute*) pianoforte-tuning, chair-seating, upholstery, etc. It is the idea of many that this school is a charitable one merely; on the contrary, it is an educational and industrial institution principally. Terms, $300 a year. (A few indigent applicants are permitted to enjoy the privileges of instruction at this school, if residents of the State, upon application to the Governor). Mr. Michael Anagos is Director of the school. (Take any line of South Boston horse-cars, from Scollay sq., Brattle st., or Park sq). (See *Kindergarten for the Blind*).

Perkins Musical Institute. (1829). 553 East Broadway, South Boston. Mr. Michael Anagos, Director. Established solely for the education of the blind, in music, etc. (See *Perkins Institution and Massachusetts School for the Blind*). This is the oldest Music School in Boston, and, it is believed, in this country. Some of the pupils have here acquired a knowledge of music and of pianoforte-tuning, etc., which has enabled them to obtain an independent livelihood in various parts of the country, as vocalists, pianoforte soloists and accompanists, vocal and instrumental teachers, band and orchestra performers and teachers, pianoforte tuners, etc. The city of Boston has arranged to have all the pianofortes in the various public schools tuned and kept in order by the pupils of this school, and the result has been extremely successful in every respect. Pupils are taught by means of raised letters, a system invented by Dr. Howe.

Petersilea Academy of Music, Elocution, Languages and Art. (1871). 281 Columbus av. This was the third great Conservatory of Music — chronologically considered — to be established in Boston. It holds, and has ever maintained a foremost rank among the renowned educational institutions of the Modern Athens. It was established by one of the most eminent of America's pianists—Carlyle Petersilea—who is still at its head, and who is assisted by a large staff of leading instructors. The noted Petersilea Method for the Pianoforte is the text-book for that instrument here. The pupils of this famous school represent every section of the United States and Canada. Many thousands of its students are to be found exemplifying the sound basis and thorough system and finish of the Petersilea School throughout the continent, in the concert-room, as teachers, or in the parlor of the home. Class and private lessons are given. Prices of tuition: Pianoforte, 20 one-hour lessons, in classes of four, $15; Harmony, 20 lessons, $15; Singing, 20 lessons, $15; Organ, 20 half-hour lessons (private), $20, 20 one-hour lessons, $50. The Pianoforte Department is pre-eminently distinguished, from the fact that the celebrated Director of this Academy is the only pianoforte *virtuoso* who has founded a large and comprehensive music school in this country. Many brilliant solo pianists have graduated from this rapidly extending Academy. (To reach the Petersilea School take Columbus av. horse-car.) *See Petersilea School of Art, School of Elocution, School of Languages*).

Petersilea School of Languages. (1871). 281 Columbus av. Latin, Greek, German, French and Italian taught by the best Professors. Among the Faculty are Signor Veneziani and Signor Ventura, the method of the latter being in the combination of the grammar of the language with the natural process. Terms: for any one of the languages, 20 hour lessons, in classes of 6, $10.

Phillips Academy. (1778). Andover. This Academy has classical and English departments. No age for admission is prescribed. Boys of 14 are sufficiently matured for taking up the courses of study here. Tuition, $60 per year. Board and lodgings from $6 to $7 per week. (Andover is twenty miles from Boston, on the Boston & Maine Railway). Principal of the Academy, Cecil F. P. Bancroft, Ph.D.

Preparatory School for Harvard University. (1828). 279 Boylston st. Education is here given in the branches of which a thorough knowledge is required for admission to America's greatest college; the classical course being arranged and modified exactly in accordance with the demands of Harvard's examination tests. During the past *fifty years* a long list of graduates have here been prepared for college. Class-work is combined with private instruction. Terms: classical course, $200. (*See Chauncy Hall School*).

Preparatory School for Institute of Technology. Rockers and Bradford's Commercial School, 18 Boylston st.

Preparatory School for Institute of Technology, 174 Boylston st. The Berkeley School is widely recognized as a thorough preparatory school for the great Institute of Technology. Pupils are required to be 16 years of age in order to take the preliminary Institute examinations. (*See Berkeley School.*)

Preparatory Schools and Teachers for Colleges and Scientific Schools. Adams Academy; Berkeley School; Chauncy Hall School, Collins, Leroy Z.; Columbus School of Languages; Humphreys, E. R.; Noble, G. W. C.

Private Schools and Teachers. Boston abounds in private schools of distinction. Among them are those of Miss H. A. Adam, 98 Chestnut st.; L. C. Atkinson Kindergarten, 17 Cazenove st.; Berkeley School, 174 Boylston st.; Mrs. A. K. Browne Kindergarten, Morton st., Jamaica Plain District, Miss A. E. Bursley, 106 Chestnut st.; Miss Carrie Bursley, 106 Chestnut st.; Chauncy Hall School, 259 Boylston st.; Children's Mission, 277 Tremont st.; Leroy Z. Collins, 23 Temple place; Elizabeth Curtis, 8 Rockland st.; M. G. Daniell, 259 Boylston st.; Miss L. E. Davis, 189 Warren st., Roxbury District; Mme. M. de Maltchyce, 16 St. James st., Roxbury District; Isaac Emerson, 41 Tremont st.; Miss Grace B. Fisher, 174 Boylston st.; Miss M. B. Foote, 23 W. Cedar st.; Gannett Institute, 69 Chester sq.; M. J. Garland and R. J. Weston (Kindergarten), 52 Chestnut st.; German Catholic School, 133 Shawmut av.; German Lutheran School, Parker st., near Tremont; German School, 29 Middlesex st.; T. B. J. L. Grady, 41 Tremont st.; Abbie L. Gunnison, Jackson pl., Dorchester District; Albert Hall, 18 Boylston pl.; Fannie Hall, 63 Chestnut st.; Mrs. S. H. Hayes, 68 Chester sq.; Mrs. John J. Heard, 6 Juniper st., Roxbury District; Heloise E. Hersey, 25 Chestnut st.; Miss J. E. Hilliard, 116 Mt. Vernon st.; Miss M. Hillard, 302 Marlborough st.; Hintz Art School, 248 Newbury st.; J. P. Hopkinson, 20 Boylston pl.; House of the Angel Guardian, 85 Vernon st.; Miss Ellen P.

Hubbard, 112 Newbury st.; E. R. Humphreys, 129 West Chester park; Miss C. I. Ireland, 9 Louisburg sq.; Mary E. James, 78 Saratoga st., East Boston; Abby H. Johnson, 18 Newbury st.; Kindergarten, 14 Cottage pl.; Kindergarten, 114 East Canton st.; Kindergarten (Normal), 29 Hanson st.; Ladd & Daniell, 259 Boylston st.; Mrs. C. B. Martin, 5 Otis pl.; Miss M. A. Matthews, 5 Charles st.; A. F. McHugh (Kindergarten), 721 Tremont st.; William Nichols, 36 Temple pl.; G. W. C. Noble, 174 Tremont st.; Annie M. Osgood, 35 Appleton st.; Lavina F. Pitcher, 7 Walnut st.; Miss M. L. Putnam, 68 Marlborough st.; Walton Ricketson, 110 Tremont st.; Miss Mary E. Rogers, 37 Tremont st.; Annie Rust (Kindergarten), 581 Warren st., Roxbury District; Sacred Heart Academy, 5 Chester sq.; Sacred Heart Parochial School, Paris st., near Brooks st., East Boston; Miss H. H. Sampson, Boylston Chapel, Main st., Charlestown District; J. C. Sharp (Sciences). Centre st., cor. Allston st., Dorchester District; Miss S. K. Shepard, Hancock st., opp. Downer ct., Dorchester District; Sisters Notre Dame, 2893 Washington st., Roxbury District, 56 Havre st., East Boston, and W. Berkeley st., cor. St. James av., Back Bay; Daniel S. Smalley, Green st., Jamaica Plain District; Mrs. Ella L. Sparks (Kindergarten), Northfield st.; Star of the Sea Parochial School, Moore st., cor. Bennington st., East Boston; St. Agnes Convent, 127 I st., South Boston; St. James, 6 Kneeland pl.; St. John's, 11 Moon st.; St. John's Ecclesiastical Seminary, Lake st., Brighton District; St. Margaret's School, 5 Chestnut st.; St. Mary's, Cooper st., cor. No. Margin st.; St. Mary's, 41 Lancaster st.; St. Thomas Parochial School, South st., Jamaica Plain District; St. Vincent de Paul, Camden st.; Charles W. Stone, 68 Chestnut st.; W. H. Titcombe, 630 Washington st.; Leonard B. Treharne, 174 Boylston st.; Trinity Parish School, Shawmut av., cor. Lucas st.; Miss Theodora W. Turner, 411 Shawmut av.; Mrs. James P. Walker, Centre st., cor. Orchard st., Jamaica Plain District; Miss S. Wesselhœft, 9 Newbury st.; Lucy Wheelock (Kindergarten), 259 Boylston st.

Rachel Noah's Lessons in Dramatic Action and Elocution. Creighton House, 245 Tremont st. Miss Noah devotes her exclusive attention to imparting instruction in elocution, dramatic action, gesture, and the other aids and essentials to proper deportment on stage and platform. Amateurs are coached by Miss Noah, and amateur performances are directed and rehearsed. Terms of tuition: 20 lessons in dramatic instruction, $40; 12 lessons in elocution and dramatic reading, $20. Miss Noah is a professional artist of distinction. Her methods of teaching have been endorsed by Edwin Booth, William Warren and Joseph Jefferson. She has the privilege of giving *practical* lessons on the Boston Theatre stage, by the courtesy of Manager Eugene Tompkins.

Reckers and Bradford's Commercial School. (1875). 18 Boylston st. This school has met with good success during the ten years that it has been in operation. Branches taught: Commercial course,—writing, arithmetic, book-keeping, commercial correspondence, practical business preparation, commercial law—fees, $35; mathematical course, $35; preparatory course, $30. Evening school (reading, writing, arithmetic, spelling, etc.), one month, $5; six months, $25; stationery free. Pupils prepared for the Institute of Technology or other scientific schools.

Rudersdorff School of Singing. Miss Jeannette Van Buren, who teaches the celebrated Rudersdorff School of Singing, was one of the principal pupils of Mme. Erminia Rudersdorff, who came to Boston from London, and for a number of years, until her death, held the foremost position among the music teachers of America. Miss Van Buren thoroughly acquired the excellent method, and has met with the greatest success in teaching it. Mme. Rudersdorff herself acknowledged the ability of Miss Van Buren to impart the system, over her own signature, and it was a deserved testimonial. Pupils from various sections of the country are studying with Miss Van Buren, at Hotel Thorndike, Boylston and Church streets. Miss Van Buren is a vocalist of eminence, and her services are in requisition at some of the best concerts given in Boston and vicinity. In her singing she demonstrates the principles of the vocal art as illustrated by Mme. Rudersdorff, of which she is so brilliant an exponent, and which she succeeds in imparting with so much ease, and with such remarkable artistic results.

Sacred Heart Academy. 5 Chester sq. An excellent school.

St. John's Ecclesiastical Seminary. Lake st., Brighton District. This institution was established principally to accommodate the clerical students of the Archdiocese of Boston, but is open to those of all other dioceses who come duly recommended and qualified. The course of studies comprises philosophy—natural and mental—; theology—dogmatic and moral—: canon law; Biblical studies, Church history, etc. The exercises of the scholastic year begin in September. All are expected to be present at that time. Tuition: for students belonging to the Archdiocese of Boston, $180; for all others, $220. (Brighton is easily reached by horse-car from Bowdoin sq).

Sauveur School of Languages. 18 Pemberton sq. German, French, Italian, Spanish and other languages taught by native teachers. Marie Mohlbach, Principal. The Sauveur method, exclusively taught here, is as follows: The instruction is given wholly in the language to be acquired, and the pupils learn to understand and to converse in the foreign tongue as practically and as easily as if they were living in a foreign country, *where English is neither spoken nor understood*. From the first lesson, the beginner's ear and organ of speech are trained by speaking about *objects* near and far, constantly progressing from the known to the unknown, from the concrete to the abstract. Then, the *ear* and *tongue* having been formed, pupils are led into grammar orally. Tuition: Twenty private hour lessons, $30; two pupils, each $20. In class, 20 lessons, $12 and $15.

Sawyer's Commercial College. (1836). 164 Tremont st. This college, the oldest of its class in the United States and having the highest standard, attracts pupils from every section of the country who desire a *thorough, practical business education*. The best advertisement for this celebrated school is the genuine success of its graduates, who are to be found in counting-rooms, offices, etc., the world over. In fact, so high does this college stand in the opinion of the leading merchants of the great cities that any young lady or gentleman vouched for by Mr. George A. Sawyer, the Principal, is almost sure to obtain an immediate and profitable position. The Faculty of the college comprises teachers of eminence, all of whom have had *successful* experience in some of the foremost educational institutions in the land. The commercial course includes the English branches, book-keeping, business correspondence, navigation, drafting and mathematics, especial attention being given to grammar, orthography, arithmetic and penmanship. Book-keeping, including commercial calculations, consists of a thorough and practical course of both single and double entry, with or without journal. Upon graduation, the pupil is *fully prepared to take charge of any set of books*. Students completing the entire course and successfully passing the required examination, are granted the Diploma of the Sawyer Commercial College, which is universally recognized throughout the country as a sufficient introduction and recommendation for any young man or woman. There is no class system here, *all instruction being given in private*. A separate department for ladies has been opened. Terms: Mercantile course, 3 months, day, $30; evening $12; until qualified, unlimited time, $30; with privilege of reviewing, $35; book-keeping till qualified, day or evening, $20; penmanship, 30 lessons, $6; evenings, $5; English branches, 3 months, (days) $25; (evenings) $12; navigation, 2 weeks, $12; complete course, 2 months, $30.

Schools of Agriculture. (See *Bussey Institute; College of Agriculture.*)

School of All Sciences. (1874.) 12 Somerset st. The instruction presented here includes all branches of knowledge adapted to the ends of a universal postgraduate school. To qualified specialists it will aim to provide thorough instruction in all cultivated Languages and their Literatures; all natural and mathematical Sciences; all Theological, Legal and Medical Studies; all Fine Arts, properly so called; all branches of special Historical Study, etc. Members of the School of All Sciences of Boston University who are Bachelors of Arts can pursue approved courses of study in the National University at Athens, Greece—*without expense for tuition*, and also in the Royal University at Rome, Italy. Degrees of Doctor of Philosophy, Doctor of Science, Doctor of Music, Doctor of Civil Law, Master of Arts, Master of Laws, Bachelor of Philosophy, Bachelor of Arts, and other degrees are conferred by the School of All Sciences. Fees, matriculation once only, $10; annual examination fee, $10; admission to Degree of Master of Arts, $25; to Degree of Master of Laws, $25; to Degree of Doctor of Philosophy, Science or Music, $50, to Degree of Doctor of Civil Law, $50. The payment of the regular tuition fee of $100 covers any selection from the courses of instruction, *without examination fee*.

School of Arboriculture, Arnold Arboretum. (1872.) Jamaica Plain District. In the year named Harvard University received from the late James Arnold a bequest of $100,000, providing for the establishment of a school for tree-cultivation, to be under the instruction of able professors and teachers, in order that the most successful *practical* results may be obtained. It was the desire of the testator that this school should be established on the grounds of the Bussey Institute See *Bussey Institute*) in the Jamaica Plain District, which is one of the most beautiful tracts in New England. Of the original estate of the Bussey Institute grounds of 360 acres, 137 have been devoted to the purposes of the Arboretum. It was Mr. Arnold's desire that every variety of tree, bush, shrub and herbaceous plant which grows in the open air should have a specimen here, and such will eventually be found growing within these naturally beautiful grounds. The professorship of tree-culture having been established, the school soon became widely known, and in consequence pupils made application for the benefit of the valuable *practical* instruc tion to be obtained here. The scientific study of arboriculture is one that is highly attractive to many, and that this department of Harvard University is a credit to that famous and foremost educational institution of America need scarcely be said. Students of the Arnold School of Arboriculture, not candidates for a degree, may join at all times without examination, and pursue such courses as may be selected. Candidates for the degrees of Bachelor of Agricultural (or Horticultural) Science are required to take a preliminary course of one year in the Lawrence Scientific School, (Cambridge), or possess equivalent knowledge. Fees: for academic year, $150; half-year, $75; for any single course, $40 a year.

School of Architecture.
Institute of Technology. 191 Boylston st. A most thorough and comprehensive school of architecture, indeed the leading school of the kind in the country, has been for some twenty years maintained by this renowned Institute. It is under the skilful direction of Prof. William R. Ware, the course of instruction being modelled, as fully as is practicable, upon that of the Ecole des Beaux Arts, of Paris. This school has in some measure been instrumental in giving Boston pre-eminence in the architecture of its buildings. The influence of this correct teaching must sooner or later affect the architectural taste of the country, as pupils now come from various sections to receive the benefits of the instruction given here.

School of Art Embroidery.
(1867). 27 East Newton st., Franklin sq. Practical instruction is here given in the art of embroidery. Not only the Kensington (as done in England) is taught here, but Kensington as done in France; chenille work,—in all the natural tints of the flowers—; portraits in silk from photographs; white French initials; monograms; black lace embroidery; Bulgarian, Moorish, and also the old Oriental work. (See *New England Conservatory*).

School of Art, Martin.
Mrs. L. Edna Martin, Principal. 81 Boylston st., corner of Winter st. Branches taught: Drawing, Painting — Water Colors and Oil, both Landscape and Flower — Tapestry, Still Life, Pottery Decorating. Mrs. Martin's ability and success in imparting instruction are well known throughout Boston and New England, her pupils coming from all sections of the Eastern States. They are her best advertisements, for the progress made by them is a strong recommendation to others with artistic taste to avail themselves of her tuition. Lessons are given in classes or privately, as desired. Terms: In classes, $2 a lesson; a monthly course of 24 lessons, $40; private lessons, given on Wednesdays only, $5 per lesson — this day being reserved exclusively for private pupils. Length of lesson, in all cases, three hours.

School of Art Needlework.
(1878). 8 Park sq. Instruction is given in every variety of needle-work, in silks, crewels, linens or gold; secular or ecclesiastical. Under the direction of Mme. Smith, from the Royal School at South Kensington, London, England. Tuition: 6 lessons in classes, $5; 12 lessons, $8. Private instruction is also given. A few free pupils are admitted to this school. (Take any Columbus av., Back Bay or Huntington av. car).

School of Art, Petersilea.
(1871). 281 Columbus av. Here are taught drawing, pottery-painting, oil, water-colors, flower, landscape, china and decorative painting. Single lessons, $1.25. Lessons by the term, 20 lessons, 10 weeks, (2 lessons weekly) $20. (See *Petersilea Academy*).

School of Blacksmith Work.
191 Boylston st. (See *School of Mechanic Arts*).

School of Church Music.
(1867). Franklin sq. A theoretical and practical course of study is arranged in this important musical field, under the direction of S. B. Whitney, George E. Whiting, H. M. Dunham and W. F. Sherwin. Instruction is given in solo singing, organization of choirs of all descriptions, and in chorals for the people, with the best models of music, the correct style of rendering them, and the proper use of the organ. (See *New England Conservatory*).

School of Church Music.
(1882). At the Tremont School of Music, 550 Tremont st., there is a Church Music class, the pupils in which are taught the proper rendering of Church music. Miss Fanny E. Bruce, Principal.

School of Drawing, Painting and Sculpture.
(1876). Museum of Fine Arts. For males and females. Two classes are engaged in drawing and one in advanced painting. The first class in drawing takes up rudimental and disciplinary studies, including ornament, still life, drapery and antique and living models. The education is practical, also, being useful to engravers, designers, lithographers, etc. Text books are used, lectures are given, study in shading, perspective, architectural and decorative form, giving students ability to make illustrative drawings and sketches. The second class is intended for those students who expect to become professional artists, the branches being much more

advanced and thorough, although free scope is allowed toward the development of the individual talent and taste of the student. Artists and draughtsmen are formed into free classes for drawing from nude models. Collateral instruction is provided by lectures and lessons at the Institute of Technology, the Lowell Institute, the Society of Decorative Art, etc. Terms of tuition: Admittance fee, $10; full term, $45; to professional artists, $25. School year from October to June. The only applicants received are those who intend to study at least three hours a day, four days of the week. (The Museum of Fine Arts faces Copley sq., at the intersection of Dartmouth st., Huntington av. and St. James av., in the most beautiful square, architecturally, in America).

School of Elocution and Dramatic Art. (1867). 27 East Newton st., Franklin sq. The course of study is divided into the following departments: Vocal Technique; Elocution; Rhetorical Oratory; Dramatic Art (the emotions and passions—mechanics and application of gesture — facial expression—pose and counterpoint—mensur and sword exercise — stage etiquette, dress modes and management — playwrights; Lyric Art and Opera (study of the principal operas — musical declamation — expression—gesticulation and stage business). Terms, ten class lessons, $15; ten private lessons, $20; school year, $200. Samuel R. Kelley, A. M., principal; Annie B. Lincoln, 1st assistant. Students are furnished weekly and semi-quarterly opportunities for appearing in public.

School of Elocution, Petersilea. (1871.) 281 Columbus av. Students fitted for the Lyceum, Forensic or Dramatic Stage, and Character Reading. The Delsarte Philosophy of Gesture and Expression, with Rhetoric and English Literature, is taught during the last year of the Graduating Course. Rapier and Broadsword Fencing taught in connection with Dramatic Action. Overton W. Barrett is the able director of the elocutionary department, which is renowned throughout the country. Terms; 20 one-hour lessons (class of four, 2 lessons per week), $15. Also, private lessons.

School of Fine Arts. (1867). 27 East Newton st., Franklin sq. Boston, with its eminent painters and sculptors, its numerous studios, its fine collections, its extensive galleries, its great Art Museum, its frequent exhibitions and genuine Old-World art atmosphere, is generally conceded to be the centre for the study of Fine Arts in America. This School has the following courses: Drawing, Painting, Advanced Portraiture (under the direction of the acknowledged master, William Willard), and other departments.

Tuition: Elementary course, in classes, $20 per term; advanced course in Painting, $25 per term; in Portrait Painting, $40 per term.

School of Forging. (See *School of Mechanic Arts*).

School of Foundry-Work. (See *School of Mechanic Arts*.)

School of General Literature. (1867). Franklin sq. Principal, Wm. J. Rolfe, A. M.; associate principal, John B. Willis, A. M. Instruction is given in advanced English studies. Fee, $5 for each term of 20 lessons.

School of Industrial Science. (1861). 191 Boylston st. The School of Industrial Science of the Massachusetts Institute of Technology provides an extended series of scientific and literary studies, and of practical exercises. The courses of study include the physical, chemical and natural sciences and their applications; pure and applied mathematics; drawing; the English, French, German and other modern languages; history; political economy, and international and business law. These studies and exercises are so arranged as to offer a liberal and *practical* education in preparation for active business pursuits, as well as a thorough training for most of the scientific professions. The following regular courses of study — each of four years' duration—have been established, and for proficiency in any one of them the degree of Bachelor of Science, (S. B.) is conferred in the course pursued: 1. Civil and topographical engineering; 2. Mechanical engineering; 3. Mining engineering; 4. Architecture; 5. Chemistry; 6. Electrical engineering; 7. Natural history, biology; 8. Physics; 9. General course. Courses 1 to 6 are distinctly professional. Tuition, $200 per year. Free evening courses of scientific and literary instruction — open to both sexes — are given each year. School of Industrial Science year begins on last Monday in September.

School of Law. (1872). 10 Ashburton pl. This is one of the departments of the great Boston University (12 Somerset st.), and is one of the most flourishing law schools in the world. Students come from far and near to obtain the advantages it offers to young men who desire to read law or to enter the legal profession. Young men of business, not intending to practice law as a profession, are admitted to the course of lectures on Commercial Law, including such subjects as agency, bills, notes, contracts, insurance, partnership, sales, etc. Expenses of a three-years' course in the School of Law, $325. If taken in two years, $275. There are a limited number of *free* scholarships for the second and third years. Board in clubs, $3.50. Room, $3.

School of Lyric Art and Opera. (1867). 27 East Newton st., Franklin sq. Connected with the New England Conservatory. Opportunities for stage practice, and for private or public appearances. Terms, ten class lessons, $15; ten private lessons, $20. Regular course, four lessons per week, for term of ten weeks, $50. Principal, Samuel R. Kelley, A. M. All the principal operas are studied, and scenes from them performed. Pupils are fully instructed in elegance of carriage, grace of manner, freedom and ease of position and attitude, proper expressions of the features, gesture and eye to convey the thought and correctness of accent.

School of Mechanic Arts. (1861.) Garrison st. Established by the corporation of the Massachusetts Institute of Technology, giving special prominence to *handiwork*, in connection with high-school studies. Instruction is given in the use of hand and machine tools for working iron and wood. The general plan of the School of Mechanic Arts is similar to that of the Imperial Technical School of Moscow; the Royal Mechanic Art School of Komotou in Bohemia; the École Municipale d' Apprentis of Paris; or that of the Ambachtsschoole of the principal cities of Holland, but has been especially adapted to the somewhat different conditions existing in the United States. The handwork is done without regard to pecuniary profit. The facilities for instruction are constantly being increased. The mechanical laboratories have a thorough equipment. The instruction in the mechanic arts, given to each regular student, embraces: 1. Carpentry and Joinery; 2. Wood-Turning; 3. Pattern-Making; 4. Foundry-Work; 5. Iron-Forging; 6. Vise-Work; 7. Machine-Tool Work. The regular course includes two years of study. Special students are received for shorter times. The training given in Grammar Schools affords suitable preparation for examination. For shop-work only, or for mechanical drawing, no examination is required. Tuition, $150 per year.

School of Medicine. (1873). E. Concord st. This school was the first in America to present in combination the essential elements of a thorough reform in medical education. Candidates must be at least nineteen years old. Examinations are held at the College Building, East Concord st., early in June and October. Students have free access to the great City Hospital, the extensive Massachusetts Homœpathic Hospital (both of which are located near the School of Medicine) as well as to the three Homœpathic Medical Dispensaries, the other various public and private hospitals of the city, the Insane Hospitals, etc. Library of two thousand volumes. Students are also allowed the full privileges of the Boston Public Library, the finest in America in extent and value. The school Museum comprises a large and rapidly increasing collection of anatomical, pathological and physiological specimens. Tuition, one year, (including three lecture terms) $125. Graduates of other medical colleges (one course), $50.

School of Modern Languages. 174 Boylston st., cor. Berkeley st. One of the departments of the renowned Berkeley School. The pupil is given a reading, writing and speaking mastery of the language studied. Older pupils are taught to translate English into French or German. Terms: either modern language, $25, half year.

School of Music. (1875). Wellesley College, Wellesley. This school has become renowned throughout the country for its elevated standard and thoroughness. Under the direction of Junius W. Hill it has become one of the great classical music schools of the country. Nearly fifty pianofortes are furnished for the use of pupils, together with an organ of 1584 pipes. Terms: *private instruction*, for college year, voice, pianoforte, organ or violin, one lesson per week, $50; two lessons, $100. (See *Wellesley College*).

School of Natural Science. 174 Boylston, cor. Berkeley st. Branches: Astronomy, physics, chemistry, botany, and mineralogy. Principals: James Brainerd Taylor, Edwin De Meritte, Walter C. Hagar. Instructors: Leonard B. Treharne, Delia Stickney. Terms: $15 half-year. (See *Berkeley School*).

School of Portrait Painting. 27 East Newton st. (See *School of Fine Arts*).

School of Physical Culture. (1867). 27 East Newton st., Franklin sq. This is one of the departments of the New England Conservatory, and is in a most flourishing state. The development of the body should keep pace with the cultivation of the mind. Here are simple gymnastic appointments and a system of exercise on the most approved plan. Fees to pupils of the Conservatory, for one half-hour lesson daily, with use of Hall and apparatus, $5 per term. For outside pupils not connected with the Conservatory, $10 per term. Use of wardrobe boxes, $1 per year.

School of Sculpture. Atelier, 161 Tremont st. Modelling in clay; designing and drawing in sepia, crayon and India ink, from casts. Classes from 9 to

12 A. M. Evening classes, Monday, Tuesday, Thursday and Friday. Life classes from 2 to 4 P. M. Stephen O'Kelley, sculptor; Clemente Biagini, modeller; D. A. Fucigna, assistant teacher.

School of Theology. (1847). 36
Bromfield st. The regular triennial course of instruction comprises: Introductory lectures; exegetical theology; historical theology; systematic theology; practical theology, and comparative theology. With the consent of the respective Deans, any student may attend upon the instruction in any class in the College of Liberal Arts, without charge. Tuition, $50.

School of Wood-Turning.
(See *School of Mechanic Arts*.)

Schools and Teachers of Art.
Academy of Art ....630 Washington st
American Academy of Arts and Sciences
.... 101 Beacon st.
Art School ....27 E. Newton st.
Bacon, Frederic Walton........43 Eliot st.
Bailey, M. A. Miss....Normal Art School
Bartlett, G. H..............27 Tremont row
Bartlett School of Modelling............
..........................394 Federal st.
Bass, E. E. Mrs.............524 Tremont st.
Berkeley School.........171 Boylston st.
Biagini, Clemente modelling............
.............................161 Tremont st.
Bird School of Art.....492 E. 4th st., S. B.
Bothe, Ida..............Wellesley College
Brackett, W. F......164 Washington st.
Bradley, L. Miss..........5 Temple pl.
Chauncy Hall School .....252 Boylston st.
Cowles Art School..... 145 Dartmouth st.
Crane, Fred. L......230 Meridian st., E. B.
Cross, A. K.............Normal Art School
Cushman, A. A.............113 Tremont s
Dabney, J. P. Miss ....17 Boylston pl.
Davis, A. F. Miss.......Tremont School
Davis, A. M. Miss ....Normal Art School
Daw, Florence, Miss..Petersilea Academy
DeCamp, Joseph R.....Wellesley College
Dudley, C Hortense.....21 Dartmouth st.
Faller, Emilie..........27 E. Newton st.
Farley, Helen S............20 Beacon st.
Farr, Ellen B Mrs......149A Tremont st.
Fucigna, D. A ....161 Tremont st.
Gannett Institute..........69 Chester sq.
Goodwin, A. J. Miss......Tremont School
Graves, Abbott F ....433 Washington st.
Greene, C. S. Miss........74 Boylston st.
Griggs, S. W ....39 Studio Building
Hale, Susan Miss..........97 Boylston st.
Hartshorne, Annie L....615 Tremont st.
Hastings, Agnes........Wellesley College
Hintz Art School..........248 Newbury st.
Hintz, W. Bertha .....248 Newbury st.
Hitchings, Henry...English High School
Hoyt, D. L. Miss......Normal Art School
Johnston, John B.......Wellesley College
Juglaris Art School......161 Tremont st.
Kenerson, Ellen P. Mrs...13 Appleton st.
Knight, Emma W. Miss...................
..................Petersilea Academy

Langerfeldt, T. O.......... 114 Charles st.
Lanza, M. P. Miss.........Tremont School
Lowell School of Design..191 Boylston st.
Martin, L. Edna .. ..130 Tremont st.
Martin School of Art......130 Tremont st.
Menard, Edmond, Mrs..281 Columbus av.
Mills, Alice............. ...Wellesley College
Morris, George E....... .Berkeley School
Morse, M. A. Miss...........Savin Hill av.
Munich Art School........19 Temple pl.
Munsell, Albert H .... Normal Art School
Museum of Fine Arts Classes ....
.........................St. James av.
N. E. Conservatory School of Art ... ..
........................27 E. Newton st.
Nolen Art School.........48 Boylston st.
Nolen, Caroline..........48 Boylston st.
Normal Art School...1679 Washington st.
Notre Dame Academy....................
..........................283 Washington st.
Notre Dame Academy......Berkeley st.
Noyes, N. N Mrs. ....36 Milford st.
O'Kelley, Stephen sculptor.............
..........................161 Tremont st.
Parsons, Lydia A. Miss....28 School st.
Petersilea Academy... 281 Columbus av.
Plaisted, L. M. Miss . ..Tremont School
Porter, Edwin Forsythe.....45 Winter st.
Putnam, Benj. W.......................
.........Alveston st., Jamaica Plain
Richardson, L. Miss...................
................40 Erie st., Cambridge
Rigby, Emily.............25 Winter st.
Rigby, Mary..............25 Winter st.
Sanbourne, G. E. Miss......2A Beacon st.
Sanders, Carrie H. Miss.Gannett Institute
Sawyer, H. A.....18 Monument et.,Chas'n
School of Modelling....... 394 Federal st.
School of Sculpture...... 161 Tremont st.
School of Sculpture...... 354 Federal st.
Sears, J. Mrs .. ..163 Tremont st.
Stevens, A. B. Miss. ....17 Boylston pl.
Springer School of Decorative Art......
..........................114 Tremont st.
Stone, J. M............666 Washington st.
Titcombe, W. H .....630 Washington st.
Tremont School of Art....550 Tremont st.
Wagner, Jacob............12 West st.
Webster, Isabel M....... Lasell Seminary
Wellesley School of Art.........Wellesley
White, Sarah D..............12 West st.
Willard, William........27 E. Newton st.
Windship, Rebecca G...Lasell Seminary

Schools and Teachers of Dramatic Art.
Abell, Edith (opera and oratorio).........
.............................Music Hall
Adams, Charles R. opera .159 Tremont st.
Atkinson, Charles F....32 Pemberton sq.
Barry, Flora E. opera and oratorio)......
..........................124 Chandler st.
Bickford School of Elocution............
..........................18 Boylston st.
Bijou Dramatic School.540 Washington st.
Blish School of Elocution................
...........................Tremont Temple
Boston School of Acting..179 Tremont st.
Boston School of Elocution...............
............................18 Boylston st.
Boston School of Expression.Freeman pl.

Boston School of Oratory....7 Beacon st.
Delsarte School...........147 Tremont st.
Kelley, (S. R.).........Music Hall Building
Lothian, Napier.........Boston Theatre
Monroe Conservatory....36 Bromfield st.
New England Conservatory..Franklin sq.
Noah, Rachel..........Hotel Creighton
Peirce, Elmore A....Music Hall Building
Petersilea Academy......281 Columbus av
Tremont School of Elocution............
.....................550 Tremont st.

Schools and Teachers of Elocution.

Alden, Silas A...........36 Bromfield st.
Atkinson, Chas. F...... 32 Pemberton sq.
Averill, Flora H. Miss....550 Tremont st.
Barrett, Overton W.....281 Columbus av.
Berkeley School...........174 Tremont st.
Bickford School of Elocution.............
...................18 Boylston st.
Bijou Dramatic School......540 Wash. st.
Bixby, Eula P. Miss.Chauncy Hall School
Bleecker, J. A..........179 Tremont st.
Blish School of Elocution..78 Tremont st.
Blood, Mary A...........36 Bromfield st.
Boston School of Acting..179 Tremont st.
Boston School of Elocution.18 Boylston st.
Boston School of Expression.Freeman pl.
Boston School of Oratory....7 Beacon st.
Brown, Moses True...........7 Beacon st.
Buell, Lillian H................70 Cedar st.
Burrill, Charles E........36 Bromfield st.
Burrill, C. W..........241 Columbus av.
Call, Annie P............Lasell Seminary
Chadbourne, E. S. Miss....Grampian way
Clark, Henrietta B........36 Bromfield st.
Craigin, Mary L...............7 Beacon st.
Currier, Mary A........Wellesley College
Curry, Samuel S.............Freeman pl.
Delsarte School............147 Tremont st.
Dolbear, Amos E............7 Tremont st.
Drew, L. W. Miss............9 Chester sq.
Eddy, M. E. Miss..........175 Tremont st.
Eldridge, Jessie..........36 Bromfield st.
Emerson, Charles W......36 Bromfield st.
Fobes, Walter K...........18 Boylston st.
Fowle, Florence A......318 Longwood av.
Harris, Abby F. Mrs.Chauncy Hall School
Heald, J. S. Mrs..........147 Tremont st.
Holden, Alice E. Miss.......................
..................Chauncy Hall School
Ireson, Jennie E........ ....69 Chester sq.
Johnston, C. C............Payson av.
Jones, Henry D......Harvard University
Kimball, Edwin F...Chauncy Hall School
Kelley, Samuel R.........Music Hall bldg.
Lothian, Napier...........Boston Theatre
Marshall, Wyzeman.......2 Pinckney st.
Monroe Conservatory of Music............
.......................36 Bromfield st.
Munson, Kate C...........32 Winter st.
New England Conservatory..Franklin sq.
Noah, Rachel..........Creighton House
Petersilea Academy.....281 Columbus av.
Pierce, Elmore A......2 Music Hall bldg.
Pote, A. C...............112 Berkeley st.
Power, Clara T. Miss..........7 Beacon st.
Powers, Leland T..........39 Hancock st.
Rogers, Susan J..........550 Tremont st.
Russell Elsie, Miss.........18 Boylston st.

Southwick, F. T...........175 Tremont st.
Stanmore, Edith......540 Washington st.
Taylor, James Brainerd...174 Boylston st.
Ticknor, Howard M.......175 Tremont st.
Tremont School............550 Tremont st.
Warner, Clara G................5 Park st.
Wasserboehr, J. L. ....Draper ct.
Webster, Lucette, Miss....43 Pinckney st.

Schools and Teachers of Languages.

Alba-Raymond and Genoud..............
........................181 Tremont st.
Ambrose, Marietta (Italian)..............
.......................616 Washington st.
Barnum, Francis (French).Boston College
Bartels, Carl..271 Ruggles st, Rox'y Dist.
Barnard, Margaret B. (French).........
......................Berkeley School
Berkeley School..........174 Boylston st.
Berlitz, Max D............154 Tremont st.
Berlitz School of Languages.............
...................154 Tremont st.
Bernard, Victor (French)...17 Juniper st.
Boston Cor. School of Greek..............
........................38 Bromfield st.
Boston School of Languages...............
........................44 Boylston st.
Buck, A. H................12 Somerset st.
Burkart, F. C............179 Tremont st.
Carrisan, Lucien (French)...............
........................616 Washington st.
Chauncy Hall School......259 Boylston st.
Cheeney, Mary H........14 Hotel Adelphi
Chesneau, Leopold...........6 Beacon st.
Choate, Isaac B....168 W. Springfield st.
Clarke, Julia C......Chauncy Hall School
Clarke, Lucia F. (Latin).Wellesley College
College Lafayette.........181 Tremont st.
Columbus School of Languages..........
.......................179 Tremont st.
Cyr, Narcisse (French)...Hotel Richwood
Daniell, M. Grant...Chauncy Hall School
Decombs, Emilie Mlle. (French)..........
.........................Tremont School
De Lestrade, G. (French)..159 Tremont st.
De Maltchyce, A. Miss....16 St. James st.
De Meritte, Edwin (Latin and Greek).....
.........................Berkeley School
De Montrachy, Mary (French)...........
..........................22 Wheeler st.
Duval, F. Miss (French).94 W. Newton st.
Duval, M. Miss(French).94 W. Newton st.
Dwelshauvers, C. Mrs......20 Willard pl.
Gardner, L. M. Miss (German)...........
........................33 Worcester st.
Godefrin, A. E. A. (French)..............
.......................40 Montgomery st.
Green, N. L. Mme.........130 Tremont st.
Harkins, Francis A. (French)............
..........................Boston College
Humphreys, E. R....129 W. Chester Park
Kelley, James V. (French).Boston College
Jansen, John A. Rev. (German)..........
..........................Boston College
Lauler, G. W. (French).....58 Rutland st.
Machado, Juan F. (Spanish).............
..........................Tremont School
Manning, Sarah E.........21 Jenkins st.
Marchal, B. M. (French)..26 Grenville pl.
Morand, Henri...............131 Dale st.

New England Conservatory..............
.....................27 E. Newton st.
Nichols, Anna.........70 Studio Building
Noble, G. W. C..........174 Tremont st.
Nolte, Heinrich (German)...............
.....................159 A Tremont st.
Noury, Leontine (French)................
....................108 Pembroke st.
O'Sullivan, Patrick J. (French)..........
... de..................Boston College
Peiffer de, Jean French)..27 E. Newton st.
Perkins, R. L. (Latin and Greek).........
....................31 Pemberton sq.
Petersilea Academy.....281 Columbus av.
Rambaud, Miss............386 Beacon st.
Rosenstein, Albert (German)..............
....................27 E. Newton st.
Sauveur School of Languages............
....................18 Pemberton sq.
Schmetzky, O............154 Tremont st.
School of French and German Languages.
.....................179 Tremont st.
Schroeder, Bernard (German)..6 Park sq.
Shandelle, Henry J. Rev. (German)......
....................Boston College
Siedhof, Carl, Jr.(German).23 Chestnut st.
Solial, Arthur French.....6 Boylston pl.
Stoddard, Helen E. Miss (German).......
.....................Berkeley School
Tappan, Mary French .Gannett Institute
Torricelli, J. B.................19 Gray st.
Tremont School.........550 Tremont st.
Ventura, L. D. (Italian and French......
.....................102 Boylston st.
Von Olker, Ida (German).8 Hotel Baldwin
Wesselhoeft, Mrs. M.......9 Newbury st.
White, Julie (German)........58 Gray st.

Schools and Teachers of Music.
Certainly no other American city presents so extended a list of good music schools and teachers as Boston; and it may be questioned whether any foreign capital can surpass it. While this city is so well provided, there can be no good reason for going elsewhere to to study the art of singing or playing. The names and addresses are as follows:
Abercrombie Oratorio School............
.....................181 Tremont st.
Adams Operatic School...159 Tremont st.
Barry (Flora E.), School of Lyric Art....
....................124 Chandler st.
Boston Conservatory of Music...........
....................154 Tremont st.
Chauncy Hall School (singing...........
....................259 Boylston st.
De la Motte Music School................
....................36 Commonwealth av.
Eichberg Violin School...154 Tremont st.
Gannett Institute..........69 Chester sq.
Harvard School of Music......Cambridge
Hayden Guitar School..146A Tremont st.
Lasell Seminary Musical Courses.........
.....................Auburndale
Mendelssohn Musical Institute..........
....................5 Columbus sq.
New England Conservatory of Music.....
....................Franklin sq.
N. E. Conservatory Violin School........
....................Franklin sq.

Parisian Academy of Music..............
.............Tremont st., cor Boylston
Perkins Musical Institute (for the Blind)
.......................South Boston
Petersilea Academy of Music............
....................281 Columbus av.
Tremont School of Music..550 Tremont st.
Truette Organ School....Tremont Temple
Van Buren (Rudersdorff) School.........
.....................Hotel Glendon
Ward Music School......707 Shawmut av.
Wellesley College Courses of Music......
......................Wellesley
Abell, Edith.........4 Music Hall Building
Abercrombie, Charles.....181 Tremont st.
Adamowski, Timothie de.27 E. Newton st.
Adams, Charles R....... 159A Tremont st
Adams, M. E. J. Mrs.2930 Washington st.
Aiken, Henry M..............Hotel Bristol
Allen, Charles N............Hotel Lafayette
Ames, Lucia T..........218 W. Canton st.
Apthorp, W. F............27 E. Newton st.
Atwood, James B.........105 Warren av.
Bacon, W. F..................89 Court st.
Baermann, Carl..........195 Tremont st.
Bagley, E. M..............112 Berkeley st.
Bailey, Emma F..............114 Main st.
Bailey, Eben H.........112 Berkeley st.
Bailey, Sara G.........................
......Dorchester av. cor. Foster st.
Baker, Theo...........149A Tremont st.
Ball, L. W.................132 Tremont st.
Ball, O. J..............178 Washington st.
Bancroft, S. A..............117 Tremont st.
Barker, George.........180 Washington st.
Barker, Geo. F........90 Eutaw st., E. B.
Barnard, Kate F..........301 Shawmut av.
Barrett, Ellen D.........281 Columbus av.
Barry, Flora E..........124 Chandler st.
Bastine, J. Mrs..............14 Terrace st.
Bean, L. F. Miss...............3 West st.
Behr, Charles........................
..Chestnut av. Jamaica Plain District
Bemis, George............31 Beacon st.
Bemis, Geo. W..............3 Hamilton pl.
Bendix, Otto..............27 E. Newton st.
Bennett, Chas. W..........121 Court st.
Benson, Harry..14 Music Hall Building
Bishop, Marie Fries, Mme..33 Boylston st.
Blodgett, J. L.........179 Washington st.
Boardman, D. W......230 Washington st.
Bowers, Kate A......................
......20 Hotel Boylston, 26 Boylston st.
Bowser, S. S. Mrs.....Hollis pl., Allston
Brackett, L. F...........152 Tremont st.
Bradshaw, Briggs..........11 North av.
Bradstreet, L. E. Miss...152 Tremont st.
Brayley, George...........125 Tremont st.
Brown, Henry C........226 Washington st.
Browne, Annie E. Miss.12 Hotel Boylston
Bruce, Fanny E..........550 Tremont st.
Buckingham, John D.....27 E. Newton st.
Bullard, M. G. Miss...36 Music Hall Bldg
Burton, Ida M..............54 Berkeley st.
Butler, Justus E.........156 Tremont st.
Callender, Nellie D....96 W. Concord st.
Campanari, Leandro,....27 E. Newton st.
Capen, C. L..............281 Columbus av.
Carney, C..................103 Court st.
Carney, Philip I............103 Court st.
Carpenter, Moses...........180 Salem st.
Carter, Mary E..........27 E. Newton st.

Carter, O. L............51 Monument av.
Carter, T. M..............................
   179 Washington st., and 34 Isabella st.
Chadwick, G. W............99 Boylston st.
Chaffee, Mrs...................3 West st.
Chandler, Fred................3 West st.
Chandler, Lillian....Home Journal Office
Cheeney, J. W...........14 Hotel Adelphi
Chelius, George A.........104 Kendall st.
Chelius, H. P............154 Tremont st.
Chenery, C................170 Tremont st.
Clark, C. A..............149 Tremont st.
Claus, J. B............27 East Newton st.
Cleaveland, M. B. Miss...2 Wise st., J. P.
Clouston, R. H. Jr..........8 Millmont st.
Cobb, J. P.............451 Washington st.
Colburn, B. F..........281 Columbus av.
Cole, S. W..............212 Columbus av.
Cole, William A.............121 Court st..
Conant, Albert F........281 Columbus av.
Corbet, Marguerite S......25 Bowdoin st.
Cowles, H. H..............Hotel Boylston
Crane, Fred L............230 Meridian st.
Crowell, Frank L..20 Music Hall building
Currier, T. P............154 A Tremont st.
Cutter, A. A..................7 Ottawa st.
Cutter, Benj............27 East Newton st.
Damm, August...........30 Buckingham st.
Daniell, M. Grant...........11 Schuyler st.
Daniell, W. H.........27 East Newton st.
Davenport, Warren........154 Tremont st.
Davis, J. W..............169 Tremont st.
DeAngelis, E. M. Mme...159 A Tremont st.
Denee, C. F............27 East Newton st.
DeSeve, Alfred............Hotel Glendon
Dewey, E................179 Tremont st.
De Witt, William E......342 Harrison av.
De Wolfe, M. B. Miss......
   ....Waverly st., Brighton
Dobson, Geo. C.........290 Shawmut av.
Donahoe, J. Frank.....149 A Tremont st.
Downes, I. H. K............
   ....60 Sullivan st., Charlestown
Driscoll, Mrs..................3 West st.
Dryden, F. L..........521 East Seventh st.
Dudley, Geo. W..........154 Tremont st.
Duffy, J. G................152 Dudley st.
Dunham, H. M.........27 East Newton st.
Duncan, A. Mrs...........143 Tremont st.
Dunn, Jennie G......Taylor st., Neponset
Eichberg, Julius..........154 Tremont st.
Eichler, Chas. H.........75 E. Brookline st.
Eichler, J. E...............61 Melrose st.
Elliot, R. M............149 A Tremont st.
Elsom, Louis C........27 East Newton st.
Eltz, Paul..................14 Milford st.
Emery, Ada P.............550 Tremont st.
Emery, S. A............149 A Tremont st.
Faelten, Carl...........27 East Newton st.
Fay, H. F..................152 Tremont st.
Fearing S. Jennie Miss....
   ....569 East Broadway, S. B.
Fenner, Thos. P........18 Claremont park
Fenollosa, W. S.............14 Winter st.
Fernald, A. H..........451 Washington st.
Fisher, Sarah C........27 East Newton st.
Finmara, Plaicide.............80 Green st.
Foote, Arthur............2 West Cedar st.
Fox, Geo................10 Common st.
Franco, Samuel.......451 Washington st.
Freeman, James O........1 Bosworth st.
French, S. E. Miss...East st., Dorchester

Fries, Wulf C. J............369 Dudley st.
Frost, S..................601 Washington st.
Fuller, Eloise L............4 Kearsarge av.
Gage, A. Louise..........86 Mt. Vernon st.
Garrett, Elizabeth M....200 Columbus av.
Gerrish, S. H............795 Washington st.
Gilder, John Francis.....451 Tremont st.
Girovano, G..............149 A Tremont st.
Gleason, F. E.............65 Indiana pl.
Goddard, N. P.........79 E. Brookline st.
Grant, E. C..................12 Davis st.
Grebe, Fannie............154 Tremont st.
Guilmette, Chas. A. Mrs..301 Shawmut av.
Gustine, L. Miss..........12 Hotel Boylston
Guttridge, James B..Garden st., Mt. Hope
Hale, F. W.............27 East Newton st.
Hall, Edna A. Mrs......206 Dartmouth st.
Hall, J. Dudley............125 Tremont st.
Hall, Lillian J................10 Lynde st.
Hamann, August.............34 West st.
Hambro, Frances...........19 Madison st.
Harding, E. M. Miss....18 Pemberton sq.
Hartwell, M. D. Miss..152 Huntington av.
Hatch, Isadore Miss......536 Tremont st.
Hawes, Charlotte W......Hotel Berkeley
Hay, C. E...............149 A Tremont st.
Hayden, W. L............146 Tremont st.
Hendl, H...................125 Tremont st.
Henry, Thomas W........Hotel Carleton
Higgins, Lottie Miss........84 Warrenton st.
Hill, E. C...................29 Dover st.
Hill, James W........21 Music Hall bldg.
Hill, Junius W..............154 Tremont st.
Hills, Joseph A..........149A Tremont st.
Hodsdon, J. L. jr......14 Hotel Boylston
Hoey, F. M. Mrs...........98 Chambers st.
Holmes, Theresa C. Miss.208 Dartmouth st.
Hooton, H.................12 Howard st.
Hopper, H. G.............181 Tremont st.
Hosmer, Lizzie Green....64 Evans House
Howard, George H.......27 E. Newton st.
Howard, John............149A Tremont st.
Howard, Nellie W......91 Weld av. Rox'y
Howell, W. I............Hotel Berkeley
Hoyt, John................157 Tremont st.
Hudson, Joseph C.....616 Washington st.
Human, Theodore.........147 Tremont st.
Hunt, Charles G............17 Cherry st.
Ide, M. W..........Downer ct. Dorchester
James, Ingles M. Mrs...218 Columbus av.
Jamieson, S. W...........14 Grenville pl.
Johnson, Herbert O.....149A Tremont st.
Kammerling, H. A........3 Creighton st.
Keach, L...............28 Music Hall bldg.
Keach, Olivia E. Mrs.....1 Rockville Park
Keene, A. W.............27 E. Newton st.
Kellogg, Fanny Miss........Hotel Pelham
Kelly, E. A................17 Beacon st.
Kelsey, E. E.............14 Music Hall
Kettele, Emma LeB......112 Berkeley st.
King, H. Adelaide Mrs........52 Eutaw st.
Kraus, Jennie Mrs...........12 Bond st.
Lanegan, Jane R. W............Grant pl.
Lang, B. J................152 Tremont st.
Lansing, George L.........74 Tremont st.
Lavallee, Calixa..........281 Columbus av.
Leavitt, W. J. D..........133 Washington st.
Leitch, John............2930 Washington st.
Lennon, J. G............149A Tremont st.
Lewis, Chas. Mrs.......11 Hotel Newton
Lewis, Fred H............27 E. Newton st.
Lichtenberg, Leopold.....41 Somerset st.

Lincoln, A. L. Miss........12 Pinckney st.
Lincoln, F. F..............27 E. Newton st.
Lindall, C. E..........180 Washington st.
Linscott, Nellie F..........2 E. Canton st.
Lissner, S. Miss...........154 Warren av.
Listemann, Bernhard. ..132 Tremont st.
Little, Minnie Mrs..   ....3 West st.
Long, J. H. Mrs.....   ....21 Holyoke st.
Lott, W. H. Mrs...........Hotel Columbus
Lowry, Louis..............Hotel Harrison
Lynes, F................149A Tremont st.
Maas, Louis................156 Tremont st.
Madden, Mary.............152 Tremont st.
Maiers, Laura A..........152 Tremont st.
Mann, S. H................28 Winter st.
Manning, C. H ....15 Music Hall bldg.
Marble, Edw. B......   ....39 Hancock st.
Marsh, C. A. Mrs.........181 Tremont st.
Marshall, L. ....169 W. Newton st.
Martin, S. C. jr......252 Webster st. E. B.
Mason L...............516 Washington st.
McGowan, M. E...........790 Parker st.
McLaughlin, James M........3 West st.
McLaughlin, Kate C.......61 Appleton st.
McLaughlin, Lillie T..........3 West st.
McLeod, N............26 Music Hall bldg.
Mead, Olive.322 Harvard st.Cambridgep't
Menzel, William A....................
.....Chestnut av. near Boylston, J. P.
Merck, George G....   .   ...1 Oak pl.
Merrill, E. L. Miss.......509 E. Seventh st.
Metcalf, William H. F....175 Tremont st.
Meyrelles, Pedro C ....Hotel Cherry
Miller, A. T. M. Miss....106 Cambridge st.
Milligan, T. M. Miss......304 Shawmut av.
Milligan, Willis...........304 Shawmut av.
Mitchell, Nellie Brown.   ....16 Mills st.
Morrill, L. P. Mrs......104 Dartmouth st.
Morse, Cora, Mrs..............3 West st.
Morse, F. E.............27 E. Newton st.
Moulton, Hattie A   .Richmond, L. M.
Munroe, S. A. D.Highland st., Dorchester
Munson, Julius S.....   ....32 Winter st.
Nichols, C. R. Mrs..............3 West st.
Noeroth, J....................76 Temple st.
Norman, T................78 Chapman st.
Norton, James H............103 Court st.
Nowell, G. M ....181 Tremont st.
Nowell, Willis E..........181 Tremont st.
O'Brien, Mary E. Miss.....Hotel Glendon
O'Neill, John ....27 E. Newton st.
Oliver, Edward B ....5 Columbus sq.
Orth, John...   ..   ..179 Tremont st.
Orth, Louise E.   ....36 Holyoke st.
Orth, Sybilla Miss.........36 Holyoke st.
Osgood, Geo. L..........149A Tremont st.
Osgood, Marion............125 Tremont st.
O'Shea, John A., jr...49 Chelsea st., E. B.
Pennell, A. E..............157 Tremont st
Park, Carrie M. Miss....................
......Linden, near Dorchester av.
Parke, Fred. W............39 Concord sq.
Parker, H. W. ....179 Tremont st.
Parker, J. C. D ....27 E. Newton st.
Parks, Gideon N....................
......18 Huntington House, Cortes st.
Parmenter, L. H..........156 Tremont st.
Pégou, Albert..............Hotel Boylston
Pégou, Mme................Hotel Boylston
Pennell, Albert E.......157 Tremont st.
Perabo, Ernst..Park st., near Anawan av.
Perry, Edward B.........179 Tremont st.

Petersilea, Carlyle......281 Columbus av.
Pflueger, Carl.............154 Tremont st.
Phippen, Joshua........149A Tremont st.
Plumer, Annie E.........9 Hotel Boylston
Poole, Lillie B.................76 Dudley st.
Porter, A. W. Mrs...... 27 E. Newton st
Porter, F. A..............27 E. Newton st.
Pray, Georgia, Miss......170 Tremont st.
Preston, J. A.   ....149A Tremont st.
Proeschold, Carl H. F ....79 Dudley st.
Pstrokonsky, Jules de.70 E. Chester Park
Purdy, Geo..................3 West st.
Rametti, Joseph...   .....40 Dartmouth st.
Rametti, Joseph Mrs.....40 Dartmouth st.
Ramsdell, Eugene C........3 Creighton st.
Reed, Albin R....   ....3 W. Cedar st.
Reid, C. E.......   ....   .3 West st.
Reilly, May C....   ....28 Milford st.
Richardson, J. H........1 Bosworth st.
Ripley, W. S   ....88 Court st.
Robinson, G   ....170 Tremont st.
Robinson, W. B..........149A Tremont st.
Roby, Charles C.... 149 Trenton st., E. B.
Rogers, Clara Doria, Mme..309 Beacon st.
Rotoli, August............27 E. Newton st.
Ryan, Alice..................
......Mill st., cor. Com'l, Dorchester
Ryder, J. G. Miss............181 Tremont st.
Ryder, Thomas P..........156 Tremont st.
Sargent, Sullivan A........175 Tremont st.
Sawyer, H. E. Mrs.........17 St. James av.
Scheidemandel, Th. Mrs..365 Tremont st.
Scheindler, Paul............ ..18 Sharon st.
Schmitt, S. M. Mrs......102 Boylston st.
Sharland, J. B. Centre st., Jamaica Plain
Shattuck, Lillian Miss....154 Tremont st.
Shaw, Franklin A   ....175 Tremont st.
Shepard, Martha D. Mrs................
......Ashland st., Dorchester
Shepard, Mary ....94 Waltham st.
Sherman, Etta R..........27 E. Newton st.
Sherwood, Wm. H ....156 Tremont st.
Shuebruk, Richard......179 Tremont st.
Simonds, M. Anna......281 Columbus av.
Siple, M. DeForrest.......154 Tremont st.
Smart, Clara E...........179 Tremont st.
Smith, Elmira ....451 Washington st.
Smith, Frank J.............39 Hancock st.
Smith, Frank T.............681 Tremont st.
Smith, Henry J......... 31 Worcester sq.
Smith, H. H...........1030 Washington st.
Smith, H. M. Mrs.... 25 Music Hall Bldg
Smith, T. J. Mrs ....Hotel Pelham
Spring, N. J ....179 Washington st.
Staats, C. L...............3 Tremont row
St. Clair, K. T.........344 Shawmut av.
Stetson, J. B ....506 Washington st.
Stoddard, H. H. Miss .....83 Shawmut av.
Stone, Minnie C...........293 Tremont st.
Stone, Nellie, Miss ....3 West st
Strater, Pauline P.   ...18 Boylston st.
Stratton, Henry W..............14 Truro st.
Suck, August P. F..........6 Catawba st.
Suck, Carl J.............10 Ferdinand st.
Sullivan, Daniel........rear 815 Albany st.
Sumner, G. W............96 Charles st.
Swan, A. W............27 E. Newton st.
Tenney, Alice L. Miss....178 Tremont st.
Thaxter, Fannie, Miss..........3 West st
Thayer, Arthur W........179 Tremont st.
Ticknor, H. M.........Evans House Block
Titus, George R........149A Tremont st.

Tolman, Olivia Miss...81 Montgomery st.
Tompson, C. H. ......179 Washington st.
Tracy, James M............152 Tremont st.
Trask, C. R. B............360½ Tremont st.
Trask, Julia, Miss.........47 Humphreys st.
Trautmann, Carl..........125 Tremont st.
Truette, Everett E.......Tremont Temple
Tucker, H. G..............152 Tremont st.
Tufts, John W..............19 Holyoke st.
Turner, A. D.............27 E. Newton st.
Turner, J. W..........3 Chelsea st., E. B.
Underwood, Mary L........604 Tremont st.
Urso, Camilla.............451 Tremont st.
Van Buren, J. Miss........Hotel Glendon
Van Raalte, Albert........154 Tremont st.
Van Walkenburg, W. B...70 Chapman st.
Vincent, M. T. M..............Evans House
Von Ette, Edward..............20 Delle av.
Von Radecki, Olga.......5 Hotel Glendon
Waddington, James....   ...7 Copeland st.
Want, Geo. W..............181 Tremont st.
Ward, C. C..................64 Clarendon st.
Ward, Julius E..........707 Shawmut av.
Washburn, A. M. Miss..433 Washington st.
Washington, R. M. Miss..........5 Smith ct.
Webber, Charles F........149A Tremont st.
Webster, Mary P..........152 Tremont st.
Wenzel, Iwan P....445 W. Broadway, S.B.
Werner, J. A. Mrs....1173 Washington st.
Weston, J. P..........451 Washington st.
Weston, Louis F..........125 Tremont st.
Wheeler, J. Harry........149A Tremont st.
Wheeler, Lyman W.......161 Tremont st.
Whelpley, B. L.............152 Tremont st.
Whyte, Frank Leroy.32 Music Hall bldg.
Whiting, Arthur..........179 Tremont st.
Whiting, Geo. E.........27 E. Newton st.
Whitney, F. P. Mrs...... 5 St. Charles st.
Whitney, H. L..............125 Tremont st.
Whitney, S. B..............125 Tremont st.
Whittier, Charles H......27 E. Newton st.
Wild, J. C..................20½ Bedford st.
Wilde, Hiram...........616 Washington st.
Woodward, L. F. Miss.....112 Berkeley st.
Wyatt, Julia Miss........100 Boylston st.
Yeomans, H. W....................150 G st.
Zerrahn, Carl...........27 E. Newton st.

Schools and Teachers of Cookery.
Boston Cooking School, 174 Tremont st. (See *Boston Cooking School*.) North Bennet Street Industrial Cooking School, 39 North Bennet st.; Ruggles Street Cooking Classes, Ruggles Street Church, Roxbury District; South End Industrial Cooking School, 45 Bartlett st., Roxbury District; Trinity House Evening Cooking Classes, 13 Burroughs pl.; Olive C. Daniell, Lasell Seminary; Mme. A. Favier, Acorn st., cor. Willow st.; Kate R. Bragdon, Lasell Seminary; Miss J. Sweeney, 113 Revere st.; Hemenway Industrial School for Girls, Starr King School House, Tennyson st.

Schools and Teachers of Dancing.
J. T. Atwood, 724 Washington st.; Banta's (J. J.) Dancing Academy, 1371 Washington st.; Emily M. Condell, 19 Baldwin st., Charlestown District; G. H. Gardner, 176 Tremont st.; Pauline Gravier, 753 Tremont st.; George A. Gustin, 79 Dartmouth st.; Miss J. C. Hunt, 72 Chapman st.; E. W. Masters, 502 Tremont st.; H. E. Munroe, Highland Hall, Roxbury District; A. L. Papanti, 23 Tremont st.; Miss C. M. Post, 4 Berkeley st.; Wm. H. Seavey, 140 Meridian st., East Boston; Slye (E. P.) and Blacqs, 176 Tremont st.; Josephine M. Thaxter, 7 Worcester pl.; Russ B. Walker, 24 Dwight st. (See *Walker's Private Dancing Academy*.)

Schools and Teachers of Dress-Cutting.
H. A. Brown, 517 Tremont st.; M. E. Church, 633 Washington st.; Mrs. E. E. Durgin, 25 Winter st.; N. P. Emery, S. Groton st.; G. M. Greenwood & Company, 179A Tremont st.; Mrs. A. A. Hewitt, Mrs. D. A. Inwood, 31 Winter st.; Miss L. F. Kendrick, 25 Winter st.; O. S. Spare, 179 Tremont st.; Mrs. B. A. Stearns, 409 Washington st.; Mrs. F. M. Tilden, 25 Winter st.; Industrial Training School, Gray st.; Hemenway Industrial School for Girls, Starr King School House, Tennyson st.; First Church, Marlborough st., cor. Berkeley st.; Girls' Industrial Club, 27 Chambers st.; South End Industrial School, 45 Bartlett st., Roxbury District.

Sears School for Young Ladies.
(1885). 140 Marlborough st. An extremely successful school of high rank. Branches taught: French, German, Latin, mathematics, natural sciences, English history and drawing. English composition is an especial feature. Ladies of extended experience in teaching are included in the Faculty of this school, which is becoming so well known among the cultivated families of New England, New York, the South and West. The natural sciences are in charge of an instructor who has made them a special study. *Native* teachers of French and German are engaged, in order that the idioms of each language may be made perfectly clear to the student. Mathematics form a strong feature of the curriculum, as a preliminary to the course in natural science. Botany, zoology and physics receive particular attention. The History of Modern Europe and of America is taught by Mr. E. H. Sears—the eminent Principal of the school — who makes this study especially interesting to those who intend to travel in foreign lands or in our own country. Drawing is taught by the most competent instructors. Pupils must not be under fourteen years of age. Special students are received. Tuition: $250; special students, $50 a year for each study. The Sears School is located in the most aristocratic quarter of the city.

Simmons Female College.
In 1870, John Simmons provided (by will) for the establishment in Boston of a great College for Young Women, wherein should be taught music, drawing, design-

ing, medicine, telegraphy, and other important branches of industry, science and art, by means of which young women might be enabled to acquire an independent livelihood. Great interest is being manifested concerning the long delay in carrying out the testator's legal provisions.

South End Free Industrial School. (1882). 45 Bartlett st., Roxbury District. Branches: book-keeping, printing, carpentry, dressmaking, sewing, chemistry, botany, drawing, cooking, etc. Reading and recreation rooms. Free Evening Classes.

Special Training School for Nurses. 24 McLean st. 6 months or 1 year. Pay: $12 per month, for 6 months; $15 afterward.

Spencer Classes in Elocution. 202 Dartmouth st.

Springer School of Decortive Art. 114 Tremont st., opposite the Common, near Temple pl. Principal, L. R. Springer. Instruction is given in the various branches of modern Decorative Art, in a practical, thorough manner. There are classes in water-colors, by a new and improved method, by which beginners are easily and quickly taught flower-painting, etc., from Nature. Other branches include crayon and pastel drawing, and enlarging by the use of the pentagraph; modelling in plastic composition, manufactured by Mrs. Springer, with no restrictions, no firing being required; diaphonie (a beautiful imitation of stained glass taught in ten minutes; photograph-coloring, in oil and water-colors, a knowledge of which will generally secure a profitable position for one. French and German decorative art — a perfect substitute for painting on silk, china, paper, or other material used for painting, by new patent process. Both processes are taught *free* on certain days.

Stall's Bicycle School. 509 Tremont st. It is an axiom of the teachers of the mind that the physical system should be developed simultaneously, that the pupil may have a sound mind in a healthy body. One of the best methods of taking healthful exercise, which is recommended by eminent clergymen, physicians, lawyers, and all following literary or sedentary professions, is by bicycle or tricycle riding. The benefits derived are the greater owing to the pleasure of viewing the country, thus diverting the mind from any labor of exercise, and resting it by change. At Stall's Bicycle School, which has been established in Odd Fellows Building, at the corner of Tremont and Berkeley sts., riding on any style of wheel, Star, Columbia,

etc., is taught, as well as tricycle riding. Lessons are also given on the road. Single lessons, 50 cents; course, $5. W. W. Stall, 509 Tremont st., 4 Warren av. (Horse-cars from all parts of the city and suburbs pass the building; also, cars to and from all railway stations.)

State Normal School. Bridgewater. Preparatory school for those intending to become teachers in Massachusetts public schools. Courses, 2 and 4 years. Tuition *free*.

State Normal School. Framingham. Preparatory school for Massachusetts public school teachers. Courses, 2 and 4 years. Tuition *free*.

State Normal School. (1854). Salem. Although this school was established principally for the preparation of women teachers to instruct in the Common and High Schools, ladies desiring to teach in other States or in private schools are admitted by paying $15 a term for tuition. Instruction is *free* to all who comply with the condition of teaching in the public schools of Massachusetts, *wherever they may previously have resided*. Salem is 16 miles from Boston, on the Eastern Railway. Daniel B. Hagar, Ph D., is the Principal of the School. The Board of Visitors comprises Edward C. Carrigan, John W. Dickinson, A.M., and Francis A. Walker, L.L.D., of Boston.

Stone Art School. (1878). 666 Washington st. J. M. Stone, Principal. Drawing and painting from life; perspective, portrait painting, etc., are here taught.

Studies at Home. (1873). Established for the purpose of assisting women over 17 years of age, by advice and correspondence, to develop intellectual habits while pursuing their ordinary occupations. Books are loaned from a library formed for the purpose. A most philanthropic work. Annual fee, $3. Address Miss Anna E. Ticknor, Secretary of the Society to Encourage Studies at Home, 41 Marlborough st.

Summer Courses in Chemistry. Boylston Hall, Cambridge. From July 5 to August 14. Branches: Chemistry for beginners; advanced students; Qualitative and Quantitative Analysis; Mineralogy. Tuition: for course, $25; $5 to $6 for material and apparatus. Places in the Harvard Chemical Laboratory are secured by addressing Arthur M. Comey, Cambridge.

Summer Normal School of Singing. H. E. Holt, Director. Mr. Holt, whose address is at Lexington, Mass., holds summer courses of music lessons for teachers.

Summer School of Art. Tomasso Juglaris, Director. The Juglaris Art School holds summer sessions which are largely attended. (See *Juglaris Art School.*)

Summer School of Oratory. (1873). 1 Somerset st., and 7 Beacon st. The Boston School of Oratory holds summer sessions of five weeks, beginning early in July. Boston being a summer city, having guests from all over the country, this School complies with a general demand and opens its rooms for instruction in the Synthetic Philosophy of Expression, according to Delsarte, supplemented by modern scientific methods. Teachers attend this Summer School largely. Tuition: $5 per week; five weeks, $20. Prof. Moses True Brown is the Principal of this School, which is renowned for excellence and thoroughness. (See *Boston School of Oratory.*)

Summer School of Philosophy. (See *Concord School of Philosophy*).

Summer Schools. (See *Concord School of Philosophy; Summer School of Art, (Juglaris); Summer (Normal) School of Singing; Summer School of Oratory; Vacation Schools*).

Teacher of Christian Science. An all-absorbing subject with many persons throughout the country just now is the "mind-cure," and classes are being formed by Dr. Clara E. Choate, to meet on Tuesdays at 3 Wellington st., (second door from Columbus av.), with free lectures every Thursday, at the same place. Dr. Choate has prepared and published several lectures on the following subjects: "The Unfolding, or Mind Understood;" "The Healing Power" and "True Christianity: The Basis of Healing with Mind," which are sold at 20 cents per copy. The Choate School of Christian Science may easily be reached by any Columbus Avenue street-car.

Teachers and Schools of Science. Berkeley School, 174 Boylston st.; Choate's School of Christian Science, 3 Wellington st., Columbus av.; Columbus School of Languages and Sciences; Joseph C. Burke, Lasell Seminary; Alice E. Freeman, Wellesley College; Lawrence Scientific School; J. C. Sharp, Centre st., Dorchester District; James B. Taylor, Berkeley School, 174 Boylston st.

Teachers of Astronomy. Observatory, Cambridge. One of the most fully equipped observatories in the world; noted throughout Europe for its thorough scientific researches. Pupils received for regular or special courses. The Time Signals of Boston and New England are largely furnished by the Time Service of this renowned Observatory.

Teachers of Natural History. Agassiz Museum, Cambridge. Special and regular courses.

Teachers' School of Science. (1839). *Free.* A School of lectures sustained by the John Lowell fund. Lectures are given on physics, geology, physiology, and various other branches of Science, on Saturday afternoons, at the Institute of Technology Building, 191 Tremont st., and are open to all public school teachers from any section of the country.

Technology Preparatory School. (1828). 259 Boylston st. As the Massachusetts Institute of Technology offers a practical training in science —as applied to the various wants of the active American life—equal to that of the noted polytechnic schools of Europe, and in the perfection of its courses of laboratory instruction *surpasses all other schools*, Chauncy Hall makes a specialty of preparing scholars for the Institute in the studies demanded for their entrance examination. English or classical course, $200. (See *Chauncy Hall School*).

Theological (Episcopal) School. (1867). Cambridge. Dean, Rev. George Zabriskie Gray, D. D. Bachelors of Arts admitted without examination; all others are required to pass one. Special courses are arranged.

Theological Seminary. (See *Andover Theological Seminary*).

Tremont School of Music. (1882). 550 Tremont st. Miss Fanny E. Bruce, Principal. Since the establishment of this fine music school several years since it has made rapid strides towards the front ranks of our great conservatories. The patronage attracted from various sections of the country demonstrates the fact that the reputation of the School is commensurate with its great merits. In the study of the Pianoforte a high standard is maintained, the pupils being required to pursue the most thorough modern system of technical training. The following course of study must be completed before graduating: Beren's 50 Piano Lessons; Kohler's Op. 50; Plaidy's Technical Studies, Heller's Op. 46 and 47; Bertini's Op. 29 and 32; Czerny's Studies in Velocity; Cramer's Studies; Clementi's Gradus ad Parnassum; Loeschorn's Studies; Mosheles' Studies; Kullak's Octave Studies; Bach's Preludes and Fugues; Chopin's Concertos, Polonaises, Etudes, etc.; the principal works of Mozart, Weber, Haydn, Beethoven, Hummel, Liszt; Selections from Clementi, Mendelssohn, Schumann, Krause, Bertini, Eschmann, and the course in Harmony and Theory. Each graduate is expected to give a recital during the last year. Organ pupils must complete studies from Whiting, Buck, Rink, Mendelssohn, Bach, Best, Hopkins, Westbrook, Warren and other composers, before graduating. Other branches of instrumental music comprise the study of the Violin, Violoncello, Guitar, Flute, Cornet, etc. Vocal music, in the study of which the true Italian method is employed, Elocution and Oratory, etc., are included in the curriculum. Private instruction is given to pupils in the latter department. Evening lessons are provided for those otherwise engaged during the day. The English branches, bookkeeping, Greek and Latin, modern languages, fine arts, decorative art, art embroidery, etc., also have departments in this great School. Tuition: (term of 20 lessons) from $10 to $20; organ, from $20 to $25; violin, $10 to $20; violoncello, $10 to $20; guitar, flute, cornet, $15 to $20; vocal music, $15 to $20, other branches, from $12 to $20. Conveniently located, at the corner of Tremont and Waltham sts., the School is easily accessible by several lines of horse cars from all parts of the city and railway stations. (Take any Tremont st. car going south.)

Tremont School of Music. Oratory Department.
550 Tremont st. By arrangement with the Monroe Conservatory of Oratory the Tremont School of Music — Miss Fannie E. Bruce, Principal — has united its Oratory Department with the former renowned institution. Tuition — for which application is to be made at 550 Tremont st. — is as follows: 20 lessons, $15 to $20.

Tufts College.
College Hill, Medford. President, Elmer H. Capen, D. D. Course of study, Freshman class: Latin, Roman History, Greek, Mathematics, Oratory. Sophomore class: Latin, French, Greek, Natural History, Physics, Mathematics, Oratory, Rhetoric. Junior class: German, Physics, Chemistry, English Literature; Psychology, Natural History, Rhetoric. Senior class: Natural History, Moral Philosophy, Political Economy, Logic, Rhetoric. There are also courses in Theology, Civil Engineering, Electrical Engineering, etc. Expenses: College charges, tuition, care of rooms, incidentals, per year, $100; half-room rent, from $15 to $50 per week; board, $3.50 to $4 per week; total, $251.50 to $306 per year. Students' board in Commons at $3.50 per week. College year begins September 17. (College Hill is three miles from Boston State House, on Boston & Lowell Railroad).

Vacation Schools.
(See *Free Schools*.).

Vinal Park Riding Academy.
West Chester Park st. cor. Newbury st. W. A. McGibbon, Instructor. Terms: single lesson, $2. Six lesson tickets, $10. Road lesson, 5. Two persons, $4 each. Exercises at Academy, single ride, $1.50. Twelve rides, $15. Tickets not transferable. Lessons of one hour for ladies, from 10 A.M. to 12 M.; and 2 to 4 P.M. For gentlemen from 8 to 10 A.M.; and 4 to 6 P.M. Exercise hours from 12 to 2 P.M.; and 4 to 6 P.M. Gentlemen not admitted during hours devoted to instruction to ladies. Special evenings for private classes.

Violin School, Allen.
Hotel Lafayette. Charles N. Allen's success as a teacher of the violin is recognized throughout the country, and his fame is based upon the possession of true merit as a musician, as well as upon the ease and facility with which he imparts his excellent method. Mr. Allen's position as a violin soloist of the first rank, as a conductor of high ability, and as a musician of great and general accomplishments, enables him to develop the musical talent of his pupils in a surprisingly rapid manner, enabling them to overcome all difficulties with ease, and to acquire the finish and style of a master. The *proficiency* of Mr. Allen's students is his best recommendation.

Violin Schools.
(See *Eichberg's Violin School, New England Conservatory Violin School, Urso (Camilla) Violin Lessons, C. N. Allen*).

Walker's Private Dancing Academy.
21 Dwight st. This is an institution familiar to the leading people in Boston society, especially among those who desire their sons and daughters to be taught a graceful carriage, and an elegant deportment. Students of the various Colleges, Seminaries, Conservatories, and other Schools in Boston and vicinity, who have received lessons here in polished manners, have carried the fame of this Academy to all sections of the country. At the head of assistants is Mr. Russ B. Walker, who impresses his faculty of imparting polite accomplishments, ease and grace to his teachers, who also share his patience with beginners. This Academy was established many years since, and is one of the most successful institutions in the city.

Ward (Julius E.) School of Vocal Culture.
Also teacher of pianoforte, organ and harmony. Mr. Ward is a *certified pupil* of Prof. John Knowles Paine, of the Harvard University School of Music, at Cambridge, (a musical course ranking with those of the foremost music schools of Europe). Mr. Ward's new Music Room is at 707 Shawmut av., where he has better facilities

than at his former rooms, and in a more favorable location for giving lessons. This artist and teacher is one of the most versatile gentlemen in the entire musical profession, excelling in the capacity of a vocalist, pianist, accompanist, organist, and choral conductor, in all of which branches of the profession he has won merited recognition from the press and public. As a teacher he is no less successful, having the rare faculty of being able to impart his knowledge and to ground his pupils upon the same thorough basis upon which he has been placed by Prof. Paine, the foremost composer America has yet produced. Among other branches not mentioned in the beginning of this article, elocution and the violin are taught at Mr. Ward's Music Rooms.

Wellesley College. (1875). Wellesley. Established to furnish young women who desire to obtain a liberal education such advantages as are enjoyed in institutions of the highest grade. By its charter, the Corporation of Wellesley College is authorized to confer such honors, degrees and diplomas as are granted or conferred by any University, College or Seminary of learning in this Commonwealth. This great College is far-famed for its extensive curriculum; its high educational standard; its healthful location; its proximity to the literary musical and art centre of the continent; its eminent board of instructors; its schools of art, languages, music, cooking; and its various other instructive, elevating and refining features. It is generally conceded that Wellesley College is not surpassed by any similar institution, and, in some important respects, it is unequalled. It has pupils at present from nearly every State in the Union, (from Massachusetts, 128; from New York State, 80) from Canada, Mexico, England, Turkey and India. Alice E. Freeman, Ph.D., is President, assisted by more than seventy instructors. Board and tuition — including heating and lights — for each student, is $300 per year. Tuition alone, $100 per year. Music extra. Collegiate year begins early in September. (Wellesley is 15 miles from Boston, on the Boston & Albany Railway).

Wellesley School of Art. (1875). Wellesley College, Wellesley. A five years' course of study in drawing, modeling, designing, painting from life models, etc. (See *Wellesley College*).

West Newton English and Classical School. West Newton. Family and Day School for both sexes. Students fitted for Colleges and Scientific Schools. Nathaniel T. Allen is the Principal. (West Newton is 9 miles from Boston, on the Boston and Albany Railway).

PLACES OF AMUSEMENT.

Boston Theatre. 537 Washington Street, between West and Avery Streets. Opened Sept. 11, 1854, with "The Rivals" and the "Loan of a Lover," Thomas Barry, Manager. (See *Eventful Playbills*). This is the largest and most magnificent of American play-houses, and its record has been a remarkably brilliant one. Opened on the grandest scale by Thomas Barry, with a superb stock company, including such artists as Julia Bennett Barrow, Mrs. John Wood, Mrs. W. H. Smith, John Gilbert, George Pauncefort and others, its first season was a marvel of artistic excellence in dramatic productions. Mr. Barry continued its sole manager for five years, maintaining the same high artistic standard. During the season of 1859-60 Mr. Barry acted as manager for the directors. The lessee and manager for 1860-1 was Bernard Ullman. Wyzeman Marshall was manager for two seasons. In August, 1863, Orlando Tompkins and B. W. Thayer became the owners of nearly all of the stock of the company, leasing the theatre to Henry C. Jarrett, for two seasons, (1864-5, 1865-6), to Edwin Booth and John Sleeper Clarke for one season (1866-7), to Junius Brutus Booth, jr., for six seasons (1867-8-9-70-71-72-73). The names of Messrs. Thayer & Tompkins first appeared upon the bills as proprietors, Sept. 1, 1873, with L. R. Shewell as manager, a position he held for five years, until June 17, 1878. Upon the death of Mr. Thayer, Noble H. Hill became the partner of Mr. Tompkins, the firm-title being Tompkins & Hill. Eugene Tompkins became the manager at the opening of the season of 1878-79, a position he has since filled, with the most brilliant success. The house being especially adapted to the production of plays of a spectacular nature, Mr. Tompkins has utilized the vast stage for bringing out in the most superb manner, pieces which he has secured abroad and elsewhere, and which have been presented here in a style of magnificence wholly unapproached by any dramatic establishment in the United States, not merely by reason of the great size of the stage, but on account of the *newness* and splendor of the entire production and strength of cast. Among the spectacles that have signalized his managerial career have been the following productions, every costume and property, and every inch of the scenery, having been entirely new, everything having been made in Europe and here especially for the production, each piece being strongly cast, and given with every accessory necessary, with a small army of auxiliaries, generally with grand ballets, the *premieres* engaged in Europe by Manager Tompkins and brought over expressly for these productions, most of which had runs extending over three months: "The Exiles," by Victorien Sardou, 1877; "Cosette," by Victor Hugo, 1878; "Andre Fortier," by Victorien Sardou, 1879; "Drink," by Charles Reade, 1879; "Voyages in Southern Seas," by Adolph D'Ennery and Jules Verne, 1880; "Michael Strogoff," by Adolph D'Ennery and Jules Verne, 1881; "The World," by Henry Pettitt, Paul Merritt and Augustus Harris, 1882; "Free Pardon," by Henry Pettitt and George Conquest, 1882; "Youth," by Paul Merritt and Augustus Harris, 1882; "£50,000," by Henry Pettitt and Augustus Harris, 1883; "Jalma," by Charles Gaylor, 1883; "The Silver King," by Herman and Jones, 1884; "Zanita," by Dexter Smith and Eugene Tompkins, 1884. The foremost dramatic and musical stars of the world have appeared upon the stage of the Boston Theatre. Rachel, Adelaide Ristori, Charlotte Cushman, Sarah Bernhardt, Jean Davenport Lander, Carlotta Leclerc, Julia Bennett Barrow, Mrs. John Wood, Fanny Janauschek, Mary Anderson, Edwin Forrest, Edwin L. Davenport, Edwin Booth, Tommaso Salvini, Charles Fechter, Henry Irving, Lawrence Barrett, William Warren, Joseph Jefferson, John Gilbert, James E. Murdoch, John Brougham, Dion Boucicault, John McCullough, James W. Wallack, James H. Hackett; Tietjens, Parepa-Rosa, Patti, Lucca, Rudersdorff, Grisi, Lagrange, Kellogg, Hauk, Nilsson, Amodio, Cary, Phillipps, Mario, Lefrane, Wachtel, Hermann, Capoul and many others have been seen here. The theatre seats 3,000. Orlando Tompkins died during the season of 1884-5, and Noble H. Hill, Sr., in that of 1885-6. In May, 1886, Eugene and Arthur G. Tompkins purchased the right of the Hill estate, becoming sole proprietors July 1, 1886. Hill & Tompkins, proprietors; Eugene Tompkins, manager; Noble H. Hill, treasurer; H. A. M'Glenen, business agent; Daniel Hurley, ticket agent; Louis S. Goulland, assistant ticket agent; stage manager, L. J. McCarty; Napier Lothian, musical director; Charles S. Getz, John Somers, J. S. Getz, Richard Gannon, scenic artists; James W. Taylor, master of auxiliaries; Miss Annie Endress, costumer; Wm. P. Prescott, machinist; J. B. Sullivan, properties; George Sevey, gas engineer; W. H. Onthank, chief usher; Andrew Willent, Amos Schaffer, Charles Harris, Cornelius D. Murphy, door-keepers. Opens at 7.15.

Globe Theatre. 596 Washington Street, between Hayward Place and Essex Street. Opened Dec. 3, 1874 (replacing the old Globe — originally Selwyn's Theatre, opened Oct. 29, 1867. See *Eventful Play-bills*). Selwyn's Theatre was built by Arthur Cheney and Dexter H. Follett. John H. Selwyn was manager. Arthur Cheney assumed the sole proprietorship in 1869. Thomas Barry became stage manager under Selwyn, 1869-70. The name of the theatre was changed with the opening of the season of 1870-71 (Sept. 12), Charles Fechter being sole manager with the beginning of that season until Jan. 16, 1871, when William R. Floyd became manager, a position he filled until the destruction of the theatre by fire, May 30, 1873. Rebuilt and reopened Dec. 3, 1874, D. W. Waller becoming manager. Sept. 13, 1875, the season opened with Mr. Floyd again manager. He continued to hold that position until the close of the season of 1876-77. John Stetson became lessee and manager, Sept. 3, 1877, and has since controlled the theatre, presenting some of the strongest combinations and most renowned stars in the dramatic firmament, including Sarah Bernhardt, Adelaide Neilson, Mary Anderson, Tommaso Salvini, Henry Irving, Patti, and other artists of the first magnitude. Mr. Stetson has expended vast sums of money in decorating and embellishing this elegant theatre until it is one of the most sumptuous playhouses in the world. Three exits are provided — on Washington and Essex Streets and Hayward Place. The theatre seats 2,200. The prices for the best seats are ordinarily $1.00, with balcony seats at 75 and 50 cents; admission tickets to lower floor being sold for fifty cents. (During special engagements of expensive combinations or grand opera the prices are increased from fifty to one hundred per cent.) One of the principal features of the front of the establishment is the smoking-room, a spacious, well-ventilated apartment which is very largely resorted to before the performance begins, as well as between the acts. Under the present enterprising management the Globe has become one of the most successful theatres in the United States. John Stetson, Manager; Frank J. Pilling, business manager; G. S. Wellman, secretary; Martin Drake, treasurer; S. J. Hamilburg, ticket agent; J. P. Cooke, stage manager; H. L. Reid, scenic artist; John Mullaly, musical director; C. A. Henry, properties; W. J. Moorhead, gas-engineer; F. L. Baker, M. Cutter, door-keepers; E. C. Battey, chief usher. Opens at 8.

Boston Museum. 28 Tremont Street, between School and Court Streets. Opened by the proprietors of the old Boston Museum (on the corner of Tremont and Bromfield Streets, Nov. 2, 1846. The original Museum was opened June 14, 1841). During the first two seasons, 1841-2-3, the bill consisted of musical pieces. The first regularly organized dramatic company was engaged for the season of 1843-4, beginning Monday, September 4, the bill comprising "The Hypochondriac," dancing and "Nature and Philosophy." One of the artists in this bill, Mrs. Jane Germon, is still on the stage. (For bill of opening of first season at the present Museum see *Eventful Playbills*). W. H. Smith was the first stage-manager, remaining in that position for sixteen years; in 1859, E. F. Keach assumed those duties. R. M. Field became sole manager of the theatre Jan. 31, 1864, and still controls its affairs. We have not the space to give the names of those of the foremost artists of the world who have graced this stage, but will enumerate a few, as follows, with the date of their first appearances: John Brougham (1843); Junius Brutus Booth, sr. (1849), his son, Edwin, making his first appearance on any stage during this engagement (Sept. 10, 1849); Julia Bennett (Barrow); Agnes Robertson (Mrs. Boucicault) (1853); Dion Boucicault (Feb. 4, 1854); C. W. Couldock (1854); E. L. Davenport (1854); Mrs. D. P. Bowers (1857); Mrs. John Drew (1862); Carlotta Leclercq (1874); John McCullough (1876); Lawrence Barrett formerly leading-man at this theatre); (1877); Adelaide Phillipps (1843); William Warren (1847). The Boston Museum is noted for its production of new plays from foreign authors for the first time on the American stage, as well as for its sumptuous revivals of the standard old and modern English comedies. This theatre has had uninterrupted success for upwards of fifty years, a condition of affairs that cannot be paralleled by the history of any other place of amusement in the United States, if in the world. The wise policy of the house appears to be grounded upon two important factors, namely: Attractions of merit and a moderate scale of prices. The simple fact that excellent seats — some of the best in the theatre — can be secured for fifty cents, draws throngs of family parties, of moderate means, who probably attend the performances here much oftener than they visit any other theatre, if, indeed, they go elsewhere at all; and the placing of the admission fee at thirty-five cents attracts crowds of young men about town who are not made so welcome at any other theatre. The Museum is fitted up elegantly and tastefully; the stage is finely equipped; and there is an air of comfort and cosiness, combined with luxury, that makes a performance here extremely enjoyable. This theatre is one of the very few in the country that adheres to the stock company plan, that having been the policy of the house since its opening, with occasional engagements of stars supported by the stock company. It may be interesting to give the dates upon which some of the favorite members began their first seasons there: William Warren, Aug. 23, 1847; Mrs. J. R. Vincent, May 10, 1852; Miss Annie Clarke, 1861; Charles Barron, 1868. The seating capacity of this theatre is 1119, distributed as follows: orchestra chairs, 289, ($1.00); parquet circle, 295, (50 cents); proscenium chairs, 68, ($1.50); first balcony, 404, (75 cents); second balcony, 85, (50 cents); six private boxes, 2, 4 and 6 persons each, $8, $10. R. M. Field is manager; William Seymour, acting and stage manager; J. R. Pitman, assistant stage manager; B. R. Ambrose, box attache; W. H. Emery, treasurer; C. B. Whittemore, ticket agent; George Purdy, musical director; Edward LaMoss, scenic artist; Miss Sarah Ormond, costumer; Frank Goodwin, properties; John Witherell, gas and calcium effects; Matt Graham, master machinist and carpenter. Time of beginning: winter, 7.45 o'clock; summer, 8. The theatre is open all the year round. The great Curiosity Hall is open every day, except Sunday, from 8 A. M. to 10 P. M.

Park Theatre. 617 Washington Street, between Avery and Boylston Streets. Opened April 14, 1879. The theatre is owned by Miss Lotta Crabtree, the celebrated actress, who appeared in " La Cigale " on its opening night. (See *Eventful Playbills*.) The theatre was built on the site of Beethoven Hall. Henry E. Abbey was the original manager of the Park Theatre. It is an elegant, richly furnished playhouse, and the successes of many of the foremost exponents of the drama are associated with its stage. Such artists as Edwin Booth, Lawrence Barrett, Clara Morris, Janauschek, and Fanny Davenport are identified with the history of this famous house, while Daly's, the Union Square, Wallack's and the Madison Square Companies of New York, have played long and brilliant engagements here. It is a combination house, of high class. The seating capacity of the house is 1181. There are two balconies and four proscenium boxes. The first balcony is divided into balcony and dress-circle seats, the first two rows being designated as the balcony. The second circle is arranged as the family circle and gallery. The prices of admission range from $1.50 for orchestra stalls to 50 cents for seats in the second balcony. The price of admission is 50 cents. John B. Schoeffel became a partner with Mr. Abbey, March 8, 1880. The present executive staff of this theatre is as follows: Abbey & Schoeffel, lessees and managers; E. R. Byram, business manager; Philip Shea, treasurer; George W. Murray, stage manager; Edward N. Catlin, musical director; J. S. Schell, scenic artist; Edwin Morse, master machinist; F. W. Alexander, property-maker; W. H. Kelly, gas-engineer; J. F. Vila, doorkeeper; B. Bonari, chief usher; J. C. McGarrey, advertising-agent.

Bijou Theatre. 545 Washington Street, between West and Avery Streets. Opened Dec. 11, 1882, with "Iolanthe," George H. Tyler, general manager. See *Eventful Playbills*. Previous to its reconstruction, it had been known as the Gaiety Theatre, having been opened by Manager Jason Wentworth, Oct. 15, 1878. The Gaiety itself had been reconstructed from the new Melodeon Hall, which had been made memorable by a season of performances by Mr. and Mrs. Henri Drayton. This was originally the site of the famous Lion Tavern. The Bijou has become one of the most popular theatres in the city for certain classes of entertainment, such as comic opera, farce-comedy, burlesque and musical plays. Its interior is elaborately and artistically decorated. The proscenium arch is of horse-shoe form. There are a number of beautiful friezes, designed by Francis Lathrop and George W. Maynard, representing a scene from the "Midsummer Night's Dream," "Study," "Declamation," etc. The principal chandelier, of Egyptian Moresque design originally made for the Khedive of Egypt, is a most elegant affair, and is lighted—as are the other chandeliers, footlights, etc.—by incandescent electric light. Portieres supply the place of doors. The theatre seats 900; 850 seats being on the main floor. For seven of the front rows, $1.00 is the price of seats; the others being sold at 75 cents. The price of admission is 50 cents. The balcony seats sell for $1.00, 75 and 50 cents, according to location. Miles & Barton are the lessees and managers; Edward H. Hastings, business manager; Henry Lewis, treasurer and ticket agent; C. A. Metcalf, secretary; John J. Braham, musical director; William H. Harrison, door keeper; Peter Henderson, master machinist; James McElroy, electrician; Joseph Sullivan, property-man. Opens at 8.

Hollis Street Theatre. 12 Hollis Street, between Washington and Tremont Streets. Opened Nov. 9, 1885, with "The Mikado"; Isaac B. Rich, Manager. See *Eventful Playbills*. Manager Rich has been identified with theatrical affairs in Boston for many years, having been manager of the Howard Athenaeum, Howard Street, as early as May 1, 1846 and having been lessee, manager or associate manager of that theatre for the larger portion of the time since, and with William Harris, manager of Oakland Garden, Blue Hill Avenue. The Hollis Street Theatre was reconstructed from the old Hollis Street Church. It has a large and elegant auditorium, beautifully decorated, and brilliantly illuminated. The stage is spacious, and the pieces produced here are well mounted. The auditorium has a seating capacity of 1,597. The prices of tickets on the lower floor are $1.50 and $1.00. First balcony, $1.00, 75 and 50 cents. Second balcony, 50 and 25 cents. Admission, 50 cents. Isaac B. Rich, manager; Charles J. Rich, assistant manager; Wm. Dixon, stage manager; John A. Thompson, scenic artist; George Loesch, musical director; H. B. Roberts, jr., treasurer; Edward C. Bellows, ticket agent, Benj. Craig, machinist; Fred. Cutter, steam and gas engineer; Wm. O'Brien, Wm. Baker, properties; S. L. Atwood, chief usher; Daniel Sutton, Emery N. Moore, doorkeepers; Mrs. Kate Ferry, ladies' cloak-room. Opens at 8.

Howard Athenæum.
28 Howard Street, near Scollay Square. Opened (after being reconstructed from Millerite Tabernacle) Oct. 13, 1845, by W. F. Johnson, W. L. Ayling, Thomas Ford and Leonard Brayley. Destroyed by fire Feb. 25, 1846. Rebuilt and reopened (Oct. 25, 1846) by James H. Hackett & Co. (It was during this season that William Warren made his first appearance on the Boston stage.) Thomas Ford became manager Feb. 23, 1847. Since then its managers have been John Brougham, W. E. Burton, Chas. R. Thorne, Sr., Wyzeman Marshall, Henry Willard, J. M. Field, Thomas Placide, E. L. Davenport, Jacob Barrow, E. A. Sothern, W. M. Fleming, Isaac B. Rich and others, as legitimate dramatic managers. Among the celebrated artists who appeared on this stage during this period (1845 to 1867) were James W. Wallack, Jr., Anderson, "The Wizard of the North," Edwin Adams, Joseph Proctor, E. L. Davenport, Mrs. Warner, the English tragedienne; Lola Montez, Matilda Heron, Maggie Mitchell, Helen Western, John Brougham, Mrs. D. P. Bowers, John E. Owens, Mr. and Mrs. W. J. Florence, and others. On the 10th of August, 1868, it was opened as a variety theatre by Isaac B. Rich and Joseph Trowbridge, Josh Hart afterward joining the firm. Jan. 1, 1870, John Stetson and Isaac B. Rich became associate managers, continuing for nearly seven years. During the next two seasons, 1876-77-78, Mr. Stetson was sole manager. During season of 1878-79, Benj. F. Tryon and Fred. Stinson were managers; 1879-80, Josh Hart and B. F. Tyron. On Aug. 23, 1880, Isaac B. Rich associated himself with William Harris, the former withdrawing to assume the management of the Hollis Street Theatre at the opening of the season of 1885-86. Mr. Harris still continues to direct the successful fortunes of the Howard, playing dramatic as well as variety combinations. The theatre seats 1,500. Seats are $1.00, 75, 50, 35, 25 cents. Admission, 50 cents. William Harris, manager. Opens at 8.

Windsor Theatre.
1132 Washington Street, corner of East Dover Street. Opened (as the Novelty Theatre) Dec. 15, 1879, with "Home," played by the stock company; F. H. Butler, Manager. (See *Eventful Playbills*). This theatre has for several years past been very successfully managed, combinations of a fair degree of merit having been presented in most cases, and such attractions as "Esmeralda," "The Shaughraun," "Pavements of Paris," etc., with stars including Katherine Rogers, Maud Granger and other favorites, proving powerful magnets, at low prices of admission. Originally called Williams Hall, it was reconstructed into the Novelty Theatre Mr. Butler was followed by R. M. Hooley, who assumed the management at the opening of the season of 1880-1, calling it Hooley's Theatre. Charles H. Thayer was the next manager, restoring the name of the Novelty Theatre. A fine presentation of "Billee Taylor" signalized his management, which was very successful. The season of 1881-2 had John A. Stevens as lessee, and D. B. Hopkins as manager. George E. Lothrop leased the theatre Oct 16, 1882, and has since continued its successful manager. Prices range from 50 to 10 cents. George E. Lothrop, lessee and manager. Executive staff: J. W. Randolph, business manager; Wm. McAvoy, stage manager; Harry McCluskey, treasurer; J. C. Wiley, machinist; King & Hagen, properties; T. C. Gray, musical director; C. F. Harmond, advertiser; H. J. Partridge, officer. Opens at 8.

Theatre Comique.
1170 Washington Street. Managers Hyde & Behman, early in 1886, arranged to construct a Theatre on the site of the Columbia Rink, at 1170 Washington Street, to be devoted to combinations, musical productions, etc., at reasonable prices of admission. The great success of the Windsor Theatre in playing combinations of a fair degree of merit, undoubtedly attracted the attention of these enterprising managers to the desirability of this populous and accessible locality as an amusement centre. It will probably not be many years before several other places of amusement will be opened in this busy section of the city. With the South End, South Boston, Roxbury, Dorchester, Brookline, Milton, Quincy, (and when the West Chester Park Bridge is completed, Cambridge, Allston, Arlington, etc.), to draw from, to say nothing of the population of the city northward and eastward, and the large suburbs in those directions, this quarter of the city will become more and more central every year, especially as the means of rapid transit are improved. There are now seventeen lines of street-cars which pass through this portion of Washington Street.

Dudley Street Opera House.

111 Dudley Street, Roxbury District. Reconstructed from Institute Hall. Opened as a theatre, 1879. Seats 700. Proprietor, N. J. Bradlee. The house is not open regularly, but is well patronized by residents of the Highlands who never good attractions are presented. If Roxbury had a theatre of sufficient size to permit combinations to play profitably at low prices, entertainments could be given here as successfully as at Chelsea and other suburban districts. (Take Norfolk House, Shawmut Avenue, Egleston Square or Oakland Garden cars).

Oakland Garden Theatre.

This is a very successful summer theatre, established in 1879. Located opposite the entrance to Franklin Park, West Roxbury. Performances of light opera, farce-comedy, musical plays, etc., are given here from about the middle of June until the first of September. It has been managed very profitably by Messrs. Isaac B. Rich (of the Hollis Street Theatre and William Harris of the Howard Athenæum, Howard Street for several seasons. Oakland Garden comprises quite a number of acres of well kept grounds upon which are restaurants, etc., and is a very popular resort on summer evenings and on Wednesday and Saturday afternoons. (Take Oakland Garden car at Temple Place). J. A. Gilbert, manager.

Germania Theatre.

(Turn Halle). 27 Middlesex Street, between Castle and Dover Street. A pretty little theatre, where performances, in the German language, are frequently given during the season, largely by amateurs, although tickets are offered for sale to the general public. Prices are usually 50 and 25 cents. Tremont and Shawmut ave. cars pass Castle st., from which runs Middlesex st.).

Cyclorama.

Cyclorama Building, 541 Tremont Street, between Berkeley and Clarendon Streets, on the site formerly occupied by the Moody & Sankey Tabernacle). Exhibition of the "Battle of Gettysburg," with lectures, etc. Open day and evening. Admission 50 cents.

Boston Music Hall.

Winter Place, Winter Street. One of the grandest halls in the world. Of vast size, great architectural beauty and perfect acoustic properties, it has surprised and delighted foreign artists who have appeared here. Opened in 1852, it was then and is to-day unrivalled in all that go to form the essential features of a music hall. It is 130 feet long 78 feet wide and 65 feet high, these proportions being admirably adapted for furnishing the best conditions for the most favorable hearing of vocal and instrumental performances given by large and well-balanced choruses and orchestras. The hall contains a majestic statue of Beethoven, a cast of Apollo Belvidere, various busts presented by Charlotte Cushman, etc. The hall is brilliantly lighted with incandescent electric lights. The concerts by the famous Boston Symphony Orchestra are given here; also the oratorios by the Handel and Haydn Society (the foremost choral organization in the United States), as well as the concerts of the Apollo, Boylston and other noted clubs. The Great Organ, erected in 1863, and which was one of the largest, best and most renowned instruments of the kind in the world, was sold and removed in 1884, with the intention of erecting a proscenium arch and stocking the stage with scenery and theatrical appointments. This has not yet been done, however. Alfred P. Peck was for many years the Superintendent of the Hall. Charles A. Ellis now fills that position. The Hall seats 2,600.

Tremont Temple.

80 Tremont Street. This is one of the largest and finest Halls in the country. Occupied on Sundays for religious services by the Union Temple Church, it is frequently used on the evenings of other days for concerts, etc. It was dedicated Oct. 17, 1880. It is 122 feet long, 72 feet wide, and 66 feet high. It seats 2,600. It is furnished with an organ of great power and beauty, having 4 manuals, 66 registers, and 3,442 pipes.

Horticultural Hall.

Corner of Tremont and Bromfield Streets. Concerts, amateur theatrical entertainments and exhibitions of various kinds are given here.

World's Museum, Menagerie, Aquarium and Theatre.

667 Washington Street, between Boylston and Lagrange Streets. A very successful low-priced place of amusement, largely patronized by ladies and children. The collection of animals comprises forty cages, some of them being fine specimens. The trick elephant, "Bijou," is a permanent attraction. On the stage performances of light opera, farces, variety, etc., are given. Ten cents is the price of admission. The auditorium seats 930. Open from 10 a. m. to 10 p. m.

Keith & Batcheller's Gayety Museum and Theatre.

565 Washington Street, between West and Avery Streets. Messrs. Keith and Batcheller, Proprietors and Managers; J. L. Littlefield, business manager. Performances of light opera, etc., are given several times during the day and evening, in addition to exhibitions of curiosities.

Austin & Stone's Museum and Theatre. 4 Tremont row, Scollay Square, near Howard Street. Messrs. Austin & Stone, Proprietors and Managers; George Milbank, business manager. Musical farces, variety performances, etc., are given here, entertainments taking place frequently during the day and evening. Curiosities of various kinds are exhibited, the admission to all being ten cents. Open from 10 a. m. to 10 p. m. Admission to all, ten cents. The auditorium seats 420. Open from 10 a. m. to 10 p. m.

MUSEUMS AND EXHIBITIONS.

Museums, Collections and Exhibitions, established permanently in Boston are briefly described here. (Occasional Exhibitions of Paintings, Fruit, Flowers, Manufactures and Mechanics are referred to in another department.)

Museum of Fine Arts. (1870). Located at the intersection of St. James Avenue, Dartmouth Street and Huntington Avenue, (Copley Square, Back Bay). One of the celebrated Art Museums of the world. The building is a magnificent one, of brick, ornamented with panels of terra cotta, representing allegorical subjects, "The Genius of Art," and "Art and Industry." These designs are on a larger and more striking scale than any hitherto attempted. Among the heads of the figures are those representing Copley, Allston, Crawford and other celebrated artists. The collection of famous paintings, statuary, tapestries, casts, mummies, pottery, etc., is a magnificent one, and in some respects is unequalled in the United States, especially in the department of casts, which is the most complete collection in America. The paintings include masterpieces by Francais, Corôt, Couture, Millet, Diaz, Doré, Stuart, Copley, Allston, Ames, Trumbull, Page and other famous artists, the works being the property of the Museum. The collection of water-colors is very large and valuable. The reproductions from objects in the South Kensington Museum, London, are especially attractive. In addition to the works owned by the Museum there are always more or less loaned paintings and other rare objects which attract visitors from far and near. The Museum is open every day. On Saturdays, from 9 to 5 o'clock, and on Sundays, from 1 to 5 o'clock, *admission is free*. On other days, from 9 to 5, the admission fee is twenty-five cents. (Take cars on any of the following lines of street-railways: Vendome, Clarendon st., Dartmouth st., Huntington av., or West End.)

Cyclorama. 541 Tremont st. Exhibition of the famous "Battle of Gettysburg." Every day and evening, except Sunday. Admission, fifty cents.

Natural History Rooms. (1831). Berkeley Street, between Boylston and Newbury Streets (Back Bay). The Building in which the Collection of the Boston Society of Natural History is exhibited is a very large and substantial edifice of brick and freestone, its front being embellished by Corinthian columns and capitals. The collection of birds, shells, insects, plants, skeletons, geological and mineralogical specimens is in some of its features unparalleled on the continent. These rooms are of great interest to students of the various great Universities and Schools of Boston and vicinity, as well as to tourists and others, who come in large numbers to examine the rare collection. The Exhibition Rooms are open to the public on Wednesdays and Saturdays, from 10 to 5 o'clock. *Admission free*. On other days, from 9 to 5, when a small admission fee is charged. (Reached by street-cars of Clarendon st., Vendome, Huntington av., Dartmouth st. and West End lines.)

Boston Public Library Collection. (1852). Bates Hall, 46 Boylston st. Here is a collection of ancient, rare and curious works, among which are the following: The Nuremberg Chronicle, (1493); Chronicles of the Kings of Hungary, (1483); Epistles of St. Jerome, in Black Letter, (1518), with autograph of Martin Luther; Benjamin Franklin's autograph, in a copy of his "Political, Philosophical and Miscellaneous Pieces"; a collection of Franklin Medals; Captain John Smith's "Generall Historie of Virginia, New England, etc."; the MS. of Rufus Choate's Eulogy on Daniel Webster; a "Dialogue between an Actor and a Critic," in the handwriting of David Garrick, the author; a collection of Madrigals, (Venice, 1546); Eggestein's Latin Bible, (Strasburg, 1468); Bay Psalm-

Book, (Boston, 1640); Eliot's Indian Bible, (Cambridge, 1663), the type having been partly set by Indians; Sermon by Increase Mather, Boston, 1675); Holy Bible, Black Letter, (London, 1572 ; Autograph letter of George Washington; Autograph letter from Martha Washington to Gen. Montgomery's widow; Thomas Moore's commonplace-book, containing notes made in the United States in 1804; Poems by John Milton, (London, 1645 ; Shakespeare's Plays, first collected edition, (London, 1623), and many other objects, arranged in the glass cases around the staircase. Open to the public every weekday. *Free.*

Boston Athenæum. (1804). 10B
Beacon Street. There is a collection of rare and valuable paintings, statuary, etc., in the grand vestibule and staircase of the Athenæum Building, which can be seen by those interested, on any week day, without charge. The Library, however, is a private one, and can only be visited upon the introduction of a member.

Old South Museum.
One of the largest and most valuable collections of Revolutionary and historical relics, is on exhibition in the Old South Meeting-House, which was opened as a place of worship, April 26, 1730. The Society removed from it to the Back Bay in 1872, and the Building is now under the control of the Old South Preservation Committee. The Museum is open on weekdays from 9 to 6. Admission, twenty-five cents. Washington St., cor. Milk.

Old State House Collection.
Washington Street, corner of State Street. This is the best preserved historical Building in the United States, remaining almost exactly as it was in olden times. The upper portion is now utilized for Exhibition Rooms of relics of historical interest, under the auspices of the Bostonian Society. Paintings, portraits, antiquities, etc., form a fine collection, of the greatest interest to strangers. Open to the public every day (except Sunday) from 9.30 to 5.30. *Admission free.*

Massachusetts Historical Museum. (1791). 30 Tremont Street.
The oldest Historical Society in the country, (the Massachusetts) has a rare collection of curiosities. Among them are the swords of Miles Standish, Sir William Pepperell, Col. Prescott and others; a phial of the tea washed ashore after its having been thrown into the Harbor at the famous tea-party; an oak chair brought over in "The Mayflower"; the diary of Judge Samuel Sewall; King Philip's samp-bowl; portraits of Governors Endicott, Winslow, Winthrop, and many other objects of interest. Open from 9 to 5. *Admission free.*

Faneuil Hall Collection of Historical Paintings.
Merchants Row and Faneuil Hall Square. This famous old "Cradle of Liberty" is annually visited by thousands of strangers from various sections of America and Europe who make pilgrimages to this shrine of American Independence as much for the purpose of standing within the building itself as to view its rare and costly treasures. The history of the old building is one identified with the first struggles of the American people to secure Freedom, and every school-boy in the land knows its story well. It is open to all every day (except Sunday) from 9 to 4 o'clock. *Admission Free.*

Historic-Genealogical Collection. (1845). 18 Somerset Street.
At the pleasant rooms of the New England Historic Genealogical Society are to be seen a large and valuable collection of rare engravings, prints, books, etc., possessing rare interest to historians, genealogists, antiquarians and especially to those interested in the local histories and genealogies of New England. The Rooms are open to the public every week day from 9 to 5 (Saturdays 9 to 2). (Somerset Street is a few steps up Beacon Street at the head of School Street). *Free.*

Warren Museum of Natural History. (1846). 82 Chestnut Street.
A notable private Museum (incorporated in 1858) formed mostly from Collections made by Dr. J. C. Warren, the famous surgeon. Among the rare and curious objects on exhibition are the skeleton of the mastodon (the only perfect specimen of the kind anywhere), and various other skeletons; casts from various objects in the British Museum; the head, brain and heart of Spurzheim; mummies; casts of eggs of mammoth birds; and hundreds of other objects of great interest. The collection is preserved in a fire-proof building, erected especially for the purpose. Cards of admission are issued upon application to Dr. J. Collins Warren, 58 Beacon Street, or to Dr. Thomas Dwight, 235 Beacon Street. *Free.*

State House Doric Hall Collection.
Beacon Street, head of Park Street. This may be styled the Westminster Abbey of Boston, from its extensive treasures in the way of Memorial stones, statues, busts, tablets, battle-flags, cannon, etc. (See HISTORICAL TABLETS; BATTLE-FLAGS and STATUARY). One can pass an hour or two with interest and profit in examining the various historical memorials. *Free.*

Boston Museum. (1841). 28 Tremont Street, between School and Court Streets.
A very large and valuable col-

lection of paintings, statuary, coins, in the Grand Hall of cabinets. Open day and evening. Admission thirty-five cents.

Public Library Art Gallery. (1852). 46 Boylston Street. Although not a particularly large collection, there is a very fine Exhibition of Works of Art at the Public Library Building, Lower Floor. It comprises paintings and statuary. *Free.*

Museum (Agassiz) of Comparative Zoology. Oxford Street, Cambridge. This great Museum, which has no equal in America, was founded under the direction of Agassiz, one of the foremost naturalists of the world, who was associated with its direction until his death. The Exhibition Rooms comprise the Synoptic Room, the Rooms containing the collections of mammals, birds, reptiles, fishes, mollusks, crustacea, insects, radiates, sponges, protozoa, faunal collections of North and South America, the Indo-Asiatic, the African and Australian Realms. Open to visitors every week-day, from 9 to 5, throughout the year; on *Sundays* (from May 1 to November 1), from 1 to 5. *Admission free.* (Street-cars from Bowdoin sq. and Park sq.)

Barnum Museum. Tufts College, College Hill, Medford. This fine Natural History Collection was the gift of P. T. Barnum, the famous amusement manager, and is destined to become one of the most interesting Museums in the United States, additions being frequently made to it. Among the unique features of the collection to be kept here permanently is the stuffed skin of the famous elephant, "Jumbo," and many other rare and curious specimens.

Arnold Aboretum. (1872). Jamaica Plain District. A Collection of trees, shrubs and herbaceous plants of great interest to students of arboriculture and all lovers of Nature. It is carried on under the auspices of Harvard University. (Near Forest Hills Station of the Boston and Providence Railway.)

Peabody Museum of American Archeology and Ethnology. (1866). Cambridge. The rare collections on exhibition here are from the mounds of North America; from ancient and modern Pueblos, of Utah, Colorado, Arizona and New Mexico; from ancient tribes of Mexico and Central America; from present Indian tribes; from ancient and present tribes of Peru, Brazil, and other parts of South America; from the Pacific Islands, Japan, China, India, Egypt, and Eastern and Southern Africa; from the Swiss Lakes, the French Caves, the Valley of the Somme and Denmark. Open to the public every day (except Sunday) from 9 to 5 o'clock. (Curator, Frederick Ward Putnam, A. M.; assistant, Lucien Carr, A. M.) *Admission free.* (Street-cars from Bowdoin sq. or Park sq).

Public Garden. The Boston Public Garden, bounded by Charles, Boylston, Arlington and Beacon Streets, is, from early in the spring until late in the autumn, a most attractive place to visit, to those who appreciate the highest degree of success in flower-gardening. There is no public ground in the United States, where the cultivation of flowers is attended with more brilliant results, and no foreign grounds in this respect eclipse this favorite resort. Here are statues, fountains, etc., and among the various attractions one may pass several very pleasant hours.

Bunker Hill Museum. At the base of Bunker Hill Monument, Charlestown District, there is kept a collection of interesting relics, etc. (Cars from Cornhill).

Botanical Garden. Cambridge. One of the largest and finest collections of plants and flowers in the country. Open to the public. (Take cars at Park sq. or Bowdoin sq.).

United States Navy Yard Museum of Naval Curiosities. Wapping Street. Charlestown District. (Cars from Cornhill; Lynn & Boston, Chelsea and Charlestown lines).

Austin & Stone's Museum. 4 Tremont Row. Curiosities. Open from 10 a. m. to 10 p. m. Admission ten cents.

World's Museum, Menagerie and Aquarium. 667 Washington Street. Large collection of living animals, including an elephant, bears, lions, tigers; also seals, fishes, reptiles, etc., together with other curiosities. Open from 10 a. m. to 10 p. m. Admission ten cents.

Keith & Batcheller's Gayety Museum. 565 Washington Street. Rare and curious collection of objects on exhibition. A popular resort for ladies and children. Open from 10 a. m. to 10 p. m. Admission ten cents. (There is also an Opera Company and a Comedy Company connected with this establishment.)

Hunnewell Gardens. Wellesley. Through the courtesy of the proprietor of these celebrated grounds, Italian terraces and remarkable perfection of landscape-gardening with rare trees and plants, visitors are admitted, on week days, under proper restrictions. (Wellesley is 15 miles out, on the Boston and Albany Railway.)

Krino Grotto, Museum and Gardens. Wellesley. William Emerson Baker has at enormous expense converted his noted Ridge Hill Farms into one of the most unique and interesting pleasure-grounds imaginable. There are rare and beautiful plants, a zoological collection, aquarium, underground gardens and forneries, grottoes, and various other novel and grotesque features. A nominal admission fee is charged. Excursion tickets for the round trip (75 cts., admission included), are to be obtained. (Wellesley is 15 miles out, on the Boston and Albany Railway.)

Locations of Places of Amusement and Public Resort.

Boston Theatre ... ...537 Washington st.
Globe Theatre ......536 Washington st.
Boston Museum...........28 Tremont st.
Hollis Street Theatre........12 Hollis st.
Park Theatre ....617 Washington st.
Bijou Theatre.........545 Washington st.
Windsor Theatre....1132 Washington st.
Howard Athenæum........28 Howard st.
Theatre Comique.....1170 Washington st.
Germania Theatre (Turn Halle)...........
...........27 Middlesex st.
Dudley Street Opera House, 111 Dudley st.
Cyclorama .... 541 Tremont st.
World's Museum, Menagerie and Theatre
..........667 Washington st.
Austin & Stone's Museum and Theatre ..
.........4 Tremont Row.
Keith & Batchelder's Museum and Theatre.....565 Washington st.
Academy of Music ....Chelsea.
Sander's Theatre............Cambridge.
Museum of Fine Arts......St. James av.
Old South Museum, Wash. st., cor. Milk st.
Oakland Garden Theatre....Blue Hill av.
Park Square Garden............Park sq.
Agassiz Museum.............Cambridge.
Faneuil Hall Collection..Merchants Row.
Historical Museum.........30 Tremont st.
Barnum Museum Tufts College, Medford
Peabody Museum ....Cambridge
Amory Garden .....Jamaica Plain
Museum of Naval Curiosities.........
........Navy Yard, Charlestown
Botanic Garden................Cambridge
Bunker Hill Collection................
........Bunker Hill, Charlestown
Boston Music Hall, Winter pl., Winter st.

Tremont Temple... ...80 Tremont st.
Chickering Hall...........152 Tremont st.
Union Hall... ....18 Boylston st.
Horticultural Hall........100 Tremont st.
Bumstead Hall...........15 Winter st.
Meionaon................80 Tremont st.
Apollo Hall..............152 Tremont st.
Miller Hall...............156 Tremont st.
Parker Memorial Hall.......Berkeley st.
Paine Memorial Hall ....Appleton st.
Old State House Collection..........
........Washington st., cor. State st.
Natural History rooms..............
........Boylston st., cor. Berkeley st.
Museum and Grotto... Krino ..Wellesley
Athenæum Paintings and Statuary...
........108 Beacon st
Hunnewell Terrace Gardens ..Wellesley
Public Library Art Gallery,46 Boylston st.
Arnold Arboretum Exhibition...........
..........Jamaica Plain
Mechanics Fair Building, Mechanics Hall
..........Huntington av.
Institute Fair Building...Huntington av.
Boston Art Club Exhibition..Newbury st.
Studio Building .... 110 Tremont st.
New Studio Building...143 Dartmouth st.
Warren Museum of Natural History.....
........82 Chestnut st.
Historic-Genealogical Collection ..
..........18 Somerset st.
Doric Hall State House Collection........
..........Beacon st.
Williams & Everett Gallery,79 Boylston st.
Chase Art Gallery ....7 Hamilton pl.
Childs Art Gallery ....352 Washington st.
Doll & Richards Art Gallery...2 Park st.
Elliott Art Rooms.....58 Washington st.
National Art Society, 361 Washington st.
Noyes & Blakeslee Gallery,127 Tremont st.
Wesleyan Hall............36 Bromfield st.
Huntington Hall Technology Building .
..........191 Boylston st.
Mechanics Hall..........Huntington av.
Association Hall....174 Boylston st.
Minot Hall............Common st.
Hawthorne Hall.....2 Park st.
Winslow Rink......rear 62 St. James av.
Highland Rink ....
.....751 Shawmut av., cor. Ruggles st.
Olympian Rink ....
.....Mechanics Hall, Huntington av.
Columbian Rink.....1172 Washington st.
Argyle Rink............888 Washington st.
Alhambra Rink..........City Point, S. B.
Paris Rink................Paris st., E. B.
Phœnix Rink..........Webster st., E. B.

(In the foregoing list no Public Halls are mentioned except those in which entertainments are given *almost every day or evening*. There are many other Halls, which are used occasionally).

EXHIBITION OF BATTLE FLAGS.

Battle Flags of the War of the Rebellion. At the State House, Beacon Street, have been placed in alcoves of Doric Hall, the flags — tattered and blood-stained — of the regiments returning home to Massachusetts at the close of the War. The survivors of the battles of the Rebellion, the descendants of the soldiers, and many others, make pilgrimages to this repository of these flags, and many a memory is quickened, many a feeling of patriotism kindled, in young and old, by these emblems of the courage and devotion of the soldiers of Massachusetts, which are to remain forever within the sight of all who choose to visit this sacred shrine of loyalty and freedom. We quote as follows from the eloquent address made to the returning heroes by John Albion Andrew, the famous War Governor of Massachusetts: "These banners returned to the Government of the Commonwealth through welcome hands, borne one by one out of this Capitol during more than four years of Civil War, as the symbols of the Nation and the Commonwealth, under which the battalions of Massachusetts departed to the fields — they come back again, borne hither by surviving representatives of the same heroic regiments and companies to which they were intrusted. Proud memories of many fields; sweet memories alike of valor and friendship; sad memories of fraternal strife; tender memories of our fallen brothers and sons, whose dying eyes looked last upon these flaming folds; grand memories of heroic virtues, sublime by grief; exultant memories of the great and final victories of our Country, our Union and the righteous cause; thankful memories of a deliverance wrought out for human nature itself, unexampled by any former achievement of arms; with immortal memories blended twine around the splintered staves, weave themselves along the warp and woof of these familiar flags, warworn, begrimed and baptized with blood." We also here record what a writer in the Boston Transcript (December 22, 1885), said: "Twenty years ago to-day was a memorable epoch in the annals of the citizen soldiery of the Old Bay State; for on that day the battle-stained banners, which spoke so eloquently of the history which had been wrought out under their folds in blood-red characters, were received into the outstretched arms of Massachusetts, in whose sheltering breast they still remain enfolded in loving embrace. When the troops were mustered out of the United States Service, the flags, with other property, were turned over to Brevet Colonel F. N. Clarke, who surrendered them to the custody of the Commonwealth. On the 22d of December, 1865, under the marshalship of Major-General Darius N. Couch, the veterans assembled upon the Common, every one of the old commands being represented, and with proud step and swelling breast the torn and tattered reminders of the thronged and tumultuous past were carried through the streets of the city, amid martial strains from scores of bands, the booming of cannon and the welcoming shouts of the multitudes. It was a day never to be forgotten. The sky was clear, and the sun's bright face seemed to gain an added lustre from the warm spirit of sympathy which beamed through its round and ruddy countenance. The procession reached the State House at one o'clock, and during the impressive exercises which followed, consisting of prayer by Rev. Dr. S. K. Lothrop and an eloquent address by War-Governor John A. Andrew, the color-bearers of each command were stationed upon the steps of the capitol. After the delivery of the colors it was found that there were more than had been given out in the morning. They were clustered around the columns in Doric Hall, where they remained until the Legislature of 1866 passed a resolve, in furtherance of a suggestion made by Governor Bullock, authorizing their being placed in the niches on the north side of Doric Hall and in the sides of the niches occupied by the Washington statue, and providing that, after having been so placed, the flags should not be removed from the State House without the permission of the Legislature; and with the exception of the flag of the Twenty-first, which was carried at the funeral of Sergeant Thomas Plunkett, who defended it so gallantly during life, no one of the flags has ever left the State House since they were gathered there twenty years ago. The flags were arranged without order, some of the infantry colors being outside the enclosure; and thus they remained until the 8th of last August, when *they drooped and fell*, as if in sadness over the death of America's great General, whose body was then being borne to its last resting-place. With characteristic promptitude, Captain Mitchell ordered that the standards be immediately set up, the work of restoration falling into the loving hands of Captain Charles O. Eaton, who had been associated with the life of these emblems of heroism from their very birth. The flags have all been repaired and systematically arranged in strong and substantial frames, the infantry colors now being inside the Washington niche, while the flags of the cavalry, batteries and heavy artillery are in the niches on the north and south sides of Doric Hall. The infantry standards are numerically arranged, the odd numbers on the left, the even on the right hand. Every flag in the building is ragged, and it is anticipated that at no distant day each niche will bear a tablet giving the names of the organizations represented within. There are in all 274 flags, 196 of which were carried by infantry regiments, and 78 by cavalry, battery or heavy-artillery organizations, and the number of engagements recorded is 246. These colors are eloquent, not only in themselves of the time which tried the nation's life, as that other time tried men's souls, but they are surrounded, also, by an atmosphere pregnant with interesting and pathetic history. This is recorded in the long list of battlefields borne upon these silken folds, in the especial inscriptions upon many of them, and in the events collated from hundreds of sources by the indefatigable Captain Eaton."

The following is a complete list of these Battle Flags, together with the number of engagements in which each organization represented took part:

First Regiment—five colors.
....................19 engagements
Second Regiment—three flags and two staffs ....14 engagements
Third Regiment—two flags.3 engagements
Fourth Regiment—two flags ....
....................3 engagements
Fifth Regiment—two flags.3 engagements
Sixth Regiment—six flags (three of them being in the Governor's room)........
....................9 engagements
Seventh Regiment—one flag.
Eighth Regiment—two flags.
Ninth Regiment—nine flags.............
....................41 engagements
Tenth Regiment—two flags..............
....................16 engagements
Eleventh Regiment—five flags...........
....................24 engagements
Twelfth Regiment—four flags...........
....................11 engagements
Thirteenth Regiment—three flags and one staff................35 engagements
Fourteenth Regiment—(afterwards First Regiment Heavy Artillery) two flags.
Fifteenth Regiment—three flags........
....................20 engagements
Sixteenth Regiment—four flags.........
....................19 engagements
Seventeenth Regiment—six flags........
....................14 engagements
Eighteenth Regiment—three flags.......
....................27 engagements
Nineteenth Regiment—six flags.........
....................23 engagements
Twentieth Regiment—four flags.........
....................27 engagements
Twenty-first Regiment—five flags......
....................22 engagements
Twenty-second Regiment—four flags....
....................23 engagements
Twenty-third Regiment—three flags.....
....................12 engagements
Twenty-fourth Regiment—two flags.....
....................23 engagements

Twenty-fifth Regiment—three flags.....
....................20 engagements
Twenty-sixth Regiment—four flags, number of engagements not given.
Twenty-seventh Regiment—three flags...
....................17 engagements
Twenty-eighth Regiment—five flags.....
....................39 engagements
Twenty-ninth Regiment—four flags.....
....................21 engagements
Thirtieth Regiment—four flags.........
....................7 engagements
Thirty-first Regiment—five flags.........
....................9 engagements
Thirty-second Regiment—two flags......
....................15 engagements
Thirty-third Regiment—five flags......
....................19 engagements
Thirty-fourth Regiment—three flags....
....................17 engagements
Thirty-fifth Regiment—four flags.......
....................16 engagements
Thirty-sixth Regiment—four flags.......
....................13 engagements
Thirty-seventh Regiment—three flags...
....................18 engagements
Thirth-eighth Regiment—four flags.....
....................7 engagements
Thirty-ninth Regiment—four flags......
....................18 engagements
Fortieth Regiment—five flags...........
....................20 engagements
Forty-first Regiment—afterwards Third Cavalry).
Forty-second Regiment—two flags.
Forty-third Regiment—two flags........
....................3 engagements
Forty-fourth Regiment—two flags.......
....................1 engagements
Forty-fifth Regiment—two flags ....
....................4 engagements
Forty-sixth Regiment—two flags.
Forty-seventh Regiment—two flags.
Forty-eighth Regiment—two flags.......
....................4 engagements
Forty-ninth Regiment—two flags.......
....................4 engagements
Fiftieth Regiment—two flags............
....................1 engagement
Fifty-first Regiment—two flags..........
....................3 engagements
Fifty-second Regiment—two flags.......
Fifty-third Regiment—two flags.........
....................3 engagements
Fifty-fourth Regiment—three flags......
....................9 engagements
Fifty-fifth Regiment—two flags.........
....................2 engagements
Fifty-sixth Regiment—three flags.......
....................9 engagements
Fifty-seventh Regiment—two flags......
....................8 engagements
Fifty-eighth Regiment—two flags.......
....................9 engagements
Fifty-ninth Regiment—four flags........
....................9 engagements
Sixtieth Regiment—two flags.
Sixty-first Regiment—two flags.........
....................1 engagement

In the outside niches are flags belonging to the First, Second, Third, Fourth and Fifth Cavalry, the four regiments of heavy artillery and the sixteen light batteries. There is also in the collection a bunting flag marked "Ninth Army Corps, First Division, Third Brigade, McLaughlin's Brigade." This is thought to be the flag carried by Napoleon B. McLaughlin, formerly of the First Massachusetts Regiment, after he became brigade commander. There are also six unidentified flags.

ART GALLERIES.

Among the Collections of Paintings and other works of Art the visitor to Boston will find the Museum of Fine Arts to be well worthy of attention. This great exhibition is more fully described on another page in this book. There are numerous other Galleries where one is always sure to find pictures of merit. We specify a few of the leading ones.

Art Club..................Newbury st.
At the rooms of the Boston Art Club are frequently held exhibitions of Paintings, to which the public are admitted. Full information regarding these exhibitions, as to time of holding, works to be seen, etc., may at any time be obtained at the Art Club House, corner of Newbury and Dartmouth sts.

Boston Athenæum. 10 B Beacon st.

Chase Art Rooms...7 Hamilton pl.
Here are generally to be seen fine paintings and other works of Art, to the inspection of which lovers of Art are cordially invited.

Childs Art Rooms....352 Wash. st.

Cyclorama..........541 Tremont st.
A gigantic painting of the Battle of Gettysburg is here exhibited. The admission fee is fifty cents. It attracts throngs of people, who are enthusiastic in praise of the great work. This is one of the permanent exhibitions of the city. All of the Tremont Street cars pass near the Cyclorama Building. Open from 9 a. m. to 11 p. m.

Doll & Richards Rooms.........
............................2 Park st.
Here may usually be seen an attractive exhibition of Paintings, etc.

Eden Musee. A company has been formed for the purpose of establishing here a permanent exhibition on a plan similar to that of Madame Taussaud's Gallery of Wax-Works, in London. Mr. F. H. Raymond is the President of the Boston Eden Musée Company, and Mr. Dudley C. Hall, Treasurer.

Elliott Art Rooms................
....................538 Washington st.

Historic-Genealogical Rooms
........................18 Somerset st.
Rare and curious collection of pictures, etc. *Free.*

Household Art Rooms.........
........................44 Boylston st.

Kensington Placque Company
........................179 Tremont st.

Mass. Historical Rooms........
........................30 Tremont st.
A collection of old paintings, etc. *Free.*

Museum of Fine Arts............
........................St. James av.
(See *Museums and Exhibitions*).

Noyes and Blakeslee Gallery
........................127 Tremont st.

Paint and Clay Club............
........................419 Washington st.
This Club holds Exhibitions at stated intervals, when the public is admitted.

Prang Art Rooms..286 Roxbury st.

Public Library Art Gallery...
........................46 Boylston st.

Williams & Everett Gallery...
........................79 Boylston st.
At this celebrated Art Gallery may always be seen a collection of choice paintings by eminent artists, which are sure to interest art-lovers, and are made to feel welcome. In a most central and easily accessible location, near Park Square, not far from the stations of several great railway lines and with street cars to various points passing the door, visitors to the city will find this Gallery a most attractive centre. In a studio above the Gallery, Hubert Herkomer makes his headquarters while in Boston.

SUMMER GARDENS.

Amory Garden. West Roxbury District. Take Jamaica Plain street-cars from Tremont House.

Maolis Garden. Nahant. Take steamer from India Wharf. Maolis Garden is a beautiful seaside enclosure, having many features of interest. The ocean view is a fine one. The Garden may also be reached by rail to Lynn and coach to Nahant.

Melville Garden. Downer Landing. Take steamboat from India Wharf. A very picturesque and romantic spot. Noted for its genuine old-fashioned clambakes and "shore dinners." A favorite resort with excursionists from all over New England.

Music Hall Garden. 15 Winter Street. During the summer months Boston Music Hall is converted into a beer-garden, where concerts of orchestral music are given every evening except Sunday. The admission-fee is twenty-five cents. Smoking is permitted, and at the refreshment-tables lager beer, ices, and other refreshments are served. It is modelled upon the beer-gardens of Germany.

Oakland Garden. Blue Hill Avenue. A very popular amusement resort. Entertainments day and evening. Here is a theatre, of good size, wherein dramatic and operatic performances are given. J. A. Gilbert, manager. Take Oakland Garden or Franklin (West Roxbury) Park street-cars at Temple Place.

Oriental Garden. Shawmut Avenue, corner of Ruggles Street. Concerts of orchestral music are given here every evening, except Sunday. Refreshments are served. Admittance to the Garden is placed at a low rate. Take any Shawmut Avenue street-car.

Park Square Garden. Park Square. This very centrally located and popular place of amusement is leased by Manager William Austin, who provides entertainments of good quality, consisting of circus and variety performances, at low prices. The auditorium seats about 4,000 persons. The price of admission is ten cents, the average price for seats being twenty-five cents.

Summer Bazaar Garden. Mechanic Hall Building, Huntington Avenue. Orchestral music, military band concerts, billiard playing, bowling, rifle practice, dancing, skating and other amusements are provided.

ARCHITECTURAL MUSEUM.

One of the most interesting and instructive collections in the city, and, as far as is known, unique in this country, is the extensive Architectural Museum of the Massachusetts Institute of Technology. It consists of thousands of photographs, casts, drawings, prints, etc., including photographs, lithographs and drawings presented to the Institute by French, English and American architects, taken from their own works, including *sets of actual* working-drawings, with details and specifications; a complete series of drawings presented by the late Ernst Benzon, of London, illustrating the course of architectural instruction in the Ecole des Beaux-Arts in Paris,—*Esquisses-Esquisses, Projets Rendus, Projets d'Ordre, Projets de Construction, Grand Prix de Rome, Envoi de Rome*. In addition to these is a very large collection of models and illustrations of architectural details and materials. (The Architectural Museum is at 191 Boylston Street. Take Back Bay cars).

MEDICAL AND METRIC MUSEUMS.

Boston University Medical School Museum. East Concord Street. A large and constantly increasing collection of anatomical, pathological and physiological specimens; preparations in wax illustrative of anatomical structures and pathological conditions; histological and microscopical cabinets, etc. Very interesting and instructive.

At 132 Hawley Street is a unique collection of charts, books, weights and measures, apparatus, etc., forming a complete Museum of illustrations of the metric system. It is well worthy of a visit from strangers visiting the city.

ARTISTS.

A very large number of eminent artists make their home in Boston. Their studios are generally open to visitors at seasonable hours. Many of them appoint regular visiting days. The following are among the best known portrait, landscape and marine painters:

Adams, S. A. Mrs........Studio building
Aitken, William..........8 Hamilton pl.
Alexander, S. B.......81 Studio building
Allen, Thos.........12 Commonwealth av.
Astrom, Carl G..................7 State st.
Attwill, L. B. Miss......149A Tremont st.
Attwood, F. G...............28 School st.
Bacon, F. W..................43 Eliot st.
Badger, T. H................11 Akron st.
Baker, Joseph E........178 Devonshire st.
Baker, M. K. Miss......54 Studio building
Barnard, Edward H...247 Washington st.
Barse, G. R. jr................22 Beach st.
Bartlett, Geo. H...........27 Tremont row
Bartlett, J. E. Miss........17 S. Russell st.
Bartoll, E. H. Miss......60 Mt. Vernon st.
Bass, E. E...................524 Tremont st.
Beaman, W. G..............5 Tremont st.
Bellows, Jennie E. Mrs....2A Beacon st.
Billings, E. T..........55 Studio building
Bixby, Helen S. Miss.......48 Boylston st.
Borris, A..................175 Tremont st.
Bothe, Ida, Miss............72 Boylston st.
Botts, A ....339 Washington st.
Bowditch, Charlotte, Miss.48 Boylston st.
Brackett, Arthur L........41 Tremont st.
Brackett, Walter M........41 Tremont st.
Bradley, L. Miss..............5 Temple pl.
Brown, H. L. Miss.....82 Studio building
Brown, J. Appleton..........6 Beacon st.
Browne, Nellie E......72 Studio building
Buhler, Augustus..........5 Hamilton pl.
Caliga, I. H................3 Hamilton pl.
Carter, J. G................159 A Tremont st.
Champney, Benj.........21 Bromfield st.
Champney, Edwin G........36 Temple pl.
Chandler, A. E. Miss..60 Studio building
Churchill, WilliamW., jr......12 West st.
Clerk, W. F......80 Munroe st., Roxbury
Closson, W. B.........149 A Tremont st.
Cobb, Darius..........149 A Tremont st.
Cobb, Frederick W.....8 Pemberton sq.
Cole, J. Foxcroft...433 Washington st.
Conover, Charles H.....4 Charlestown st.
Cook, Henry..........53 Studio building
Coolidge, Baldwin......154 Tremont st.
Coolidge, M. E. Mrs....149 A Tremont st.
Copeland, C. W........17 Pemberton sq.
Corbett, K. F. Miss...30 Music Hall bldg.
Cowles, F. M... ... 143 Dartmouth st.
Crowningshield, F.........Dartmouth st.
Curtis, Leslie L............14 Temple pl.
Cushing, F. K..........10 Pemberton sq.
Cushman, A. A. Miss.....143 Tremont st.
Dabney, J. P. Miss........17 Boylston pl.
Damoreau, Madame......125 Tremont st.
Dana, Charles G........9 Pemberton sq.
Day, Henry..........149 A Tremont st.
Dean, Walter L........31 Pemberton sq.
DeBlois, F. B................48 Winter st

DeCamp, J. R............110 Chauncy st.
Dee, R. H..................193 Dudley st.
Defrees, Thaddeus..........33 School st.
Devitt, J. J.............595 Washington st.
Dickerman, Albert.......40 Chester Park
Dobinson, V. A. Miss......85 Studio bldg.
Dole, E. F. Mrs..........19 Pemberton sq.
Dow, Grace L.............48 Studio bldg.
Draper, Francis, jr.........44 Boylston st.
Drew, Clement............10 Copeland st.
Duffee, P. Edwin............63 Court st.
Eaton, Clarissa, Miss, River st., Mattapan
Eksergian, C................175 Tremont st.
Eldred, L. D............76 Studio building
Ellis, Lucy................154 Tremont st.
Elwell, D. Jerome.........175 Tremont st.
Enneking, John J........174 Tremont st.
Faller, Emilie, Miss......27 E. Newton st.
Farley, H. S. Mrs..............20 Beacon st.
Farr, Ellen B. Mrs..... 149 A, Tremont st.
Farr, F. M. Mrs........29 Music Hall bldg.
Fernald, E. L.Mrs,6 Rockland pl.Roxbury
Fletcher, Harold........149 A Tremont st.
Foley, S. L. Miss........149 A Tremont st.
Fraser, J. A............Adams st., Dorch.
Gallison, H. H.........44 Studio building
Garratt, J. H................24 Temple pl.
Garrett, Edmund H............. 3 Park st.
Gaugengigl, I. M.......45 Studio building
Gilbert, James, Mrs....24 Studio building
Giles, H. P...................12 West st.
Goodale, M. S., Miss....7 Mt. Pleasant pl.
Goodridge, J. F...........4 Pemberton sq.
Goodyear, Clara.......23 Studio building
Gorham, Annie L........149 A Tremont st.
Gould, M. S............58 Studio building
Grant, C. R...................34 School st.
Green, Charles E. L.........33 School st.
Greene, C. S., Miss........74 Boylston st.
Greenough, Charlotte G. 145 Tremont st.
Gregory, A. M., Miss..........12 West st.
Griggs, S. W............39 Studio building
Grundmann, Otto..........6 Bedford st.
Guild, Samuel..............114 Dudley st.
Hale, E. D., Miss..........74 Boylston st.
Hale, Martha............4 Pemberton sq.
Hallett, Hendricks A......... 42 Court sq.
Halsall, W. F............174 Tremont st.
Hammond, N. C. Miss... 39 Studio bldg.
Hanlon, E. L........17 Music Hall building
Harlow, Louis K..............6 Beacon st.
Hassam, F. C...........282 Columbus av.
Henry, A. M. Mrs........ 1 Mt. Vernon pl.
Hill, Edward................12 West st.
Hill, Robert............251 Bennington st.
Hills, L. C. Mrs........ 26 Studio building
Hobbs, A. S. Miss........3 Hamilton pl.
Hollingsworth, Mark...143 Dartmouth st.
Hollis, L.....................12 West st.
Houston, F. C. Mrs..154 W. Chester park.
Humphrey, L. B. Miss..149 A Tremont st.
Jackson, William H.........48 Winter st.
Jenks, Phœbe A......52 Studio building.
Johnson, Marshall, jr..........12 West st.
Johnston, John B........154 Tremont st.
Jordan, R. S. Miss.....42 Studio building.
Joslyn, M. E. Miss............4 Park sq.
Juglaris, Tomaso..........161 Tremont st.

Knight, G. Hollis..............94 Court st.
Knowlton, Helen M........169 Tremont st.
Knox, Edw.......6 Winthrop block, E. B.
Lane, S. M. Miss.........154 Tremont st.
Langerfeldt, T. O............114 Charles st.
Lansil, W. F..Milton avenue, Dorchester.
Lawton, E. H..........30 Studio building.
Leighton, Scott........433 Washington st.
Leonard, Charles W..........152 Dudley st.
Lee, Misses....................6 Beacon st.
Linton, Hobart........47 Studio building.
Loring, G. A.........66 Studio building.
Lyndon, Wm. M.............7 Cottage pl.
Magoun, C. J............521 Washington st.
Manning A. A. Miss....32 Mt. Vernon st.
Mansfield, J. W............31 School st.
Martin, L. Edna..........130 Tremont st.
McAuliffe, James J..........42 Court st.
McLean, N. Wallace.....15 Pemberton sq.
Means, James Mrs....51 Studio building.
Merriam, A. L., Miss...7 Mt. Pleasant pl.
Merrill, E. F............30 Studio build'ng.
Merrow, C. E. A..........10 Pemberton sq.
Miles, S. S...............10 Pemberton sq.
Miller, Frank.....26 Music Hall building.
Morris, F. A.............55½ Sudbury st.
Morse, May..........24 Studio building.
Moulton and Barry, Misses.44 Boylston st.
Munzig, George C..........48 Boylston st.
Myrick, Frank............... 28 School st.
Nichols, Edwin M.............5 Temple pl.
Niles, G. E................ 33 School st.
Noa, Jessie............33 Studio building.
Nolen, Caroline, Miss......48 Boylston st.
O'Connell, John J.....595 Washington st.
Nowell, Annie C........149A Tremont st.
Onthank, N. B..........35 Hotel Clifton
Ordway, Alfred........29 Studio building
Oudinot, A. F.........145 Tremont st.
Page, Samuel.......37 Somerset st.
Parker, Edgar.........433 Washington st.
Parmenter, J. G............28 School st.
Parsons, C. L..........32 Studio building
Parsons, L. A............28 School st.
Pennock, S. C.........16 Pemberton sq.
Perkins, S. E.........86 Studio building
Perrin, Julia, Miss.........74 Boylston st.
Phillips & Randall..........26 Somerset st.
Pierce, C. F................12 West st.
Poor, James W..............20 Beacon st.
Porter, B. C..............48 Boylston st.
Porter, Edwin F............45 Winter st.
Primus, Nelson A....123 Sumner st., E.B.
Purdie, Miss...............12 West st.
Putnam, A. C. Miss........11 Hamilton pl.
Ransom, M. S. Mrs.........171 Tremont st.
Reed, E. V. R............469 Tremont st.
Rhees, M. J................2A Beacon st.
Rich, J. Rogers..........167 Tremont st.
Robbins, Ellen................6 Beacon st.
Rogers, F. W.........419 Washington st.
Russell, Geo. D...........125 Tremont st.

Ryder, J. S............595 Washington st.
Sabine, Wm. L............20 Beacon st.
Sanderson, Charles W.......20 Beacon st.
Sandham, Henry.....11 Hotel Edinburgh
Sandys, Louis.............Hotel Boylston
Schroff, A. H............8 Pemberton sq.
Scudder, J. M. Miss....32 Studio building
Seaton, Annie............171 Tremont st.
Seavey, G. W........28 Studio building
Segitz, Fred............34 Studio building
Selinger, J. P.............3 Hamilton pl.
Shapleigh, Frank H....79 Studio building
Shields, A. B.....Rosseter st., Dorchester
Shute, A. B...........178 Devonshire st.
Skinner, E. G. Mrs..............5 Park sq.
Slafter, Theodore S.....87 Studio building
Smith, Frank Hill........62 Boylston st.
Starbuck, F. M., Miss...................
............45 Bartlett st., Roxbury
Stevens, A. B. Miss........17 Boylston pl.
Stiefil, I. H.............3 Hamilton pl.
Stillings, S. Vinton.......54 Bromfield st.
Stokes, John.............43 Hammond st.
Stone, J. M..............666 Washington st.
Strain, Daniel J..........175 Tremont st.
Stuart, R. A............3 Hamilton pl.
Stubbs, W. P.............3 Mt. Vernon st.
Sturtevant, A. L. Miss....Hotel Berkeley
Taylor, Mattie M..........3 Tremont row
Teeling, Joseph A..........79 Sudbury st.
Thompson, Albert.....433 Washington st.
Titcomb, W. H..........630 Washington st.
Triscott, S. P. R......433 Washington st.
Tryon, S. C. Mrs. Hancock st., Dorchester
Turnbull, F. M. Dr....433 Washington st.
Turner, Charles H..........12 West st.
Turner, E. Winslow.......2 Hamilton pl.
Turner Ross...........48 Boylston st.
Turner, W. F..........2 Hamilton pl.
Villiers, Chas. F..........3 Pemberton sq.
Vinton, Frederick P..............1 Park sq.
Vonnoh, R. W............62 Boylston st.
Wagner, Jacob.........169 Tremont st.
Wainwright, T. F......206 Dartmouth st.
Walker, H. O...........9 Somerset st.
Warren, A. R. Miss....81 Studio building
Waterman, Marcus....616 Washington st.
Webber, Wesley......1 Pemberton sq.
Weber, Otis S..............31 Beacon st.
Welch, G. B. Mrs.........181 Tremont st.
Wellington, Leah N. Mrs..74 Boylston st.
Wenige, Gustav. E........26 Village st.
Wentworth, George A....Centre st., J. P.
Whipple, Chas. A..........48 Winter st.
White, Sarah D............12 West st.
Wilkie, Robert D..........152 Dudley st.
Willard, Wm............27 E. Newton st.
Wright, F. E................6 Beacon st.
Wyman, F. A....38 Warren st., Roxbury
Wynne, M. V..........11 Hamilton pl.
Young, Fred Grant........Evans House
Young, J. Harvey..........12 West st.

PUBLIC HALLS.

Adams Hall........144 Meridian st., E. B.
Administration Hall.....Huntington av.
Allston Hall..............116 Tremont st.
Alpha Hall..................18 Essex st.
American Hall........Sanford st., Dorch.
Amory Hall............503 Washington st.
Anawan Hall.......Anawan av., W. Rox.
Apollo Hall................151 Tremont st.
Appleton Hall, Appleton st., cor. Ber'k'ly
Armory Hall......Dorchester av., Dorch.
Arcanum Hall...... Allston st., Brighton
Association Hall..........174 Boylston st.
Athenæum Hall..........Pond st., Dorch.
Bacon Hall..........2185 Washington st.
Banta Hall..........1371 Washington st.
Bartlett Hall.....389 W. Broadway, S. B.
Bay State Hall...........197 Shawmut av.
Berkeley Hall...............4 Berkeley st.
Boston Hall................176 Tremont st.
Bowdoin Hall................. Bowdoin sq.
Boylston Hall....Wash. st., cor. Boylston
Brunswick Hall..........241 Tremont st.
Bumstead Hall..................15 Winter
Caledonia Hall................15 Chauncy
Caledonia Hall..............43 Eliot st.
Casino Hall..Shawmut av., cor. Lucas st.
Chandler Hall.................18 Essex st.
Chapel Hall...........820 Washington st.
Chauncy Hall...........259 Boylston st.
Chickering Hall...........151 Tremont st.
Chickering Hall,cor. Apple. and Berk.sts.
City Hall........................School st.
City Hall............City sq., Charlestown
Cockerel Hall................Hanover st.
Codman Hall........ .....176 Tremont st.
College Hall..................34 Essex st.
Columbia Hall............Davenport av.
Concert Hall...................7 Green st.
Concord Hall............ 75 W. Concord st.
Congress Hall........360 Main st., Chas'n
Conservatory Hall.......27 E. Newton st.
Curtis Hall................Jamaica Plain
Covenant Hall............ 515 Tremont st.
Cyclorama Hall............541 Tremont st.
Decker Hall..........286 Dorchester, S. B.
Dorchester Hall ....Adams st., Dorch.
Doric Hall...................State House
Eagle Hall..........616 Washington st.
Eaton Hall.................18 Boylston st.
Eliot Hall......... Eliot st., Jamaica Plain
Elks Hall..........24 Hayward Place
Elmwood Hall..................Oriole st.
Elson Hall.........Station, Jamaica Plain
Emmet Hall.............28 Kneeland st.
Encampment Hall........ 515 Tremont st.
Evans Hall..................3 Tremont row
Evening Star Hall......7 City sq., Chas'n.
Everett Hall................Davenport av.
Faneuil Hall...............Faneuil Hall sq.
Federhen Hall.........107 Cambridge st.
Foresters' Hall........2373 Washington st.
Freemasons' Hall............Thompson sq.
Friendship Hall...........515 Tremont st.
Friendship Hall..............187 Cabot st.
Friendship Hall......Bowdoin st., Dorch.
Garfield Hall..cor. Wash'n and Dover sts.
Germaina Hall.....193 Maverick st., E. B.
Goldsmith Hall..........1418 Tremont st.

Gospel Hall...............34 Essex st.
Grand-Army Hall......735 Washington st.
Grand-Army Hall.......25 Main st. Chas'n
Grand-Army Hall....2389 Washington st.
Gray's Hall.........619 E. Broadway, S. B.
Guild Hall...Washington st., cor. Dudley
Hancock Hall........Hancock sq., Chas'n
Harmonia Hall.....Rockland st.,W. Rox.
Hawthorne Hall..................2 Park st.
Highland Hall..............191 Warren st.
Hitchcock Hall................7 Beacon st.
Hobah Hall................National st., S. B.
Horticultural Hall........100 Tremont st.
Hospitaller Hall.......712 Washington st.
Howe's Hall........376 W. Broadway, S. B.
Huntington Hall.............191 Boylston st.
Hutchinson Hall............Forest Hill av.
Independent Hall..6 Hancock st., Chas'n
Investigator Hall............Appleton st.
Ivanhoe Hall...........2 Main st., Chas'n
Ivy Hall..................1371 Washington st.
Jacob Sleeper Hall.........12 Somerset st.
John A. Andrew Hall.Chauncy st. c. Essex
Kneeland Hall................Appleton st.
Knights-of-Honor Hall.730 Washington st.
Knights-of-Honor Hall.144 Meridian, E. B.
Knights-of-Pythias Hall...2 Main, Chas'n
Kossuth Hall.............1093 Tremont st.
Lawrence Hall.........724 Washington st.
Lincoln Hall............69 W. Concord st.
Lurline Hall....................3 Winter st.
Lusitana Hall................Hanover st.
Lyceum Hall................East st., Dorch.
Lyceum Hall........198 Sumner st., E. B.
Masonic Hall.........33 Central sq., E. B.
Masonic Hall.................Dudley st., Rox.
Masonic Hall............Adams st., Dorch.
Masonic Hall....Warren bldg., Brighton
Masonic Hall................20 Blossom st.
Masonic Hall.........Bartlett bldg., J. P.
Maverick Hall....Maverick Square, E. B.
Mechanic Hall..............Huntington av.
Mechanic Hall...............40 Bedford st.
Mechanic Hall........212 Main st., Chas'n
Mechanic Hall......Dorchester st., S. B.
Meionaon Hall.............78 Tremont st.
Memorial Hall..........Old State House
Memphis Hall...............34 Essex st.
Meridian Hall......140 Meridian st. E. B.
Miller Hall.................156 Tremont st.
Minot Hall......................Common st.
Minot Hall..............68 W. Springfield st.
Mishawum Hall...11 City Square, Chas'n
Montgomery Hall.389 W. Broadway, S. B.
Monument Hall..........Hancock Square
Mozart Hall...................369 Hanover st.
Music Hall..................15 Winter st.
Myrtle Hall..............1221 Washington st.
Mystic Hall..............70 Main st., Chas'n
Mystic Hall................91 Hanover st.
Nassau Hall.........833 Washington st.
National Hall.................South Boston
National Bank Hall...............Brighton
New England Hall....987 Washington st.
New Era Hall...................176 Tremont st.
Norcross Hall................18 Boylston st.
Oakland Hall..................River st.
Oasis Hall................515 Tremont st.

Odd-Fellows Hall,515 Tremont st., c. Berk.
Odd-Fellows Hall.......25 Main st., Chas'n
Odd-Fellows Hall........6 Winthrop Block
Odd-Fellows Hall....2298 Washington st.
Odd-Fellows Hall...........River st., Dorch.
Odd-Fellows Hall.......Elson Block, J. P.
Orienta Hall..........2156 Washington st.
Osmer Hall.........144 Meridian st., E. B.
Paine Hall.....................Appleton st.
Palladio Hall.................54 Warren st.
Papanti Hall..................23 Tremont st.
Papineau Hall..........180 Green st., J. P.
Park Hall..................176 Tremont st.
Park Street Hall..............Park, Dorch.
Parker Memorial Hall......Berkeley st.
Pierce Hall................Clayton, Dorch.
Pilgrim Hall.................7 Beacon st.
Preble Hall..............176 Tremont st.
Pulaski Hall..........Fourth st., Dorch.
Pythian Hall..............176 Tremont st.
Pythian Hall......364 W. Broadway, S. B.
Quincy Hall.............South Market st.
Raymond Hall.....172 Main st., Chas'n
Revere Hall....................7 Green st.
Rockland Hall..........2343 Washington st.
St. Omer Hall.....376 W. Broadway, S. B.
Samaritan Hall..cor. Chambers & Camb.
Science Hall.............718 Washington st.
Shawmut Hall............176 Tremont st.
Sheil Hall....................287 Hanover st.
Sherwood Hall........Hunneman st., Rox.
Sleeper Hall................27 E. Newton st.

Spelman Hall.....136 W. Broadway, S. B.
Stacy Hall ....186 Washington st.
Stickney Hall........212 Main st., Chas'n
Sullivan Hall. ....River st., Dorch.
Sumner Hall.............Elbow st., E. B.
Sutton Hall.............Masonic Temple
Templar Hall....Osborn Block, Brighton
Temple Hall ....Norfolk st., Dorch.
Thorndike Hall.......560 Main st., Chas'n
Town Hall..........Washington st., Dorch.
Tremont Hall..............1435 Tremont st.
Tremont Temple............78 Tremont st.
Trimountain Hall............8 Boylston st.
Turn Halle (Germania Theatre).
........................29 Middlesex st.
Union Hall................18 Boylston st.
Union Hall......Cambridge st., Allston
Union Park Hall...........Union Park st.
United Fellowship Hall......26 Union st.
Vernon Hall ....1180 Tremont st.
Wadman Hall ....176 Tremont st.
Wait's Hall ....390 W. Broadway, S. B.
Washington Hall .....133 Blackstone st.
Washington Hall ..Dorchester av., S. B.
Washington Hall.....Maverick sq., E. B.
Waverley Hall...........City sq., Chas'n
Webster Hall...........Webster st., E. B.
Wells Hall ....387 Washington st.
Wesleyan Hall..............36 Bromfield st.
Winthrop Hall......406 Main st., Chas'n
Winthrop Hall....14 Hancock st., Dorch.
Woolsey Hall..............Jamaica Plain

PUBLIC BUILDINGS.

Adams Building..............23 Court st.
Advertiser Building...246 Washington st.
Angelo Building..........48 Congress st.
Artisan's Block..........Union Park st.
Athenæum, Boston.......10B Beacon st.
Athenæum................Pond st., Dorch.
Atlantic Building......Forster's Wharf
Bacon Building........102 Harrison av.
Bartlett Building,Green st., Jam'ca Pl'n
Bay State Block............8 Essex pl.
Bickum Block............Ferdinand st.
Blanchard Block,Court st., near Hanover
Board of Health (City)..32 Pemberton sq.
Board of Health (State).....Beacon st.
Board of Trade..............53 State st.
Boston Art Club, Newbury st., c. D'rtm'h
Boston Athenæum.........10B Beacon st.
Boston Post Building..........17 Milk st.
Bowdoin Building............31 Milk st.
Bowdoin Square Block......179 Court st.
Bradlee Building,c. Dudley & Warren sts.
Brazer's Building............27 State st.
Brower Building........186 Devonshire st.
Bristol Block...................Bristol st.
Carney Hospital Bldg...National st., S.B.
Census Office..............20 Beacon st.
Chamber of Commerce.....So. Market st.
Chandler Building......47 Devonshire st.

Channing Building......141 Franklin st.
Chapman Block..............Chapman st.
Charity Building............Chardon st.
Chester Block ...Cambridge st., Allston
Children's Hospital Bldg. Huntington av.
City Hall ....School st.
City Hall......City Square, Charlestown
City Hospital Bldg...........Harrison av.
Civil Service Commission,5 Pemberton sq.
Claflin Building...........20 Beacon st.
Commonwealth Block...1697 Washing. st.
Commonwealth Building..65 Bowdoin st.
Congregational House........7A Beacon st.
Congress Building........4 Post-Office sq.
Continental Block....1293 Washington st.
Coolidge Building...........Bowdoin Sq.
Court House....................Court Sq.
Court House (U. S.)......Post-Office sq.
Cox Bldg....cor. Dudley and Bartlett sts.
Cruft Block................16 Pearl st.
Custom House... cor. India and State sts.
Custom House Block..........177 State st.
Cutter Block.....No. Beacon st., Brighton
Dentist Block,Shawmut av. cor. Dover st.
Denvir Block.........Market st., Brighton
Diamond Block .....2293 Washington st.
Equitable Bldg., cor.Milk and Devon. sts.
Evans Building............175 Tremont st.

Exchange Building.. 2343 Washington st.
Farmers' Market Block...Central Wharf.
Fellows Athenæum...........Millmont st.
Folsom Block..................15 King st.
Gore Block......cor. Green and Pitts sts.
Greenleaf Block..........Cazenove Place.
Green's Block..........Walnut st., Chas'n
Hastings Building......... 165 Tremont st.
Hayes Block.........47 Walnut st., Chas'n
Head Building............ 181 Tremont st.
Hemenway Bldg.,cor.Trem.and Court sts.
Herald Building......257 Washington st.
Hichborn Block..............83 North st.
Holmes Block..............Haymarket sq.
Howard Bank Bldg........19 Congress st.
Institute of Technology Building.........
....................191 Boylston st.
James Block....Centre st., Jamaica Plain
Jones Block...........30 Colony st., S. B.
Journal Building..... 264 Washington st.
Kast Building.............100 Hanover st.
Knickerbocker Bldg......178 Tremont st.
Lawrence Block. Wash. cor. Kneeland st.
Lawrence Bldg....Tremont, cor. West st.
Lexington Building.......174 Tremont st.
Liberty Building..............30 Kilby st.
Liberty Tree Block..Wash. cor. Essex st.
Madison Block......1098 Washington st.
Mariners' Exchange ....
..... Cor. Hanover and N. Bennet sts.
Marlborough Bldg...391 Washington st.
Mason Building..............Liberty sq.
Masonic Temple..........................
......Cor. Tremont and Boylston sts.
Master Builders' Exchange...............
....................164 Devonshire st.
McLaughlin Building.........Endicott st.
Mechanics' Block............Waltham st.
Mechanics' Exchange......35 Hawley st.
Merchants' Bank Bldg........28 State st.
Merchants' Building......40 Bedford st.
Merchants' Exchange.........53 State st.
Minot Buildings. Court st., head Sudbury
Monks Building.........35 Congress st.
Monks Building......366 W. B'way, S. B.
Morgue........ ....North Grove st.
Museum of Fine Arts Bldg.St. James av.
Music Hall Building.........15 Winter st.
Mut. Life Insurance Bldg.....95 Milk st.
Natural History Building................
......Cor. Berkeley and Boylston sts.
New England Block........Blackstone st.
New England Institute Building..........
....................Huntington av.
New Eng. Mut. Life Ins. Bldg..87 Milk st.
New Studio Building...143 Dartmouth st.
Newman Block.......rear 172 Pleasant st.
Niles Block..................33 School st.

Oakman Block......Walnut st , Neponset
Odd Fellows Building.....515 Tremont st.
Old State House. Cor. Wash. and State sts.
Osborn Block.......Wash'n st., Brighton
Paine Memorial Bldg........Appleton st.
Parker Memorial Bldg....................
........cor. Berkeley and Appleton st.
Pelham Studios...........44 Boylston st.
Phœnix Building.........52 Devonshire st.
Plimpton Building...1075 Washington st.
Probate Building.......28 Court Square
Public Library Bldg........46 Boylston st.
Railroad Block.cor. Lincoln & Beach sts.
Railroad Exchange..........Court Square
Reed Block..........51 Meridian st., E. B.
Reed Block...............460 Harrison av.
Rialto...................131 Devonshire st.
Richardson Building...178 Devonshire st.
Roberts Building...........11 Chardon st.
Rogers Building......209 Washington st.
Roxbury Athenæum.....Dudley st., Rox.
Sanderson Block..........110 Pleasant st.
Sargent Block................19 Lincoln st.
Sears Building..........................
......cor. Washington and Court sts.
Seaver Block....Centre st., Jamaica Plain
Shillaber Building. ....61 Court st.
Shurtleff Building.........2A Beacon st.
Sidney Buildings..........Union Park st.
Simmons Building...........40 Water st.
Smith Block..........1727 Washington st.
Snow Block.cor. Federal & Matthews sts.
Soren Block................113 Dudley st.
State House..Beacon st., head of Park st.
Stevenson Block............Central sq., E. B.
Studio Building..........110 Tremont st.
Tilden Block.................83 Broad st.
Transcript Building...324 Washington st.
Traveller Building.............31 State st.
Tremont Bank Bldg., c. Cong's & St'e sts.
Tremont Temple..........78 Tremont st.
Union Building.................40 State st.
V Block........................Waltham st.
Walworth Block........E. First st., S. B.
Warren Building................2 Park st.
Warren Building, Washington st., B'gt'n
Warrenton Block........ 4 Warrenton pl.
Washington Building......383 Wash. st.
Waverley Block...........City sq., Chas'n
Wells Memorial Building, 987 Wash'n st.
Winsor Block..................Dover st.
Winthrop Block......Maverick sq., E. B.
Winthrop Block...... 2167 Washington st.
Woolsey Block..............Jamaica Plain
Wyman Block............795 Devonshire st.
Y. M. C. A. Building......174 Boylston st.
Y. M. C. U. Building......18 Boylston st.
Y. W. C. A. Building........Appleton st.

BACK BAY DIRECTORY.

ABOUT the year 1857, the filling-in of the so-called Back Bay, lying between Charles st., Charles River, Parker st. and the Boston and Providence Railway, was begun in good earnest, and to-day that enormous territory of made-land is almost entirely covered. Grand, wide streets have been laid out, — notably Commonwealth avenue, two hundred feet in width, with a park running its entire length, — and hundreds of the most magnificent dwellings have been erected thereon by opulent merchants of Boston. Practically, a new city has risen, almost magically, and the Back Bay (or new West End, as it is now commonly being termed) rivals in magnificence the most sumptuous quarters of the cities of the Old World. Take, for example, the group of buildings on Copley Square, at the junction of Huntington av. with Boylston st., including the Museum of Fine Arts, Trinity Church, the new South Church, and other buildings; where can such a combination of architectural grandeur be surpassed? The private residences of Oliver Ames, at the corner of Commonwealth av. and West Chester Park st.; John F. Andrew, at the corner of Commonwealth av. and Hereford st., with its Tuileries balcony; John P. Phillips, corner of Marlborough and Berkeley sts.; Charles A. Whittier and F. L. Higginson, 270 and 274 Beacon st., are elegant structures. The Hotel Vendome, Commonwealth av., corner of Dartmouth st., is a fine building, and the numerous apartment houses are superb structures. The accompanying complete list of the residents of this beautiful quarter will be of value to strangers as well as citizens, and may prove of service to future genealogists, biographers and historians. (This section is reached by either line of Back Bay street cars — Vendome or Clarendon — from Scollay Square).

Arlington Street. (From opposite 95 Beacon st. to opposite 113 Boylston st.). This is one of the finest streets in the city, overlooking the Public Garden. The residents are:

1 ....Leonard R. Cutter
2 ....Mrs. Charles Faulkner
5 ....Charles B. Porter, M. D.
6 ....Nathaniel F. Goldsmith
7 ....Peter C. Brooks, Jr.
8 ....Charles B. Cory
9 ....James Austin
10 ....George A. Miner
11 ....Charles J. Morrill
12 ....J. Montgomery Sears
13 ....James W. Bartlett, M. D.
14 ....George W. Harding
15 ....H. W. Williams, M. D.
16 ....Ralph Warner
 ....James B. Kellock
17 ....W. O. Grover
18 ....Reginald H. Fitz, M. D.
19 ....Charles S. Bates

Beacon Street. (From 63 Tremont st., to Newton line). Hotels on this street: Albion (1), Bellevue (17), Royal (295), Tudor (34B). Among the eminent persons living on this street are Oliver Wendell Holmes (286), William D. Howells (302), and Julia Ward Howe (241). The residents from Park st., to the Mill dam are as follows:

28 ....Mrs. Mary R. Plympton
29 ....Mrs. Mary Brewer
 ....Miss Caroline A. Brewer
 ....Miss Susan Weld
30 ....Mrs. T. E. P. Beebe
 ....E. Pierson Beebe
 ....Frank H. Beebe
 ....Miss Emeline B. Beebe
31 ....Mrs. John E. Lodge
32 ....David Nevins
33 ....Geo. F. Parkman
34 ....Mrs. Joseph S. Cabot
 ....Miss Elizabeth Howes
35 ....T. O. H. P. Burnham
36 ....George F. Fabyan
37 ....Mrs. George B. Blake
38 ....Thomas L. Winthrop
39 ....William S. Appleton
40 ....Martin B. Inches
 ....George B. Inches
41 ....William Amory
 ....Francis I. Amory
42 ....Somerset Club
44 ....Alexander Cochrane
45 ....Edward Austin
46 ....Eben D. Jordan
47 ....Martin Brimmer
48 ....Mrs. T. B. Williams
 ....Benjamin Clark
49 ....John L. Braman
50 ....Charles Amory
51 ....Fred. R. Sears
52 ....Henry J. Bigelow, M. D.
54 ....Von L. Meyer
55 ....Franklin G. Dexter
56 ....Mrs. Franklin Dexter
 ....Arthur Dexter
57 ....Mrs. George N. Black
58 ....John C. Warren, M. D.
59 ....Mrs. Turner Sargent
60 ....William S. Bigelow, M. D.
61 ....Mrs. E. B. Bryant
 ....Henry Bryant
 ....William S. Bryant
62 ....James C. Jordan
63 ....William B. Swett
64 ....Mrs. William F. Cary
65 ....Powell Parkman
66 ....M. H. Richardson, M. D.
67 ....Mrs. George Gardner
68 ....Mrs. Mary L. Putnam
 ....Miss G. L. Putnam

69	Mrs. Louisa Chadwick	127	William C. Wharton
70	James Dwight	128	Mrs. A. Thompson
72	Miss Mary Russell	129	John W. Wheelwright
73	Daniel Sargent		A. W. Wheelwright
74	Edward A. Abbott	130	H. H. Hunnewell
75	Mrs. E. J. Holmes		Henry Hunnewell
76	Mrs. E. W. Appleton	131	William Brewster
	William Appleton, M. D.	132	Knevet W. Sears
77	Henry Sigourney	133	Mrs. Matthew Bartlett
78	George G. Hall	134	Otis Kimball
79	William Sohier	135	Samuel H. Russell
80	Mrs. S. E. Guild	136	Mrs. W. P. Winchester
	Samuel E. Guild	137	Charles H. Gibson
81	Mrs. H. M. Wigglesworth	138	Thomas B. Winchester
82	Mrs. Seth E. Pecker	139	William C. Otis
	Frank S. Pecker		Miss Margaret S. Otis
	Edward E. Pecker		Miss Violet Otis
83	J. Arthur Beebe	140	A. Wentworth
84	William G. Prescott		W. H. Stewart
86	Mrs. David Sears	141	Miss Eunice Hooper
87	William A. Burnham		Mrs. F. A. Hooper
88	S. R. Payson	142	G. W. Wales
89	Henry S. Grew	143	Mrs. Horace Gray
90	Mrs. Lucy R. Read		Russell Gray
92	Shepherd Brooks	144	G. F. Upham
93	T. Jefferson Coolidge	145	Nathan Matthews
94	William C. Fay		Albert Matthews
95	Sidney Bartlett	146	George C. Richardson
96	Henry Lee	147	J. Randolph Coolidge
97	Francis Brooks		J. Randolph Coolidge, Jr.
98	T. Quincy Brown	148	John T. Coolidge, Jr.
99	Mahlon D. Spaulding	149	Mrs. S. H. Bullard
100	Henry S. Hovey	151	Mrs. George C. Lowell
101	Percival L. Everett	152	John L. Gardner
102	Mrs. Joseph Whitney	153	John T. Morse
103	Henry M. Clark		Charles J. Morse
104	James H. Beal	154	Peleg W. Chandler
105	Mrs. Edward B. Everett	155	Sewall H. Fessenden
106	George M. Barnard	156	H. P. Arnold
107	F. W. Bradlee	157	Thomas Goddard
108	John T. Coolidge		Mrs. Anne Campbell
109	Richard H. Weld	158	E. A. Boardman
110	Mrs. W. J. Niles	159	Francis C. Lowell
111	Mrs. Eben Dale	161	John Homans, M. D.
	Charles D. Temple	163	Roger N. Allen
	Mrs. Mary N. Temple	165	Mrs. Southworth Shaw
112	Augustus T. Perkins		Frank A. Shaw
113	J. T. Bradlee	166	George O. Shattuck
	J. R. Bradlee	167	Charles A. Welch
114	John T. Coolidge, Jr.	168	Robert M. Cushing
115	Miss E. Collamore	169	A. B. Wilbor, M. D.
	Miss H. Collamore	170	Mrs. John P. Cushing
116	Samuel Hammond	171	Joseph B. Moors
117	Mrs. J. B. Silsbee		A. W. Moors
	Arthur B. Silsbee		John F. Moors
118	R. Lockwood		Francis J. Moors
120	Benjamin C. Boardman	172	Mrs. Richard S. Fay
121	Mrs. J. M. Waldron	173	Mrs. J. Willard Peele
	Mrs. H. L. Hawes	175	Richard T. Parker
	Miss F. R. Hawes	176	John C. Gray
	J. W. Hawes	177	Henry C. Weston
	Philip Winn	178	William G. Russell
	Clarence W. Barron		Thomas Russell
	Mrs. J. H. Bradley	179	Alfred B. Hall
	Miss Grace A. Bradley	180	Mrs. Benjamin T. Reed
	Mrs. Maria S. Porter	181	Arthur J. Parsons
122	Fredrick R. Sears, Jr.	184	Lucius M. Sargent
124	Mrs. Charles Stoddard	185	John F. Anderson
125	William P. Sargent		Edward H. Leighton
126	John Jeffries		Mrs. James Tays
	Walter L. Jeffries	186	George P. Gardner
	William A. Jeffries	187	F. W. Andrews

188	E. Wigglesworth, M. D.
189	Miss Mary L. Bangs
	Miss Fanny Bangs
190	Frederick H. Prince
191	Mrs. Alice Thayer
192	Charles S. Storrow
193	James H. Blake
194	George Von L. Meyer
195	Nathaniel W. Curtis
	Hamilton R. Curtis
197	John W. Brigham
	Arthur F. Brigham
198	Mrs. R. S. Prescott
199	James T. Eldredge
200	Francis Skinner
201	George H. Warren
202	William Perkins
203	Francis W. Hunnewell
204	Mrs. Harvey Jewell
	George Sanger, Jr.
205	William C. Rogers
206	George M. Browne
208	Francis Braggiotti
	Isidor Braggiotti
210	Mrs. N. D. Hubbard
	Gorham Hubbard
211	John T. Ellis
	Augustus H. Ellis
	Mrs. F. Josceylon
212	William R. Robeson
213	Chase Langmaid
	Charles Kenney
214	William B. Clarke
215	Henry C. Hutchins
	Mrs. Julia Hale
217	Charles Davis, Jr.
	Mrs. W. Freeland
218	Mrs. Alanson Tucker
219	George Mixter
	Mrs. William Mixter
220	Aaron H. Allen
221	Mrs. Charles L. Thayer
	Lowell L. T. Field
222	Waldo Adams
223	Mrs. John R. Blake
	Frank Dumaresq
224	W. W. Eastham
225	Miss E. M. Iasigi
226	Jacob M. Haskell
227	Dudley B. Fay
228	Nathaniel D. Turner
229	Charles F. Shimmin
230	Francis Peabody
231	Charles Head
232	Joseph S. Lovering
233	Mrs. Thomas Brewer
234	George B. Chase
235	Thomas Dwight, M. D.
236	Francis Bartlett
237	Francis A. Walker
238	J. H. Walcott
239	Prof. Henry W. Haynes
240	Edward Bangs
241	Mrs. Julia Ward Howe
	Miss Maud Howe
242	Charles P. Hemenway
243	George C. Davis
244	T. D. Boardman
245	Joseph A. Iasigi
247	Robert H. Bancroft
249	Henry W. Pickering
	Henry G. Pickering
251	Pierre C. Severance
252	Prof. Bennet H. Nash
	Miss Abbie Tuxbury
253	George L. Deblois
254	Francis L. Lee
255	Francis W. Palfrey
	John H. Lee
256	Carleton H. Lee
258	Mrs. S. Frothingham
260	Mrs. Charles Mifflin
263	Eben. D. Jordan, Jr.
264	Nathaniel Hooper
	John F. Hooper
	Arthur W. Hooper
	A. G. Bowles
267	Edward Frothingham
269	Henry H. Brown
270	Charles A. Whittier
271	L. Cushing Kimball
273	George F. Putnam
274	F. L. Higginson
275	Charles E. Powers
276	J. S. Allen
277	John Goldthwait
	Charles B. Goldthwait
	Samuel Davis
279	Robert Amory, M. D.
280	John W. Shepard
281	Miss Caroline Bartlett
	Miss Mary H. Bartlett
282	Caleb A. Curtis
284	William F. Matchett
286	S. F. Robinson
287	Henry K. Horton
288	Daniel C. Holder
289	William Rotch
290	Mrs. Thomas E. Chickering
	Gordon Prince
291	Daniel H. Lane
292	Joseph L. Stackpole
293	Edward Gray
294	William Bacon, Jr.
296	Oliver Wendell Holmes, M. D.
298	Lewis S. Dabney
300	Edward Burgess
301	George E. Niles
302	William D. Howells
	Mrs. H. A. Bridge
303	John H. Rogers
304	Charles E. Fuller
305	William A. Rust
306	John E. Atkins
307	Miss M. E. Torrey
	Miss F. T. Sturgis
308	David Hunt
	William D. Hunt
309	Henry M. Rogers
310	Joshua B. Richmond
	B. Ruberia
311	Frederick O. Prince
312	Edward B. Haven
313	F. R. Thomas
314	Mrs. G. F. Williams
	Robert W. Williams
315	Edwin A. Hills
316	George M. Dana
317	William B. Kehew
318	Mrs. H. A. Hildreth
	Mrs. Elizabeth Welch
319	Elliott W. Pratt
320	Charles J. Whitmore
321	William N. Mills

321	William H. Mills
322	Robert D. Evans
323	Walter I. Bigelow
325	Augustus N. Loring
327	T. E. Proctor
328	Henry H. Fay
330	Mrs. F. A. Hall
331	Walter Dabney
332	David L. Webster
	Augustus F. Webster
333	Robert B. Forbes
334	Franklin W. Smith
335	H. L. Dalton
336	Edwin Morey
	Walter G. Morey
338	Henry Stackpole
339	Nathaniel W. Pierce
340	Mrs. Sarah Washburn
341	Charles W. Leonard
342	Daniel C. Knowlton
343	George H. Norman
	Mrs. Rufus B. Kinsley
344	Lucien Carr
345	Elwell Parks
	Charles F. Allen
347	James W. Converse
	Isaac W. Chick
351	George D. Oxnard
353	Mrs. John Tyler
	Mrs. Addie Hawes
	Mrs. Mary Foote
354	William W. Vaughan
355	Mrs. George Bancroft
356	Francis H. Manning
357	Henry R. Dalton
361	Thomas K. Cummins
	Thomas K. Cummins, Jr.
365	William F. Johnson
377	Charles F. Morse
	G. M. Randall Morse
379	Isaac B. Mills
	Isaac B. Mills, Jr.
	James C. Mills
381	George Hayward, M. D.
383	Mrs. James A. Roberts
386	Henry J. Barnes, M. D.
387	Charles B. Perkins
388	William J. Cutler
389	Ellis L. Motte
390	Howard Stockton
391	Mrs. Mary S. Langley
	Miss A. D. Williams
392	Stephen R. Niles
393	Mrs. C. T. Randall
394	Calvin A. Richards
395	George H. Thayer
396	Albert O. Smith
397	W. K. Blodgett
398	Elijah B. Phillips
	Cyrus A. Page
400	M. H. Griffith
401	Charles H. Andrews
403	James R. Gregerson
405	Samuel Jackson, M. D.
407	Miss A. B. Henshaw
	Miss Laura Henshaw
409	Matthew Bolles
411	Mrs. Roxanna Dabney
413	H. C. Wainwright
415	Miss Annie W. Davis
	Mrs. Ellen Read
417	J. J. Storrow
421	Robert Lilly
423	John M. Washburn
425	Linus M. Child
429	Rev. Wm. C. Winslow
431	Samuel H. Savage
	Henry Savage
433	Ira L. Moore, M. D.
435	J. Brooks Young
	Harrison B. Young
443	Jarvis D. Braman
	Dwight Braman
445	Peter Duvernet
449	Oliver L. Briggs

Boylston Street. (From Wash'n to Back Bay Park). Boylston st. is rapidly becoming a business street; hotels, schools, and stores having already threatened the residences well towards Berkeley st. If but a few months' time has been sufficient to wholly change the character of this street from Park sq. to Church st., what may not be expected to take place during the next few years? Business is fast working Back Bay-ward, rather than South End-ward; Columbus av. is being rapidly converted into a street of manufactories; and altogether it looks very much as if dwelling-houses were to be pushed farther back year by year. The once fashionable character of a portion of Boylston st. has almost departed, and many of its former residents have sought homes elsewhere. Hotels on this street are as follows: Berkeley (158), Boylston (26), Bristol (231), Brunswick (198), Cluny (233), Kensington (291), Pelham (34), Puritan (29), Thorndike (91), Vivian (283), Vercelli Italian Restaurant (87). Schools: Berkeley, Boston School of Elocution, Chauncy Hall School, French's Commercial School, Institute of Technology, etc. As will be seen by the following list of residents, many of the houses are now occupied by physicians:

113	Henry I. Bowditch, M. D.
	V. S. Bowditch, M. D.
114	Miss Lucy Ellis
115	A. P. Lighthill, M. D.
	Wm. H. L. Briard, M. D.
116	Henry O. Marcy, M. D.
117	Mrs. E. Manton
118	V. C. Pond, M. D.
	M. E. Webb, M. D.
	H. P. Bellows, M. D.
	Miss Mary W. Lincoln
	Miss Mary Willard
	Miss Edith L. Chase
	F. Stanhope Hill
119	Mrs. John W. James
	Henry W. Daniell
	Miss Maria Daniell
120	George Babson
	Frank B. Babson
121	G. H. Lyman, M. D.
122	George T. Hawley
123	George F. Jelly, M. D.
124	George W. Sears
	Henry C. Sears
	Charles Overman
	Miss Ellen Beal
	Miss Eliza Beal

124	Thomas Lovell	167	W. H. Bowman, M. D.
125	William J. Clark		Tyler B. King
126	J. D. W. Joy		E. Stanton
	Frank L. Joy		J. E. Stanton, M. D.
127	Francis S. Watson, M. D.		Frederick W. Stanton
	William N. Bullard, M. D.		George E. Wilder
	Michael C. Shields		A. W. Spencer
128	Richard M. Matthews		O. D. Witherell
	Prosper Bender, M. D.		Frank H. Briggs
129	S. W. Langmaid, M. D.		G. S. Reed, M. D.
130	Francis A. Brooks		George B. Bodwell
131	Frederick I. Knight, M. D.		John M. Welch
132	D. M. Parker, M. D.		Mrs. Herbert Beach
	Charles E. Dearborn		Miss C. S. Eaton
	Jere. E. Stanton, M. D.		Miss L. H. Eaton
133	Samuel G. Webber, M. D.		Oliver Stevens
	George E. Newton		Frank H. Jenney
134	T. M. Dillingham, M. D.		Joseph T. Brown, Jr.
	Thomas Fillebrown, M. D.		William G. Preston
	William H. Kehew		John B. Osborne
	Miss Elene B. Kehew		Mrs. A. H. Nelson
	Gen. Robert Dalton		Mrs. James Simonet
135	Mrs. Mary A. Haradon		Ambrose Eastman
136	Edward S. Niles, M. D.		Joseph T. Brown, Sr.
	A. L. Kennedy, M. D.		Mrs. J. H. Patterson
	G. R. Southwick, M. D.		Dwight F. Boyden
137	James E. Dodd		Mrs. E. E. Boyden
	Arthur H. Dodd		Mrs. E. W. Weston
	Perham H. Dodd		Miss Charlotte W. Hawes
138	A. N. Blodgett, M. D.		Joseph B. Spiller
139	O. F. Wadsworth, M. D.		Miss M. D. Stowe
140	Edward A. White		Mrs. H. W. Warren
141	Mrs. Harvey D. Parker		Henry D. Warren
142	Charles S. Bartlett, M. D.		Miss C. L. Fairbanks
143	Mrs. F. E. Stevens		Miss Kate Fairbanks
	George H. Monks, M. D.		Mrs. L. L. Burns
	H. W. Cushing, M. D.		Miss Cora Burns
144	Charles L. Austin		Mrs. Edward P. Parker
145	Jacob Pfaff		Miss Sarah J. Brown
	Charles Pfaff		Miss F. C. Batcheller
	Mrs. Adrianne White		Miss Sarah H. Hooker
146	Thomas Waterman, M. D.		Miss Sarah Dunn
	Claude L. Kettle		H. R. Gardner
	Robert Tabraham		A. D. Barnes
147	George Flagg		Miss A. P. Andrews
148	W. H. Carpenter, M. D.		Miss E. L. Andrews
	Alzaman Sawyer, M. D.		Miss Ellen Andrews
	Mrs. E. J. Winslow		Mrs. Abbie Hooper
149	David Hunt, M. D.		Miss L. R. Staniford
151	William Quirin		W. I. Howell
153	Joseph M. Gibbens		Joshua Nye
	Edward E. Pope		Miss A. L. Sturtevant
155	Samuel Wells		Mrs. E. M. Francis
157	Mrs. E. H. Winslow		Mrs. E. L. Lincoln
	Edward Winslow		Sterling Colby
	Mrs. H. Winslow		Richard Clark
159	Henry L. Shaw, M. D.		Mrs. H. J. Davis
	Frederick L. Jack, M. D.		J. P. Oliver, M. D.
	Edwin Everett Jack		E. H. Bradford, M. D.
	Lafayette Jack		William L. Edwards
161	F. Gordon Morrill, M. D.		Edward W. Dale
163	William Pitkin		Herbert Radclyffe
	Charles Pitkin	178	Isaac Cruft
165	Leslie A. Phillips, M. D.	180	Miss H. O. Cruft
	Homer Albers		Miss A. P. Cruft
167	HOTEL BERKELEY:	182	D. H. Storer, M. D.
	Hon. Charles Allen		Prof. F. H. Storer
	John R. Hall		Robert W. Storer
	William H. Hall		Malcolm Storer
	Mrs. A. Bigelow		Miss A. M. Storer
	J. R. Cummings, M. D.		Miss M. G. Storer
	Miss H. S. Ware	184	R. H. White

186 ....Luther A. Wright	196 ....T. A. Hall
188 ....Mrs. John G. Webster	....................Charles L. Butler
190 ....Mrs. C. M. Richardson	........................C. S. Butler
............Miss Sarah Richardson	........................G. L. Goodwin
192 ....Gedney K. Richardson	........................E. Robinson
194 ....Charles A. Browning	........................J. W. Bowen
196 HOTEL BRUNSWICK	....................Mrs. James Bowen
....................H. H. Atkins	........................Miss Bowen
................Miss Emma J. Fitz	....................Miss H. K. Bayley
....................E. C. Fitz	....................Mrs. Wales Tucker
................Mrs. M. Bartlett	....................Miss H. Raymond
................Misses Bartlett	........................C. B. Raymond
....................G. W. Terrill	........................E. C. Briggs
....................R. S. Covell	....................W. A. Haskell
................George E. Downes	....................Coburn Haskell
....................Misses Davis	....................Mrs. H. M. Carney
....................E. L. Davis	....................Miss Carney
................Maturin M. Ballou	....................M. S. Crehore
................Mrs. Frederick Almy	....................Lawrence Barr
....................C. C. Gilbert	........................G. R. Barrett
....................A. Lawrence	....................Mrs. T. M. Holmes
....................F. W. Emery	....................Mrs. Dexter Clapp
....................W. B. Thomas	....................Miss Brownlow
................Philip C. Lockwood	....................Miss E. K. Bates
................Miss Jennie Lockwood	....................Mrs. D. H. Hayden
....................G. L. Thayer	....................Misses Ward
................Miss M. J. Eaton	....................George F. Godfrey
................Miss C. J. Robinson	....................James Schouler
................Mrs. Alexander Strong	....................Miss T. E. Holmes
................Miss H. M. Robinson	....................Miss E. T. Holmes
................J. L. Williams, M. D.	....................Miss Mary Bigelow
....................O. J. Lewis	....................James C. Barr
....................G. H. Peters	....................H. Davenport
................Miss E. W. Peters	....................Mrs. J. C. Putnam
................Mrs. J. P. Bayley	....................Amos Barnes
....................H. H. Mawhinney	....................Frederick Barnes
................Miss Mawhinney	....................Herbert H Barnes
....................W. A. Hall	....................J. W. Dunklee
................Mrs. S. H. Bertram	....................Miss Dunklee
................Joseph L. Richards	....................M. P. Robinson
....................N. H. Cotton	....................John H. McCue
................Mrs. J. F. Bumstead	....................Mrs. Edward Harris
................Willis Bumstead	....................Misses Harris
................Mrs. F. B. White	....................Mrs. J. H. Chace
................Mrs. Andrew L. Bates	....................J. Mason
....................G. B. Du Bois	....................A. L. Hollingsworth
....................R. M. Pulsifer	....................William Ware
................George P. Messervy	....................Charles L. Smith
....................W. A. Shields	....................Miss F. Addicks
....................J. E. Addicks	....................Miss E. A. Goodwin
................Mrs. C. H. Pickman	....................Mrs. G. Granger
....................Miss Head	....................Misses Granger
................Miss M. W. Head	....................George H. Chickering
....................J. P. Ellicott	....................Mrs. H. M. Kent
................Miss Josephine Ellicott	HOTEL BRISTOL:
....................E. R. Hunnewell	....................Levi Tower, Jr.
....................Miss Linzee	....................Samuel F. Ham, M. D.
................T. J. Alexander	....................Dwight Whiting
....................C. H. Fiske	....................Mrs. Rebecca Whiting
................Richard G. Haskell	....................Mrs. Orlando Tompkins
................Charles A. Vialle	....................Arthur G. Tompkins
....................C. H. Venner	....................William W. Warren
................Mrs. Charles B. Whiting	....................Mrs. Eleanor Bennett
....................Misses Sturdevant	....................Miss C. I. Wilby
....................T. M. Drown	....................William D. Thayer
....................Lyman P. French	....................Henry M. Aiken
................Mrs. R. A. Sturdevant	....................Joshua Bates
....................H. R. Dalton	....................Frank C. Bates
....................Alfred W. Fitz	....................Thomas H. Chandler, M. D.
....................Mrs. Downes	....................T. O. Loveland, M. D.
....................Miss Downes	....................Miss S. E. Bingham
....................Henry Hall	....................J. Augustus Felt

HOTEL BRISTOL:
......................Matthew Crosby
......................William Tebbetts
......................Albert W. Bliss
......................George Albree
......................Mrs. A. B. Swaim
......................Moses B. Wildes
......................Fred B. Wildes
......................Miss E. G. Wildes
......................Miss Marion R. Wildes
......................Miss K. R. Wildes
......................Alfred Hill
......................Mrs. M. E. Hayden
......................Mrs. Josiah Bacon
......................Prof. C. W. Holman
229 HOTEL CLUNY:
......................George R. Fisk
......................Frank W. Page, M. D.
......................Wm. H. H. Newman
......................Joshua K. Bigelow
......................Charles E. Bigelow
......................Channing Lilly
......................Alexander Moseley
......................Miss E. F. Moseley
......................Miss E. C. Jewett
......................Miss M. D. Whitney
......................Charles S. Eaton
......................Robert F. Straine
......................Lewis W. Tappan
......................Mrs. M. A. H. Ayer
......................Grace Walker, M. D.
......................L. V. Ingraham, M. D.
235 ....Samuel C. Cobb
......................G. Arthur Hilton
237 ....M. L. Chamberlain, M. D.
239 ....D. W. Cheever, M. D.
241 ....Solomon Lincoln
243 ....Samuel B. Hopkins
261 ....John C. Balderston
263 ....D. Webster King
265 ....Samuel A. Carlton
283 HOTEL VIVIAN:
......................Mrs. E. A. Bowman
......................H. V. Dillenback
......................Joseph Ness
......................Dr. T. S. Very
291 THE KENSINGTON:
......................Andrew G. Greeley
......................Gardner C. Hawkins
......................Alexander Henderson
......................Edward Henderson
......................Benjamin Hosford
......................John Little
......................Mrs. J. H. Towne
......................S. B. Whittemore
......................Henry B. Williams
399 ....Charles Harrington, M. D.
401 ....Mrs. Nathaniel Hooper
......................Horace N. Hooper
......................Arthur Hooper
......................C. W. Romney

Commonwealth Avenue Residents. (From 12 Arlington st. to Brookline av.) Following are the names of those residing on the street that *Harper's Weekly* has termed the most magnificent avenue in America: (Hotels: Agassiz, (191) Vendome (166).)
1 ....Mrs. James S. Amory
......................Frederick Amory
......................Harcourt Amory

2 ....James L. Little
......................Arthur Little
......................Mrs. Grace A. Oliver
3 ....Mrs. Annie B. Rotch
......................Arthur Rotch
......................Abbott L. Rotch
4 ....John L. Manning
5 ....Abbott Lawrence
......................William P. Lawrence
6 ....William G. Weld
7 ....Samuel Johnson
......................Wolcott H. Johnson
......................Arthur S. Johnson
8 ....Mrs. E. B. Bigelow
9 ....Mrs. Otis Norcross
......................Miss Laura Norcross
......................Miss Nellie Stevens
10 ....R. M. Pomeroy
......................Daniel Ahl, Jr.
11 ....Mrs. Henry W. Abbott
......................Miss L. W. Abbott
......................Henry W. Abbott
12 ....Thomas Allen
13 ....Frederick H. Bradley
14 ....Mrs. J. H. Wright
......................Lyman Nichols
15 ....William D. Pickman
16 ....Charles Woodbury
......................Albert R. Whittier
17 ....William M. Hilton
18 ....Charles H. Dorr
......................George B. Dorr
19 ....Thomas C. Amory
20 ....Charles P. Curtis
......................Charles P. Curtis, Jr.
21 ....Mrs. John A. Burnham
......................Henry D. Burnham
......................Charles Frye
22 ....Edward Motley
......................Edward P. Motley
......................Miss Jessie Motley
23 ....Eugene V. R. Thayer
24 ....Samuel G. Snelling
......................Rodman H. Snelling
......................John L. Snelling
26 ....Henry Saltonstall
27 ....Thornton K. Lothrop
28 ....H. H. A. Beach, M. D.
29 ....Mrs. N. I. Bowditch
30 ....Mrs. Jonas Fitch
......................John Wallace
31 ....Joseph Sawyer
......................Walter L. Sawyer
32 ....L. Miles Standish
......................Miss Addie Standish
33 ....Charles H. Dalton
34 ....Miss Susan E. Dorr
35 ....Charles Marsh
......................Miss Mabel M. Marsh
36 ....Mlle. G. de la Motte
37 ....Elisha Atkins
40 ....Isaac D. Farnsworth
......................John Revere
41 ....William H. Horton
42 ....Jonathan French
......................J. D. W. French
43 ....Irving O. Whiting
......................Daniel G. Grafton
44 ....Royal E. Robbins
......................Miss Fannie Horton
45 ....Charles G. Patterson
......................Miss Kate W. Kirby

46	Frank M. Ames	117	Charles M. Baker
	Miss Alice M. Ames		Ezra H. Baker, Jr.
	Oakes Ames	118	Mrs. William H. Harding
47	Joseph Peabody	119	Samuel N. Brown
48	David P. Kimball		Miss Grace H. Haskell
49	Charles Torrey	120	James B. Case
	Harry B. Torrey	121	Joseph N. Fiske
50	John Hogg	122	Richards Bradley
	Robert W. Hogg		Richards M. Bradley
	C. P. Searle		J. Dorr Bradley
51	George A. Gardner	123	George H. Perkins
52	Edward I. Brown	124	E. P. Bradbury, M. D.
	Frank B. Brown		H. F. Hamilton, M. D.
	Miss Harriet T. Brown		J. S. Mason, M. D.
54	John C. Sharp	125	Joseph H. Gray
	John C. Sharp, Jr.	126	Elias Merwin
	Arthur R. Sharp	127	Mrs George L. Pratt
55	Joseph T. Bailey		Miss L. S. Pratt
	Walter B. Ellis	128	Col. Jonas H. French
56	W. Arnold Buffum		Miss Fanny French
57	John A. Burnham, Jr.		Harry G. French
58	Lyman Hollingsworth	129	Mrs. F. C. Manning
59	Amory A. Lawrence		Miss Abby Manning
60	George Allen		Miss Annie Manning
62	William S. Eaton	130	Edmund H. Bennett
	William S. Eaton, Jr.		Samuel C. Bennett
63	Mrs. J. M. Warren	131	Gideon Scull
	Miss Annie C. Warren	133	William F. Wharton
64	Charles W. Pierce	135	Francis Jaques
	George A. Pierce	144	William Atherton
	Rev. A. Lee Holmes	146	Stephen E. Westcott
65	Charles Rollins	148	Mrs. Franklin L. Fay
	Charles H. Rollins		A. W. Hobart
	Henry A. Lewis	150	Orlando W. Doe, M. D.
66	Joseph W. Clark	151	Robert G. Shaw
	Charles Van Brunt	152	Mrs. Richard Baker
68	D. R. Whitney		Richard Baker
70	W. W. Blackmar	161	John D. Bates
72	J. R. Brewer	163	William A. Tower
	Frank Brewer	165	George B. Clapp
74	Mrs. Isaac Butters	167	E. R. Morse
	George P. Butters	169	Joseph S. Fay, Jr.
	William H. Butters	171	Augustus Lowell
	Mrs. W. B. Cobb		Percival L. Lowell
76	Allen M. Sumner, M. D.	173	Roger Wolcott
78	William A. Prescott	175	Charles Merriam
80	William Duff		HOTEL VENDOME:
82	Edward Page		Mrs. George E. Adams
84	Mrs. Theresa A. Dodge		E. D. Bangs
	Miss Theresa B. Dodge		Mrs. E. D. Bangs
86	Mrs. William Thomas		L. Bassett
88	Mrs. H. Keyes		Mrs. L. Bassett
	H. W. Keyes		Miss Bassett
	Mrs. I. F. Keyes		Miss M. J. C. Becket
	Miss M. G. Keyes		Wesley Bigelow
90	Nathaniel Walker		G. W. T. Braman
	Grant Walker		Mrs. G. W. T. Braman
107	J. Murray Forbes		Misses Braman
109	Caspar Crowninshield		Mrs. William M. Bremer
111	Henry Whitwell		John F. Brooks
	S. H. Whitwell		Misses Brooks
113	Jacob H. Hecht		Miss Abby C. Brown
	Louis Hecht		Miss Rebecca W. Brown
114	David H. Coolidge		I. W. Brown
	Charles A. Coolidge		Mrs. I. W. Brown
	David H. Coolidge, Jr.		James F. Brown
	Miss Isa Coolidge		G. I. F. Bryant
115	Mrs. William F. Weld		Miss Burt
	Miss M. M. Weld		S. Cabot
	George W. Weld		Mrs. S. Cabot
116	Mrs. H. L. Daggett		James A. Campbell
117	Ezra H. Baker		F. S. Chick

HOTEL VENDOME:
- Mrs. F. S. Chick
- H. A. Church, Jr.
- George D. Clapp
- Miss Mabel Clapp
- Mrs. E. P. Clark
- Ed. S. Clark
- Mrs. Ed. S. Clark
- John M. Clark
- George L. Clark
- E. S. Converse
- Mrs. E. S. Converse
- C. C. Converse
- Mrs. C. C. Converse
- H. E. Converse
- C. Coon
- Mrs. C. Coon
- Miss S. K. Cox
- S. W. Cummings
- Mrs. Frank Cutting
- Miss Cutting
- Henry L. Daggett
- Mrs. Henry L. Daggett
- Daniel Denny
- Mrs. Daniel Denny
- Clarence H. Denny
- Mrs. H. M. Dexter
- S. C. Dizer
- Mrs. S. C. Dizer
- I. F. Dobson
- Mrs. I. F. Dobson
- Miss C. B. Dobson
- Miss G. A. Dobson
- Miss I. K. Dwight
- W. Tracy Eustis
- George F. Farley
- George A. Furlow
- C. H. Fitch
- Mrs. C. H. Fitch
- Mrs. C. A. Goodnow
- Miss Goodnow
- Miss H. E. Goodnow
- R. B. Greene
- Mrs. R. B. Greene
- Miss Greene
- Miss Nellie Greene
- Henry Guild
- George S. Hall
- Mrs. George S. Hall
- Henry Hastings
- Henry Hastings, Jr.
- Misses Hastings
- D. W. Hitchcock
- Mrs. D. W. Hitchcock
- Lemuel C. Hitchcock
- Mrs. Charles W. Howard
- Miss Howard
- T. R. Hoyt
- E. C. Hoyt
- Mrs. E. C. Hoyt
- Joseph L. Keith
- Mrs. Joseph L. Keith
- Miss Keith
- H. W. Kimball
- George P. King
- Mrs. King 176
- I. W. Lefavour 177
- Mrs. I. W. Lefavour 178
- Mrs. Leland 179
- O. G. Lundell
- Mrs. O. G. Lundell 180
- Emil Marqueze 181

HOTEL VENDOME:
- Mrs. E. Marqueze
- Miss I. F. Marqueze
- Captain N. Maxwell
- Miss Mary McHugh
- H. R. Merrill
- Mrs. H. R. Merrill
- Mrs. Lansing Millis
- H. L. Millis
- Mrs. H. L. Millis
- H. F. Mills
- Mrs. H. F. Mills
- Mrs. E. W. Morton
- Galloupe Morton
- Gen. C. B. Norton
- B. F. Nourse
- Mrs. B. F. Nourse
- Miss Pomeroy
- Miss Porter
- W. Porter
- Mrs. W. Porter
- George A. Priest
- Mrs. George A. Priest
- Frank K. Priest
- E. E. Rice
- Mrs. E. E. Rice
- Charles F. Rice
- Arthur Richardson
- M. W. Richardson
- Mrs. M. W. Richardson
- C. H. Richardson
- W. I. Riley
- Mrs. W. I. Riley
- Mrs. E. C. Roberts
- Prof. Sanborn
- Mrs. Sanborn
- Miss Kate Sanborn
- S. B. Sargent
- I. P. Seliyer
- R. Sherburne
- Mrs. R. Sherburne
- Nelson Skillings
- Mrs. Nelson Skillings
- Charles F. Smith
- Mrs. Thomas C. Sullivan
- Miss Sullivan
- Mrs. E. B. Taylor
- W. L. Towey
- D. A. Varney
- Mrs. D. A. Varney
- Miss Varney
- Miss Bertha Von Hillern
- August Weil
- Mrs. August Weil
- D. Wheeler
- Mrs. D. Wheeler
- C. Whitney
- Mrs. C. Whitney
- Miss Whitney
- Miss Lillian Whiting
- E. R. Wiggin
- Mrs. E. R. Wiggin
- R. C. Wiggin
- B. C. Wright
- Mrs. B. C. Wright
- W. P. Wesselhoeft, M. D.
- John Quincy Adams
- James Bell, M. D.
- William L. Bradley
- Ross Coe
- J. M. Latter
- Charles C. Jackson

182	Oliver M. Wentworth	240	Col. Henry G. Parker
183	Frank Merriam	244	Asa P. Potter
190	Mortimer B. Mason	246	Charles Buffum
	Mrs. Sarah E. Mason		Walter N. Buffum
	Miss Sarah D. Mason	247	Uriel H. Crocker
191	HOTEL AGASSIZ.	248	William G. Means
	H. L. Higginson		James Means
	Charles Peirson	249	Charles U. Cotting
	Charles Fairchild		Charles E. Cotting
	Miss E. G. Parker	250	John H. Hubbell
	Lewis H. Parker		Miss C. Dana
	William Houghton	251	Joseph S. Bigelow
	Clement Houghton	252	George H. Richardson
	Miss Lizzie Houghton		George O. Richardson
	A. L. Coolidge		Jeffrey Richardson
	Edward Jackson	253	N. B. Mansfield
	Miss Ellen Jackson	254	Mrs. Susan G. Page
	Miss Lucy L. Russell	255	Miss E. L. Borland
	Miss Adeline L. Jones	256	Fred A. Haserick
	Miss Ellen M. Jones		Arthur A. Haserick
192	Frank B. Fay	258	Charles C. Poor
196	Mrs. Daniel N. Spooner	260	John O. Poor
	Miss Nellie Spooner	261	Walter Hunnewell
	Miss May Spooner	262	Charles H. Dill
197	T. M. Rotch, M. D.		Miss Annie A. Dill
198	William Matthews, Jr.	263	Charles T. Lovering
	Frank H. Matthews	264	Mrs. John S. Hitchcock
	William A. Matthews		Miss F. E. Hitchcock
	Edward C. Matthews	265	Frank H. Appleton
200	Mrs. John J. French		Mrs. Sewall Tappan
	Frederick W. French	266	J. Reed Whipple
202	Mrs. C. E. Stratton	267	Mrs. Charles Boyden
	Charles E. Stratton	269	Thomas Mack
	Nathaniel Wales	278	William Emerson Baker
203	Leopold Morse		Edward F. Baker
	Godfrey Morse		Walter F. Baker
205	Samuel E. Peabody		Mrs. C. A. Baker
206	Mrs. Dennis F. Flagg	284	Mrs. S. R. Mead
207	Winthrop H. Sargent	286	Edwin L. Sanborn
211	William P. Mason	288	Alfred H. Batcheller
	Miss Fannie Mason		Francis Batcheller
212	Benjamin W. Munroe		Robert Batcheller
213	Charles T. White		Alfred Batcheller
214	George H. Quincy	291	W. H. Allen
	Mrs. Caroline Sweetser		William L. Allen
215	John F. Andrew	294	John S. Day
216	Andrew Fisk		Stanton Day
218	George H. Mackay	296	Wallace F. Robinson
220	Robert C. Mackay	298	Thomas N. Hart
222	Benjamin F. Guild		C. W. Ernst
223	Charles E. Perkins		Frederick B. Taylor
	Robert F. Perkins	302	Samuel P. Mandell
224	Truman J. Doe		William D. Mandell
	Charles C. Doe		Miss Lydia W. Dutton
	Miss Nellie Doe		Miss Mary M. Dutton
	Miss May Doe	307	Mrs. Nathaniel Thayer
225	W. L. Richardson, M. D.	311	Thomas Dana
226	Charles M. Carter		William F. Dana
227	Mrs. Martha Bartlett	313	Warren D. Hobbs
	Miss Mary Bartlett	316	R. C. Flower, M. D.
	Miss Fannie Bartlett		Benjamin O. Flower
228	Charles W. Parker		J. S. Manfull
	Miss Mary Parker	317	Fletcher M. Abbott
229	Francis P. Sprague, M. D.	318	Edward O. Shepherd
230	B. W. Taggard	319	Uriel Crocker
	Henry Taggard	320	Edward A. Taft
235	George Wheatland, Jr.	321	Mrs. E. B. Kendall
	Philip B. Wheatland		Miss Alice L. Kendall
236	H. W. Wadleigh	322	William H. Sands
	William L. Alden	323	Horace Billings
238	Mrs. Sarah D. Wilson	324	Augustus P. Martin
	Miss Hattie McCarter	325	Mrs. M. Day Kimball

COM—HER 115

326	Lewis B. Bailey
327	Mrs. M. L. Hall
	George G. Hall
	Mrs. F. T. Hooper
	Miss S. M. Stetson
330	Benjamin Fitch
332	William Noble
	Arthur G. Noble
	Walter I. Noble
334	Frederic Warren
336	J. B. Lincoln
337	Thomas S. Nowell
	Willis Nowell
	George M. Nowell
338	George L. Damon
339	Henry S. Shaw
340	William V. Hutchins
	George H. Williams
341	Nehemiah W. Rice
342	James H. Payne, M. D.
	James H. Payne, Jr.
343	George G. Crocker
348	Arthur B. Gove
352	George F. Wood
353	Oliver Ames
354	Mrs. F. Smith
	J. G. Nickerson
356	A. B. Turner
358	D. B. Flint
378	Albert A. Pope
380	Henry D. Hyde

Exeter Street. (From 299 Beacon to Huntington av.) Here reside:
1	Edward A. Adams
3	Miss Abby W. May
	Miss E. G. May
5	George S. Hale
7	Miss C. C. Thomas
	Mrs. Delano Goddard
9	Miss E. Frothingham
11	S. A. B. Abbott
19	H. C. Haven, M. D.
	Rev. H. F. Allen
25	William Bliss
30	A. L. Thorndike

Fairfield Street. (From 345 Beacon st. to Boylston st.) Residents:
1	Mrs. E. A. Hinkley
	Holmes Hinkley
	Mrs. Preston West
3	Alfred P. Rockwell
5	Augustus L. Soule
7	Mrs. S. M. Stackpole
	William Stackpole
8	James Jackson
9	Horatio Bigelow
10	Charles White
12	Miss Georgina Lowell
16	John T. Morse, Jr.
20	Francis R. Allen
21	George P. King
22	Nathaniel Thayer
30	W. G. Saltonstall
31	Herbert L. Perry
32	Charles I. Thayer
33	A. D. W. French
34	A. H. Alden
35	Ferdinand Strauss
36	Mrs. Addie Wetmore

37	W. A. Foster
38	Edward Maynz
39	George W. Coleman
41	Mrs. L. T. Craigin
	Miss Maida Cragin
	George A. Cragin

Gloucester Street. (From 397 Beacon st., to Boylston st.) The following are the names of residents, with the numbers of their houses:
1	Frederick D. Hussey, M. D.
3	James H. Reed
4	W. P. Walley
5	William Winslow
6	Frederick Stone
7	Samuel T. Ames
8	Mrs. John A. Blanchard
9	Robert F. Clark
10	John Lathrop
11	John B. Swift, M. D.
12	Charles M. Reed
13	Arthur Lincoln
14	Francis C. Welch
15	Willard T. Sears
29	Mrs. J. M. Manning
30	Albert S. Bigelow
31	Mrs. Charles T. Ward
	John M. Ward
32	Frederick W. Payne, M. D.
33	Arthur W. Sawyer
34	Charles W. Smith
36	Thomas P. Beal
42	Clarence H. Poor
44	George M. Baker
46	Alexander Williams, Jr.,
48	George S. Forbush
	Mrs. A. C. Shipley
49	Mrs. William P. Grier
50	Edwin D. Hathaway
51	Robert C. Poor
52	Gordon E. Denison
	James G. Denison
	Mrs. Mary Denison
53	Alden E. Viles
55	Charles B. Edgerly
56	James M. Olmstead
	William H. Leatherbee

Hereford Street. (From 433 Beacon st., to Boylston st.) Here reside:
7	Arthur Hobart
9	Mrs. James Tolman
11	Miss Elizabeth Upton
13	Eben Dale
14	A. Forbes Freeman
15	James R. Bayley
	Edward B. Bayley
16	Miss E. Whitney
	Miss M. Whitney
17	Frank A. James
	Albert S. Woodworth
	Arthur V. Woodworth
18	Mrs. J. W. Chamberlin
	Mrs. John Bigelow
20	William C. Loring
27	James W. Preston
	George W. Preston
29	Mrs. T. B. Curtis
31	Edwin L. Sprague
35	Frank G. Macomber

46 HOTEL FRANCESCA.
..................John H. Dane
47 ....Walter R. Goodnow
49 ....F. B. Wentworth
51 ....George H. Tilton
52 HOTEL HERFORD.
..................George S. Priest
..................James F. McNeil
53 ....Moses Burlen

Huntington Avenue. (From Dartmouth st., Copley sq., to Tremont st). On this fine Avenue are located the Mechanics Building (containing the vast Mechanics' Hall, used for opera, oratorio, concerts, lectures, meetings, balls, fairs, dog-shows, exhibitions of hens, cats, etc., and for gatherings where great space is required), the Institute Fair Building (now owned by the Metropolitan Street Railway Company), the Hotel Copley, the Hotel Huntington, the Hotel Oxford, the Children's Hospital, Free Surgical Hospital for Women, etc. Residents are as follows:

1 ....F. R. Stoddard
..................Thomas L. Nelson
18 HOTEL COPLEY:
..................F. E. Allen
..................Alfred D. Heard
..................Peleg C. Chase
..................Mrs. E. M. Stevens
..................Arthur D. McClellan
..................Alfred T. Hartwell
..................William W. Palen
..................Frank A. Sawyer
..................Arthur S. Austin
..................A. H. Hayes, M. D.
..................Charles H. Ward
..................Augustus P. Loring
..................Miss Maud Hutcheson
..................Miss Mary Hutcheson
HOTEL HUNTINGTON:
..................Nathaniel N. Thayer
..................W. N. Hill
..................A. G. Weeks, Jr.
..................Edward L. Tead
..................Mary A. Smith, M. D.
..................Emma Culbertson, M. D.
..................Fred D. Flagg
..................R. S. Whitney
..................Mrs. S. S. Whitney
..................Albert I. Croll
..................J. A. Dresser, M. D.
..................Myron W. Joslin
..................John P. Woodbury
..................William P. Shreve
..................Eugene Tompkins
..................Abner J. Moody
..................Gardner S. Lamson
..................Mrs. Mary S. Lamson
..................Warren Sawyer
..................Eugene B. Abbott
..................Miss M. J. Jackson
..................Mrs. J. C. Hoyt
..................Miss H. Jackson
..................Frank E. Simpson
..................Mrs. H. C. Hasbrooke
HOTEL OXFORD:
..................H. E. Woodward
..................Henry Waterman
..................James Bogle

HOTEL OXFORD:
..................Harry M. Howe
..................Daniel Lothrop
..................William T. Brigham
..................Mrs. William Brigham
..................Miss Gertrude Franklin
..................Mrs. M. E. Beattie
..................Dr. Gibbs
..................Mrs. C. B. Sawyer
..................Mrs. Sarah M. Eldredge
..................Isaac H. Bromley
..................Samuel W. Clifford
..................Samuel W. Clifford, Jr.
..................Fisher Howe, Jr.
..................Mrs. M. Merrill
..................Mrs. Eben C. Stanwood
..................Mrs. M. L. Horton
..................F. E. Boden
..................Mrs. D. A. Sheldon
..................Mrs. T. E. Warden
..................Walter B. Adams
..................W. Lincoln Sage
..................Henry B. Jackson
..................Miss I. Colby
..................Mrs. Richard Arnold
..................Charles E. Grinnell
..................Mrs. S. C. Osborne
..................L. V. S. Peck
..................Mrs. M. Peck
..................Charles P. Hall
..................L. C. Briggs
..................Miss McCate
..................E. C. Sherburne
..................Henry A. Thomas
..................F. A. Swallow
..................F. B. Swallow
..................Sidney Clementson
..................Charles O. Stearns
..................Miss Swett
..................William M. Thompson
..................Rev. T. R. Lambert
..................William T. Lambert
..................L. B. Greenleaf
..................F. W. Nickerson
..................Lyman W. Wheeler
..................Mrs. E. M. Kilvert
..................Mrs. M. E. York
..................Miss Anna York
..................Mrs. Gershom Cox
..................Miss M. T. Washburn
..................Miss Lucy Washburn
..................Edward H. Hastings
..................B. O. Kinnear, M. D.
..................C. M. Caverly
..................J. H. Hasbrouck
..................Mrs. Lucy C. Mitchell
..................Frank W. Adams
..................Mrs. John MacMahon
..................Mrs. Israel
..................Louis P. Roberts
..................D. T. Timayenis
..................W. C. Thairlwall
..................William B. Tilton
..................Mrs. L. B. Robinson
..................Miss Robinson
..................George B. Bigelow
..................John D. Sargent
..................E. H. Sampson
..................Rev. J. W. Olmstead
..................William Thornton, M. D.
..................Mrs. M. B. Wood
..................Mrs. M. T. Vose

HOTEL OXFORD:
..................Mrs. M. C. Goddard
..................Miss Goddard
..................Mrs. A. G. Wason
..................Miss Susan Flowers
..................E. W. Wason
..................Hollis B. Page
..................Henry Guild
..................Miss Nellie Guild
..................H. F. Guild
..................W. H. Wade
..................Miss Wade
..................Mrs. F. M. Wainwright
..................Misses Wainwright
144 ....Mrs. C. W. Kimball
..................Charles A. Kimball
..................Walter Kimball
..................D. P. K. Loring
..................George Cutler
..................Charles F. Butler
..................Edwin E. Snow
150 ....W. G. Benedict
152 ....Mme. E. de Combes
154 ....Frederic C. Herrick

Marlborough Street. (Runs from 7 Arlington st. to West Chester Park st.,) on the Back Bay. Reached by either line (Clarendon st., or Vendome) line of Back Bay cars. On this street is located the Algonquin Club, at No.164, corner of Dartmouth st. Among the prominent persons residing on Marlborough st. are Hon. Robert C. Winthrop, Richard Olney, George L. Osgood, Dr. Isaac T. Talbot, Robert Grant, Rev. O. B. Frothingham, Thomas F. Cushing, Ex. Gov. William Gaston, and others. There are no Apartment Hotels on this street. The complete list of residents is as follows:

1 ....William T. Glidden
2 ....William R. Richards
..................Mrs. W. B. Richards
3 ....A. T. Cabot, M. D.
4 ....F. F. Patch, M. D.
5 ....Mrs. H. W. Sargent
7 ....J. S. Hooper
8 ....Lewis W. Tappan
9 ....Edward A. Kelly
10 ....George Wigglesworth
11 ....Henry P. Bliss
..................Henry W. Bliss
12 ....Samuel T. Morse
13 ....Henry A. Rice
14 ....Henshaw Walley
..................Bates Walley
15 ....Charles F. Folsom, M. D.
16 ....Albert H. Hoyt
17 ....George D. Howe
18 ....Miss A. D. Torrey
19 ....Causten Browne
..................Alexander P. Brown
20 ....Mrs. C. C. A. Linzee
..................John T. Linzee
21 ....L. N. Kettle
22 ....William Minot
..................Harry D. Minot
23 ....Mrs. J. C. Phillips
24 ....G. B. Shattuck, M. D.
25 ....John Foster
26 ....Rev. J. H. Morrison
27 ....Frederick L. Richardson
28 ....Benjamin S. Shaw, M. D.
29 ....Mrs. C. A. Johnson
30 ....Mrs. Henry F. Durant
31 ....James H. Freeland
32 ....Benjamin P. Cheney
33 ....Miss E. M. Pierce
..................Miss A. W. Lawrence
35 ....George A. Newell
..................Edward A. Newell
37 ....Miss Isabel Williams
..................Miss Susan Williams
39 ....Buckminster Brown, M. D.
41 ....Miss Annie E. Ticknor
53 ....E. W. Codman
57 ....William S. Dexter
..................George T. Dexter
59 ....Mrs. R. C. Hooper
..................F. H. Hooper, M. D.
..................Miss. I. R. Hooper
61 ....Matthew Luce
63 ....Charles P. Putnam, M. D.
..................J. J. Putnam, M. D.
65 ....Francis Minot, M. D.
66 ....Isaac T. Talbot, M. D.
67 ....Richard M. Hodges, M. D.
..................William D. Hodges, M. D.
68 ....Miss Mary L. Putnam
70 ....Robert Henry Eddy
71 ....Monton French, M. D.
72 ....Alexander S. Wheeler
..................Henry Weeeler
73 ....A. L. Lowell
74 ....Arthur G. Stanwood
75 ....John W. Eliot, M. D.
76 ....Robert T. Edes, M. D.
77 ....Charles B. Amory
78 ....Charles M. Green, M. D.
79 ....Mrs. E. R. Fitz
80 ....Edward J. Lowell
81 ....A. Coolidge, M. D.
..................Sidney Coolidge
..................A. Coolidge, Jr.
82 ....John M. Glidden
83 ....Mrs. Charles Armory, Jr.
85 ....George H. Mifflin
86 ....Charles H. Joy
87 ....Thomas Motley, Jr.
88 ....Mrs. Charles Jackson
89 ....Jacob C. Rogers
90 ....Robert C. Winthrop
91 ....Augustus Hemenway
92 ....Joseph B. Thomas, Jr.
103 ....Miss. C. L. Hill
..................Miss A. Hill
101 ....Robert Grant
..................Patrick Grant
105 ....Oliver W. Peabody
106 ....Mrs. Rufus Ellis
..................Arthur B. Ellis
107 ....William Watson
108 ....W. H. Gorham, M. D.
..................Charles H. Abbott, M. D.
109 ....Reuben E. Demmon
110 ....Rev. Geo. E. Ellis
111 ....Charles B. Barnes
112 ....Miss E. S. B. Danforth
..................Miss Mary S. Danforth
113 ....E. W. Hutchings
114 ....E. G. Cutler, M. D.
115 ....Robert Ferguson
116 ....Mrs. James B. Dow
117 ....Mrs. William B. Rogers

118	Rev. O. B. Frothingham
119	Nathaniel F. Tenney
	William P. Tenney
	Henry W. Tenney
120	Miss M. C. Mixter
121	Mrs. B. R. Curtis
	Allen Curtis
122	George H. Tilden, M. D.
123	Edward C. Johnson
124	Joseph C. Whitney
125	George Lewis
126	Brenton H. Dickson
127	Mrs. David Buck
	Henry H. Buck
128	Mrs. Calvin G. Page
	Hollis B. Page
129	Mrs. Oscar Iasigi
130	Avery Plummer
131	Thomas O. Richardson
133	Arthur Amory
134	Eugene Battelle
135	F. C. Shattuck, M. D.
136	Thomas E. Moseley
	Edward C. Moseley
140	Edmund H. Sears
	John Cullen
142	Joseph C. McKay
	Richard C. McKay
144	Edward L. Adams
146	J. Otis Wetherbee
148	Mrs. E. C. Sherman
163	Thomas F. Cushing
164	Algonquin Club
166	Herbert Dumaresq
167	Mrs. C. U. Gordon
168	Theodore Chase
169	Mrs. S. Parkman Shaw
170	Mrs. George Holden
171	George B. Upton
173	George S. Cushing
174	Samuel D. Warren, Jr.
175	G. Q. Thorndike
176	Miss Effie Ellis
177	William Gaston
	William A. Gaston
178	John V. Apthorp
179	Horatio G. Curtis
180	S. J. Mixter, M. D.
181	John L. Thorndike
182	Mrs. A. C. Knowlton
	Harry M. Knowlton
183	Frank W. Sargent
184	Charles D. Homans, M. D.
	George Homans
185	Edward S. Grew
188	J. J. Minot, M. D.
190	Russell Sturgis, M. D.
191	Edward Dwight
192	George H. Davenport
193	O. H. Sampson
	Charles E. Sampson
194	Mrs. J. L. Richardson
195	Frank W. Chandler
225	Harold Williams, M.D.
226	Clarence J. Blake, M. D.
	John H. Blake
227	Mrs. Charles R. Train
228	W. F. Whitney, M. D.
229	William I. Holmes
230	Fred. A. Whitwell
	Fred. S. Whitwell
231	Mrs. W. O. Taylor
	Fred. S. Taylor
232	John W. Cummings
233	W. E. Boardman, M. D.
234	A. F. Hervey
235	Samuel A. Hopkins, M. D.
236	Francis A. Osborn
237	Darwin E. Ware
238	John Parkinson
239	George Whitney
240	Mrs. N. Silsbee
	William E. Silsbee
241	Richard Olney
242	Joseph H. Meredith
244	Mrs. G. W. Simmons
	George W. Simmons
	Miss M. H. Simmons
245	George R. Minot
246	Emory K. Benson
247	Josiah Bradlee
249	Otis Norcross
250	Wilbur P. Parker, M. D.
	W. H. Rollins, M. D.
253	James F. Curtis
	Barnet C. Preston
	Frank G. Curtis
255	Robert S. Bradley
257	William Sines
259	James C. White, M. D.
	Donald E. White
	Perrin E. White
272	Nelson S. Bartlett
274	Edward L. Fuller
277	Edward W. Kinsley
279	Benjamin F. Smith
282	George H. Binney
284	W. H. H. Hastings, M. D.
285	Mrs. C. R. Anthony
	S. Reed Anthony
286	Charles C. Smith
287	James Means
288	E. W. Warren, M. D.
289	Mrs. Edward Gardner
	Edward G. Gardner
290	Lewis E. Jenks
291	Mrs. W. W. Goddard
	William Goddard
292	Charles S. Tuckerman
293	Edward W. Winslow
294	John H. Butler
295	J. Henry Sleeper
296	Samuel Carr, Jr.
297	William West
298	Loren G. Du Bois
299	William W. Greenough
300	John A. Remick
301	Mrs. T. J. Lee
303	William Dexter Smith
	Albert A. Smith
	Frank G. Smith
304	Horace Dupee, M. D.
306	George A. Sawyer
	Frederick Sawyer
308	Mrs. B. W. Thayer
	Henry B. Thayer
309	F. W. Freeborn
310	Mrs. L. Skinner
	Frederick Skinner
311	Edward E. Newell
	Otis K. Newell, M. D.
	Frederick E. Newell
312	Thomas S. Perry
313	James P. Safford
314	Mrs. E. F. Waters
315	Mrs. H. D. Thomas

#	Name
315	Miss E. D. Thomas
	J. B. Thomas
317	William B. Williams
319	Charles A. Rogers
	Alvin H. Rogers
320	W. H. Reynolds
321	William Minot, Jr.
322	Charles W. Seabury
	Frank Seabury
	William H. Seabury
323	Charles A. Morss
334	John E. Hudson
336	William G. Brooks
337	George M. Coburn
338	William A. Means
339	William L. Parker
340	Frederick A. Turner
341	Miss Susan M. Wells
342	Eben Sears
343	Solomon B. Stratton
344	Richard J. Monks
345	Edward T. Russell
346	Mrs. I. D. Hayward
347	Charles F. Dowse
348	Mrs. S. A. Heath
	John A. Heath
	Nathaniel Heath
349	Dr. G. A. Leland
350	Frank S. Sherburne
351	William S. Butler
352	Mrs. Alfred Rodman
353	J. C. Inches
354	Nathan Matthews
355	Mrs. Harriet Putnam
	Miss Ellen Putnam
356	Rev. Daniel P. Noyes
	Edward P. Noyes
357	George L. Osgood
358	Barrett Wendell
360	Mrs. W. S. Lincoln
	Mrs. F. U. Tracy
362	James B. Billings
	George B. Billings
364	Stephen M. Crosby
	Miss G. E. Hayden
365	Spencer W. Richardson
369	Edward R. Tyler
370	William C. Williamson
371	Elliott Russell
372	Frank H. Skinner
373	John L. Emmons
	George D. Wheeler
374	Albert E. Harding
375	Miss A. F. Odin
	Miss H. L. Odin
376	Miss A. D. Sever
377	Isaac T. Burr, Jr.
378	Francis B. Jones
379	S. A. Williams
380	L. L. Scaifo
	C. J. Sprague
	C. Sprague
381	Benjamin S. Calef
382	James M. Hubbard
383	Charles B. Southard
384	W. L. P. Boardman
385	Mrs. J. J. Clark
	Mrs. M. L. Mulliken
386	Charles E. Hubbard
387	Morton Dexter
388	Alexander P. Sears
389	Miss Augusta Brown
	Miss Louisa Brown

#	Name
391	Lemuel R. How
399	W. H. Rollins, M. D.

Newbury Street.

(Running from 15 Arlington st. to Brookline av.) On this street are the Massachusetts Bicycle Club Building, the Boston Art Club Building, the Hollis Church, Emmanuel Church, Hotel Harold, Prince School, Hintz Art School, the Wesselhoeft School, the First Spiritual Temple, the Normal Art School Building, etc.

#	Name
2	Mrs. Henry P. Kidder
	Nathaniel T. Kidder
	Charles A. Kidder
3	Joseph C. Stevens
5	Edwin Sheafe
6	George C. Shattuck, M. D.
8	J. N. Denison
9	Mrs. Minna Wesselhoeft
	Miss Selma Wesselhoeft
10	Benjamin French
11	Mrs. M. C. Dexter
	Conrad Reno
	Amos P. Tapley
12	John A. Dodd
13	G. W. A. Williams
14	Andrew G. Weeks
	Warren B. P. Weeks
16	Miss M. A. Carney
	Eugene H. Sampson
	Henry Wing
	William Marshall
18	Miss A. H. Johnson
20	William B. Byrnes
22	Frank T. Bemis
	Frank B. Bemis
26	Joshua D. Ball
27	Henry C. Snow
28	R. C. Greenleaf
29	Charles L. Flint
	Charles L. Flint, Jr.
31	Mrs. George C. Crehore
32	Edward A. Studey
	Cyrus B. Fuller
33	James Paul
34	Benjamin R. Curtis
35	Alexander D. Sinclair, M. D.
36	Nathaniel Knowles
38	Mrs. O. H. Badger
	Oliver H. Badger
40	Thomas T. Bouvé
42	George H. Leonard
44	Edward A. Dana
	Miss E. B. Hathaway
46	William C. Lovering
69	Mrs. Florence R. Hersey
71	H. W. Suter
73	Mrs. H. B. Mather
75	Charles W. Dexter
77	Miss E. L. Henshaw
79	Charles Carruth
81	Isaac Cushing
83	Constantine F. Hutchins
85	C. P. Wilson, M. D.
	E. E. Hopkins, M. D.
91	Benjamin B. Newhall
93	Henry S. Rowe
95	P. Francis Wells
	Benjamin W. Wells
97	Mrs. A. H. Bundy
	Wilfred C. French
99	Staples Potter

101	Charles C. Lauriat	216	Miss M. J. Aldrich
103	Edward Jewell		Henry H. Kelt
110	Henry A. Green	217	David C. Percival
	William L. Green	218	Mrs. Martin Hayes
112	Mrs. W. J. Hubbard	219	Mrs. W. D. Richards
113	George R. Shaw	220	Charles T. Carruth
114	Charles B. Gookin	221	Mrs. Samuel W. Luce
116	Timothy Remick	222	Cornelius Gray
	Hoffman Davidson		J. Converse Gray
118	Alphonso Ross	223	Mrs. James R. Hill
119	Charles J. Underwood		J. Edward Hill
	Charles J. Underwood, Jr.	225	George Willcomb
	William L. Underwood		George Morgan
	Francis L. Underwood	227	J. Dudley Richards
121	Stevens Palmer	228	Frederick A. Leigh
123	Nathan Morse	229	Warren B. Hopkins
125	William Beals	230	A. Pierce Green
127	C. A. W. Crosby	231	James B. Richardson
128	William B. Garrett	232	Francis G. Webster
129	Henry C. Richards	234	Samuel Watts
130	Henry A. Rogers	242	Benjamin H. Fabens
	William P. Brigham	244	Lewis J. Elkan
131	Edwin F. Waters	245	Herbert Nash
	Hazen Clement	246	John P. Rogers
132	F. H. Smith		William S. Rogers
133	Stephen G. Deblois	247	Andrew G. Webster
134	Wallace D. Dexter	248	Miss W. Bertha Hintz
135	Richard H. Stearns		Henry W. Nye
	Richard H. Stearns, Jr.	249	Charles W. Sargent
136	Francis Moseley		William C. Denney
	C. Alger Hawes	250	Miss Julia M. Dutton
137	James M. Shute		Mrs. Harriet Scudder
	Walter Shute		Miss Vida Scudder
138	John B. Bugbee	251	Miss R. A. Goddard
139	Alexander Williams		Matilda Goddard
	Robert Williams	252	W. M. Conant, M. D.
	Charles C. Williams	253	Prescott C. Hall
140	Samuel Smith		Clarence P. Hall
	Morrill A. Smith		Arthur C. Hall
	F. Langdon Smith	254	David K. Horton
141	Charles F. Perry	255	Mrs. J. B. Tilton
143	George F. Hall		Joseph B. Tilton
149	HOTEL AUBREY:	256	H. A. Royce
	George K. Guild		Francis T. Kimball
	G. M. Garland, M. D.	257	Edward H. Goff
	Thomas F. Patterson		Homer J. Goff
	Miss Marion F. Pelton	258	Lewis S. Dixon, M. D.
	Nathaniel W. Cumner		Rufus E. Dixon, M. D.
	Harry W. Cumner	259	Caleb Chase
153	Frank N. Lord	260	Mrs. George F. Williams
155	Henry Whittemore		A. T. Williams
162	Horace H. Coolidge	261	Charles S. Kendall
	Charles C. Coolidge		Dana W. Kimball
164	R. Gardner Chase	262	Thomas W. Emerson
	E. G. Chase	263	Walter D. Eaton
165	George Hayward, M. D.	264	Mrs. E. Metcalf
166	Joseph W. Hayden	265	Josiah H. Benton, Jr.
167	Stanley Cunningham	266	John S. Alley
168	Ernest W. Cushing, M. D.	267	Mrs. Elvira Hamblin
169	Charles U. Thomas	268	Charles Weil
170	Thomas Cushing	269	W. Whitney Lewis
	Herbert B. Cushing	270	W. H. Kennard
171	Frederick H. Tappan		Francis E. Fitz
173	Francis E. Peabody	272	Alexander Stowell
179	Rollin H. Allen	273	Francis Jones
205	Charles E. Thayer	274	Charles H. Whiting
	Edward K. Thayer	275	Horace B. Wilbur
207	Francis J. Coburn		Charles D. Cobb
209	Nathaniel S. Hotchkiss	276	Edmund J. Folsom
211	Lucius W. Smith	277	John O. Teele
213	Charles F. Fairbanks	278	William M. Scott
215	George F. Brown	280	Mrs. Moses H. Day
216	Mrs. Sarah Aldrich	282	Alvah A. Burrage

284	George D. Sargent
	Arthur H. Sargent
	G. Winthrop Sargent
286	A. G. Van Nostrand
288	Mrs. William H. Sherwood
290	Robert L. Means
293	George H. Edwards
295	Francis G. Post

(West) Berkeley Street. (From Boylston St. to 147 Beacon St.) On this street is the fashionable Hotel Kempton, at No. 237. The following are the names of the residents:

237	HOTEL KEMPTON:
	Walter Burgess
	Miss A. Cheever
	Miss Mary Cheever
	Hartwell B. Colby
	Mrs. Alfred Ely
	Joel Goldthwait
	Mrs. J. Newell
	G. E. Richards, M. D.
	Warren B. Potter
	Mrs. B. F. Thomas
	Miss Mary Thomas
	Mrs. C. A. Whiting
247	F. H. Peabody
249	Frederick S. Leonard
	Rev. Edmund F. Slafter
	Alexander Jackson
	Thomas W. Davis
	Mrs. Rebecca Crafts
	Mrs. Nathaniel Smith
	Mrs. Eliza Crafts
	Mrs. E. C. Taylor
	Miss Eliza Taylor
297	Mrs. J. C. Phillips
299	Charles H. Minot
300	Charles S. Dana
302	Henry Winsor, Jr.
	Mrs. F. H. Jackson
304	Mrs. F. B. Ellison

(West) Clarendon Street. From 201 Beacon st. to St. James av. Hotels Guildford (220) and Hamilton (260), are upon this street. Rev. Phillips Brooks' parsonage is at No. 233, and there are several physicians within its three blocks. The residents are as follows:

220	HOTEL GUILDFORD:
	Miss Isabella Dodd
	William D. Hodges, M. D.
	Miss S. Cunningham
	Howard M. Buck, M. D.
	Mrs. E. C. Drew
	Miss Kittie Drew
	Mrs. Lombard
	W. P. P. Longfellow
	John W. Magruder
	Charles Lewis
	John B. Sweet
	Newton Talbot
320	Charles A. Cummings
232	Mrs. H. B. Goodwin
233	Rev. Phillips Brooks
234	John W. Farlow, M. D.
236	John P. Reynolds, M. D.
260	HOTEL HAMILTON:
	Alonzo Boothby, M. D.
	Henry W. Dodd
	Edward H. Dunn

	HOTEL HAMILTON:
	Arthur F. Estabrook
	G. W. Hammond
	Frederick H. Higginson
	Miss E. W. Perkins
	Mrs. R. Roach
	Miss. C. Spring
	Mrs. J. D. W. Williams
	Mrs. S. Witherell
	John A. Higginson
261	Mrs. Randolph Clark
263	Thomas H. Perkins
265	A. L. Mason, M. D.
267	Mrs. Andrew Robeson
270	James R. Chadwick, M. D.
273	Mrs. F. Cunningham
274	Augustus Flagg
275	Frederick A. Lovering
279	George Lyman, Jr.

(West) Dartmouth Street. (From 10 Boylston st. to 255 Beacon st.)

277	Mrs. J. P. Putnam
	Miss Sally Putnam
	Mrs. C. F. Fearing
279	J. Heber Smith, M. D.
280	A. S. Mansfield
	F. S. Mansfield
	Lott Mansfield
281	Dexter T. Mills
282	George A. Smith
	Alexander Martin
283	E. H. Smith, M. D.
	Samuel J. Shaw, M. D.
	F. E. Banfield, M. D.
284	John P. Knight
	Cyrus W. Alger
303	Arthur Hunnewell
306	Frederick L. Ames
312	Mrs. Richard S. Fay
314	Mrs. George Tyson
315	Mrs. H. H. Hunnewell
317	John M. Little
326	Mrs. M. E. Wright
	Charles H. Wright
	Miss E. F. Wright
328	Joseph G. Beals

Westland Avenue. (From West Chester Park st. to Parker st.)

	HOTEL WESTLAND:
	George Lowell Tracy
	H. J. Butler
	Albert D. Kilham
	E. G. Chamberlin
	Mrs. C. M. Seymour
	Frederick M. Newcomb
	T. H. Chandler, M. D.
	Henry F. Knowles
	John R. Ainsley
	George B. Upham
	Edwin C. Miller
	B. Leighton Beal
	Charles H. Pope
	Ezra B. Parker
	Augustus F. York
	Mrs. W. H. Hollister
	Mrs. M. T. Batchelder
	Herbert H. Bangs
	Charles B. Gardner
	Arthur P. French
	Lyman Boynton
	Roscoe Kilham

CABS AND HACKS.

Cabs. Boston is well supplied with public carriages: the Boston Cab Company (which succeeded the Boston Hotels Coach Company); the Crystal Cab Company; the Gurney Cab Company; the Hansom Cabs; the Herdic Phæton Company; the Standard Cab Company, etc., in addition to the fine public carriages furnished from the well-known stables of Barnard & Co., Maynard, Timmins and various other establishments. There are abundant facilities for transportation to all parts of the city and suburbs at any hour of the day or night, at most reasonable prices. Public carriages are always to be found at the various railway stations, steamship piers, etc., in large numbers.

Boston Cab Company. Central office, 100 Arch st.; other offices and standings at 211 Washington st., 129 Eliot st., and 105 Arch st.

Crystal Cab Company. 368 Atlantic av., foot of Hanover st., Utica st., cor. Kneeland st., B. & M. R'y Station, and 425 Hanover st.

Gurney Cab Company. Standings are as follows:
124 E. Dover st.
50 Washington st.
123 Washington st.
  East Concord st.
7 Boylston st.
103 Purchase st.
  East Concord st., cor. James.
124 Harrison av.
3 Tremont Row.
103 Tremont st.
  Tremont st., cor. Berkeley.
  Tremont st., cor. Bosworth.

Herdic Phæton Company, (1881.) Office, 35 Congress st., standings:
55 State st.
  B. & Prov. R'y Station.
55 Court st.
21 Exchange pl.
  Bowdoin sq. church.
  Mechanics Hall.
  Mason b'ld'g, Liberty sq.
  N. Y. & N. E. R'y Station.
  Winthrop sq.
  Summer st., cor. Lincoln.
  Central st., cor. Broad.
  Lincoln st., cor. Kneeland.
4 Post Office sq.
  B. & M. R'y Station.
  Scollay sq.
119 Causeway st.
55 Causeway st.
  N. E. Institute b'ld'g.
93 Causeway st.
  Washington st., cor. Milk.
  South st., cor. Kneeland.
  Falmouth hotel, Causeway st.
  Washington st., cor. Avon.
  B. & A. R'y Station.
245 Friend st.
  Revere Beach R'y Station.
  Haverhill st., cor. Causeway.
  Tremont st., cor. Temple pl.
  Bosworth st.
  Washington, cor. Eliot st.
61 Court st.
  Tremont st., cor. Boylston.

Hansom Cabs. (1884). The London Hansom is evidently destined to become eventually the most popular cab in Boston, owing to its manifest advantages over every other form of public vehicle. It has been steadily gaining in public favor for a number of years, and there are numbers of persons who will ride in no other public carriage, unless a Hansom cannot be procured. For business purposes, for making calls, for shopping and for pleasure rides, nothing can equal the Hansom. The passenger can enter and leave them easily, without crushing hat or clothing; one can have a full view of either side of the street, the driver being at the top of the Cab, in the rear; the cushions and linings of this carriage are always well aired,—(which is quite a consideration, as four-wheeled, close cabs are sometimes used for the conveyance of fever patients and others to the Hospital) —and as the Hansoms are well lighted at night by side lamps, there is scarcely any danger by collision or other accident. The Hansom is the only public carriage that may be said to have survived almost all the others that have been tried in London, in which city there are upwards of 20,000 in use. The Hansom has unquestionably come to Boston to stay.

Hansom Cab Standings are at 24 Hayward Place, (from 582 Washington st.), at 32 North st., and at various other points. Telephone orders for Hansoms can be sent to 32 North st., or calls by messenger to 24 Hayward Place.

Standard Cab Company. Central Office, 8 Post-Office sq. Other standings are as follows:
  N. Y. and N. E station.
  6 and 8 High st.
217 South st.
110 Washington st.
93 Court st.
29 Boylston st.
  Boston & Maine station.
216 Devonshire st.
103 Commercial st.
107 Kneeland st.

52 Kilby st.
30 Chardon st.
678 Harrison av.
40 Water st.
61 Essex st.
   Kneeland st., cor. Albany.
47 Court st.
109 Pearl st.
4 Bosworth st.
116 Franklin st.
147 Federal st.
43 Kingston st.
   Boston & Providence station.
149 Tremont st.
2 Franklin st.
   Hayward place.
14 Summer st.
   Park Square Hotel.
   Boylston st., cor. Carver.
   Hampton Hotel, Haymarket sq.
   Falmouth House.
   Doane st., cor. Kilby.
   Court st., cor. Cornhill.
   Berkeley st., cor. Boylston.
29 Kneeland st.
17 Harvard st.
   Beacon st., cor. Charles.
   Hawley st., cor. Franklin.
   Pearl st., cor. High.
   Washington st., cor. Brattle.
165 Tremont st.
   Water st., cor. Devonshire.
   Tremont st., cor. Boylston.
61 Court st.
118 West Brookline st.

Cab Fares. Within the Sections, A, B, C and D, 25c. is charged. From A to B, 25c. To Section C, 50c.; two, 75c. To Section D, $1; two, $1.25, to Roxbury (Walk Hill), $1.50, two, $1.75. To South Boston Dorchester st., 75c.; two, $1. To East Boston, Porter st., 75c.; two, $1. (tolls to be paid by passenger). To Dorchester, (Preston st.), $1.50; two, $2. To Charlestown, 50c.; two, 75c. To Brighton, $2; two, $2.25. To West Roxbury, (Walk Hill st.), $2.50; two, $2.75.

Cabs by Telephone. Cabs, and all other public vehicles, can, at all hours of the day or night, be ordered by telephone.

Cab Service by the Hour. Cabs can be taken by the hour, $1.00 for one, two, three or four passengers.

Ferry Tolls. Cab passengers pay all ferry tolls.

Suburban Rides. Parties of eight are taken from the city proper to Revere, Malden, Medford, Arlington, Belmont, Watertown, Newton, West Roxbury, Dorchester, Hyde Park, Milton or Quincy, and return to the city for $6. Other excursions may be arranged. Office, 35 Congress st.

Hack Fares. The city proper is divided into the following sections:
SECTION A includes all that part of the city proper lying north of a line drawn through the centre of State, Court, and Cambridge sts. Fare, within this section, 50c. for each adult passenger; to Section B, one passenger, 50c.; two $1; to Section C, $1; two, $1.50; to Section D, $2, for one or three; to Roxbury, $2.50, for one or four; to South Boston, $2 for one or four, to East Boston, $2 and tolls, for one or four; to Dorchester, $3, for one or four; to Charlestown, (Lincoln st.,) $1; beyond, $1.50; to any point in Brighton, $4, for one or four; to West Roxbury north of Walk Hill, $1.50, for one or four; beyond, $6, for one or four.
SECTION B includes all that part of the city proper lying south of a line drawn through the centre of the streets named as forming the southerly boundary of Section A, and north of a line drawn through the centre of Dover and Berkeley streets.
SECTION C includes all that part of the city proper lying south of a line drawn through the centre of the streets named as forming the southerly boundary of Section B, and north of a line drawn through the centre of Chester Park and Chester Square.
SECTION D includes all that part of the city proper lying south of a line drawn through the centre of the streets named as forming the southerly boundary of Section C, and north of a line beginning at Willow Court; thence running through the centre of Boston and Dudley sts., Eliot sq., Roxbury, Pynchon, Tremont and Francis sts.
Between twelve o'clock, midnight, and six a. m., 50c. is added to each passenger fare.
Children under four pay no fare; a child over four, and under twelve, accompanied by an adult, pays half-fare.
One trunk is carried free. For each additional trunk, 25c. is charged.

STREET CARS AND COACHES.

Boston's First Horse Railway was laid on Tremont st., running from the head of Bromfield st., to the South End only, in 1856, by the Metropolitan Street Railway Company. Previous to that time, omnibuses—lines known as "King's" and "Hawthorne's"—had had a monopoly of passenger transportation. Other horse-railway lines were subsequently organized, and there are now seven great lines, carrying an enormous number of passengers daily.

Cambridge Horse Railway.
(1856). Stations, Bowdoin sq., and Park sq. Time-table:
To Brighton,	every 15 min.
Harvard sq. (Main st.,)	5
Harvard sq. (Camb. st.,)	30
Harvard sq. (Prov. sta.,)	8
Prospect st.,	15
North av.,	10
E. Cambridge,	15
Fresh Pond,	15
Mount Auburn,	15
W. Somerville,	15
Arlington,	30
Watertown,	30
Newton,	30

Charles River Horse Railway.
(1882). Stations, 29 Cambridge st., and Park sq. Leaving Bowdoin sq.:
To Porter station,	every 30 min.
Harvard sq.,	15
Somerville,	30
Cottage Farm,	30

Leaving Park sq.:
Somerville,	30
Porter station,	30

Highland Street Railway.
(1872). Office, 827 Shawmut av.:
To Grove Hall,	every 8 min.
Dudley st.,	8
Warren st.,	9
Mt. Pleasant,	9
Blue Hill av.,	9
Northern Depots,	10
Post Office sq.,	10
Columbus av.,	5

The Oakland Garden line runs regularly through Hampden st. every 15 minutes, and through Shawmut av. every 20 minutes, except during the summer season at Oakland Garden Theatre, when cars run from Temple pl. every 3 minutes. Omnibuses run from Oakland Garden to Mount Hope Cemetery, every day during the summer, every hour, beginning at 11 A. M., connecting with the Highland-st. railway.

Lynn and Boston Horse Railway. Office, 13 Tremont row. Central passenger station, 71 Cornhill.

To Charlestown, every 10 min.	
Lynn,	60
Chelsea,	10
Peabody,	60
Swampscott,	60
Woodlawn,	60
Revere Beach,	15

Connects at Peabody sq. with horse cars for Salem and Beverly.

Metropolitan Horse Railroad. (1856). Office, 16 Kilby st.
To Norfolk House, every 7 min.	
Mt. Pleasant,	10
Warren st.,	8
Tremont st.,	3
Back Bay,	5
West End,	10
Jamaica Plain,	10
Grove Hall,	15
Meeting House Hill,	30
Fields Corner,	30
Atlantic av.	8
Dartmouth st.,	10
Chelsea,	7
Chelsea Ferry,	15
Washing'n Village,	15
E. Boston Ferry,	7
Atlantic av.,	10
Forest Hills,	15
Egleston sq.,	10
Depots,	15
Brookline,	10
Dorchester,	15
Town Hall,	15
Geneva av.,	30
Upham Corner,	30
Northern Station,	8
Chester Park Ext'n	20
East Boston,	7
Winthrop Junct.,	30
Milton	30

Cars for Fields Corner, Washington Village and Milton leave head of Milk st.; for Meeting-house Hill leave head of Bedford st., cor. of Washington.

Middlesex Horse Railway.
Office, 27 Tremont Row.
To Charlestown, every 5 min.	
Bunker Hill,	7
Malden,	30
Everett,	30
Somerville,	15
Winter Hill,	15
Medford,	30
Woodlawn,	30

South Boston Horse Railway. Office, 715 Broadway, So. Boston.
To So. Boston, via Dover st. every 10 min.	
Federal st.	5
Northern, and Southern Railway Stations	10

The Federal st. line starts from Brattle st., and the Dover st. line from Park sq.

Four-Cent Fares. The Main st. line of the Charles River Railway, from Bowdoin sq. to Harvard sq. has four-cent fares.

Horse Railways to the Stations. Horse cars to the northerly and southerly railway stations run frequently. For the Boston and Maine, Eastern, Lowell and Fitchburg stations, take car on Tremont st. going north, marked "Depots." For New York & New England, and Boston, Revere Beach & Lynn stations, take Atlantic av. horse cars. For Old Colony and Boston & Albany stations, take Charlestown or South Boston cars going south. For Boston & Providence station, any Columbus av. car going south, or any Back Bay, Dartmouth st., West End or Huntington av. car going south, getting off at Church st. opposite the Public Garden.

Night Cars. Cars leave Tremont crossing every hour, (12.30 to 5.30) during the night; Tremont House, every hour from 12, midnight, till 6 a. m. going down Cornhill; Bartlett st. every hour from 12, midnight, to 6 a. m.; State st., every half hour during the night; South Boston night cars run between K st. and Milk st., city, on every hour.

Railway to Steamboat Piers. Horse cars leave the head of Franklin st. (from 380 Washington st.) every few minutes for the various steamship piers.

Tariff. The fare in the city is five cents on any line; to Dorchester, 5c.; to Milton, 10c.; to Oakland Garden, 5c.; to West Roxbury Park, 5c.; to Upham Corner, 5c.; to Mount Auburn, 5c.; to South Boston, 5c.; to Harvard sq., 5c.; to Chelsea, 5c.; to Lynn, 14c.; to Bunker Hill, 5c.; to Malden, 9c.; to Peabody, 25c.; to Swampscott, 14c.; to Back Bay, 5c.; to Brookline, 5c.; to Jamaica Plain, 5c.; to Mount Pleasant, 5c.; to Newton, 10c.; to Watertown, 10c.; to Arlington, 10c.; to Marblehead, 25c.; to Revere, 7c.; to Everett, 7c.; to North av., 5c.; to Medford, 10; to Brighton, 5c.; to Somerville, 5c.

The Distances of Horse-Car Routes. To Brighton, 5 miles; Arlington, 6m.; Newton, 7m.; Watertown, 8m.; Mt. Auburn, 6m.; Cottage Farm, 3m.; Lynn 12m.; Chelsea, 4m.; Revere, 6m.; Peabody, 15m.; Swampscott, 12m.; Milton, 6m.; Brookline, 3m.; Jamaica Plain, 3m.; Cambridge, 3m.; Medford, 5m.; Somerville, 2m.; Bunker Hill, 1½m.; Charlestown sq., 1m.
TIME between Bowdoin sq. and Harvard sq., 30 minutes.

Omnibuses. Omnibuses were never a popular passenger vehicle in Boston, and since 1856 — when the horse cars were first introduced — the demand for them has been steadily on the decline. There is no doubt, however, that before a great many years, the horse car tracks on Washington and Tremont sts., between Cornhill and Dover sts. will be taken up, and omnibuses of the London and Paris patterns substituted. As the traffic continues to increase on these busy thoroughfares, year by year, blockades of horse cars will be more and more frequent, and as horse cars cannot turn out for other carriages, omnibuses, which very seldom become blockaded, owing to the facility with which they can be made to take short turns, will naturally be put in the place of the cars. Along Cheapside and the Strand, in London, two of the most crowded thoroughfares in the world, omnibuses run at a good rate of speed, much faster, in fact, than our horse cars, and blockades are almost unknown. From the top of these omnibuses one can get a better idea of the city than in any other way. Boston will never know what perfect street transit is until lines of omnibuses are placed in her principal streets. Horse cars may be used, as in foreign cities, for suburban service. Following are the lines of omnibuses now in operation in the city:

Citizen's Omnibus Line. From Northampton st. (off Washington st., South End,) Boston, to foot of Salem st., Charlestown district, every three minutes, from 5:30 a. m., to 9:30 p. m.; returning every three minutes, from 6:15 a. m., to 10:30 p. m. (Fare, 5c., by ticket, 4c.)

Mount Hope Omnibus Line. From head of Columbia st., Grove Hall, daily, at 11 a. m., 1, 2, 3, 4, 5, and 6, p. m., connecting with Grove Hall street cars. Coaches also connect with trains on the Boston and Providence railway, leaving Boston at 11:40 a. m., 1:15, 2:40, 4:05, and 5:10, p. m.; also connecting with Forest Hills street cars, which leave Temple Place at 11, a. m., and half-hourly until 4:30 p. m.; (except on Sundays).

People's Omnibus Line. From Field's Corner (Dorchester,) to Neponset district, at 9:30, 10:30, a. m., 1:30, 2:30, 5:30, p. m. From Neponset district, at 9:00, 10:00, a. m., 1, 2, 5, p. m. Sunday, leave Field's Corner, at 10:40, a. m., 1:30, 2:30, 3:30, 4:30, 5:30, 7:30, 8:30, 9:30, p. m. From Neponset for Field's Corner, at 10, a. m., 1, 2, 3, 4, 5, 7, 8, 9, p. m.

CHURCHES IN BOSTON.

Baptist. Baptist Bethel, Hanover st., cor. North Bennet.
Bowdoin-Square Church, Bowdoin sq.
Brighton Avenue Baptist, Brighton av., junc. Cambridge st., Allston. F. T. Whitman.
Bunker Hill Baptist Church, Bunker Hill, cor. Mystic st., Chas'town. R. B. Moody.
Central-Square Church, Meridian st., near Central sq., E. B. J. K. Richardson.
Clarendon-Street Church, Clarendon st., cor. Montgomery. Adoniram J. Gordon.
Day-Star Baptist Church, 1607 Wash. st.
Dearborn-Street Church, Dearborn st. Francis J. Bellamy.
Dudley-Street Baptist Church, 137 Dudley st. Albert K. Potter.
Ebenezer Baptist Church, 85 W. Concord st.
First Baptist Church, Clarendon st., cor. Commonwealth av. Philip H. Moxom.
First Baptist Church, Charlestown, Lawrence st., cor. Austin. G. E. Horr, Jr.
First Baptist Church, Roslindale, South st., opp. Poplar. J. M. Wyman.
First Free Baptist Church, Shawmut av., cor. Rutland sq. F. L. Hayes.
First German Church, Vernon st., near Cabot. W. Papenhausen.
Fourth-Street Baptist Church, W. Fourth st., cor. L. C. H. Spalding.
Harvard-Street Church, Harrison av., cor. Harvard st. J. H. Gunning.
Independent Baptist Church, Smith ct. Peter Smith.
Jamaica Plain Baptist Church, Centre st., cor. Myrtle, Jamaica Pl. D. H. Taylor.
Neponset-Avenue Church, Chickatawbut st., Neponset.
Ruggles-Street Baptist Church, Ruggles st. Robert G. Seymour.
South Baptist Church, W. Broadway, cor. F st., S. B. David B. Jutten.
Stoughton-Street Church, Stoughton st., cor. Sumner, Dorchester.
Trinity Baptist Church, Trenton st., E. B. Nelson B. Jones, Jr.
Twelfth Baptist Church, 3 Tremont row. Lemuel G. Walden.
Union Temple Church, Tremont Temple. Emory J. Haynes.
Warren-Avenue Church, Warren av., cor. W. Canton. O. P. Gifford.

Catholic Apostolic. Catholic Apostolic Church, 227 Tremont st. B. F. Treadwell.

Christian. Church of Christ, Shawmut av., cor. Madison. J. H. Garrison.
First Christian Church, Tyler st., cor. Kneeland. Edward Edmunds.

Christian Scientist. Church of Christ, Scientist, Chickering Hall. M. B. G. Eddy.

Churches of the Advent. Messiah's Church, Shawmut av., near Williams. Cyrus Cunningham.
Seventh Day Advent, A. L. Wright. 21 Boylston pl.

Congregational Trinitarian. Berkeley-Street Church, Berkeley st., cor. Warren av. William Burnet Wright.
Boylston Congregational Church, Boylston st., cor Amory, Boylston station, Jamaica Plain. S. Sherberne Mathews.
Brighton Evangelical Congregational Church, Washington st., cor. Winship pl., Brighton. Wm. Hayne Leavell.
Central Church, Berkeley st., cor. Newbury. Joseph T. Duryea.
Central Congregational Church, Elm st., cor. Seaverns av., J. P. G. M. Boynton.
Dorchester Second Church, Washington st., cor. Centre, Dor. Ed. N. Packard.
Eliot Church, Kenilworth st. A. C. Thompson, B. F. Hamilton.
First Parish Church and Society, Harvard sq., Charlestown. G. W. Brooks.
Highland Church, Parker st., cor. Oscar. Wm. R. Campbell.
Immanuel Church, Moreland st., cor. Copeland.
Maverick Church, Central sq., E. B. Samuel E. Herrick.
Mount Vernon Church, Ashburton pl
Old South Church, Dartmouth st., cor. Boylston. Geo. A. Gordon.
Olivet Church, W. Springfield, near Tremont. Daniel M. Stearns.
Park-Street Church, Tremont st., cor. Park. John L. Withrow.
Phillips Church, W. Broadway, near Dorchester st., S B. Francis E. Clark.
Pilgrim Church, Stoughton st., Upham's Corner. John W. Ballantine.
Shawmut Church, Tremont st., cor. Brookline.
South Evangelical, Centre st., cor. Mt. Vernon, W. Rox. Clarence A. Beckwith.
Swedish Church, N. sq. John Hagstrom.
Trinity Church, Walnut st., Neponset. John L. Harris.
Union Church, 485 Columbus av. R. R. Meredith
Village Church, River st., near Temple, Lower Mills, Dorchester. S. P. Fay.
Walnut-Avenue Church, Walnut av., cor. Dale. Albert H. Plumb.
Winthrop Church, Green st., Charlestown. Alexander S. Twombly.
Hope Chapel, 15 Shawmut av.
Maverick Chapel, 331 Chelsea st., E. B.
Old Colony Chapel, Tyler st, near Harvard. Robert F. Gordon.
Park-Street Auxiliary, 175 Hanover st.
Phillips Chapel, 538 E. Seventh st.
Shawmut Chapel, 642 Harrison av. D. W. Waldron.
Shawmut Mission Chapel, Rockland st., near Dedham line, W. Rox.

Congregational Unitarian.

Appleton-Street Chapel, Parker Memorial building. Wm. G. Babcock.
Arlington-Street Church, Arlington st., cor. Boylston. Brooke Herford.
Bulfinch-Place Chapel, Bulfinch st. Samuel H. Winkley.
Church of Our Father, 54 Meridian st. George M. Bodge.
Church of the Disciples, West Brookline st., cor. Warren av. James Freeman Clarke.
Church of the Unity, 91 West Newton st. Minot J. Savage.
Church of the Unity, Walnut st., cor. Oakham, Neponset. Henry H. Woude.
First Congregational Society, Centre st., cor. Eliot, Jamaica Plain. Charles F. Dole.
First Parish, Centre st., cor. Church, West Roxbury. Augustus M. Haskell.
First Parish of Brighton, Washington st., cor. Market, Brighton. Wm. P. Tilden.
First Parish, Winter st., cor. East, Meeting House Hill, Dorchester. Christopher R. Eliot.
First Religious Society, Eliot sq. James De Normandie.
Harrison Square Unitarian Church, Neponset av., cor. Mill, Dorchester. Caleb Davis Bradlee.
Harvard Church, Main st., cor. Green, Charlestown. Pitt Dillingham.
Hawes Place Congregational Society, K st., cor. Emerson, S. Boston. Charles B. Elder.
Hollis Street Church, Newbury st., cor, Exeter. H. Bernard Carpenter.
King's Chapel, Tremont st., cor. School. Henry W. Foote.
Mt. Pleasant Congregational, 221 Dudley st. William H. Lyon.
New South Church, Camden, cor. Tremont st. George H. Young.
Parmenter Street Chapel, 24 Parmenter st. Wm. S. Heywood.
Second Church, Copley sq., near Dartmouth. Edward A. Horton.
Second Hawes Congregational, E. Broadway, bet. G and H sts. Edward F. Hayward.
South Congregational, Union Park st. Edward E. Hale.
Third Religious Society, Richmond st., Lower Mills, Dorchester. William I. Lawrence.
Warren Street Chapel, 10 Warrenton st. E. R. Butler.
Washington Village Union Church, Dorchester st. Wm. H. Savary.

Congregational.
First Church, Marlboro', cor. Berkeley st.
Twenty-Eighth Congregational Society, Berkeley, cor. Appleton st. James Kay Applebee.
West Church, Cambridge, cor. Lynde st. Cyrus A. Bartol.

Episcopal.
Rev. Benjamin H. Paddock, Bishop of Massachusetts.
All Saints Church, Dorchester av., near Ashmont st., Dorchester. George S. Bennitt.
Christ Church, Salem st., Wm. H. Munroe.
Church of the Advent, 30 Brimmer st., C. C. Grafton.
Church of the Good Shepherd, Cortes st. George J. Prescott.
Church of the Messiah, Florence st., Henry F. Allen.
Emmanuel Church, Newbury st. Leighton Parks.
Grace Church, Dorchester st. Washington Village. George C. Buck.
St. Andrews Church, 27 Chambers st. Reuben Kidner.
St. Ann's Chapel, Cottage, near Dudley st. J. R. Peirce.
St. Augustine's Mission, 37 Anderson st. Edward Osborne.
St. James Church, St. James st. Percy Browne.
St. John's Church, Devens st., cor. Rutherford av., Charlestown. Philo W. Sprague.
St. John's Church, Roanoke av., cor. Revere, J. P. Sumner C. Shearman.
St. John's Church, Paris, cor. Decatur, E. B. N. H. Chamberlain.
St. John's Church, Tremont st., between Vernon and Clay. George S. Converse. B. S. Sanderson, assistant.
St. John the Evangelist, Bowdoin st. A. C. A. Hall.
St. Margaret's, Washington, cor. Church, Brighton. Augustus Prime.
St. Mark's Church, West Newton, cor. Newland, L. B. Baldwin.
St. Mary's Church, Bowdoin st., Dorchester. L. W. Saltonstall.
St. Matthew's Church, 408 Broadway, S. Boston. John Wright.
St. Paul's Church, 134 Tremont st. Frederick Courtney.
Trinity Church, Boylston, cor. Clarendon st. Phillips Brooks and Frederick B. Allen.
Reformed Episcopal Church, Dartmouth, cor. Harwich. James M. Gray.

Friends.
Friends' meeting at Wesleyan Hall, Bromfield st. Sunday A. M. and Wednesday P. M.

Jewish.
Beth Abram, 287 Hanover. Jacob Diamondstein.
Gates of Prayer, 139 Pleasant st. M. Klatchkin.
House of Prayer, 231 Hanover st. Mendel Silvermann.
Mishkan Israel, Ash st. S. S. Cohen.
Ohabei Sholom, 76 Warrenton st. Raphael Lasker.
Shomrey Shabos, 287 Hanover st.
Temple Adath Israel (German), Columbus av., cor. Northampton st. Solomon Schindler.
Zion's Holy Prophets of Israel (Orthodox) Church, cor. Winchester. L. Schnitkin.

Lutheran.
Emmanuel's (Swedish), Emerald st. C. F. Johansson.

Evangelical Lutheran Zion Church, Shawmut av., cor. Waltham. F. Lindeman.
Immanuel's German Lutheran Church, 77 Chelsea st., E. B. Adolf Biewend.
Norwegian Lutheran Church, Shawmut av., cor. Waltham. John Koren.
Trinity Church (Ger.), Parker st., near Tremont. Adolf Biewend.

Methodist Episcopal. Rev. Randolph S. Foster, Resident Bishop.
Allston M. E. Church, Harvard av. cor. Farrington av., Allston. W. W. Le Seur.
Appleton Church, Walnut, near Neponset av., Neponset. George H. Perkins.
Bethel Church, Meridian, cor. Decatur, E. B. L. B. Bates.
Broadway Church, West Broadway, near F, S. B. George A. Crawford.
Bromfield-Street Methodist Episcopal Church, Bromfield st. David H. Ela.
City Point Mission, Emerson, cor. L. Charles Tilton.
Dorchester Church, Washington, near Richmond, Dorchester. T. C. Watkins.
Dorchester-Street Church, Dorchester st., cor. Silver, S. B. M. E. Wright.
Egleston-Square Church, Washington st., cor. Beethoven. Samuel L. Brengle.
German M. E. Church, 777 Shawmut av. Frederick W. Boese.
Grace Church, Temple st. Horace W. Bolton.
Harrison-Square M. E. Church, Parkman st. B. J. Johnston.
Highland Church, 160 Warren st. Wm. T. Worth.
Jamaica Plain M. E. Church, Elm st., cor. Newbern, Jamaica Plain. George S. Butters.
Mattapan Methodist Episcopal Church, Norfolk st., Mattapan. J. P. Kennedy.
Monument-Square M. E. Church, Charlestown. G. S. Chadbourne.
Mt. Pleasant Church, Howard av. W. J. Hambleton.
People's Church, Columbus av., cor. Berkeley st. C. E. Davis.
Revere-Street Methodist Episcopal Church, 79 Revere st. D. W. Shaw.
Roslindale M. E. Church, Ashland st., cor. Sheldon. Garret Beckman.
Saratoga-Street M. E. Church, Saratoga st., E. B. Stephen L. Baldwin.
Swedish M. E. Church, Isabella st., cor. Ferdinand. H. Olson.
Tremont-Street M. E. Episcopal, Tremont st., cor. W. Concord. S. F. Jones.
Trinity M. E. Church, High st., Charlestown. R. L. Greene.
Washington Village Church, Washington Village. Joseph Jackson.
Winthrop-Street M. E. Church, Winthrop st., Rox. A. B. Kendig.

Methodist. African Union Church, 3 Southac pl.
First African Church, 68 Charles st. J. T. Jenifer.
Morgan Memorial Church, 87 Shawmut av. N. W. Jordan.

Union Am. M. E. Church, 119 Cambridge st. W. A. Jackson.
Zion Church, No. Russell st. John W. Brown.

New Church, (Swedenborgian)
First New Jerusalem Church, Bowdoin st. James Reed.
Roxbury Church of the New Jerusalem, St. James st., cor. Regent. Julian K. Smyth.

Presbyterian. First Presbyterian, Berkeley st., cor. Columbus av. V. A. Lewis.
First Presbyterian of East Boston, Meridian st., cor. London. John L. Scott.
First Reformed Presbyterian, Ferdinand st., cor. Isabella. William Graham.
Fourth Presbyterian, E. Fourth st., bet. G and H, South Boston. Andrew Burrows.
Highland Hall, Warren st. J. W. Sanderson.
Second Reform Presbyterian, 33 Chambers st. David McFall.
Springfield-Street Presbyterian Church, W. Springfield st., n. Tremont. P. M. Macdonald.
United Presbyterian, Berkeley st., cor. Chandler. John Hood.

Reformed Church. German Reformed Church, 13 Shawmut st. Louis B. Schwarz.

Roman Catholic. Most Rev. John J. Williams, Archbishop.
Cathedral of the Holy Cross, Washington st., cor. Malden. Lawrence J. O'Toole.
Church of Gate of Heaven, 606 E. Fourth st. M. F. Higgins.
Church of the Assumption, Sumner st., E. B. Joseph H. Cassin.
Church of the Holy Trinity, 140 Shawmut av. (German). Francis X. Nopper.
Church of the Immaculate Conception, Harrison av., cor. E. Concord. Edward V. Boursaud.
Church of the Most Holy Redeemer, Maverick st., cor. London, E. Boston. L. P. McCarthy.
Church of the Sacred Heart, Brooks st., cor. Morris, E. Boston. Michael Clarke.
Church of Our Lady of the Rosary, 98 W. Sixth st., S. Boston. J. J. McNulty.
Mission Church, 1545 Tremont st. Joseph Henning.
Notre Dame des Victoires, Freeman pl. Louis Touche.
Star of the Sea, Saratoga st., n. Moore, E. B. Hugh R. O'Donnell.
St. Ann's, Minot st., n. Neponset av. Wm. H. Fitzpatrick.
St. Augustine, Dorchester st., n. Eighth. Dennis O'Callaghan.
St. Columbkille, Market st., cor. Arlington, Brighton. A. J. Rossi.
St. Francis de Sales, Bunker Hill st., Charlestown. M. J. Supple.
St. Francis de Sales, 110 Vernon st. John Delahunty.

St. Gregory, 2222 Dorchester av., Dor. W. H. Fitzpatrick.
St. James, Harrison av., n. Kneeland st. Matthew Harkins.
St. John the Baptist, No. Bennet st. (Portuguese). Henry B. M. Hughes.
St. Joseph's, Chambers st. Wm. Byrne.
St. Joseph's of Roxbury, Circuit st. H. P. Smyth.
St. Leonard's of Port Maurice, (Italian), Prince st. F. Boniface.
St. Mary's, Endicott st., cor. Thatcher. William H. Duncan.
St. Mary's, Rutherford av., Charlestown. John W. McMahon.
St. Patrick's, Dudley st., cor. Magazine. J. H. Gallagher.
St. Peter and St. Paul, 55 W. Broadway. Wm. A. Blenkinsop.
St. Peter's, Meeting House Hill, Dor. Peter Ronan.
St. Stephen's, Hanover st., cor. Clark. Michael Moran.
St. Theresa, Spring st., W. Roxbury.
St. Thomas, South st., cor. Jamaica, Jamaica Plain. T Magennis.
St. Vincent de Paul, E. cor. W. Third. William J. Corcoran.

Spiritualist. First Spiritual Temple, Newbury st., cor Exeter.
Spiritual Temple, Horticultural Hall.

Union. Beacon Hill Church, Beacon Hill pl. Charles Cullis.
Grove Hall Church, Warren st., cor. Blue Hill av. Edward D. Mallory.

Lenox-Street Chapel. W. L. Lockwood.
Mariners' Bethel, 287 Hanover st. S. E. Breen.
North End Mission, 201 North st.
North-Street Union Mission, 2029 Washington st. Philip Davies.
Union for Christian Work, Centre st., cor. Walden, Rox. William Bradley.
Western-Avenue Union Church, Western av., cor. Waverley, Brighton. W. W. Le Seur.

Universalist. Central Square Universalist, Central sq., E. B. Sanford P. Smith.
Church of Our Father, E. Broadway, near G, S. B. John J. Lewis.
First Universalist Church, Warren st., Charlestown. C. F. Lee.
First Universalist, Guild row, cor. Dudley. Adoniram J Patterson.
Grove Hall Universalist Church, Blue Hill av., c. Schuyler. I. P. Coddington.
Second Universalist, Columbus av., cor. Clarendon st. Alonzo A. Miner.
Shawmut Universalist, Shawmut av., below Brookline st. Geo. Landor Perin.
St. John's Universalist Church, Adams st., cor. Gibson, Dor. R. T. Polk.
Universalist Church, Cambridge st., Union sq., Allston.

Salvation Army. Federhen Hall, 107 Cambridge st.
Argyle Hall, 888 Washington st.

ASSOCIATIONS AND SOCIETIES.

Societies in Boston seem to be almost without number. We have endeavored to give as complete a list as possible, classifying them under several convenient and appropriate heads. Many of these Societies hold Anniversary Meetings in this city, in May, notice of which will be found in the daily papers.

Societies for Benevolent Works.

Am. Seaman's Friend Society, 7 Beacon st.
Am. Society of Hibernians, 96 Leverett st.
Am. Order Un. Workingmen.
Associated Charities, 41 Charity Building, Chardon st.
Ass. Evan. Luth. Church.
Association for Protection of Destitute Catholic Children, Harrison av.
Auxiliary Visitors, State Board of Charity, State House.
Baldwin Place Home, for Little Wanderers, Baldwin pl., Salem st.
Bay State Benevolent Association, 176 Tremont st.
Benevolent Fraternity of Churches, 5 Worcester sq.
Boston Benefit Society.
Ben. Order of Elks, 24 Hayward pl.
Boffin's Bower, 1031 Washington st.
Boston Children's Aid Society, H. D. Chapin, Sec., 40 State st.
Boston Children's Friend Society, 48 Rutland st.
Boston Episcopal Char. Soc., Sec. Edw. N. Perkins.
Boston Fatherless and Widows' Society, Mrs. Geo. W. Ware, Pres.
Boston Female Asylum, 1008 Washington st.
Boston Flower and Fruit Mission, 33 Pleasant st.
Boston Home for Incurables, Codman st.
Boston Industrial Temporary Home, 17 Davis st.
Boston Lying-in Hospital, 24 McLean st.
Boston Marine Society, 13 M's Exchange.
Boston Masonic Mut. Ben. Association, Masonic Temple.
Boston Musicians' Relief Fund Society, T. M. Carter, Sec., 179 Washington st.
Boston North End Mission, 201 North st.
Boston Pilots' Relief Society, E.G.Martin, Sec., 41 Lewis whf.
Boston Police Relief Association, Charity Building, Chardon st.
Boston Port and Seaman's Aid Society, 11 North sq.
Boston P. O. Relief Association.
Boston Provident Association, 32 Charity Building.
Boston Reading Charity, B. R. Jewell, Col., 36 Bromfield st.
Boston Seaman's Friend Society, 7 Beacon st.

Boston Sewing Circle, Charity Building, Chardon st.
Boston Widow and Orphan Association, 3 Tremont Row.
Boston Widows' and Orphans' Assoc'n, 3 Tremont row.
Boylston Relief Fund, Overseers of the Poor.
British Charitable Soc., Henry Squire, Sec.
Carney Hospital, Old Harbor st., So. B.
Channing Home, 30 McLean st., S. A. Green, Pres.
Charity Association Fire Department, 36 Summer st., Charlestown.
Charitable Irish Society, Jere. W. Fogarty, Sec.
Charlestown Free Disp'y, 27 Harvard sq.
Charlestown Infant School Association, 36 Austin st.
Charlestown Poor Fund, City Hall, Charlestown.
Children's Hospital, Huntington av.
Children's Mission, 277 Tremont st.
Church Home for Orphans, N st., S. B.
Columbian Charitable Society, 448 Atlantic av.
Conference of Charities, 141 Franklin st.
Congregational Charitable Soc. Henry B. Rogers, Pres.
Consumptives' Home, Grove Hall, Dr. Chas. Cullis.
Co-operative Society of Visitors among the Poor, 48 Charity Building.
Co-operative Soc. of Visitors among Poor, Charity Building.
Country Week Fund, 18 Boylston st.
David Sears Charity, Overseers of the Poor.
Dexter Fuel Fund, Overseers of the Poor.
Doane Fund for Nurses, Miss M. Goddard. 251 Newbury st.
Dorcas Committee, Emmanuel Church, Newbury st.
Devens' Benevolent Society, 52 Monument av.
Dispensary for Children, 18 Staniford st.
Dispensary for Women, 18 Staniford st.
Emergency Asssoc'n, 155 Boylston st.
Episcopal City Mission, 6 Tyler st.
Emmet Benevolent Association, T. W. Murray, Sec., 11 Jerome pl.
Episcopal City Mission, 6 Tyler st.
Eye and Ear Infirmary, 176 Charles st.
Female Benevolent Firm, for Colored Women.
Ferry Relief Association, C. E. Pearson, Sec., E. B., North Ferry.
First Spiritualists' Ladies' Aid Society, 1931 Washington st.
Franklin Fund, City Hall.
Fragment Society, Mrs. C. Van Brunt, Sec., 66 Commonwealth av.
Fraternal Association of Colored Men.
Free Hospital for Women, 60 E. Springfield st.

French Mutual Benev. Soc., C. Lavallee 281 Columbus av.
Friendly Hand, 2 Main st., Charlestown.
German Aid Society, G. J. Walther, sec., 128 Tremont st.
German Lutheran Aid Society, F. Schrepel, Pres., 131 Warwick st.
Girls' Friendly Society, 51 Temple st.
Goodnow Poor Fund, Overseers of the Poor.
Guild of the Good Samaritans, Newbury st., cor. Exeter.
Harbor Free Ticket Fund, 18 Boylston st.
Hebrew Ladies' Sewing Society, Mrs. J. H. Hecht.
Highland Aid Society, 107 Warren st.
Highland Aid Society, 117 Warren st.
Holton Pauper Fund, Overseers of the Poor.
Holton Poor Fund, Overseers of the Poor.
Home for Aged Colored Women, 27 Myrtle st.
Home for Aged Couples, 431 Shawmut av.
Home for Aged Men, 133 W. Springfi'd st.
Home for Aged Women, 108 Revere st.
Home for Aged and Friendless Women, 19 Common st.
Home for Destitute Catholic Children, Harrison av.
Home for Little Wanderers, Baldwin pl.
Homoeopathic Medical Dispensary, 11 Burroughs pl.
Hospital Newspaper Soc., 113 Revere st.
House of the Angel Gua: rd., 85 Vernon st.
House of the Good Samaritan, 6 McLean st.
House of the Good Shepherd, 1752 Tremont st
Howard Benevolent Society, C. F. Wyman, treas., 58 India sq.
Humane Soc. of Mass., 7 Exchange pl.
Industrial Aid society, 256 Charity Build'g.
Industrial School for Girls, Centre st., Dorchester.
Indian Aid Fund, State House.
Italian Char. Soc., P. Pastene, 23 Central st.
Italian Benefit Society, 78 Lowell st.
Italian Mutual Relief Soc., 153 North st.
Jamaica Plain Relief Society, Curtis Hall.
Ladies' Aid Soc, 1031 Washington st.
Little Sisters of the Poor, 424 Dudley st.
Liversidge Orphan Institute, River st., Mattapan.
Lowell Institute, Aug. Lowell, Trustee, 60 State st.
Lunatic Hospital, E. First st., S. B.
Mariners' House, 11 North sq.
Martin Luther Orphan Home, W. Rox.
Mass. Baptist Char. Association, 14 Tremont Temple.
Marcella-St. Home for Children, Marc. st.
M. ss. Char. Fire Soc., H. H. Sprague, Clerk, 14 Pemberton sq.
Mass. Char. Soc., T. Restieux, Sec., 29 Tremont st.
Mass. Cong. Char. Soc., Ezra Farnsworth, Treas.
Mass. General Hospital, Blossom st.
Mass. Infant Asylum, Chestnut av.
Mass. Medical Benev. Soc., R. Amory, sec., 279 Beacon st.

Mass. School for Feeble-Minded, 723 E. 5th st., South Boston.
Mass. Soc. for Aiding Discharged Convicts, 35 Avon pl.
Mass. Soc. for Prevention of Cruelty to Animals, 19 Milk st.
Mass. Soc. for Prevention of Cruelty to Children, 1 Pemberton sq.
Mass. Soldiers' Emp. Bureau, 34 Pemberton sq.
Mass. Working People's Aid Soc., 777 Washington st.
Mechanics' Mutual Aid Society.
Methodist Ministers' Relief Associa., 38 Bromfield st.
Mission House of St. Paul's Church, 6 Tyler st.
Mount Hope House, Bourne st., Forest Hills.
Murdock Free Hospital for Women, Huntington av.
Needle-Woman's Friend Soc., 149 Tremont st.
New Day Nursery, 35 Blossom st.
New England Aid Soc., 431 Shawmut av.
N. E. Hospital for Women and Children, Dimock st.
N. E. Hospital Dispensary, 29 Fayette st.
N. E. Hosp. Med. Soc., Mary A. Smith, M. D., Sec., Hotel Huntington.
N. E. Moral Reform Soc., 6 Oak pl.
N. E. Scandinavian Benevolent Society, 93 State st.
N. E. Scandinavian Soc., 131 Federal st.
N. E. Soc. for Suppression of Vice, 13 Pemberton sq.
Newsboys' and Bootblacks' Reading-Room, 16 Howard st.
Nickerson Home for Children, 11 Tyler st.
North End Diet Kitchen, r. 34 Lynde st.
North End Indus. School, 39 No. Bennet st.
North End Nursery, 39 No. Bennet st.
Pawn Fund, 414 Charity Building.
Penitent Females' Refuge, 32 Rutland st.
Perkins Institution for the Blind, 589 E. Broadway.
Police Charitable Fund, A. T. Turner, City Hall.
Poor Children's Excursions, Treas. 35 Congress st.
Poor Widows' Fund, Portland St. Mission, 90 Portland st.
Poor Widows' Fund. Apply to any Alderman.
Preachers' Aid Society, (Methodist), 36 Bromfield st.
Provident Wood Yard, S. B.
Portuguese Benev.Society,164 Hanover st.
Public Library of Boston, 10 Boylston st.
Roxbury Char. Soc., 118 Roxbury St.,
Roxbury Female Benevo'ent society, Boston Highlands.
Roxbury Home for Children and Aged Women, Copeland st.
Sailor's Snug Harbor, Quincy, H. C. Brooks, Pres.
Scots' Charitable Society, 77 Camden st.,
Shaw Asylum for Mariners' Children, Brookline.
St. Elizabeth Hospital, 78 Waltham st.
St. John's Home for Dest. Chil., 2 Elmo st., Dorchester.

St. Joseph's Home for Females, 43 E. Brookline st.
St. Luke's Home for Convalescents, 149 Roxbury st.
St. Margaret's Home, 17 Louisburg sq.
St. Mary's Infant Asylum, Cushman av.
St. Vincent de Paul Society, J. J. Mundo, sec., 89 Emerald st.
St. Vincent Orphan Asylum, Camden st.
Scandinavian Benev. Rel. Soc., 3 Tremont row.
Scots Charitable Soc., 77 Camden st.
Seashore Home, Winthrop; office, 40 State st.
Shaw Asylum for Mariners' Children, R. G. Shaw, Pres., 17 Congress st.
Sheltering Home for Animals, Lake st., Brighton.
Small pox Hospital, Canterbury st., W. Roxbury.
Society for Relief of Destitute Clergymen,
Society for Relief of Episcopal Clergymen's Widows and Orphans. H. W. Foote, Sec., 25 Brimmer st.
Society for Relief of Sick Poor.
Society Franco-Belge de Secours, 309 Washington st.
Soldiers' Messenger Corps, 34 Pemberton sq.
South Boston Samaritan Society, 377 W. Fourth st.
South End Day Nursery, 341 Harrison av.
South End Diet Kitchen, 37 Bennet st.
Summer Street Fire Fund.
Spiritualists' Ladies' Aid Society, 503 Washington st.
Swiss Benevolent Society, 20 Conant st.
Temp. Asylum, Dedham.
Temporary Home, Chardon st.
Temp. Home for Destitute Children, 46 Worcester st.
Temp. Home for Destitute Women, Chardon st.
Temp. Home for Working Women, 126 Pleasant st.
Training Schools for Nurses, Mass. Gen. Hospital.
Union Benevolent Society, of N. E., 172 Main st., Charlestown.
United Hebrew Benevolent Association, 13 Charity Building.
Universal Benefit Association, 110 Tremont st.
Waiters' Benevolent Association, T. Dunn, Sec., 162 F st.
Wayfarers' Lodge, Hawkins st.
Wells' Workingmen's Inst., 987 Wash. st.
West End Nursery, 37 Blossom st.
Widows' Society, Miss S. L. Whitwell, Sec., 111 Commonwealth av.
Winchester Home for Aged Women, 10 Eden st., Charlestown.
Women's Education Association, Mrs. James Brown, Treas.
Women's Educational and Industrial Union, 74 Boylston st.
Working Boys' Home, (Father Roche), 113 Eliot st.
Young Men's Benevolent Society, Charity Building.

Societies for Educational Purposes.

Am. College and Ed. Society, 7 Beacon st.
Association of Collegiate Alumnæ, M. Talbot, A. M., Sec., 66 Marlborough st.
Boston Latin School Association, G. H. Norcross, Sec., 35 Congress st.
Boston Library Society, 18 Boylston pl.
Catholic Literary Assoc., 1180 Tremont st.
Chautauqua School, 38 Bromfield st.
General Theolog. Library, 9 Somerset st.
Horace Mann School for the Deaf, 63 Warrenton st.
Industrial School for Girls, Centre st. Dorchester.
Mass. Institute of Technology, 191 Boylston st.
Mass. Metaphysical College, 571 Columbus av.
Mass. Society for University Education of Women, Miss C. C. Barrell, Sec.
Mercantile Library Association, 674 Tremont st.
Moral Education Association, Susan C. Vogl, Treas., 1 Hamilton pl.
N. E. Education Society, 36 Bromfield st.
New West Education Commission, 7 Beacon st.
Roxbury High School Association, C. D. Barrett, Sec., 10 Laurel st.
Roxbury Latin School Association, Henry W. Putnam, Pres.
St. John's Ecclesiastical Seminary, Lake st. Brighton.
Society to Encourage Studies at Home, Miss Ticknor, 41 Marlborough st.
Women's Education Association, 4 Otis pl.

Societies of a Religious Nature.

Advent Christian Publication Society, 144 Hanover st.
Am. Advent Mission Soc., 144 Hanover st.
Am. Baptist Home Mission Society, Tremont Temple.
Am. Baptist Missionary Union, Tremont Temple.
Am. Baptist Publication Society, 256 Washington st.
Am. Board Com., for Foreign Missions, 7 Beacon st.
Am. Congregational Association, 7 Beacon st.
Am. Millennial Assoc., 19 Harrison av.
Am. Missionary Association, 7 Beacon st.
Am. Peace Society, 7 Beacon st.
Am. Tract Society, 52 Bromfield st.
Am. Unitarian Association, 7 Tremont pl.
Association of Evangelical Lutheran Church, Sec., 716 Parker st.
Baptist Social Union, W. H. Vialle, Sec., 132 Fulton st.
Baptist Sunday School Superintendents Association, A. A. Blair, Sec., 197 Devonshire st.
Boston Branch Inst. Tract and Missionary Society, 21 Boylston pl.
Boston Wesleyan Association, 36 Bromfield st.
Boston Y. M. C. Assoc., 174 Boylston st.
Boston Y. M. C. Union, 18 Boylston st.

Boston Y. M. Catholic Association, 761 Harrison av.
Boston Y. M. Hebrew Association, Washington st.
Boston Y. W. C. Association, 68 Warren ton st.
Catholic Union of Boston, 1371 Wash. st.
Charlestown Y. M. C. Association, Union st., cor. Lawrence.
City Missionary Society, 7 Beacon st.
Congregational Club, Horticultural Hall.
Congregational Sunday School and Pub. Society, 7 Beacon st.
Congregational Sunday School Superintendent's Union, S. B. Pratt, Pres.
Episcopal Church Assoc., 5 Hamilton pl.
Episcopal City Missionary Society, 5 Hamilton pl.
Evangelist Baptist Benevolent and Missionary Society, Tremont Temple.
Evang. Ministers' Assoc., Rev. J. L. Scott, Pres.
Evang. Sunday School Union, George Bed, Sec., Tremont Temple.
Faith Training College, 2 Beacon Hill pl.
Female Auxiliary Bible Soc., Mrs. T. E. Proctor, Treas.
Free Church Assoc., 5 Hamilton pl.
Free Religion Assoc., 44 Boylston st.
German Luth'n Bible Soc., 716 Parker st.
Margaret Coffin Prayer-Book Soc., H. M. Upham, Treas.
Mass. Bapt. Convention, 11 Trem. Temple.
Mass. Bible Soc., 8 Beacon st.
Mass. Church Miss'y Soc., Martin L. Bradford, Pres.
Mass. Conv. Cong. Ministers, Rev. E. N. Packard, Sec.
Mass. Evang. Miss'y Soc., Rev. Henry F. Jenks, Sec.
Mass. Home Miss'y Soc., 7 Beacon st.
Mass. New Church Union, 16 1/2 Tremont st.
Methodist Social Union, 36 Bromfield st.
Northern Bapt. Education Soc., C. S. Kendall, Treas., 91 Federal st.
Parker Fraternity, Berkeley st.
Sisterhood of the Holy Nativity, 16 Brimmer st.
Sisters of the Holy Name, 24 Cortes st.
Soc. for Prom. Christian Knowledge, 2 Mt. Vernon st.
Soc. for Prom. Theolog. Education, H. W. Foote, Sec., 25 Brimmer st.
Soc. for Prop. the Gospel among Indians, S. C. Cobb, Treas.
Soc. for Emp. Bible Readers, Miss M. C. Woods, 69 Mt. Vernon st.
Union for Christian Work, Rev. W. Bradley, Pres.
Unitarian Club, H. H. Edes, Sec. 87 Mi'k st.
Unitarian Sun. School Soc., 7 Tremont pl.
Universalist Sun. School Union, Chas. F. Potter, Pres.
Woman's Am. Bapt. Home Mission Soc., 14 Tremont Temple.
Woman's Bapt. For. Mission Soc., 33 Tremont Temple.
Woman's Board of Missions, 7 Beacon st.
Woman's Methodist For. Miss'y Soc., 36 Bromfield st.
Woman's Home Miss'y Assoc., 7 Bea'n st.

Young Men's Union, Ruggles-St. Church, E. G. Miller, Sec.

Societies of Arts and Sciences.

Am. Academy of Arts and Sciences, 10 B Beacon st.
Am. Academy of Dental Science, E. E. Hopkins, Sec., 85 Newbury st.
Am. Metric Bureau, 32 Hawley st.
Am. Social Science Association, F. B. Sanborn, Sec., 13 Beacon st.
Am. Society for Psychical Research, N.D. C. Hodges, Sec.
Am. Statistical Assoc., 19 Boylston pl.
Archæological Institute, Chas. E. Norton, Pres.
Boston Art Club, Dartmouth st.
Boston Numismatic Soc., 18 Somerset st.
Boston Scientific Society, 419 Wash. st.
Boston Society of Civil Engineers, H. L. Eaton, Sec., City Hall.
Boston Soc. of Decorative Art, 8 Park sq.
Mass. Normal Art School, 167 Wash. st.
Museum of Fine Arts, Copley sq.
School of Expression, Freeman pl., Beacon st.
Society for Ethical Culture, Parker Hall, Berkeley st.
Society of Arts, Inst. of Technology, Boylston st.
South Boston School of Art, 4th st., S. B.

Societies of Colored Men and Women for Mutual Relief.

Alexander Dumas Association, (men), 17 Beach st.
Female Benevolent Firm (women), Mrs. Emma Gray, 21 Phillips st.
Fraternal Association (men), 255 Washington st.
United Daughters of Zion (colored women), Liza A. Gardner, Treas., 20 N. Anderson st.

Societies of Commerce and Trades.

Am. Carpenters and Joiners, 43 Eliot st.
Boston Board of Trade, 53 State st.
Boston Chamber of Commerce, F. H. Market.
Boston Co-Operative Building Co., 5 Park st.
Boston Cooking School, 174 Tremont st.
Boston Culinary and Confectory Society, 8 Boylston st.
Boston Druggists' Association, H. Canning, Sec., 100 Green st.
Boston Fish Bureau, 3 Long whf.
Boston Fruit and Produce Exchange, 43 So. Market st.
Boston Merchants' Assoc., 40 Bedford st.
Boston Ret. Grocers' Association, J. H. Wright, Sec., 43 Causeway st.
Boston Tariff Association, 70 Kilby st., Room 61.
Boys' Institute of Industry, 375 Harrison av.
Central Ret. Grocers' Association, J. C. McCready, Sec., 52 So. Market st.

Cigar Maker's Union, 43 Eliot st.
Citizens' Trade Association, (E. B.) A. H. Lewis, Sec., 3 Winthrop Block.
Expressman's League, H. L. Jackson, 32 Court sq.
Industrial Aid Society, Chardon st.
Industrial Home, 39 North Bennet st.
Lumber Dealers' Association, W. H. Stearns, Sec., 2 P. O. sq.
Mass. Charitable Mechanic Association, Mechanics Hall.
Master Builders' Association, 164 Devonshire st.
Nat. Association Wool Manufacturers, J. L. Hayes, Sec., 70 Kilby st.
N. E. Cotton Manuf. Association, 68 Sear's Building.
N. E. Saddlery Hardware Association, W. P. Hill, Sec., 90 Federal st.
N. E. Shoe and Leather Association, 79 Bedford st.
Newsdealers' and Stationers' Union, 186 Devonshire st.
South End Industrial School, 45 Bartlett st., Roxbury.

Societies of Employes and Mechanics for Mutual Relief.

Alfred Mudge & Son Mutual Benefit Association (1883). 24 Franklin st.
Amalgamated Society of Carpenters and Joiners (1860). Sec., G. W. Comstock, 1445 Washington st.
A. Schuman & Co. Mutual Benefit Association (1880). 440 Washington st.
Boiler Makers' Benevolent and Protective Union (1882). Pres., Edwin T. Dando, Maverick st., E. B.
Boston and Maine Railroad Relief Association (1883). Eastern Railway Station, Causeway st.
Boston and Providence Railroad Relief Association (1877). B. & P. Railway Station, Park sq.
Boston Chapel Benevo'ent Order of Printers (1883). Sec., Geo. F. Clark, 10 Boylston pl.
Boston Firemen's Mutual Relief Association (1872). Treas., Wm. A. Green, City Hall, Court sq.
Boston Herdic Drivers' Union (1884). Rear of 7 Tremont st.
Boston Lamplighters' Benefit Association (1875). Lamp Department, City Hall.
Boston Longshoremen's Provident Union (1884). Treas., A. Lowrey, 25 Charter st.
Boston Marine Society (1742). 13 Merchants Exchange.
Boston Pilots' Relief Society (1866). Sec., E. G. Martin, 41 Lewis Wharf.
Boston Police Relief Association (1871). Clerk, G. A. Walker, Police Station 13, Jamaica Plain.
Boston Theatrical Mechanics' Association (1883). Sec., C. E. B. Tyler, 90 Newland st.
Carriage Drivers' Protective Association (1882). Pres., D. P. Nichols, 118 W. Brookline st.
Carriage Drivers' Union Association (1862). Sec., L. B. Fitts, B. & M. Railway Station.
Charitable Association of the Boston Fire Department (1829). Treas., Wm. A. Green, City Hall.
Cigar Makers' Association of Boston. (1883.) Pres., I.G. Elsthaver, 19 Rollins st.
City Ferries' Mutual Benefit Association, (1884.) East Boston Ferries.
Coachmen's Benevolent Association,(1879) James Tighe, 8 Stanhope st.
Columbian Charitable Society of Shipwrights and Caulkers, Treas., W. L. Dolbeare, 522 Atlantic av.
Franklin Typographical Society (1824), Hon. Hugh O'Brien, Treas.
Highland Mutual Aid Society (1874), Highland Railway office, 827 Shawmut av.
Journeymen Horseshoers' Benvolent Association.
Massachusetts Charitable Mechanic Association (1795), Huntington av.
Mechanics' Mutual Aid Society (1842), Sherman House, Court sq.
Metropolitan Mutual Aid Association (1882), 16 Kilby st.
New England Commercial Travellers' Association (1877), 177 Devonshire st.
N. E. Railway Pass. Conductors' Ben. Association, Sec., C. E. Dyer, 48 Perkins st., Charlestown.
Old Colony Railroad Beneficial Association (1878), Kneeland st., cor. South.
State Firemen's Benefit Association (1883), Sec., H. H. Easterbrook, 20 Hawley st.
Walters' Benevolent Association (1865), Sec., T. Dunn., 162 F st.

Societies of Freemasons for Mutual Relief.

Boston Masonic Mutual Benefit Association, Masonic Temple, Room 30.
Eastern Mass. Masonic Relief Association. Pres. E. H. Brainard, 12 Summer st.
Suffolk Masonic Mutual Relief Association. Masonic Hall, E. B.

Societies of Medical Men and Women.

Boston Dental College, 485 Tremont st.
Boston Dist. Ecl. Medical Society, P. E. Howes, Sec., S. B.
Boston Ecl. Gynecological Society, P. E. Howes, Sec., S. B.
Boston Homœop. Medical Society, Dr. A. L. Kennedy, Treas.
Boston Medical Library Association, 19 Boylston pl.
Boston Med. Association, 19 Boylston pl.
Boston Society for Medical Imp't., 19 Boylston pl.
Boston Society for Medical Observation, 19 Boylston pl.
Boston Veterinary Medical Society, 50 Village st.
College of Physicians and Surgeons, 34 Essex st.
Gynecological Society of Boston, 19 Boylston pl.
Harvard Dental School, ft. North Grove st.

Harvard Medical School, Boylston st., cor. Exeter.
Harvard Odontological Society, A. J. Colgan, Sec.
Ladies' Physiological Institute, 36 Bromfield st.
Mass. College of Pharmacy, 1151 Wash. st.
Mass. Dental Society, W. E. Page, Sec., 110 Tremont st.
Mass. Eclectic Med. Soc., J. P. Bills, Pres.
Mass. Homœop. Medical Society, Dr. H. C. Clapp, Treas., 11 Columbus sq.
Mass. Medical Society, 19 Boylston pl.
Mass. Surgical and Gyne'l Society, Dr. L. A. Phillips, Sec., 165 Boylston st.
N. E. Medical Society Specialists, 34 Temple pl.
Obstetrical Society of Boston, Dr. C. M. Green, Sec., 78 Marlborough st.
Suffolk Dist. Med. Society, 19 Boylston pl.

Societies of Military.
A. and H. Artillery, Faneuil Hall.
Charlestown Artillery Vet. Association, J. W. Rose, Sec., 17 Congress st.
Eleventh Regt. Association, Wm. H. Ward, Pres.
First Mass. Battery Association, E. Baxter, Sec., 432B Tremont st.
First Mass. Cavalry Association, Charles G. Davis, Pres.
First Mass. Infantry Vet. Association, W. L. Candler, Pres.
Forty-Fourth Regt. Association, W. G. Reed, Sec., 24 Exchange pl.
Forty-Third Regt. Association, J. Guild, Sec., 95 Milk st.
K Association, 25th Mass. Vols., W. E. Murdock, Pres., 155 Franklin st.
Mass. Association, Prisoners of War, J. G. Bovey, Sec., State House.
Mass. Rifle Association, J. E. Leach, Sec. 40 Water st.
Nims' Battery Association, J. R. Smith, Sec., 94 Kilby st.
N. P. Banks' Army and Navy Vet. Corps, 7 City sq.
Roxbury Artillery Vet. Association, L.W. Bixby, Clerk, 33 Summer st.
Third Mass. Cavalry Association, C. T. Emery, Sec., 121 Leverett st.
Thirty-Eighth Mass. Regt. Association, B. F. Kelly, Sec., 76 Tyler st.
Twenty-Eighth Mass. Regt. Association, J. Hatton, Sec., 358 Bunker Hill st.
Twenty-Fourth Mass. Regt. Association, F. A. Osborn, Pres.
Twenty-Ninth Mass. Regt. Association, S. C. Wright, Sec., Custom House.
U. S. Vet. Signal Corps, Association, C. D'W. Marcy, Sec., 155 Franklin st.

Societies of Musicians and Musical Persons for Mutual Relief.
Beneficent Society of the New England Conservatory, Franklin sq.
Boston Musicians' Relief Fund Society, T. M. Carter, Sec., 179 Washington st.

Societies for Mutual Relief.
Ætna Mutual Aid Society. James Howey. 1324 Tremont st.
Alexander Dumas Association (Colored men.) Robt. Ransom,Treas., 17 Beach st.
American Society of Hibernians. Martin Dowling, Sec., 73 Harrison av.
Banded Brothers Mutual Benefit Association. Isaac Cohen, Pres., 18 Harris st.
Benevolent Order of Elks, 24 Hayward pl. (Dramatic profession largely).
Boston Caledonian Club, 43 Eliot st.
Boston Episcopal Charitable Society.
Boston Musicians' Relief Society. T. M. Carter, Sec., 179 Washington st.
Boston Turnverein. (German). 29 Middlesex st.
City Point Mutual Aid Society. R. P. Boss, Sec., Daily Globe office.
Columbia Aid Association. 375 Washington st.
Eastern Associates. 31 Milk st.
Emmet Benevolent Association. T. W. Murray, Sec., 244 E st., S. B.
Equitable Mutual Relief Society of Mass. 131 Devonshire st.
Female Benevolent Firm. (Colored women), 24 Phillips st.
Fraternal Association. (Colored men). J. C. Chappelle, 255 Washington st.
Good Templars Mutual Benefit Asssciation of New England.
Home Mutual Aid Association. 18 Post Office sq.
Independent Fraternal Union. W. H. Preble, Pres., 291 Bunker Hill st., Charlestown.
Italian Charitable and Mutual Relief Society of Boston. P. Pastene, 23 Central st.
Knights of Pythias (Bunker Hill) Mutual Benefit Association. F. M. Reed, Sec., 21 Main st., Charlestown.
La Prévoyance Société. C. Lavallee, Pres., 281 Columbus av.
Loyal Orange Institution, T. Milligan, Sec., 18 Ontario st.
Mass. Benefit Association. 36 Tremont Temple.
Mass. Charitable Society. T. Resticaux, Sec., 29 Tremont st.
Mass. Fraternal Benevolent Union. S. C., Dr. O. B. Sanders, 376 Columbus av.
Mass. Life and Accident Association, Amos E. Hall, Treas., 31 Milk st.
Mass. Medical Benevolent Society, F. Minot, M. D., Treas., 65 Marlborough st.
Mass. Mutual Accident Association, 131 Devonshire st.
Mass. Relief Association, 31 Milk st., Room 50.
Mass. Standard Benefit Company, 28 School st., Room 69.
Mass. United Benevolent Association, F. G. Wallbridge, G. D., 23 Washington st.
Methodist Ministers' Relief Association, 38 Bromfield st.
Mercantile Mutual Accident Association, 18 Post Office sq.
National American Association, 152 Dudley st.
New England Mutual Accident Association, 31 Milk st., Room 9.
New England Mutual Aid Society, 31 Milk st., Room 9.

New England Relief Assoc'n, 31 Milk st.
New England Scandinavian Benevolent Society, R. Anderson, 131 Federal st.
Northern Mutual Relief Association, C. M. Crofoot, 19 Tremont st.
Norwegian Society of Boston, Turn Hall, 29 Middlesex st.
Pilots' Relief Society, E. G. Martin, Sec., 41 Lewis' Wharf.
Portuguese Benevolent Society, Lusitana Hall, 164 Hanover st.
Saint Andrew's Mutual Benefit Society.
Sons of St. George (English), J. H. Kerrison, Pres., 255 Washington st.
Swedish American Society, J. A. Ostberg, 26 Warren st.
Swiss Benevolent Society of Boston, F. Von Euw, 20 Conant st., Roxbury Dist.
Unabhaengiger Gegenseitiger Kranken Unterstuetzungs Verein Von Boston Highlands, 55 Elm st.
Union Mutual Benefit Association, 85 Devonshire st.
United Daughters of Zion (Colored Women), Eliza A. Gardner, Treas., 20 No. Anderson st.
United States Benefit Association, 199 Washington st.
United States Mutual Accident Relief Company, 186 Washington st.

Societies of Odd Fellows for Mutual Relief.
Odd Fellows Beneficial Association of Mass, 515 Tremont st.
Odd Fellows Mutual Benefit Association, 21 Main st., Charlestown Dist.
Odd Fellows Mutual Ben fit Assoc'n, Neponset av., Dorchester.
United Order Ind. Odd Ladies, Osmer Hall, East Boston.

Societies of Scotchmen for Mutual Relief.
Caledonian Club, 43 Eliot st.
Scots' Charitable Society, 77 Camden st.

Societies to Promote Historical Researches.
Appalachian Mountain Club, 9 Park st.
Beacon Soc., J. W. Hayden, Sec., 78 Pearl.
Boston Memorial Association, P. Cummings, Sec., 82 Devonshire st.
Boston Soc. of Natural History, Berkeley st.
Boston Tablet Society.
Boston Zoological Soc., 3 Pemberton sq.
Bostonian Society, Old State House.
Bunker Hill Monument Association, 13 Doane st.
Dorchester Historical Society, 18 Somerset st.
Massachusetts Historical Society, 30 Tremont st.
Methodist Historical Society, 36 Bromfield st.
Military Historical Society, S. M. Quincy, Sec., 5 Mt. Vernon pl.
N. E. Historic-Genealogical Society, 18 Somerset st.
Webster Historical Society, Old South Church.

Societies to Promote Temperance.
Boston Woman's Christian Temp. Union, 515 Tremont st.
Catholic Total Abstinence Union.
Citizens' Law and Order League, 28 School st.
East Boston Women's Christian Temp. Union, 16 Paris st.
Mass. Branch Church Temp. Soc., Rev. E. Osborne, 44 Temple st.
Mass. Home for Int. Women, 41 Worcester street.
Mass. Social Temperance Union, 36 Bromfield st.
Mass. Soc. for Prom. of Temperance, R. Scott, Sec., 63 Court st.
Mass. Temp. Alliance, 28 School st.
Mass. Tem. Society, W. J. Barber, Sec., 265 Washington st.
Mass. Total Abstinence Soc., 36 Bromfield st.
Mass. Women's Christian Temp. Union, 36 Bromfield st.
Temperance Republican Headquarters, 36 Bromfield st.
Washingtonian Home, 41 Waltham st.
Young Men's Temp. Soc., Odd Fellows Hall.

Societies with Political Aims.
Am. Woman's Suffrage Assoc'n, H. B. Blackwell, Sec., 5 Park st.
Civil Service Reform Assoc'n, 68 Devonshire st.
Mass. School Suffrage Assoc'n, 5 Park st.
Mass. State Reform Club, S. R. McCready, Pres.
Mass. Tariff Reform Assoc'n, 40 State st.
Mass. Woman's Suffrage Assoc'n, 5 Park st.
N.E. Woman's Suffrage Assoc'n, 5 Park st.
Republican City Committee, 375 Washington st.
Republican State Committee, 106 Washington st.

Various Societies:
American Society of Hibernians, M. Dowling, Sec., 73 Harrison av.
Bank Presidents' Association, C. Guild, Sec., 88 Summer st.
Bar Assoc., R. Grant, Sec., 39 Court st.
Bicknell Association, E. Bicknell, Sec., 79 Milk st.
Bohemians, 43 Eliot st.
Boston Athenæum, 10B Beacon st.
Boston Base-Ball Assoc., 765 Wash. st.
Boston Bicycle Club, 87 Boylston st.
Boston Board of Marine Underwriters, 18 Merchant's Exchange.
Boston Chess Club, 53 Pemberton sq.
Boston Colored Improvement Assoc., 47 Hanover st.
Boston Commercial Base-Ball Association, 580 Washington st.
Boston Deaf Mute Society, 70 Kilby st.
Bost. Fire Underw'r's Union, 70 Kilby st.
Boston Marine Society, 13 Merchant's Ex.
Boston Soc. of Architects, 6 Beacon st.

Boston Terra Novins, 43 Eliot st.
Boston Theat'l Mech. Assoc., 616 Wash. st.
Boston Turnverein, 20 Middlesex st.
Bost. Typographical Union, 176 Trem. st
Boston Veteran Firemen Association, 4 Prescott st., E. B.
Bost. Young Men's Congress, 54 Essex st.
Boylston Schulverein, Boylston station.
Cape Cod Assoc., Eben Bacon, Treas.
Charlestown Vol. Vet. Firemen's Association, Geo. O. Wiley, Pres.
City Press Association, 242 Wash. st.
Eliot School Association, G. F. Hosea, Sec., 264 Washington st.
English High School Association, W. H. Moriarty, Sec., 680 Washington st.
Fire Notification Association, J. H. Ryan, manager, 5 Hamilton st.
Franklin Typographical Society, Hon. Hugh O'Brien, Treas.
Fraternity of the White Cross, 12 Pemberton sq.
German Social Club, 61 Maverick st. E.B.
Harvard Musical Assoc., Park Place.
Ingersoll Secular Society, Paine Hall.
Institute Canadien-Français, 18 Essex st.
Institut of Heredity, D. Needham, Pres.
Knights of St. Patrick, P. C. Conway, Sec.
Knights of the Wrench, 860 Wash. st.
Maritime Provincial Assoc., 241 Trem. st.
Mass. Bicycle Club, 152 Newbury st.
Mass. Fish and Game Protective Association, H. J. Thayer, Sec., 216 Wash. st.
Mass. Grange P. of H., Geo. Noyes, Sec., 45 Milk st.
Mass. Horticultural Society, Horticultural Hall, Tremont st.
Mass. Indian Association, Mrs. G. J. Fiske, Treas.
Mass. Mutual Fire Ins. Union, A. L. Barbour, Sec.
Mass. Society for Promoting Agriculture, 23 Court st.
Mass. State Fireman's Association, 20 Hawley st.
Nat'l League, 36 Bromfield st., Room 22.
N. E. Agricul. Soc., D. Needham, Sec., 45 Milk st
N. E. Associated Press, R. M. Pulsifer, Sec., 255 Washington st.
N. E. Ch's and Checker Clubs, 15 Pem. sq
N. E. Commercial Travellers' Association, 178 Devonshire st.
Orpheus Musical Soc., 724 Wash. st.
Paine Hall Liberal League, Paine Hall, Appleton st.
Parker Fratery, Parker Hall, Berkeley st.
Philharmonic Society, L. H. Wightman, Sec., 170 Washington st.
Phil-sec'tic Society, 114 Chauncy st.
Prince Society, 18 Somerset st.
Social Law Library, 13 Court House.
Society of the Cincinnati, F. W. Palfrey, Sec., 34 Equitable Building.
Sons of St. George, 176 Tremont st.
Spartans, 81 Seaverns av., Jamaica Plain.
Swedish American Soc., 176 Tremont st.
United Press, 242 Washington st.
Working Union of Prog. Spiritualists, Exeter st.
Young Men's Social Union, 54 Meridian st., E. B.

(See *Orders and Secret Societies.*)

ORDERS AND SECRET SOCIETIES.

American Legion of Honor.
Supreme Council. A. Warnock, Supreme Secretary, 20 Beacon st. Grand Council of Massachusetts, James K. Odell, Grand Commander, Boston; S. H. Jackson, Grand Secretary, 20 Beacon st; Norton Folsom, Grand Treasurer, Cambridge. Boston Councils are held as follows:
Alpha, 1, 1371 Washington st...1-3 Thurs.
Harmony, 6, 70 Sullivan st., Ch'n.2-4 Mon.
Morning Star, 7, Arcanum Hall...2-4 Fri.
Lincoln, 11, 2319 Wash. st........1-3 Mon.
Highland, 12, Tremont Hall....2-4 Thurs.
E. Boston, 15, Osmer Hall.........1-3 Wed.
Howe, 24, 285 W. Fifth st., S. B..1-3 Wed.
Warren, 29, 616 Wash. st.........1-3 Mon.
Suffolk, 37, 375 Columbus av.....2-4 Mon.
Egleston, 42, Egleston sq.........2-4 Mon.
Equity, 50, Tolman Hall, Matta...2-4 Mon.
Oriental, 72, Webster pl., Br'n...2-4 Wed.
Taylor, 87, O. F. Hall, S. B........1-2 Fri.
Windsor, 91, Parker Hall..........2-4 Fri.
Boston, 93, 2 Hayward pl.........1-3 Tues.
Amity, 108, Jamaica Plain........1-3 Tues.
Tremont, 128, 2319 Wash.........2-4 Thurs.
Dudley, 130, 2319 Wash..........2-4 Thurs.
Standish, 141, S. Boston..........1-3 Wed.
Star of the East, 161, O.F. Hall, S.B.2-4 Ths.
Odell, 394, Charles st............2-4 Thurs.
Social, 421, 1 Russia Wharf.....2-4 Thurs.
Garfield, 720, Bart. Hall, S. B...2-4 Thurs.
Bay State, 1145, 1783 Wash......2-4 Fri.
Columbian, 1188, 616 Wash. st...1-3 Tues.
Puritan, 1199, 18 Essex st.......2-4 Tues.

Ancient Order of Foresters.
S. R. Anderson, E. Cambridge, Secretary of the New England United District. The Boston Courts are held at the following places:
Ct. Commonwealth, 176 Tremont st., Sec., T. C. Kelleher, 10 Indiana pl.
Ct. Liberty, 197 Shawmut av., Sec., A. R. Billings, 112 W. Seventh.
Ct. St. Andrews, 3 Tremont row, Sec., O. T. Andrews, 48 Canal st.
Ct. Charles Sumner, 47 Hanover st., Sec., J. H. McEleney, 27 Corey st., Charles'n.
Ct. Maverick, 144 Meridian st., E. B., Sec., C. S. Provost, 154 Bremen, E. B.
Ct. Bonnie Dundee, 2319 Washington st., Sec., J. Shepherd, 1 Greenwich pl.
Ct. Evening Star, 2 Main st., Charlestown, Sec., J. Mahoney, 12 Moulton st.
Ct. Welcome, 3 Tremont row, Sec., G. McCarthy, 34 Broad st.
Ct. City of Boston, 616 Washington st., Sec., H. Quinn, 12 Cherry st.
Ct. Mass., 164 Hanover st., Sec., P. Daly, 45 Sudbury st.
Ct. Tremont, 176 Tremont st., Sec., J. P. Abbott, Cambridgeport.
Ct. Will Scarlet, 2373 Washington st., Sec., J. J. Kearns, 238 Centre st., Rox.
Ct. Good Shepherd, 376 Broadway, S. B., Sec., T. Ronald, 77 Jenkins st.

Ct. Highland, 2373 Washington st., Sec., H. Steeger, 270 Eustis st.
Ct. Edward Lasker, 176 Tremont st., Sec., H. Hanheimer, 4 G st.
Ct. Winthrop, O. F. Hall, E. B., Sec., N. Depner, 214 E. Eagle st.
Ct. Wendell Phillips, 3 Tremont row, Sec., W. T. Bibby, 7 Vernon pl.
Ct. Paul Revere, 197 Shawmut av., Sec., J. Sheehy, 54 Melrose st.
Ct. Bay State, 197 Shawmut av., Sec., H. J. Andrews, Hotel Cabe.

Ancient Order of Hibernians.
Division No. 2, Odd Fellows' Hall, E. B., 1st & 3d Wed.
Division No. 11, 59 Cambridge st. Mark Leonard, President.

Ancient Order of United Workmen. Grand Lodge. J. Edward Burtt, G. M. W. Charles B. Boothe, G. F. James Weymouth, G. O. Hugh Doherty, M. D. G. Recorder. Thomas F. Temple, G. Receiver. W. S. Thompson, G. G. John A. Farrell, G. W. The Boston Lodges are herewith given:
Beacon, 31 Essex st ....2-4 Mon.
Mass. Highland Hall ....1-3 Mon.
Unity, Hobah Hall, S. B..........2-4 Fri.
Everett, Upham Corner..........1-3 Tues.
Dearborn, Highland Hall........1-3 Tues.
Temple, Field Corner............1-3 Thurs.
Metropolitan, Parker Hall......1-3 Fri.
Archimedes, Garfield Hall......2-4 Tues.
Monticello, 212 Main st., Ch'wn..1-3 Tues.
Central, 144 Meridian st., E. B...1-3 Tues.
Prescott, Grand Army Hall Ch'n 2-4 Mon.

Catholic Order of Foresters.
High Court of Massachusetts. James J. McLaughlin, High Chief Ranger; James J. Barry, High Vice Chief Ranger; Bernard J. O'Daly, High Court Sec.; James F. Supple, High Treasurer. The Boston Courts are given as follows:
Cathedral Ct..............1221 Washington
Fenwick....................164 Hanover.
St. Francis.................187 Cabot
Leo.........................144 Meridian, E. B.
Cheverus..................Lusitana Ha'l
St. Patrick's ....Howe's Hall
Sherwood.................Caledonian Hall
Columbus.................854 Washington
St. Joseph's..............Camb. cor N. Russell
Fulton.....................197 Shawmut av.
Fitzpatrick................164 Hanover
SS. Peter and Paul....136 Broadway, S. B.
Hamilton.................172 Main, Charlestown
St. Peter.................H. School Ho., Dorch.
Williams..................Maverick sq., E. B.
Mt. Pleasant............Highland Hall
St. Alphonsus..........187 Cabot
St. Gregory............Sullivan Hall, Dorch.

Erin..................1221 Washington
Americus................Parker Hall
Shell........Hanover, cor. Blackstone
Friendship..................187 Cabot
St. Joseph............Foresters' Hall
Star of the Sea......... Bennington, E. B.
St. Augustine,...Howe's Hall, S. Boston
Constantine..........197 Shawmut av.
Lyndon...............Washington Hall
Holy Trinity...............Parker Hall
Highland..............1693 Tremont
St. James................176 Tremont
Carroll, Royal Arcanum Hall, Jamaica Pl.

Catholic Total Abstinence Union.
Archdiocese of Boston. President, Jeremiah G. Fennessey. Secretary, William H. Brine, 40 Houghton st., Somerville, Suffolk County; Vice President, Patrick J. Guerin.
Catholic Total Abstinence Society, 1st and 3d Wed. Cathedral.
St. James' T. A. and M. R., 1st Sun., St. James' Church, Harrison av.
St. James' Young Men's T. A. Union, 786 Washington st.
St Stephen's Total Abstinence, 1st and 2d Sun., Church.
St. Valentine's T. A., 2d and 3d Mon., Boston College Hall.
St. Joseph's Total Abstinence Society, 2d and 4th Sun., 59 Cambridge st.
SS. Peter and Paul T. A. and B. S., 1st Thurs., Broadway, near B, South Boston.
St. Vincent T. A. and M. R., South Boston, 3d Sun., Church.
St. Augustine M. R. and T. A. Society, Boston, Wed.
Father Mathew Total Abstinence, 4th Sun., Broadway Hall, South Boston.
Catholic T. A. and B., Sun., Webster Hall, East Boston.
St. Mary's Y. M. T. A. and L. A., Tues., Main st., Charlestown District.
St. Francis de Sales, Tues., Main st., Charlestown District.

Daughters of Liberty.
Lady Putnam Council, No. 5, Fridays, 212 Main st., Charlestown District.

Daughters of Rechab.
Massachusetts Encampment meets at 176 Tremont st. Secretary, Mrs. S. A. Bickner, 42 Lawrence st.; Treasurer, Mrs. Elizabeth Roberts.
North Star Tent, No. 6, Wed., 176 Tremont st.
Olive Branch Tent, No. 7, Wed., 176 Tremont st.

Druids.
United Ancient Order, William H. Lee, D. D. G. A. Sylvan Grove, No. 1, Frid., Boston Hall, 176 Tremont st.

Elks.
Benevolent and Protective Order, Elks' Hall, 24 Hayward pl. John H. Dee, E. R., Jos. Robertson, E. L. K., Willis R. Russ, E. L. K., Bennet Benari, E. L. K., R. L. Frampton, J. G., Edwin

Stearns, Sec., Louis L. Jones, Treas., J. B. G. McElroy, Tiler. Every Sunday night, from September to June.

Freemasonry.
Masonic Temple, Tremont st., cor. Boylston. A. H. Howland, Jr., Grand Master; Samuel Wells, G. Treas., 31 Pemberton sq.; Sereno D. Nickerson, G. Secretary, Masonic Temple. Meetings of Grand Lodge, 2d Wed. in December, March, June, September and December 27. Blue Lodges:

St. John's Lodge................1st Mon.
Mt. Lebanon....................2d Mon.
Massachusetts..................3d Mon.
Germania.......................4th Mon.
Revere.........................1st Tues.
Aberdour.......................2d Tues.
Joseph Warren..................4th Tues.
Joseph Webb....................1st Wed.
Zetland........................2d Wed.
Columbian......................1st Thurs.
St. Andrews....................2d Thurs.
Eleusis........................3d Thurs.
Winslow Lewis..................2d Fri.
Mt. Talor, E. B.)..............3d Thurs.
Baalbec, E. B..................1st Tues.
Hammatt, E. B.)................4th Tues.
Temple, E. B...................1st Thurs.
St. Paul's, S. B...............1st Tues.
Gate of the Temple, S. B.......4th Tues.
Baldoni, S. B.)................2d Tues.
Adelphi, S. B..................3d Tues.
Washington, Rox.)..............2d Thurs.
Lafayette, Rox.................2d Mon.
Union, Dore....................Tues.
Eliot, Jamaica Plain...........3d Wed.
Bethesda, (Brighton............Tues.
King Solomon, Charlestown......2d Tues.
Henry Price, Charlestown.......4th Wed.
Faith Lodge, Charlestown.......2d Fri.

Freemasonry.
Grand Royal Arch Chapter. Frederick R. Cotace, G. H. P.; Richard Briggs, G. Treas., Masonic Temple.
St. Andrew's Chapter...........1st Wed.
St. Paul's.....................3d Tues.
St. John's, J. B...............4th Mon.
St. Matthew's, S. B............2d Mon.
Mt. Vernon Chap., Rox..........2d Thurs.
Chapter of the Signet, Chas'tn..2d Thurs.
St. Stephen's, Quincy).........Tues.

Freemasonry.
Grand Council Royal and Select Masters; Scrants Bowen, G. Master. Grand Commandery of Knights Templars; Alfred F. Chapman, G. Rec., 223 Washington st. Convention of High Priests; John W. Dadmun, Pres. Ancient and Accepted Scottish Rite; Boston Lodge of Perfection, Masonic Temple, last Mon. in Jun., Meh., Sept. and Nov., L. M. Averill, T P. G. Master. A. and A. Scot. Rite, under jurisdiction Sup. Grand Council, Lawrence Hall, 724 Washington st. Prince Hall Grand Lodge (colored), Andrew M. Bush, M. W. Grand Master, 20 Blossom st. (See *Masonic Relief Associations*.)

Foresters. (*See Ancient Order of Foresters and Catholic Order of Foresters.*)

Good Templars. Independent Order, Grand Lodge of Massachusetts. Sarah A. Leonard, G. W. Sec., 28 School st. Lodges in Boston:
Florence, 1, S. B........................Mon.
Ray of Hope, 2, E. B. ....Thurs.
Commonwealth, 4....................Mon.
Leonard, 23, Charlestown...........Mon.
Tremont, 59, 1221 Washington st...Thurs.
Undine, 55..............................Fri.
Equity, 71..............................Fri.
Allston, 78, Brighton..............Thurs.
Stowe, 104, 465 Washington st.......Sat.
Light of World, Camb. st............Tues.
Monumental, 217, 212 Main st........Sat.
Boston, 300, 18 Essex................Mon.
Amiette, 138, 3 Tremont Row......Thurs.
Trimountain, 465 Wash.............Tues.

Golden Rule Alliance. 4 Exchange Place. J. S. Damrell, President; C. J. Spencely, Secretary. Chapters:
Alpha, Lenox St. Chapel............Wed.
Day Star, 84 W. Springfield st......Tues.
Gilbert Haven.......................Thurs.
Mt. Lebanon, Eg. Sq................Thurs.
Beulah, S. B. ....Mon.
Mt. Zion, Charlestown ....Tues.

Grand Army of the Republic. Headquarters Department of Massachusetts, 12 Pemberton sq. Commander, John W. Hersey. Boston Posts:
Dahlgren, 361 Broadway, S. B.......Wed.
Charles Russell Lowell, 735 Wash.....Fri.
Abraham Lincoln, Charlestown....Tues.
John A. Andrew, 1151 Washington...Fri.
Friedrich Hecker, 29 Middlesex.....Sun.
Joseph Hooker, E. B................Tues.
Thomas G. Stevenson, Roxbury....Mon.
Washington, S. B....................Wed.
Ben. Stone, Jr., Dorchester........Tues.
Francis Washburn, Brighton.......Mon.
E. W. Kinsley, 1682 Washington....Wed.
Robt. A. Bell, 59 Cambridge st.....Thurs.
G. L. Stearns, Charlestown..........Fri.
John A. Hawes, E. B.................Fri.

Harugari. German Order. Grand Lodge meets 1st week in August and February. G. Rothfuss, G. B. Lodges:
Eintracht, 176 Tremont............Thurs.
Kossuth, 1093 Tremont...............Sun.
Monument, 176 Tremont............Thurs.
Humboldt Mannie.....................Sun.
Goethe, E. B.......................Thurs.
Blucher, Roxbury....................Tues.

Hibernians. (*See Ancient Order of Hibernians.*)

Home Circle. (Inc. Jan. 13, 1880.) Supreme Council meets 2d Tuesday in Oct. Joel Seaverns, Sup. Leader; Thos. Waterman, M. D., Sup. Medical Ex., 146 Boylston St. Grand Council meets 4th Tuesday in Sept. Rodney P. Woodman, Grand Leader; F. M. Forbush, Grand Sec., 95 Milk St. Subordinate Councils:
Commonwealth ....1-3 Thurs.
Myrtle, (Jamaica Plain)........2-4 Thurs.
Jos. Warren, (Chas'n)..........2-4 Thurs.
Starlight...........................1-3 Wed.
Bay State, (Allston Dis't\.......2-4 Tues.
Dudley, 10 Warren st.............1-3 Wed.
Harvard (Chas'n) ....1-3 Mon.
Welcome, (S. B.)...................2-4 Fri.
Columbia, (Up. Corner)...........2-4 Wed.
Phenix (Allston)...................2-4 Wed.

Independent Order of Red Men. Meets 1st Sunday in Feb. and Aug. John Kirchgassner, South Boston, G. O. Ch. New England Encampment, meets at 1093 Tremont st., (Kossuth Hall,) 1st Sunday of each month.
Massachusetts, 1093 Tremont st.....Tues.
Bay State, 361 Broadway............Wed.
Massasoit, 176 Tremont st..........Mon.
Bismarck, 1093 Tremont st..........Sun.

Independent Order United Essenians. Supreme Lodge, S. B. Gilbert, S. C.
Pioneer Lodge, No. 1, Eagle Hall, 616 Washington st., 1st-3d Fri. Frank Baxter, sec.

Jewish Societies. I. O. Sons of Benjamin.
Kossuth, 176 Tremont st. ....Sun.
Mordecai, 176 Tremont st..........Tues.
Bay State, E. Berkeley st..........Sun.
Boston, 176 Tremont st.............Sun.
Eva, 176 Tremont st.................Sun.
Liberty, 176 Tremont st............Wed.
 I. O. B'NAI B'RITH:
Jegar Sahdutha......................Sun.
Amos, Eagle Hall ....Tues.
Boston, Minot Hall..................Sun.
Pinchas, 176 Tremont st............Sun.
Mosenthal, (E. B.)..................Tues.
 KASHER SHEL BARSEL :
Gal Ed, 176 Tremont st..............Wed.
Pinchas, 176 Tremont st.............Sun.
 I. O. FREE SONS OF ISRAEL :
Moses Mendelssohn...................Sun.
Bay State ....Sun.
 (Both at Wells' Memorial Hall, 987 Washington st.)
 ORDER B'RITH ABRAHAM :
Boston, 176 Tremont st...............Sun
Wendell Phillips, 176 Tremont st...Sun.
 (New Era Hall is at 176 Tremont st., Eagle Hall at 616 Washington st., corner Essex st.)

Knights of Labor. District E, No. 30. G. A. Carlton, chairman ; G. McNeill, secretary. Headquarters, 186 Devonshire st., room 4.

Knights of Honor. Knights of Honor Hall, 730 Washington st. Grand

Lodge meets 2d Wednesday in April.
Lodges, places and times of meeting :
Boston Lodge, 730 Washington st...Wed.
Charlestown, 2 Main st... ...Tues.
Amo, K. of H. Hall, E. B.)............Fri.
Roxbury, O. F. Hall.................Mon.
Golden Rule, 735 Washington st....Thurs.
Highland, 2243 Washington st.....Thurs.
Union, 730 Washington st............Mon.
Bellevue, Roslindale...............Tues.
Mattapanock, S. B.)................Wed.
Eagle, 730 Washington st..........Thurs.
Dorchester Up. cor................Mon.
Stony Brook Jamaica Plain.........Wed.
Paul Revere Charlestown ....Wed.
Chickering, 1783 Washington st....Tues.
Scandia, 730 Washington st.........Sat.
Brighton, O. F. Hall..............Thurs.
Broadway S. B.....................Thurs.
Commonwealth, 2519 Washington ...Wed.
Mass., 2419 Washington st..........Wed.
Sumner, Appleton st................Mon.
Mercantile, 616 Washington st.....Thurs.
King Arthur, 616 Washington st....Thurs.
Tremont, 1425 Tremont st..........Mon.
W. Roxbury, Cent. Sta..............Mon.
Peter Parenil ....Tues.
City Point (S. B.)................Tues.

Knights and Ladies of Honor.
Grand Lodge meets in Boston 2d Wed. in Oct. F. F. Boylen, Grand Protector, Samuel Hathaway, Grand Secretary, 150 Falmouth st. Lodges:
Jewel, 2543 Washington st..........Wed.
Unity, 730 Washington st...........Fri.
Island L. B........................
Magnet.............................Thurs.
Friendship S. B...................Thurs.
Waverly, 616 Washington st........Tues.
Shulman, Bartlett Hall..............Mon.
Vine Rock W. Roxbury...............Wed.
New England, 26 Union Park st.....Tues.

Knights of Pythias.
Grand Lodge is held at 150 B Tremont st. 2d Wednesday in February. James A. Fox, G. V.C.; Francis A. Chase, G. K. of R. and S., 149 B Tremont st., Lodges are held as follows:
Schiller, Park Hall................Mon.
Tutonia, Park Hall................Fri.
Commonwealth, 176 Tremont........Thurs.
Boston, 34 Essex st................Wed.
Webster, 18 Essex st...............Mon.
King Solomon, 18 Essex st.........Tues.
Foresters, 18 Essex st..............Fri.
Unity, 987 Washington st..........Mon.
King Philip, L. B.................Tues.
Mass., 2243 Washington st.........Mon.
Washington, 301 Broadway, S. B....Mon.
Ivanhoe, 2 Main, Charlestown.....Thurs.

Knights of the Golden Eagle.
Grand Castle meets 1st Tuesday in March. Grand Chief, George Otis Wiley, Charlestown district; Grand Master of Records, Albert G. Fray, 57 Congress st. Castles are located as follows:
Mizpah, 212 Main st., Charlestown..Tues.
Kenilworth, 616 Washington st....Thurs.

Windsor, 212 Main st ....Tues.
Columbia, Charlestown.............Mon.
Barbage, 987 Washington ....Mon.
Harmony, O. F. Had, E. B.........Mon.
Ivanhoe, O. F. Hall, Jamaica Plain, Tues.
Battalion, Armory, Charlestown ...Wed.

Masons. (See Free Masons.)

Military Order of Loyal Legion.
Commander, Charles R. Codman; Recorder, Arnold A. Rand, 53 Tremont st. Meetings at Young's Hotel, 1st Wednesday of every month.

Mystic Brothers.
Independent Order. Mystic Hall, 91 Hanover st. Meets 2d Tuesday in May. Subordinate Councils are held at the following places:
Winslow, Mystic Hall..............Fri.
Trimountain Council, Mystic Hall..Sat.
True Fellowship, Eagle Hall......Fri.

National American Association.
State Association meets 4th Wednesday in April, Sec., Henry H. Page, Warren st., corner Dudley st., Boston Highlands. Associations meet as follows:
Washington, K. of H Hall, Rox....Thurs.
Atlantic, Palladio Hall, Rox......Fri.
Warren, Palladio Hall, Rox........Fri.
Tremont, 2519 Washington st.......Fri.

Odd Fellows.
Odd Fellows' Building, 515 Tremont st. Grand Lodge meets second Thursdays in February and August. Edwin L. Pilsbury, Grand Master, Charlestown District. Places and times of Encampment and Lodge meetings:
Mass. Lodge, O. F. Hall............Mon.
Unity Lodge, O. F. Hall...........Tues.
Tremont Lodge, O. F. Hall.........Wed.
Siloam, O. F. Hall................Thurs.
Franklin, O. F. Hall..............Fri.
Washington, O. F. Hall............Tues.
Orient, O. F. Hall................Wed.
Mary Washington, O. F. Hall.....Thurs.
Suffolk Lodge, 21 Hayward pl.....Wed.
Massasoit Enc., 515 Tremont st...1 3 Fri.
Trimount Enc., 515 Tremont st...2 4 Fri.
Boston Enc., 515 Tremont st.....2 4 Mon.
Paul Revere Enc., 515 Tremont st.1 3 Mon.
Shawmut Camp, 515 Tremont st...3 Wed.
Mt. Washington Enc. S. B......2 4 Thurs.
Bethesda Lodge, S. B..............Mon.
Holah Lodge Dorch................Tues.
Last. Star Lodge, O. F. Hall E. B..Wed.
Ridgeley Enc., O. F. Hall E. B 1 3 Tues.
Loyal Rockett 730 Wash. st......2 4 Thurs.
Warren Lodge, 2330 Washington st. Tues.
Highland Enc., 2501 Wash. st .1 3 Thurs.
Olive Branch L. 25 Main st.,Ch'n ..Wed.
Mystic L. 25 Main st., Ch'n ....2 4 Thurs.
Hermann, O. F. Hall...............Fri.
Montezuma, O. F. Hall.............Mon.
Boston, O. F. Hall................Tues.
Commercial, O. F. Hall...........Thurs.
Commonwealth, O. F. Hall..........Fri.
Covenant, 987 Washington st.....Thurs.
Mt. Sinai, 987 Washington st.....Wed.

An. Landmark, 616 Washington st..Mon.
Putnam Lodge, 1435 Tremont st.....Tues.
Nonantum Lodge (Brighton).........Wed.
Rebekah Deg. Lodge(Brighton)1-3 Thurs.
Norfolk Lodge (Dorchester).........Wed.
Shalom Enc. (Dorchester).........1-3 Fri.
Neponset Lodge (Neponset District).Mon.
Dorchester Lodge (L. Mills).........Mon.
Azar Reb. D. Lodge (Dorchester).2-4 Fri.
Mt. Pleasant Lodge (Up. Corner)..Thurs.
Ellison Enc. (Fields Corner)......1-3 Fri.
Quinobequin Lodge (J. Plain).......Mon.
Bunker Hill Lodge (Charlestown)...Mon.
Howard Lodge (25 Main st.).........Fri.
Bunker Hill Enc. (25 Main st.,) Thurs.
Prescott U. D. Camp (Ch'n)........Wed.

Odd Fellows.
International Order. Sovereign Grand Lodge meets at 987 Washington st., 1st Monday in January, April, July and October. W. S. Swett, S. G. M.; P. McCabe, S. G. S., Chapman st.; P. Dacey, S. G. M. Boston Lodge No. 1, 987 Washington st., 2d and 4th Mondays of each month.

Odd Fellows.
Grand United Order, Federhen Hall, Cambridge st.
Boston Patriarchs..................Mon.
Sumner Lodge......................Wed.
Council 23........................Mon.
Bay State Lodge...................Tues.
Plymouth Rock Lodge, 20 Blossom..Tues.
Boston Lodge, 987 Washington st....Wed
Irving Lodge, 176 Tremont st.......Fri.

Odd Ladies.
United Order, Independent:
Amity Lodge (E. B.)..............Thurs.
Friendship Lodge (Charlestown)......Fri.
Olive Branch Lodge (Charlestown)..Wed.
Irvin Lodge, 176 Tremont st........Tues.
Fidelity Lodge (Ch'n District).......Mon.

Pilgrim Fathers.
Supreme Colony. Subordinate Colonies are as follows:
Highland Colony, 2298 Wash. st.....Wed.
John Winthrop, 1435 Tremont st...Thurs.
John Alden (E. B.)................Thurs.
Mt. Washington (S. B.).............Tues.
Gov. Dudley, 26 Union Park st......Mon.
Commonwealth, Wash. st., c. Essex.Wed.
Boston, 987 Washington st..........Mon.
Waverley (2 Main st., Ch'n).........Wed.
Revere Colony, 26 Union Park st.....Wed

Reform Clubs.
52 S. Market st., Samuel R. McCready, Pres.; W. S. McDonald, Sec. Clubs:
Boston Ref. Club, 3 Tremont row...Tues.
Faneuil Hall Club, 3 Tremont row...Sun.
People's Club, Berkeley st..........Fri.
Temple-St. Club....................Wed.
Lewis-st. Club......................Fri.
Monumental Club (Ch'n).............Sun.
Osgood Club (Ch'n)................Thurs.
Bunker Hill Club (Ch'n)............Mon.
Olive Branch Club, G. A. R. Hall..Wed.
(The Boston Reform Club also meets at 187 Atlantic av., on Sunday, 3 P. M.)

Royal Arcanum.
Headquarters, 7 Exchange pl., Congress st. Supreme Council yearly meeting, 1st Tues. in June, A. E. Tripp, S. R.; E. A. Skinner, S. T.; W. O. Robson, Sup. Sec. Office, Mass. Grand Council, 43 Kilby st. Henry Goodwin, G. R., Wm. N. Swain, G. Sec., A. D. Turner, Jr., (117 Milk st.), G. Treas. Annual meeting, 3d Wed. in March. Boston Subordinate Councils are held as follows:
Alpha, 735 Washington st. ......1-3 Thurs.
Eliot (Rox.) ....1-3 Fri.
Boston (18 Essex st.) ....1-3 Thurs.
Washington, Sumner Hall........2-4 Wed.
Temple, Sumner Hall............2-4 Wed.
Monument (Ch'n) ....1-3 Thurs.
Howard, Friendship Hall........1-3 Mon.
Bay State, (Rox.) ....2-4 Tues.
Bradley, (34 Essex st.) ....1-3 Fri.
Suffolk, (Rox.)...................1-3 Fri.
Forest, (J. Plain).................1-3 Thurs.
Lincoln (389 Broadway, S. B.)...1-3 Mon.
Warren, 987 Washington ....2-4 Tues.
Maverick (E. B.).................1-3 Fri.
Star, 730 Washington............2-4 Thurs.
Allston (Allston Dist.)............2-4 Fri.
Shawmut (Milton)...............2-4 Fri.
Tri-Mountain ....2-4 Mon.
Dorchester (Upham Cor.).......2-4 Mon.
John Hancock (18 Essex st.).....2-4 Fri.
Parker Hill 1435 Tremont st.,....2-4 Fri.
Winthrop (S. B.)................1-3 Tues.
Charlestown (2 Main st.) ......2-4 Mon.
Charles Sumner, 616 Washing'n 2-4 Thurs.
Jamaica Pl'n (Arcanum Hall,J.P.)2-4 Mon.

Royal Society of Good Fellows.
Assemblies in Boston.
Boston, 616 Washington st........3d Fri.
Puritan, 389 Broadway.......... 2-4 Wed.

Scottish Clans.
Grand Clan of Massachusetts. Alexander McKay, Grand Chieftain; Wm. J. Boyd, Grand Secretary, 33 Summer st. Clan McKenzie, No. 2 Eagle Hall, Essex st., cor. Washington st., 1st and 3d Wed.

Sons of Temperance.
Annual Sessions Grand Div. are held in Boston, 3d Wed. in April. J. W. Cameron, G. W. P.; C. E. Dennett, 36 Bromfield st., Grand Scribe. Division meetings are held as follows:
John Brown, 59 Cambridge st....... Mon.
Harmony 140, Meridian st. (E. B.)... Mon.
Evening Star (212 Main st., Ch'n.)...Mon.
Crystal Fount (Harrison sq.) ....Mon.
Norfolk (Dorchester Dist.)..........Tues.
Mass. (34 Essex st.)................Tues.
Signal Light, 2373 Washington st....Wed.
Crystal Wave (S. B.)................Wed.
Dorchester (L. Mills)................Wed.
Old Bay State, 34 Essex st.,.........Wed.
Mutual (Neponset Dist.)............Wed.
Ever True (Washington Vil.).......Thurs.
St. Mark (Dorchester Dist.).......Thurs.
Ocean Spray (S. B.)................Thurs.
Caledonia, 987 Washington st........Sat.

Templars of Honor. Subordinate Temples:
Trimount, 176 Tremont st............Fri.
Tremont, 144 Meridian ....Wed.
Phoenix (E. B.) ....Mon.
St. John (Charlestown).............Wed.
(Grand Council meets in June and Dec.)
Amo Council.........................Sat.
Shawmut Temple, 176 Tremont st.....Fri.
Washington Council (E. B.)........Mon.
Phoenix Section (E. B.)...........Tues.

Union Veteran Army. Headquarters, 63 Court st., Emmet J. Patterson, Pres.; J. S. W. Chapman, Sec.; B. F. Kelley, Treas.; Wilbur F. Lane, Asst. Recruiting Officer.

United American Mechanics.
C. S. Litton, S. C.; C. C. Littlefield, Box 27, South Boston, S. C. Sec. Annual meeting, Boston, Feb. 22. Charlestown Council, 212 Main st., Thursday.

United Fellowship. Sup. Council, 26 Union Park st. Henry Damon, Sup. Director. Councils:
Ivy, 26 Union Park st..............Mon.
Excelsior, 121 Washington st......Tues.
Eagle, 26 Union Park st............Tues.
Harmony, 26 Union Park st..........Wed.
Pearl, 26 Union Park st...........Thurs.
Hawthorne, 26 Union Park st........Fri.
Beacon Hill, 5 Park st............Thurs.
Lincoln, 1471 Washington st........Mon.
Althea (Dorchester) ....Thurs.
Park, 29 Upton st.................Mon.
Council No. 9, Osmer Hall (E. B.)..Thurs.

United Friends. Annual meeting of Grand Council, 2d Wednesday in April. Chris. J. Spenceley, G.C.; Edw. H. Studley, 127 Broad st., G. Rec. Boston Councils:
Cosmos, 18 Essex st...............Wed.
Dearborn, 2798 Washington st......Fri.
Aldine, 18 Essex st..............Tues.
Signet, 389 Broadway S. B.).......Fri.
Wendell Phillips 389 Broadway,(S.B.) Wed.
Boston, 1221 Washington st........Fri.
Trimountain, 176 Tremont st......Tues.
Kismet (Jamaica Plain)...........Thurs.

United Order Golden Cross.
E. Hartshorn, Grand Commander. Boston Commanderies:
Boston, 34 Essex st................Mon.
Mt. Washington, 389 W. Broadway..Thurs.
Mt. Pleasant, 2373 Washington st..Mon.
Highland ....Fri.
Charlestown 212 Main st...........Wed.
Commonwealth, 1371 Washington st. Wed.
Oriental (E. B.)................Thurs.
Beacon Light, 18 Essex st.......Thurs.
Brighton (Allston Dist.) ....
John A. Andrew, 91 Hanover st....Mon.
Gen. Warren (Charlestown Dist.)...Fri.

Women's Relief Corps. Mrs. M. S. Goodale, Pres.
Dahlgren Corps (S. B.)............Tues.
John A. Hawes Corps (E. B.).......Tues.
Chas. Russell Lowell Corps........Fri.
Abraham Lincoln Corps (Charlest'n) Tues.

(For addresses of officers in orders and Secret Societies, see *Addresses*.)

FIRE ALARM AND SERVICE.

Fire Department. The present fire-system was established during Mayor Henry L. Pierce's administration, in 1883. The Fire Commissioners are Henry W. Longley, chairman; John E. Fitzgerald, (term expiring in May, 1888); William A. Green, (term expiring in May, 1887). The Commissioners are nominated by the Mayor, and confirmed by the City Council. Salary of each, $3000 per annum. Clerk,—appointed by the commissioners, Frederick W. Smith, Jr. Salary $1200. Chief Engineer, Lewis P. Webber. Salary, $3000. Office, City Hall. There are ten Assistant Engineers; salary, $1600 each; three Clerks, and three Call Engineers. John W. Regan, Inspector of Hose and Harness; Henry R. Demary, Superintendent of Apparatus Repairs.

Fire Alarm Telegraph. The fire-alarm telegraph was invented by Dr. William F. Channing, of Boston, in 1845. In 1851 the City Government—after numerous experiments, appropriated $10,000 toward a final test of the system. Boston was the first city to employ the Fire-Alarm Telegraph, adopting it and putting it into successful operation in 1852. A constant watch is kept in the office, City Hall, night and day, by the operators. Accurate accounts are kept of the time of giving every alarm, and from the station whence it is sent. It takes but about half a minute to strike the alarm after receiving it from the box operated upon. Superintendent, Brown S. Flanders. Salary, $2800. Asst. Supt., Cyrus A. George. Salary, $4.75 per day. There are three operators, each receiving $4 per day.

Fire Alarm Telegraph. The Numbers and Locations of the Fire Alarm Boxes are as follows:

2 ....Phipps pl., Charter st.
3 ....Prince st., cor. Salem
4 ......Boston & Maine Freight Depot
4 ..(Dup.) Endicott st., cor Charlestown
5 ....Causeway st., cor. Lowell
6 ....Leverett st., cor. Willard
7 ....Poplar st., cor. Spring
8 ....Merrimac House, Merrimac st.
9....Constitution whf., Commercial st.
9 ....(Dup.) Hanover st., cor. Clark
12 ....Cooper st., cor. No. Margin
13 ....Richmond st., near Hanover
14 .....Eastern Av., cor. Commercial st.
15 . Richmond st., cor. Commercial. st.
16 ....East End of Faneuil Hall
17 ....Hanover st., cor. Endicott
18 ....Brattle st., opp. Quincy House
19 Haymarket sq.,(Boston & Me.Station)
21 ....Sudbury st., cor. Hawkins
23 ....Cambridge st., cor. Moss pl.
24 ....No. Russell st. Church
25 .....West City Stables, No. Grove st.
26 .....West Cedar st., near Cambridge
27 ....River st., (Engine House 10)
28 ....N. E. House, Clinton st.
29 ....Beacon st., cor. Clarendon
31 ....Beacon st., cor. Beaver
32 ....Pinckney st., cor. Anderson
33 ....State House, Mt. Vernon st.
34 ....Joy st., cor. Myrtle
35 ....Tremont st., cor. School
36 ....Old State House, N. W. cor.
37 ....India st., cor. Central Wharf
38 ......Atlantic Av., cor. Long Wharf
39 ....Mason st., (Engine House 26)
41 ....Washington st., cor. Milk
42 ....Tremont st., cor. Winter
43 ....Washington st., cor. Bedford
45 ....Federal st., cor. Franklin
46 ....Milk st., cor. Oliver
47 ....Fort Hill sq., (Engine House 25)
48 ....Atlantic av., junc. Federal st.
49 ....Summer st., opp. Hawley
51 ....Purchase st., cor. Pearl
52 ....Bedford st., cor. Lincoln
53 ....Washington st., cor. Boylston
54 ....Beach st., cor. Hudson
56 ....Old Colony Station, Kneeland st.
57 ....Quincy School, Hudson st.
58 .....Gasometer, near Federal st. Br.
59 ....East st., School House
61 ......Tremont st., junc. Shawmut av.
62 ....Pleasant st., cor. Eliot
63 ....Berkeley st., cor. Commonw'l av.
64 ....Washington st., cor. Indiana pl.
65 ....Broadway, cor. Albany st.
67 ....Washington st., cor. Common
68 ....Harrison av., cor. Wareham
68 (Private,) Loco. Works, Harrison av.
69 ....Dover st., cor. Albany
69 (Dup.) Engine House 3, Harrison av.
71 ....Warren av., cor. Berkeley
72 ....Washington st., cor. Waterford
73 ....Shawmut av., cor. Waltham
74 ....Dedham st., (Police Station 5)
75 ....Shawmut av., (Hose 5)
76 ....Tremont st., cor. Rutland sq.
77 ....Albany and Dedham sts.
78 ....So. City Stables, Albany st.
79 ....Marlborough st., cor. Exeter
81 ....W. Canton st., cor. Appleton
82 ....Northampton st. (Eng. Ho. 25)
83 ....Tremont st., cor. Camden
84 ....Beacon st., cor. W. Chester Park
85 ....Tremont st., cor. Castle
86 ....Washington st., cor. E. Concord
87 ....Shawmut av., cor. Lenox
88 ....Columbus av. and W. Newton
89 ....Boylston st., cor. Clarendon
91 ....Brighton and Brookline avs.
92 Huntington av., opp. Mechanic Hall
93 ....Tremont st., cor. Dartmouth
94 ....Dartmouth st. (Eng. Ho. 22)
95 ....Boylston st., cor. Arlington
96 ....Columbus av., cor. Berkeley
97 ....Spruce st., near Beacon
98 ....Columbus av., cor. Chester sq.
99 ....Newbury and Hereford sts.

FIR 145

SOUTH BOSTON:
112 . . . . Dorchester av. and Swan st.
113 . . . . B st., cor. First
114 . . . . D st., cor. Third
115 . . . . A st., cor. First
116 . . . . Eng. Ho., 15 Broadway
117 . . . . Broadway (Pol. Sta. 6.)
118 . . . . Dorchester av. and Dorr st.
119 . . . . Broadway and F st.
120 . . . . E st., cor. Eighth
121 . . . Dorchester av. and Dorchester st.
122 . . . . (Dup.) Hose 10, Dorchester st.
123 . . . . B st., cor. Sixth
124 . . . . G st., cor. Eighth
125 . . . . Dup.) Eighth st., near Mercer
126 . . . . Dorchester and Fourth sts.
127 . . . . D st., cor. Fifth
128 . . . . K st., cor. Eighth
129 . . . . K st., cor. First
130 . . . . Hose Ho. 12, Fourth st.
131 . . . . . (Dup.) I and Insts., Broadway
132 . . . . House of Correction Gate
133 . . . . H st., cor. Second
134 . . . . Boston Wharf, off Granite st.
135 . . . . (Dup.) Standard Sugar Refinery
136 . . . . P. st.'s Mills, First st.
137 . . . . Dorchester and Seventh sts.
138 . . . . Broadway and P st.
139 . . . . Eng. Ho. No. 2, O st.
140 . . . . Boston Cordage Co., N st.
141 . . . . . . (Dup.) Idiot Asylum, Fourth st.
142 . . . . Story st., near G
143 . . . . Congress and A sts.
144 . . . . Freight Sheds, Boston Wharf
EAST BOSTON:
151 . . . . South Ferry House
152 . . . . Sumner and Lamson sts.
153 . . . . Eng. Ho. 11, Orleans st.
154 . . . . Maverick st., near sq.
156 . . . . Sumner and Border sts.
157 . . . . Decatur and Liverpool sts.
158 . . . . Decatur and Paris sts.
159 . . . . E. Machine Shop, Marginal st.
160 . . . . Marginal st., Freight Sheds
162 . . . . Central sq.
163 . . . . Chelsea and Marion sts.
164 . . . . Simpson Dock
165 . . . . Eng. Ho. 5, Marion st.
167 . . . . Forge Works, Maverick st.
168 . . . . Grand Junction Yard
169 . . . . Webster and Lewis sts.
171 . . . . Dyewood Wharf, Border st.
172 . . . . 146 Condor st.
173 . . . . Eagle and Glendon sts.
174 . . . . Brooks and Saratoga sts.
175 . . . . Hose Ho. 6, Chelsea st.
176 . . . . Saratoga and Pope sts.
178 . . . . Saratoga and Moore sts.
179 . . . . Winthrop Junction
182 . . . . Sumner and Paris sts.
183 . . . . Cottage and Everett sts.
184 . . . . . Meridian and Princeton sts.
185 . . . . Putnam and Lexington sts.
186 . . . . Meridian and Eutaw sts.
187 . . . . Mav. Oil Works, Chelsea st.
188 . . . . Deer Island
189 . . . . Chelsea
ROXBURY DISTRICT.
211 . . . . . . Westminster and Williams sts.
212 . . . . Albany and Hampden sts.
213 . . . . Hampden st. and Norfolk av.
214 . . . . Washington and Arnold sts.
215 . . . . Tremont and Cabot sts.
216 . . . . Ruggles and Parker sts.
217 . . . . Tremont and Ruggles sts.
218 . . . . Washington and Warren sts.
219 . . . . Huntington and Longwood avs.
221 . . . . Clay and Elmwood sts.
223 . . Huntington av. and W. Chester pk.
224 . . . . Albany and Hunneman sts.
225 . . . . Eustis st., near Washington
229 . . . . Eustis and Dearborn sts.
233 . . . . George and Langdon sts.
234 . . . . Police Station 9, Dudley st.
235 . . . . Warren and Dudley sts.
236 . . . . Engine House 13, Cabot st.
237 . . . . Gas Co. Office, Dudley st.
238 . . . . Swett st., near Old Hospital
239 . . . . Shawmut av. (Horse R'y stable)
241 . . . . . Warren st. and Walnut av.
242 . . . . Clifford st. and Blue Hill av.
243 . . . . Engine House 14, Centre st.
244 . . . . Met. Stables, Bartlett st.
245 . . . . Police Station 11, Pynchon st.
246 . . . . Longwood av.
247 . . . . Tremont and Francis sts.
248 . . . . B. & P. R. R. Repair Shop
249 . . . . . . (Dup.) in State Fair Building
250 . . . . Burkhardt's Brewery
251 . . . . Highland and Cedar sts.
252 . . . . Dale and Washington sts.
254 . . . . Warren st. and Blue Hill av.
254 . . . . Pynchon and Heath sts.
255 . . . . . . Winthrop and Greenville sts.
256 . . . . Schoolhouse, Heath st.
257 . . . . Engine House 21, Warren st.
258 . . . . Tremont and Downer sts.
259 . . . . Centre and Parker sts.
261 . . . . . Washington st. and Codman av.
262 . . . . (Dup.) N. E. Hosp., Codman av.
263 . . . . Lodge of Marcella st. Lodge
268 . . . . Centre and Creighton sts.
269 . . . . Walnut av. and Munroe sts.
265 . . . . Warren and Dale sts.
266 . . . . Walnut av. and Dale st.
267 . . . . Parker and Alleghany sts.
268 . . . . Moreland st., opp. Fairland
269 . . . . Alpine and Regent sts.
270 . . . . (Pri.) Tag Factory, Vale st.
272 . . . . Crawford st., near Williams av.
273 . . . . Columbia and Blue Hill av.
274 . . . . Cherry and Quincy sts.
275 . . . . Columbia and Stanwood av.
DORCHESTER DISTRICT.
312 . . . . Boston and Mt. Vernon sts.
313 . . . . Dor. av. and Pond st.
314 . . . . Engine House 21, Boston st.
315 . . . . Dudley and Cottage sts.
316 . . . . Meeting House Hill
317 . . . . Bird and Ceylon sts.
318 . . . . . . Dudley st., near Meinadnock
319 . . . . Norfolk av., R'y Bridge
321 . . . . Savin Hill, R'y Station
322 . . . . McNeil Mills, Commercial st.
323 . . . . Clever corner
324 . . . . Green and Bowdoin sts.
325 . . . . Field corner
326 . . . . Harrison sq., Railway station
327 . . . . . . Neponset av. and Adams st.
328 . . . . Port Norfolk
329 . . . . Pleasant and Stoughton sts.
331 . . . . Hancock and Trull sts.
332 . . . . Old Harbor Point
334 . . . . Quincy and Bellevue sts.

Box	Location
335	Ashmont and Adams sts.
336	Mt. Bowdoin Station
337	Howard av. and Sargent st.
338	Cushing av.
341	Commercial and Freston sts.
342	Neponset av. and Minot st.
343	Walnut and Water sts.
345	Adams and Granite sts.
346	Dorchester av. and Codman
347	Washington and Fuller sts.
348	Richmond and Adams sts.
349	Dorchester av., near Fuller st.
351	Washington st. and Dorchester av.
352	Eng. Ho. 16, Temple st.
353	Eng. Ho 19, Norfolk st.
354	Norfolk and Madison sts.
356	Washington and Norfolk sts.
357	Eng. Ho. 18, Harvard st.
358	Dorchester av., cor. Centre st.
359	Austin Farm
361	Harvard st. and Blue Hill av.
362	Mt. Hope Cemetery
364	Washington st., near Coffee ct.
365	Small-pox Hospital
367	Norfolk st. and Thetford av.
368	Blue Hill av. and Walkhill
371	Clayton st. and Harrison sq.
372	Neponset st. and Boutwell av.

CHARLESTOWN DISTRICT:

Box	Location
412	School and Main sts.
413	Washington and Union sts.
414	Fitchburg Freight House
415	Fitchburg Railway
416	Harvard and Main sts.
417	Rutherford av.
417	Old Prison Yard
418	Fitchburg Yard, Warren av.
419	Dunstable st.
421	City sq. and Chelsea st.
423	Chelsea st. and Henley pl.
424	Bunker Hill and Vine sts.
425	Bunker Hill and Concord sts.
426	Hose Ho. 3, Winthrop st.
427	Chelsea and Prospect sts.
428	Chelsea Bridge
431	Bunker Hill and Webster sts.
432	Walker and Russell sts.
435	Medford st.
436	Bunker Hill and Auburn sts.
441	Eng. Ho. 27, Elm st.
442	Navy Yard Gate
443	Dock Elevator, Water st.
451	Medford st., opp. Tufts
452	305 Medford st.
453	Bunker Hill and Medford sts.
454	Arlington av. and Alford st.
461	Gardiner and Main sts.
462	H. & L. House, No. 9
463	Main st., foot of Baldwin
465	Grain Elevator, Cambridge st.

WEST ROXBURY DISTRICT:

Box	Location
512	Centre and Spring Park
513	Boylston st., Railway Station
514	Egleston sq.
516	Washington and A sts.
517	Harris av. and Alveston
518	Chestnut av. and pl.
519	Washington st. and Greenwood av.
521	Jamaica pl. R'y Station
523	Engine House 28, Centre st.
524	Prince and Perkins sts.
525	Pond and Prince sts.
526	May and Centre sts.
527	South and Key sts.
528	Forest Hill R'y Station
529	Walnut st. and Glen Rd.
531	Scarborough st.
532	Canterbury st., School House
534	Mt. Hope R'y Station
535	Poplar st.
537	Roslindale st.
542	Central R'y Station
543	Engine House 30, Vernon st.
546	Spring and Gardiner sts.
547	Germantown

BRIGHTON DISTRICT.

Box	Location
561	Cottage Farm Station
562	Brighton av., near Malvern
563	Allston st.
564	Barry Corner
565	Abattoir
567	N. Beacon and Market sts.
568	Oak sq.
569	Washington, opp. Oakland st.
571	Engine House 29
572	Washington st., near Union
573	North Harvard st.
574	Everett and Pleasant sts.
575	Western av.
576	Union sq.
578	Brooks and Newton sts.
579	Beacon st. and Chestnut Hill av.
581	North Harvard st.
582	Western Av.

Special Fire Alarm Boxes.

Box	Location
612	City Hospital
621	City Hall
631	Mass. Gen. Hospital
643	Mass. Hom. Hospital
731	Howard Athenæum
732	Boston Museum
734	Park Theatre
735	Globe Theatre
736	Public Library
741	Boston Theatre
742	Boston Music Hall
743	Masonic Temple
745	R. H. White & Co.
746	Jordan, Marsh & Co.
812	Mechanics' Hall, Huntington av.

Keys of the Alarm Boxes.

Police officers and one person residing near each station have keys to the Boxes. Alarms should not be sent in unless there is POSITIVE evidence of the existence of a fire.

Salaries of the Force.

The annual cost of maintaining the general Fire Department is about $500,000. Salaries are as follows:

Fire-Commissioners (each)	$3,000
Chief Engineer	3,000
Supt. Fire-Alarms	2,800
Assistant Engineers	1,400
Call Assistant Engineers	300
Assistant Foremen	1,250
Assistant Foremen	1,000
Enginemen	1,200
Assistant Enginemen	1,100
Hosemen	1,000
Laddermen	1,000
Chemical Enginemen	1,000

Hostlers	720
Veterinary Surgeons	1,500
Fire-Boat Captain	1,270
Mate of Fire-boat	1,800
Fire-Boat Engineman	1,500
Assistant Engineman	1,110
Deck Hands	1,880
Foreman Call-Force	1,000
W. Roxbury Foreman	1,002
Call Foreman	500
Engineman	1,200
Assistant Engineman	1,100
Drivers	1,000
Hosemen	150
Chemical Hosemen	100
Driver Chemical Engine	1,000
Laddermen	150
Brighton Foreman	1,000
Engineman	1,200
Assistant Engineman	1,100
Chemical Engine Driver	1,000
General Driver	1,000
Call Foreman	150
Hosemen	100
Laddermen	100
Fire-Alarm Operators	2,000
Batterymen	600

Noon Bells. Forty-nine bells, one hundred and ninety-six gongs, forty two tappers, and six vibrators, in various localities, on churches, school houses, engine houses and railway stations, are struck from the Fire-Alarm Office, precisely at noon every day. Correct time is furnished by telegraph from Cambridge Observatory, thus securing absolute accuracy.

School Bells. When there is a heavy storm raging, alarms (22) struck at twelve o'clock, indicate that there is to be no afternoon session.

Boston Fire Data. Following are dates of important events, relating to fires, etc., in Boston, chronologically arranged:

First engine imported	1676
Eight fire companies organized	1679
First engine house built	1711
Fire-wards established	1711
First church-bell alarms	1715
First hand-engine built	1765
Faneuil Hall burned out	1767
John Hancock gave engine	1772
Watchmen's-rattle alarms	1791
Federal-Street Theatre burned	1798
Columbian Museum burned	1807
Exchange Coffee House burned	1818
Beecher's Hanover-St. Ch'ch burned	1830
Morse telegraph invented	1832
First-paid fire department	1837
Telegraph fire-alarm invented	1845
Experiments with alarms	1848
Telegraph alarm adopted	1851
Tremont Temple destroyed	1852
Old National Theatre burned	1853
First steam-fire engine	1854
Miles Greenwood bought	1854
Hand-engines abolished	1860
Noh'nt H'tel destroyed	1861
New National Theatre burned	1863
Morris Bros. Opera House burned	1864
Winthrop House destroyed	1864
Parker House damaged	1865
Adelphi Theatre burned	1871
Great fire (65 acres)	1872
Globe (Selwyn's) Theatre burned	1873
Fire commission established	1873
Present system organized	1873
State Prison Workshops burned	1874
Tremont Temple burned	1879
Journal Building damaged	1880
American House damaged	1886

Great Fires have occurred in Boston in the years 1676, 1679, 1711, 1787, 1825, 1835, 1847, 1846 and 1872. The latter was the most disastrous, financially, that ever occurred in America, 65 acres of granite, iron and brick blocks, in the business heart of the city having been burned, at a loss of over one hundred millions of dollars. It broke out at the corner of Summer and Kingston sts., Nov. 9th, at 7.15 P. M. It spread with wonderful rapidity. Buildings were blown up to check its progress, but nothing availed, and it was only extinguished after the finest wholesale stores in the country were laid in ruins. In 1873, several acres, at the corner of Washington and Essex sts., were burned over.

Location of Steam Fire-Engines.

1	Dorchester and Fourth sts., S. B.
2	Fourth and O sts.
3	Harrison av., cor Bristol
4	Bulfinch st.
5	64 Marion, E. B.
6	Wall st.
7	East st.
8	114 Salem st.
9	Paris st., E. B.
10	River st., Mt. Vernon
11	Sumner st., E. B.
12	Dudley st.
13	Cabot st.
14	57 Centre st., Roxbury
15	Dorchester av.
16	Temple st., Dorchester
17	Meeting House Hill, Dorchester
18	Harvard st., Dorchester
19	Norfolk st., Dorchester
20	Walnut st., Dorchester
21	Boston st., Dorchester
22	Dartmouth st.
23	Northampton st.
24	Warren and Quincy sts.
25	Fort Hill sq.
26	Mason st.
27	11 Elm, Charlestown
28	Centre st., Jamaica Plain
29	Chestnut Hill av., Brighton
30	Mt. Vernon, W. Roxbury
31	India Wharf, (Fire Boat)
32	Bunker Hill, Charlestown

Chemical Engine Houses.
1 ....Bulfinch st.
2 ....Church st.
3 ....Longwood av.
4 .... Poplar st., W. Roxbury
5 ....Near Egleston sq.
6 .... So. Harvard av., Allston

Hose Companies.
1 .... Main st., Charlestown
3 .... Winthrop st., Charlestown
4 ...... 51 Bunker Hill st., Charlestown
5 ....368 Shawmut av.
6 ....301 Chelsea st., E. B.
7 ....1046 Tremont st.
8 ....North Grove st.
9 ....116 B st., S. B.
10 .... Washington Village
12 .... Fourth st., S. B.

Ladder Companies.
1 ....Friend st.
2 .... Sumner st., E. B.
3 .... Harrison av. and Bristol st.
4 .... Dudley st., cor. Winslow
5 ....W. Fourth st., S. B.
6 ....Temple st., Dorchester
7 ....Meeting House Hill
8 .... Fort Hill sq.
9 .... Main st., Charlestown
10 ....Centre st., Jamaica Plain
11 ....Chestnut Hill av., Brighton
12 .... 1046 Tremont st.
13 ....1171 Washington st.
14 ....Fort Hill sq.
.... Water Tower, Bulfinch st.

TELEGRAPH AND TELEPHONE.

Telegraph. Boston, from the time of the invention of the telegraphic system, has been closely identified with the progress of the service. It could scarcely be otherwise, as the inventor of the telegraph, Samuel F. B. Morse, was a native and citizen of the Charlestown District, having been born in the family homestead at the foot of Breed's (Bunker) Hill, 1791. The Telegraph having been invented in 1832, it was but a few years later that Boston capitalists began to invest largely in the stock. Several companies were organized here previous to 1840. Among the companies formed have been the Northern the first, Boston and Vermont, New York and Boston, the Magnetic, Union, American, Independent, People's, Insulated Air Line between Boston and Washington, International, Franklin, Atlantic, United States, and, later, the Western Union, with which have been merged the Atlantic and Pacific and American Union. To-day there is no city better supplied with facilities for telegraphing than Boston. Offices are numerous and conveniently located, rates are extremely reasonable, especially for night messages to the principal cities, and altogether there is nothing lacking to make the service completely satisfactory. Indeed, so well pleased with it are many business men and theatrical managers that with them the telegraph has almost superseded the postal service.

Telegraph Offices. One has not far to go on week-days to find an office, at any reasonable hour. If one is down town, he will find offices which are *never closed* day or night, Sundays included, at 109 State st., cor. Federal and Milk sts., Old State House, 177 Devonshire st., 31 Milk st., and up to midnight on weekdays the following offices are open: Hotel Brunswick, 12 Worcester st., Traveller's Building 31 State st., International Hotel (623 Washington st.), Washington st., cor. Waltham; while at the leading hotels offices are open until 10.30 p. m. The cable offices are *never closed*. The service of the various lines is quite efficient, and the tariff reasonable. Following are the locations of the offices of the different lines, with hours of closing:

Atlantic Cable. Commercial Mackay-Bennett, 4 Arch st., never closed. Direct, 109 State st., never closed.

Baltimore and Ohio.
33 Milk st.,	never closed.	
Chamber of Commerce	5.30	p.m.
Stock Exchange	5.30	"
26 No. Market st.	6	"
Hotel Vendome	8	"

9 Bennet st.	8	p.m.
175 Atlantic av.	8	"
T Wharf, Atlantic av.	8	"
242 Columbus av.	8	"
Boston Hotel	8	"
211 Washington st.	8	"
28 Central st.	8	"
65 High st.	8	"
1382 Tremont st.	8	"
42 Springfield st.	8	"
386 Broadway, S. B.	8	"

Multiplex. 78 Devonshire st., 8 a.m. to 5.30 p. m.

Mutual Union.
Federal st., cor. Milk	Never closed	
Old State House	"	"
Produce Exchange	5.30	p.m.
Board of Trade	5.30	"
34 Broad st.	6.00	"
109 Atlantic av.	6.00	"
International Hotel	12.00	"
Washington, cor. Waltham	12.00	"

United Lines.
177 Devonshire st.	Never closed	
84 Devonshire st.	5.30	p.m.
110 High st.	5.30	"
7 Merchants Row	5.30	"
38 Broad st.	5.30	"
T Wharf	5.30	"
Stock Exchange	5.30	"
105 Summer st.	6.00	"

Western Union.
109 State st.	Never closed	
State House	5.00	p.m.
Stock Ex., 53 State st.	5.30	"
Produce Ex., Quincy Market	5.30	"
197 Atlantic av.	6.00	"
Shoe & Leather Ex.	6.00	"
101 High st.	6.00	"
B. & M. R. R. Station	6.00	"
Old Colony Station	6.00	"
N. Y. and N. E. Station	6.00	"
Fitchburg Station	6.00	"
Commercial st., cor. S. Market	6.00	"
105 Chauncy st.	6.00	"
Boston & Lowell Station	6.00	"
23 Commercial Wharf	6.00	"
Eastern R. R. Station	7.00	"
Revere House	8.00	"
Hotel Vendome	8.00	"
East Boston P. O.	8.00	"
South Boston P. O.	8.00	"
City sq., Chsn.	8.00	"
United States Hotel	8.00	"
Young's Hotel	8.00	"
American House	8.00	"
Quincy House	8.00	"
Crawford House	8.00	"
Adams House	8.00	"
Boston P. O.	10.00	"
2340 Washington st.	10.00	"
Boston & Providence Station	10.30	"

Boston & Albany Station......10.30 p.m.
Tremont House.................11.00 "
Hotel Brunswick................12.00 "
12 Worcester st................12.00 "
Traveller Building, (31 State)...12.00 "

Messenger Service. The District Telegraph offices (Messenger Service) is used in connection with all of the Telegraph offices named.

Night Rate Messages.—Messages to be forwarded at night rates (which are sent at about one-half the tariff for day messages) can be filed at any time of day.

Night Rates.—The night rates of the United Lines are: To all points north of — and including Virginia, Kentucky and Missouri — 15 words for 15 cents; south of this line, one-half of the day rate.

Tariff for Mexico, (10 words, or less): City of Mexico, $3; Chihuahua, $1.80; Guaymas, $1.64; Tampico, $3.50; Tuxpan, $4.25; Vera Cruz. $3. All other places in Mexico (via Galveston) $3.50.

Tariff to Great Britain,—(England, Ireland, Scotland, Wales), France and Germany, by Atlantic Cable, 40 cents per word. Rules for Cable Messages — all lines — are as follows: 1. The maximum length of a chargeable word is fixed at *ten letters*. Should a word contain more than ten letters, every ten (or fraction of ten) will be counted as a word. 2. Code messages must be composed of words in the English, French, German, Spanish, Italian, Dutch, Portuguese and Latin languages. Proper names (names of persons and places) will not be permitted in the text of Code Messages, except in the manner used in ordinary private messages. 3. Groups of figures (or letters) will be counted at the rate of three figures (or letters) to a word, and one word for any excess.

Tariff to Havana. The rate to Havana, Cuba, is 50 cents for each word.

Gold and Stock Telegraph Company, 7 Merchants' Exchange, 53 State st.

Boston's First Telegraph Office, that of the Northern Telegraph Company, was opened in 1839, in Court square, corner of Williams ct., in the building now used by the Second Station of Police.

Telephone. It is interesting to note the fact that the telephone now in general use almost everywhere, was first developed as a transmitter of conversation by Prof. A. Graham Bell, of Boston University, 12 Somerset st. He had a laboratory in Exeter pl., Chauncy st. On Feb. 13, 1877, the first messages ever sent by telephone were received at the Exeter pl. Laboratory, in Boston, from Prof. Bell, who had gone to Salem, 16 miles out, for that express purpose. His dispatches were published Feb.14 (the next morning), the Boston Daily *Globe* of that date being the first newspaper on record to publish telephone messages. Prof. Dolbear, of Tufts College, College Hill, about this time invented what is known as the Dolbear Telephone. The first telephone established in Boston was the Bell, the formation of the American Bell Telephone Company rapidly bringing the system into general use.

Telephone Tariff to New England Cities and Towns. The tariff to Biddeford, Me., is 25c; Kittery, Me., 25c; Portland, Me., 25c; Amherst, N. H., 25c; Concord, N. H., 25c; Dover, N. H., 25c; Exeter, N. H., 25c; Farmington, N. H., 25c; Gilmanton, N. H., 35c; Great Falls, N. H., 25c; Keene, N. H., 25c; Manchester, N. H., 25c; Nashua, N. H., 25c; Portsmouth, N. H., 25c; Abington, Mass., 25c; Athol, Mass., 35c; Attleboro, Mass., 25c; Brockton, Mass., 25c; Brookfield, Mass., 35c; Fall River, Mass., 40c; Falmouth, Mass., 50c; Fitchburg, Mass., 25c; Gardner, Mass., 30c; Gloucester, Mass., 25c; Haverhill, Mass., 25c; Lawrence, Mass., 25c; Lowell, Mass., 25c; Lynn, Mass., 25c; Milford, Mass., 25c; New Bedford, Mass., 40c; Newburyport, Mass., 25c; Osterville, Mass., 50c; Oxford, Mass., 35c; Peabody, Mass., 25c; Petersham, Mass., 35c; Plymouth, Mass., 25c; Salem, Mass., 25c; Swampscott, Mass., 25c; Taunton, Mass., 35c; Webster, Mass., 35c; Worcester, Mass., 30c; Bristol, R. I., 25c; Newport, R. I., 45c; Pawtucket, R. I., 25c; Providence, R. I., 25c; Woonsocket, R. I., 25c.

Telegraph Companies in Boston. Baltimore & Ohio Telegraph Co., 33 Milk st.; Boston District Telegraph Co., 33 Milk st.; Boston Electric Protective Association, 56 Summer st.; Boston Multiplex Telegraph Co.,—Eastern District,—78 Devonshire st.; Commercial Cable Co., 4 Arch st.; Direct Cable, 109 State st.; Financial Telegram Co., 54 Devonshire st.; Gold and Stock Telegraph Co., 7 Merchants Exchange; Mutual District Messenger Co., basement Old State House, State st., cor. Washington; Mutual Union Telegraph Co., 77 Milk st.; New England Telegraph Co., 266 Washington st.; United Line Telegraph Co., 141 Devonshire st.; Western Union Telegraph Co., 109 State st.

Associated Press. 109 State st. This is an Association of Newspaper Publishers, made some years ago, for the purpose of securing exclusive privileges in telegraphic news. The Association is limited to certain daily and weekly publishers, no new members now being admitted.

Messengers may be obtained from the office, Old State House, by Telephone, at all hours of the day or night.

New England Telephone and Telegraph Company.
Boston offices: The great Central Telephone Office is at 50 Pearl st., with branch offices at 485 Tremont st., South End, and at 52 Warren st., (Boston Highlands).

New England Telephone City Pay Stations.
The City Pay Stations are at the following points:
Central Office.................... 50 Pearl
Up Town Branch............... 485 Tremont
Highland Branch.............. 52 Warren
Adams House... ....555 Washington
Young's Hotel................ 3 Court av.
Revere House................Bowdoin sq.
B. & Lowell sta.............92 Causeway
Hotel Bristol ....Boylston
Hotel Vendome.................Back Bay
Parker House ....School
Hotel Clifton......485 Columbus av.
South End.............1386 Washington
South End .... 1523 Washington
South End..............89 Chester sq.
South End.............151 W. Canton
North End....Washington, cor. Hanover
North End..................386 Hanover
Adams Bui'ding................3 Court
Old Colony sta...............Kneeland st.
Horse-car sta................Bowdoin sq.
Mt. Pleasant.............. 1 Blue Hill av.
Roxbury. .... 5 Pyncheon
South Boston ....N st., City Point

New England Telephone Company Executive Officers.
President of the Company, Thomas Sherwin; President's Assistant, David B. Parker; Treas., Wm. R. Driver; Sec., F. J. Boynton; General Manager, J. N. Keller; Assistant General Manager, W. J. Denver; Cashier, Charles B. Wells. Executive Offices, 50 Pearl st.

New England Telephone Exchange.
The Telephone Exchange, at 50 Pearl st., is a most interesting point to visit. Strangers are always welcome.

Telephone Companies in Boston.
American Bell Telephone Co., 95 Milk st.; Anti-Bell Telephone Co., 82 Devonshire st.; Continental Telephone Co., 95 Milk st.; Dolbear Telephone Co., 51 State st.; Inter-Continental Telephone Co., 95 Milk st.; Mexican Telephone Co., 53 Devonshire st.; New England Telephone and Telegraph Co., 50 Pearl st.; Tropical American Telephone Co., 95 Milk st.

Telephone for Police Assistance.
There is no direct Telephonic communication with the Police Stations from Pay stations or private residences; but by sending a message to the Central Telephone Station messengers can be despatched to the nearest Police Station, and any information given.

Telephone Messengers.
Messengers are furnished from the following City Pay Stations only: 50 Pearl st.; 485 Tremont st.; 52 Warren st. Messengers are sent from the following Suburban Pay Stations only: Chestnut Hill; Clarendon Hills; Dedham; Weymouth.

Telephone Suburban Offices:
Suburban Offices have been established at Brookline, Cambridge, Canton, Charlestown, Chelsea, Dorchester, East Boston, Hyde Park, Jamaica Plain, Malden, Medford, Milton, Newton, Newtonville, Quincy, Somerville, Waltham, Woburn.

Telephone Suburban Pay Stations:
Allston ....Beck & Harris
Bedford..................Bedford House
Brighton .... Warren's
Chestnut Hill............Railway sta.
Clarendon Hills..............Colby's
Dedham ....Smith's
East Milton................
East Weymouth..............Cutter's
Everett......................Kimball's
Harvard Square............Bartlett's
Highlandville..............Whetton's
Hingham... ....Cushing House
Hingham Centre..........Fearing's
Hollbrook ....White's
Malden ....W. End Store
Mattapan..............Mattapan House
North Cambridge....Maccabee & Long's
North Weymouth..............Orcutt's
Quincy Point...............Post-Office
Reading ....Danforth's
South Weymouth..............Nash's
Stoneham..................Gordon's
Upham Corner..............Upham's
Watertown....................Taylor's
W. Newton..................Fleming's
W. Somerville...............Studley's
Weston....................Cutting's
Weymouth................. Smith's
Wollaston................Railway sta.
Wyoming..................Gilman's

Telephone Tariff.
For five minutes' or less use of the Telephone at any of the City Pay Stations, for the sending of messages to city subscribers, the fee is 15 cents.

Telephone Tariff to Subscribers.
The cost of using the Telephone by subscribers is $10 per month; $30 per quarter; $120 per year.

Telephone Telegraph Service. Telegrams may be sent by Telephone to the main office of the Western Union Telegraph Company, 109 State st., or to its Suburban Branch Offices at Brookline, Cambridge, Canton, Harrison sq., Hyde Park, Somerville and Woburn.

Telephone to Cab and Carriage Standings. Cabs, carriages, etc., may be ordered by Telephone at any Pay Station.

Telephone to Messengers. Messengers for any service may be called by Telephone, by giving full particulars to the Central Station concerning the manner of service required.

Telephone to New York City. An office for Telephone service for Long Distances has been opened at the Adams House, 555 Washington st. The line extends to New York City, and points in Rhode Island and Connecticut. The rate to New York City is one dollar.

Telephone to the Suburbs. What is known as the Suburban Sub-Division (George E. Hanson, Superintendent, Somerville), comprises Arlington, Bedford, Braintree, Brighton, Brookline, Cambridge, Canton, Charlestown, Chelsea, Dedham, Dorchester, East Boston, Everett, Hingham, Holbrook, Hyde Park, Jamaica Plain, Lexington, Lincoln, Malden, Medford, Melrose, Milton, Needham, Newton, Norwood, Quincy, Randolph, Reading, Revere, Sharon, Somerville, Stoneham, Stoughton, Wakefield, Waltham, Watertown, West Roxbury, Weymouth, Wilmington, Winchester, Winthrop, Woburn.

MESSENGER SERVICES.

Soldier-Messenger Corps. For the delivery of letters, circulars, messages, small packages, etc., in Boston and near suburbs. Stations are as follows:

1............Boston and Maine R'y sta.
2............Tremont, cor. Berkeley sts.
3............Scollay sq.
4............Union Park and Concord sq.
5............Merchants' row, cor. State st.
6............Cor. Milk and Washington sts.
7............Cor. Summer and Washington sts.
8............Boston and Albany sta.
9............Boston and Providence sta.
10 State cor. Washington. Old State House
11............Cor. Winter and Tremont sts.
12............Front Merchants Bank, 28 State st.
13............Boylston Market
14............Cor. Charles and Beacon sts.
16............Cor. Arlington and Beacon sts.
17............Congress st., cor. Post Office sq.
18............Liberty sq.
19..Opp. Horticultural Building, 100 Tremont st.
20............Cor. Devonshire and Milk sts.
21............Lowell and Eastern sta's.
22............State House
23 Front Merchants' Exchange,55 State st.
24..Front of Parker House, on School st.

Mutual District Messenger Company. Principal Office, Old State House, Washington st., cor. State st. Branch offices at the various hotels and railway stations. General Manager, D. J. Hern; Superintendent, W. H. Smith. Neatly uniformed messengers are furnished to deliver letters, packages, etc., and to perform all kinds of commissions, errands, etc., as well as to stand in line and secure amusement tickets at the various theatres and music halls, in advance. The delivery of circulars, handbills, etc., is attended to, and the Company will also take charge of the folding and addressing of such matter. Messengers can be had at *all hours of the day or night*, at a general rate of 30 cents per hour.

MILITARY ORGANIZATIONS.

Militia. *Commander-in-Chief*, His Excellency, Governor George D. Robinson. Staff: *Adjutant-General, Quartermaster-General, and Inspector-General*, Brig.-Gen. Samuel Dalton. *Asst. Adjutants Gen.*, Cols. Geo. A. Flagg, Ed. H. Gilbert. *Ast. Inspectors Gen.*, Cols. H. T. Rockwell, Ed. E. Currier. *Asst. Quartermasters General*, Cols. Ed. E. Metcalf, H. E. Boynton, Ephraim Stearns. *Judge-Advocate-General*, Brigadier-General Edward P. Nettleton. *Surgeon-General*, Brigadier-General Alfred F. Holt. *Aides-de-camp*, Cols. Edward J. Russell, William S. Greenough, Charles H. Allen, John J. Whipple.

First Brigade. Headquarters, 608 Washington st. *Brigadier-General*, Nathaniel Wales. *Asst. Adjutant-General*, Lieut.-Col. William M. Olin. *Medical Director*, Lieut.-Col. George E. Pinkham. *Asst. Inspector-General*, Major John W. Sanger. *Brig. Quartermaster*, Capt. John B. Osborn. *Aide-de-Camp*, Capt. Benjamin F. Field, Jr., of Boston; Joseph H. Lathrop. *Engineer*, Capt. L. T. Boyce. *Judge Advocate*, Capt. Bowdoin S. Parker. *Provost Marshal*, Capt. F W. Reynolds. *Signal Officer*, Charles H. Cutler.

Second Brigade. Headquarters, 26 Pemberton square. *Brigadier-General*, Benj F. Peach, Jr., Lynn. *Asst. Adjutant-General*, Lieut.-Col. Charles C. Fry, Lynn. *Medical Director*, Lieut.-Col. Thomas Kittredge, Salem. *Asst. Inspector-General*, Maj. Joseph A. Ingalls, Swampscott. *Brig. Quartermaster*, Capt. George W. Preston, Boston. *Aides-de-Camp*, Captain A. N. Sampson, Capt. Ezra J. Trull, Boston. *Engineer*, Capt. Wm. T. Lambert, Boston. *Judge Advocate*, Captain Elijah George, Boston. *Provost Marshal*, Capt. Aaron A. Hall, Boston. *Signal Officer*, C. Merton Haley, Boston. *Ambulance Officer*, Samuel B. Clarke.

First Corps of Cadets. Headquarters, 130 Columbus avenue. *Lieutenant-Colonel*, Thomas F. Edmands. *Major*, George R. Rodgers. *Adjutant*, E. R. Hill. *Quartermaster*, Charles E. Melcher. *Paymaster*, Capt. Charles E. Stevens. *Surgeon*, Dr. Wm. L. Richardson. *Asst. Surgeon*, Chas. M. Greene. This Corps has a Battalion organization, with the following Company Officers: Francis H. Appleton, W. H. Alline, Andrew Robeson, H. B. Rice, each with the rank of Captain. William A. Hays, T. B. Ticknor, Robert C. Heaton, William B. Clarke, rank of First Lieutenants.

First Regiment of Infantry. Headquarters, 605 Washington Street. *Colonel*, Austin C. Wellington, Boston. *Lieut. Colonel*, A. B. Hodges, Taunton. *Majors*, T. R. Mathews, Boston; J. F. Jackson, Fall River; Charles L. Hovey, Boston. *Adjutant*, Fred'k G. King, Boston. *Quartermaster*, Francis Batcheller, Boston. *Paymaster*, W. W. Kellett, Boston. *Surgeon*, Otis H. Marion. *Chaplain*, M. J. Savage.

Fifth Regiment of Infantry. Headquarters, 6 Ashburton pl. *Colonel*, Wm. A. Bancroft, Cambridge. *Lieutenant-Colonel*, Alonzo L. Richardson, Woburn. *Majors*, G. F. Frost, Waltham; J. H. Whitney, Medford. *Adjutant*, Leon H. Batemen, Boston. *Quartermaster*, Fred'k P. Barnes, Newton. *Paymaster*, Everett W. Burdett, Boston. *Surgeon*, R. B. Dixon, Boston. *Asst. Surgeon*, John A. Mead, Watertown. *Chaplain*, Samuel J. Barrows, Boston.

Ninth Regiment of Infantry. Headquarters, 3 Park st., room 14, *Colonel*, William M. Strahan, of Boston. *Lieut. Colonel*, Lawrence J Logan, of Boston. *Majors*, Patrick J. Grady, of Boston; Fredrick B. Bogan, of Boston. *Adjutant*, David McGuire, of Boston. *Quartermaster*, James A. Nugent, of Boston. *Paymaster*, John Hogan, of Boston. *Surgeon*, William H. Devine, of Boston. *Chaplain*, James Lee, of Boston.

First Battalion of Cavalry. Headquarters, 27 Tremont st. *Major*, Horace G. Kemp, of Cambridge. *Adjutant*, J. P. Frost, of Boston. *Captains*, Henry D. Andrews, Lemont G. Burnham. *Lieut.*, Isaac H. Allard. *Quartermaster*, S. B. Newton, of Boston. *Paymaster*, Samuel Noyes, jr., of Cambridge. *Surgeon*, H. L. Burrell, of Boston. *Asst. Surgeon*, T. M. Durrell, of Boston. *Chaplain*, William H. Rider, of Gloucester.

Light Artillery. Battery A. Headquarters, cor. Wareham st. and Harrison av. *Captain*, John C. Potter. *First Lieutenant*, James R. Murray. *First Lieutenant*, Charles D. White. *Second Lieutenant*, Alfred A. Mercer.

Ancient and Honorable Artillery Company. (1638.) The oldest military organization in the United States. Headquarters, Faneuil Hall. Officers: *Captain*, Ezra J. Trull, Charlestown District. *First Lieut.*, Henry E. Smith, Worcester. *Second Lieut.*, Isaac D. Dana, Boston. *Adjutant*, Edward L. Wells,

Boston. *First Sergt. of Infantry*, Lyman S. Hapgood, Boston. *Second Sergt. of Infantry*, Aaron A. Hall, Dorchester District. *Third Sergt. of Infantry*, F. F. Olney, Providence. *Fourth Sergt. of Infantry*, William H. Marsh, Boston. *Fifth Sergt. of Infantry*, William J. Smith, Boston. *Sixth Sergt. of Infantry*, Charles H. Betteley, Roxbury District. *First Sergt. of Artillery*, Jacob Fottler, Boston. *Second Sergt. of Artillery*, Daniel H. Smith, North Attleboro'. *Third Sergt. of Artillery*, Albert E. Lockhart, East Cambridge. *Fourth Sergt. of Artillery*, Charles B. Barrett, Boston. *Fifth Sergt. of Artillery*, Thomas L. Churchill, Chelsea. *Sixth Sergt. of Artillery*, Charles T. Robinson, Taunton. *Treasurer and Paymaster*, Vincent La Forme, Boston. *Clerk and Asst. Paymaster*, George H. Allen, Boston. *Armorer and Quartermaster*, George P. May, Boston.

Boston Light Infantry.

Veteran Corps. (1852.) *Lieutenant-Colonel*, Ezra J. Trull. *Adjutant*, Albert C. Betteley. *Quartermaster*, James C. Laughton. *Surgeon*, Joseph T. Brown. *Paymaster*, John D. Lilley. *Commissary*, Chas. T. Hough. *Sergeant-Major*, Lewis F. Foster. *Quartermaster-Sergeant*, Caleb L. Pope. *Chaplain*, Edward A. Horton. *Captains*, B. Appleton, Jacob Bensemoil. *Lieuts.*, W. G. Shillaber, Frank H. Little, Edwin D. W. Wardrop, Joshua M. Cushing, Geo. Warner, John McDonough. *Trustees*, C. G. Attwood, Samuel Hichborn, Charles W. Wilder.

HOTELS IN BOSTON.

Public Hotels. This city is distinguished for its numerous large and elegant hotels, which are by travellers pronounced to be unsurpassed in all that pertains to luxurious furnishing, comfort, a good table, reasonable prices and accessibility, by those of any capital of the world. The names and locations of some of the principal Hotels are:

Adams, 553 Washington st., George G. Hall.
American, 50 Hanover st., H. B. Rice & Co.
Boston, Harrison av., cor. Beach, Baxter & Young.
Brunswick, 198 Boylston st., Barnes & Duncklee.
Clarendon, 521 Tremont st., J. P. Draper.
Commonwealth, 1697 Washington st., R. W. Carter & Co.
Coolidge, Bowdoin sq., I. N. Andrews & Co.
Crawford, 83 Court st., Stumcke & Goodwin.
Creighton, 245 Tremont st., Robertson & Long.
International, 623 Washington st., Mrs. K. Reichardt.
Maverick, 24 Maverick sq., E. B., Charles Moore.
Metropolitan, 1162 Washington st., John McKay.
Oxford, Huntington av., T. B. Gaskell.
Park, 4 Bosworth st., Wm. D. Park & Son.
Parker, 60 School st., Beckman & Punchard.
Quincy, 1 Brattle sq., J. W. Johnson & Co.
Revere, Bowdoin sq., John F. Merrow & Co.
Richwood, 258 Tremont st., D. F. Robinson.
Sherman, 16 Court sq., Milo H. Crosby.
Thorndike, 91 Boylston st., A. L. Howe.
Tremont, Tremont st., cor. Beacon, Silas Gurney & Co.
United States, Beach st., cor. Lincoln, Tilly Haynes.
Vendome, 165 Commonwealth av., Barnes & Duncklee.
Victoria, 273 W. Dartmouth st., Barnes & Duncklee.
Young's, 3 Court av., J. Reed Whipple.

There are numerous other smaller, and, in most instances, well kept Hotels, among them being the following:

Abbey, 71 Harrison av.
Albany, No. Beacon, Brighton, J. S. Blanchard.
Allston, Hichborn st., Brighton, J. H. Walsh.
Almar, 69 Essex st., B. R. Woods.
American, 56 Sumner st., L. B., Richard Hinchcliffe.
Arlington, Causeway st., corner Canal, L, Richards.
Atlantic, E. Sixth st., S. B., Wm. E. Brewster.
Avenue, 131 Dorchester Av., Plant & Leavitt.
Avenue, Beacon st., Brighton av., J. L. Paine.
Bangor, 350 Commercial st., S. H. Jones.
Bay State, 382 Hanover, A. B. Clark.
Beach, 878 E. 6th, S. B., F. F. Eibber.
Beacon, Beacon av., P. J. Ryan.
Bowdoin, Cambridge, n. Bowdoin sq., E. A. Dore & Co.
Brighton, Washington, cor. Winship, Br., Mrs. H. Kelly.
Bromfield, 55 Bromfield, E. M. Messenger.
Bulfinch, 3 Bulfinch st.
Cambria, 63 Beach st.
Carlton House, 5 Hanover, H. Stumcke.
Carrolton, Providence, cor. Church, A. W. Worcester.
Centennial, Cambridge, cor. Gordon, Allston, J. H. Walsh.
Center, Washington, junc. Friend, M. Pearson & Co.
Central, 114 Commercial, Dorch., John Hagerty.
Charles River, Market, cor. Western av., North Brighton, Lou Palmer.
Chauncy, 105 Chauncy, Fred Evans.
City, Atlantic av. cor. India, George A. Davis.
Continental, 119 Causeway.
Cunard, 78 Marginal, E. Francy.
Derby, 25 Cambridge st.
Dew Drop Inn, 831 East Sixth.
Earley, 11 La Grange, T. Earley.
Edgerly Hotel, 6 Norfolk pl., C. E. B. Edgerly, prop.
Eliot, 16 and 18 Eliot, Geo. Everett.
Essex, 27 and 31 Essex, G. W. Mark & Co.
Eureka, Cambridge, near Beacon park, Allston, C. H. Colgan.
Falmouth, 70 Causeway, C. F. Clark.
Faneuil, Washington, cor Market, Br., F. E. Bach.
Farwell, 801 Tremont, H. D. Reed.
Ford's, 71 Beach, W. H. Ford.
Franklin, 416 Tremont, Nahum Poole.
Glendon, 461 Chelsea, E. B., Leander Smith.
Granite, 32B Leverett, J. F. Beaman.
Grant, foot E. Sixth, George Grant.
Granville, 57 and 59 Green, Mrs. E. Otto.
Guenther's, 6 Indiana pl., A. Guenther.
Hampton, 189 Blackstone, Z. T. Favor.
Hancock, 1 Corn ct., Alexander Clarkson.
Hazelwood, T. J. Heaphy, 105 Eliot.
Highland, 209 Roxbury, Mrs. Geo. White.
Hill Side, 1680 Tremont, Charles Curtis.
Ingleside, Washington, cor. Camden.
Irving, 29 Howard, Mrs. M. E. Lincoln.
Jefferson, 18 North, M. J. Flatley.
Lancaster, 1249 Washington, D. O. Gatchell.
Lefevre, 1119 Tremont, Henry J. Lefevre.

Lowell, 73 Causeway.
Lyons, 55 Harrison av., H. O. Lyons.
Mansion, 699 Washington, I. M. Southwick.
Mariners', 11 North sq., J. P. Hatch, Supt.
Mark's, 668 Main, C. H. Marks.
Marshall, 19 Marshall, J. Wadsworth.
Massachusetts, Endicott, c. Cross, Chas. Warren Baker.
Mattapan, junc. Blue Hill av. and Norfolk, Mat., L. E. Francis.
Merchants', 13 Change av., H. W. Cottle.
Merchants' Exchange, 57 and 59 Portland, J. F. Maguire.
Merrimac, Merrimac, cor. Friend, Parker Spinney.
Miller, 1135 Washington st.
Miller, 143 Court, J. C. Miller.
Milliken, 347 Washington, F. Milliken.
Millward's, 14 and 16 Beach, B. F. Millward.
Milton, 1205 Washington, L. M., W. F. Ablott.
Moldenhauer's, 850 Washington, J. Moldenhauer.
Montreal, 44 Portland, O. C. Merrill.
Moore's, 35 Green, W. H. Moore.
Narragansett, 691 Washington, Geo. H. Royce.
National, 30 Chelsea, Chsn., H. M. Lewis.
Nautilus, O, cor. East Eighth, J. Golden.
Nelson, 274 Marginal, Francis Nelson.
Nelson, 36 Causeway st., N. W. Haskell.
New England, Blackstone, cor. Clinton, J. T. Wilson.
New Marlboro', 736 Washington, Alex. Torrey.
Norfolk, Eliot sq., Mrs. C. A Jones.
Oakland, Blue Hill av., T. H. Carr.
Orient Lake, Saratoga, near Winthrop Junc., L. J. & Joseph White.
Park Square, 251 Pleasant, G. W. Bixby.
Pequossette Hotel, 157 Green, J. P., B. McSherry.
Phenix, 23 Green, I. M. Southwick.
Plymouth, Kneeland, cor. South, W. J. Anderson.
Prescott, 11 Lawrence, Chsn., Mrs. S. A. Downer.
Providence, 239 Pleasant, H. P. Line.
Province, 325 Washington and 11 Province ct., C. P. Conant.
Puritan, 29 Boylston, C. Jacobs.
Reservoir, Washington, Brighton, Thos. Mullen.
Riverside, Cambridge, op. Beacon park, Allston, Charles Witz.
Robertson, 181 Hanover, C. W. Baldwin, manager.
Rockingham, 1204 Washington, Philip Yeaton.
Rockland, Washington, cor. Rockland, W. R., William Saunders.
Russ, 495 Tremont.
Sea-Side, 855 East Sixth, F. J. McElroy.
Seaver, 255 Tremont, Frank H. Hamblin.
Seyter's, 100 Boylston and 178 Lamartine, J. P., Wm. G. Seyter.
Shawmut, 644 Shawmut av., Orin Fairbanks.
Sinclair, 235 Pleasant, F. W. Fisher, manager.

Stanley, 8 and 9 Bowdoin sq., Noah B. Smith.
St. Julien, No. Beacon, c. Market, Brighton, A. Nussbaum.
St. Marc, 7 Ashburton pl.
St. Nicholas, 8 to 14 Province, A. B. Clark.
Strangers' Home, 180 Marginal, Edward Wood.
Sudbury, 97 Sudbury, N. A. T. Jones.
Temple, 1143 and 1145 Washington, H. M. Temple.
Union, 4 Cambridge, Chsn., Henry Sheppard.
Van Ness, 243 Pleasant, Eldridge & Doane.
Vienna, 1239 Washington st.
Walcott, 797 East Sixth, Henry Walcott.
Warrenton, 60 Warrenton, A. E. White.
Webster, 182 Sumner, F. N. Maine.
Welden, Tremont, cor. Berkeley, T. D. McEnay.
White Star Line, 54 Marginal, M. Brady.
Windsor, 6 Bowdoin, J. H. Grout.
Winthrop, Bowdoin, cor. Allston, Mrs. L. F. Cobb.

Apartment Hotels. The first apartment hotel erected in the United States was the Hotel Pelham, at the corner of Tremont and Boylston sts. Boston has now a large number of these hotels, as the following list will show; and numerous others are in process of construction:

Acme, 86 Harrison av.
Addison, 422 Tremont st.
Adelphi, 2161 Washington st.
Agassiz, 151 Commonwealth av.
Albany, 1 Bulfinch st.
Albemarle, 282 Columbus av.
Albert, 62 Emerald st.
Albion, 1 Beacon st.
Albion, 80 Albion st.
Aldine, 561 Columbus av.
Alexandra, 1761 Washington st.
Alison, W. Cottage, cor. Brook av.
Allston, 18 Bulfinch st.
Anderson, 4 N. Anderson st.
Angelo, 534 Columbus av.
Anthony, 142 Warren av.
Appleton, Appleton, near Tremont st
Argyle, 185 West Chester park.
Arlington, 1413 Washington st.
Arnold, 49 Hammond st.
Arnold, 646 Shawmut av.
Arthur, 63 Emerald st.
Ashburton, 1 Ashburton pl.
Ashton, 995 Washington st.
Ashton, Beacon, cor. Maitland st.
Atherton, Gray, near Berkeley st.
Atlantic, 130 Castle st.
Aubry, 151 Newbury st.
Austin, 130 Dartmouth st.
Baldwin, 396 Northampton st.
Ballard, 804 Washington st.
Bartlett, 63 Pleasant st.
Bellevue, 17 Beacon st.
Belmont, 1890 Washington st.
Benedict Chambers, 3 Spruce st.
Bennett, 120 Dartmouth st.
Berkeley, 158 Boylston st.
Berkshire, 190 Dartmouth st.

Berlin, 35 Village st.
Berwick, Columbus av., cor. Holyoke st.
Bismarck, 139 Dartmouth st.
Blackstone, 423 Shawmut av.
Blethen, Mayo st.
Boylston, 26 Boylston st.
Brackett, 28 Harvard, and 67 Tyler sts.
Bradford, 101 Union Park st.
Brigham, 358 Main st.
Bristol, 231 Boylston st.
Bristow, Harrison av., cor. E. Dedham st.
Brookline, 128 W. Brookline st.
Burleigh, 88 Berkeley st.
Burlington, 32 Wellington st.
Burney, Burney, near Belle av.
Burton, 82 Albion st.
Byron, Berkeley, cor. Cortes st.
Cabe, 8 Appleton st.
Carbry, 67 Middlesex st.
Carlisle, 23 Warren av.
Carter, 269 Tremont st.
Carver, 7 Blossom st.
Cary, 84 Hammond st.
Castle, 128 Castle st.
Chapman, Chapman, cor. Tremont st.
Charter, 21 Charter st.
Chatham, W. Concord, cor. Washington st.
Chatham, Worcester, cor. Tremont st.
Cherry, Cherry st., ward 16.
Chester, 545 Shawmut av.
Chestnut, 804 Tremont st.
Clifford, Cortes st.
Clifton, 455 Columbus av.
Cluny, 233 Boylston st.
Clytie, 11 Emerald st.
Columbia, 173 Eliot st.
Columbus, 415 Columbus av.
Comfort, Washington, cor. Williams st.
Continental, 1323 Washington st.
Copley, 18 Huntington av.
Dale, Dale, cor. Regent st.
Dartmouth, 141 Dudley st.
Dearborn, 237 Dudley st.
Decatur, Decatur, cor. Washington st.
De Paris, Wellington st.
Dexter, Lenox, near Tremont st.
Dighton, 1460 Washington st.
Dixon, Mayo st.
Dorchester, Hancock st., Upham Corner.
Douglas, 78 Albion st.
Dover, 71 Dover st.
Dudley, 231 Dudley st.
Eddy, 10 Willard pl.
Edinburgh, Columbus av.
Edison, 236 Columbus av.
Ellingham, Cortes st.
Eliot, Bartlett, cor. Blanchard, Rox.
Eliot, 133 Eliot st.
Elizabeth, 101 Union Park st.
Elizabeth, 17 Cortes st.
Enfield, 28 Adams pl., Rox.
Ernest, 67 Emerald st.
Ethel, 8 Middlesex st.
Everton, 62 Shawmut av.
Exeter, 81 West Rutland sq.
Falmouth, Columbus av.
Farwell, Cumberland st.
Felker, 540 to 525 Dudley st.
Florence, Florence, cor. Washington st.
Florence, Forest pl., Roxbury.
Florentine, 80 Berkeley st.
Francesca, 46 Hereford st.

Francis, 25 Hammond st.
Francis, 139 Hampden st.
Franklin, 716 Harrison av.
Fred, 72 Sawyer st.
Garfield, 80 W. Rut. and sq.
Geneva, 72 Albion st.
Geneva, Tremont st.
Girard, 1194 Tremont st.
Glendon, Columbus av.
Glencoe, 73 Village st.
Gloucester, 5 Gloucester place.
Glover, 335 Shawmut avenue.
Goldsmith, 1418 and 1422 Tremont st.
Grafton, 282 Columbus av.
Greely, 24 Hammond st.
Grenville, Clifton, Dor.
Greylock, 53 Village st.
Guildford, 220 Clarendon st.
Hamilton, 260 W. Clarendon st.
Hamlet, 15 Middlesex st.
Hammond, 47 Hammond st.
Hampton, 224 Northampton st.
Harold, 76 Albion st.
Harold, 316 Newbury st.
Harrison, 720 Harrison av.
Harvard, 140 Harrison av.
Harwich, 12 Harwich st.
Helen, Castle, cor. Mayo st.
Henderson, 76 Hammond st.
Hereford, 52 Hereford st.
Hoffman, Berkeley st.
Holbro, Holborn st., ward 21.
Holden, 121 Dartmouth st.
Hosmer, 52 Hammond st.
Howard, Oak, cor. Oak pl.
Howland, 218 Columbus av.
Hudson, 79 Church st.
Humboldt, Holborn st.
Humphreys, Humphreys sq., Dorchester.
Huntington, Huntington av.
Huntington, Cortes, n. Ferdinand.
Ideal, Waterford st.
Johnson, 258 Shawmut av.
Johnson Block, Meander st
Kempton, 237 W. Berkeley.
Kendall, 8 Kendall st.
Kensington, 33 Wellington st.
Kensington, 291 Boylston st.
Kingston, 87 Kingston st.
Kirkland, 66 Pleasant st.
Kramer, 84 Warrenton st.
Lafayette, Columbus av.
Lagrange, 218 Tremont st.
Langdell, 804 Washington st.
Langham, 172 St. James av.
Lawrence, Model Houses, E. Canton.
LeBrun, 17 Cazenove st.
Lisle, Mayo st.
Lovejoy, Cumberland st. c. St. Botolph st.
Lucerne, Tremont st.
Lynde, 40 Lynde st.
Lyndeboro', Isabella st.
Lyndhurst, 6 Alston st.
Madison 1048 Washington st.
Madison Park, Sterling, c. Warwick st.
Madison Place, 1100 Washington st.
Mason, 74 Albion st.
Mayo, Mayo st.
Medfield, 23 Wellington st.
Melita, 771 Dudley st.
Middlesex, 23 Middlesex st.
Milford, 3 Milford st.

Milton, Zeigler, near Washington st.
Mineola, 129 Lenox st.
Morse Mansion, 105 Union Park st.
Mt. Pleasant, 62 Forest st., Roxbury
Nassau, 17 Nassau st.
Neufchatel, Tremont st.
Newbury, 633 Washington st.
Newton, E. Newton st.
Nightingale, 637 Dudley st.
Normandy, 86 Berkeley st.
Northwood, Hancock, Upham Corner.
Norwood, 8 Oak st.
Ophir, 593 Tremont st.
Oregon, 1290 and 1300 Washington st.
Ormond, Holden pl., Dorchester.
Osborn, 4 Osborn pl.
Oxford, Huntington ave.
Oxford Terrace, Huntington av.
Pacific, 132 Castle st.
Palmer, Hampden st.
Palmerston, 177 West Chester park.
Parthia, 690 Shawmut av.
Pelham, 34 Boylston st.
Pembroke, 67 Pembroke st.
Pierpont, 36 Essex st.
Pierson, 46 Harvard st.
Prescott, 24 Cazenove st.
Putnam, 20 Cazenove st.
Putnam, 93 Warren, Rox.
Rand, 76 West Rutland sq.
Reen, 65 Middlesex st.
Regent, Regent, cor. Dale.
Richmond, 70 Shawmut ave.
Ritchie, 64 Emerald st.
Rochdale, Blue Hill av., cor. Irving av.
Rockdale, Burney, near Delle av.
Rockford, Delle av., near Burney st.
Rockwood, 50 Perry st.
Rossmore, 159 W. Chester park.
Roxbury, Roxbury, cor. King st.
Royal, 295 Beacon st.
Rutland, 701 Tremont st.
St. Belmar, 854 Washington st.
St. Botolph, 780 Dudley st.
St. Clare, 98 West Brookline st.
St. Cloud, Tremont st.
St. George, 1389 Washington st.
St. Marc, 7 Ashburton pl.
St. Omer, 265 Shawmut av.
Salem, The, Pearl, cor. High, Chsn.
Sanford, 75 Albion st.

Sharon, Sharon, cor. Harrison av.
Shawmut, 80 Village st.
Sherwood, Kendall, cor. Tremont st.
Shirley, 131 Dudley st.
Sidney Building, Union Park st.
Siloam, 10 Middlesex st.
Spencer, 260 Columbus av.
Star, 13 Emerald st.
Strathmore, 77 Village st.
Sumner, 78 Carver st.
Sun, 73 W. Brookline st.
Sunnyside, 144 Blue Hill av.
Tempest, 17 Middlesex st.
Temple, 35 and 37 Temple st.
Tennyson, Tennyson, cor. Church st.
Thornton, 494 Tremont st.
Tremont, 297 Tremont st.
Truro, 12 Truro st.
Tudor, 34B Beacon st.
Tyler, 70 Oak st.
Union, 301 Shawmut av.
Upton, 70 Albion st.
Upton, 14 Upton st.
Van Rensselaer, 219 A Tremont st.
Vernon, 56 River st.
Victor, 736 Harrison av.
Vine, Vine st., Roxbury st.
Vivian, 285 Boylston st.
Waltham, 5 Waltham st.
Waquoit, 247 Columbus av.
Warren, 6 Warren st., Roxbury.
Warwick, 11 Marble st.
Waterford, 1 and 2 Waterford st.
Waterston, 8 Bulfinch pl.
Wave, 13 Middlesex st.
Waverly, City sq., Charlestown.
Wayland, 75 Pleasant st.
Wellington, 1818 Washington st.
Wentworth, 112 Berkeley st.
Western, 17 Norman st.
Westland, Westland av.
Westminster, Marble st.
Weston, 61 Weston st., Roxbury.
Wilson, E. Newton st., cor. Harrison av.
Wilton, 977 Washington st.
Winchester, 4 Winchester st.
Windsor, 103 Shawmut av.
Woolsey, Woolsey sq., J. P.
Worcester, Tremont, cor. Worcester st.
Yarmouth, Yarmouth, cor. Truro st.
Zurich, Centre, opp. Linwood, Roxbury.

COURTS IN BOSTON.

Supreme Judicial Court. Court House, Court sq. Court Terms, first Tuesday of April; second Tuesday of September. *Chief Justice*, Marcus Morton; salary, $6,500. *Associate Justices*, Walbridge A. Field, Charles Devens, William Allen, Charles Allen, Oliver Wendell Holmes, Jr., William S. Gardner; salary, $6,000. *Attorney General*, Edgar J. Sherman; salary, $4,000. *Ass't Attorney General*, Harvey N. Shepard; salary, $2,000. *Reporter of Decisions*, John Lathrop. *Clerk for the Commonwealth*, George W. Nichols; salary, $3,000. *Clerk*, John Noble; salary, $5,500, and fees. *Ass't Clerk*, Henry A. Clapp; salary, $2,500.

Superior Court.—Court House, Court sq. Civil Session. Court Terms, first Tuesdays of January, April, July and October. *Chief Justice*, Lincoln F. Brigham; salary, $5,500. *Associate Justices*, Julius Rockwell, Robert C. Pitman, John W. Bacon, P. Emory Aldrich, Hamilton B. Staples, Marcus P. Knowlton, Caleb Blodgett, Albert Mason, Jas. M. Barker, Chas. P. Thompson. Salary, $5,000 each. *Clerk*, Joseph A. Willard. Salary, $3,500, and one-half the excess of fees above that sum. *Asst. Clerk*, Edwin A. Wadleigh. Salary, $2,500. *Second Ass't*, Edward A. Willard. Salary, $2,000. Criminal Session. Terms, first Monday in every month. *District Attorney*, Oliver Stevens. Salary, $4,500. Elected by the people. Term expires first Wednesday in January, 1887. *First Assist.*, T. J. Dacey; salary, $2,400. *Second Assist.*, M. O. Adams. Salary, $2,000. Appointed by the District Attorney. *Clerk*, John P. Manning. Salary, $3,000 and half the excess of fees above that sum. Elected by the people.

Municipal Court.—Court House, Court square. *Chief Justice*, William E. Parmenter. Salary, $3,000. *Associate Justices*, William J. Forsaith, John H. Hardy. Salary, $3,000 each. *Special Justice*, Geo. Z. Adams. *Clerk, Civil Business*, William T. Connolly. Salary, $3,000. *Assistants*, O. G. Sleeper. Salary, $1,800. Henry E. Bellew. Salary, $1,600. *Clerk, Criminal Business*, John C. Leighton. Salary, $3,000. *1st Asst. Clerk*, Fred. C. Ingalls. Salary, $2,000. *2d Asst. Clerk*, Otis V. Waterman. Salary, $1,800. *3d Asst. Clerk*, William W. Davis. Salary, $1,600. *4th Asst. Clerk*, John C. L. Sanborn. Salary, $1,400. *5th Asst. Clerk*, Edward J. Lord. Salary, $1,400. COURT TERMS: Civil, every Saturday, at 9 A. M.; Criminal, every day, except Sundays and holidays, at 9 A. M.

Municipal Courts are also held in the following Districts: South Boston, Dorchester st.; Dorchester, Field's Corner; Brighton, Town Hall; Roxbury, Roxbury st.; East Boston, Meridian st.; West Roxbury, Seaverns av.; Charlestown,

Medical Examiners.—Frank W. Draper, Francis A. Harris, George Stedman, (associate).

Probate and Insolvency Courts.—28 Court sq., (entrance also at 32 Tremont st). Terms—Probate Court, every Monday, except 1st, 2d and 4th Mondays of August. Insolvency, every Friday in every month, except August. *Judge of Probate and Insolvency*, John W. McKim. Salary, $4,000. *Register of Probate and Insolvency*, Elijah George. Salary, $3,000. *Asst. Register*, John H. Paine. Salary, $2,000. *Clerks*, James L. Crombie. Salary, $1,200; and Ebenezer Gay. Salary, $1,000. *Constable*, W. A. Fort.

Registry of Deeds, 28 Court sq. Register of Deeds, Thomas F. Temple. *Asst. Register*, Charles W. Kimball.

Sheriff and Deputies.—*Sheriff and Jailer*, John B. O'Brien. Salary, $2,500. Office, Court House, Court sq. Elected by the people. Term expires first Wednesday in January, 1887. *Deputy Sheriffs*, Harum Merrill, William D. Martin, John B. Ingalls, Fred H. Seavey, Thos. Fee, Jr., John B. Fitzpatrick, Henry F. Spach, Geo. B. Munroe, of Boston.

United States Circuit Court, United States Building, Post Office sq. Terms—May 15, October 15. Rule day—1st Monday of each month. *Associate Justice U. S. Supreme Court*, Horace Gray. *Circuit Judge*, Le Baron B. Colt. *Attorney of the U. S. for Mass. District*, George P. Sanger. *Assistants*, Chas. Almy, Jr., [Vacancy]. *Clerk*, John G. Stetson. *Deputy Clerk*, A. H. Trowbridge. *Crier*, Wm. M. H. Copeland. *U. S. Marshal of the District of Mass.*, Nathaniel P. Banks. *Chief Deputy Marshal and Clerk*, William D. Pool. *Deputy Marshals*, Antonio Enos, Frederick D. Gallupe, Charles H. Snow, Wm. M. H. Copeland. *Commissioners*, Elias Merwin, C. H. Hill, Chas. P. Curtis, Caleb William Loring, William S. Dexter, Henry L. Hallett, Winslow Warren, Jr., Edwin H. Abbot, Fisher Ames, John G. Stetson, Charles H. Swan, Charles L. Woodbury, Boston; William L. Smith, Springfield; J. H. Hill, Thomas G. Kent, Worcester; Charles Warren Clifford, New Bedford; Edgar M. Wood, Examiners, J. Henry Taylor, Wm. P. Preble, Jr.

United States District Court, United States Building, Post Office square. Terms—3d Tuesday in March; 4th Tuesday in June; 2d Tuesday in September; 1st Tuesday in December. *District Judge*, Thomas L. Nelson. *Clerk*, Clement Hugh Hill. *Deputy Clerks*, Elisha Bassett and Francis S. Fiske. Terms of the Court—March, the 3d Tuesday; June, the 4th Tuesday; September, the 2d Tuesday; December, the 1st Tuesday. *Registers in Bankruptcy*, S. Lothrop Thorndike, Sam'l B. Noyes, F. W. Palfrey, of Boston; Edgar J. Sherman, of Lawrence; Benjamin C. Perkins, of Salem; Peter C. Bacon, of Worcester; Timothy M. Brown, of Springfield; H. M. Knowlton, of New Bedford; Charles F. Howe, of Lowell; Charles G. Delano, of Greenfield.

UNITED STATES SUPREME COURT.

The Supreme Court is held in the city of Washington, and has one session annually, commencing on the second Monday in October, and such adjourned or special terms as may be necessary for the despatch of business. There are now nine Judicial Circuits, in each of which a Circuit Court is held twice every year, for every State within the Circuit, by the Circuit Judge appointed for the Circuit, or by the District Judge of the State or District in which the Court sits. Each Justice of the Supreme Court must every two years attend at least one term of the Circuit Court in each District of his Circuit. The Judges are appointed for life, or during good behavior. Any Judge who has held his commission ten years, and resigns after reaching the age of seventy, shall receive the same salary during the rest of his life.

By the act of Congress of July 23d, 1866, the several circuits are thus constituted, to wit: *First*, The Districts of Maine, New Hampshire, Massachusetts, Rhode Island. *Second*, Vermont, Connecticut, New York. *Third*, New Jersey, Pennsylvania, and Delaware. *Fourth*, Maryland, Virginia, West Virginia, North Carolina, and South Carolina. *Fifth*, Georgia, Florida, Alabama, Mississippi, Louisiana, and Texas. *Sixth*, Ohio, Michigan, Kentucky, and Tennessee. *Seventh*, Indiana, Illinois, and Wisconsin. *Eighth*, Minnesota, Iowa, Missouri, Kansas, Arkansas, and Nebraska. *Ninth*, California, Oregon and Nevada.

By the act of April 10, 1869, the Supreme Court is made to consist of the Chief Justice and eight Associate Justices, any six of whom make a quorum. Justices have been assigned to the circuits as follows:

4th Circuit. *Chief Justice*, Morrison R. Waite, Toledo, O. Appointed, 1874. Salary, $10,500. *Associate Justices*, 1st Circuit, Horace Gray, Massachusetts. Appointed, 1881. Salary, $10,000. 2d, Samuel Blatchford, New York. Appointed, 1882. Salary, $10,000. 3d, Joseph P. Bradley, Newark, N. J. Appointed, 1870. Salary, $10,000. 5th, William B. Woods, Montgomery, Ala. Appointed, 1881. Salary, $10,000. 6th, Stanley Matthews, Ohio. Appointed, 1881. Salary, $10,000. 7th, John M. Harlan, Louisville, Ky. Appointed, 1877. Salary, $10,000. 8th, Samuel F. Miller, Keokuk, Iowa. Appointed, 1862. Salary, $10,000. 9th, Stephen J. Field, San Francisco, Cal. Appointed, 1863. Salary, $10,000. Sam'l F. Phillips, *Solicitor-General*, Washington, D. C. Appointed, 1870. Salary, $7,500. James H. McKenney, *Clerk*. John G. Nicolay, *Marshal*.

By the same act of April 10, 1869, provision is made for the appointment of a Circuit Judge for each of the nine Circuits, to reside in the Circuit and receive an annual salary of $6,000, with the same power and jurisdiction in his Circuit, as the Judge of the Supreme Court allotted thereto. The following are the Circuit Judges: 1st Circuit, Le Baron B. Colt, of Bristol, R. I.; 2d, William J. Wallace, of Syracuse, N. Y.; 3d, Wm. McKennan, of Washington, Pa.; 4th, Hugh L. Bond, of Baltimore,Md.; 5th, Don A. Pardee, of New Orleans, La.; 6th, John Baxter, of Knoxville, Tenn.; 7th, W. Q. Gresham, of Wisconsin; 8th, David J. Brewer, of Kansas; 9th, Lorenzo Sawyer, of San Francisco, Cal.

COURT OF CLAIMS.—Wm. A. Richardson, *Chief Justice*. C. C. Nott, Glenni W. Scofield, Lawrence Weldon, John Davis, *Judges*. Archibald Hopkins, *Chief Clerk*. The Court holds its sessions in the Capitol, at Washington, D. C.

TREASURER OF THE UNITED STATES.—C. N. Jordan.

INTERNAL REVENUE.—J. G. Miller, *Commissioner*.

COMMISSIONER OF AGRICULTURE.—Norman J. Colman.

COMMISSIONER OF PENSIONS.—John C. Black.

COMMISSIONER OF PATENTS.—M. V. Montgomery.

COMMISSIONER OF LAND OFFICE.—Wm. A. J. Sparks.

COMMISSIONER OF INDIAN AFFAIRS.—J. D. C. Atkins.

PUBLIC PRINTER.—S. P. Rounds.

LIBRARIAN OF CONGRESS.—A. R. Spofford.

SUPT. CENSUS OFFICE.—Charles W. Seaton.

FERRIES AND WHARVES.

Ferries. The first row-boat Ferry (Winnisimmet, now Chelsea) was opened May 14, 1631, by Thomas Williams; a Charlestown Ferry was opened June 14, 1631, by Edward Carver; East Boston (Noddle's Island) had row-boats in 1637, steamboats in 1832.

Boston, Revere Beach and Lynn Railway Ferry. 340 Atlantic av., foot of High st. (Take streetcars at head of Franklin st., corner of Washington st). This Ferry runs usually on each hour. In summer, to accommodate the vast travel to Beachmont, Crescent Beach, Revere Beach, Point of Pines, Lynn Beach, Swampscott, Nahant, and other sea-side resorts, the Ferry and connecting trains run oftener.

Chelsea Ferry. (1631). Foot of Hanover st. First boat leaves Chelsea, foot of Winnisimmet st., 4.45 a. m., then every 30 min. to 6.15 a. m., every 15 min. to 7.45 p. m., every 30 min. to 11.15 p. m. First boat from Boston 5 a. m.; last boat 11.30 p. m.
SUNDAY.— First boat leaves Chelsea 6.15 a. m., every 30 min. to 8.15 a. m., every 15 min. to 7.45 p. m., then every 30 min. to 11.15 p. m.; last boat from Boston 11.30 p. m.

East Boston (North Ferry). (1637). Foot of Battery st. Leave at 4.07 a. m., every 15 min. to 6.00 a. m., every 7½ min. to 8.00 p. m. (Sat. 9.00 p. m.), every 15 min. to 12.00 p. m., every 30 min. to 4.00 a. m.
SUNDAY.—Leave 12.00 midnight, Saturday, every 30 min. to 6.30 a. m., every 15 min. to 9.30 a. m., every 7½ min. to 10.00 p. m., every 30 min. to 12.00 p. m.

East Boston (South Ferry). Foot of Fleet street. Leave at 4.00 a. m., every 15 min. to 6.00 a. m., every 7½ min. to 8.00 a. m., every 9 min. to 6.30 p. m., every 7½ min. to 8.00 p. m. Sat. 9.00 p. m.), every 15 min. to 12.00 p. m., every 30 min. to 4.00 a. m.
SUNDAY.—Leave 12.00, midnight, Saturday, every 30 min. to 6.30 a. m., Sunday, every 15 min. to 12.00 midnight.

Wharves. Liverpool Wharf—then called Griffin's — was the scene of the famous Boston Tea-Party, Dec. 16, 1773. From the following complete list of wharves in Boston, one can readily find the points from which the various steamers depart and arrive:

Abbott's....................370 Charles st.
Adams'......lower end Chelsea st., Chsn.
Adams'............Hilton st., near Sweet
Alger's....Fourth, cor. Foundry st., S. B.
Aspinwall's Mast Yard.419 Commercial st.
Atkins...............521 Commercial st.
Atlantic..............72 Border st., E. B.
Bacon's..................402 Albany st.
Bailey & Draper's..........242 Albany st.
Bartlett's........501 & 511 Commercial st.
Batchelder's..............478 Atlantic av.
Battery ....379 Commercial st.
Bay State Iron Co's.E. First st., n. I, S. B.
Bay State............Albany st., c. Dover
Bayside..........E. First st., n. I., S. B.
Boole's..............Jeffrey's Point, E. B.
Boston.....................................
First, Granite and Mt. Wash. av., S. B.
Boston Dyewood and Chemical Co.'s ....
....................310 Border st., E. B.
Boston Gas Co.'s.............................
..563 Com'l st. to Charles-river bridge
Bowker's..........186 Border st., E. B.
Bradley's ....278 Albany st.
Brooks'.....285 Medford st., Charlestown
Bullard's.................548 Albany st.
Burnham's.E.Ninth st.,c.Old Harbor,S. B.
Burnham & Co.'s...........132 Charles st.
Burns'......313 Medford st., Charlestown
Calef's..................408 Federal st.
Carleton's...........119 Sumner st., E. B.
Carter's....Albany st., opp. City Hospital
Caswell's........97 Water st., Charlestown
Central...................241 Atlantic av.
City.........Albany st., opp. East Newton
City........251 Medford st., Charlestown
Clark's....................564 Albany st.
Clark & Smith's...231 Medford st., Chsn.
Comey's...............Commercial st.
Commercial........84 and 98 Atlantic av.
Constitution............411 Commercial st.
Craft's.............266 to 274 Albany st.
Crosby's (Robert)..........................
...Coleridge st., n. Wordsworth, E. B.
Crowley's..........104 Condor st., E. B.
Cunard...Marginal st.,opp. Orleans, E. B.
Curtis'......Albany st., cor. Chester park
Curtis'..............374 Border st., E. B.
Curtis'...................250 Federal st.
Cushing's....W. First st., foot of C, S. B.
Cutter's..............Commercial Point
Cutter & Ward's............................
......Condor st., cor. Meridian, E. B.
Dana's......487 Medford st., Charlestown
Darton's..............270 Border st., E. B.
DeButts & Daggets..........................
...........New st., n. Sumner, E. B.
Dillaway's.......foot of Sumner st., E. B.
Dodge's. Medford st., opp. Webster,Chsn.
Dorchester Yacht Club......................
...............Commercial st., opp. Mill
Eames & Stimson's..........................
............Medford st., opp. Cook, Chsn.
East Boston Dry Dock......86 Border st.
Eastern Packet Pier......128 Atlantic av.
Eastern R. R Marginal st., n. Lewis, E. B.

Eddy's................Commercial, H. S.
Edmand's.........455 Medford st., Chsn.
Edmand's............41 Medford st.,Chsn.
Edmonds'..................392 Federal st.
Emery's................... 288 Federal st.
Fall's..............195 Medford st., Chsn.
Ferguson's...............34 New st., E. B.
Ferry.............foot of Lewis st., E. B.
Fitchburg R. R............Warren Bridge
Fisk's..................463 Commercial st.
Fort Hill..................448 Atlantic av.
Fort Hill Dry Dock........464 Atlantic av.
Foster & Leighton's..280 Border st. E. B.
Foster's...................366 Atlantic av.
Foster's Coal..............n. Chelsea Ferry
Foundry..............W. First, n. C., S. B.
Frame's...................32 New st., E. B.
Francis.................256 Federal st.
Franklin Coal.....32 Dorchester av., S. B.
Fulton Iron Foundry........................
........Foundry st., jc. Dor. av., S. B.
Furber......................254 Albany st.
Gage's...........85 Water st., Charlestown
Gibson's...............110 Lewis st., E. B.
Glendon...Glendon st., ft. Trenton, E. B.
Goodnow's................294 Causeway st.
Googin's....Eagle st., n. Gas Works, E. B.
Grand Junction........Marginal st., E. B.
Gray's............481 and 489 Commercial st.
Green's Dry Dock....270 Border st., E. B.
Greenleaf's.....527 Main st., Charlestown
Griffith's..................232 Cambridge st.
Gutterson's........Lehigh st., cor Albany
Hall's...............170 Border st., E. B.
Hallowell Granite...49 Medford st., Chsn.
Hamblen's..491 Medford st., Charlestown
Ham's......Northampton st., cor. Albany
Holmes'.....119 Medford st., Charlestown
Hoosac Tunnel D. & E. Co. Water st.,Chsn.
Howe's....................342 Federal st.
Howe's..................5 Sumner st., E. B.
Huckins'..............192 Border st., E. B.
India......................288 Atlantic av.
Jackson's Ship Yard..230 Border st., E. B.
James'.............306 W. First st., S. B.
Jenney's.........W. First st., near E, S. B.
Johnson's......513 Main st., Charlestown
Jones'...............180 Border st., E. B.
Kelly's.....Marginal st., n. Jeffries, E. B.
Kelly's Marine Railway....................
....................63 Sumner st., E. B.
Kendrick.....................98 Condor st.
Keyes'......243 Medford st., Charlestown
Knight & Co's.....149 Medford st., Chsn.
Ladd's Dock...........11 Sumner st., E. B.
Leatherbee's (A. F.)........376 Albany st.
Leatherbee's (J. W.)........390 Albany st.
Leighton's....from 109 Sumner st., E. B.
Lewis...................32 Atlantic av.
Lincoln's............... 365 Commercial st.
Litchfield's................468 Atlantic av.
Liverpool..................512 Atlantic av.
Lockwood's.........Charles-River av.
Long....206 Atlantic av., foot of State st.
Loring's...E. First st., bet. L and M, S. B.
Lovejoy's.................182 Causeway st.
Lowell R. R......... Chelsea bridge, Chsn.
Martin's......E. Ninth st., foot of H, S. B.
Maverick............37 Sumner st., E. B.
Maynard's..............50 New st., E. B.
Mayo's..........New st., opp. Cross, E. B.
McKay's (New).......420 Border st., E. B.
McKay's (Old)........ 334 Border st., E. B.
Meany's..................534 Albany st.
Merrill & Edmand's.....18 Mt. Wash. av.
Monument..................................
...Medford st., opp. Lexington, Chsn.
Morse's....................880 Harrison av.
Munn's....................438 Federal st.
Mystic...... Chelsea bridge, Charlestown
National Dock and Warehouse wharf....
.....................Lewis st., E. B.
New England & Fire Brick Co.'s.........
..............K st., near E. First, S. B.
Nickerson's........Congress-street bridge
Norway Iron Co's.......363 Dorchester av.
O'Brien's..................498 Albany st.
Odiorne's............81 Sumner st., E. B.
Old Colony..........25 Foundry st., S. B.
Osgood's....Chester Park, cor. Albany st.
Otis'......................404 Atlantic av.
Oxbow......Chester Park, cor. Albany st.
Page's........ .....W. First st., foot of E.
Parker's.....85 Medford st., Charlestown
Parker & Son's.............142 Charles st.
Park's...... 175 Medford st., Charlestown
Payne's........Albany st., opp. Wareham
Pearl Street Wharf.......518 Atlantic av.
Pearson's.................. 398 Atlantic av.
People's Ferry Wharf.55 Sumner st., E. B.
Perry's......................99 Lehigh st.
Pierce's............Sixth st., near P, S. B.
Pierce's, (lumber).415 Dorchester av., S. B.
Plummer's.Jefferies st., opp. Everett,E.B.
Pond's................ 372 W. First st., S. B.
Pope's...........280 Albany st., foot of Troy
Pope's...Commercial st., near Park, Dor.
Porter's...............296 Border st., E. B.
Powers'....................390 Atlantic av.
Prentice's..................564 Atlantic av.
Prison Point Wharf.......................
..at Prison Point bridge, Charlestown
Rich's.................Jeffries Point, E. B.
Ripley's................473 Commercial st.
Robinson's.............445 Commercial st.
Roby's.................. 280 Causeway st.
Rogers Bros..W. First st., foot of F, S. B.
Rogers & Hankey.........................
.............Sixth st., near P, City Point
Rowe's.....................340 Atlantic av.
Russell's....................438 Federal st.
Russia......................550 Atlantic av.
Sargent's.................295 Commercial st.
Shackford & Co's.....256 Border st., E. B.
Shepard's...........Swett st., near Albany
Shepard's...............Commercial, H. S.
Simpson's Dry Dock.....273 Marginal st.
Slade's..........New st., near Sumner, E. B.
Slate.....................529 Commercial st.
Snelling's...Albany st., foot of E. Canton
Snelling's Dock...........24 New st., E. B.
Snow's............foot of Mt. Washington av.
Snow's Arch Wharf.........430 Atlantic av.
South Boston Gas Light Co's..............
...W. First st., cor. Dorchester, S. B.
So. Boston Iron Co's.......................
26 Dorch. av. and 57 Foundry st., S. B.
South Boston Yacht Club's................
.................E. Sixth st., near P, S. B.
Souther's.....E. First st., foot of H, S. B.
Stearn's.....................470 Albany st.
Stetson's & Pope's..304 W. First st., S. B.
Stetson's..........498 East First st., S. B.
Stewart & Co's......65 Medford st., Chsn.

Stone's..... 199 Medford st., Charlestown
Sturtevant's..........322 Border st., E. B.
Suffolk Glass Co's.....foot of Lowland st.
Sumner Street wharf, ft. Sumner st., E. B.
T Wharf...................178 Atlantic av.
Teneau................Commercial Point
Tileston's.................608 Atlantic av.
Tilton's.....................412 Albany st.
Tirrell's.,.....................304 Federal st.
Tucker's, Medford st., opp. Belmont, Chsn.
Tudor's........Charles-river Bridge, Chsn.
Tuft's..................37 Foundry st., S. B.
Tuft's.........Lewis st., opp. Webster, E. B
Tuft's...541 and 553 Main st., Charlestown
Union.................323 Commercial st.
Wales's.....................272 Federal st.
Ward's......................418 Federal st.
Warren's....................326 Charles st.
Waterman's....... 425 Medford st., Chsn.

Way's......................450 Federal st.
Weeks' (John S.).....210 Border st., E. B.
Weeks' (E.)...........1 Sumner st., E. B.
Wellington's...............................
    bet. Charles-river av. & War. br.,Chsn.
Whidden's Dock, Sumner st., n. New, E.B.
White, Frame & Company's . New st., E.B.
Whorf's...Jeffries st., cor. Maverick, E. B.
Williams'..........267 Medford st., Chsn.
Wilson's.................................
    ..Northampton st., near Harrison av.
Winnisimmet ferry...foot of Hanover st.
Winslow & Co's..........278 Causeway st.
Winsor's......................324 Albany st.
Wiswall's...................254 Federal st.
Woodbury's...............122 Border st., E. B.
Wood's............400 and 410 Charles st.
Wooley's............176 Condor st., E. B.
Young's....Condor st., n. the bridge, E. B.

RAILWAY STATIONS AND BRIDGES.

Boston Railway Stations.

There are 54 Railway Stations in Boston, as follows:
Boston & Albany............Kneeland st.
Boston & Lowell..........92 Causeway st.
Boston, R. B. & Lynn....340 Atlantic av.
Boston and Providence........Park sq.
Central Mass.............92 Causeway st.
Eastern Div. (B. & M.)...110 Causeway st.
Fitchburg................152 Causeway st.
N. Y. & N. E. (Woon. Div) B....Beach st.
N. York & N. England...foot Summer st.
Old Colony..................Kneeland st.
Boston & Maine...........Haymarket sq.
Allston (B. & A.)...............Linden st.
Ashmont (O. C.).............Dorchester av.
Bird (N. Y. & N. E.)............Ceylon st.
Boylston (B. & P.)............Boylston st.
Brighton (B. & A.)............Market st.
Cedar Grove (O. C.)..............Adams st.
Central (Dedham Br.).......Anawan av.
Charlestown (B. & M).........Austin st.
Charlestown (Fitch.)..........Austin st.
Chickering (B. & P.)............Ward 18
Columbus (B. & A.).........Columbus av.
Cottage Farm (B. & A.)... ..Brighton av.
Crescent (O. C.)............Crescent av.
Dorchester (N. Y. & N. E.)....Lauriat av.
Dudley (N. Y. & N. E.).........Dudley st.
East Boston (East.).........Maverick st.
East Boston (R. B.)...........Marginal st.
East Somerville (B. & M.)..Cambridge st.
East Somerville (East.).....Cambridge st.
Faneuil (B. & A.)...............Brooks st.
Field Grove (O. C.).............Charles st.
Forest Hills (B. & P.)....Washington st.
Forest Hills (N. Y. & N. E.)..Forest Hills
Granite Bridge (O. C.).........Granite st.
Harrison sq. (O. C.)............Dickens st.
Harvard (N. Y. & N. E.)......Harvard st.
Heath (B. & P.)...............Old Heath st.
Highland (Dedham Br.)..........Corey st.
Huntington (B. & A.).....Huntington av.
Jamaica Plain (B. & P.)..........Green st.
Mattapan (O. C.)............Blue Hill av.
Mattapan (N. Y. & N. E.)... Blue Hill av.
Mount Bowdoin (N. Y. & N. E.)..Erie av.
Mount Hope (B. & P.).........Florence st.
Neponset (O. C.)..............Taylor st.
Roslindale (Dedham Br.).........South st.
Roxbury (B. & P.).........1369 Tremont st.
Savin Hill (O. C.).............Savin Hill av.
Shawmut (O. C.).................Centre st.
South Boston (O. C.)..........Foundry st.
South Boston (N. Y. & N. E.), W. First st.
Spring (Dedham Br.)...........Spring st.
West Roxbury (Ded. Br.)....Lagrange st.

Bridges.

Broadway...............to South Boston
Cambridge....... Brighton to Cambridge
Cragie................to E. Cambridge
Charles River............to Charlestown
Chelsea..........Charlestown to Chelsea
Chelsea st.........East Boston to Chelsea
Commercial Point....................
Congress st........over Fort Hill Channel
Dover st................to South Boston
Essex st..........Brighton to Cambridge
Federal st.............to South Boston
Granite............Dorchester to Milton
Malden..........Charlestown to Everett
Meridian st.......East Boston to Chelsea
Mount Washington av...to South Boston
Neponset............Dorchester to Quincy
North Beacon st..Brighton to Watertown
Prison......Charlestown to E. Cambridge
Warren..............................
West Boston............to Cambridgeport
Western av.................to Watertown
Winthrop......Breeds Island to Winthrop

ASYLUMS, HOMES AND HOSPITALS.

Asylums. The spirit of charity is never better expressed than when it provides asylums for the intemperate, the insane and the orphan. Following are the names and locations of Boston's Asylums:
Adams Nervine Asylum, Centre st., Jamaica Plain.
Boston Asylum and Farm School, Thompson's Island.
Boston Female Asylum, 1008 Washington st.
Feeble-Minded; Asylum for, 723 East 8th st., South Boston.
Massachusetts Infant Asylum, Chestnut av., cor. Wyman st.
McLean Asylum for the Insane, Somerville.
New England Moral Reform Asylum, 6 Oak place.
St. Mary's Infant Asylum, Cushman av., Dorchester.
St. Mary's Infant Asylum, Old Harbor st., South Boston.
St. Vincent Orphan Asylum, Camden st.
Temporary Asylum for Discharged Female Prisoners, Dedham.

Homes. Boston has many homes for the aged, indigent and unfortunate, as follows:
Appleton Temporary Home, 15 Davis st.
Baldwin Place Home for Little Wanderers, Baldwin pl., Salem st.
Bethesda Home for Infants and Foundlings, President, Lucius W. Smith.
Boffin's Bower, Jennie Collins, 1031 Washington st.
Boston Home for Incurables, Dorchester av., Dorchester District.
Boston Industrial Temporary Home, 17 Davis st.
Boston Young Women's Christian Association Home, 68 Warrenton st.
Cancer Home (for women only), Dr. Chas. Cullis, Beacon Hill pl.
Channing Home, 30 McLean st., C. P. Curtis, Clerk.
Charity Building, Chardon st.
Children's Lodging House, 7 Crescent pl., Green st.
Children's Home, Auburndale, Melrose st. near Station.
Children's Home, Charlestown, 36 Austin st.
Children's Mission Home, 277 Tremont st.
Church Home for Orphans, N st., S. B.
Consumptives' Home, Grove Hall.
Convalescent Home, Belmont.
Father Roche's Working Boys' Home, 113 Eliot st., or 34 Bennett st.
Friendly Hand, 2 Main st., Ch'ton Dist.
Girls' Friendly Society Home, 51 Temple st.
Home for Aged and Friendless Women, 19 Common st.
Home for Aged Colored Women, 27 Myrtle st.
Home for Aged Couples, 431 Shawmut av.
Home for Aged Men, 133 West Springfield st.
Home for Aged Women, 108 Revere st.
Home for Deaf Mutes, Beverly.
Home for Destitute Catholic Children, Harrison av., cor. Concord st.
Home for Little Wanderers, Baldwin pl., Salem st.
Home for the Aged Poor, 424 Dudley st., Highland Dist.
Home of the Boston Children's Friend Society, 48 Rutland st.
House of the Angel Guardian, 85 Vernon st.
House of the Good Samaritan, 6 McLean st.
House of the Good Shepherd, 1752 Tremont st.
Industrial Home, 39 North Bennet st.
Industrial Temporary Home, 17 Davis st.
Industrial School and Home for Girls, Centre st., Dorchester.
Inebriate's Home, Sec., 63 Court st. Room A.
Jane Marshall Dodge Memorial Home, Humarock Beach, Scituate.
Little Sisters of the Poor, 424 Dudley st.
Liversidge Institute, River st., Mattapan District.
Marcella Street Home for Children, Marcella st.
Mariner's House, 11 North sq., J. P. Hatch, Supt.
Martin Luther Orphan Home, Baker st., West Roxbury.
Massachusetts Home for Intemperate Women, 44 Worcester st.
Massachusetts Infant Asylum, Chestnut av., cor. Wyman st.
Mission House of St. Paul's, 6 Tyler st.
Mount Hope Home, Bourne st., Forest Hills.
National Sailors' Home, Quincy. Treas., Joshua Crane, 10 Tremont st.
New England Home for Intemperate Women.
Nickerson Home for Children, 14 Tyler st.
North End Mission Home, 201 North st.
Old Farm Home for Boys, Blue Hill, Milton.
Old Farm Home for Girls, Blue Hill, Milton.
Penitent Females' Refuge, 32 Rutland st.
Perkins' Institute, 553 E. Broadway, S. B.
Pine Farm Home, Ass't Agent, C. W. Birtwell, 35 Temple st.
Portland Street Home, Supt., 61 Court st.
Rebecca Pomroy Home for Orphan Girls, Mrs. J. Sturgis Potter.
Roxbury Home for Aged Women, Burton av., Copeland st.

Sailors' Snug Harbor, Germantown, Quincy.
St. John's Home for Destitute Children, 2 Elmo st., Dorchester.
St. Joseph's Home for Servant Women, 43 East Brookline st.
St. Luke's Home for Convalescents, 149 Roxbury st
St. Margaret's Home, 17 Louisburg sq
Scots' Temporary Home, 77 Camden st.
Seashore Home, Winthrop. Office, 40 State st.
Shaw Asylum for Mariners' Children, B. G. Shaw, President.
Sheltering Home for Animals, Lake st., Brighton.
Society of St. Margaret Home, 17 Louisburg sq.
Soldiers' Home, Powder-horn Hill, Chelsea. 12 Pemberton sq.
Spinal Home, Blue Hill av., Roxbury District.
Temporary Home for Discharged Female Prisoners, Dedham.
Temporary Home for Children, Chardon st.
Temporary Home for the Destitute, 1 Pine pl.
Temporary Home for the Destitute, 46 Worcester st. For children.
Temporary Home for Working Women, 126 Pleasant st.
Temporary Home for Fallen Women, 6 Oak pl.
Two Homes for Children, Blue Hill av., Grove Hall, Roxbury.
Wayfarers' Lodge, Hawkins st.
Washingtonian Home, 41 Waltham st.
Wellesley Home, Y. M. C. Union, 18 Boylston st.
Wesleyan Home for Orphan and Destitute Children.
Winchester Home for Aged Women, 10 Eden st., Charlestown
Working Boys' Home, Father Roche's, 31 Bennet st.

Hospitals and Dispensaries

are located as follows:
Boston Dispensary (free), Bennet st., cor. Ash.
Boston City Hospital, Harrison av., opp. Worcester sq.
Boston Home for Incurables, Dorchester av., Dorchester.
Boston Lunatic Hospital, East First st., South Boston.
Boston Lying-in Hospital, 24 McLean st.
Cancer Hospital for Women, Dr. Chas. Cullis, Beacon Hill pl., Bowdoin st.
Cancer Hospital for Women, 58 East Springfield st.
Carney Hospital, Old Harbor st., South Boston.
Carney Hospital, Ear Dispensary, South Boston.
Carney Hospital, Eye Dispensary, South Boston.
Channing Hospital, 30 McLean st.
Charlestown Free Dispensary and Hospital, 27 Harvard sq.
Children's Hospital, Huntington av.
College of Physicians and Surgeons' Free Dispensaries, 34 Essex st., and 712 Washington st.
Consumptives' Home, Blue Hill av., Grove Hall.
Convalescent Home, Belmont.
Convalescents' Home, Wellesley. Receives patients from Children's Hospital.
Dental Infirmary (free) of Boston Dental College.
Dental College, 485 Tremont st.
Dental Infirmary (free) of Massachusetts Gen. Hospital, Blossom st., foot of No. Grove st.
Dental Infirmary (free), of the Homœopathic Dispensary, 14 Burroughs pl.
Dispensary (free) for Eye and Ear patients, 14 Burroughs pl.
Dispensary (free) for Heart and Lungs Treatment, 14 Burroughs pl.
Dispensary (free) for Nervous Patients, 14 Burroughs pl.
Dispensary (free) for Throat Affections, 14 Burroughs pl.
Dispensary for Children, 18 Staniford st.
Dispensary (free) for Skin Diseases, 14 Burroughs pl.
Dispensary of Mass. Gen. Hospital, Blossom st.
Epileptic Children's Cottages, Baldwinsville.
Eye and Ear Infirmary, 176 Charles st., out-patient treatment free.
Free Hospital for Women, 58 East Springfield st.
Homœopathic Free Dispensary, 14 Burroughs pl.
Hospital Cottages for Children, Baldwinsville.
House of the Good Shepherd, 1752 Tremont st.
House of the Good Samaritan, 6 McLean st., for Women and Children.
Infirmary of Boston Dental College, 485 Tremont st.
Jamaica Plain Free Dispensary, Everett st., cor. Gordon.
Lunatic Hospital, East First st., South Boston.
Massachusetts General Hospital, Blossom st., foot of McLean st.
Massachusetts Hospital Ambulance Service, Blossom st.
Massachusetts Homœopathic Hospital, East Concord st., near Albany st.
McLean Asylum for the Insane, Washington st., Somerville.
Murdock Free Surgical Hospital for Women, Huntington av., cor. Camden.
New England Hospital for Women and Children, Codman av., Roxbury Dist.
New England Hospital Dispensary, 29 Fayette st.
North End Diet Kitchen, 2 Staniford pl.
Out-patient Department (free), 37 Blossom st.
Seashore Summer Hospital for Children, Winthrop.
Small-pox Hospital, Canterbury st.
Society of St. Margaret Hospital, 17 Louisburg sq.

Soldiers' Hosp., Powderhorn Hill, Chelsea.
South End Diet Kitchen, 37 Bennet st.
Spinal Home and Hospital, Blue Hill av.
St. Elizabeth Hosptl., 61 West Brookline st.
St. Joseph's Hospital, 43 East Brookline st.
St. Luke's Hospital, 149 Roxbury st.
United States Marine Hospital, Chelsea.
United States Naval Hospital, Chelsea.
University (Harvard) Dental Infirmary, foot of North Grove st.
West End Nursery, Hospital, 37 Blossom st.
Women's Dispensary, 18 Staniford st.
Women's Dispensary, 27 Hollis st.
Working People's Dispensary, 777 Washington st.

ALMSHOUSES.—CEMETERIES.

Almshouses. The Directors of Public Institutions, 30 Pemberton Square, have charge of four City Almshouses, viz: Austin Farm, Charlestown District, Deer Island and Rainsford Island.

Austin Farm Almshouse, West Roxbury District. For aged and infirm women, having a legal settlement. The cost of the maintenance of each inmate is $1.87 per week.

Charlestown Almshouse, Charlestown District. Here are supported adult poor, free lodgings to wayfarers, and over a thousand persons receive meals annually. It costs $1.51 per week for the support of each pauper.

Deer Island Almshouse, Deer Island, Boston Harbor. Almshouse, for women and children, including pauper school (for girls) and nursery.

Rainsford Island Almshouse, Rainsford Island, Boston Harbor. Support given to adult male paupers. Those able to work are employed in cutting stone. Expense of each inmate per week, $2.19.

Cemeteries. The cemeteries in and around Boston are noted for their natural and artistic features of beauty. Mount Auburn, Cambridge, was the first in the United States to be laid out as a "garden cemetery," is the most widely known burial-place, and is probably more largely visited by strangers from Europe and elsewhere, than any similar enclosure in this country. (See *Mount Auburn*). Cemeteries are located as follows:

Bunker Hill Burial Ground ....
..............Bunker Hill, Charlestown
Catholic Burial Ground...................
..............Bunker Hill, Charlestown
Catholic Cemetery...Fenwick st., Rox'y
Cedar Grove Cemetery....Adams st., Dor.
Central Burying Ground, Boston Common
Codman Burial Ground..Norfolk st., Dor.
Copp's Hill Burial Ground...............
..............Cor. Charter and Hull sts.
Dorchester Old Burial Ground ....
......Stoughton st., Upham's Corner
Dorchester South Burial Ground........
..............Dorchester av., Dorchester
East Boston Cemetery....Swift st., E. B.
Evergreen Cemetery.....................
..........near Chestnut Hill Reservoir
Forest Hills Cemetery...Morton st., J. P.
Gethsemane Cemetery...................
..............Brook Farm, W. Roxbury
Granary Burying Ground....
........Tremont st., opp. Bromfield
Hand-in-Hand (Jewish) Cemetery........
..............Grove st., W. Roxbury
King's Chapel Burying Ground..........
...Tremont st., bet. School and Court
Mount Auburn Cemetery......Cambridge
Mount Benedict Cemetery................
..............Arnold st., W. Roxbury
Mount Calvary Cemetery..................
..............Mt. Hope st., W. Roxbury
Mount Hope Cemetery....................
..............Walk Hill st., W. Roxbury
Ohabei Shalom Burial Ground ....
..............Wordsworth st., E. B.
Old Burial Ground.....Phipps st., Chas'n
Old Catholic Burial Ground ....
..............Norfolk st., Dorchester
Roxbury Cemetery........................
..............Washington st., cor. Eustis
St. Augustine Cemetery....South Boston
South Burial Ground ....
..............Washington st., above E. Newton
Tifareth Israel (Jewish)......W. Roxbury
Warren Cemetery....Kearsage av., Rox'y
Woodlawn Cemetery..............Everett

STREET GUIDE.

The absence of initials indicates that the Street is in the City proper; the letters E. B. denote East Boston; C,—Charlestown; S. B.,—South Boston; R,—Roxbury; W. R.,—West Roxbury; D,—Dorchester; B,—Brighton.

A Street..........210 Dorchester av., S. B.
A Street,Boylston to Spring Park av.W.R.
Abbott....................Blue Hill av. D.
Aberdeen..Beacon to N. Y. & N. E. Ry. R.
Acorn........ ....2 Willow st.
Acton................1251 Washington st.
Adams........Winthrop to Chelsea st. C.
Adams....................105 Hampden, R.
Adams........Bowdoin st. M. H. Hill, D.
Adams......................Everett st. B.
Adams Place................9 Lincoln, C.
Adams Place..........15 North Anderson
Adams Place...........342 E street, S. B.
Adams Place........2135 Washington, R.
Adams Sq.,..Wash., Brattle and Cornhill
Addison,Sar't'ga to Ch'lsea-st. B'dge, E.B.
Ætna Place...................69 Kingston
Akron....................... 22 Alpine, R.
Akron Place................ 22 Akron, R.
Alaric..........Centre to Spring, W. R.
Alaska..............129 Blue Hill av., R.
Alban....................Welles av., D.
Albano, Washington to Roslin av., W. R.
Albany.........................83 Beach
Albany Avenue.............235 Dudley, R.
Albany Place..............103 Albany
Albert......Old Heath, near Railroad, R.
Albion..........................12 Dover
Albion.....................538 Dudley, R.
Albion Place..................415 Main, C.
Alden.........................149 Court
Alden Court....................4 Alden
Alden Place.....Green near Wash., W. R.
Alexander Avenue......681 Dudley, R.
Alford.....587 Main to Malden Bridge, C.
Alfred......Green to Seaverns av., W. R.
Alger......... 468 Dorchester av., S. B.
Allandale, Centre to Brookline line, W.R.
Allard Court.............16 Pynchon, R.
Allbright Court....Boston to Sumner, D.
Alleghany.................71 Terrace, R.
Allen........................452 Main, C.
Allen.............opposite 74 Chambers
Allen..... Brown Avenue to Rowe, W. R.
Allen Court........................Allen
Allen-street Court...........11 Allen, C.
Allen Place......................37 Allen
Allen Place.............103 Roxbury, R.
Allen Place ...Washington near Lake, B.
Allen's Court..............103 Havre, E. B.
Allerton......................Gerard, C.
Allston................247 Bunker Hill, C.
Allston.... ....24 Somerset
Allston...........Mather to Centre, D.
Allston.................Brighton av., B
Allston Heights, Camb'ge opp. Gordon, B.
Allston Place......................6 Allston
Allston Square..Allston to Washburn, B.
Alna Place..............217 Webster, E. B.
Alpine... ....46 St. James, R.

Alpine Place ....52 Alpine, R.
Alveston............33 Seaverns av., W. R.
Ames......Dorr to O. C. R. R., at E, S. B.
Ames..............Dix av. to Madison, B.
Ames Court...................Ames, S B.
Amherst.....Brandon to Prospect, W. R.
Amory......................248 Centre, R.
Anawan Av., Park to Central Sta., W. R.
Anderson................150 Cambridge
Anderson Court..............18 Anderson
Anderson Place............20 Anderson
Andrews......72 E. Canton to E. Dedham
Anthony Place........ N. Hanover Court
Appian Way...... Vernon to Pleasant, B.
Apple Place............. Washington, D.
Appleton....................441 Tremont
Appleton Place.....Brookline Avenue, R.
Arcadia........School to Atherton, W. R.
Arcadia...Adams, near Dorchester av., D.
Arch..............35 Milk to 50 Summer
Arch Place..................217 Hanover
Argyle............ Dorchester Avenue, D.
Arklow......................Walden, R.
Arlington............ opposite 95 Beacon
Arlington, Market opposite Sparhawk, B.
Arlington Av.Alford to Somerville line,C.
Arlington Place.............83 Tremont, C.
Arlington Place............Arlington, B.
Armandine., Washington to Milton av., D.
Arnold .... 1979 Washington, R.
Arnold.......Weld to Newton line, W. R.
Arrow........ 52 Bow to Eastern R. R., C.
Arrow-street Court...........11 Arrow, C.
Arthur Place...................328 Main, C.
Ash..................29 Bennet to 16 Oak
Ash Place..................52 Myrtle
Ashburton Place............. 14 Somerset
Ashford........... Malvern to Linden, B.
Ashland......................88 Leverett
Ashland......Washington to Back, W. R.
Ashland............... Park to Mill, D.
Ashland Av., Granite nr. Spring-st.,W. R.
Ashland Place..............1206 Washington
Ashmont... Washing. to Neponset av., D.
Ashton Place..................267 Charles
Asylum...................1020 Washington
Athens..................W. 11 Second, S. B.
Atherton .... 3071 Washington, W. R.
Atherton Av. Albano to Washington,W.R.
Atherton Place... foot of Atherton, W. R.
Atkins ....Haven Avenue, D.
Atlantic............473 East Fourth, S. B.
Atlantic Avenue,jun. Com'l and East. av.
Atwood Avenue...............89 Day, R.
Auburn........................399 Main, C.
Auburn........................99 Poplar
Auburn.................66 Ruggles, R.
Auburn ... Washington to Bellevue av. R.
Auburn............ Pleasant to Vernon, B.
Auburn Court............80 Cambridge
Auburn Place...............15 Auburn, C.
Auburn Place ....15 Auburn, R.
Auburn Square..Auburn opp. Russell, C.
Auckland.................Savin-hill av. D.
Augustus Avenue..........Poplar, W. R.
Austin....148 Main to Prison Point br. C.
Austin.......Bellevue to Brookline av. R.

Autumn....386 Longwood av. to Park, R.
Autumn..... Centre, near Granite, W. R.
Avery..........585 Washington to Mason
Avery Place........................7 Avery
Avon......................472 Washington
Avon......Centre to Brookline line, W. R.
Avon Place................. 79 Sullivan, C.
Avon Place................263 Ruggles, R.
Avondale Court............Richmond, D.
B Street..........282 Dorchester av. S. B.
Babcock Court...............593 Main, C.
Back.................Blue-hill av. W. R.
Badger Place..................67 Green, C.
Bailey....................Dorchester av. D.
Bailey's Court...............872 Albany, R.
Bainbridge..................155 Chelsea, C.
Bainbridge..................122 Dale, R.
Baker........Centre to Newton line,W. R.
Baker..Boylston, near Washington,W. R,
Baker Avenue............Washington, D.
Baker Place......................Bird, R.
Baker's Alley.....................192 North
Baker's Alley................48 South Margin
Baker's Court...Wash. at Lower Mills, D.
Baldwin......433 Main to 502 Medford, C.
Baldwin............Granite to 144 A, S. B.
Baldwin...Parker, near B. & A. R. R., R.
Baldwin Place...................118 Salem
Baldwin Place............6 Baldwin, S. B.
Baldwin Place...........Washington, B.
Ball..................2009 Washington, B.
Ballinakill Avenue..........Baker, W. R.
Ballou Avenue.........Lauriat av. W. R.
Bancroft Place................33 Hawkins
Barber's Alley...................312 North
Barnard Place..........540 E. Third, S. B.
Barre Place.......................53 Eliot
Barrett ....8 Fulton to 79 North
Barry........Bellevue to Hamilton av. D.
Barry Court...............1252 Washington
Bartlett......north cor. Monument sq. C.
Bartlett...2503 Washington to Eliot sq. R.
Bartlett Court..........170 Norfolk av. R.
Bartlett Place....................98 Salem
Barton...............91 Lowell to 8 Milton
Barton Court...................65 Barton
Bateman Place.............183 N st. S. B.
Bates................40 Bunker Hill, C.
Bates Place....................9 Kneeland
Bates Place................205 Roxbury, R.
Bath......................Post-Office sq.
Bath Avenue ....Savin-hill av. D.
Battery....499 Hanover to People's Ferry
Batterymarch................Liberty sq.
Baxter...................C to 80 E, S. B.
Baxter Place...................25 Harvard
Baxter Square.................207 E, S. B.
Bay................crosses Fayette at 56
Bay............................Leed's pl. D.
Bay-state Place..........545 E. First, S. B.
Bay-view Place........558 E. Eighth, S. B.
Bay-view Place..............Rogers av. R.
Beach....................555 Medford, C.
Beach......672 Washington to 301 Federal
Beach.............Commercial to Park, D.
Beach Place..................24 Beach, C.
Beacham.......West to Mystic River, C.
Beacon............63 Tremont over Milldam
Beacon-hill Place...............65 Bowdoin
Beale....Dorchester av., near Fuller, R.
Bearse Avenue.........River-view av. D.
Beaumont....................Adams, D.

Beaver.........................91 Beacon
Beckler Avenue.....................134 K
Bedford...500 Washington to 115 Summer
Beech............Centre to Poplar, W. R.
Beech-glen Avenue......173 Highland, R.
Beethoven, Washington to Arcadia, W. R.
Belcher Lane............ 353 Atlantic av.
Belfort......Dorchester av. to Saxton, D.
Belknap Place....................68 Joy
Bell Court....................104 D, S. B.
Belle Avenue, Baker, near Railr'd, W. R.
Bellevue............ 374 Longwood av., R.
Bellevue........Centre, near Park, W. R.
Bellevue............Columbia to Bowdoin, D.
Bellevue Av., junc. Wash. & Beech, W. R.
Bellows Place...............20 Walnut, C.
Bellows Place..........Dorchester av., D.
Belmont................297 Bunker Hill, C.
Belmont.....116 Ruggles to 99 Vernon, R.
Belmont Place............122 Everett, E. B.
Belmont Square........188 Webster, E. B.
Bendalls Lane........40½ Faneuil Hall sq.
Bennet....................774 Washington
Bennet Avenue.................47 Prince
Bennet Place....................42 Bennet
Bennett............Market to Parsons, B.
Bennett Place, White, opp. Marion, E. B.
Bennington..........20 Central sq., E. B.
Benton...........983 Tremont to 63 Berlin
Berkeley........(See E. and W. Berkeley)
Berkeley Court......... 7 Berkeley pl., R.
Berkeley Place............760 Dudley, R.
Berlin.......Walpole to 38 Davenport, R.
Bernier....Brookline av. to Plymouth, R.
Berry......Canterbury to Ashland, W. R.
Berry.....................Central av., W. R.
Berwick Park..........437 Columbus av.
Bessom Court..........92 Webster, E. B.
Bethel Place..................35 Anderson
Beverly....................44 Charlestown
Bickford............80 Heath to Centre, R.
Bickford Avenue............105 Heath, R.
Bicknal Avenue............81 Roxbury. R.
Bigelow........Washington to Brooks, B.
Billerica....................54 Causeway
Bills Court................303 Ruggles, R.
Binney........Francis to Longwood av. R.
Binney Place.... ....862 Albany, R.
Birch........Brandon to Prospect, W. R.
Bird........Magnolia to 55 Columbia, R.
Bird's Avenue.Centre, opp. Bellevue,W.R.
Bird's Lane.......................River, D.
Bishop.............Newbern to Call, W. R.
Bismarck.......Messinger to Oakland, D.
Blaban Place..................94 Pearl, C.
Blackstone....2 Fulton to Haymarket sq.
Blackstone Square..1533 to 1549 Washing.
Blake...Boston st. to Dorchester av. S. B.
Blanchard....66 Bartlett to 40 Norfolk, R.
Blandon.......South to Dudley av. W. R.
Bleiler Court................4 Heath pl. R.
Blossom ....135 Cambridge
Blossom Court....................7 Blossom
Blossom Place................15 Blossom
Blue Hill Avenue....403 Dudley to Milton
Board Alley.................237 Hanover
Bodwell Park......Bird near Railroad, R.
Bolton......91 W. Second to 45 Dor. S. B.
Bolton Court................7 Bolton, S. B.
Bolton Place................135 High, C.
Bolton Place...............2 Bolton, S. B.
Bond..........4 Milford to 1 Hanson

Border........... People's Ferry av. E. B.
Boston 587 Dorchester av. to 800 Dudley
Boston Common. Trem., Boyl., Chas., Bea.
Boston Place........ 329 Dorchester, S. B.
Bosworth................. 98 Tremont
Bourne...Walk Hill to Canterbury, W. R.
Boutwell........Neponset av. to Train, D.
Bow...........City sq. to 18 Washington, C.
Bow-Street Court......... 60 Devens, C.
Bowditch Court.......... 547 Warren, R.
Bowdoin.......6 Cambridge to 27 Beacon
Bowdoin...Washington opp. Harvard, D.
Bowdoin Avenue...Bowdoin to Columbia
Bowdoin Square........... 187 Court
Bowdoin Square.............Bowdoin, D.
Bowe....300 Centre to Chestnut av. W. R.
Bowen..................west of 36 C, S. B.
Bower..................... 384 Warren, R.
Bowker.........49 Sudbury to 49 Chardon
Boylston....643 Washington to Back Bay
Boylston....Washington to Centre, W. R.
Boylston Avenue. Green to Boylston, W.R.
Boylston Place............ 54 Boylston
Boylston Square......... 657 Washington
Bradford................... 49 Waltham
Bradford Place .... 6 Mason
Bradstreet Court............. 2. Park, C.
Bragdon....3903 Wash. to Armory, W. R.
Branch........Butler to River View av. D.
Branch Avenue . 17 Charles to 4 Spruce
Brandon...... South to Dudley av. W. R.
Brattle........ 77 Court to 137 Washington
Brattle Square........51 Brattle to 15 Elm
Bread .... 82 Broad to 36 India
Breck..........Warren to Washington, B.
Breen Place..30 Livingston to 382 Charles
Bremen................. 232 Sumner, E. B.
Bremen Place........... 16 Bremen, E. B.
Brewer..........Burroughs to Eliot, W. R.
Brewster..........501 East Seventh, S. B.
Bridge Court..........21 North Anderson
Briggs Place............ 242 Shawmut av.
Brighton..... Cambridge to Columbia, C.
Brighton........... 101 Lowell to 67 Allen
Brighton Avenue...Beacon, Brookline av.
Brighton-street Avenue..... 105 Brighton
Brighton-street Place......... 66 Brighton
Brimmer........102 Pinckney to 86 Beacon
Brimmer Place............... 12 Essex
Bristol.................... 349 Albany
Broad .... 117 State to 333 Atlantic av.
Broadway................. 906 Washington
Broadway Court.....East Broadway, S. B.
Bromfield..309 Washington to 102 Tremont
Bromley ...42 Heath to Bromley Park, R.
Bromley Park .....Albert to Bickford, R.
Brook ....Bellevue to Hill, W. R.
Brook Avenue,497 Dudley to 573 Dudley,R.
Brook Farm Av.,Baker to Newt.line,W.R.
Brook Place............ 498 Dudley, R.
Brookford....Blue Hill av., to Howard av.
Brookline..(East and West Brookline) R.
Brookline Av...Beacon op. Bright. av., B.
Brooks...272 Bremen to 107 Condor, E. B.
Brooks........Faneuil to B. & A. R. R., B.
Brooks Place............ 142 Cambridge
Brooks Place, Washington nr. Oak sq. B.
Brookside Av...Green to Boylston, W. R.
Brown.................48 Hunneman, R.
Brown Ave.......Florence to Poplar, W. R.
Brown Place..14 Seaverns Avenue, W. R.
Brown's Court............40 Lawrence, C.

Browning Avenue..........Warner, D.
Brunswick Av. Centre to W. Walnut pk.
Buchanan Ct. South, nr. White av. W. R.
Buchanan Place............ 657 Parker, R.
Buckingham......267 Columbus Avenue
Buckingham Place....... 40 Buckingham
Buena Vista Avenue ...... 214 Warren, R.
Bulfinch ....166 Court to 9 Allston
Bulfinch Place.............5 Bulfinch
Bumstead Court........... 23 Boylston
Bumstead Lane........ 1715 Tremont, C.
Bunker Hill ...183 Chelsea to 507 Main, C.
Bunker Hill Court ....318 Bunker Hill, C.
Burke.....1007 Tremont to 47 Berlin, R.
Burk's Court............ 84 Everett, E. B.
Burlington Av. Prookline Av. to Beac., R.
Burney . ....1482 Tremont to Belle av. R.
Burnham. East Ninth to Lowland, S. B.
Burr. Boylston to Spring Park Av. W. R.
Burrell Place............... 163 I, S. B.
Burroughs.........Centre to Pond, W. R.
Burroughs Place............. 15 Hollis
Burton Avenue..........10 Copeland, R.
Bush.................... 92 E. Canton
Bussey...........South to Centre, W. R.
Bussey Place........... 101 Arch
Butler, Brookline Avenue to N. Y. & N.
E. R. R., R.
Butler, Richmond to River View av., D.
Butler Square........... 56 Chatham
Butler's Row .... 3 Chatham Row
Buttonwood... Crescent av., S. B. & D.
Buttonwood Court......Buttonwood, D.
Buttrick Place........... 53 North Margin
Byrnes Place........... 72 Havre, E. B.
Byron..............Bennington, E. B.
Byron .... 10 River
Byron Court............ 16 School, W. R.
C Street.............49 W. Seventh, S. B.
C Street..Boylston to Spring Park, W. R.
Cabot, 1000 Tremont to E. Linden Park, R.
Cabot Place, 116 Cabot to 97 Warwick, R.
Cabler.........Canterbury to Back, W. R.
Call......... 51 Park to 40 Chelsea, C.
Call ...... Jamaica Plain Station, W. R.
Call-street Place. 12 Call to 33 Henley, C.
Colver Place .... Rear 230 Dover
Cambridge ...774 Main to Somerville, C.
Cambridge Bowdoin sq. to Cambridge
Cambridge .Cambridge line to Wash., B.
Cambridge-street Avenue, 201 Cambridge
Cambridge-street Pl., 217 & 221 Cambridge
Camden..... 1817 Wash. to B. & P. R. R.
Camden Place............ 1822 Washington
Campbell Place............. 224 Eustis, R.
Canal.......Haymarket sq. to Causeway
Canal Bank.....Beacham to Dorrance, C.
Canny Place .... 31 Webster av.
Canterbury, Blue Hill av. to Poplar, W. R.
Canton........See E. and W. Canton
Canton-street Court.....27 West Canton
Canton-street Place..... 28 West Canton
Capen...........Norfolk to Fuller, D.
Carey Court......18 Maudlin to Water, C.
Carlton....West Newton to Berwick Park
Carlton..............Crescent av. D.
Carnes Place............ 14 Hawkins
Carolina Avenue..South to Wash., W. R.
Carrigg's Court.............4 Ice ct., C.
Carroll Place .. ..112 Salem
Carruth..........Ashmont to Codman, D.
Carter, Camb'dge, near Som'ville line, C

Carter Place................65 Charter
Carver........74 Boylston to 113 Pleasant
Carver Place................40 Carver
Cary....13 Tremont pl. to 230 Ruggles, R.
Cary Place................127 High, D.
Castle................935 Washington
Castle Court............168 Everett, E. B.
Catawba.....37 Sherman to 10 Laurel, R.
Causeway................27 Leverett
Cazenove.75 Chandler to 254 Columbus av.
Cedar..............27 High to 8 Bartlett, C.
Cedar.2663 Washington to 138 Pynchon, R.
Cedar..Washington to Bellevue av. W. R.
Cedar................River, D.
Cedar Avenue..Chestnut to Oak pl. W. R.
Cedar Avenue..Union av. to Bowdoin, D.
Cedar Place................Bird, R.
Cedar Square..bet. Ced., Jun., Thorn., R.
Cemetery Street. Norfolk to Cath. Cem. D.
Central.32 Kilby, ac. India to Atlantic av.
Central Avenue...Wash. n. Beech, W. R.
Central Avenue......450 Blue Hill av. D.
Central Court............446 Washington
Central Place............106 Main, C.
Central Square............Border, E. B.
Centre............Eliot sq. to Dedham
Centre............Washington, Adams, D.
Centre Avenue........Dorchester av, D.
Centre Court.....Centre, near Adams, D.
Centre Place..61 Preble to the marsh, S. B.
Centre Place................61 Centre, R.
Centre Place................Centre, W. R.
Ceylon...........Preble to Hyde, S. B.
Ceylon................Quincy to Bird, R.
Chadwick................37 Hampden, R.
Chadwick Court..........66 Chadwick, R.
Chadwick Place....19 Chad. to 842 Alb. R.
Chamber................26 City sq. C.
Chambers......63 Cambridge to 24 Spring
Chamber-street Court........26 Chambers
Champney....Newman to Lowland, S. B.
Champney Court........Champney, S. B.
Champney Place............43 Anderson
Champney Place............18 Madison, R.
Chandler...431 Tremont to 332 Colum. av.
Change Avenue..56 Sta. to 13 Fan. Hall sq.
Channing......82 Federal to 167 Congress
Channing Place............25 Leather sq.
Chapel........24 Milford pl. to 59 Weston
Chapel Place................167 Friend
Chapel Place................93 Albany
Chapin Avenue........LaGrange, W. R.
Chapman........202 Main to Washington
Chapman............1063 Washington D.
Chapman Avenue........Blue Hill av. C.
Chapman Place............68 Chapman, C.
Chapman Place..52 School to 6 Bosworth
Chardon.....Bowdoin sq. to 118 Portland
Chardon Court................7 Chardon
Chardon-street Place............20 Chardon
Charles........479 Main to 426 Bunker Hill, C.
Charles........76 Boylston. opp. Park sq.
Charles............Poplar, near Dale, W. R.
Charles................Dorchester av., D.
Charles Place............124 Foundry, S. B.
Charles-street Place............7 Charles. C.
Charles-river Avenue........33 City sq., C.
Charlestown. Haym't sq. to 279 Causeway
Charter........394 Hanover to Commercial
Chatham...21 Merchants Row to 8 Com'l.
Chatham Row....136 State to 57 Chatham
Chaucer............Pope to Moore, E. B.

Chauncey Place............90 Decatur, C.
Chauncy................53 Summer
Chauncy Place...Wash., n. School, W. R.
Cheever Court..........359 Summer, E. B.
Chelsea, Maverick sq. to Chelsea Br. E.B.
Chelsea......23 City sq. to Chelsea, Br. C.
Chelsea Court............156 Chelsea, E. B.
Chelsea Place............88 Chelsea, E. B.
Chemical Av.. Wash. to Brookside, W. R.
Cheney..Blue Hill av. to Elm Hill av., R.
Cherry................1045 Washington
Cherry............112 Quincy to Dove, R.
Cherry Court................Cherry, R.
Cheshire................Green, W. R.
Chessman Place............250 Hanover
Chester......Blue Hill av. to Oakland, D.
Chester................Brighton av., B.
Chester Park............1756 Washington
Chester Place............538 Shawmut av.
Chester Square............1755 Washington
Chestnut................72 Chelsea, C.
Chestnut.....15 Walnut to Charles River
Chestnut Avenue............59 Chestnut
Chestnut Avenue, Wyman to Green, W. R.
Chestnut Grove, Centre, opp. Pond, W. R.
Chestn't Hill Av.,Wash. to B'kline line, B.
Chestnut Place............42 B, S. B.
Chestnut Place........Chestnut av., W. R.
Chestnut Square........Chestnut av., W. R.
Chickatawbut .Neponset av. to Glide, D.
Chickering Place........570 Washington
Child................South, W. R.
Chilson Place................17 Lyman
Chipman............Norfolk to Torry, D.
Church....351 Tremont to 2 Columbus av.
Church........Centre, opp. South, W. R.
Church............Adams to Winter, D.
Church....Washington to Mt. Vernon, B.
Church Avenue...355 W. Broadway, S. B.
Church Court............109 Warren, C.
Church Place............190 Cabot, R.
Church Place......Wash. near Centre, D.
Churchill Place............Washington, D.
Circuit............27 Walnut av., R.
City Hall Avenue............35 School
City Point Court, E. First, above O, S. B.
City Square..........junc. Main, Park, C.
Clapp................176 W. Eighth, S. B.
Clapp................Boston, R.
Clapp Place...Boston, opp. Dexter ct., D.
Claremont Park........535 Columbus av.
Clarence....436 Dudley to 113 George, R.
Clarence, Spring, nr. D'm line to Bell,W.R.
Clarence Place......Wash. near Park, D.
Clarendon.....(See E. and W. Clarendon)
Clarendon....Roslin av. to Poplar, W. R.
Clarendon Pk. Poplar to Metro., Av. W.R.
Clark.....395 Hanover to 292 Commercial
Clark........Bellevue to Hamilton av., D.
Clark Place............Lamartine, W. R.
Clark's Court..........316 Bunker Hill, C.
Clay................1288 Tremont, R.
Clayton........Commercial to Park, D.
Clayton Place............25 Magazine, R.
Cleveland Place............17 Snowhill
Cliff................139 Warren, R.
Cliff Place................32 Cliff, R.
Clifford................298 Warren, R
Clifford Place................26 Fleet
Clifton................Cottage to Taylor, R
Clifton,Kittredge, crossing Albano, W.R.
Clifton Place............1921 Washington, R

Clinton ... ..35 Merchants Row
Clinton Place ...... Cambridge, C.
Clyde........ ....61 Marginal, E. B.
Cobb............. ......1011 Washington
Cobden ....2988 Washington, R.
Coburn Court ....26 Phillips
Coburn Place.................... Reed
Codman........... Forest-Hills av., D.
Codman Park........... 2926 Washington
Codman Place........2956 Washington, R.
Coffee Place ... .Washington, D.
Colby Place ....2002 Washington, R.
Coleman.... Bellevue to Hamilton av., D.
Coleridge ...Wordsworth to Swift, E. B.
Collamore Place.... ....85 Salem
Collins .... Blue Hill av., D.
Colony .....18 Swan to 208 Foundry, S. B.
Colony Place ....859 Albany, R.
Columbia................ 660 Main, C.
Columbia..................87 Bedford
Columbia,Hancock to Blue Hill av.,R.& D.
Columbia Court ....rear 662 Main, C.
Columbus Avenue .... Park sq.
Columbus Place .... 189 Eliot
Columbus Square.......... Columbus av.
Commerce ....3 Commercial
Commercial..................170 State
Commercial,Hancock to Neponset av. D.
Commercial Court .....446 Commercial
Commercial Point ......Commercial, D.
Common .....37 Winthrop to Adams, C.
Common........... .....827 Washington
Commonwealth Avenue ... 12 Arlington
Conant......645 Parker to Whitney, R.
Conant Court ....31 King, R.
Conant-street Place..........28 Conant, R.
Concord (see E. Concord and W. Concord)
Concord ....25 Monument sq. C.
Concord Avenue. ...2 Lex. to Jeff. av. C.
Concord Place .... 109 Worcester
Concord Square.............723 Tremont
Condor..foot of Border to Glendon, E. B.
Confirmed Place ....93 Rutherford av. C.
Congress................31 State to A st.
Congress-street Place..........192 Congress
Congress Square............29 State
Cook..............259 Bunker Hill, C.
Cook......Washington, near Harvard, D.
Cook Place ....386 Commercial
Cook-street Court.............23 Cook, C.
Cook-street Place ....41 Cook, C.
Coolidge Avenue.............31 Temple
Coolidge Avenue..........Standish av. D.
Coolidge Place...........114 Bolton, S. B.
Cooper ....104 Salem to 45 Charlestown
Cooper-street Court ....36 Cooper
Copeland............260 Warren, R.
Copeland Place........22 Copeland, R.
Copley.......School, near Arcadia, W. R.
Copley Square......Boylston, Dartmouth
Coral Place................92 Pearl, C.
Corbet......Norfolk to Forest-hills av. D.
Cordis......93 Warren to 34 High, C.
Cordis-street Avenue..........21 Cordis, C.
Cordis-street Place............29 Cordis, C.
Corey..................11 Moulton, C.
Corey ....Weld to Park, W. R.
Corey Avenue..........11 Ash to 37 Bennet
Corey Court............58 Corey, C.
Corinth...............Washington, W. R.
Corn Court............10 Faneuil Hall sq.
Cornhill..............151 Washington

Cornhill Court............201 Washington
Cortes .... 6 Ferdinand
Cottage... ....118 Marginal, E. B.
Cottage,167 Bunker Hill to 210 Medf'd, C.
Cottage.... ....167 W. Ninth, S. B.
Cottage..... ....550 Dudley, R. & D.
Cottage Av., Centre, near Spring, W. R.
Cottage Court ....4 Rand sq., R.
Cottage Place ..... 1238 Washington
Cottage Place..........1261 Tremont, R.
Cottage Row............Medford, C.
Cottage Side..Cottage, near Pleasant, D.
Cottage-street Place.....33 Cottage, E. B.
Cotting ....41 Lowell
Cotting Place ....14 Chambers
Cotton Alley ....463 Atlantic av.
Court .... 193 Washington
Court Avenue.......... 217 Washington
Court Square, 24 and 28 Court to City Hall
Courtland............. ....380 Parker, R.
Cove..................23 East to Furnace
Cove Place...........106 Cove to Furnace
Coventry..............1033 Tremont, R.
Cowper........... Moore to Short, E. B.
Crab Alley................8 Batterymarch
Craft........320 Heath to Kimball, R.
Crawford ....627 Warren, R.
Crawshaw Place.......97 Hampshire, R.
Creek.......Dorchester av. to Pleasant, D.
Creek Square.................Union
Creighton ....369 Centre, R.
Crescent Av., Dorch. av. opp. Pond, D.
Crescent Court ....274 Friend
Crescent Place................33 Green
Crest Avenue...... ...Riverview av., D.
Crimmen Place .... 35 Corey, C.
Crocker Place ....188 Albany
Crosby Place ....64 W. Canton
Crosby Place.......................Reed
Crosby Place .... 1 Adams, R.
Cross ....16 Border to 15 New, E. B.
Cross .....41 High to 20 Bartlett, C.
Cross .... Haymarket sq.
Cross ....Corey to Maple, W. R.
Cross-street Avenue ...... 33 Cross, C.
Cross-street Court..... ......29 Cross, C.
Crossin Place ....28 King, R.
Crystal Place ....20 Mead, C.
Culbert Place ... .101 Pynchon, R.
Culvert...... 224 Ruggles to 195 Cabot, R.
Culvert Court.......Culvert to Vernon, R.
Cumston....79 W. Concord to 14 Rutland
Cumston Place............460 Shawmut av.
Cunard ....65 Cabot to 17 Berlin, R.
Curtis..664 Saratoga to 553 Chelsea, E. B.
Curve.....266 Harrison av. to 168 Albany
Cushing Avenue,Hancock to Sawyer av.D.
Cushman ..Madison av. to Lexington, B.
Cushman Avenue..101 Leverett to 9 Wall
Cusson Place...............32 South Margin
Custer...... South, near Centre, W. R.
Custom House Street,70 Broad to 31 India
Cypress....1-1 Cambridge to 44 Parkman
Cypress.........Beech to Bellevue av. W. R.
Cypress........... Spring to Baker, W. R.
D Street ....440 Dorchester av. S. B
Dabney Place...............34 Regent, R.
Dale............ ....299 Warren, R.
Dale.........Poplar to Hyde Park, W. R.
Dallas Place................180 Cabot, R.
Dalton........ Falmouth to B. & A. R. R.
Damon Place.................19 Bennet

Dana..................219 W. Ninth, S. B.
Dana Place..................135 Dudley, R.
Danforth......Boylston to Wyman, W. R.
Danforth Place...........30 St. James, R.
Dartmouth...(See E. and W. Dartmouth)
Dartmouth Place...........65 Dartmouth
Davenport... 967 Tremont to 81 Berlin, R.
Davenport Avenue..........Columbia, R.
Davenport Place... 23 Davenport, R.
Davis.................1040 Washington
Davis Court..............207 London, E. B.
Davis Court.............6 North Grove
Davis Place.................30 Webber, R.
Day..............186 Heath to 389 Centre, R.
Dayton Avenue..............30 Mall, R.
Deacon..................78 W. Concord
Dean..............Warren to Breck. B.
Dearborn....922 Albany to 254 Dudley, R.
Dearborn Place.........28 Dearborn, R.
Dubois..................480 Shawmut av.
Decatur...115 Border to 94 Bremen, E. B.
Decatur..11 Bunker Hill to 18 Medford, C.
Decatur................1076 Washington
Decatur Avenue..........83 Pynchon, R.
Decatur Court...........58 Decatur, C.
Dedham........(See E. and W. Dedham)
Dell Avenue......528 East Seventh, S. B.
Delle Avenue..............743 Parker, R.
Dennis....................457 Dudley, R.
Dent. Mt.Vernon to Dedham Br.R.R.W.R.
Derby Court........556 East Second, S. B.
Derby Place........1941 Washington, R.
Derne..........47 Bowdoin to 46 Hancock
Devens......23 Washington to 92 Main, C.
Devon....580 Warren to Blue Hill av., R.
Devonshire.......Dock sq. to 92 Summer
Dewerson Court............118 Silver, S. B.
DeWolf....Commercial opposite High, D.
Dexter..........559 Dorchester av., S. B.
Dexter Court, ...Boston op. Clapp pl., R.
Dexter Row, Thompson sq., cor Green. C.
Dickens, Adams, near Dorchester av., D.
Dimock, 2933 Wash. to 82 Amory, R.&W.R.
Dingley Place...............33 Fayette
Ditson............Charles to Westville, D.
Division............ Dorchester av., S. B.
Division..Northampton and Chester Park
Dix..........Adams to Dorchester av., D.
Dix Avenue...................Union, B.
Dix Place..............737 Washington
Doane............... 10 Kilby to 7 Broad
Dock Sq.,Washington st. Faneuil Hall sq.
Doherty Court..........180 Everett, E. B.
Dolan Court...........279 Norfolk av., R.
Dorchester..........423 West First, S. B.
Dorchester Av., Federal-st. Brid. to Wash.
Dorchester Square, bet. Hancock,Church
 and Winter, D.
Dorr........448 Dorchester Avenue, S. B.
Dorr.................. 66 Highland, R.
Dorrance.......651 Main to Gas Works, C.
Dorset.........Dorchester Avenue, S. B.
Douglass.......455 East Eighth, S. B.
Douglass Av......20 Mall to 15 Webber, R.
Douglass Court..............137 Endicott
Dove........383 E to 15 Dorchester, S. B.
Dove..242 Blue Hill Avenue to Cherry, R.
Dove Court....................Dove, R.
Dover....494 Tremont to Dover-st. bridge
Downer, Tremont near Brookline line, R.
Downer Avenue...Pleasant to Sawyer, D.
Downer Court, Hancock, nr. Bellevue, D.

Downer Place...............Hancock, D.
Draper......................Arcadia, D.
Draper's Court, Hancock nr. Bellevue, D.
Draper's Lane.................5 Newland
Drew Place............205 Ruggles, R.
Drisko....................400 Parker, R.
Dudley................... Eliot sq., R.
Dudley Av., from Wash. to South, W. R.
Dudley Place...............46 Dudley, R.
Duncan...................200 Ruggles, R.
Duncan..........Greenwich to Leonard, D.
Duncan Place.................Duncan, D.
Dunlow..... 219 Roxbury to Elmwood, R.
Dunlow Place..Dunlow near Elmwood, R.
Dunmore.......382 Dudley to Magazine, R.
Dunreath Place............228 Warren. R.
Dunstable..Main to 211 Rutherford av. C.
Dunster......Brookline av. to Binney, R.
Durham............ ....14 St. Botolph
Dutton Place..................51 Phillips
Dwight................227 Shawmut av.
Dyer.................. Capen to Evans, D.
E Street..................O. C. R. R., S. B.
Eagle............(See E. and W. Eagle)
Eagle Place...... rear 332 Bunker Hill, C.
Eagle Mill Place.....River opp. Cedar, D.
Earl................... 143 W. Ninth, S. B.
East.........................102 South
East...........Adams to Dorchester av., D.
East-street Place................11 East
East Berkeley................497 Tremont
E. Broadway...con. of W. Broadway, S. B.
East Brookline...........1532 Washington
East Canton.............1494 Washington
East Chester Park............774 Albany
East Clarendon...............557 Tremont
East Concord............1636 Washington
East Dartmouth..............607 Tremont
East Dedham............1456 Washington
East Eagle.........opp. 45 Putnam, E. B.
East Eighth...238 Dor. to City Point, S. B.
East Fifth........61 G to City Point, S. B.
East First ....H to City Point, S. B.
East Fourth..124 Dor. to City Point, S. B.
East High....................Fort Hill sq.
East Lenox..............1872 Washington
East Newton............1550 Washington
East Ninth .... 254 Dorchester, S. B.
East Second..............City Point, S. B.
East Seventh....110 G to City Point, S. B.
East Sixth.......86 G. to Q, City Point, S. B.
East Springfield..........1718 Washington
East Third...... 54 Dor., City Point, S. B.
East Windsor........675 Shawmut av., R.
Eastern Av..Commercial and Atlantic av.
Eaton.....................54 Chambers
Eaton Court..............16 North Bennet
Eaton Place.................166 Cedar, R.
Eaton Place..................20 Norman
Eaton Sq..Church, Bowdoin & Adams, R.
Eddy Place....................139 Tyler
Eden.........341 Main to 74 Russell, C.
Eden Place...................23 Eden, C.
Eden-street Court..............,19 Eden, C.
Edgerly Place..............44 Winchester
Edgewood................348 Warren, R.
Edgeworth...........50 Bunker Hill, C.
Edgeworth Place...........24 Paris, E. B.
Edinboro'......................93 Essex
Edmands Court.......105 Rutherford av.
Edmund Place.........36 North Russell
Egleston Square..(changed to Seaver st.)

Eighth....(see E. Eighth and W. Eighth)
Elbow..................35 Meridian, E. B.
Elder Place..................136 Brighton
Eldon..................Washington, D.
Eldridge..........Metropolitan av. W. R.
Eliot......................707 Washington
Eliot..............Centre to Pond, W. R.
Eliot Place......................67 Eliot
Eliot Square..Rox. Dudley & Putnam, R.
Ellery..........Dexter to Boston st. S. B.
Ellery Court..............46 Ellery, S. B.
Ellicott........Walnut to Morton, W. R.
Ellis......................61 Thornton, R.
Ellsworth..............Dorchester av. D.
Ellsworth Place..........18 School, W. R.
Elm..........................69 High, C.
Elm............69 Hanover to 13 Dock sq.
Elm..............Walker to Green, W. R.
Elm..............Exchange to Everett, D.
Elm Hill Avenue..........535 Warren, R.
Elm Place....................34 Portland
Elmer Place....................121 Salem
Elmo..................Blue Hill av. D.
Elmore..................217 Walnut av. R.
Elmwood..................293 Roxbury, R.
Elmwood Court............2 Elmwood, R.
Elmwood Place............9 Elmwood, R.
Elton....,Dorchester av. to Sagamore, D.
Emerald............110 Castle to 44 Dover
Emerson..................Dorchester, S. B.
Emmet............526 East Third, S. B.
Emmet Place........ ....17 Everett, E. B.
Emmet Place....................9 Blossom
Endicott......................158 Hanover
Endicott Court..............178 Endicott
Enfield..............Spring Park av. W. R.
Englewood Avenue...Chestnut-hill av. B.
Episcopal Av., Centre near Myrtle, W. R.
Ericsson............Walnut to Fulton, D.
Erie Avenue.....Wash., Mt. Bowdoin, D.
Erie Place..............64 School, W. R.
Erin Alley..............62 Liverpool, E. B.
Essex..................Main and Mill, C.
Essex..................622 Washington
Essex.... Brighton av., Cottage Farm, B.
Essex Place....................141 Essex
Euclid......Washington. Withington, D.
Eustis........ 2120 Wash. to Magazine, R.
Eustis Place..................259 Eustis, R.
Eutaw......................319 Border, E. B.
Eutaw Place..............43 Marion, E. B.
Evans............Nelson to Milton av. D.
Evelyn Place..........Dorchester av., D.
Everett............69 Orleans, E. B.
Everett..................157 Bunker Hill, C.
Everett..............Elm to Call, W. R.
Everett..................Park to Mill, D.
Everett..................North Beacon, B.
Everett Avenue............Stoughton, D.
Everett Court..........250 Everett, E. B.
Everett Court..............45 Everett, C.
Everett Court..................322 North
Everett Place..........238 Everett, E. B.
Everett Place...Vernon, near Everett, B.
Everton..........Olney to Geneva av., B.
Ewer..................131 West Ninth, S. B.
Exchange..........38 State to 30 Dock sq.
Exchange.......... Park to the water, D.
Exchange Place..............32 Congress
Exeter..........................299 Beacon
Exeter Court..............47 Sullivan, C.
Exeter Place..............51 Sullivan, C.

Exeter Place..................87 Chauncy
Export......................116 Broad
F Street........ 198 West Eighth, S. B.
Fabin......................19 Newland
Fairfield..................345 Beacon
Fairfield Place..................14 Harris
Fairland........ 91 Mt. Pleasant av., R.
Fairmount..............Walnut, W. R.
Fairmount..............Washington. D.
Falcon..................Border, E. B.
Falmouth........West Newton to Camden
Faneuil........Market to Washington. B.
Faneuil Hall Square..........Faneuil Hall
Farnham..................76 Hampden, R.
Farnum Place............2 Rogers av., R.
Farrell Place..........379 West First, S. B.
Farrington..............Anawan av., W. R.
Farrington Avenue........Harvard av., B.
Farwell Avenue..................56 Poplar
Favre.......... Messinger to Oakland, D.
Faxon..................1463 Tremont, R.
Fay..................413 Harrison av.
Fayette..................112 Pleasant
Fayette Court............603 Washington
Federal........................75 Milk
Federal Court..................121 Federal
Federal Place.................. 235 Federal
Feiling Place..............1196 Tremont, R.
Fellows..................28 Northampton
Fellows Court..................7 Fellows
Fellows Place..............81 Fellows, R.
Felton Place..........2174 Washington, R.
Fenco Place............Field's Corner, D.
Fenton............. Duncan to Clayton, D.
Fenton Place......Fenton to Greenwich, D.
Fenwick..................60 Circuit, R.
Ferdinand..................429 Tremont
Ferrin..................132 Chelsea, C.
Ferry........ 54 Fulton to 127 North
Ferry Court..................24 Ferry
Fessenden Court........90 Webster, E.B.
Fifth....(See East Fifth and West Fifth)
Fifth..................26 Lynde to R. R., C.
Fifth-street Place..........21 W. Fifth, S. B.
Fillmore Place..................489 Hanover
First.....(See East First and West First)
First............Austin, corner Lynde, C.
Fisher Avenue............ 885 Parker, R.
Flagg.....From Lake, near Kendrick, B.
Fleet......................361 Hanover
Floral Place..................849 Washington
Florence..................1060 Washington
Florence..........Poplar to Bourne, W. R.
Follen......St. Botolph to B. & P. R. R.
Forbes Avenue..........Chestnut av., W. R.
Forest............14 Mt. Pleasant av., R.
Forest Avenue..................202 Warren, R.
Forest Hills..............Washington, W. R.
Forest Hills Avenue..........Worton, W. R.
Forest Hills Avenue..........18 River, R.
Forest Place....................26 Eden
Forest Place..................62 Forest, R.
Forster's Court............17 Union
Fort Avenue..............421 Harrison av.
Fort Avenue..............145 Highland, R.
Fort Hill Square................Oliver
Foss..................61 Chelsea, C.
Foster......47 Charter to 476 Commercial
Foster..................Dorchester av. D.
Foster..............Washington to South, B.
Foster Court..................17 Foster
Foster Place..................13 Foster

Foundry............47 Dorchester av. S. B.
Foundry Avenue......120 Foundry, S. B.
Foundry Square....51 West Fourth, S. B.
Fountain..................38 Regent, R.
Fountain Hill.............16 Fountain, R.
Fountain Place.............422 Hanover
Fountain Place............6 Fountain, R.
Fountain Square.........Walnut av. R.
Fourth....(See E. Fourth and W. Fourth)
Fourth-street Court..166 W. Fourth, S. B.
Fourth-street Place...533 E. Fourth, S. B.
Fox Avenue....Adams to Percival av. D.
Francis................1643 Tremont, R.
Francis Place.................196 Hanover
Frankfort.................cemetery, E. B.
Franklin..................305 Main, C.
Franklin..................380 Washington
Franklin............Taylor to Fulton, D.
Franklin................Cambridge st. B.
Franklin Avenue...............31 Court
Franklin Avenue, Spr., n. Ded. line,W.R.
Franklin Court............Norfolk av. R.
Franklin Square.........1534 Washington
Franks Court................9 South May
Fred.....................Arlington av. C.
Frederick............171 West Ninth, S. B.
Frederika........Adams near Codman, D.
Freeman............Charles to Foster, D.
Freeman Place................15 Beacon
Fremont........River to Blue Hill av. D.
Fremont Avenue..............36 Mall, R.
Fremont Court............Fremont pl. C.
Fremont Place............50 Medford, C.
Fremont Place.............201 Dudley, R.
French's Square....59 West Fourth, S. B.
Friend..........8 Union to 111 Causeway
Friend-street Place.............272 Friend
Front...................Warren av. C.
Frothingham Avenue.........306 Main, C.
Fruit....................5 Bunker Hill, C.
Fruit....................32 Blossom
Fruit-street Court................7 Fruit
Fruit-street Place...............31 Fruit
Fuller......Carruth to Forest Hills av. D.
Fulton.............34 Clinton to 7 Lewis
Fulton............Walnut to Ericsson, D.
Fulton Court..................111 North
Fulton Place.......70 Fulton to 149 North
Furbush Court...............490 Main, C.
Furnace....................401 Federal
G Street....Dorchester n. E. Third, S. B.
Garaux Place..............37 Portland
Garden......124 Cambridge to 63 Myrtle
Garden............Maple to Corey, W. R.
Garden.................Brom av. W. R.
Garden-court Street.........3 North sq.
Garden Place..............18 Eden, C.
Garden-street Arch.............19 Garden
Garden-street Court...........45 Garden
Gardner....................624 Main, C.
Gardner...................294 Roxbury, R.
Gardner....Spring to Dedham line,W. R.
Gardner....................Malvern, B.
Gardner Avenue.........298 Roxbury, R.
Gardner Place....162 W. Broadway, S. B.
Garfield Avenue.......Washington, W. R.
Garland.................1095 Washington
Garrison................Huntington av.
Gaston.................530 Warren, R.
Gates............156 Dorchester, S. B.
Gay....................161 Roxbury, R.
Genesee..............340 Harrison av.

Geneva Avenue........476 Blue Hill av. D.
George...............Hamblen to Fred, C.
George..................154 Hampden, R.
Georgia................471 Blue Hill av. R.
Gerard............. Swett to George, R.
Germain...................Norfolk av. R.
German......Washington to Grove, W. R.
Germania............Baker to Jess, W. R.
Gibbon Place..............621 Washington
Gibbs Court..................498 Main, C.
Gibson..................Dorchester av. D.
Gifford Place.............16 Ward st. S. B.
Gilbert............Centre to Wyman, W. R.
Gilbert Avenue......Hamblen to Fred, C.
Gilman Place.................214 Friend
Gilson Court.............106 W. Cedar
Glen........Boylston, Washington, W. R.
Glen........Glen Road to Greenwood, D.
Glen.................Glendale to Trull, D.
Glenarm..Washington to New Seaver, D.
Glen Road...Forest Hills st., W. R. & D.
Glendale.......Bird to Hancock, R. & D.
Glendon...............East Eagle, E. B.
Glendon Place..........491 Chelsea, E. B.
Glenn Avenue............Blue Hill av., D.
Glenside Avenue......Glen Road, W. R.
Glenvale Terrace.......Lamartine, W. R.
Glenway Avenue........Savin Hill av., D.
Glenwood..................75 Warren, R.
Glenwood Place........24 Glenwood, R.
Glide................Chickatawbut, D.
Globe Alley............428 Commercial
Gloucester...................397 Beacon
Gloucester Place...........377 Harrison av.
Glover................28 Woodward, S. B.
Gold........................11 A, S. B.
Goodwin Court..........36 Ward st., S. B.
Goodwin Place................73 Revere
Gordon, Elm to Jamaica Plain Sta.,W. R.
Gordon..................Cambridge st., B.
Gore Avenue.............728 Parker, R.
Goreham....Washburn to Holmes av., B.
Gorham Place............1279 Washington
Gouch-street Place............24 Norman
Gould's Court.........130 Orleans, E. B.,
Grafton.................Dorchester av., D.
Graham......................Clapp, R.
Grampian Way........Savin Hill av., D.
Granger............Duncan to Clayton, D.
Granger Place................Duncan, D.
Granite................66 W. Second, S. B.
Granite............Centre to Spring, W. R.
Granite Av., Adams to Norfolk bridge, D.
Grant....................Crescent av., D.
Grant Place..................12 Camden
Grant Place................Washington, D.
Grant's Court...........19 North Mead, C.
Granville Place...........89 Brook av., R.
Grape Place..................23 Spring
Gray..........47 Chelsea to 58 Water, C.
Gray......................30 Berkeley
Green.............Main, 6 Dexter Row, C.
Green.................Bowdoin Square
Green....Centre, near Starr Lane, W. R.
Green Hill......................Mill, D.
Green Hill Avenue..........Centre, W. R.
Green-street Court...............Olney, D.
Green-street Place.............30 Green
Greenleaf..............414 Parker, R.
Greenough Av., Centre, near South, W.R.
Greenough Lane............24 Charter
Green's Alley.........33 West First, S. B.

Greenville................213 Dudley, R.
Greenville Place..........25 Greenville, R.
Greenwich................11 Westminster, R.
Greenwich................Dorchester av., D.
Greenwich Park...........515 Columbus av.
Greenwich Place..........Dorchester av., D.
Greenwood................Brunswick av., R.
Greenwood................Glen Road, D.
Greenwood Avenue...Washington, W. R.
Grenville Place...........72 Church
Gridley..................117 High
Griggs..................Washburn, B.
Griggs Place..............Allston, B.
Grimes..........179 West Seventh, S. B.
Grinnell.................Milford Place, R.
Grosvenor Place.....2448 Washington, R.
Groton.................1191 Washington
Grotto Glen.............37 Day, R.
Grove..................172 Cambridge
Grove Place ....17 Grove
Grove Place.........Lawrence av., W. R.
Grove Square..............106 Myrtle
Grove Terrace.............13 Grove
Guild..................2581 Washington, R.
Guild Row................14 Roxbury, R.
Gurney.................1419 Tremont, R.
H Street............451 East First, S. B.
Hagar.............Thomas to Eliot, W. R.
Hall Place................263 Hanover
Hallock.................31 Station. R.
Hall's Court.......2245 Washington, R.
Hall's Court......Adams near Linden, D.
Hamblen................Arlington av. C.
Hamburg..................7 Mystic
Hamilton..............47 Batterymarch
Hamilton Avenue, Bowdoin to Columbia, D.
Hamilton Court..........418 Main, C.
Hamilton Place............123 Tremont
Hamlen Place..............206 Pleasant
Hamlet........Boston to 21 Berkeley pl. R.
Hamlin.................469 East Eighth
Hammond................659 Shawmut av.
Hammond Avenue.........123 Chambers
Hampden....802 Albany to 380 Dudley, R.
Hampden Place..........141 Hampden, R.
Hampshire.................150 Ruggles
Hampshire Court..........Hampshire, R.
Hampshire Place.......62 Hampshire, R.
Hampton Court..........156 Northampton
Ham's Court...............514 Main, C.
Hancock........77 Green to 61 Elm, C.
Hancock................48 Cambridge
Hancock..783 Dudley to Bowdoin, R. & D.
Hancock..................Ashland, W. R.
Hancock Avenue.28 Bea. to 8 Mt. Vernon
Hancock Place.............18 Blossom
Hancock Row.....9 Marshall to Creek sq.
Hancock Square..Main, Mill & Essex, C.
Hanover........95 Court to Chelsea Ferry
Hanover Avenue............423 Hanover
Hanover Place..........212 Hanover
Hanson................269 Shawmut av.
Harbor View.............Coleridge st. E. B.
Harbor View Street...Dorchester av. D.
Harcourt................Huntington av.
Harding Court......166 West Fifth, S. B.
Harley..................Welles av. D.
Harlow...............Woodward Park, R.
Harmony................Bennington, E. B.
Harmony Place.....37 Lexington, E. B.
Harrington Avenue......55 Centre, R.
Harris..................413 Hanover

Harris Avenue.............W. R.
Harrison..................Green Hill, D.
Harrison Avenue............25 Bedford
Harrison Place.............236 Friend
Hart's Yard..............28 Lawrence, C.
Hartford..................Wendell
Hartford..............Howard av. R.
Hartopp Place..........922 Albany, R.
Hartwell................13 Schuyler, R.
Harvard..................City sq. C.
Harvard................740 Washington
Harvard..Washington to Blue-hill av. D.
Harvard Avenue.......Cambridge st. B.
Harvard Court..............13 Harvard
Harvard Place..........20 Harvard, C.
Harvard Place..........311 Washington
Harvard Place.........Washington, B.
Harvard Square..........27 Harvard, C.
Harwich..................29 Yarmouth
Hathaway................South, W. R.
Hathon Square............263 Main, C.
Hautevale................Poplar, W. R.
Haven.................446 Shawmut av.
Haven Avenue............Blue Hill av. D.
Haverhill...............636 Main, C.
Haverhill..............Haymarket sq.
Havre..................148 Summer, E. B.
Hawes...................52 Congress
Hawkins.................73 Sudbury
Hawley ....25 Milk to 22 Summer
Hawley Place.....38 Hawley to 45 Arch
Hawthorn..............186 Highland, R.
Hawthorn Avenue...2491 Washington, R.
Hawthorne..Florence to Sycamore, W. R.
Hawthorne Place........1183 Washington
Haymarket Place............20 Avery
Haymarket Square...........Union
Haynes.................9 Orleans, E. B.
Hayward................466 Warren, R.
Hayward Place........582 Washington
Hazel........Enfield to Rockview, W. R.
Hazel Place................Maywood, R.
Head Place,..............35 Boylston
Heath..................201 Centre, R.
Heath Place.............120 Heath, R.
Hemlock..Washington to Bellevue, W. R.
Henchman................37 Charter
Henley.............27 Harvard sq., C.
Henry..............16 Maverick sq., E. B.
Herbert..............Clarence pl., D.
Hereford................433 Beacon
Hersey.................Haven av., D.
Hersey Place..............21 Essex
Hickory Avenue.............Ferrin, C.
High.........West, Monument sq., C.
High....................128 Summer
High...Washington nr. LaGrange, W. R.
High...........Commercial to Highland, D.
High..................Water to Ericsson, D.
High...................Bigelow, B.
High-street Place............68 High
Highland..............Eliot sq., E.
Highland..........East to Winter, D.
Highland Avenue..........28 Centre, R.
High'd Av., Waln't to Blue H'l av, W. R.
Highland Avenue..........Minot, D.
Highland Avenue.........Cambridge, B.
Highland Park..........16 Fort av., R.
Highland Park Avenue....31 Fort av., R.
Highland Place........12 Highland, R.
Hildreth Place..............72 Charter
Hill....................27 Webster

Hill	Central av., W. R.
Hill Avenue	Franklin, Allston, B.
Hillburn	Poplar, W. R.
Hill's Court	85 Revere
Hillside	Parker, R.
Hillside Avenue	Poplar, W. R.
Hillside Place	54 Haynes, E. B.
Hilton	Swett, R.
Hingham	201 Shawmut av.
Hoffman	Lamaratine to Gilbert, W. R.
Hogg Bridge	Centre, R. & W. R.
Holbrook	Centre, W. R.
Holden Court	398 Commercial
Holden Place	728 Dudley, R.
Holden Row	Wesley, C.
Holland Place	58 Tyler
Holley Square	10 Hollis
Hollis	779 Washington
Hollis Place	23 Hollis
Hollis Place	111 Roxbury, R.
Hollis Place, Allston, nr. Brighton Av., B.	
Holmes Avenue	Harvard Avenue, B.
Holmes Place	Mill, D.
Holyoke	415 Columbus av.
Homer	Moore to West, E. B.
Homer Place	52 Moreland, R.
Homes Avenue	Adams, D.
Homes Place	642 Main, C.
Homestead	Walnut av., R.
Homestead Place	174 Main, C.
Hooten Court	167 Everett, E. B.
Hope Place	10 North Russell
Houghton	Clay, D.
Houghton Place	326 Centre, W. R.
Houston Place	1368 Tremont, R.
Hovey Avenue	Blue Hill Avenue, D.
Hovey's Court	rear 444 Main, C.
Howard	84 Court
Howard	138 Hamden, R.
Howard	Howard Avenue, R.
Howard Avenue	599 Dudley, R.
Howard Place	13 Elm, C.
Howard Place	Union, B.
Howe Avenue	153 H, S. B.
Howe Place	20 Quincy, C.
Howe's Court	1134 Tremont, R.
Howland	583 Warren, R.
Hoyt Place	80 Joy
Huckins	32 Blue Hill Av., R.
Hudson	37 Chelsea, C.
Hudson	67 Beach
Hudson	516 Dudley, R.
Hudson Place	33 Hudson
Hulbert	2672 Washington, R.
Hull	27 Bunker Hill, C.
Hull	176 Salem
Hull-street Court	4 Hull
Hull's Row	Mill, C.
Humboldt Avenue	Seaver, R.
Humboldt Place	545 Dorchester av. S. B.
Humphrey Court	162 West Fourth, S. B.
Humphrey Square	740 Dudley, R.
Humphreys	668 Dudley, R.
Humphreys Place	Humphreys, R.
Hunneman	2032 Washington, R.
Hunneman Place	2062 Washington, R.
Hunnewell Place	123 Marion, E. B.
Huntington Avenue	Boyl. to Tremont
Huntington Avenue	Canterbury, W. R.
Huntoon	Riverview av., D.
Hutchings	Williams av., R.
Hyde	620 Dorchester av. S. B.
Hyde Park	Harvard, W. R.
Hyde Park Avenue	Walk Hill, W. R.
I Street	489 East First, S. B.
Ice Court	92 Water, C.
Independence Square	E. Broadway, S. B.
India	135 State
India Square	120 Broad
Indiana	940 Washington
Indiana Place	935 Washington
Irving	104 Cambridge
Irving	Anawan av. W. R.
Irving Place	421 Main, C.
Irving Place	19 Irving
Isabella	18 Ferdinand
Island	38 Hampden, R.
Ivanhoe	46 Upton
Ivory	Dent to Temple, W. R.
Jackson	66 Bunker Hill, C.
Jackson	Boston to Dorchester av. S. B.
Jackson Avenue	73 Charter
Jackson Avenue	Chestnut Hill av., B.
Jackson Place	10 Winter
Jackson Place	School, D.
Jamaica	South, W. R.
James	East Brookline
James Avenue	123 G, S. B.
James Place	37 Anderson
Jarvis Place	106 George, R.
Jasper Place	195 North
Jay	534 East Fifth, S. B.
Jefferson	325 Tremont
Jefferson Avenue	164 Bunker Hill, C.
Jefferson Place	35 Bennet
Jeffries	304 Marginal, E. B.
Jenkins	326 Dorchester, S. B.
Jenkins Place	520 Commercial
Jenner	8 Bow, C.
Jennings Place	234 Medford, C.
Jerome	Hancock, D.
Jerome Place	83 Bunker Hill, C.
Jess	Boylston, W. R.
Jewell Place	Ottawa, R.
John	4 Fulton
John A. Andrew	Newbern, W. R.
Johnson Avenue	196 Main, C.
Johnson Place	12 River, D.
Joiner	25 Park, C.
Jones Avenue	Blue Hill av., D.
Jordan	Dent to La Grange, W. R.
Joy	34 Beacon
Juniper	Cedar, R.
K Street	559 East First, S. B.
K Street Place	60 K, S. B.
Kearsarge Avenue	92 Warren, R.
Keith's Alley	170 North
Kelley Court	42 Cook, C.
Kelley's Lane	Western av., B.
Kemble	98 Hampden, R.
Kemble Place	9 P, S. B.
Kemp	688 Dorchester av., S. B.
Kendall	637 Shawmut av., R.
Kendrick	Lake, B.
Kenilworth	71 Dudley, R.
Kenna Place	38 Grove
Kennard Avenue	61 Allen
Kennard Court	4 Kennard av.
Kensington	Elmore, R.
Kensington Park	287 Warren, R.
Keyes	Washington, W. R.
Keyes Place	W. R.
Kilby	67 State
Kilton	Harvard, D.

Kimball	Tremont, R.
King	229 Roxbury, R.
King	Dorchester av., D.
King-street Court	22 King, R.
Kingsbury	Bainbridge, R.
Kingston	Cambridge, C.
Kingston	81 Summer
Kingston Court	110 Kingston
Kingston Place	15 Kingston, C.
Kingston Place	134 Kingston
Kirkland	66 Pleasant
Kittredge	Washington, W. R.
Knapp	15 Beach
Kneeland	706 Washington
Kneeland Place	25 Kneeland
Knights Avenue	Green, W. R.
Knower Place	2342 Washington, R.
Knowlton	25 Telegraph, S. B.
Knox	18 Church
L Street	609 East First, S. B.
La Fayette Avenue	138 Prince
La Fayette Place	4 Rand, R.
La Grange	679 Washington
La Grange	Washington, W. R.
La Grange Place	29 Blue Hill av., R.
Lake	Washington, B.
Lakeville Place	Centre, W. R.
Lamartine	Centre, W. R.
Lamartine Court	Lamartine, W. R.
Lamartine Place	Lamartine, W. R.
Lamartine Square	Green, W. R.
Lambert	36 Highland, R.
Lambert Avenue	Kenilworth, R.
Lamson	132 Webster, E. B.
Lamson Court	3 Lamson, E. B.
Lancaster	101 Merrimac
Land's Court	223 North
Langdon	416 Dudley, R.
Langdon Court	Langdon pl.
Langdon Place	215 North
Lansing	373 Warren, R.
Lark	179 W. Eighth, S. B.
Lathrop Place	315 Hanover
Laurel	Monument sq., C.
Laurel	48 Dale, R.
Laurel	Norfolk, D.
Lauriat Avenue	Blue Hill av., D.
Lawn	231 Heath, R.
Lawn	Mt. Hope st., W. R.
Lawrence	30 Union, C.
Lawrence	62 Berkeley
Lawrence Avenue	324 Blue Hill av. D.
Lawrence Court	28 Lawrence, C.
Lawrence Court	107 W. Third, S. B.
Lawrence Place	155 Cambridge
Lawrence-street Place	27 Lawrence, C.
Learnard	Norfolk, D.
Leather Square	5 Channing
Lebanon	24 Magnolia, R.
Lee	Carolina av. W. R.
Lee Place	79 Phillips
Leeds	12 Woodward, S. B.
Leeds	Adams, D.
Leeds Place	Savin Hill av. D.
Lehigh	214 Albany
Leighton Park	1024 Dartmouth
Leland Place	1283 Washington
Lenox	1873 Washington, R.
Lenox Court	rear 914 Harrison av.
Leonard	Duncan, D.
Leslie Park	101 Walnut av. R.
Lester Place	Centre, W. R.
Leverett	93 Green
Leverett Avenue	98 Leverett
Lewis	203 Sumner, E. B.
Lewis	208 Commercial
Lewis Park	55 Highland, R.
Lewis Place	451 Dudley, R.
Lexington	271 Border, E. B.
Lexington	15 Monument sq. C.
Lexington Avenue	126 Bunker Hill, C.
Lexington Avenue	Washington, B.
Lexington Place	53 Lexington, E. B.
Liberty	77 Preble, S. B.
Liberty Square	Kilby
Lily	187 Tudor, S. B.
Lime	48 River
Lime Alley	88 Charter
Lime-street Place	Lime
Lincoln	324 Main, C.
Lincoln	115 Summer
Lincoln	Adams, D.
Lincoln	Cambridge, B.
Lincoln Place	23 Elm, C.
Lincoln Place	38 Winchester
Lincoln Place	12 Worcester
Lindall Court	83 Phillips
Lindall Place	188 Cambridge
Linden	501 E. Fourth, S. B.
Linden	Beech, W. R.
Linden	Brandon, W. R.
Linden	Adams, D.
Linden	Cambridge, B.
Linden Avenue	23 Linden Park
Linden Park	119 Roxbury, R.
Linden Place	29 Allen
Linnet	Bellevue, W. R.
Linwood	82 Centre, R.
Linwood Place	255 Main, C.
Linwood Place	26 South
Linwood Square	27 Linwood, R.
Litchfield Court	346 Sumner, E. B.
Liverpool	86 Sumner, E. B.
Livingston	85 Brighton
Locust	Dorchester av., S. B.
Lombard Place	82 Prince
Lombard Place	54 Ellery, S. B.
London	112 Sumner, E. B.
London Court	135 London, E. B.
Longwood	Longwood av., B.
Longwood Avenue	619 Parker, R.
Longwood Park	Park, R.
Lotus Place	Washington, W. R.
Louisburg Square	80 Pinckney
Louisiana Place	51 Princeton, E. B.
Lovedeed Court	9 Chadwick, R.
Lovering Place	1000 Washington
Lovett Place	30 Poplar
Lovis	187 Gold, S. B.
Lowder's Lane	Centre, W. R.
Lowell	40 Causeway
Lowell Court	2 Tamworth
Lowell Square	Cambridge st.
Lowland	293 E. Eighth, S. B.
Lowland Place	99 Everett, E. B.
Lubec	Swift, E. B.
Lucas	1035 Washington
Luteman Place	Texas av., R.
Luther Place	416 Commercial
Lyman	73 Corvis
Lyman Place	14 Lyman
Lynde	8 Arrow, C.
Lynde	37 Cambridge
Lynde Avenue	168 Main, C.

Lynde-st. Place .... 32 Lynde
Lyndeboro' .... 23 Essex
Lyndeboro' Place .... 100 Carver
Lyon Place .... 570 Shawmut av., R.
Lyons .... Lauriat av., D.
M Street .... E. First, S. B.
Madison .... 2035 Washington, R.
Madison .... Norfolk, D.
Madison Avenue .... 12 Tremont
Madison Avenue .... Madison, D.
Madison Avenue .... Washington, B.
Madison Court .... 456 Parker, R.
Madison Park .... Marble and Warwick, R.
Madison Place .... 1100 Washington
Magazine .... 420 Dudley, R.
Magnolia .... 661 Dudley, R. & D.
Magog Place ......,........ 875 Albany, R.
Mahan Avenue .... 53 Hampshire, R.
Mahan Place .... 223 Pleasant
Maiden Lane .... 66 Hampden, R.
Main .... 14 City sq. C.
Maitland .... Beacon, R.
Malhon Place .... 169 Roxbury, R.
Malden .... 1428 Washington
Malden Court .... 48 Malden
Mall .... 36 Eustis, R.
Malvern .... Adams, D.
Malvern .... Brighton av. B.
Mansfield .... Cambridge, B.
Maple .... 280 Seaver, R.
Maple .... Centre, W. R.
Maple Avenue .... Brookline av. R.
Maple Grove Avenue ...... Bowdoin av. D.
Maple Park .... 30 Dale, R.
Maple Place .... 219 Harrison av.
Maple Place .... Seaverns av. W. R.
Marble .... 99 Westminster, R.
Marble Court .... 40 Lynde
Marcella .... 2841 Washington, R.
March Avenue .... Bellevue av. W. R.
Margaret .... 83 Prince
Marginal .... 60 Lewis, E. B.
Marion .... 1 White, E. B.
Marion .... 65 Bunker Hill, C.
Marion Court .... Marion, E. B.
Marion Place .... 197 Marion, E. B.
Market .... 103 Portland
Market .... Washington, B.
Market Place .... 1240 Tremont, R.
Marlborough .... 7 Arlington
Marsh .... Adams, D.
Marsh Lane .... 35 Union
Marshall .... 149 Hanover
Marshall Place .... 32 Walnut
Marshall Place .... 76 Charter
Marshall's Court .... 29 Bow, C
Marston Place .... 91 Chambers
Martin .... LaGrange, W. R.
Mason .... 12 Bow, C.
Mason .... 28 West
Mason Court .... 63 Sullivan, C.
Mason Place .... Rear Mason
Matchett .... Washington, B.
Mather .... Dorchester av., D.
Mattapan .... Blue Hill av., D.
Matthews .... 118 Federal
Maudlin .... 17 Wapping, C.
Maverick .... 41 New, E. B.
Maverick Square ...... 202 Sumner, E. B.
Maxwell .... Milton av., D.
May .... Centre, W. R.
May .... Glen Road, D.

May Place .... 26 Oak
May Place .... 283 Ruggles, R.
Mayfair .... Elmore, R.
Mayfield .... Pleasant, D.
Mayo .... 60 Castle
Maywood .... 366 Warren, R.
McClellan Avenue .... Blue Hill av., D.
McGee .... Norfolk av., R.
McLean .... 66 Chambers
McLean .... Blue Hill av., D.
McLean Court .... 24 McLean
McManus Court .... 30 Quincy, C.
Mead .... 367 Main, C.
Mead-street Court .... 26 Mead, C.
Meander .... 46 East Dedham
Mechanic .... 15 Putnam, C.
Mechanic .... 221 Hanover
Mechanic .... 319 Ruggles, R.
Mechanic .... Brighton av.. B.
Mechanic Court .... 10 Mechanic
Mechanic's Place .. 651 East Seventh, S. B.
Medford .... 185 Chelsea, C.
Medford .... 92 Charlestown
Medford Court .... 1 Medford
Medford Court .... 1231 Washington
Melbourne .... Centre, D.
Melrose .... 126 Pleasant
Melrose Place .... 37 Poplar
Melville Avenue .... Washington, D.
Melville Place .... 29 Spring
Mennig Court .... 26 Hampshire, R.
Mercantile .... Clinton
Mercer .... 172 Dorchester, S. B.
Merchants Row .... 88 State
Meridian .... Maverick sq., E. B.
Meridian Place .... 169 Meridian, E. B.
Merrill .... Eric av., C.
Merrimac .... Haymarket sq.
Merrimac Place .... 156 Merrimac
Merton Place .... 145 Centre, R.
Messinger .... Rockville, D.
Metropolitan Avenue, Washington, W. R.
Michigan Avenue .... Blue Hill av., D.
Middle .... 341 Dorchester, S. B.
Middlesex .... 398 Main, C.
Middlesex .... 96 Castle
Midland .... Savin Hill av. D.
Milford .... 251 Shawmut av.
Milford Place .... 1087 Tremont, R.
Milk .... 320 Washington
Mill .... 161 Sumner, E. B.
Mill .... 346 Main, C.
Mill .... Adams, D.
Mill-street Court .... 34 Mill, C.
Miller .... 214 Main, C.
Millet .... Park, D.
Millmont .... 48 Highland, R.
Mills .... 12 Rockland, R.
Milner Place .... 762 Washington
Milton .... Moore, E. B.
Milton .... 35 Spring
Milton .... Adams, D.
Milton Avenue .... Norfolk, D.
Milton Place .... 147 Federal
Minden .... Bickford, R.
Mindoro .... 34 Prentiss, R.
Miner .... Beacon, R.
Minot .... 119 Leverett
Minot .... Neponset av. D.
Minot Place .... Minot, D.
Minton .... Savin Hill av. D.
Model Place .... 161 Havre, E. B.

MOD—NOR 179

Model Place	171 Pleasant
Monadnock	Dudley to Bird, R.
Monmouth	377 Meridian, E. B.
Monmouth Square	Monument, E. B.
Montana	Mt. Seaver av. R.
Montgomery	557 Tremont
Montgomery	Spring, W. R.
Montgomery Park	74 Montgomery
Montgomery Pl..(ch. to Bosworth st. 1883)	
Montrose Avenue	216 Warren, R.
Monument	21 Monument sq. C.
Monument Avenue	71 Main, C.
Monument Court	Monument sq. C.
Monument Court	H, S. B.
Monument Lane	144 Bunker Hill, C.
Monument Sq..around the Monument, C.	
Monument Square	Centre, W. B.
Moon	1 North sq.
Moon-street Court	11 Moon
Moore	Pope to Cowper, E. B.
Moreland	140 Warren, R.
Morland Place	Pond, W. R.
Morni Court	201 W. Ninth, S. B.
Morris	224 Marion, E. B.
Morrison	Gardner, W. R.
Morton	56 Salem
Morton	South, W. R.
Morton Place	1438 Tremont, R.
Moseley Avenue	Crescent av., D.
Moss Place	5 Cambridge
Motte	299 Harrison av.
Moulton	33 Bunker Hill, C.
Moulton Court	42 Moulton, C.
Mt. Everett	Hamilton av., D.
Mt. Hope	Canterbury, W. R.
Mt. Ida	Bowdoin
Mt. Pleasant Avenue	253 Dudley, R.
Mt. Pleasant Place	291 Dudley, R.
Mt. Seaver Avenue	485 Blue Hill av., R.
Mt. Vernon	25 Adams, C.
Mt. Vernon	Beacon
Mt. Vernon	Boston, S. B. & D.
Mt. Vernon	Centre, W. R.
Mt. Vernon	Rockland, B.
Mt. Vernon Avenue	8 Mt. Vernon, C.
Mt. Vernon Avenue	101 Mt. Vernon
Mt. Vernon Place	95 Chelsea, B.
Mt. Vernon Place	1 Hancock av.
Mt. Wachusett Avenue, Hyde Park av.,B.	
Mt. Warren	23 Walnut av., R.
Mt. Washington Avenue	356 Federal
Mt. Washington Place, 413 E. Eighth,S. B.	
Mulberry Place	59 Portland
Mulberry Place	321 Dudley, R.
Munroe	407 Warren, R.
Munroe Place	38 Tyler
Munroe Place	26 Vernon, R.
Munson	Beacon, B.
Murdock	Cambridge, B.
Murray Avenue	95 Blue Hill av., R.
Murray Court	37 Orleans, E. B.
Murray Place	55 Prince
Music Hall Place	15 Winter
Myrtle	57 Hancock
Myrtle	Centre, W. R.
Myrtle Place	Magnolia, R.
Myrtle Place	7 Glenwood, R.
Mystic	223 Bunker Hill, C.
Mystic	9 Malden
Mystic Avenue	653 Main, C.
Mystic Place	54 Walnut, C.
Mystic Place	34 Cook, C.

N Street	East First, S. B.
Napier Place	56 Barton
Narragansett	Chickatawbut, D.
Naseby	Crawford, R.
Nash Court	397 West First, S. B.
Nashua	72 Causeway
Nason Place	33 Conant, R.
Nassau	191 Harrison av.
Nassua Place	12 Nassua
National	465 East Fourth, S. B.
Nawn	2076 Washington, R.
Nawn Place	1001 Harrison av., R.
Nawn Court	39 King, R.
Neal's Court	5 Short, C.
Nelson	Norfolk, D.
Neponset	Commercial, D.
Neponset Avenue..Hyde Park av., W. R.	
Neponset Avenue	Adams, D.
New	22 Sumner, E. B.
Newbern	1076 Tremont, R.
Newbern	Carolina av. W. R.
Newbern Court	7 Newbern, R.
Newbern Place	57 Carver
Newbury	15 Arlington
Newbury	Canterbury, W. R.
Newcomb	1904 Washington, B.
Newhall	Pierce av. D.
New Heath	153 Centre, R.
Newland	12 Upton
Newman	Dorchester, S. B.
Newman Court	Champney, S. B.
Newman Place	349 Dudley, R.
Newport	Crescent av. D.
New Seaver	Columbia, D.
Newton...(see E. Newton & W. Newton)	
Newton	Brooks, B.
Newton Court	127 Tyler
Newton Place..(changed to Knapp st.1879)	
Nichols Court	Phillips, R.
Ninth...(see East Ninth and West Ninth)	
Nixon Avenue	Centre, D.
Noble Court	372 Sumner, E. B.
Nonantum	Washington, B.
Norfolk	26 Highland, R.
Norfolk	Washington, D.
Norfolk Avenue	116 Hampden, R.
Norfolk Place	552 Washington
Norman	53 Green
North	1 Union
Northampton	801 Albany
Northampton Place	224 Northampton
North Anderson	165 Cambridge
North Avenue	521 Dudley, R.
North Beacon	con. of Brighton av. B.
North Bennet	38 Hanover
North Bennet Avenue	26 North Bennet
North Bennet Place	8 North Bennet
North Brimmer Place	173 North
North Centre	163 Hanover
North Chapel Place	167 Friend
North Ferry Avenue	59 Sumner, E. B.
Northfield	818 Tremont, R.
North Grove	187 Cambridge
North Hanover Court	228 Hanover
North Harvard	Cambridge st. B.
North Hudson	54 Snowhill
North Margin	90 Salem
North Margin Place	47 North Margin
North Margin-street Court...93 N. Margin
North Market	24 Commercial
North Mead	327 Bunker Hill, C.
North Mead-street Court... 6 N. Mead, C.

North Russell...............95 Cambridge
North Square....................Moon
North Townsend Place...516 Commercial
Norwich........................3 Mystic
Notre Dame............Codman av., W. R.
Noyes Place...................128 Salem
O Street...................E. First, S. B.
O-street Place...............151 O, S. B.
Oak..........................383 Main, C.
Oak.......................870 Washington
Oak...........................Beech, W. R.
Oak Avenue......................Adams, D.
Oak Place.........................13 Oak
Oak Place......................Green, W. R.
Oak Square.....................Faneuil, B.
Oakes......................Norfolk av., R.
Oakland...............2701 Washington, R.
Oakland..........................River, D.
Oakland.....................Washington, B.
Oakland Place...........Blue Hill av., D.
Oakland Place................Oakland, B.
Oakman.........................Walnut, D.
Oakville Avenue.........59 St. James, R.
Ocean......................Welles av., D.
Ohio........................927 Washington
Old Harbor..............140 Dorchester, S. B.
Old Harbor Place....90 Old Harbor, S. B.
Old Heath..................(See Heath)
Olive Place................1352 Washington
Oliver.........................131 Milk
Oliver Court..............19 Webster av.
Oliver Place....................83 Essex
Olney......................Geneva av., D.
Olney-street Place.............Olney, D.
Oneida..................320 Harrison av.
Ontario.....................40 Swan, S. B.
Ontario-street Place..........8 Ontario
Orange......................957 Washington
Orange Court.............20 Fellows, R.
Orange Lane...............966 Washington
Orchard.....................41 Yeoman, R.
Orchard......................Centre, W. R.
Orchard Park..............34 Orchard, R.
Orchard Place..................Boston, D.
Ordway Place............347 Washington
Oregon......................90 Conant, R.
Orient Heights......Breed's Island, E. B
Oriental Court..............12 Phillips, R.
Oriole....................352 Walnut av., R.
Oriole.........................Park, W. R.
Orleans...................48 Marginal, E. B.
Osborn Place.................46 Pleasant
Oscar.....................754 Parker, R.
Osgood Court..........2653 Washington, R.
Osgood Place.............rear 38 Poplar
Oswego...................330 Harrison av.
Otis.......................217 Devonshire
Otis Place.....................321 Main, C.
Otis Place....................45 Brimmer
Ottawa....................51 Sherman, R.
Ottawa Place..(changed to Temple Park)
Otter........................99 Beacon
Oxford.........................69 Essex
Oxford Place.............26 Harrison av.
P Street...................East First, S. B.
Pacific...................East Fourth, S. B.
Page's Court......................358 North
Page's Court.........322 W. Broadway, S. B.
Paine Place...............782 Washington
Palmer...................2234 Washington, R.
Palmer Place...........65 Palmer, R.
Paris......................176 Sumner, E. B.

Paris Court.................79 Paris, E. B.
Park..........................18 City sq. R.
Park........................126 Tremont, R.
Park........................Brookline av.
Park........................Centre, W. R.
Park........................Washington, D.
Park Place.................53 Yeoman, R.
Park Place.................10 Myrtle, W. R.
Park Square.................Boylston
Parker..........................Perkins, C.
Parker...............West Chester Park
Parker Hill Avenue....1752 Tremont, R.
Parker Place................72 Terrace, R.
Parker's Alley.......222 W. Fourth, S. B.
Parker's Court......223 W. Fourth, S. B.
Parkman....................40 N. Russell
Parkman..................Dorchester, D.
Parkman......................Brooks, B.
Parkman Place.............220 Hanover
Parkman Place..............Parkman, D.
Parley Vale................Centre, W. R.
Parmenter..................266 Hanover
Parnell....................68 Lenox, R.
Parsons....................Washington, B.
Paul..........................392 Tremont
Paul Gore..................Centre, W. R.
Payson Avenue..Hancock to Glendale, D.
Payson Court..312 West Broadway, S. B.
Payson Place..................9 Elm, C.
Peabody..............Brookline avenue, R.
Peabody Place............Lamartine, W. R.
Peaceable....................Rockland, B.
Pearl.........................103 High, C.
Pearl...........................97 Milk
Pearl........................Pleasant, B.
Pearl.........................Franklin, B.
Pearl Place............132 Marginal, E. B.
Pearl-street Place............90 Pearl, C.
Pelham..................1431 Washington
Pelton......................Park, W. R.
Pemberton Square.............1 Tremont
Pembroke..................421 Shawmut av.
Pembroke Court..........23 Pembroke
Pepperell Place..143 Dorchester av. S. B.
Percival Avenue..............Church, D.
Percival Place.........106 Orleans, E. B.
Percy Place.................155 Roxbury, R.
Perham........Dedham Br. R. R., W. R.
Perkins..................55 Cambridge, C.
Perkins..........................170 Congress
Perkins................Centre, R. & W. R.
Perkins Place..............58 Roxbury, R.
Perrin....................87 Moreland, R.
Perry......................168 Chelsea, R.
Perry...................1226 Washington
Perry Place..............33 Pleasant, C.
Pevear Place..............197 Dudley, R.
Phillips......................25 Irving
Phillips...................1499 Tremont, R.
Phillips Court..............70 Phillips
Phillips Place..........60 W. Fourth, S. B.
Phillips Place............748 Dudley, R.
Phipps.......................248 Main, C.
Phipps....................Blue Hill av. D.
Phipps Place.................50 Charter
Phoenix Place.............75 Hampden, R.
Pickering Avenue.......90 Walnut av. R.
Piedmont...................158 Pleasant
Pierce Avenue..................Adams, D.
Pierce Place................Hancock, D.
Pierpont...................22 Prentiss, R.
Pike......................831 Albany, R.

Pinckney	10 Joy
Pine	19 Bunker Hill, C.
Pine	892 Washington
Pine	Brown av. W. R.
Pine Island	Swett st. R.
Pine Place	1 Pine
Pitts	82 Merrimac
Pitts Court	30 Pitts
Pitts Place	34 Pitts
Plain	Chickatawbut, D.
Pleasant	99 Main, C.
Pleasant	907 Washington
Pleasant	Mt. Vernon, W. R.
Pleasant	Commercial, D.
Pleasant	South, D.
Pleasant	Franklin, B
Pleasant-street Court	35 Pleasant, C
Pleasant-street Court	65 Pleasant
Pleasant-street Place	209 Pleasant
Plummer Place	33 Middle, S. B.
Plymouth	385 Longwood av. R.
Plymouth	Commercial, D.
Plymouth Court	979 Harrison av., R.
Plymouth Place	(ch. to Knapp st. 1879)
Plympton	640 Harrison av.
Polk	189 Bunker Hill, C.
Pond	Centre, W. R.
Pond	Dorchester av., D.
Pond Avenue	Perkins, R. & W. R.
Pond-street Place	111 Endicott
Pope	580 Saratoga, E. B.
Pope's Hill Street	Neponset av., D.
Poplar	98 Chambers
Poplar	Washington, W. R.
Poplar Avenue	101 Poplar
Poplar Court	72 Poplar
Poplar Place	43 Poplar
Porcelain Place	100 Poplar
Porter	19 Central sq., E. B.
Porter	72 Pleasant
Porter	Boylston av., W. R.
Porter Place	134 Porter, E. B.
Portland	84 Hanover
Portland Place	51 Portland
Posen	Minden, R.
Post-Office Avenue	20 Congress
Post-Office Square	Congress
Power	Boston st., S. B.
Powers Court	378 North
Pratt	Ballou av., D.
Pratt	Linden, B.
Pratt's Court	12 Weston, R.
Preble	588 Dorchester av., S. B.
Prentiss	1283 Tremont, R.
Prentiss Place	77 Linden Park, R.
Presby Place	58 Winthrop, R.
Prescott	372 Bremen, E. B.
Prescott	Bow and Harvard, C.
Prescott	198 Eustis, R.
Prescott Place	8 Prescott, R.
Prescott Place	Winter, R.
Prescott Square	Eagle, E. B.
Preston	Mill, D.
Price Avenue	Blue Hill av., D.
Primus Avenue	82 Phillips
Prince	5 North sq.
Prince	Pond, W. R.
Princeton	271 Meridian, E. B.
Princeton	53 Lexington, C.
Princeton Place	233 Princeton, E. B.
Prospect	108 Chelsea, C.
Prospect	192 Merrimac
Prospect	Birch, W. R.
Prospect	Norfolk, D.
Prospect Avenue	Albion, W. R.
Prospect Hill	Br'n and Prosp't av.,W. R.
Prospect Place	396 Meridian, E. B.
Providence	Park sq.
Province	38 School
Province Court	331 Washington
Public Garden	Boylston
Pulaski Avenue	356 Athens, S. B.
Purchase	165 Broad
Putnam	189 Condor, E. B.
Putnam	58 Henley, C.
Putnam	16 Dudley, R.
Putnam	Griggs, B.
Putnam Place	118 Roxbury, R.
Putnam Square	Eagle, E. B.
Pynchon	1400 Tremont, R.
Q Street	E. Second, S. B.
Quiet Place	77 Purchase
Quincy	371 Bunker Hill, C.
Quincy	432 Warren, R. & D.
Quincy Court	185 North
Quincy Place	Quincy, C.
Quincy Place	17 Quincy, R.
Quincy Row	79 Clinton
Rand	170 Blue Hill av., R.
Rand Place	28 Rand, R.
Rand Square	24 Rand, R.
Randall	972 Harrison av., R.
Randlett Place	54 Rand, R.
Randolph	514 Harrison av.
Ransom Court	18 Cotting
Ravenswood Park	Glen Road, W. R.
Ray	Hulbert, R.
Read	Glen Road, D.
Reading	Kemble, R.
Redesdale	Brighton av., B.
Reed	76 Northampton
Reed's Court	11 Yeoman, R.
Regent	139 Warren, R.
Regent Court	57 Regent, R.
Regent Place	19 Regent, R.
Regent Square	90 Regent, R.
Reims Place	1 Ward st., R.
Renfrew	19 Eustis, R.
Renfrew Court	15 Renfrew, R.
Renfrew Place	17 Renfrew, R.
Revere	51 S. Russell
Revere	Elm to Alveston, W. R.
Revere Place	10 Charter
Revere-st. Place	79 Revere
Reynolds	Addison, E. B.
Richards	Granite
Richards	Washington, B.
Richards Avenue	Hyde Park av., W. R.
Richards Court	Green, D.
Richardson Place	491 Saratoga, E. B.
Richmond	109 Atlantic av.
Richmond	Washington, D.
Ridgeway Lane	36 Cambridge
Rill	Hancock, D.
Ringgold	4 Hanson
River	69 Beacon
River	49 Washington, D.
River Place	72 River st.
River-street Place	75 River
Riverside	1189 Tremont, R.
Riverview Avenue	Adams, D.
Roanoke Avenue	Elm, W. R.
Robinson	Adams, D.
Robinson Avenue	Robinson, D.

Robinson Court..........Savin-hill av., D.
Robinson Place..........93 Brook av., R.
Rochester..............350 Harrison av.
Rockingham Court.....136 Orleans, E. B.
Rockingham Place..........248 Cabot, R.
Rockland..................267 Warren, R.
Rockland..............Washington, W. R.
Rockland.................Washington, B.
Rockland Avenue..........20 Rockland, R.
Rockland Court........136 Everett, E. B.
Rockland Place............7 Rockland, R.
Rockview..........Spring Park av., W. R.
Rockville..............Blue Hill av., D.
Rockville Place............186 Warren, R.
Rockwell..............near Bailey, D.
Rockwood..................Pond, W. R.
Rocky Hill Avenue........26 Hancock, R.
Rogers...............376 Dorchester, S. B.
Rogers Avenue............241 Ruggles, R.
Rogers Court............Rogers av., R.
Rollins.................1308 Washington
Rollins Place...................25 Revere
Romsey...............Dorchester av., D.
Roslin...............from 504 Warren, R.
Roslin..................Washington, D.
Roslindale Avenue..........Beach, W. R.
Rosseter..................Union av. D.
Rowe................Canterbury, W. R.
Rowe Place.................90 Chauncy
Roxbury..............2349 Washington, R.
Roxbury Avenue.....Chestnut-hill av., B.
Roy......................Hulbert, R.
Roys................Lamartine, W. R.
Ruggles..............2195 Washington, D.
Ruggles Place..........Washington, D.
Ruggles-street Court......312 Ruggles, R.
Russell...................36 Pearl, C.
Russell Court........34 North Russell
Russell Court.............289 Ruggles, R.
Russell Place..................59 Russell
Russell Place.........32 North Russell
Rutherford Avenue............66 Bow, C.
Rutland..................1591 Washington
Rutland Place..................Haven
Rutland Square..............703 Tremont
Rutledge..................Park, W. R.
Sagamore..............Savin Hill av., D.
St. James................141 Warren, R.
St. James Avenue............194 Berkeley
St. James Place..........62 St. James, R.
St. Mary..............Brighton av., R.
Salem....................271 Main, C.
Salem....................160 Hanover
Salem.................Washington, W. R.
Salem Court...................181 Salem
Salem-hill Court.............8 Pearl, C.
Salem Place..................28 Salem
Salem-street Avenue..........8 Salem, C.
Salt Lane.....................25 Union
Salter Place..................48 Prince
Salutation..................439 Hanover
Salvisberg Avenue........Hampshire, R.
Samoset Place.............43 Prince
Sanford.................Washington, D.
Sanford Place..............10 East Lenox
Saratoga............36 Central sq., E. B.
Saratoga Place..........12 Saratoga, E. B.
Sargent.................Howard av., R.
Sargent..............Canterbury, W. R.
Savage Court..........160 Chelsea, E. B.
Savin...................396 Warren, R.
Savin-hill Avenue..........Pleasant, D.
Sawyer..............623 Shawmut av., R.
Sawyer Avenue.........Savin Hill av., D.
Saxon Court................150 Paris, E. B.
Saxton.........................Romsey, D.
Sayward.........................Bird, R.
Sayward Place........43 Woodward, S. B.
Scarborough...............Walnut, W. R.
School....................285 Washington
School...................231 Main, C.
School.....................Walnut, W. R.
School...............Washington, W. R.
School......................Market, E. B.
School-street Place..........60 School, C.
School-street Place......41 School, W. R
Schoolhouse Court..........13 Charles, C.
Schuyler............505 Blue Hill av., R.
Scollay Square..............Tremont Row
Scotts Court...............195 Chelsea, C.
Seabury Place................33 Blossom
Sear's Place.................34 Anderson
Seaver................188 Webster, E. B.
Seaver..3076 Washington, R., W. R. & D.
Seaver Place............... 251 Tremont
Seaverns Avenue............Centre, W. R.
Second....(See E. Second and W. Second)
Second......................66 Lynde
Sedgwick..........J. A. Andrew, W. R.
Selden..................Milton av., D.
Seminary Place........ 11 Lawrence, C.
Seneca..................308 Harrison av.
Seventh.(See E. Seventh and W. Seventh)
Seventh-st. Court....776 E. Seventh, S. B.
Sever....................20 Haverhill, C.
Sewall Place..................16 Milk
Sewall Place...............1468 Tremont, R.
Sewall's Court............Arlington av., C.
Shailer Avenue..............139 Roxbury, R.
Shamrock............Dorchester av., D.
Sharon..................726 Harrison av.
Sharon..................Brown's av., W. R.
Sharon Court...............186 Havre, E. B.
Shaving....................310 Federal
Shawmut................182 Pleasant
Shawmut Avenue............290 Tremont
Shawmut Place......698 Shawmut av., R.
Shawmut Terrace.....560 Shawmut av.
Sheafe.....................10 Cook, C.
Sheafe.....................160 Salem
Shelburne............Buttonwood, S. B.
Shelby...............335 Princeton, E. B.
Sheldon......Ashland to Florence, W. R.
Shelton....................Adams, D.
Shepard.................Washington, B.
Shepton Terrace.rear 681 E. Eighth, S. B.
Sherbrook Place............1489 Tremont, R.
Sheridan...............386 Centre, W. R.
Sheridan Court...............48 Tufts, C.
Sheridan Place......59 West Fifth, S. B.
Sheridan Place..............Minot, D.
Sherman..................Mystic av., C.
Sherman..................8 Rockland, R.
Sherman Court...338 W. Broadway, S. B.
Sherman Square............Mystic av., C.
Shirley....................486 Dudley, R.
Short.......................Homer, E. B.
Short..................218 Everett, E. B.
Short..............419 Bunker Hill, C.
Short....................28 Middle, S. B.
Short....................Maple av., C.
Short.................Washington, W. R.
Short-street Court..............5 Short, C.
Short-street Place..............6 Short, C.

Shreve........Norfolk to Madison av., D.
Sigourney....................Walnut, W. R.
Sigourney Place........Rear 476 Hanover
Silva Place.....................Munroe, R.
Silver..........146 Dorchester av., S. B.
Silver-street Place..........6 Silver, S. B.
Simmons....................164 Vernon, R.
Simpson Court.......5 Van Rensselaer pl.
Simpson's Court...............99 Pearl, C.
Simpson's Court......874 E. Second, S. B.
Sixth..................(See E. Sixth and W. Sixth)
Sixth......................10 Lynde, C.
Sixth-street Alley.....148 W. Sixth, S. B.
Smith......................695 Parker, R.
Smith Court.......................48 Joy
Smith Place........................66 Joy
Smith-street Place........68 Smith, R.
Smith's Avenue..........106 Kendall, R.
Smyrna..................Brookline av., R.
Snelling Place......................7 Hull
Snowhill....................103 Prince, C.
Snowhill Place................11 Snowhill
Soley......................57 Warren, C.
Somerset........................9 Beacon
South.................137 Summer
South....................Centre, W. R.
South....................Commercial, D.
South.............Chestnut Hill av., B.
Southac Place.................78 Phillips
South Cedar-st. Place......20 Winchester
South Eden....................538 Main, C.
South Margin....................54 Pitts
South Market..........29 Merchants Row
South May..................1286 Washington
South Russell...............92 Cambridge
Southwood..........199 Blue Hill av., R.
Sparhawk...................Cambridge, B.
Spear Alley................83 Purchase
Spear Place..................16 Pleasant
Spencer......................Park, D.
Spice Court..............60 Cambridge, C.
Spring......................100 Leverett
Spring....................Centre, W. R.
Spring...................Savin Hill av., D.
Spring Court.............124 Fellows, R.
Spring Garden............Crescent av., D.
Spring Lane.............278 Washington
Spring Lane............Lamartine, W. R.
Spring Park Avenue......Centre, W. R.
Spring-st. Court................57 Spring
Springer Court....... 514 E. Eighth, S. B.
Springfield,(See E. S'ng'ld & W. Sp'ng'ld)
Springvale Avenue........Spring, W. R.
Spruce......................49 Beacon
Stafford..........82 Blue Hill av., R.
Standish Avenue..............Harvard, D.
Standish Court..................36 Pitts
Stanhope....................146 Berkeley
Stanhope Place..............18 Phillips
Staniford..................27 Cambridge
Staniford Place................9 Staniford
Stanley Place.................43 Bow, C.
Stanmore Place...........233 Warren, R.
Stanton Avenue................Norfolk, D.
Stanwood Avenue...........Columbia, D.
Stark....................Cambridge, C.
Starr Lane.................Centre, W. R.
State....................206 Washington
Station.................1339 Tremont, R.
St. Botolph....................Fairfield
St. Charles...............65 Chandler
Sterling.............695 Shawmut av., R.

Stetson Court................44 Henley, C.
Stetson Place................96 W. Cedar
Stevens.................500 Shawmut av.
Stewart................Boston st., S. B.
Stillman......................76 Salem
Stillman Place................47 Stillman
Stoddard......................25 Howard
Stone....................14 Princeton, C.
Stone Place.............3 Edgeworth, C.
Stony Brook Place..........238 Centre, R.
Story..........................76 G, S. B.
Stoughton................768 Harrison av.
Stoughton.....................Dudley, D.
Stoughton-street Place.....Stoughton, D.
Strong Place............160 Cambridge
Studley Place..................215 Eliot
Sudan.....................Sydney, D.
Sudbury..................Haymarket sq.
Sudbury Place..............48 Weston, R.
Sudbury Square................Sudbury
Suffolk Place.................15 Bedford
Sullivan......................297 Main, C.
Sullivan Place.............107 Federal
Sullivan Square..................Main, C.
Summer........................14 Elm, C.
Summer..................428 Washington
Summer.........Spring to Centre, W. R.
Summer....................Warren, B.
Summit....................25 Circuit, R.
Summit........Metropolitan av., W. R.
Summit Avenue..............Breck, B.
Sumner..............Week's Wharf, E. B.
Sumner..................Stoughton, D.
Sumner Court................Sumner, D.
Sumner Place..........385 Sumner, E. B.
Sumner Place.............204 Cabot, R.
Sumner-street Place........Sumner, D.
Sun-court Street...............232 North
Sunderland............624 Warren, R.
Swallow........................N, S. B.
Swan......... 187 Dorchester av., S. B.
Swan Place................45 Swan, S. B.
Swan's Court..................Olney, D.
Swett..................800 Albany, R. & D.
Swift..................601 Saratoga, E. B.
Sycamore................Florence, W. R.
Sydney..................Crescent av., D.
Sydney Place................Harvard, D.
Tabor....................20 Warren, R.
Taft's Place.............South, W. R.
Tamworth..................20 Boylston
Taylor......................12 Dwight
Taylor......................Clifton, R.
Taylor................Neponset av., D.
Taylor.........................Lake, R.
Teevan Place.... 581 Shawmut av., R.
Telegraph..........222 Dorchester, S. B.
Temple....................20 Cambridge
Temple......Dedham Br. R. R., W. R.
Temple.......................River, D.
Temple Park............1272 Washington
Temple Place..............140 Tremont
Temple Place..............Temple st., D.
Templeton...................Adams, R.
Tenean..................Commercial, D.
Tennis Court..........49 Buckingham
Tennyson.................212 Pleasant
Terrace...............1424 Tremont, R.
Terrace Avenue...33 Sheridan av., W. R.
Terrace Place...........173 Webster, E. B.
Texas Avenue..........1350 Tremont, R.
Texas Court..................Texas av., R.

Thacher....................... 98 Prince
Thacher Avenue..... .... 34 Thacher
Thacher Court................. 29 Thacher
Thayer................. 456 Harrison av.
Thetford Avenue.............. Norfolk, D.
Third...................... 54 Lynde, C;
Third........ (Sec E. Third and W. Third)
Third-street Court.... 259 W. Third, S. B.
Third-street Place..... 239 W. Third, S. B.
Thomas................... Centre, W. R.
Thomas Park................. 77 G, S. B.
Thompson................. 119 Main, C.
Thompson Square.. Main and Warren, C.
Thompson's Court............. 51 Revere
Thorn................... 114 E. Canton
Thorndike................. 472 Main, C.
Thorndike........... 1944 Washington, R.
Thornley............. Dorchester av., D.
Thornton....................... Guild, R.
Thornton Place.......... 102 Thornton, R.
Thwing Place.............. 211 Highland, R.
Tibbets..................... 20 Mill, C.
Tilden Place................ 8 Auburn, R.
Tileston.................... 352 Hanover
Tileston............... Blue Hill av., D.
Tileston Avenue........... Walk Hill, D.
Tileston Place............. 15 Tileston
Tileston Place.......... Neponset av., D.
Tolman Place............... 169 Warren, R.
Torrey................. Washington, D.
Town-hill Court......... 9 Harvard sq., C.
Townsend.......... 2878 Washington, R.
Townsend Place............... 8 Carver
Train......................... Mill, D.
Trainer Court............... 76 Lenox, R.
Transit..................... Cabot, R.
Travers................. 81 Merrimac
Tremont............. 14 Monument sq., C.
Tremont........ 48 Court to Brookline
Tremont................. Washington, B.
Tremont Court............. 38 Tremont
Tremont Court......... 5 Tremont pl., R.
Tremont Place............. 26 Tremont
Tremont Place.................Beacon
Tremont Place........ 1233 Tremont, R.
Tremont Row................. 2 Howard
Trenton............ 325 Meridian, E. B.
Trenton.................. 15 Bartlett, C.
Trinity Place........... 70 St. James av.
Troy.................... 360 Harrison av.
Trull....................... Hancock, D.
Trumbull................. Reynolds, E. B.
Trumbull................ 37 Newland
Truro.................. 25 Yarmouth
Tucker Place.................. 52 Joy
Tuckerman......... 327 Dorchester, S. B.
Tudor..................... 11 B, S. B.
Tufts................. 51 Bunker Hill, C.
Tufts........................ 105 South
Tufts Court............... 55 Tufts, C.
Tupelo.................... 9 Savin, R.
Tyler........................ 55 Beach
Tyler Place................. 30 Tyler
Ulmer..................... Minden, R.
Union.................. 116 Main, C.
Union......................... Dock sq.
Union................ Commercial, D.
Union................. Washington, B.
Union Avenue........ Washington, W. R.
Union Avenue............... Bowdoin, D.
Union Court........... 202 Everett, E. B.
Union Court.............. 110 Main, C.

Union Park............. 313 Shawmut av.
Union Park Street....... 314 Shawmut av.
Union Place........... 305 Princeton, E. B.
Union Place.......... 117 Porter, E. B., C.
Union Place..................... 33 Wall
Union Square............. Brighton av., B.
Union Terrace............. Morton, W. R.
Unity..................... 24 Charter
Unity Court.................... 9 Unity
Upham Avenue............. Hancock, D.
Upham Corner. Hancock, Dudley, R. & D.
Upham Court.................. Boston, D.
Upland Place............. Norfolk av., R.
Upton................. 333 Shawmut av.
Upton's Lane............. Western av., B.
Utica......................... 12 Tufts
Utica Place....................... 46 Utica
Vale.................. Dorchester st., S. B.
Vale................... 117 Thornton, R.
Valentine............. 2797 Washington, R.
Vancouver................. 151 Ward, R.
Van Rensselaer Place........ 215 Tremont
Van Winkle............. Dorchester av., D.
Vaughan............... Blue Hill av., D.
Vaughan Avenue.......... Geneva av., D.
Vernon............. 2293 Washington, R.
Vernon..................... Franklin, B.
Vernon Place................. 23 Charter
Vernon Place............. 98 Vernon, R.
Vernon Place.................. Vernon, B.
Vicksburg........... 572 E. Second, S. B.
Victoria............. Dorchester av., D.
Vila..................... Francis, R.
Village.................. 134 Castle
Vine................. 143 Chelsea, C.
Vine................. 329 Dudley, D.
Vine-street Place.............. 5 Parkman
Vinton............. 340 Dorchester, S. B.
Vinton Court............. 48 Henley, C.
Virginia................... 741 Dudley, R.
Vose..................... Crest av., D.
Wabeno.................. Wyoming, C.
Wabon............... 507 Warren, R.
Wadleigh Place............. 1 Ellery, S. B.
Wait................... Hillside st., R.
Wakullah................ 42 Rockland, R.
Walden................. 150 Heath, R.
Walden Park........... 33 Highland, R.
Wales................ Blue Hill av., D.
Wales Place............... Columbia, D.
Walford................... 32 Bow, C.
Walker.................. 315 Main, C.
Walker Avenue............ 36 Walker, C.
Walker Place......... 146 Northampton
Walker-street Court..... 8 Walker av., C.
Walk Hill............. Morton, W. R. & D.
Walk Hill Avenue...... Walk Hill, W. R.
Wall................... 70 Sullivan, C.
Wall....................... 11 Minot
Wallace Court........... 67 Winthrop, C.
Wall's Place............. 64 Henley, C.
Walnut............... 387 Bunker Hill, C.
Walnut..................... 38 Beacon
Walnut, continuation of Walnut av., W.R.
Walnut................. Neponset av., D.
Walnut Avenue........... 183 Warren, R.
Walnut Court............ 62 Walnut, C.
Walnut Court......... 98 Walnut av., R.
Walnut Park........ 3044 Washington, R.
Walnut Place......... 1846 Washington
Walnut-street Court......... Walnut, D.
Walpole............. 1073 Tremont, R.

Walsh Place	19 Clark
Walter	Bussey, W. R.
Waltham	551 Harrison av.
Walton	Washington, D.
Wapping	65 Chelsea, C.
Ward	360 Dorchester, S. B.
Ward	Parker, R.
Ward Court	28 Ward, S. B.
Ware	Trull, D.
Wareham	614 Harrison av.
Warland Place	43 Hanover
Warner Avenue	Harvard, D.
Warren	Park and Henley, C.
Warren	2250 Washington, R.
Warren	Cambridge, B.
Warren Avenue	34 City sq., C.
Warren Avenue	14 Berkeley
Warren Place	84 Warren, R.
Warren Place	Washington, R.
Warren Sq	jun. Merrimac and Friend
Warren Square	Green, W. R.
Warrenton	877 Washington
Warrenton Place	58 Warrenton
Warwick	98 Hammond, R.
Washburn	Boston st., S. B.
Washburn	Harvard av., B.
Washburn Place	74 Charter
Washington	32 Harvard, C.
Washington..Haym'k't sq.to Dedham line
Washington	Warren to Milton line, D.
Washington	Commercial, D.
Washington.Brookline line to Newton line
Washington Avenue	Minot, D.
Washington Court	197 Roxbury, R.
Washington Park.Dale and Bainbridge,R.
Washington Place	E. High
Washington Place	39 Washington, C.
Washington Place	57 Silver
Washington Place	95 Roxbury, R.
Washington Square	43 Washington, C.
Wason Place	39 Everett, C.
Water	26 Warren av. C.
Water	270 Washington
Water	Taylor, D.
Waterford	1079 Washington
Waterlow	Harvard, D.
Waumbeck	531 Warren
Waverley	270 Warren, R.
Waverley	Market, B.
Waverley Place	38 South
Way	288 Harrison av.
Way Place	16 Copeland, R.
Wayne	529 Blue Hill av. R.
Webber	1012 Harrison av. R.
Webster	24 Lewis, E. B.
Webster	285 Bunker Hill, C.
Webster	Spring, W. R.
Webster	Bigelow, B.
Webster Avenue	349 Sumner, E. B.
Webster Avenue	374 Hanover
Webster Avenue	Brighton av. B.
Webster Court	40 Webster, R.
Webster Place	251 Webster, E. B.
Webster Place	18 Fleet
Webster Place	65 West Fifth, S. B.
Weekes Place	224 Centre, R.
Weld	Centre, W. R.
Weld Avenue	Egleston sq. W. R.
Weld Park	Centre, W. R.
Well	15 Custom-House st.
Welles Avenue	Washington, D.
Wellington	561 Columbus av.
Wellington Place	32 Quincy, C.
Wells Place	1271 Washington
Wendell	58 Pearl
Wendell	49 Preble, S. B.
Wendell Place	73 Preble, S. B.
Wentworth	Norfolk, D.
Wentworth Place	162 Northampton
Wesley	30 Chelsea, E. B.
Wesley	4 Pearl, C.
Wesley	23 Preble, S. B.
Wesley Avenue	Savin Hill av., D.
Wesley Place	288 Hanover
West	Reynolds, E. B.
West	Alford, C.
West	509 Washington
West Broadway	Dorchester av., S. B.
West Brookline	1531 Washington
West Canton	1495 Washington
West Cedar	57 Chestnut
West Chester Park	781 Tremont
West Concord	1635 Washington
West Cottage	551 Dudley, R.
West Dedham	1457 Washington
West Eagle	Border, E. B.
West Eighth	114 D, S. B.
West Fifth	212 Dorchester av., S. B.
West First	Foundry crossing, S. B.
West Fourth	Dover-St. Bridge, S. B.
West Haven	77 Newland
West Newton	1549 Washington
West Ninth	101 D, S. B.
West Park	Warner, R.
West Rutland Square	495 Columbus av.
West Second	100 Dorchester av., S. B.
West Seventh	282 Dorchester av., S. B.
West Sixth	252 Dorchester av., S. B.
West Sixth-street Place, 62 W. Sixth,S. B.
West Springfield	1717 Washington
West Third	61 West Second, S. B.
West Walnut Park 3045 Washington,W.R.
West Windsor	211 Ruggles, R.
Western Av., Camb'port to Watertown,B.
Westfield	819 Tremont, R.
Westland Av.,W.Chester P'k to Parker,R.
Westminister	46 Hammond, R.
Westminister Avenue,3032 Washington,R.
Weston	109 Warwick, R.
Westville	Bowdoin, D.
Wharf	102 Broad
Wheatland Avenue	Washington, D.
Wheeler	67 Shawmut av.
Wheelock Avenue	Hancock, D.
White	389 Border, E. B.
White-street Place	20 White, E. B.
Whitfield	Park, D.
Whitney	Tremont, R.
Wicklow	Market, B.
Wiggin	31 North Bennett
Wigglesworth	Tremont, R.
Wilbur Court	319 Sumner, E. B.
Wilder	Washington, D.
Wilford Court	75 Fellows, R.
Willard	131 Leverett
Willard Place	1853 Washington, R.
Willard Place	North Harvard, B.
Williams	262 Main, C.
Williams	2119 Washington, R.
Williams	Washington, W. R.
Williams Court	239 Washington
Willoughby Place	4 Blanchard, R.
Willow	37 Chestnut
Willow	Centre, W. R.

Willow Court...155 Boston st., S. B. & D.
Willow Park.........737 Shawmut av., R.
Wilson..........Walnut to Suffolk, W. R.
Wilton... ....Cambridge st., B.
Winchester...................142 Pleasant
Windham Place...............Warren, B.
Windsor.........(see E. and W. Windsor)
Winfred Court...............7 Sawyer, R.
Winship..................Washington, B.
Winship Avenue..............Market, B.
Winship Place............Washington, B.
Winslow.....................49 Eustis, R.
Winslow....................Dent, W. R.
Winslow Place...............81 Chambers
Winslow Place.......2153 Washington, R.
Winter...................439 Washington
Winter......................Hancock, D.
Winter Place................24 Winter
Winthrop..........30 Maverick sq., E. B.
Winthrop.....................53 Main, C.
Winthrop..................108 Warren, R.
Winthrop Place.........2165 Washington
Winthrop Sq., Win., Adams & Com.st., C.
Winthrop Square.........217 Devonshire
Wirth Place.................20 Camden, R.
Wistar Place....................44 Elm, C.
Withington..................Norfolk, D.
Wood.......................185 Main, C.
Wood.......................Walnut, D.
Wood-street Court...........Walnut, D.

Woodbine..................326 Warren, R.
Woodbury..........1923 Washington, R.
Woodman...................Custer, W. R.
Woodside Avenue......Forest-hills st., B.
Woodstock.................Maple av., R.
Woodville Square.......53 W. Cottage, R.
Woodward.......... 361 Dorchester, S. B.
Woodward Avenue..........26 Dudley, R.
Woodward Park......opp. 638 Dudley, R.
Worcester...............1677 Washington
Worcester Place.....1907 Washington, R.
Worcester Square.......1678 Washington
Wordsworth..................Pope, E. B.
Worthington.................Tremont, B.
Wren....................Rutledge, W. R.
Wright's Court...350 W. Broadway, S. B.
Wyman..................346 Centre, W. R.
Wyman Place.................11 Common
Wyman Place..........288 Centre, W. R.
Wyoming.................485 Warren, R.
Yarmouth..............363 Columbus av.
Yendley Place............ 35 Coventry, R.
Yeoman..................878 Albany, R.
Yeoman Court............33 Yeoman, R.
Yeoman Place............ 38 Yeoman, R.
York......................Glen Road, D.
Young's Court................ 124 North
Zeigler.............2348 Washington, R.
Zeigler Place..............115 Zeigler, R.

BOSTON POST-OFFICE.

Post-Office and Sub-Treasury Building. Situated on the square bounded by Post-Office Square, Milk, Devonshire and Water Streets. The principal entrance is from Post-Office Square. There are also entrances on Devonshire, Milk and Water Streets. The building, architecturally, is grand and imposing, and is of the Renaissance style, built of granite. Up to the construction of this building the Post-Office in Boston has been located in quarters leased by the United States Government for that purpose. During the siege of Boston, 1776, the Post-Office was removed to Cambridge, having previously been located on Washington Street, near what is now Cornhill. It has at different periods been located on State Street; in the Old State House; in Summer Street (corner of Chauncy Street); in Faneuil Hall and in the Old South Church. The present building was largely the means of arresting the progress of the Great Fire of 1872, not, however, until the flames had damaged the building to the extent of $175,000. Traces of the fire are yet to be seen in the stone, although the blocks badly defaced were removed and new ones substituted.

Offices are open as follows: Cashier's office, rooms 50-51 (from Water st. side) from 9 to 3; Superintendent of Newspaper and Periodical Postage, payment of Box Rent, 36, main floor (from Water st. side), 9 to 5; Superintendent of Unpaid Postage, (Water st.) 9 to 5; Superintendent of Inquiry Room (from Devonshire st.) 9 to 5; Superintendent of Stamp Office, Section 18 (from Devonshire st.) stamps at wholesale, 8 to 6; retail, 7 a. m. to 9 p. m. (Sundays, 8 to 5.30); Superintendent Carriers' Delivery, 1 and 2 (from Water st.) main floor, 7 a. m. to 9 p. m. Sundays, 9.30 to 10.30 a. m.; Box Delivery, 3 and 4 (from Water st.) main floor, 7 a. m. to 9 p. m. Sundays, 9 to 11 a. m.; Newspaper Delivery, 57, (from Post-Office sq.) main floor, 7.30 a. m. to 7 p. m.; General Delivery, 51, 52, 53 and 54 (from Post-Office sq.), main floor, 7.30 a. m. to 7 p. m. Sundays, 9 to 10 a. m.; Special Delivery, 7 a. m. to 12 p. m. Mailing Division, 30 (from Milk st.) main floor, 9 to 5; Foreign Branch, 32 (from Milk st.) main floor; Registered Letter Division, 45, 46, 47 (from Post-Office sq.) main floor, 9 to 6; Money Order Division, 41, 42, 43 (from Milk st.) main floor, 10 to 6; Railway Mail Service, 79, 80, 81, 82, (from Post-Office sq.) second floor, 9 to 5; Post-Office Inspector's Department, 78 (from Post-Office sq.) second floor, 9 to 4.

Stamp Agents. Agencies for the sale of postage stamps at retail have been appointed as follows: Archer, F.W., Dorchester Lower Mills; Blake, George W., 536 Columbus Avenue, Station A; Boyden, E. C., corner Joy and Myrtle Streets; Brown, M. F., Brookline; Crane, C. H., 154 Perkins Street, Somerville; Croucher, Mrs. E. W., Chapel Station, Brookline; Curtis, Bracey, 184 Washington Avenue, Chelsea; Day, C. H. & F. B., 235 Meridian Street, East Boston; Freeman, Simon A., 559 Main Street, Charlestown; Godding, John G., corner Newbury and Dartmouth Streets; Gove, Ezra C., Main Street, Cambridgeport; Jewett, Amory, Winter Hill, Somerville; Jones, James T., corner Fourth and O Streets, South Boston; Mowrey, A. B., Grove Hall, Roxbury; Shepard, S. A. D., corner Dover and Washington Streets; Tucker, Frank, Roxbury Crossing, Roxbury; Webster, S. & Co., 63 Warren Avenue, Station A; Williard, Sidney F., Woods Block, Neponset.

Postal Rates and Conditions. Letters, and all other written matter, whether sealed or unsealed, and all other matter sealed, nailed, sewed, tied, or fastened in any manner, so that it cannot be easily examined, two cents per ounce or fraction thereof. All manuscript matter designed for publication, manuscript music, and manuscript maps, unless accompanied by proof-sheets or corrected copies thereof, and also drawings, plans, and designs, are first-class matter. When only a single copy of a reproduction by any other process than ordinary type, plate, and lithographic printing is offered for mailing, and it does not appear from internal evidence that it is being sent in identical terms to several persons, it is subject to letter rates of postage. All *sealed* packages, except packages of seeds in sealed *transparent* envelopes; all packages *sewed* up except in the case of seeds, where the absence of any other matter can be ascertained by feeling; and all packages *in any way so closed against inspection* that their contents cannot be fully ascertained without breaking the seal, or without undue delay in opening the same, are subject to first-class postage. The use of the hand stamp for printing personal communications, as the stamping of a receipt or credit on a bill or account, constitutes the matter first-class. The use of a printed signature to partly written and partly printed papers does not alter their character as first-class matter. Deeds, mortgages, promissory notes, insurance policies, drafts, and checks, cancelled or uncancelled, and all matter of the same general character wholly or partially in writing, are subject to first-class rates of postage. Diaries and bank books with entries in writing, and autograph albums filled in with written signatures or miscellaneous writing, are first-class matter. Written visiting cards, envelopes, and tags with written addresses thereon, are first-class matter. Matter produced by the typewriter or caligraph and similar processes is first-class matter and subject to letter rates of postage.

Postal Cards. The object of the postal card is to facilitate correspondence and provide for the transmission through the mails, at a reduced rate of postage, of short communications, either printed or written in pencil or ink. They may, therefore, be used for orders, invitations, notices, receipts, acknowledgements, price-lists, and other requirements of business and social life: and the matter desired to be conveyed may be either in writing or in print, or partially in both. In using postal cards, care should be taken not to paste, gum (except an address tag or label), or attach anything to them, or to write anything on the address side other than the address. They are unmailable as postal cards when these suggestions are disregarded, but are mailable as letters when additional stamps are affixed thereto to prepay letter postage, viz., one cent for a single rate, and two cents for each additional rate. Postal cards are issued exclusively by the Post-Office Department, and may be used either for printed or written, or partly printed and partly written, communications. "Postal cards" issued by private parties are subject to letter rates of postage when they contain any written matter whatever in addition to the date and name of the addressed and of the sender, and the correction of mere typographical errors therein. In getting up such cards, care should be taken not to imitate the cards issued by the Post-Office Department, or have the words "Postal Card" printed thereon, or they may render themselves liable to prosecution. When any one is annoyed or expects to be annoyed by postal cards sent from any particular place or from any known person, he may direct the postmaster at the point named to destroy all postal cards addressed to him, or cards from any person named so addressed, and so far as the duties of the post-office permit sufficient examination, the postmaster should comply with the request. The same request may be made of the receiving postmaster. The direction to the postmaster should be in writing and should be placed on the files of his office.

Newspaper Rates. The postage on newspapers is at the rate of one cent for each four ounces or fraction thereof.

Foreign Rates. The rates for the countries and places which belong to the Postal Union, are as follows: Prepayment optional, except for registered articles, but on printed matter and samples postage must be at least partially prepaid. Letters — 5 cents per 15 grammes, a weight very slightly over one half ounce. Post cards — 2 cents each. Printed Matter. — 1 cent for each two ounces or fraction. Limit of weight, 4 lbs. 6 oz. Commercial Papers (Insurance Documents, Way Bills, Invoices, Papers of Legal Procedure, Manuscripts of works, &c.)— The same as for printed matter, but the lowest charge is 5 cents.

Boston Postal Districts.
Station A.............1638 Washington st.
Roxbury Station............49 Warren st.
South Boston Station...... 474 Broadway
East Boston Station........5 Maverick sq.
Charlestown Station...........23 Main st.
Chelsea Station.............268 Broadway
Cambridge Station...........Harvard sq.
Mount Auburn Station.......Harvard sq.
Cambridgeport Station.......611 Main st.
East Cambridge Station.129 Cambridge st.
North Cambridge Station...150 North av.
Somerville Station.............10 Bow st.
Jamaica Plain Station....Elsom Building
Dorchester Station........Dorchester av.
Neponset Station..........Dorchester av.
Brighton Station................Brighton
Allston Station..................Brighton
Mattapan Station..............Blue Hill av.
West Roxbury Station..........Centre st.
Roslindale Station.............Roslindale
Winthrop Station..............Winthrop
Revere Station....................Revere
Brookline Station..............Brookline

Postal Money Orders. Fees for issuing money orders are as follows: on orders not exceeding $10, 8 cents; over $10 and not exceeding $15, 10 cents; over $15 and not exceeding $30, 15 cents; over $30 and not exceeding $40, 20 cents; over $40 and not exceeding $50, 25 cents; over $50 and not exceeding $60, 30 cents; over $60 and not exceeding $70, 35 cents; over $70 and not exceeding $80, 40 cents; over $80 and not exceeding $100, 45 cents.

International Money Orders. To Canada, Great Britain and Ireland, Germany, France, Algeria, Switzerland, Austria, Norway and Sweden, Denmark, Belgium, Portugal, Jamaica, New Zealand, New South Wales, Victoria, Queensland, Tasmania, Hawaiian Islands, Windward Islands, Cape of Good Hope, Constantinople, Hong Kong and Egypt, Japan and British India. On orders not exceeding $10, 10 cents; over $10 and not exceeding $20, 20 cents; over $20 and not exceeding $30, 30 cents; over $30 and not exceeding $40, 40 cents; over $40 and not exceeding $50, 50 cents.

Postal Notes. All postmasters at money-order offices are authorized to issue postal notes for sums less than five dollars, payable to bearer at any time within three months from the last day of the month of issue. The fee for a postal note is *three cents*.

Suggestions. Do not address letters " B. H. District." If Boston Highlands is intended use " Roxbury District;" if Bunker Hill is the desired destination use " Charlestown District." Do not place newspapers on the top of the street boxes. The collectors are not required to carry them to the Central Office, the boxes being intended for the reception of *letters only*. Some of the papers and packages left in this careless way are stolen by tramps, who are tempted by the stamps, while others have the stamps washed off and the enclosures ruined by sudden rains, or are blown away.

STATUES AND MONUMENTS.

Adams Bust. Doric Hall, State House, Beacon Street. A marble bust of Samuel Adams.

Adams Statue. (1880). Adams Square, at the intersection of Washington Street, Cornhill and Brattle Street. A bronze statue of Samuel Adams, of Revolutionary fame, by Miss Anne Whitney. The inscriptions on the pedestal—of granite—are as follows:

SAMUEL ADAMS
— 1722 — 1803 —
A PATRIOT.
HE ORGANIZED
THE REVOLUTION
AND SIGNED THE
DECLARATION OF
INDEPENDENCE.

GOVERNOR
A TRUE LEADER
OF THE PEOPLE.

ERECTED A. D. 1880.
FROM A FUND BEQUEATHED
TO THE CITY BY
JONATHAN PHILLIPS.

A STATESMAN
INCORRUPTIBLE AND FEARLESS.

This Statue cost $6,856, and was unveiled July 5, 1880.

Adams Statue. Chapel, Mount Auburn, Cambridge. A statue of John Adams, second President of the United States.

Andrew Statue. (1871). Doric Hall, State House, Beacon Street. A fine marble statue of John Albion Andrew, the War Governor of Massachusetts. Thomas Ball was the sculptor, and he succeeded in reproducing the familiar features of Andrew with the utmost fidelity to nature. It cost $10,000. It was placed here Feb. 14, 1871. In writing of "Our Portrait Statues," George B. Woods said: " It is not only a faithful portraiture—always Mr. Ball's strong point—but there is something better than literal likeness about it—an incorporation into the marble of the noble nature of the man, which is the highest achievement of Art. Altogether the statue moves the spectator to hearty liking; and we feel sure that it will grow into the popular heart as it stands close by where the Governor toiled and thought through five exhausting years surrounded by the tattered flags of the thousands of Massachusetts boys, who, like him, gave their utmost effort for nationality and liberty, and many of whom, like him, sealed the sacrifice with death."

Aristides Statue. (1849). Louisburg Square, between Pinckney and Mount Vernon Streets. An Italian marble statue of Aristides "the Just," presented by the late Joseph Iasigi to the city. Placed here December, 1849.

Army and Navy Monument. (1877). Monument (or Flagstaff) Hill, Boston Common. The monument is of granite, in the form of a Doric column, surmounted by a bronze emblematic statue of the Genius of America; at the base are four statues representing respectively the Soldier, the Sailor, History and Peace. Bas-reliefs in bronze are placed between these statues, representing the Departure of the Regiment, a Naval Action, the Sanitary Commission and the Return from the War and Surrender of the Battle-Flags to the Governor at the State House. Portraits of John Albion Andrew, Wendell Phillips, Phillips Brooks, D. D., A. H. Vinton, D. D., Archbishop Williams, Henry W.

Longfellow and others are to be seen in the bas-relief of the Departure of the Regiment, standing upon the steps of the State House, while with the troops are Generals Charles Russell Lowell and Benjamin F. Butler, Colonels Cass and Shaw. The Sanitary Commission bas-relief has portraits of Alexander H. Rice, James Russell Lowell, Marshall P. Wilder, Ezra H. Gannett, D. D., George Ticknor, Rev. Edward Everett Hale and others. In the Return from the War group is represented a regiment halting in front of the State House, with Generals Devens, Bartlett, Banks and Underwood mounted. Upon the steps of the State House are represented Governor Andrew, Charles Sumner, Henry Wilson and others. The monument is 70 feet high. It was the work of Martin Milmore. It cost $75,000. It was dedicated Sept. 17, 1877, the President of the United States and nearly all of his cabinet being present at the ceremonies. The oration was pronounced by General Charles Devens. There was a grand procession, with upwards of 30,000 persons — military and civic bodies — in line. The inscription on the monument — written by Charles W. Eliot, President of Harvard University — is as follows:

TO THE
MEN OF BOSTON
WHO DIED
FOR THEIR COUNTRY
ON LAND AND SEA
IN THE WAR WHICH
KEPT THE UNION WHOLE
DESTROYED SLAVERY,
AND MAINTAINED
THE CONSTITUTION,
THE GRATEFUL CITY
HAS BUILT THIS MONUMENT
THAT THEIR EXAMPLE
MAY SPEAK TO
COMING GENERATIONS.

It may be interesting if not instructive to record here the opinion of Wendell Phillips on this work: "No Ball or Greenough hand ever lifted that proud column which crowns Frogpond Hill (Boston Common); the drapery of its figures so flowing and graceful, that, without hiding, it adorns them; costumes and figures neither violent nor clumsy, but easy, lifelike, natural and suggestive, each telling its own story; no sense of weariness in gazing at them; no drawback on your satisfaction. It has only one peer, that living figure at Concord, so full of life and movement that one fears he shall not see it again if he passes that way the next week. This otherwise perfect column (the Army and Navy Monument) has one defect, the one I have noticed in every city and town monument raised since the war. For anything these marble records tell, the war might have been, like that of 1812, for 'free trade and sailors' rights,' or for a northeastern boundary. You search in vain through them all for the broken chain or the negro soldier. Milmore has done better than his fellows; for he gives us, in one bas-relief, the stern and earnest face of J. B. Smith, a suggestion welcome and honorable. He should have done more. Perhaps sometime it can be mended, and a broken chain and negro form tell what really saved the Union."

Ballou Statue. Mount Auburn, Cambridge. A fine statue of Rev. Hosea Ballou. By Edward A. Brackett, the well-known sculptor.

Beethoven Statue. Boston Music Hall. The majestic statue of Ludwig Von Beethoven, in bronze, on the stage of Music Hall, was the work of Thomas Crawford, an American sculptor, so grateful to the citizens of Boston who gave him a commission for an ideal statue (that of Orpheus, now at the Boston Museum of Fine Arts), that when Charles C. Perkins gave him an order for a bronze statue of Beethoven, Crawford accepted the commission but declined to accept any payment whatever for his work. Mr. Perkins therefore paid the expense of casting, founding and shipment to Boston, and had it placed in its present position. It is a grand statue; in fact, there are few works by American sculptors that equal it. It is greatly admired by all who behold it.

Boy and the Eagle. Vestibule of Boston Athenæum, 10B Beacon Street. Bronze. By Richard S. Greenough.

Bowditch Statue. (1847). Mount Auburn, Cambridge. One of the most noted statues in Boston or vicinity is this bronze statue of Nathaniel Bowditch, representing the famous scientist seated, with globe and quadrant at his feet, holding a book. It was designed by Ball Hughes, and was cast in Boston. It attracts great attention from visitors to Boston, who pronounce it a fine work of art.

Bowditch Statue. Vestibule of Boston Athenæum, 10B Beacon Street. Statue of Nathaniel Bowditch, the celebrated writer on navigation. (Cast.)

Brewer Fountain. (1868). A beautiful bronze fountain placed on the Common, near Park Street, in 1868. It was the gift of the late Gardner Brewer. At the base are figures of Neptune, Amphitrite, Acis and Galatea. Liénard, the eminent French artist, made the design, which received a gold medal at the Paris Exposition of 1855.

Brighton Soldiers' Monument. (1866). Evergreen Cemetery, Brighton District. Dedicated July 26, 1866. It is of granite, and is 30 feet high. The cost was $5,000. Rev. F. A. Whitney delivered the dedicatory oration.

Bunker Hill Monument. (1843). This obelisk of granite, so conspicuous a land mark for many miles around Boston, was erected upon Bunker Hill, in the Charlestown District, to commemorate the first great battle of the American Revolution, which was fought here, June 17, 1775, when 4,000 British troops and 3,000 Americans (commanded by Prescott, Putnam and Warren), for four or five hours hotly contested the possession of the breastworks erected by the American troops during the previous night. The monument is 220 feet high. The cornerstone was laid by Lafayette. Fairs, subscriptions and other means were applied toward raising funds for its completion, Fanny Ellsler, the celebrated dancer, contributing liberally. On June 17, 1843, Daniel Webster (who had made the address at the laying of the corner-stone by Lafayette), delivered the dedicatory oration, in the presence of John Tyler, the President of the United States, and his entire cabinet. (Webster was then Secretary of State). A historical writer says of the impressive event: "Webster was himself that day, and his apostrophe to the gigantic shaft was as grand and noble as the subject was lofty and sublime. Waving his hand toward the towering structure he said: *'The powerful speaker stands motionless before us!'* He was himself deeply moved. The sight of such an immense sea of upturned faces—he had never before addressed such a multitude—he afterwards spoke of as awful and oppressive. The applause from a hundred thousand throats surged in great waves around the orator, completing, in his mind, the parallel of Old Ocean." (To reach Bunker Hill take Charlestown street-cars from Cornhill, Scollay Square).

Ceres Statue. (1865). Surmounting Horticultural Hall, at 100 Tremont Street, is a fine granite statue, representing Ceres, from the hand of the late Martin Milmore. The strength and freedom of the figure are supremely artistic.

Charlestown Soldiers and Sailors' Monument. (1872). Winthrop Square, Charlestown District. Martin Milmore was the designer. Erected on what was in colonial times the training-ground of the militia. On a pedestal are three figures, one — the ideal Genius of America—crowning the soldier and sailor with laurel wreaths. It was here that the Fifth Maryland Regiment coming to Boston to participate in the celebration of the centennial anniversary of the Battle of Bunker Hill, June 17, 1875, marched, and without any escort or announcement of their intention, placed upon this monument a most elaborate and beautiful floral shield, inscribed:

MARYLAND'S
TRIBUTE TO
MASSACHUSETTS,

their band playing a dirge, while the regiment stood around the monument, forming three sides of a square. This tribute was really the first demonstration of Southern troops in honoring the memory of the Northern heroes of the Rebellion, and the beautiful ceremony is still warmly remembered and cherished by the people of Boston, who honor the soldiers of the Fifth Maryland Regiment for so graceful and magnanimous an expression of good-will. No political demagogues can destroy a friendship between the people of the North and South that is based upon such noble and generous impulses as those from which sprang the execution of the act here recorded.

Columbus Statue. (1849). Louisburg Square, between Mount Vernon and Pinckney Streets. A statue of Christopher Columbus, in Italian marble. Presented to the city by the late Joseph Iasigi.

Dorchester Soldiers' Monument. (1867). Meeting-House Hill, Dorchester District. A granite obelisk, 31 feet high, resting upon a ledge. Tablets, giving the names of the soldiers of Dorchester who fell in the War of the Rebellion, are upon its base. B. F. Dwight was the architect. Rev. Chas. A. Humphreys delivered the oration on the occasion of its dedication, Sept. 17, 1867.

Emancipation Group. (1879). In Park Square, Dec. 6, 1879, there was unveiled a bronze group of statuary, representing Abraham Lincoln standing over a prostrate freedman with his shackles broken. On the pedestal is inscribed

EMANCIPATION.

On the base are the following words:
- A RACE SET FREE -
- AND THE COUNTRY AT PEACE -
- LINCOLN -
- RESTS FROM HIS LABORS -

The group, costing $17,000, was the gift of Moses Kimball. Mayor F. O. Prince delivered the dedicatory oration.

Ether Monument. (1868). The monument erected in 1868 on the Public Garden, near Arlington Street, was the gift to the city of Thomas Lee. It is of granite and red marble, and the two ideal figures surmounting the shaft represent the Good Samaritan and the sufferer. The inscriptions are as follows:

TO COMMEMORATE
THE DISCOVERY
THAT THE INHALING
OF ETHER CAUSES
INSENSIBILITY TO PAIN
FIRST PROVED
TO THE WORLD
AT THE
MASS. GENERAL HOSPITAL
IN BOSTON,
OCTOBER, A. D. MDCCCXLVI.

"NEITHER SHALL THERE BE
ANY MORE PAIN"—REVELATION.

IN GRATITUDE
FOR THE RELIEF
OF HUMAN SUFFERING
BY THE
INHALING OF ETHER
A CITIZEN OF BOSTON
HAS ERECTED
THIS MONUMENT.
A. D. MDCCCLXVII.

"THIS ALSO COMETH FORTH
FROM THE LORD OF HOSTS
WHICH IS WONDERFUL
IN COUNSEL
AND EXCELLENT
IN WORKING."
—ISAIAH.

The celebrated sculptor, Truman H. Bartlett, says of this statue: "It produces an excellent effect as a whole." The large number of visitors proves that the work is interesting in itself, as well as for the important discovery it commemorates, the illustration of the parable appealing to the sentiment of all.

Everett Statue. (1867). Public Garden, near Beacon Street. This statue, in bronze, by William W. Story, was unveiled November, 1867. It has the merit of bearing the closest resemblance to Everett in features, although the pose has been severely criticised. It is said that the right arm was placed in an upright position at the wish of the committee having in charge the work of having it designed, and against the desire of the artist. Bartlett says of it: "It is the only portrait-statue in Boston that has a defined and undistracted intention as the basis and structure of its composition." Wendell Phillips wrote of this celebrated statue as follows: "And so we come in our walk to Everett, in trousers too large for him, and a frockcoat which he has slightly outgrown. It requires consummate genius to manage the modern costume. But this figure also seems toppling over backwards, as, with more energy than Everett ever showed in his lifetime, he exclaims, '*That is the road to Brighton!*' pointing with lifted arm and wide-spread fingers to that centre of beef and the races. Story's friends say *he* never lifted that weary arm, but yielded to a committee's urging, as no true artist ever should do."

Flora Statue. (1865). An ideal statue of Flora, by Martin Milmore, in granite, ornaments the façade of the Building of the Massachusetts Horticultural Society, at the corner of Tremont and Bromfield Streets.

Franklin Statue. (1856). City Hall Yard, School Street. This, the first statue to be placed in the public squares and parks of the city, was unveiled Sept. 17, 1856. Richard S. Greenough, the famous Boston artist, was its designer. Upon the sides of the pedestal are bas-reliefs illustrating events in Franklin's career. Bartlett considers the pose "happy, human and effective." Wendell Phillips, however, thought it represented a "*dilapidated roue!*" This statue (whatever may be its artistic shortcomings) owing to its proximity to one of the most largely-travelled thoroughfares in the city, is almost constantly an object of great interest to numbers of persons, and it is seldom that it is not surrounded by a score of strangers.

Garrison Statue. (1886). A bronze Statue of William Lloyd Garrison, the famous anti-slavery agitator of Boston, was placed on the Commonwealth Avenue Parkway, May 13, 1886, without any formal services. It stands between Dartmouth and Exeter Streets, in front of the Hotel Vendome. The statue is of colossal size, and represents Garrison seated in his chair, his head turned slightly to the right, and uncovered. In his right hand are some sheets of manuscript. The face is a good likeness of the celebrated reformer, the pose is easy, and the work is strong, simple and natural. It is the largest piece of casting ever done in America in one piece, the weight being 2600 pounds. The inscriptions are as follows:

WILLIAM LLOYD GARRISON.
1805 — 1879

I AM IN EARNEST—I WILL NOT EQUIVOCATE—I WILL NOT EXCUSE—I WILL NOT RETREAT A SINGLE INCH, AND I WILL BE HEARD.

MY COUNTRY IS THE WORLD;
MY COUNTRYMEN ARE
ALL MANKIND.

Glover Statue. (1875). Standing on the Commonwealth Avenue Parkway is the celebrated John Glover statue, which has attracted so much attention from those interested in sculpture. It is of bronze, and the artist, Martin Milmore, has here exhibited to the fullest extent his disregard of old traditions and ventured upon new ground in his strong and heroic treatment. Gen. Glover commanded a regiment formed in Essex County during the Revolution. The statue was the gift of Benjamin Tyler Reed. Its pedestal bears the following inscription:

> JOHN GLOVER,
> OF MARBLEHEAD,
> A SOLDIER OF THE REVOLUTION.
>
> HE COMMANDED A REGIMENT
> OF ONE THOUSAND MEN
> RAISED IN THAT TOWN, KNOWN
> AS THE MARINE REGIMENT,
> AND ENLISTED TO SERVE
> THROUGH THE WAR;
> HE JOINED THE CAMP
> AT CAMBRIDGE, JUNE 22, 1775,
> AND RENDERED DISTINGUISHED
> SERVICE IN TRANSPORTING
> THE ARMY FROM BROOKLYN
> TO NEW YORK, AUG. 28, 1776,
> AND ACROSS THE DELAWARE,
> DEC. 25, 1776.
> HE WAS APPOINTED BY
> THE CONTINENTAL CONGRESS
> A BRIGADIER GENERAL
> FEB. 21, 1777,
> BY HIS COURAGE, ENERGY,
> MILITARY TALENT AND
> PATRIOTISM HE SECURED
> THE CONFIDENCE OF
> WASHINGTON
> AND THE GRATITUDE
> OF HIS COUNTRY.
> Born, Nov. 5, 1732.
> Died, Jan. 30, 1797.

The statue was erected in 1875.

Hamilton Statue. (1865). The first of the statues to be placed on Commonwealth Avenue Parkway was that of Alexander Hamilton. It is said to have been the first statue to be made of granite. It was the work of William Rimmer. The following are the inscriptions upon the pedestal:

> ALEXANDER HAMILTON,
> BORN IN THE ISLAND OF
> NEVIS, WEST INDIES,
> 11 JANUARY 1757.
> DIED IN NEW YORK
> 12 JULY 1804.
>
> ORATOR, WRITER, SOLDIER,
> JURIST, FINANCIER.
> ALTHOUGH HIS PARTICULAR
> PROVINCE WAS THE TREASURY,
> HIS GENIUS PERVADED THE
> WHOLE ADMINISTRATION
> OF WASHINGTON.

The Hamilton statue was presented to the city by Thomas Lee, and was placed in its present position in 1865. It is much visited by students of the late Dr. Rimmer, the sculptor, and by many who admire the treatment of the subject.

Harvard Monument. (1828). Grateful graduates of Harvard University erected in the old graveyard in the Charlestown District—near the State Prison—a shaft of granite to the memory of John Harvard, the founder of the great University bearing his name. The shaft is inscribed as follows:

> ON THE TWENTY-SIXTH DAY
> SEPTEMBER, A. D. 1828
> THIS STONE WAS ERECTED
> BY THE GRADUATES
> OF THE
> UNIVERSITY AT CAMBRIDGE
> IN HONOR OF
> ITS FOUNDER,
> WHO DIED AT CHARLESTOWN,
> ON THE TWENTY-SIXTH DAY
> SEPTEMBER, A. D. 1638.

Edward Everett delivered the oration at the dedication of this monument.

Lincoln Bust. Doric Hall, State House. A bust of the late President Lincoln.

Lincoln Statue. (1879). Abraham Lincoln. (See *Emancipation Group*).

Lyman Fountain. (1885). Eaton Square, Meeting-House Hill, Dorchester District. This elegant fountain—the largest and most imposing in or about Boston—was erected in honor of Theodore Lyman, Jr., Mayor of Boston 1834-5. Designed and constructed by M. D. Jones. It is 28 feet high. It is built of bronzed iron. At the base are four figures representing the seasons. A figure, of zinc, illustrating Leda and the Swan, surmounts the structure. The fountain cost $7,000. Erected by means of a subscription. Dedicated, with musical and oratorical exercises, Oct. 24, 1885.

Mann Statue. (1865). Terrace of State House Grounds, Beacon Street. This bronze statue of Horace Mann, the most conspicuous figure in the development of the general educational system of Massachusetts, was the work of Emma Stebbins, an American artist. The cost of the statue was defrayed by a subscription of the teachers and children of the public schools of the State, who presented it to the Commonwealth in 1865. The dedication addresses were made by Samuel G. Howe, John A. Andrew and others. Criticism on this statue is at variance. Truman Bartlett thinks "There is a great deal of earnest thought and work in the execution." Arthur Dexter considers it "a mass of bad drapery." It is visited much by students of art from various parts of the country, as are the numerous other statues and monuments of the city.

Military Memorial. Mount Hope Cemetery. This is formed of heavy ordnance, contributed by the United States Government. On a stone base, of triangular shape, are placed three cannons, arranged as a pyramid, supporting a fourth cannon, while underneath is a pyramid of cannon balls. Charles Russell Lowell Post 7, Grand Army of the Republic, erected the Memorial.

Martineau (Harriet) Statue. By Anne Whitney. This statue, placed in the Old South Church some time since, is now at Wellesley College.

Orpheus Statue. (1844). Museum of Fine Arts, St. James av. An ideal statue of great beauty. Through the efforts of Charles Sumner a sum of money was subscribed and sent to Thomas Crawford, then a needy and struggling American artist at Rome, with a commission for the Orpheus. It was the first encouraging hand held out to the young artist, and he keenly appreciated it. The Orpheus is one of the best works of any American artist, and together with his Beethoven, at Boston Music Hall, will keep Crawford's memory green in the hearts of his countrymen. The Orpheus statue was purchased in 1844.

Otis Statue. Chapel, Mount Auburn, Cambridge. A statue of James Otis, the patriot.

Pomona Statue. (1865). Upon the Horticultural Society's Building, at 100 Tremont Street, corner of Bromfield Street, is an ideal statue of Pomona, by the late Martin Milmore, forming one of a group of three, namely, Ceres, Flora and Pomona.

Prescott Statue. (1881). On the Bunker Hill Monument grounds, in the Charlestown District, is a striking statue of Colonel William Prescott, by W. W. Story. It is erected on the spot where the hero is supposed to have stood when he spoke the memorable caution to his men: "Don't fire until you can see the whites of their eyes!" The statue was erected June 17, 1881. Robert C. Winthrop was the orator at the unveiling. The front panel of the pedestal is inscribed:

COLONEL
WILLIAM PRESCOTT,
JUNE 17, 1775.

Quincy Statue. (1879). City Hall Enclosure, School Street. By Thomas Ball. A bronze statue of Josiah Quincy, second Mayor of Boston (1823), and one of the most progressive men the city has ever possessed. It was owing to his enterprise that Quincy Market was established, and many other improvements had their inception in his far-seeing mind. Had all of his suggestions been carried out, Boston would have been a far handsomer city even than it is to-day. It was his wish to have laid out a wide avenue from Roxbury Neck to Chelsea Ferry, which would have been the Washington Street, instead of the narrow, crooked thoroughfare in which people, cars and cabs to-day get almost hopelessly and inextricably "blocked" at nearly every hour of the day; and what is to be done there in ten years from now in the way of transit nobody will dare to predict, unless the method of London is followed. Quincy foresaw that Boston was to become a great metropolis, and endeavored to make others realize it, but he could not break the shell of conservatism which has always enclosed Boston, and which still impedes its natural progress. This fine statue portrays the able Mayor at his best, and represents him at a time when he said, in his inaugural address: "The destinies of the City of Boston are of a nature too plain to be denied or misconceived. The prognostics of its future greatness are written on the face of Nature too legibly and too indelibly to be mistaken. The indications are apparent from the location of our city, from its harbor, and its relative position among rival towns and cities; above all from the character of its inhabitants, and the singular degree of enterprise and intelligence which are diffused through every class of its citizens."

Roxbury Soldiers' Monument. (1867). Forest Hills Cemetery. A bronze statue; the work of Martin Milmore. It was cast at Chicopee.

Soldiers' Monument. Mount Hope Cemetery. Erected by the City of Boston to commemorate the services of her fallen heroes.

Sphinx. Mount Auburn, Cambridge. One of the greatest works of one of Boston's famous sculptors, the late Martin Milmore, and one that will, of itself, long perpetuate his name, is the widely-celebrated Sphinx, placed in Mount Auburn. Directly in front of the Chapel, it stands as a permanent memorial of the War of the Rebellion. A writer has said: "It is an Egyptian symbol of might and intelligence combined; but, in its human features, modern or American, not brooding on Death, but looking forward to the larger life." Its inscription is:

AMERICAN UNION PRESERVED;
AFRICAN SLAVERY DESTROYED
BY THE UPRISING OF
A GREAT PEOPLE;
BY THE BLOOD OF
FALLEN HEROES.

Story Statue. Chapel, Mount Auburn, Cambridge. A marble statue of Joseph Story, the eminent jurist, designed and executed by his son. In a sitting position, the left hand holding a book, and the right hand slightly raised.

Sumner Bust. Doric Hall, State House, Beacon Street. A bust of the late Charles Sumner.

Sumner Statue. (1878). Public Garden, near Boylston Street, opposite Church Street. This statue, of bronze, by Thomas Ball, was placed here Dec. 23, 1878. Its cost was $15,000. Among the artists who competed for the three prizes of $500 each were Thomas Ball, Anne Whitney and Martin Milmore, each receiving one, and the design of Mr. Ball was selected as that most pleasing to the committee having in charge the erection of the statue. Wendell Phillips had his fling at this statue, but his "criticism" was so hasty and so much overdrawn that it had the effect of creating sympathy and fair treatment for the artist and of acting as a boomerang on the writer: "If this bronze pyramid on Boylston Street be a cask made of staves, why is it set on human legs? and if it is really Sumner, why do his chest and shoulders rise out of a barrel? Is his broadcloth new felt, too stiff for folds, or is he dressed in shoe-leather? That matters little, however. But no angry Southerner would have needed to smite those overfed cheeks, which may have faced many a snowstorm on the locomotive, or many a Northeaster on our coast, but surely must have been far too innocent of thought and passion ever to anger senates or rouse nations to war." Eminent European critics have highly praised this statue.

Venus Statue. On the Public Garden, near the Arlington Street entrance, from Commonwealth Avenue Parkway, is a marble statue of Venus,— sometimes called "The Maid-of-the-Mist"—standing in one of the fountain-basins near the equestrian statue of Washington. When the water is let into the fountain a shower of spray is made to fall upon the pretty statue, making a very pleasing effect. On summer days it is quite a centre of attractions to the throngs of people who visit this great pleasure garden.

Washington Equestrian Statue. (1869). Public Garden, facing the Arlington Street entrance, opposite the Commonwealth Avenue Parkway. Among the earliest promoters of the movement to erect this statue, which is said by competent art critics to be the most artistic work of the kind on the continent, was William Willard, the eminent portrait painter. Robert C. Winthrop handed over the proceeds of an oration at Boston Music Hall, as a contribution to the fund, in 1859; the city donated $10,000; a great fair was held in aid of the project, and the balance remaining after the purchase of the Everett statue— $5,000—being added, the sum was ample for its cost. The commission for its execution was given to Thomas Ball, Boston's famous sculptor, in 1859, and on July 3, 1869, it was unveiled to the gaze of admiring thousands. In conception, freedom, strength, and all the elements that combine to form a complete artistic whole, this statue may unreservedly be ranked among the world's greatest works of art, and Boston was indeed fortunate in securing so magnificent a creation. Students of what is really true and great in sculpture may here find a model worthy of their best thoughts and aspirations. This colossal and imposing work will be better appreciated day by day and year by year, as the artistic sense of the general public becomes more highly educated and refined, and its many beauties will appear correspondingly conspicuous. Truman Bartlett, himself a sculptor of eminence, and therefore the better qualified to judge of the efforts of another in the same field of art, says this statue is "the most important and best specimen of monumental decoration in New England. The horse has a personality; the ears being thrown forward, the eyes and action of the head indicating that he is attracted by some object. This personality is an essential quality in a composition like this. Whatever may be said against this statue from the standpoint of the great equestrian statues of the world, it is certain that as time goes on, and the circumstances surrounding its production are fully understood, it will lose neither interest nor admiration." As an amusing foil to this magnanimous and well-grounded criticism of a brother-artist, let us turn to the scolding paragraph of Wendell Phillips, the beloved late silver-voiced orator, who placed on record the following diatribe, which is certainly antagonistic to the criticism of every real artist who has written of this grand work: "But who is this riding-master, on a really good horse, staring so heroically up Commonwealth Avenue? Washington? Well, then, my worthy George, drop your legs closer to your horse's side; it must fatigue you to hold them off at that painful distance. Rest yourself, General; subside for a moment, as you used to do at Mount Vernon, into the easy *pose* of a gentleman; don't oblige us to fancy you are exhibiting, and rather caricaturing, a model 'seat' for the guidance of some slow pupil. Cannot you see, right in front of you, Rimmer's Hamilton? Let that teach you the majesty of repose." It is a matter of congratulation that this statue was in every respect a home product. Designed and modelled by a Boston artist (in a studio in the rear of the Chickering Pianoforte Manufactory, Tremont Street), it was cast by the Ames Company, of Chicopee, in this State, and it is equally as satisfactory as any work from foreign countries.

Washington Statue. (1858). Doric Hall, State House, Beacon Street. By Chantrey. This is one of the best statues to be seen in Boston. There is a dignity, strength and repose blended in its composition that fully satisfies the artistic sense. The work was obtained through the efforts of the Washington Monument Association, who placed it here.

Webster Statue. (1859). Terrace of State House Grounds, Beacon Street. This statue, of bronze, heroic size, was the work of Hiram Powers, the features having been modelled from life by the artist. Edward Everett, who delivered the oration at the unveiling of this statue, said: "His imperial gaze is directed, with the hopes of the country, to the boundless West." The work cost $10,000. It was dedicated Sept. 17, 1859. Whatever may be its blemishes, it has, at least, the merit of excellence as a portrait. Truman Bartlett, in his "Civic Monuments," says of this work: "It is an illustrative statue in its fullest and nearly its flattest sense. It is as near a work of art as bronze can make it." Wendell Phillips said of it, in his vigorous style: "Then, Webster, that mass of ugly iron at the State House! which cheers us as we climb those endless steps, robbing the effort of half its weariness by resting us with a laugh; of which a journal said, with undue frankness, that Everett, well knowing how hideous it was, let it be raised to revenge himself on the man who overshadowed and eclipsed him! But they have supplied him with a foil, which half redeems its shapelessness. It is Horace Mann, waked up so suddenly that in his hurry he has brought half his bed-clothes clinging to his legs and arms." It is easy to ridicule, and the greater the work, the more strong and original the thought, the more easily may a critic who has no practical knowledge of the art, call the attention of the public to what seems absurd, but what is often an attempt on the part of the artist to get out of the beaten track.

West Roxbury Soldiers' Monument. (1871). Corner of Centre and South Streets, Jamaica Plain, West Roxbury District. A Gothic monument of granite, designed by W. W. Lummus. Upon the monument are inscribed the names of Lincoln, Andrew, Thomas and Farragut. The structure is 34 feet high. It is surmounted by a statue of a soldier. Rev. James Freeman Clarke delivered a memorial address at its dedication, Sept. 14, 1871.

Will-o-the-Wisp. Museum of Fine Arts, St. James Avenue. By Harriet Hosmer.

Wilson Bust. Doric Hall, State House, Beacon Street. A bust of the late Henry Wilson.

Winthrop Statue. (1880). Scollay Square. Placed in one of the most crowded squares in the city, where one who wishes to pause and look at it is in danger of being run over by street cars or cabs, stands the statue of Governor John Winthrop, by Richard S. Greenough. It is of bronze. The inscriptions upon its pedestal are in the following simple and modest words:

JOHN WINTHROP.
FOUNDER OF BOSTON,
17 SEPTEMBER, 1630.

FIRST PRESIDENT
OF THE
NEW ENGLAND CONFEDERATION,
THE
EARLIEST AMERICAN UNION.

GOVERNOR OF
MASSACHUSETTS,
30 OCTOBER, 1629.
ARRIVED
WITH THE CHARTER,
22 JUNE, 1630.

HE WAS BORN
NEAR GROTON,
SUFFOLK, ENGLAND,
22 JANUARY, 1588.
HE DIED IN
BOSTON,
5 APRIL, 1649.

The cost of the statue was $7,300. It was unveiled Sept. 17, 1880.

Franklin Monument. Granary Burying Ground, Tremont Street, opposite Bromfield Street. This monument has the following inscription, composed by Benjamin Franklin:

JOSIAH FRANKLIN
AND ABIAH, HIS WIFE
LIE HERE INTERRED.
THEY LIVED LOVINGLY TOGETHER IN
WEDLOCK FIFTY-FIVE YEARS, AND
WITHOUT AN ESTATE, OR ANY GAINFUL
EMPLOYMENT, BY CONSTANT LABOUR
AND HONEST INDUSTRY, MAINTAINED
A LARGE FAMILY COMFORTABLY, AND
BROUGHT UP THIRTEEN CHILDREN
AND SEVEN GRANDCHILDREN RESPECTABLY. FROM THIS INSTANCE, READER, BE ENCOURAGED TO DILIGENCE IN THY CALLING, AND DISTRUST NOT PROVIDENCE.
HE WAS A PIOUS AND PRUDENT MAN;
SHE A DISCREET AND VIRTUOUS WOMAN.
THEIR YOUNGEST SON
IN FILIAL REGARD TO THEIR MEMORY
PLACES THIS STONE.
J. F. Born 1655 — Died 1744 — Æ 89.
A. F. —— 1667 — —— 1752 — Æ 85.

Boutwell (George S.) Bust. State Library, State House.

Franklin (Benjamin) Bust. 15 Milk Street.

Latin School Monument. Latin School Building. A marble monument, designed by Richard S. Greenough. Erected in memory of the graduates of this School who fell in the War of the Rebellion. A beautiful work of art.

Peabody (George) Bust. By Powers. Massachusetts Historical Society Rooms. 30 Tremont Street.

Scott (Sir Walter) Bust. By Chantrey. Massachusetts Historical Society Rooms. 30 Tremont Street.

Warren (William) Bust. Boston Museum.

Winthrop Statue. Chapel, Mount Auburn, Cambridge. A marble statue of Governor John Winthrop in a sitting position. By Richard S. Greenough.

Young Columbus. Museum of Fine Arts, St. James Avenue. By Giulio Monteverde.

EXPRESS OFFICES.

Principal Companies.

Adams Express Company, 38 Court st., 77 Kingston st., Lincoln st., corner Beach st., 226 Federal st.
American-European Express Company, 127 State st.
American Express Company, 40 Court sq., 43 Franklin st., 244 Washington st., 67 Devonshire st., 122 Canal st., Lincoln st., corner Kneeland st., 25 Merchants Row, 69 Kilby st.
Armstrong Transfer Company, 211 Washington st., and at the various Railway Stations
Atlas Parcel Express. (Foreign.) 105 Arch st.
Boston & Bangor Express, 76 Kingston st., 75 Kilby st., 26 Devonshire st., 1 Merchants Row.
Boston & Nashua Express, 33 Court sq.
Boston & Worcester Express, 91 Kilby st.
Canadian Express Company, 40 Court sq.
Cheney, A. W. & Co., 75 Kilby st., 135 Arch street, 25 Merchants Row, 76 Kingston st.
Eastern Express Company, (American Express Company, Proprietors, 244 Washington st., 67 Devonshire st., 122 Canal st., 25 Merchants Row.
Hoosac Tunnel Express Company, 40 Court sq., 77 Bedford st.
Hoyt & Company (Maine), 77 Kilby st., 77 Kingston st.
Merchants Express, 91 Kilby st.
New Express Company, Lincoln st.
New England Despatch Company, 26 Devonshire st., 75 Kilby st., 76 Kingston st.
New York and Boston Despatch Express Company, 105 Arch st., 25 Merchants Row.
New York and Philadelphia New Express Line, Lincoln st.
New York and New England States Express, Lincoln st.

Ocean Express (Foreign), 105 Arch st.
Snow's European Express, 40 and 42 Court st.
United States and Canada Express, 43 Franklin st., 30 Court sq., 77 Kingston st., 112 Canal st.
United States Express Company, 4 Arch st.
Wells, Fargo & Company, 244 Washington st.
Williams & Company (Foreign) 105 Arch st.

Local Expresses.

Abbott, 36 Court sq.
Abbott, 7 Merchants row (Cambridgeport)
Abbott & Co., 155 Congress st....(Beverly)
Aberle, 174 Washington st..(Charlestown)
Adams, A. W., 105 Arch st.
Adams, T. W., 26 Devonshire st.
Adams, 17 No. Market......(East Boston)
Aid, ich, 65 Lincoln st.
Alger & Co., 34 Court sq.
Allen, C. T., 26 Devonshire st....(Chelsea)
Allen, E., 34 Court sq. ....(Roxbury)
Allen & Co., 32 Court sq........(Haverhill)
Amesbury Express Company, 34 Court sq.
Andrews & Fenver, 96 Kingston st.
Austin, 78 North st............(Somerville)
Austin & Winslow, 34 Court sq.
Atwood, 77 Kingston st.
Ayer & Co., 36 Court sq........(Haverhill)
Ayer & Son, 34 Court sq......(Winchester)
Babb & Bolam, 7 Merchants Row.
Bachelder, 33 Court sq.
Bailey, 91 Kilby, 34 Court sq.
Baker, 34 Court sq............(Dedham)
Baker & Co., 34 Court sq.... (Weymouth)
Bancroft, 174 Washington st., 34 Court sq.
Barker & Tibbetts, 26 Devonshire st.
Beal, 174 Washington st......(Gloucester)
Beals, 25 Merchants Row....(Dorchester)
Beal, 34 Court sq., 75 Kilby st, (Nantasket)
Bell, 174 Washington st ....(Danvers)
Bell, 82 Bedford st.............(Roxbury)

Belatty, 77 Kingston st.
Benjamin & Vaughan, 34 Court sq.
Bettinson, 32 Court sq.
Bettis, 32 Court sq., 77 Kingston st.
Billings, 26 Devonshire st......(Brighton)
Blackall, 7 Merchants Row.
Blake & Co., 34 Court sq.
Bourke, 174 Washington st.
Bowman, 34 Court sq.
Bradford & Co., 36 Court sq.
Bragdon & Son, 36 Court sq.
Breed, J., 25 Merchants Row, 102 High st.
Brewer & Co., 36 Court sq.
Brock & Crane, 53 South Market st.
Brown's, 60 Washington st......(Chelsea)
Brooks, 34 Court sq.
Brooks & Davis, 32 Court sq.
Brooks & Co., 34 Court sq.
Buck, 38 Broad st.
Bullard, 91 Kilby, 91 Federal sts.
Burrell, 26 Devonshire st.
Butland & Son, 25 Merchants row.
Butler, 38 Broad st., 10 Faneuil Hall sq.
Buzzell, 34 Court sq.
Byam Bros., 34 Court sq., 91 Kilby st.
Calden, 25 Merchants row, 77 Kingston st.
Calley, 25 Merchants row, 41 High st.
Carter & Co., 26 Devonshire st.
Cashman, 77 Kingston st., 25 Merchants row.
Cate, 7 Merchants row, 90 Blackstone st.
Chandler & Gleason, 174 Washington st.
Chase, 91 Kilby.........(Cambridgeport)
Chase, 34 Court sq.............(Brookline)
Cheney & Son, 32 Court sq.
Childs & Kent, 75 Kilby st.
Clark, 25 Merchants row.
Cobb & Son, 25 Merchants row.
Cogswell & Co., 32 and 34 Court sq.
Collins, 81 Franklin, 12 Bromfield sts.
Connaughton, 32 Court sq.
Cook, 27 and 29 Arch st.
Coolidge, 96 Kingston st.....(Cambridgeport)
Coolidge & Holbrook, 174 Washington st.
Corson, 75 Kilby, 76 Kingston, 43 N. Market sts.
Costello, 96 Kingston st.
Coughlin, 91 Kilby, 27 N. Market sts.
Coverly, 174 Washington st.
Cox, 38 Broad, 44 N. Market sts.
Crane, H., jr., 7 Merchants row.
Critchett, 91 Kilby st., Cellar 3 Quincy Market.
Cronin, 25 Merchants row.
Cummings, 174 Washing. st., 34 Court sq.
Cunningham, 75 Kilby st......Wakefield)
Cunningham & Co., 76 Kingston st. (Medford)
Currier, 33 and 36 Court sq.........(South Boston)
Currier Bros., 36 Court sq.....(Maplewood)
Currier & Co., 132 Central st......(Everett)
Currier & Co., 36 Court sq....(Gloucester)
Cushing, 174 Washington st.
Cushing, 91 Kilby st......(East Weymouth)
Cushman & Co., 91 Kilby st., 34 Court sq.
Dame, Cellar 3 Quincy Market.
Danehy, 7 Merchants Row, 15 Blackstone st.
Dart & Co., 34 Court sq.
Davis, 33 Court sq.............(Brighton)

Davis, 24 Faneuil Hall sq.(Cambridgep't)
Davis, 25 Merchants Row..........(Lynn)
Davis, 31 North Market st.(South Boston)
Day, G. T., 25 Merchants Row.
Day, L. L., 26 Devonshire st., 44 No. Market st.
Deane, 25 Merchants Row.
Decatur, 32 Court sq., 19 Faneuil Hall sq.
Delano, 36 Court sq., 91 Kilby st., 46 No. Market st.
Dennie, 32 Court sq., 105 Arch st., 77 Kingston st.
Devir, 43 North Market st., 148 Blackstone st.
Dexter, 38 Broad st., 40 Bromfield st., 67 North st.
Dodge, 33 Court sq.
Dolhe ty & Co., 32 and 33 Court sq.
Dorchester Express Co., 32 Court sq.
Douglas, cor. Faneuil Hall Market.
Dow, 77 Kingston st.....(Cambridgeport)
Drayton, 105 Arch st.
Drew, 174 Washington st.
Dunn, 38 Faneuil Hall sq.
Durnam, 174 Washington st.
Dyer, 36 Court sq.
Eames, 34 Court sq.
Earle & Prew, 34 Court sq.
East Boston, 32 and 34 Court sq.
Eastman, 32 Court sq.
Eaton, 174 Washington st......(Needham)
Eaton, 34 Court sq............(Wakefield)
Elder, 44 North Market st.
Elms, G. W., 77 Kingston st.
Elms, R. N., 91 Kilby st., 10 Faneuil H'l sq.
Elwood, 91 Kilby st., 76 Kingston st.
Emerson, 174 Washington st.
Emerton, 26 Devonshire st.
Esau, 32 Court sq., 92 Blackstone st.
Fairbanks, 38 Broad, 38 Commercial sts.
Farrar & Co., 91 Kilby st.
Farwell, 27 North Market st.
Faunce, 174 Washington st.
Fears & Bray, 32 Court sq.
Fenner, 77 Kingston st., 25 Merchants row.
Field, 26 Devonshire st........(South End)
Fields, 25 Merchants row..........(Lynn)
Fisher, 34 Court sq............(Stoughton)
Fisher, 96 Kingston, 38 Broad st. (Wellesley)
Fisk, D. D., 82 Bedford st.
Fiske, G. W., 30 Brattle, 44 No. Market sts.
Fitch, 76 Kingston st.
Flint, 33 Court sq............(No. Reading)
Fluent, 10 Faneuil Hall sq., 102 Blackstone st.
Foster, 26 Devonshire st.
Fox, 33 Court sq.
Frye & Co.,105 Arch, 174 Washington sts.
Fuzzard, 82 Bedford st., 30 N.F.H.Market.
Gallagher, 36 Court sq., 92 Blackstone st.
Garrigan, 39 North Market st.
Garrity, 174 Washington st.
Gavett, 75 Kilby st.
Gay, 91 Kilby st., 34 Court sq.
Gerald, E., 75 Kilby st.
Gibbs & Co., 34 Court sq.
Gifford, 7 Merchants row, 76 Kingston st.
Gillett & Co., 32 Court sq.
Gilman & Co., 36 Court sq.

Glazier, 105 Arch st.
Gilmes, 96 Kingston st.
Goodwin & Co., 34 Court sq., 105 Arch st.
Gove, 174 Washington, 105 Arch, 100 High sts.
Grimes, 96 Kingston, 121 Clinton sts.
Grose, 174 Washington, 115 High sts.
Hall, 10 Faneuil Hall sq. ....(Highlands)
Harmon, 40 Fort Hill sq., 40 Merch. row.
Harris, 26 Devonshire, 18 India sts.
Hart, B.. 33 Court sq...........(W. Quincy)
Hart & Co., 75 Kilby st..........(Woburn)
Hartshorn, 174 Washington st. (Neponset)
Hartshorne, 39 and 40 Court sq....(Berlin)
Hatch, 34 Court sq..............(Belmont)
Hatch & Co.. 36 Court sq.....(Cambridge)
Hawes Brothers, 36 Court sq.
Hawkins, 174 Washington, 91 Kilby sts.
Hayes, 32 Court sq.
Hayward, 36 Batterymarch st.
Hayward & McMullen, 10 Faneuil Hall sq.
Hazen & Co., 7 Merchants row.
Henderson, C., 34 Court sq.
Henry, 36 Court sq.
Higgins, 115 Water st.
Hill, 9 Merch. row, 10 Faneuil Hall sq.
Hill & Co.. 26 Devonshire st....(Methuen)
Hill & Co., 75 Kilby st.
Hilton & Sons, 91 Kilby st.
Hobbs, 77 Kingston st.
Hollis, 33 Court sq.
Holman, 88 Faneuil Hall Market.
Holmes, 10 Faneuil Hall sq....(S. Boston)
Holmes & Co., 91 Kilby st....... (Sharon)
Holton & Co., 32 Court sq.
Hosie, 91 Kilby st.
Houghton, 34 Court sq.
Howard, 7 Merchants Row, 27 North Market st.
Howard & Co., 74 Kilby st.....(Highland)
Howe & Co., 174 Wash'gton st.(Hingham)
Howe & Co., 91 Kilby st..........(Natick)
Howes & Winchester, 33 and 36 Court sq.
Hume, 38 Broad st., 50 North Market st.
Hull, 33 Court sq.
Hunting, 174 Washington st., 34 Court sq.
Hurd, 34 and 36 Court sq.
Hussey, 35 Court sq.
Hyland, 174 Washington st.
Jackson & Co., 32 Cou.t sq.
Jenison, 34 Court sq., 91 Kilby st.
Jenkins, 36 Court sq.
Jenness & Twombly, 34 Court sq.
Jewett, 34 Court sq.
Jennings, 75 Kilby st.
Johnson, 32 Court sq., 105 Arch.(Andover)
Johnson, 38 Broad.............(Brookline)
Johnson & Co., 105 Arch st. .... (Nahant)
Jones, 91 Kilby st...(Newton Upper Falls)
Jones, 33 Court sq.............(Campello)
Jones, 26 Devonshire st.... (Charlestown)
Jones & Co., 44 No. Market st.(E. Boston)
Joslyn, 34 Court sq.............(Brockton)
Josselyn, 33 Court sq....... (No. Andover)
Kavanagh, 38 Broad st., 27 No. Market st.
Keith, 17 and 31 North Market st.
Kendall, 38 North Market st., 24 Faneuil Hall sq.
Kenney, 33 Court sq.
Kilbraith, 96 Kingston st., 223 Washington st.
King, 7 Merchants Row......(Dorchester)

King, 38 Broad st.............(Cambridge)
Knight, 27 North Market st.
Knight & Son, 27 Cornhill, 12 Bromfield st.
Lakeman, 127 Milk st., 71 Clinton st.
Lane, 174 Washington st.
Lang, 33 Court sq.
Lathrop & Keyes, 105 Arch st., 34 Court sq.
Lawrence & Co., 67 Devonshire st.
Leslie, 36 Court sq.
Libby, 26 Devonshire st.
Linnell & Co., 174 Washington st., 105 Arch st.
Litchfield, 26 Devonshire st.
Little, 33 Court sq.............(Merrimac)
Littlefield, 7 Merchants Row, 15 Oliver st.
Locke, 34 Court sq., 25 Merchants Row.
London, 33 Court sq., 96 Kingston st.
Lovejoy & Co., 33 Court sq.
Lovett, 34 Court sq.
Lowell, 91 Kilby st.
Lufkin, 36 Court sq.
Macomber, 49 Friend st.
Manchester, 7 Merchants Row.
Magee, 96 Kingston st...... (East Boston)
Magee & Co., 36 Court sq.
Marble, 34 Court sq........(North Easton)
Marean, 75 Kilby st.
Marshall, 36 Court sq..........(Rockport)
Marshall & Moulton, 32 Court sq.
Marston, 91 Kilby st.............(Medway)
Marston, 75 Kilby st.............(Danvers)
Martin, 91 Kilby st.........(East Douglas)
Martin, L., 25 Merchants Row.
McClellan, 36 Court sq., 27 No. Market st.
McConarty, 38 Broad st., 10 Faneuil Hall sq.
McCrillis, 33 Court sq.
McCuen & Davis, 105 Arch st.
McDonald, 7 Merchants Row.
McGee, 96 Kingston st.
McIntosh, 174 Washington st.
McKee, 34 Court sq.
Merrill, 35 Merchants Row.. (Beachmont)
Merrill & Co., 33 Court sq.......(Nashua)
Merritt, C. C., 174 Washington st.
Merritt & Co., 25 Merchants Row.
Messenger, 91 Kilby st.. 1 Merchants Row.
Messer, 10 Faneuil Hall sq.
Meserve, 32 Court sq.
Middleton, 33 Court sq., 91 Kilby st.
Milliken, 26 Devonshire st., 82 Bedford st.
Mitchell, 7 Merchants Row.
Moody, 7 Merchants Row.
Moore, 26 Devonshire st.
Morrill & Co., 76 Kingston st.
Morrison, 36 Court sq., 118 Blackstone st.
Morse, 105 Arch st.
Moses, 31 Brattle st., 10 Faneuil Hall sq.
Moulton, 91 Kilby st.............. (Salem)
Moulton, 26 Devonshire st.(No. Weymouth)
Munroe & Arnold, 174 Washington st.
Nay, 38 Broad st.
Neal, 75 Kilby st.
Needham, 105 Arch st.
Newhall & Marston, 34 Court sq.
Newton, 39 Court sq.
Niles & Co., 34 Court sq.
Norton, 81 Blackstone st., 110 State st.
North Cambridge Express, 33 Court sq.
Noyes & Co., 33 Court sq., 105 Arch st.
O'Brien, 75 and 91 Kilby st. ......(Malden)
Osborn, 107 Commercial st.

Page & Saville, 75 Kilby st., 33 Court sq.
Paine, 174 Washington st....(Marblehead)
Paine, 174 Washington st... (Charlestown)
Parker, 34 Court sq............ (Medfield)
Parker, 75 Kilby st....(West Roxbury and Roslindale)
Parker, 91 Kilby, 7 South Market sts. (Saugus),
Parmenter, 44 North Market st.
Patterson, 26 Devonshire st.
Pearson, 33 Court sq.
Penniman, 174 Washington st.....(South Abington)
Penniman & Co., 34 Court sq.....(Lowell
Perham, 75 Kilby st.
Perkins & Co., 33 Court sq.(Exeter, N.H.
Perry, 36 Court sq., 91 Kilby st.
Peters, 33 Court sq.
Pettengill, 32 Court, 91 Kilby sts.
Peyser, 34 and 36 Court sq.
Pickett, 91 Kilby st.
Pierce, 28 and 40 Court st.
Pierce, 65 Lincoln st........(S. Boston)
Pierce, 36 Court sq.............(Duxbury)
Pinkham, 75 Kilby st.
Plumer & Fogg, 105 Arch st., 33 Court sq.
Polson & Co., 32 Court sq.
Pope, 38 Broad, 30 Brattle sts.
Pratt, 75 Kilby st..............(Campello)
Pratt & Babb, 32 and 34 Court sq.
Pratt & Co., 34 Court sq.
Pressey, 32 Court sq.
Presson, 32 and 34 Court sq.
Prevaux, 33 Court sq., 25 Merchants row.
Prime, 33 Court sq.
Prince, 34 Court sq., 77 Kingston st.
Proctor, 32 Court sq.
Purcell & Fowle, 43 North Market st.
Randall, 174 Washington st....(Rockland)
Razor & Sanborn, 91 Kilby st.
Readel, 25 Merchants Row.
Reed & Co., 33 Court sq.
Rendall & Howard, 75 Kilby st.
Rich, 38 Broad st.
Richardson, W. H., 31 Court sq.
Riley, 36 Court sq., 50 No. Market st.
Robbins, 91 Kilby st., 45 No. Market st.
Roberts, 34 Court sq.
Robinson, 34 Court sq.
Rollins, 36 Court sq......(Cambridgeport)
Rollins, 36 Court sq...........(Mattapan)
Rollins, 91 Kilby, 90 High, (W. Newbury)
Russell, Sayward & Co., 34 Court sq.
Ryan & Co., 36 Court sq.
Safford, 25 Merchants Row, 31 North Market st.
Saunders & Son, 91 Kilby st., 34 Court sq.
Savage & Son, 34 Court sq.
Savory & Co., 32 and 34 Court sq.
Sawin, 33 and 34 Court sq.
Sawyer, 174 Washington st.
Seaver, 76 Kingston st.
Shaughnessy, 31 North Market st.
Shaw, 77 Kingston st........(Watertown)
Shaw, 27 N. Market st....(West Medford)
Sherburne & Wishart, 96 Kingston st.
Simonds, C. J., 7 Merchants Row(H'hl'ds)
Simonds, C. S., (Fitchburg R. R. Station)
Simpson, 174 Washington st.
Skillings, 36 Court sq.
Skinner, 15 Devonshire st.
Smith, A. D., 91 Kilby st.
Smith, D. B., 32 Court sq..........(Exeter)
Smith, H. C., 34 Court sq....(Manchester)
Smith, 75 Kilby st..............(Medford)
Smith & Co., 91 Kilby st......(Fitchburg)
Smith & Co., 33 Court sq.....(Lexington)
Smith & Welch, 25 Merchants Row.
Somes, 10 Faneuil Hall sq., 33 Bedford st.
Soule, 77 Kingston st., 10 Faneuil Hall sq.
Spooner, 33 Court sq., 44 No. Market st.
Stilphen & Co., 30 Brattle st.
Stone, 33 Court sq., 17 Chauncy st.
Stout, 118 Blackstone st.
Straw, 33 Court sq.
Sweet, 75 Kilby st.
Swett, 75 Kilby st.
Tainter, E., 105 Arch st.
Tarbox, 7 Merchants Row.
Tay, 38 Broad st.
Taylor, 174 Washington st... (Marshfield)
Taylor, 38 Broad st........ (South Boston)
Taylor, 34 Court sq.............(Woburn)
Tenny, 32 Court sq.
Tewksbury Bros., 105 Arch st.
Tewksbury, 105 Arch st....(East Boston)
Thayer, 174 Washington st., 91 Kilby st.
Thompson, 96 Kingston st.
Thorpe, 91 Kilby st., 110 Union st., 82 Bedford st.
Thurston, 174 Washington st.
Townsend, 32 Court sq.
Tracy, 174 Washington st.
Trask, 91 Kilby st., 105 Arch st.(Gloucest'r)
Trowbridge, 34 Court sq.
Twombly, 10 Faneuil Hall sq.
Vance, 174 Washington st.
Wadsworth, 75 Kilby st.
Walker, 105 Arch st., 25 Merchants Row.
Ward, 7 Merchants Row.
Warner, 36 Court sq.
Watson, 36 Court sq.
Webb, 26 Devonshire st.
Weeks & Co., 174 Washington st.
Weeks & Kent, 34 Court sq.
Welch, 17 North Market st.
Wells & Co., 32 and 34 Court sq.
Wentworth & Lord, 91 Kilby, 60 Union sts.
Weston, 34 Court sq.
Whall, 91 Kilby st., 34 Court sq., 105 Arch st.
Wheeler & Co., 33 Court sq.
White, 36 Court sq............(Stoneham)
Whitney, 174 Washington st...(Norwood)
Whitney, 36 Court sq........... (Malden)
Wilcomb, 32 Court sq., 105 Ar. E. st.
Williams, 31 Court sq.
Willis & Beal, 77 Kingston st.
Winn, 34 and 36 Court sq......(Winthrop)
Winn, W. N., 33 Court sq.....(Arlington)
Winslow & Co., 34 Court sq.,(Westboro')
Winslow, 105 Arch st., 75 Kilby st.(Quincy)
Winslow, 96 Kingston st........(Walpole)
Woodbridge, 25 Merchants Row.
Woodsum, 174 Washington st., 14 High st.
Wright, 26 Devonshire st.
Yeaton, 96 Kingston st., 30 Brattle st.

LIBRARIES AND READING ROOMS.

No City in America compares with Boston in the number, extent and value of its public and private libraries. Upon meeting frequently in Boston a gentleman of literary taste, a resident of New York, we asked him why he came to Boston so often. His reply was: "Boston's great libraries bring me here. I cannot find the works I desire to consult in any other libraries in the United States. The people of Boston cannot fully realize what a grand treasure-house of literature they possess in the Public Library, and the great Free Library of Harvard University has a completeness and system that is amazing to a New Yorker, accustomed to meagre facilities in this direction. I can now easily comprehend why the people of Boston and vicinity are endowed with a more general air of culture than other communities, and the reason is obvious why Boston has become the seat of so many great educational institutions. Colleges and libraries are usually to be found in juxtaposition, and in both of these educators Boston is immeasurably in advance of the rest of the United States."

Boston Public Library. (Free).

(1854). 46 Boylston Street, near Tremont Street. This is the largest free-circulation Library in the country. It contains over a million books and pamphlets, the bound volumes alone numbering nearly half a million, or in actual figures, 4,5,000. But it is not merely for its size that it is remarkable; its value lies in the character of its books, their variety and completeness upon subjects of interest to thinkers and educators, their rarity and usefulness. It is very easy to accumulate books, and especially cheap volumes of American manufacture, but to carefully select a library of works, in all languages, with as much taste, knowledge and caution as one would get together in a private collection for a scholar's use is a more difficult task. The latter, however, is what has been done in the case of the Boston Public Library, and it has been well done. In fact, the nucleus of this great collection was actually the combined private libraries of eminent scholars, while the large and valual le libraries of Nathaniel Bowditch, Theodore Parker (11,061 volumes, mostly rare works), Geo. Ticknor (a famous collection of Spanish and Portuguese works gathered at great expense and labor during the lifetime of the historian, together with other volumes, making about 8,000 in all), Thomas Prince (rich in rare New England Histories), Thomas P. Barton (comprising the largest and most complete collection of Shaksperian literature, 12,000 volumes), and numerous others. Donations in money and bequests have been extremely large. Joshua Bates gave $50,000 in cash (and $50,000 worth of books); Jonathan Phillips, $30,000; Abbott Lawrence, $10,000, and others have been generous in their gifts. The li rary, in 1854, was opened in Mason Street. In 1858 it was removed to its present building, which cost to construct nearly $400,000. On the lower floor are a distributing room, the lower library-room, two free reading-rooms and an art gallery; on the second floor is the large and elegant room devoted mainly to the reference library, named Bates Hall, in compliment to Joshua Bates, one of its most liberal donors. In the reading-room on the lower floor one may consult almost any magazine or periodical published abroad or at home. Books in Bates Hall may be read within the building by any one, while for the privilege of taking volumes home it is simply necessary for any resident of Boston above the age of 16 to subscribe to certain reasonable rules. The Library is open to all.

Central Library.

The Central Library is open every week day (except holidays) from 9 to 9. Bates Hall Reference Library is open, October to April, from 9 to 6 o'clock; April to September, 9 to 7 o'clock, on week-days. The reading-room is open every day in the year *including Sundays*, excepting on legal holidays, till 10 p. m. There are fourteen branches and deliveries of the Public Library, the names and locations of which are appended.

Bates Hall Desk Works of Reference.

For the convenience of visitors to the Public Library we subjoin a complete list of the standard works of reference which may be consulted at the Desk of Bates Hall:

Abbott's Law Dictionary.
Adams, C. K......... Manual of Historical Literature.
Adler, Dictionary of German and English
Allen....... American Biographical Dict.
Allibone........... Dictionary of Authors
American Almanac.
American Encyclopædia.
Annual Cyclopædia.
Andrews.......... Latin-English Lexicon
Anthon............ Classical Dictionary
Appleton, Cyclopædia of Applied Mechs.
Appleton........ Dictionary of Mechanics
Atlantic Monthly.................. Index

Bartlett, John........Familiar Quotations
Bartlett.....Dictionary of Americanisms
Best Reading......................Perkins
Bible.
Bibliotheca Sacra..................Index
Blackwood's Magazine.............Index
Blake............Dictionary of Biography
Boston Public Library Bulletins.
Boston Public Library,ForeignCatalogues
Boston Revised Ordinances.
Boston Statutes and Ordinances.
Brewer..............Reader's Handbook.
Bryan.............Dictionary of Painters
Burke............United States Peerage
Cassell.........Biographical Dictionary
Chambers'......Encyclopædia and Atlas
Chambers'....Information for the People
Christian Examiner................Index
Clarke......Concordance to Shakspeare
Colange............United States Gazeteer
Colange...Zell's U. S. Business Directory
Colton's Atlas of the World.
Cruden.................... Concordance
Cyclopædia of Commerce.........Homans
Drake..............American Biography
Dunglison........ Medical Dictionary
Duyckinck......Cyclo. of Am. Liter. ture
Eclectic Magazine.................Index
Eggleston......How to Educate Yourself
Encyclopædia Americana.
Encyclopædia Brittanica.
English History Notes.
Ewald.....Last Century of Univ. History
Fairholt........Dictionary of Art Terms
French Dictionary.
Gazeteer of the World.
German Dictionary................Adler
Globe Encyclopædia.
Greek Lexicon.
Hale......Biog. of Distinguished Women
Harper's Magazine.................Index
Harvard University Catalogue.
Haydn........... Un. Index of Biography
Haydn.................Book of Dignities
Haydn............ ...Dictionary of Dates
Hole............Biographical Dictionary
Imperial Dict. of Univ. Biography.
International Review..............Index
Irving.............Annals of Our Times
Italian Dictionary.
Johnson's Atlas of the World.
Johnson's Cyclopædia.
Johnson............Gazeteer of the World
Journal of Archæological Assoc'n.
Kitto Cyclo. of Biblical Literature.
Knight........Am. Mechanical Dictionary
Knight........Cyclo. of Arts and Science
Knight..............Cyclo. of Biography
Knight.............Cyclo. of Geography
Knight.........Cyclo. of Natural History
Latin Lexicons...........(Smith) (Andrew)
Law Dictionary..................Abbott
Library Atlas.
Lippincott's Biographical Dictionary.
Lippincott's Magazine.............Index
Littell's Living Age...............Index
Littré Dictiomaire Francaise.
Lucas Wörtezbuch..............(Ger-Eng).
MacClintock Cyclo. of Biblical Lit.
MacCulloch..........Geographical Dict.
MacPherson........Handbook of Politics
Martin.....Handbook of Contemp. Biog.

Massachusetts.................Atlas of
Massachusetts Census.
Massachusetts General Statutes.
Massachusetts Public Statutes.
Massachusetts Revised Statutes.
Massachusetts Special Statutes.
Medical Dictionary.
Meyer's Konversations.
Moore..............Cyclopædia of Music
Nation............................Index
New Englander....................Index
North American Review...........Index
Notes and Queries................Index
Penny Encyclopædia.
Perkins...................Best Reading
Poetical Concordance.
Political Register.
Popular Science Monthly ....Index
Pich......Dict. Roman and Greek Antiq.
Rowell...American Newspaper Directory
Scribner's Monthly................Index
Scudder........Cat. of Scientific Serials
Smith...................Bible Dictionary
Smith...............Classical Dictionary
Smith......Dict. Greek and Roman Biog.
Smith....Dict. Greek and Roman Antiq.
Smith............Dict. of Christian Antiq.
Smith..Dict. of Greek and Roman Geog.
Smith..........English-Latin Dictionary
Smith....Glossary of Terms and Phrases
Smith.........Latin-English Dictionary
Spamer Illus. Handel's-Lexikon.
Spamer Illus. Conversations-Lexikon.
Spanish Dictionary.
Statesman's Year Book.
Thomas.......Comp. Dict. of Biography
Thomas......Univ. Dict. of Biography
Ticknor Catalogue.
Tomlinson Cyclo. of Useful Arts.
Tosti Engravings..............Catalogue
United States Census................1880
U. S. Revised Statutes.
U. S. Business Directory.
Ure................Dictionary of Arts
Velasquez............Spanish Dictionary
Watts............Dictionary of Chemistry
Webster's Dictionary of Eng. Language
Wheeler..............Familiar Allusions
Wheeler........Noted Names of Fiction
Wheeler...................Who wrote it?
Winsor...Reader's Hand-book of Revol'n
Worcester's Dictionary of Eng. Language.

Brighton Branch Free Library. (1874). Rockland Street. 15,000 volumes.

Charlestown Franch Free Library. City Hall Building, Charlestown District. 25,000 volumes.

Dorchester Branch Free Library. Field's Corner, Dorchester District. 12,000 volumes.

Dorchester Lower Mills Branch Free Library.

East Boston Branch Free Library. (1870). Meridian st. 12,000 volumes.

Jamaica Plain Branch Free Library. (1877). Curtis Hall. 9,000 volumes.

Mattapan Branch Free Library.

Neponset Branch Free Library.

North End Branch Free Library. (1882). School Building, Parmenter Street.

Roslindale Branch Free Library. (1878). Florence Street.

Roxbury Branch Free Library. (1873). Corner of Millmont Street and Lambert Avenue. 20,000 volumes.

South Boston Branch Free Library. (1872). Savings-Bank Building, corner Broadway and E Street. 12,000 volumes.

South End Branch Free Library. (1877). English High School Building, Montgomery Street. 10,000 volumes.

West Roxbury Branch Free Library. (1880). Westerly Hall, Centre Street.

The Commonwealth of Massachusetts, in 1880, presented the City of Boston with a large plot of land on the corner of Dartmouth and Boylston Streets, fronting Copley Square, upon which to erect a Public Library Building, and it is intended to make the new structure a magnificent, spacious and fire-proof repository. It is probable that the present building at 46 Boylston Street will be retained as a Central Distributing Library, as at present, while the Bates Hall collection will be removed to the new quarters, where a Back Bay distributing station will be established.

Harvard University Free Library. (1638). Cambridge. Next in extent, value and importance to the Public Library is the great Library of Harvard University, which, in some departments is unrivalled. It would be strange indeed if an educational institution founded in 1638—eight years after the settlement of Boston—and the only really great University of the land, had not accumulated a Library of immense size and value. The following are the libraries of the University, the number of bound volumes being given:

Gore Hall	232,890 volumes
Lawrence Scientific Sch'l	2,500 "
Bussey Institute	2,700 "
Phillips Observatory	3,300 "
Botanic Garden	4,000 "
Law School	21,000 "
Divinity School	17,400 "
Medical School	1,500 "
Zoological Museum	17,000 "
Peabody Museum	800 "

Total number of bound volumes 304,890
Pamphlets 325,000

629,800

The Harvard University Library may be consulted *by all persons, freely*, whether connected with the University or not. The privilege of borrowing books is also granted, under special regulations, to persons not connected with the University.

State Free Library. State House. This very large and valuable Library, although provided for the use of the State officials and members of the Legislature, is open for reference to any proper person, every week-day. It contains upwards of 60,000 volumes, which have been collected with great care and judgment. Here may be found the statutes of all the States and Territories; Acts of British Parliament; French Parliamentary Archives; works on Social Science, Political Economy, etc. This was the first State Library to be established in the country.

American Academy of Arts and Sciences Library. 10B Beacon Street. An extremely valuable collection.

American Baptist Missionary Union Library. Tremont Temple Building, 73 Tremont Street. A large collection, comprising thousands of volumes on theological subjects

American Statistical Association Library. 19 Boylston Place. 8,000 volumes.

Boston Art Club Library. Art Club Building, corner of Newbury and Dartmouth Streets.

Boston Athenæum Library. 10B Beacon Street. (1804). Originally located in Scollay Building, Scollay Square, thence being removed to Tremont Street (near King's Chapel Burying Ground), and afterward to Pearl Street. It was placed in its present commodious quarters in 1849, the building costing upwards of a quarter of a million of dollars. Among the collections that have been absorbed is the library of George Washington. The Library numbers about 150,000 volumes. Although the property of shareholders, it is simply necessary to obtain a card from one of the members to obtain the full privileges of the library and reading-room.

Boston College Library. (1864). Harrison Avenue. A very fine library, selected with scholarly taste and judgment, and containing many rare and valuable works. Open to students of Boston College.

Boston Dental College Library. 485 Tremont Street.

Boston Library. 18 Boylston Place. 35,000 volumes.

Boston Medical Library. (1875). 19 Boylston Place. 10,000 volumes and 6,500 pamphlets.

Boston Society of Natural History Library. Corner of Berkeley and Boylston Streets. 15,000 volumes and 6,000 pamphlets.

Boston University Law Library. 10 Ashburton Place.

Boston University Medical School Library. College Building, East Concord Street. 2,500 volumes.

Boston University School of Theology Library. University Building, 12 Somerset Street. 5,500 volumes.

Boston Young Men's Christian Association Library. (1851). 174 Boylston Street. 6,500 volumes.

Boston Young Men's Christian Union Library. (1851). 18 Boylston Street. 6,500 volumes.

Boston Young Women's Christian Association Library. Appleton Street, corner of Berkeley Street. 4,500 volumes.

Cambridge Public Library. 639 Main Street, Cambridge. 20,000 volumes.

City Hospital Library. Harrison Avenue. A library of works on medical subjects.

Congregational Library. (1853). Congregational House, 1 Somerset Street, corner of Beacon Street. 31,000 volumes and more than 100,000 pamphlets.

Directory Library. Boston Directory Office. 155 Franklin Street. Here may be consulted the directories of the various cities.

General Theological Library. (1860). 12 West Street. 13,500 volumes.

Handel and Haydn Society Library. Park Square. Many thousand rare and valuable musical works are here collected.

Lasell Seminary Library. Auburndale. A large and varied collection.

Massachusetts College of Pharmacy Library. 1151 Washington Street. One of the largest and most valuable pharmaceutical libraries in the United States.

Massachusetts General Hospital Library. Blossom Street. A valuable library of medical works.

Massachusetts Historical Society Library. 30 Tremont St. 31,000 volumes and 55,000 pamphlets.

Massachusetts Horticultural Society Library. Horticultural Hall. 5,000 volumes.

Massachusetts Institute of Technology Library. 191 Boylston Street. This not ed library includes several hundred volumes from the library of the late President Rogers.

Massachusetts New-Church Free Library. 169 Tremont Street. Comprises Swedenborgian publications.

Missionary Library. Congregational House, 1 Somerset Street, corner of Beacon Street. 7,000 volumes; the property of the American Board of Foreign Missions.

Museum of Fine Arts Library. St. James Avenue. A large and valuable collection.

New England Conservatory Library. 27 East Newton Street. A choice and expensive collection of rare works on music.

New England Historic-Genealogical Society Library. (1845). 18 Somerset Street. 18,000 volumes and 65,000 pamphlets.

Roxbury Athenæum Library. Dudley Street, corner of Warren Street.

Social Law Library. Room 14, Court House, Court Street. 18,000 volumes.

Tufts College Library. College Hill, Medford.

Wellesley College Library. Wellesley. 26,500 bound volumes.

Wells Memorial Library. (1884). 987 Washington Street. For the use of working men.

Circulating Libraries are numerous and well stocked. Among the largest and best known are the following:

Berwick Library..........Hotel Berwick
Bird, T. H.................... 775 Dudley st.
Blick, A. & Son........1695 Washington st.
Brown, J. E. & Co.... 873 Washington st.
Carter, H. H. & Karrick..... 3 Beacon st.
Corning, E. Etta............131 Warren st.
Daly, John J ....635 Tremont st.
Gilday, Ellen F........123 Bunker Hill st.
Gill, E. H............218 W. Broadway, S. B.
Hallett, C. S....... 661 E. Broadway, S. B.
Learned, R. L.............490 Tremont st.
Lindsey, G. W..........1175 Washington st.
Loring, A. K...............9 Bromfield st.
Marno, John.......145 Meridian st., E. B.
Mendum, J. O. Mrs.......697 Tremont st.
Merrill, C. H.........1575 Washington st.
Mudie Library............3 Hamilton pl.
Osgood, J............. 352 Dorchester st.
Payne, H. B. & Co... 738 E. B'dway, S. B.
Quinn, M. H......... 1909 Washington st.
Rich, H. B........477 W. Broadway, S. B.
Sage, William...........263 Columbus av.
Shattuck Library...106 Main st., Chas'n
Shawmut Library........383 Washington st.
Thayer, W. H............463 Blue Hill av.
Walker, John B..........1392 Tremont st.
Walker, T. O.............. 8 Bosworth st.
Weston, G. H........... 525 Tremont st.

The first circulating library established in Boston was that of John Mein, a Scotchman, in 1764. His collection comprised 1,200 volumes.

Among the libraries absorbed by the Boston Public Library, where the latter has assumed the functions of the local libraries thus disestablished, have been the Mercantile Library Association Library, at the South End; the Sumner Library, East Boston; Mattapan Library, South Boston; Fellowes Athenæum Library, Roxbury; Charlestown Public Library, Holton Library, Brighton; the West Roxbury Library, etc.

Boston Public Library's Opening. The trustees of the Boston Public Library opened its first reading-room in the building on Mason Street, March. 20, 1854. The Library was first opened May 2, 1854. The corner-stone of the building at 46 Boylston Street was laid Sept. 17, 1855, and the Library was dedicated Jan. 1, 1858.

Harvard University's Library was begun in 1638 with a collection, a bequest of three hundred and twenty volumes, from John Harvard.

Mather Library. At the time of the Battle of Bunker Hill, the collection of books which had been accumulated by Increase Mather and Cotton Mather was destroyed. There were about 8,000 volumes. Of this event John Adams wrote, July 7, 1775: "The loss of Mr. Mather's library, which was a collection of books and manuscripts made by himself, his father, his grandfather and great grandfather, and was really very curious and valuable, is irreparable."

Private Libraries in 1850. Among the private libraries of Boston in 1850 were the following: Charles Francis Adams, 18,000 volumes; George Ticknor, 13,000; Theodore Parker, 13,000; Abbott Lawrence, 10,000; Edward Everett, 8,000; Dr. John C. Warren, 6,000; Francis C. Gray, 4,000; Franklin Haven, 4,000; David Sears, 4,000; Richard Frothingham, 4,000; W. H. Prescott, 6,000; Rufus Choate, 7,000; E. A. Crowninshield, 3,000; Nathaniel Bowditch, 3,000; Samuel G. Drake, 6,500; Jared Sparks (Cambridge) 6,000; Thomas Dowse (Cambridge) 5,500.

OTHER READING ROOMS.

Boffin's Bower........1031 Washington st.
Colored Improvement Association........
..........................47 Hanover st.
Harvard Street Reading Room............
...........................49 Harvard st.
Lewis Street Mission ....1B Lewis st.
Longshoremen's Reading Room ....
................220 Commercial st.
Mariners' Reading Room..................
......cor. Hanover and N. Bennet sts.
Merchants' Reading Room....53 State st.
Newsboys' Reading Room..16 Howard st.
North End Mission..........201 North st.
Republican Reading Room........3 Park st.
Ruggles Street Reading Room............
................................165 Ruggles st.
Safe Deposit Reading Room..............
...........................Devonshire st.
Women's Ed. and Indus. Union..........
.......................74 Boylston st.

NEWSPAPERS.

Daily Publications.

Boston Daily Advertiser. Morning edition. 4 cents per copy. $12 per annum. E. B. Hayes, Publisher, 248 Washington st.

Boston Evening Record. Evening editions. 1 cent per copy. $3 per annum. E. B. Hayes, 248 Washington st.

Boston Evening Transcript. Evening editions. 3 cents per copy. $9 per annum. Boston Transcript Company, 324 Washington st.

Boston Evening Traveller. Evening editions. 3 cents per copy. $9 per annum. Roland Worthington & Co., 31 State st.

Boston Flour, Grain and Produce Market Report. Daily. C. M. Barrows & Co., 2 North Market st.

Boston Globe. Morning and Evening editions. 2 cents per copy. $6 per annum. Globe Newspaper Company, 238 Washington st.

Boston Herald. Morning and Evening editions. 2 cents per copy. $6 per annum. R. M. Pulsifer & Co., 255 Washington st.

Boston Journal. Morning and Evening editions. 2 cents per copy. $6 per annum. W. W. Clapp, 264 Washington st.

Boston Post. Morning edition. 2 cents per copy. $6 per annum. Post Publishing Company, 15 Milk st.

Boston Telegraph. (German). Evening edition. 1 cent per copy. $3 per annum. P. L. Schriftgiesser, 46 La Grange st.

Daily Law Record, 266 Washington st.

Daily Commercial. 1 cent per copy. 3 Williams ct.

Sunday Papers.

Boston Budget. Sunday morning edition. 5 cents per copy. $2.50 per annum. Budget Publishing Company, 220 Washington st.

Boston Courier. Sunday morning edition. 5 cents per copy. $2.50 per annum. J. F. Travers, 303 Washington st.

Boston Globe. Sunday morning edition. 5 cents per copy. $2 per annum. Globe Newspaper Company, 238 Washington st.

Boston Herald. Sunday morning edition. 5 cents per copy. $2 per annum. R. M. Pulsifer & Co., 255 Washington st.

Saturday Evening Gazette. Sunday morning edition. 5 cents per copy. $3.50 per annum. Henry G. Parker, 2 Bromfield st.

Sunday Times. Sunday morning edition. 5 cents per copy. $2 per annum. D. S. Knowlton, 20 Hawley st.

Weekly and Other Papers.

A. B. C. Pathfinder Railway Guide (monthly), $2.50. New England Railway Publishing Company, 67 Federal st.

American Advocate of Peace (monthly), 50 cents. American Peace Society, 7 Beacon st.

American Architect (weekly), $6 per annum. Ticknor & Company, 211 Tremont st.

American Botschafter (monthly), 50 cents. American Tract Society, 52 Bromfield st.

American Cabinet Maker (weekly), $3.50 per annum. J. Henry Symonds, 93 Water st.

American Cultivator (weekly), $2. George B. James, 220 Washington st.

American Exchange and Mart (weekly), $1.50. Percival Gassett, 17 Congress st.

American Florist and Farmer, $1. W. E. Bowditch, 645 Warren st.

American Hotel Budget (weekly), $2. American Hotel Budget Publishing Co., 186 Devonshire st.

American Journal of Numismatics (quarterly), $2. Boston Numismatic Society. Jeremiah Colburn, 18 Somerset st.

American Journal of Railway Appliances (weekly), $2. 8 Exchange pl.

American Legion of Honor Journal (monthly), 50 cents. 20 Beacon st.

American Messenger (monthly), 30 cents. American Tract Society, 52 Bromfield st.

American Missionary (monthly), 50 cents. Rev. C. L. Woodworth, Dist. Secretary. 7 Beacon st.

American Teacher (monthly), $1. N. E. Pub. Company, 3 Somerset st.

American Traveller (weekly), $1.50 per annum. 31 State st.

Andover Review (monthly), $3. Houghton, Mifflin, & Co., 4 Park st.

Angel of Peace (monthly), 15 cents. Am. Peace Soc., 6 Cong. House.

Apples of Gold (weekly), 50 cents per year. American Tract Society, 52 Bromfield st.

Appleton's Railway Guide (monthly), $3. D. Appleton & Co., 6 Hawley and 5 Arch sts.

Atlantic Monthly, $4. Houghton, Mifflin & Co., 4 Park st.

Babyland (monthly), 50 cents. D. Lothrop & Co., 32 Franklin st.

Baby Pathfinder, 5 cents. N. E. Railway Pub. Co., 67 Federal st.

Ballou's Monthly Magazine, $1.50. G. W. Studley, 23 Hawley st.

Banker & Tradesman (weekly), Thursday, $5. Levi B. Gay, 31 Milk st.

Banner of Light (weekly), $3. Colby & Rich, 9 Bosworth st,

Baptist Missionary Magazine (monthly), $1. Tremont Temple, W. G. Corthell.

Baptist Teacher (monthly), 75 cents. Am. Baptist Soc., 256 Washington st.

Bay State Monthly, $3. J. N. McClintock & Co., 43 Milk st.
Beacon (The), illustrated (weekly), $2.50. Beacon Pub. Co., 295 Washington st.
Bicycling World (weekly), $2. E. C. Hodges & Co., 8 Pemb. sq.
Bivouac Monthly, $1.50. E. F. Rollins, manager, 222 Franklin st.
Blessed Hope (quarterly), 24 cts. a year. Advent Ch. Pub. Society, 144 Han over st.
Boot and Shoe Recorder (weekly), $2.50. 105 Summer st.
Boston Advertiser (weekly), $1. L. B. Hayes, 248 Washington st.
Boston Advocate (weekly), $2. Grandison & Powell, 47 Hanover st.
Boston Almanac and Business Directory (annually), $1. Sampson, Murdock & Co., 155 Franklin st.
Boston Book Bulletin (quarterly), 30 cents. D. Lothrop & Co., 32 Franklin st.
Boston Commonwealth (weekly), $2.50. D. N. Thayer & Co. 25 Bromfield st.
Boston Culinary and Confectoy Journal (weekly), $4. B. C. & C. J. Publishing Co., 8 Boylston st.
Boston Home Journal (weekly), $2.50. S. T. Cobb & Co., 403 Washington st.
Boston Household Journal (weekly), $1. M. M. Wing, 35 Hanover st.
Boston Hygienia (monthly). Dr. H. W. Libby, 55 Rutland sq.
Boston Journal of Commerce and Cotton, Wool and Iron (weekly), $3. 128 Purchase st.
Boston Medical and Surgical Journal (weekly), $5. Cupples, Upham & Co., 283 Washington st.
Boston Reference Book (monthly), $3. F. W. Dodge & Co., Publishers, 79 Milk st. and 10 Federal st.
Boston Sentinel (weekly), $2. Edward Fitzwilliam, 4 State st.
Boston Turner Zeitung (weekly), 50 cents. Boston Turnverein, 3 La Grange st.
Bostoner Rundschau (weekly), $2. M. H. Heerde, rear 130 Eliot st.
Brighton Independent (weekly), $1. Edgar W. Knights, Savings Bank building, Washington st., Brighton.
Bunker Hill Times (weekly), $1.50. E. Gerry Brown, 16 City sq.
Cambridge Chronicle (weekly), $2.50. A. F. Pollock, manager, 28 Winter st.
Carpet, Wall Paper and Curtains, (weekly), Monday, $1.50. J. Henry Symonds, 93 Water st.
Charlestown Enterprise (weekly), $1.50. 25 City sq.
Charlestown News (weekly), Saturday, $2.00. Charles R. Byram, 8 City sq.
Chatterbox (monthly), $1. Estes & Lauriat, 301 Washington st.
Chautauqua Young Folks Journal (monthly), 75 cents. D. Lothrop & Co., 32 Franklin st.
Children's New Church Magazine (monthly), $1. 169 Tremont st.
Childs' Paper (monthly), 30 cents. American Tract Society, 52 Bromfield st.
Christian (The) (monthly), $1.00. H. L. Hastings, 47 Cornhill.

Christian Advocate (weekly), $2.50. J. P. Magee, agent, 33 Bromfield st.
Christian Leader (weekly), $2.50. Universalist Publishing House, 16 Bromfield st.
Christian Register (weekly), $3. Christian Register Association, 141 Franklin st.
Christian Safeguard (monthly), 50 cents. H. L. Hastings, 47 Cornhill.
Christian Union (weekly), $3. S. Fowler, manager, 3 Hamilton pl.
Christian Witness (semi-monthly), $1. McDonald & Gill, 36 Bromfield st.
Coach, Harness, and Saddlery (weekly), $2. 129 Summer st.
Commercial Bulletin (weekly), Saturday, $4. Curtis Guild & Co., 275 Washington st.
Commercial Reporter (weekly), $2. The M'Cready Credit Register Co., 52 South Market st.
Commercial Travellers' R. R. Guide and Hotel Register (monthly), $1. E. Nickerson & Co., 3 Hamilton pl.
Commercial and Shipping List and Prices Current (semi-weekly), $8. Appleton, Tompson, & Co., 5 Chatham row.
Common People (monthly), 50 cents. H. L. Hastings, 47 Cornhill.
Congregationalist (weekly), $3. W. L. Greene & Co., 7 Beacon st.
Contributor (monthly), $1. Jas. H. Earle, 178 Washington st.
Cottage Hearth (monthly), $1.50. Cottage Hearth Co., 11 Bromfield st.
Decorator and Furnisher (monthly), $4. F. W. Dodge & Co., N. E. agents, 79 Milk st.
Deutscher Volksfreund (weekly), $2.25. American Tract Society, 52 Bromfield st.
Dial (weekly), $2. H. Dodd, 265 Washington st.
Dial Express List (quarterly), 20 cents each. H. Dodd, 265 Washington st.
Dial Postal Guide (quarterly), 15 cents each. H. Dodd, 265 Washington st.
Donahoe's Magazine (monthly), $2. T. B. Noonan & Co., 21 Boylston st.
Dorchester Beacon (weekly), $2. Geo. E. Todd & Co., 1416 Dorchester av.
East Boston Advocate (weekly), $2. A. H. Lewis, editor and publisher, 3 Winthrop block, E. B.
East Boston Argus (weekly), $2. J. B. Maccabe, 33 Central sq., E. B.
Edinburgh Review (quarterly), $4. Houghton, Mifflin & Co., 4 Park st.
Engineering and Mining Journal (weekly), $4. A. R. Brown, jr., agent, 38 Water st.
Every Other Saturday, $2. H. P. Chandler, 47 Devonshire st.
Every Other Sunday (fortnightly), 10 cents. Unitarian S. S. Society, 7 Tremont pl.
Express Pathfinder (quarterly), 20 cents each. 117 Franklin st.
Folio (monthly), $1.60. White, Smith & Co., 516 Washington st.
Français (Le) (monthly), October to June, $2. Jules Levy, lock box 3, Roxbury P. O.

Gleason's Monthly Companion, $1. F. Gleason & Co., 46 Summer st.
Golden Cross (monthly), 75 cents. Dr. E. Hartshorn, 71 Blackstone st.
Golden Rule (weekly), $2. S. A. Tucker, 3 Somerset st.
Greek Student (quarterly). A. A. Wright, 38 Bromfield st.
Guardian (semi-monthly), $2. 54 Devonshire st.
Handicraftsman (monthly), $1. Miss M. S. Devereux, 45 Bartlett st., Roxbury.
Heathen Woman's Friend (monthly), 50 cents. Miss P. J. Walden, agent, 36 Bromfield st.
Helping Hand (monthly), 40 cents. Woman's Baptist Miss. Society, Tremont Temple.
Home (monthly), $1.00. Peoples' Publishing Co., 409 Washington st.
Home Circle (weekly), $2 per annum. F. Gleason & Co., 46 Summer st.
Home Guardian (monthly) $1.25. N. E. Moral Reform Society, 6 Oak pl.
Hotel Gazette (weekly), $2. F. M. Haskell, 11 Court st.
Household Companion (monthly), $1.50. Geo. B. James, 220 Washington st.
Household and Farm (monthly), 50 cts. Mason & Co., 29 Oliver st.
Illustrated Christian Weekly, $2.50. American Tract Society, 52 Bromfield st.
Illustrated Press (weekly). Illustrated Press Co., 25 Bromfield st.
Imperial (monthly), $1. G. G. Stacy, 3 Tremont row.
Index (weekly), $3. W. J. Potter and B. F. Underwood, 44 Boylston st.
Industrial Review (monthly), $2 F. P. Payson, manager, 131 Devonshire st.
Industrial and Art Journal (weekly), $4. J. B. Morrison & Co., 25 Bromfield st.
Inventors' and Manufacturers' Gazette (monthly), 50 cents. C. J. Smith & Co., 147 Milk st.
Investigator (weekly), $3. J. P. Mendum, Paine Memorial Bldg., Appleton st.
Journal of Christian Science (bi-monthly), $1. Mary B. G. Eddy, 571 Columbus av.
Journal of Prophecy (quarterly), 40 cents. 144 Hanover st.
Knights of Honor Reporter (monthly), 50 cents per annum. J. A. Cummings & Co., 252 Washington st.
Law and Order (weekly), Saturday, $3. Law and Order Pub. Co., 28 School st.
Leader, Musical (monthly). Jean White, 226 Washington st.
Legal Bibliography (quarterly). C. C. Soule, 26 Pemberton sq.
Liberal Freemason (monthly), $2. Alfred F. Chapman, 223 Washington st.
Life and Light for Women (monthly), 60 cents. Woman's Board of Missions, 7 Beacon st.
Literary World (fortnightly), $2. E. H. Hames & Co., 1 Somerset st.
Littell's Living Age (weekly), $8. Littell & Co., 31 Bedford st.
Little Christian (The), (semi-monthly), 30 cents. H. L. Hastings, 47 Cornhill.

Little Helpers, 20 cents. Woman s Bap. Miss. Soc., Tremont Temple.
Little Pilgrim Lesson Paper (weekly), 25 cents. Mrs. W. F. Crafts, Beacon st., cor. Somerset st.
Little Wanderer's Advocate (monthly), $1. Baldwin pl.
Lutherischer Anzeiger (semi-monthly), 50 cents. Ger. Luth. Bible Soc., 716 Parker st.
Manufacturers' Gazette (weekly), $2.50. Manufacturers' Gazette Publishing Co., 220 Washington st.
Manuf. etuaers' Review and Industrial Record (monthly), 27 Kilby st.
Masonic Truth (monthly), $1. J. M. Aguayo, 4 P. O. sq.
Mason's Monthly Illustrated Coin Magazine, $2. Mason & Co., 235 Washington st.
Mass. Eclectic Medical Journal (monthly), $1. R. A. Reid, 31 Cornhill.
Massachusetts Ploughman (weekly), Saturday, $2.50. George Noyes, 45 Milk.
Matrimonial Times (fortnightly).
Messiah's Herald (weekly), $2. American Millennial Association, 19 Harrison av.
Methodist Quarterly Review, $2.50. J. P. Magee, agent, 38 Bromfield st.
Metric Advocate, 25 cents per year. 32 Hawley st.
Mining Record (weekly), $4. Philip Highley, agent, 60 Devonshire st.
Mission Day Spring (monthly), 20 cents. 1 Cong. House.
Missionary Herald (monthly), $1, including postage. C. Hutchins, general agent, A. B. C. F. M., 1 Somerset st.
Monthly Cabinet of Illustrations, $1. Howard Gannett, 24 Tremont Temple.
Monthly Companion, $1. F. Gleason & Co., 46 Summer st.
Morning Light (monthly), 30 cents. Am. Tract Society, 52 Bromfield st.
Musical Record (monthly), $1. Dexter Smith, editor. O. Ditson & Co., 451 Washington st.
Myrtle (weekly), 75 cents. Univ. Publishing House, 16 Bromfield st.
National Builder, $3. George E. Blake, 19 Doane st.
New England Bibliopolist (quarterly), 25 cents a year. N. E. Historic-Genealogical Society, 18 Somerset st.
New England Farmer (weekly), $2.15. Darling & Keith, 34 Merchants row.
New England Grocer (weekly), $2. Benj. Johnson, 20 Central wharf.
New England Historical and Genealogical Register (quarterly), $3. N. E. Historic-Genealogical Society, 18 Somerset st.
New England Illustrated Magazine (weekly), $5. J. Swigert, 10 Bond st.
N. E. Medical Gazette (monthly), $1. O. Clapp & Son, 3 Beacon st.
New England Newspaper Union. 88 Purchase st.
New England Real Estate Journal (monthly), $1.00. James Gray, 1 Pemberton sq.
New England Staaten Zeitung (weekly),

$2. P. L. Schriftgiesser & Co., 46 La Grange st.
New England Workman (monthly), 50 cents. 376 West Broadway, S. B.
New Jerusalem Magazine (monthly), $2. 169 Tremont st.
New West Gleaner (monthly), 15 cents. 6 Congregational House.
Newsman (monthly), $1. Newsman Publishing Co., 186 Devonshire st.
North American Review (monthly), $5. 283 Washington st.
North End Mission Magazine, 50 cents. 201 North st.
Northwestern Lumberman, $4. George E. Blake, 19 Doane st.
Novelette, G. W. Studley, 23 Hawley st.
Once a Week (weekly), $3. New England Railway Publishing Co., 67 Federal st.
Our Dumb Animals (monthly), 50 cents. Massachusetts Society for Prevention of Cruelty to Animals, 21 Milk st
Our Home (monthly), 50 cents. J. A. Cummings & Co., 252 Washington st.
Our Little Men and Women (monthly), $1. D. Lothrop & Co., 32 Franklin st.
Our Little Ones (weekly), 50 cents. American Baptist Publishing Society, 256 Washington st.
Our Little Ones, and Nursery (monthly), $1.50. Russell Publishing Co. 36 Bromfield st.
Our Message (Monthly), 25c. Woman's Christian Temperance Union.
Our Young People (monthly), 50 cents. Amer. Bap. Pub. Soc., 256 Washington st.
Outing (monthly), $3. The Wheelman Co., 175 Tremont st.
Pansy (monthly, also weekly), $1. D. Lathrop & Co., 32 Franklin st.
Pilgrim Lesson Paper (monthly). Beacon, cor. Somerset st.
Pilgrim Quarterly. 20 cents a year, and Pilgrim Teacher (monthly), 65 cts. a year. Beacon, cor. Somerset st.
Pilot weekly, $2.50. Pilot Publishing Co., 597 Washington st.
Police News (weekly), $4. Police News Publishing Co., 4 Alden ct.
Popular Educator (monthly), $1. Educational Publishing Co., 3 Hamilton pl.
Popular Science Monthly, $5. D. Appleton & Co., 92 Franklin st.
Popular Science News and Journal of Chemistry (monthly), $1. Popular Science News Co., 19 Pearl st.
Postal Guide (quarterly), 25 cts. New England Publishing Co., 67 Federal st.
Power (monthly), $1 per annum. 8 Exchange pl.
Quarterly Review, $4. Houghton, Mifflin & Co., 4 Park st.
Railroad Advertiser (weekly), $1. Advertiser Publishing Co., 105 Summer st.
Reporter, Law (weekly), $10. Houghton, Mifflin & Co., 4 Park st.
Republic (weekly), $2.50. Republic Publishing Co., 243 Washington st.
Rifle (monthly), $1. A. C. Gould, 4 Exchange pl.
Roxbury Advocate (weekly), Saturday $2. Holman Bros., 2336 Washington st.

Roxbury Gazette and South End Advertiser (weekly), Thursday, $2. Stephen P. O'Donnell & Co., 2239 Washington st.
Scholar's Quarterly, 20 cents. Howard Gannett, 24 Tremont Temple.
Science Observer. Boston Scientific Society, P. O. box 2725.
Shippers' Guide (quarterly), 50 cents. New England Railway Publishing Co., 67 Federal st.
Shoe and Leather Reporter (weekly), Thursday, $3.50. 141 Summer st.
Social Visitor (monthly), 50 cents. 106 Sudbury st.
South Boston Inquirer (weekly), $2. Fred C. Floyd, editor, 376 West Broadway, S. B.
South Boston News (weekly), $1.25. Western & Co., 452 W. Broadway, S. B.
Sports and Pastimes (weekly), $2. H. B. Stephens, 101 Milk st.
State, The (weekly), $2. State Publishing Co., 246 Washington st.
Standard (weekly), $3. Standard Publishing Co., C. M. Ransom, president, 70 Kilby st.
Street Railway Journal (monthly), $1. 8 Exchange pl.
Stuff (monthly), 50 cents. Lewando, publisher, 17 Temple pl.
Sunday School Advocate (semi-monthly), 25 cents. J. P. Magee, 38 Bromfield st.
Sunday School Classmate (semi-monthly), 25 cents. J. P. Magee, agent, 38 Bromfield st.
Sunday School Helper (monthly), $1, with six lesson sheets, $1.50; Universalist Publishing House, 16 Bromfield st.
Sunday School Journal (monthly), 65 cents. 38 Bromfield st.
Sunday School Myrtle (weekly), 75 cents. Universalist Pub. Co., 16 Bromfield st.
Tech (The), Institute of Technology. 187 Boylston st., alternate Wednesdays. $2.
Temperance Cause (monthly), 35 cents. Massachusetts Total Abstinence Society, 36 Bromfield st.
Temple Star (monthly), 75 cents. A. H. Lewis, 3 Winthrop block, E. B.
Textile Record of America (monthly), $3. C. F. White, 19 Pearl st.
Times of Refreshing (monthly), $1. Willard Tract Repository, 2 Beacon Hill place.
Town and Country Musician (monthly), 50 cents. E. A. Samuels, 25 Congress st.
True Flag (weekly), $2.50. William U. Moulton, 50 Bromfield st.
Unitarian Review and Religious Magazine (monthly), $3. Office 141 Franklin st.
Unity Pulpit (weekly), $1.50. 241 Franklin st.
Universalist Quarterly, $2. Universalist Publishing House, 16 Bromfield st.
Universalist Register (yearly). Universalist Publishing House, 16 Bromfield st.
U. S. Building Trade Register (monthly), $3; F. W. Dodge & Co., 79 Milk and 10 Federal st.
Wade's Fibre and Fabric (weekly), $2. Joseph M. Wade & Co., 185 Summer st.
Watchman (weekly), $2.50. Watchman Publishing Co., 8 Tremont Temple.

Watchword (monthly), $1.00. Howard Gannett, 24 Tremont Temple.
Waverley Magazine (weekly), $4. Moses A. Dow, Waverley Publishing House, City sq., Charlestown.
Wedding Bells (monthly), 50 cents. E. Smith, 31 Boylston st.
Well-Spring (weekly), 60 cents; (monthly), 12 cents; (semi-monthly), 24 cents. Beacon, cor. Somerset st.
Western Shoe & Leather Review (weekly), $3. 39 High st.
West Roxbury Advertiser (weekly), $1.50. J. P. Forde, Woolsey block, J. P., and 64 Federal st.
West Roxbury News (weekly), Saturday. $2. Jones & Barrows, J. P.
Wide Awake (monthly), $3. D. Lothrop & Co., 32 Franklin st.
Woman's Journal (weekly), $2.50. Lucy Stone, editor. 5 Park st.
Word of Life (monthly), 50 cents. Willard Tract Repository, 2 Beacon Hill pl.

Work at Home (monthly), 25 cents. Woman's Home Missionary Association, 20 Cong. House.
Working Boy (monthly), 25 cents. Rev. D. H. Roche, 113 Eliot st.
World's Crisis (weekly), $2. Advent Christian Publication Society, 144 Hanover st.
Yankee Blade (weekly), $2. E. C. Davis, 20 Hawley st.
Young Folks Library (monthly), $3. D. Lothrop & Co., 32 Franklin st.
Young Pilgrim (semi-monthly), 35 cts. Advent Ch. Publication Society, 144 Hanover st.
Young Reaper (monthly), 24 cents. 256 Washington st.
Youth (monthly), $1. Youth Publishing Co., 147 Milk st.
Youth's Companion (weekly), $1.75. Perry Mason & Co., 41 Temple pl.
Zion's Herald (weekly), $2.50. A. S. Weed, publisher, 36 Bromfield st.

REAL BOSTON.

The Actual Boston of to-day is by no means to be measured by the population crowded within the circumscribed area of the city limits. Thousands upon thousands of people transacting business in Boston—or closely identified with its vast real-estate, railway, commercial, hotel, club, theatrical, banking, school, stock, telegraph, library, musical, literary, artistic, social and multitudinous other interests—reside, or, at least, pass the night, in the numerous cities, towns and villages within a radius of twenty-five miles from the heart of the city. All of these great suburbs are within easy access by steam-railways, street-cars, etc., and—as rapid transit is now one of the foremost issues of the day in Boston--the time required for reaching these environs (which is even now quite brief) will be lessened more or less year by year. In order to substantiate the claims of Boston to a really very large population, as far as all practical identification of interests and other conditions are concerned,—*of over a million of people* (and of half a million within her borders and in her immediate suburbs) the following list of cities and towns within this radius, with their population, is given, in order that one may judge correctly of the great importance of the metropolis of New England as a commercial, business, railway, steamship, hotel and theatrical centre:

City or town.	Railway.	M.	Pop.
BOSTON			401,987
Abington	O. C.	19	3,693
Andover	B. & M.	23	5,711
Arlington	B. & L.	6	4,673
Ashland	B. & A.	21	2,633
Bedford	B. & L.	15	930
Belmont	Fitch.	6	1,030
Beverly	Eastern	17	9,186
Billerica	B. & L.	19	2,161
Braintree	O. C.	10	4,010
Brockton	O. C.	20	20,920
Brookline	B. & A.	3	19,102
Cambridge	Fitch.	3	60,123
Canton	B. & P.	14	4,380
Chelsea	Eastern	4	26,119
Cohasset	O. C.	19	2,216
Concord	Fitch	19	3,903
Danvers	B. & M.	21	7,048
Dedham	B. & P.	10	6,729
Dover	N.Y.&N.E.	16	667
Easton	O. C.	22	4,003
Everett	Eastern	3	5,375
Framingham	O. C.	21	8,275
Hanson	O. C.	24	1,227
Hingham	O. C.	17	4,375
Holbrook	O. C.	25	2,334
Holliston	B. & A.	25	3,101
Hull	O. C.	25	473
Hyde Park	B. & P.	7	8,400
Lawrence	B. & L.	25	39,173
Lexington	B. & L.	11	2,718
Lincoln	Fitch.	17	901
Lowell	B. & L.	25	65,117
Lynn	Eastern	10	46,133
Lynnfield	B. & M.	13	706
Malden	B. & M.	5	16,437
Manchester	Eastern	24	1,638
Mansfield	B. & P.	24	2,939
Marblehead	Eastern	17	7,518
Medford	B. & M.	5	9,059
Medway	N.Y. & N.E	25	2,777
Melrose	B. & M.	7	6,101
Millis	N.A. & N.E.	22	683
Milton	O. C.	6	3,579
Nahant	Eastern	16	637
Natick	B. & A.	17	8,460
Needham	N.Y. & N.E.	12	2,586
Newton	B. & A.	7	19,759
Norfolk	N.Y. & N.E.	23	825
No. Abington	O. C.	18	1,258
No. Reading	B. & M.	10	878
No. Scituate	O. C.	23	1,030
Norwood	N.Y. & N.E.	14	2,923
Peabody	Eastern	16	10,111
Quincy	O. C.	8	12,273
Randolph	O. C.	15	3,807
Reading	B. & M.	12	3,539
Readville	B. & P.	8	700
Revere	Eastern	6	3,639
Rockland	O. C.	18	4,784
Salem	Eastern	16	28,217
Saugus	Eastern	9	2,855
Scituate	O. C.	25	2,350
Sharon	B. & P.	17	1,328
Somerville	B. & M.	2	30,113
So. Abington	O. C.	21	3,921
Springdale	B. & P.	15	1,116
Stoneham	B. & M.	7	5,652
Stoughton	O. C.	18	5,183
Sudbury	O. C.	24	1,165
Swampscott	B. & M.	12	2,471
Tewksbury	B. & L.	23	2,323
Topsfield	B. & M.	25	1,141
Wakefield	B. & M.	10	6,060
Walpole	N.Y. & N.E.	19	2,443
Waltham	Fitch	10	14,609
Watertown	Fitch	8	6,238
Wayland	Ms. Cent.	17	1,946
Wellesley	B. & A.	15	3,013
Wenham	B. & M.	22	871
W. Bridgewater	O. C.	24	1,707
Weston	Ms. Cent.	13	1,427
Weymouth	O. C.	12	10,740
Wilmington	B. & M.	16	1,003
Winchester	B. & L.	8	3,802
Winthrop	B. & R. B.	5	1,370
Woburn	B & L.	10	11,793

Total population of Boston
and 86 cities and towns: 1,154,088

It will be seen that within the short distance of *three miles* there are *more than half a million* population:

BOSTON			401,987
Brookline	B. & A.	3	19,102
Cambridge	Fitch.	3	60,123
Everett	Eastern	3	5,375
Somerville	B. & M.	2	30,113

Total 507,700

Within a radius of *five miles* is the following population:

BOSTON			401,987
Brookline	B. & L.	3	10,102
Cambridge	Fitch	3	60,123
Chelsea	Eastern	4	26,119
Everett	Eastern	3	5,375
Malden	B. & M	5	16,437
Medford	B. & M	5	9,059
Somerville	B. & M	2	30,113
Winthrop	B. & R. B.	5	1,370

Total 560,685

Within a radius of *ten miles* there are nearly three-quarters of a million people:

BOSTON			401,987
Arlington	B. & L.	6	4,673
Belmont	Fitch	6	1,630
Brookline	B. & A.	3	10,102
Cambridge	Fitch	3	60,123
Chelsea	Eastern	4	26,119
Dedham	B. & P.	10	6,729
Everett	Eastern	3	5,375
Hyde Park	B. & P.	7	8,400
Lynn	Eastern	10	46,133
Malden	B. & M.	5	16,437
Medford	B. & M.	5	9,059
Melrose	B. & M.	7	6,101
Milton	O. C.	6	3,579
Newton	B. & A.	7	19,759
No. Reading	B. & L.	10	878
Quincy	O. C.	8	12,273
Readville	B. & P.	8	700
Revere	Eastern	6	3,639
Saugus	Eastern	9	2,855
Somerville	B. & M.	2	30,113
Stoneham	B. & M.	7	5,052
Wakefield	B. & M.	10	6,060
Waltham	Fitch	10	14,609
Watertown	Fitch	8	6,238
Winchester	B. & L.	8	3,802
Winthrop	B. & R. B.	5	1,370
Woburn	B. & L.	10	11,793

Total 726,197

BOARDING HOUSES.

For the convenience of those at a distance who contemplate coming to Boston for a visit, or to reside during a course of study at any of the various Colleges, Conservatories or Schools of the city, the following revised list of boarding-houses has been prepared for this work. One can live economically, or expensively, as may suit the taste or pocket of the visitor. Prices range according to location, size and number of rooms required, etc., and one can obtain board in respectable neighborhoods at from $6 to $15 per week, according to accommodations. One can, of course, find cheaper or dearer rates, but would hardly expect satisfactory table and rooms at less than $6. It would be well for our readers who propose making a stay in Boston to address a letter to several of the parties here named, a week or two before coming, asking for particulars as to prices and rooms (mentioning this book):

Barton, M. J. Mrs........18 Ashburton pl.
Berry, Sarah, Mrs...Union st., Dor. Dist.
Bigelow, H. W............472 Blue Hill av.
Billings, John.........36 West Newton st.
Brooks, Charles B.........10 Bulfinch pl.
Brown, Misses............43 Bowdoin st.
Bryent, James.....136 West Chester Park
Campbell, A. Mrs.........2 Ashburton pl.
Chase, E. N. Mrs...........350 Tremont st.
Clough, Jason............28 Hanson st.
Clough, S. A............357 Columbus av.
Clough, S. L. Mrs.........361 Tremont st.
Coffin, A. L. Mrs............. 27 Hollis st.
Crouse, Eliza, Mrs..........33 McLean st.
Cushing, George.....1866 Washington st.
Drake, S. A. Mrs..........680 Tremont st.
Erskine, D. Mrs........383 Columbus av.
Goddard, M. G. Mrs..........1 Allston st.
Gordon, Robert, Mrs......339 Tremont st.
Hall, Henry................12 Boylston pl.
Hardy, John............329 Tremont st.
Harris, A. F. Miss....14 E. Brookline st.
Hildreth, G. W.............54 Myrtle st.
Hill, Jonathan, Mrs.......42 Tennyson st.
Holt, A. A. Mrs............16 Carver st.
Hubbard, George .... 109 Charles st.
Johnson, D. F.............352 Tremont st.
Marston, M. J. Mrs........11 Bowdoin st.
McGowan, C. F.............16 Boylston pl.
McGregor, J. T. Mrs........8 Bowdoin st.
Osborn, Mary, Mrs........4 Burroughs pl.
Pickens, A. J..............23 Beacon st.
Potter, W. H..............15 Bowdoin st.
Price, Sarah J. Miss.......12 Bowdoin st.
Roberts, A. D. Mrs......2 E. Brookline st.
Sargent, C. A. Mrs........22 Bowdoin st.
Sargent, F. J.............11 Boylston pl.
Stewart, Helen M..........8 Allston st.
Swan, M. B. Miss............2 Derne st.
Twiss, Mary J............61 Hancock st.

The exact location of any of these boarding-houses may easily be ascertained by consulting the Street Directory given in this book, and the Street Map furnished with it. (See *Hotels*).

SHOPPING GUIDE.

For the convenience of ladies and gentlemen visiting Boston the following list of leading dealers in dry-goods, fancy-goods, jewelry, diamonds, books, furnishing-goods, laces, embroideries, gloves, music, pianofortes, shoes, etc., in the central shopping-district of Boston, has been prepared. It will prove of particular value to strangers in the city.

Washington Street.

225 Merrill Bros. Men's Furnishing Goods
254 Little, Brown & Co............Books
256 Springer, G. H.................Books
266 Newcomb, Jesse P...Boots and Shoes
277 Bradshaw, E........Boots and Shoes
283 Cupples, Upham & Co..........Books
298 Keeler, F. M., & Co....Fancy Goods
301 Estes & Lauriat................Books
321 Pray, John F.& Sons, Boots and Shoes
329 St. Joachim............Fancy Goods
333 Tilton, S. W. & Co............Books
340 Clarke, W. B. & Carruth.......Books
341 Donaldson, Donovan & Co...........
...........................Boots and Shoes.
349 Smith Brothers.........Fancy Goods
365 DeWolfe, Fiske & Co............Books
371 Small Brothers......Boots and Shoes
374 Dame, Stoddard & Kendall..........
.................................Fancy Goods
403 Harrington, J. A...........Diamonds
408 Trifet, F...............Fancy Goods
411 Bell, Theo. H......Boots and Shoes
426 Noyes Bros., Men's Furnishing Goods
432 Shreve, Crump & Low.........Jewelry
435 Tuttle, H. H. & Co..Boots and Shoes
450 Jordan, Marsh & Co........Dry Goods
451 Ditson, Oliver & Co............Music
459 Wark, Henry...................Books
444 Wood, N. G. & Son............Jewelry
465 Beethoven Piano Rooms.Pianofortes
469 Moseley, T. E. & Co...Boots & Shoes
477 Beal, Higgins & Henderson.........
...............................Dry Goods
484 Schwarz, R..............Fancy Goods
485 Jones, R. F...................Gloves
488 C. D. Blake & Co..............Music
493 Alden, C. E...............Pianofortes
497 Partridge, Horace......Fancy Goods
501 Zinn, W. H.............Fancy Goods
505 Keon, L................Fancy Goods
511 Bigelow, Kennard & Co....Jewelry
509 Ray, John J.Men's Furnishing Goods
518 White, R. H. & Co..........Dry Goods
521 Bijou Piano Rooms......Pianofortes
535 Vose & Sons............Pianofortes
592 Berry, H. W.............Pianofortes
601 Wheelock, W. E. & Co...Pianofortes
602 Benari, Joseph......Boots and Shoes
604 Norris, G. W............Pianofortes
608 Woods, George, Co......Pianofortes
608 Hunt Bros...............Pianofortes
615 Bailey & Co...........Fancy Goods
616 Rogers, C. E. Co........Pianofortes
630 McPhail, A. M. & Co....Pianofortes
630 Clapp, C. M.............Pianofortes

630 Richardson, R. B........Pianofortes
633 Newhall, A..............Pianofortes
637 Rowe, B. S. & Co...Boots and Shoes
666 Bourne, Wm. & Son......Pianofortes
701 Graham, M. H. & Co..Boots & Shoes
755 Bath, John H..........Boots and Shoes
787 Adams, E. H...............Diamonds

Tremont Street.

43 Doyle, Wm. E................Flowers
55 Houghton & Dutton...Fancy Goods
59 Jackson & Co........Hats and Furs
61 Galvin, Thos. F..............Flowers
69 Hovey, C. H., & Co...........Flowers
70 Brine & Norcross......Fancy Goods
90 Butler, Wm. S. & Co........Dry Goods
102 Dodge, James S.........Fancy Goods
104 Dee Brothers.................Flowers
104 Pollard & Alford.............Books
126 Russell, Joseph M.............Music
128 Walther, G. J..................Laces
140 Stearns, R. H. & Co......Trimmings
144 Schoenhof, Carl................Books
144 Toppan, F. B..........Fancy Goods
146A Emerson Piano Co.....Pianofortes
146 Palmer, Batchelder & Co....Jewelry
147 Gerrish, W. H............Pianofortes
152 Chickering & Sons.......Pianofortes
154 Mason & Hamlin...................
...............Organ and Piano Company
156 Miller, Henry F. & Sons.Pianofortes
157 Hallett & Cumston........Pianofortes
158A Harwood & Beardsley...Pianofortes
158 Ruggles, Otis A...............Flowers
159 Estey....Organ and Piano Company
161 Twombly & Sons.............Flowers
167 Hallet & Davis...................
...............Piano Manuf'g Company
169 Swedenborgian Book Store...Books
175A Woodward & Brown....Pianofortes
175B Guild, Church & Co....Pianofortes
177 Harvey, C. C............Pianofortes
178 Knabe, Wm..............Pianofortes
181 Ivers & Pond........Piano Company
181 Witherell, Julian F....Pianofortes
195 Steinert, M. & Sons.....Pianofortes
211 Ticknor & Co.................Books

Winter Street.

3 Mills & Gibbs.................Laces
4 Gillaume Glove Store.........Gloves
5 Gilchrist, R. & J..........Dry Goods
14 Goldenberg, Bros. & Co........Laces
15 Parker Bros..............Fancy Goods
17 Bon Marche................Millinery
17 Tilton, S..................Millinery
20 Conrad, David................Laces
21 Kelley, M. E................Millinery
24 Stowell, A. & Co............Jewelry
26 Shepard, Norwell & Co....Dry Goods
27 Chandler & Co.............Dry Goods
30 Stevens, John J..............Laces
43 Sidenberg, G. & Co............Laces
44 Gross & Strauss...............Laces
47 Bates, C. Miss..Ladies' Fur'n'g Goods
48 Costello, L................Millinery
48 Simpson & Weisner...........Gloves
58 Levy, Benj. & Co.........Perfumery

Temple Place.
3 Chanut, J. M. & Co............Gloves
5 Wilson, D. & Co............Jewelry
12 Fisk, M. F. Miss............Gloves
20 Forgeot, M. Mme............Millinery
20 Paris Glove Store............Gloves
21 Wethern, Geo. M............Millinery
22 Le Bon Ton............Millinery
32 Rothschild............Millinery
39 Cushman, E. F............Dry Goods
45 Cleaves, McDonald & Co........Books
47 Thayer, McNeil & Hodgkins..........
............Boots and Shoes
49 Creed, Kellogg & Co............Jewelry
51 Ford, J. G..Ladies Furnishing Goods
52 Reed, Gowell & Co............Gloves
58 Wentworth, Hall & Co......Millinery
65 Allen, W. J. & Co............Gloves

West Street.
3 Ross, Louis H. & Co............Music
3 McCormick, William......Stationery
13 Schmidt, Arthur P. & Co......Music
34 Prufer, Carl............Music
37 Stevens & Manchester.....Stationery
41 Clark, Edward E.......... Stationery
51 Grimmer, Charles P.......... Flowers

Summer Street.
33 Hovey, C. F. & Co..........Dry Goods
56 Stens, Wm. & Co..............Laces

Bromfield Street.
9 Loring, A. K..................Library
11 Belden Bros..................Books
13B Noyes, H. D. & Co. .... Books
17 Fords, Howard & Hulbert......Books
21 Adams, Putnam & Co..........Books

22 Mason, D. W.....................Books
25 Wilde, W. A. & Co............Books
36 Harris, Rogers & Co............Books
38 Magee, James P................Books
45 Hardwick, W. E......Boots and Shoes
51 McGrath Bros........Boots and Shoes

School Street.
10 Power, Thomas & Co..................
.... Boots and Shoes
11 McDonald, Alex..............Trunks
14 Harrington............ ....Hats
15 Harrington, Mrs. G. F....Restaurant
18 Smith, C. A. & Co........... Clothing
23 Clifford..................Perfumery
24 Goodyear Rubber Co...Rubber Goods
25 Bodenbrown, Wm...Boots and Shoes
26 Whittemore, John M.& Co.Stationery
29 Bensemoil, J...................Tailor
30 Hale, Alfred & Co....Rubber Goods
32 Eldridge, J. F. & Co... Rubber Goods
40 Nash & Bowers............Groceries
44 Brazilian Rubber Co... Rubber Goods

Beacon Street.
2 Boston Music Company ....Music
3 Clapp, Otis & Son..............Books
3 Carter, H. H. & Karrick..Stationery
6 Ryder, W. Scott............Millinery
22 Bunker, Michael B..........Flowers

Many of the foregoing firms do a large business by mail and express, especially the dealers in books, stationery, music, etc. A number of dry goods houses also send articles by post. In addressing any one of the parties named for lists of goods, catalogues, prices, etc., please mention this book.

BUSINESS EXCHANGES.

Boston Board of Trade........53 State st.
Chamber of Commerce....Quincy Market
Charitable Mechanics' Association........
....................Mechanics' Hall
Furniture Board of Trade.188 Hanover st.
Mass. Fish Exchange..........T Wharf
Master Builders' Exchange..............
................164 Devonshire st.
Mechanics' Exchange.......35 Hawley st.
Mining and Stock Exchange..............
................14 Exchange pl.
Nat. Association of Wool Manufacturers.
....................70 Kilby st.
Nat. Shoe and Leather Exchange........
................178 Devonshire st.

New England Cotton Manufacturers Association..............Sears building
New England Furniture Exchange.......
....................174 Hanover st.
New England Insurance Exchange.......
....................Mason building
New England Shoe and Leather Association..................79 Bedford st.
Shoe and Leather Exchange.............
....................48 Hanover st.
Stationers' and Printers' Exchange......
................250 Devonshire st.
Stock and Exchange Board....53 State st.
Waiters' Union..............10 Brattle st.

MARKETS.

Boston has long been renowned for the number, size and variety of its markets. The first market is said to have stood on ground now occupied by the Old State House, at the corner of Washington and Court Streets. It was opened there March, 1634.

Quincy Market. (1826). Between North and South Market Streets, facing Faneuil Hall, is the famous Quincy Market, so called in honor of Mayor Josiah Quincy, (1823-28), through whose commendable enterprise the great movement was inaugurated and successfully completed. The corner-stone was laid in 1825, and in 1826 was opened the present commodious market, which is justly regarded by strangers as one of the principal "sights" of the city. Early on Saturday morning, or on Saturday at any time, one may witness scenes bustling with activity, amid vast quantities of food which is being distributed in every direction throughout the great city. Quincy Market covers 27,000 feet of land. The length of the building, which is two stories in height, is 535 feet. A wide corridor, running the entire length of the building, is bordered by stalls, in which the most tempting display of meats, vegetables, fish, fruit, etc., is made.

Other Markets. The other Markets of the city, several of which are large, and all being more or less attractive, are the following:

Blackstone Market... 72-92 Blackstone st.
Boylston Market.......649 Washington st.
Central Market................ 50 North st.
Central Market....388 W. Broadway, S.B.
Clinton Market.........106 So. Market st.
Faneuil Hall Market, Under Faneuil Hall
Fulton Market,c.North andBlackstone st.
Globe Market................. 42 North st.
Lakeman Market...........Blackstone st.
Mercantile Market............Atlantic av.
St.Charles Market, Beach and Lincoln st.
Suffolk Market, Portland and Sudbury st.
Union Market.........15 Washington st.
Washington Market..1883 Washington st.
Williams Market..... 1138 Washington st.

CUSTOM-HOUSE.

United States Custom House. This public building is at the corner of State and India Streets, at the foot of the former street. The building is in the form of a Greek cross. The construction was begun in 1837 and finished in 1847. It is of granite, and is one of the most substantial and imposing public buildings in the country. It cost the government $1,000,000. There are 32 Doric columns, weighing 42 tons each. The building is 140 feet in length, and varies in width from 75 feet at the ends to 95 feet in the centre. The first Custom House was located near Congress Street.

FREE BATHS.

Boston led the way in promoting the sanitary condition of the people of the great cities, being the first city to establish free baths for the public. The experiment of placing a few of these houses at easily accessible locations worked so well that the great system was soon completed and in good working order. The baths are open early, from June 1 to September 30, for males, on week-days from 5 a. m. to 9 p. m.; and on Sundays from 5 a. m. to 9. a. m.; for females, on week-days from 6 a. m. to 8 p. m.; and on Sundays from 6 a. m. to 9 a. m. Boys and girls under fifteen years of age are not admitted to the bathing-houses after 7 p. m., the decision of the Superintendent against admission being final. All the houses are closed at 10 p. m. on week-days and at 9.30 a. m. on Sundays. The floating swimming-baths are located as follows:

FOR MEN AND BOYS.

W. Boston Bridge...foot of Camb'dge st.
Craigie Bridge........foot of Leverett st.
Charles River Bridge.. near Causeway st.
E. Boston Sect. Dock........96 Border st.
Mt. Washington Av. B'dge.nr. Feder'l st.
South Boston.. foot of L st., Dorch'r Bay
Dover St. Bridge...........at South Pier
East Boston....Maverick st., Jeffries Pt.
Charlestown...............Chelsea Bridge
Charlestown...............Malden Bridge

FOR WOMEN AND GIRLS.

Warren Bridge.........near Causeway st.
East Boston.....Sect. Dock, 96 Border st.
South Boston........... foot of Fifth st.
Dover Street................at South Pier
Dorchester............Commercial Point
Charlestown..............Chelsea Bridge
Charlestown..............Malden Bridge

SOCIAL CLUBS.

Algonquin Club. (1885). Club-House, 164 Marlborough Street, corner of Dartmouth Street. Organized by a number of gentlemen representing various business interests, largely residing on the Back Bay, for the object of social intercourse. Admission fee, $100. Annual assessment, $100. It has a membership of over three hundred gentlemen, including Augustus P. Martin, Edward A. Taft, John O. Poor, Edward Jewell, Waldo Adams, Stillman B. Allen, Oliver Ames, John F. Andrew, Charles H. Andrews, Henry H. Atkins, Nathaniel J. Bradlee, George O. Carpenter, John M. Clark, Oliver Ditson, Benjamin F. Guild, Richard G. Haskell, Wm. V. Hutchings, Eben D. Jordan, John M. Little, Emile Marqueze, Henry Mason, S. R. Niles, John C. Paige. Henry G. Parker, Thos. E, Proctor. A. A. Ranney, Eugene Tompkins, and William Ware.

Central Club. (1868). Club-House, 64 Boylston Street. Organized by leading business men for social purposes. Admission fee, $50 Annual assessment, $50. One of the by-laws reads thus: "The Club shall never be called upon to act in its official or corporate capacity as a Club, upon any political question." Among well-known members of this Club are Aquilla Adams, Linus M. Child, Asa P. Potter, Charles E. Powers, C. A. B. Shepard, Edward A. White, Samuel D. Crane, Charles H. Taylor and Calvin A. Richards.

Puritan Club. Club House corner of Joy and Mt. Vernon Streets. Admission $25. Annual assessment $25. Membership limited to 300. Members include John C. Ropes, P. Curtis, Jr., T. Jefferson Coolidge, Jr., Richard M. Saltonstall, Federick W. Lincoln, Jr., Robert Grant, Jr., William A. Gaston and J. G. Thorp, Jr. This is one of the most thriving of Boston's younger Clubs.

St. Botolph Club. (1880). Club House, 85 Boylston Street. Admission-fee $50. Annual assessment, $30. According to the constitution of this club it was established "for the promotion of social intercourse among authors and artists, and other gentlemen connected with or interested in literature or art." The Clubhouse is very elegantly furnished, having an art gallery, etc. The membership — limited to 350 — includes Brooks Adams, Martin Brimmer, Phillips Brooks, Lawrence Barrett, James Freeman Clarke, William D. Howells, John Boyle O'Reilly, J. Foxcroft Cole, Arthur B. Ellis. Among its distinctive features are its fine exhibitions of paintings (from the easels of its members), and its receptions to prominent men from other cities.

Somerset Club. (1852). Club House, Beacon Street, opposite the Common, between Spruce and Walnut Streets. Admission fee, $100. Annual assessment $100. Membership limited to 600. Occupies a fine building, its wide front being quite imposing, despite the somewhat squatty appearance of its towers. Among its members are Charles Francis Adams, Jr., Frederick L. Ames, Alexander Agassiz, Nathan Appleton, Causten Browne, Henry Cabot Lodge, F. O. Prince, F. J. Stimpson. J. Montgomery Sears, William F. Weld, Jacob C. Rogers, James Jackson and F. C. Loring. The Club has a ladies' restaurant, which is also open to non-members accompanying ladies on Club order.

Suffolk Club. (1845). Club-House, 4B Beacon Street. Its membership is unlimited, and includes Leopold Morse, Jonas H. French, Thomas E. Moseley, C. H. Andrews, Alexis Torrey, and others.

Tavern Club. Club-House, Corner of Boylston Street and Park Square. Admission fee, $25. Annual assessment, $30. Membership limited to 100. Among the objects of the Club is to furnish excellent meals to its members, at reasonable prices, where they can enjoy each other's society at such times as they may come together. Among the members are William D. Howells, Timothie d'Adamowski, George C. Munzig, B. C. Porter, T. Russell Sullivan and others well known in literature and art. Receptions to prominent gentlemen are often given by the Club. Among those who have accepted the hospitalities of the Club have been Henry Irving, Tommaso Salvini and James Russell Lowell.

Temple Club. [1829]. Club-House, 37 West St. The oldest and formerly the most fashionable Club of Boston. It is simply a social organization, and its membership is kept small and exclusive. Admission fee. $50. Annual assessment, $100. The Club possesses a fine collection of paintings. Its members include Peter Butler, Eben D. Jordan, Nathaniel Hooper, Charles Marsh, Otis E. Weld and B. F. Stevens. The fine bowling-alleys of the Club afford much pleasure to the members and their lady and gentlemen friends.

Union Club. (1863). Club House, Park Street. Admission fee, $100. Annual assessment, $50. Edward Everett, the first president of the Club, said, at its inauguration, Oct. 15, 1863: "As I contemplated the views from this house the other day, gazing, under the dreamy light of an Indian Summer, on the waters in the centre of the Common, sparkling through the tinted maples and elms; the line of surrounding hills, Brighton, Brookline, Roxbury and Dorchester; the islands that gem the harbor; the city, stretched like a panorama around and beneath, — I thought my eye had never rested on a more delightful prospect." This Club has a fine membership, including: Frederick Amory, John F. Andrew, Wm. Gaston, Alexander H. Rice, Charles Allen, Robert Treat Paine, Martin Brimmer, Edmund Quincy, William Warren, John Lowell. Table d'hote dinners are a feature of the Club. Membership is limited to 500.

ART CLUBS.

Boston Art Club. (1854). Club-House, Newbury Street, corner of Dartmouth Street. The house occupied by this Club — built expressly for it — is an elegant one, of a Romanesque form of architecture, of brick and stone, costing, with the land, nearly $100,000. The interior is furnished luxuriously and artistically. There is a fine exhibition gallery, 47 feet by 47, and 18 feet high, to which the public can be admitted. The objects of this Club are to advance the knowledge and love of Art through the exhibition of its works; the acquisition of books and papers for an Art library; lectures upon Art subjects, and social intercourse. Among those identified with the official administration of the Club have been C. C. Perkins, Alexander H. Rice and George P. Denny.

Paint and Clay Club. (1880). Club-House 419 Washington Street. Composed of gentlemen identified with the professions of art, literature or music. Initiation-fee, $15. Annual dues, $15. Membership limited to forty. The club-room is beautifully decorated with paintings by the members, who occasionally give exhibitions of their work.

MUSICAL CLUBS.

Apollo Club. (1871). 151 Tremont Street. A club of gentlemen formed with the object of singing part-songs, etc., an associate-membership being assessed for certain annual fees, receiving in return a number of tickets to the performances of the club. These concerts are of a high order. No tickets are sold, admission being by tickets furnished to members. B. J. Lang is the director of the Club.

Arlington Club. (1879). This is a society of gentlemen for the purpose of giving concerts, having an associate membership on a similar plan to that of the Boylston and Apollo Clubs. William J. Winch was the organizer of the club.

Boylston Club. (1873). Through the artistic and earnest efforts of George L. Osgood, its director, this singing-club has attained high renown for the perfection with which it interprets cantatas, masses, psalms and four part compositions. Discipline, promptness of attack, and rare effects of light and shade are the striking characteristics of this body of singers, as would naturally be expected from the exalted reputation of Mr. Osgood as a conductor, teacher and soloist. The concerts of this Club are given at Music Hall. No tickets are sold, and admission can only be secured through the courtesy of a member. There is generally so great a demand for places that it is considered a rare privilege to obtain a ticket.

Cecilia Club. (1874). An outgrowth of the Harvard Musical Association. It has an associate membership similar to that of the Boylston and Apollo Clubs, and tickets are only to be obtained of them. B. J. Lang is director.

Dorchester Glee Club. A Club formed of good material, and one destined to attain a foremost position among our singing societies. Its concerts are given at Winthrop Hall, Upham Corner, Dorchester District.

Euterpe Club. (1878). A Club organized for the cultivation of chamber music. Four or five concerts are given every season. The club was founded principally through the efforts of Francis H. Jenks.

Orpheus Club. (1853). Club-Rooms, No. 27 Boylston Street. Founded by August Kreissman, for musical and social purposes. Originally composed exclusively of Germans, it now has many American members. It was the first glee-club established here. President, A. F. Gaensslen; Secretary, Leo Schlegelmilch.

ACTORS AND AUTHORS CLUBS.

Ace of Clubs. A dining club, composed of members of the journalistic, musical and dramatic professions. Its membership includes William T. Adams ("Oliver Optic"), Eugene Tompkins, Myron W. Whitney, Willie Edouin, Benjamin F. Tryon, W. Wallace Waugh, Sol Smith Russell, Truman H. Bartlett, Charles H. Hoyt, Henry C. Barnabee, Charles Mackintosh, George Makepeace Towle, Herndon Morsell, Frank Carlos Griffith, J. B. Mason, William Seymour, Charles H. Thayer, Luther L. Holden, George F. Babbitt, Edward H. Hastings, William Harris, William H. Fessenden, Charles J. Capen, Edwin Stearns, Frazer Coulter, Charles W. Thomas, Francis Chase, Robert G. Fitch, and others. It meets monthly at the Parker House.

Elks Club. Club House, 24 Hayward Place. Composed principally of actors and those identified with the dramatic profession.

Macaroni Club. A social organization of actors, singers, literary and society gentlemen, meeting monthly at the Revere House at dinner. Among its prominent members are D. J. Maguinnis, Arthur Leach, Dr. Frank A. Harris, Frazer Coulter and others.

Papyrus Club. An organization having for its purpose the promotion of good-fellowship and literary and artistic tastes among its members. Composed of journalists, authors, publishers, artists, architects, physicians, editors and members of various professions. Eminent actors and literary men are frequently guests of the Club. The members meet on the first Saturday of every month of the "season" to dine at the Revere House, the banquet being followed by a literary entertainment. Prominent members are Geo. Makepeace Towle, Robert Grant, John Boyle O'Reilly, Nathaniel Childs, George F. Babbitt and others. Admission fee, $10 for literary members; $25 for non-literary members. Annual assessment, $5.

PRESS CLUBS.

Boston Newspaper Club. (1886). This is a social organization comprising gentlemen connected with various newspapers in this city. Officers of the club; *Editor-in-chief,* Edward E. Edwards; *Managing Editor,* Charles E. L. Wingate; *Reporter,* Charles I. Bond. *Members;* William V. Alexander, Edwin S. Crandon, Edward L. Alexander, Samuel S. Kingdon, Joseph F. Barker, Fred. W. Ford, Arthur Colburn, Edward W. Hazewell, W. A. Ford, Benjamin F. Priest, F. H. Jenks, Benjamin A. Appleton, H. L. Southwick, William D. Sullivan, W. H. Randall, Henry E. Burbeck, Francis M. Weeks, J. Irving Estes, Henry R. Chamberlain. Meetings on the third Friday of every month.

Boston Press Club. (1886). Club-Rooms, 61 Court Street. A club of gentlemen actively engaged in the profession of journalism. E. A. Perry, president; Stephen O'Meara, 1st vice-president; C. M. Hamlin, 2d vice-president; E. L. Alexander, Secretary; B. A. Appleton, treasurer; the foregoing in addition to W. G. Maker, M. H. Cushing, W. D. Sullivan, B. Leighton Beal, F. C. Hills and E. H. Farnsworth, constituting the executive committee. It is the purpose of the club to extend courtesies to gentlemen of the press from other cities.

COMMERCIAL CLUBS.

Merchants Club. (1878). An offshoot of the Commercial Club. It is composed of representatives of the different branches of business. It holds monthly meetings on Saturdays, at Young's Hotel.

Commercial Club. (1868). An organization of gentlemen interested in various branches of business for social purposes, and for the promotion of commercial matters. Among the members are Curtis Guild, George O. Carpenter, Charles M. Clapp, and other well-known citizens. The Club meets at Young's Hotel for its monthly dinners.

AGRICULTURAL CLUBS.

Agricultural Club. An association of prominent gentlemen, interested in agriculture and cognate subjects, for social purposes, as well as to promote the interests of these objects. This Club dines at Parker's, School st., on Saturday.

Cereal Club. A dining Club holding its meetings at the Quincy House.

The nature of its membership is expressed by its name. It entertains visitors in the same line of thought from other cities.

Farmers' Club. Ploughman Hall. A weekly meeting of New England farmers is held at 45 Milk st., every Saturday, to discuss agricultural matters.

DINING CLUBS.

Beside the Clubs having their own Club-Houses, there is a large contingent meeting weekly, fortnightly or monthly, dining at one of the leading hotels. It is almost impossible to present a complete list of these; but the following comprise the majority of them, with their places of dining, as far as are known:

Ace of Clubs...............Parker House
Acis Club..................Quincy House
Acme Club..................Young's Hotel
Acton Club.................Revere House
Alpha Delta Phi............Parker House
Alphabetian Club...........Young's Hotel
American Antiquarian Society............
........................Parker House
Amity Club.................Young's Hotel
Amphion Club...............Quincy House
Am. Soc. Mechanical Engineers.........
........................Parker House
Ancient and Honorable Artillery.........
........................Young's Hotel
A Republican Institution..Parker House
Athenian Club..............Young's Hotel
Bank Presidents' Association ....
........................Parker House
Barton Club................Young's Hotel
Bay State Club.............Parker House
Beacon Society.............Parker House
Bean Club ....Charlestown
Belvidere Club.................Vercelli's
Bennett Club...............Parker House
Beethoven Club.................Roxbury
Bird Club..................Parker House
Bismarck Club..............Young's Hotel
Boot and Shoe Association.Parker House
Boot and Shoe Travellers' League........
........................Parker House
Bon Vivant Club....................Taft's
Boston Club................Parker House
Brimmer School Associa'n.Parker House
British Charitable Society..Parker House
Brookline Club.............Parker House
Bunker Hill Club......................
Cedar Lodge Shooting Club.Parker House
Cereal Club .... Young's Hotel
Clefs ....
Clover Club ....Quincy House
Commercial Club...........Young's Hotel
Delsarte Club.............................
Democratic Club............Parker House
Denver Club..............................
Dry Salters' Club..........Parker House
Easel Club...............................
Emmet Club................... ....S. B.
English High School Association........
........................Parker House
Eta Pi.....................Parker House
Essex Club.................Young's Hotel
Examiner Club..............Parker House
Eurydia Club.............................
Exchange Club..............Parker House
Exeter Club................Quincy House
Fish and Game Protect. Assoc'n.........
........................Parker House
Franklin Club............................
Fraternity Club............Quincy House
Friendly Club..................Vendome

Governor Rice Staff Association.........
..................................Parker House
Grover Cleveland Club......Young's Hotel
Hamilton Association.......Parker House
Hammer and Tongs Club..Young's Hotel
Hasty Pudding Club........Quincy House
Hawes School Association.Quincy House
Homœopathic Medical Association......
..................................Parker House
Hub Club..................Young's Hotel
Independent Club......................
Irish Charitable Society....Parker House
Israel Putnam Club....................
Jeffries Winter Club.......Parker House
Jenkins Club..............Young's Hotel
Jenny Lind Club...............Dorchester
Joseph Warren Club....................
Josiah Quincy Club....................
Kingsley Post Association..Parker House
Kittery Club..............Young's Hotel
Latin School Association...Parker House
Lawrence Club.............Parker House
Liberal Union Club........Young's Hotel
Literary Club.............Parker House
Macaroni Club...............Revere House
Massachusetts Club.......Young's Hotel
Mass. Battery Association. Parker House
Mass. Reform Club.........Parker House
Mass. Regiment Assoc'n...Parker House
Master Builders' Assoc'n.. Parker House
Merchants' Club...........Young's Hotel
Mechanic Apprentices Literary Association..................Parker House
Middlesex Club............Young's Hotel
Momus Club............................
Mozart Club...................Roxbury
Mushroom Club.............Parker House
New England Club.........Young's Hotel
Newetowne Club...........Young's Hotel
Newspaper Club.................Vercelli's
Norfolk Club..............Young's Hotel
O. K. Club................Parker House
Old Point Comfort Club....Parker House
Orpheus Club..............Parker House
Oxford Club...............Parker House
Oxon Club.............................
Paint and Oil Club........Young's Hotel
Papyrus Club..............Revere House
Patti Club.................West Roxbury
Pendennis Club...........Young's Hotel
Phillips Academy Alumni .Parker House
Pibroch Club..........................
Pickwick Club.............Parker House
Pine Tree Club.............Quincy House
Quiz Club.................Young's Hotel
Reform Club...............Parker House
Review Club...............Parker House
Round Table Club.........Young's Hotel
Saturday Club.............Parker House
  At a meeting of the Saturday Club not long since there were assembled Oliver Wendell Holmes, James Russell Lowell, Charles Francis Adams, Jr., James Freeman Clarke, Phillips Brooks, Charles Eliot Norton, E. Rockwood Hoar and others.
Royal Club............................
Shakspeare Club..........Young's Hotel
Sheepskin Club............Parker House
Society of Cincinnati......Parker House
Stable Keepers' Assoc'n...Quincy House
Stoughton Club............Parker House
Suffolk Associates.........Parker House
Tablet Society............Young's Hotel
Thalia Club...............Young's Hotel
Threottyne Club...........Young's Hotel
Travellers' Club...........Parker House
Vermicelli Club.......................
Victoria Club.........................
Vision Club................Parker House
Vista Club.................East Boston
Warren Club..............Young's Hotel
Wasp Club.............................
Washington Lodge..........Parker House
Wendell Phillips Club......Quincy House
Williams Alumni...........Parker House
Wilson-Andrew Club......Quincy House
Windsor Club..........................
Zeta Psi..................Parker House
  (The foregoing list does not include numerous classes of Harvard University who have frequent class or club dinners at Young's Hotel, at the Parker House, and elsewhere.)

RECREATION CLUBS.

Apalachian Mountain Club. Ticknor Building, 9 Park st., Col. T. W. Higginson, president. This is an association of ladies and gentlemen for the purpose of making mountain excursions after the manner of the Alpine clubs of Europe. All interested may here find a library, maps and various other matter bearing on the subject. The rooms of the club are open from 2.30 to 5 o'clock every afternoon.

Boston Base Ball Club. (1871.) Grounds at South End, near Tremont Street. The game of Base Ball is nowhere more popular than in Boston, where the excitement over a match often reaches an exceedingly high point. Boston is the only city that has sustained a professional team since the establishment of a professional association in 1871. In that year the Athletics of Philadelphia held the championship. In 1872, however, the Bostons captured the pennant and held it in 1873, 1874, 1875 (losing it in 1876 to the Chicagos), and again were champions in 1877 and 1878. In 1883 they again held it. The Bostons have therefore retained the championship for seven years out of the fifteen. The Chicagos rank next, having been champions for five years. The Providence (R. I.) club were champions in 1879, 1884. The best record ever made in one season was that of the Bostons in 1875, when they won 71 games and lost 8 only. Following is the championship record:

1871..............Athletics, Philadelphia
1872, 1873, 1874, 1875...............Bostons
1876.........................Chicagos
1877, 1878......................Bostons
1879........Providences, Providence, R. I.
1880, 1881, 1882..................Chicagos
1883..............................Bostons
1884............................Providences
1885.............................Chicagos

It will thus be seen that the championship has remained in the hands of four clubs for fifteen years.

Boston Bicycle Club. (1878). 87 Boylston Street. This is the oldest bicycle club in the city, having been organized Feb. 11, 1878, its first President having been C. E. Pratt. Formerly located at the corner of Tremont Street and Union Park, it is now established on Boylston Street, and is more easily accessible to its members. Fronting the Public Garden, which is one of the most beautiful parks of the city, and being near the fine streets of the Back Bay leading to the Milldam, Longwood, Brookline, Chestnut Hill and other attractive suburbs for cyclists, it is especially convenient for its members.

Boston Blues Baseball Club.

Boston Chess Club. 33 Pemberton Square.

Boston Yacht Club. A noted club, having a large and well-appointed club-house at South Boston.

Boston Cricket Club. This noted Club comprises Thomas Pettitt, W. Rolfe, E. O'Hair, George Lockhardt, W. Pettitt, Dr. Middleton, Taylor, Seylor, Gladhill, Hickey and Loeridge.

Boston Ice-Skating Club. (1886). Union Athletic Exhibition Grounds, Huntington av. An association of ladies and gentlemen having for an object the encouragement and practice of skating upon ice. President, Geo. H. Richards; secretary, Samuel M. Quincy; treasurer, Arthur B. Silsbee. Non-members of the club are admitted to its privileges upon payment of a small fee.

Boston Lacrosse Club.

Country Club. A gentlemen's riding club, having a club-house and extensive grounds at Clyde Park, where frequent meetings are held during the summer months.

Court Tennis Club. Buckingham Street.

Dorchester Lacrosse Club.

Dorchester Yacht Club.

Harvard (or University) Boat Club.

Harvard Cricket Club.

Independent Lacrosse Club.

Longwood Cricket Club.

Massachusetts Bicycle Club. (1879). Club House, 152 Newbury Street, corner of Dartmouth Street. The original members of this great Club, which was organized March 8, 1879, at 87 Summer Street, were Albert A. Pope, Edward W. Pope, Frank W. Freeborn, H. E. Parkhurst, George G. Hall, C. H. Corken, Wm. H. Ames, Augustus F. Webster, H. Winslow Warren, Winfield S. Slocum and Albert S. Parsons. It now has the largest active membership of any bicycle club in America, if not in the world, and has the finest club-house of any cycling club on this continent or in Europe. The Club was organized for the the general promotion of bicycling. It allows no liquor in its house, and no betting or gambling is permitted. The ground floor of the club-house is entirely occupied by a large wheel-room, ninety feet in length, with every convenience for cleaning wheels, setting tires, etc. On the second floor is an elegantly-furnished parlor, reading-room, etc. On the third story is a large gymnasium, etc. In the basement is a bowling-alley, a billiard-room, etc. The building is owned by the Club. The President of the Club is Thomas Wentworth Higginson. The members number about 275. The Club is essentially a *riding* organization, over 300,000 miles having actually been ridden by the members. The average age of the members is 30 years. Members must be 18 years of age.

Myopia Club. A riding-club of gentlemen.

Olympian Club. A club for roller-skating, at Mechanics' Building, Huntington Avenue.

Shawmut Rowing Club. (1869). Dover Street Bridge.

South Boston Lacrosse Club.

South Boston Yacht Club. A large club, having a club-house here.

Union Boat Club. (1851). A large and prosperous club, having a fine club-house on Charles River, at the foot of Chestnut Street. It is strictly an amateur organization. No member is permitted to row in any race where money is awarded. Admission fee, $10. Annual assessments, $5 to $25.

West End Boat Club. East Cambridge Bridge, Charles River. Admission-fee, $5. Monthly dues, $1. The boat-house is built upon floating spars.

VARIOUS OTHER CLUBS.

Boston Liberal Club. Paine Memorial Building, Appleton Street.

Boston Sewing Circle. Charity Building, Chardon Street.

Boston Whist Club. 70 Boylston Street.

British and American Club. (1886). Organized by gentlemen representing the English, Scotch, Irish, Welsh and Canadian elements of the community for the purpose of promoting friendly relations between the people of Great Britain and the United States. The only qualification for membership is the avowal of a desire to secure the object already named. President, Wm H. Ruddick, M. D.; vice-president, James Wemyss, Jr.; treasurer, James Stark; secretary, George B. Perry.

Caledonia Club. 43 Eliot Street.

Cape Cod Association. George Thacher, Secretary.

Catholic Literary Association. 1180 Tremont Street.

Congregational Club. Horticultural Hall.

Germania Social Club. 61 Maverick Street, East Boston.

Kennel Club. (1877). An organization of dog-fanciers, who give exhibitions of dogs in Boston in April or May. These bench-shows were formerly held in Music Hall, but Mechanics Hall, on Huntington Avenue, has latterly been used for this purpose. Mechanics Hall is vastly superior to the other Halls in every respect, for such exhibitions as these. A large number of owners of dogs in all sections of the country attend these bench-shows. The Massachusetts Kennel Club is doing much for improvement in the breeding, health, care and training of the dog, by awarding prizes for the best exhibits in various classes.

Massachusetts Colored League. (1885). 47 Hanover Street.

Organized Nov. 11, 1885, for the purpose of promoting the interests of the colored people of Boston. President, John L. Ruffin.

Massachusetts State Reform Club. S. R. McCready, President.

Metaphysical Club. Mrs. Julia Ward Howe, President.

Nautilus Club. An organization for social and dining purposes. The members include Leopold Morse, Peter Butler, Chas. H. Andrews and others.

Political Clubs. Bird, Boston, Essex, Middlesex, Wilson-Andrew Clubs, etc.

Putnam Club. East Boston. The membership includes Jesse M. Gove, Walter F. Burke, Peter Morrison, J. Henry Stevenson, H. J. Derby, Henry D. Andrews, Frank E. Martin, George W. Hargrave, Harry B. Tindall and Harry J. Cook.

Rhydonian Club. Broadway, South Boston. A social organization.

Roxbury Club. A social organization, of which leading residents of Roxbury are members.

Saturday Morning Club. An association of ladies for literary and social purposes.

Thursday Club. A literary and social organization.

Unitarian Club.

Universalist Club. Formerly known as the Murray Club.

Wednesday Evening Century Club. A literary and social organization.

Workingmen's Club. Wells Memorial Hall, 987 Washington Street.

SUBURBAN EXCURSIONS.

Andover 20 miles from Boston. Boston & Maine Railway. A charming old town, often called Andover-on-the-Hill, is noted as the seat of three well-known institutions of learning, the Andover Theological Seminary, Phillips Academy and Abbott Academy. Andover is beautifully and healthfully situated, on a high and dry location, and the views in every direction are picturesque. The Mansion House is a favorite old, comfortable hotel, largely patronized by Bostonians in the summer. Trains run at almost every hour in the day from Boston, making the town very accessible to merchants who wish to get out of the city during any day or night of the heated term.

Beverly. 18 miles, on the Eastern Railway. A busy shoe-manufacturing town. Along the shore are many summer residences of Boston's wealthy men.

Brookline. 3 miles. Adjoins the city limits. Easily accessible by steam-trains on the Boston and Albany Railway, or by lines of street-cars on Huntington Avenue or Tremont Street. One of the most beautiful suburbs. Its residents are mostly families of wealth, whose mansions are substantial and elegant and are surrounded by well-kept lawns, flower beds, etc. The territory greatly resembles certain out-lying districts near London. The streets, sidewalks, and all that relate to the comfort and convenience of the inhabitants are in the most perfect condition. For driving, 'cycling or walking there is no more beautiful or picturesque locality in the country. The better direction for pedestrians, cyclists and drivers of carriages is out over Beacon Street and the Milldam, through Longwood, another charming suburb. Street-cars may be taken on Tremont Street, at the head of Bromfield Street, furnishing in the summer, when open cars are run, one of the most attractive excursions possible for the trifling expenditure of ten cents for the round trip.

Chelsea. 4 miles. Here is a flourishing city. Reached by ferry from foot of Hanover Street, by ferry from Atlantic Avenue (Boston & Revere Beach Railway), by street-cars of the Lynn and Boston horse-railway, or by street-cars via East Boston ferry. The famous Lowe Tile-Works and the celebrated Chelsea Potteries are here. On Powderhorn Hill is the Soldiers' Home. The United States Naval Hospital is also located here. An elegant theatre, the Academy of Music, is successfully conducted by Manager J. B. Field. The Soldiers' Monument is well worthy of a visit.

Chestnut Hill Reservoir and Park. One of the most beautiful drives, walks or bicycle routes out of Boston is the avenue (Beacon Street) from the Milldam to Chestnut Hill Park, where the great Reservoir of the city is located. The distance is about five miles, and the entire length is bordered by grand old country mansions surrounded by fine old trees and lawns, amid hills and dales. This whole picturesque district more closely resembles an English landscape than any section of country to be found in America. Many Queen Anne cottages peep through the foliage, the closely-shaven lawns, and beds of beautiful flowers, the well-kept roads, etc., combine to complete the great natural resemblance to "the green lanes of England." Foreigners are sure to note the similarity, and with surprise, especially when they catch a glimpse of "the winding Charles," which they liken to England's beautiful Thames. The road to Chestnut Hill is the most fashionable drive in New England, the horses and carriages to be found there on any pleasant afternoon indicating by their numbers and expensiveness the great wealth of their owners, the merchant princes of Boston. Equestrians are also to be seen here somewhat numerously, although many of them make detours by way of bridle-paths and lanes leading from the main road. The grounds about the Reservoir are laid out as a park, and in summer are very attractive. The Reservoir is one of the "sights" of the suburbs. It has an area of 125 acres, has a capacity of about 800,000,000 gallons, and is two and a half miles in circumference. (This is one of the most popular bicycle routes.)

Concord. 19 miles from Boston. Fitchburg Railway. Also, Boston & Lowell Railway. Tourists cannot fail to find most attractive objects of historical and literary interest in this picturesque old town. Here lived Nathaniel Hawthorne (in a house now standing about a mile from the Common); Thoreau and Emerson. Here is the summer home of Louise Alcott, in the house once occupied by Thoreau. On the shore of Lake Walden, one of the most beautiful sheets of water in New England, is a pile of stones marking the spot where was located the hut in which Thoreau lived for some time. The Summer School of Philosophy attracts many persons from various sections of the United States and Canada to Concord. This school is held in a chapel, which is particularly well adapted for the purpose. Near the Old Manse is "the rude bridge that arched the flood," the Concord monument, and the graves of the British soldiers who fell in the memorable battle of April 19, 1775. In the Unitarian Church building, near the Wright Tavern, the first Provincial Congress was held. The Concord Library, at the junction of Sudbury and Main Streets, is a valuable collection of books. The Davis Museum of relics is in the Old Court House. Thoreau, in his "Walden," describes the lake as follows: "It is so remarkable for its depth and purity as to merit a particular description. It is a clear and deep green well, half a mile long and a mile and three-quarters in circumference; it contains about sixty-one and a half acres; a perennial spring in the midst of pine and oak woods without any visible inlet or outlet, except by the clouds and evaporation. The surrounding hills rise abruptly from the water to the height of forty to eighty feet, being exclusively woodland. The water is so transparent that the bottom can easily be discerned at the depth of twenty-five or thirty feet." At the completion of the Concord Monument, April 19th, 1836, a hymn written by Emerson, entitled "Concord Fight," was sung. The following is the first stanza:

"By the rude bridge that arched the flood
Their flag to April's breeze unfurled,
Here once the embattled farmers stood
And fired the shot heard round the world."

Hawthorne wrote in his note-book: "The scenery of Concord, as I beheld it from the summit of the hill, has no very marked characteristics, but has a good deal of quiet beauty in keeping with the river. There are broad and peaceful meadows, which I think are among the most satisfying objects in natural scenery. The heart reposes on them with a feeling that few things else can give, because almost all other objects are abrupt and clearly defined; but a meadow stretches out like a small infinity, yet with a secure homeliness, which we do not find either in an expanse of water or air. The hills which border these meadows are wide swells of land, or long and gradual ridges, some of them densely covered with wood." Emerson wrote:

"Because I was content with these poor fields,
Low, open meads, slender and sluggish streams,
And found a home in haunts which others scorned,
The partial woodgods overpaid my love
And granted me the freedom of their state.
*   *   *   *   *
And through my rocklike, solitary went
Shot million rays of thought and tenderness."

In the principal cemetery of the town are the graves of Emerson, Thoreau and Hawthorne.

Danvers. (Salem Village of 1692.) 20 miles from Boston, on Boston & Maine Railway. This was the scene of the notorious witchcraft delusion, which exhibited the ignorance and superstition of the people of that place and period. Danvers is a pleasant town. Here is the Peabody Library, which, like the Peabody Institute at Peabody—once a portion of Danvers—was established through the munificence of George Peabody, the London banker, who was born in Peabody (South Danvers). In Danvers is still standing the house in which Gen. Israel Putnam, "Old Put," was born.

Ipswich. 26 miles from Boston, on the Eastern Division of the Boston and Maine Railway, is one of the most beautifully located towns in New England. Its great, productive farms, its old mansions, and its general thrift tempt many a Boston merchant prince to seek a summer home within its beautiful and recreative domain.

Jamaica Plain. One of the outlying Districts of Boston (West Roxbury) 3½ miles from State Street, on the Boston & Providence Railway. It was named in honor of Cromwell's conquest of the island of Jamaica from Spain. It was originally known as Pond Plain, from the famous beautiful pond within its limits, covering 70 acres and having a depth in places of from 60 to 70 feet. It is one of the most attractive sections of the city, having broad avenues lined with fine old trees, and has been a favorite location for summer residences since the days of Hancock, Bowdoin and other Governors and distinguished men who formerly resided here amid great pomp and ceremony. (John Hancock used to ride from his country-seat here to his town mansion, his equipage being princely, and preceded and followed by a body-guard of mounted soldiers fifty in number, with drawn sabres, as an illustration of republican simplicity, probably!) In this District are located the famous Bussey Institute and Arnold Arboretum, (*Colleges and Schools*); the Adams Nervine Asylum; the West Roxbury Soldiers' Monument (dedicated Sept. 14, 1871); the Allandale Springs, a place of resort of great and rapidly-growing popularity; Curtis Hall; and various other objects of interest. (In the summer open cars are run on the street-railway to Jamaica Plain, starting from the head of Bromfield st., forming a very pleasant means of communication, and, during a portion of the route, passing many fine estates, with grand mansions, well-kept lawns, etc. The roads will be found good for bicycle-riding).

Lexington. 11 miles from Boston. Boston & Lowell Railway. (Bicyclists will find the route by way of the Mill dam, Brighton Avenue, Harvard Square, Porter Station, Arlington, a good one). The poet Whittier thus sings of the Lexington of olden days: (1775).

"No Berserk thirst of blood had they,
No battle-joy was theirs, who set
Against the alien bayonet
Their homespun breasts in that old day.

Their feet had trodden peaceful ways;
They loved not strife, they dreaded pain,
They saw not — what to us is plain —
That God would make man's wrath his praise.
  *   *   *   *   *
Swift as their summons came they left
The plow mid-furrow standing still,
The half-ground corn grist in the mill,
The spade in earth, the axe in cleft.
  *   *   *   *   *
Of man for man the sacrifice,
All that was theirs to give they gave.
The flowers that blossomed from their grave
Have sown themselves beneath all skies."

Lynn. 12 miles, on the Eastern division of the Boston & Maine Railway. A great shoe-manufacturing centre. One of the most thriving cities in Massachusetts. It has many points of interest to strangers, among them its Beaches, Dungeon Rock (or Pirates' Cave), High Rock, etc. Here was formerly the abode of Moll Pitcher, the celebrated fortune-teller, whose habitation was near the base of High Rock. About sixty years ago she attracted many people from far and near — largely sea-going persons — who desired her aid in looking into futurity. Her full name was Mary Dimond Pitcher. She died in 1813, aged 75 years. She has been described as having been connected with some of the best families of Essex County, and has respected descendants now living in the vicinity of Boston. In 1832, John Greenleaf Whittier wrote a poem relating to her, from which we make the following excerpt:

"She stood upon a bare, tall crag
Which overlooked her rugged cot, —
A wasted, gray and meagre hag,
In features evil as her lot.
She had the crooked nose of a witch,
And a crooked back and chin,
And in her gait she had a hitch,
And in her hand she carried a switch
To aid her work of sin."

High rock is the name given to an elevation which commands a fine view of the city and surrounding country, as well as of the sea. From Elizabeth F. Merrill's poem, "High Rock," we transcribe the following lines:

"When the tide comes in on a sunny day
You can see the waves beat back in spray
From the splintered spurs of Phillips Head,
Or tripping along with dainty tread,

As of a million dancing feet
Shake out the light in a quick retreat
Or along the smooth curve of the beach
Snowy and curling, in long lines reach
An islet, anchored and held to land
By a glistening, foam-fringed ribbon of sand;
That is Nahant, and that hoary ledge
To the left is Egg Rock, like a blunted wedge
Cleaving the restless ocean's breast,
And bearing the lighthouse on its crest."

Dungeon Rock is noted as having been the retreat of pirates in days gone by. There is a tradition that Captain Kidd buried some of his treasure here. The huge rock is in a wild and picturesquely beautiful region, although a good carriage-road has been constructed to it from the city lying below. For many years, under "spiritual" guidance, excavations were continuously, slowly and laboriously made in expectation of discovering buried treasure, by Mr. Marble and his son, both of whom passed away without realizing their hopes. Descent into the dark, winding stairway, cut from the solid rock, may be made by the visitor upon payment of a small fee. Since the death of the zealous and industrious men who doubtless sacrificed their lives in toiling in the damp, unwholesome cavern, work upon the excavation has been entirely suspended.

Malden is a thriving and very pretty suburb, 5 miles out, on the Boston & Maine Railway. Here is the studio and home of the famous American artist, George Loring Brown, whose paintings embellish so many elegant residences. There is a very old burial-ground here, known as the Sandy Creek or Bell Rock Cemetery, and was used for purposes of interment as early as 1650. The following is copied from the oldest stone:

ALICE BRACKENBURY,
WIFE OF WM. B. BRACKENBURY.
AGED 70 YEARS.
DIED DECEMBER 28, 1670.

Here also was buried Rev. Michael Wigglesworth, noted as the author of "The Day of Doom," a poem.

Manchester-by-the-Sea. 24 miles from Boston. Eastern Railway. This is one of the most picturesque and romantic spots along the entire New England Coast. The roads are excellent, and one can find every description of drives. There are roads through the open country, along hillsides, through the woods or by the sea. Here is the famed singing beach. Manchester has for many years been the summer home of a noted colony of theatrical people, among them Mrs. Agnes Booth (Schoeffel), Mrs. D. P. Bowers, John Gilbert, Joseph Proctor, John B. Schoeffel, and others. Here is located the celebrated Masconomo House, a favorite resort of Bostonians, New Yorkers, Philadelphians, and others from the south and west, during the summer months, the cool, clear air of this region being extremely beneficial to those exhausted by over-work or illness. Rev. Dr. Bartol, the eminent Boston clergyman, has done much toward developing the resources of this beautiful town. It was called Manchester-by-the-Sea in order to distinguish it from Manchester, N. H.

Marblehead. 17 miles. (Eastern Railway to Salem, then Marblehead Branch.) This is the quaintest old seaport town imaginable. When the celebrated Whitefield visited Marblehead and saw scarcely anything but bare rocks, he asked in amazement, "Where do they bury their dead?" Here is yet standing the old Bank Building, built in 1768, and there are a number of other curious old ante-Revolutionary houses. Old Fort Sewall is an interesting feature of the locality.

Milton. 6 miles. This is one of Boston's most beautiful suburbs. It is easily reached by way of the Old Colony Railway (trains running both ways sixteen times daily), or by street cars from the head of Franklin street, corner of Washington street. The roads are good for bicycles. (Milton was a portion of Suffolk County, previous to 1793). Here is standing what is known as the Suffolk Resolves Mansion, an inscription on a tablet on the front of the building reading in part as follows:

IN THIS MANSION, ON THE NINTH DAY OF SEPTEMBER, 1774, AT A MEETING OF THE DELEGATES OF EVERY TOWN AND DISTRICT IN THE COUNTY OF SUFFOLK, THE SUFFOLK RESOLVES WERE ADOPTED. THEY WERE REPORTED BY MAJOR GENERAL WARREN WHO FELL IN THEIR DEFENCE AT THE BATTLE OF BUNKER HILL, JUNE 17, 1775.

Here, in the Cemetery, are laid the remains of Wendell Phillips, removed from the Granary Burying-ground (where they had temporarily been placed at his death) in April, 1886. There are numerous objects of interest to strangers. There is a bright local paper, the Milton News, published by W. A. Woodward.

Newton Circuit. One of the most pleasant excursions into the beautiful suburbs of Boston may be made by what is known as the Newton Circuit of the Boston & Albany Railway, opened May 16, 1886. As is well known the group of villages comprising the city of Newton, and the other towns between Newton and Boston, are among the most picturesque and charming localities to be found in America, rivalling the beautiful settlements along the banks of the Thames above London, the river Charles being no less worthy of admiration than the English river, and, in fact, there are various points of resemblance between them. By means of the new Newton Circuit one may find frequent and rapid transit to this delightful suburban region. The Circuit Line from Boston to Boston —via Main Line Circuit and Brookline Circuit—has the following stations: Cottage Farm (3m.), Allston (4), Brighton (5), Faneuil (6), Newton (6¼), Newtonville (8), West Newton (9), Auburndale (10), Riverside (11) (the farthest point of the Circuit, a branch line running from here to Newton Lower Falls), Woodland (11), Waban (10½), Eliot (10), Newton Highlands (9), Newton Centre (8), Chestnut Hill (7), Reservoir (6), Cypress Street (4½), Brookline (4), Longwood (3), Chapel (2 3-4), Beacon Street, and ending in Boston, where it begins. Trains are run every day, Sundays included, almost every half hour, upwards of 20 trains per day, each way, being made up.

Peabody. 18 miles, on the Eastern Railway. Here is the house where George Peabody was born. The Peabody Institute and Library, given by Peabody to the town, are well worthy of a visit. The Institute contains a remarkably fine oil portrait of Queen Victoria, and many other highly interesting objects. Here, also, is Harmony Grove Cemetery, where Peabody was buried, and an old burying-ground, where Eliza Wharton, "the Coquette," was buried. In this town is also the noted "Ship Rock." (Peabody can be reached by street-cars from Cornhill, via Lynn & Boston horse-railway.)

Quincy. 8 miles from Boston. Old Colony Railway. One of the most attractive suburbs of the city. This town was called after John Quincy, who died in 1767. Here are a number of historic old mansions, among them the houses in which the Presidents of the United States, John Adams and John Quincy Adams, were born and also the house in which both of them died. Their remains were placed in the portico of the Stone Temple. The house in which John Hancock lived is also standing. It was here that the first railway in this country was laid, in 1826, the line being three miles in length. The noted Adams Academy is located here. Among the interesting features of the town are the Sailors' Snug Harbor and the National Sailors' Home. The great granite quarries are objects of wonder to strangers. In fact, the town abounds in interesting localities. At the dedication of the Sailors' Snug Harbor, Lunt's fine poem, containing the following lines, was read:

"Here may the veteran mariner repose
When on his craft the life-storm fiercely blows;

Here let him turn aport, and, furling sail,
Run for a harbor through the driving
  gale;
Here, rounding to, drop anchor near the
  shore,
And ride in safety till life's voyage is
  o'er.
From cape to cape, search round our
  noble Bay,
No lovelier sight than here can eye sur-
  vey;
From yonder hill, when sunsets blazing
  sheen
Sets in a golden frame the pictured
  scene,
Let the eye wander freely as it will —
Landward or seaward — all is beauty
  still."

North of Germantown is Hough's Neck, granted to Atherton Hough, of Boston, in 1637. The road from Quincy was laid out in 1673. The view from Hough's Neck, or "Bay-side Park," is one of great beauty and diversity.

Salem. 16 miles from Boston. Reached by Eastern division Boston & Maine Railway. Also by street cars via Lynn and Peabody. Lynn & Boston horse-railway, office Cornhill, near Scollay Square. Good bicycle roads. (Bicycle route is over the Milldam, through Brighton Avenue to Harvard Square, Cambridge, to Porter's Station, to Medford, Malden, Maplewood, East Sangus, Lynn, and Salem.) Salem is an extremely interesting old city. It is the county seat of Essex County. The Essex House is on the principal street, Essex Street. Here is a State Normal School; the Essex Institute, (with a library of 25,000 vols.); the Salem Athenaeum, (with 14,000 vols.); the East India Marine Hall, containing the fine ethnological museum of the Marine Society, (open to the public *free* every day except Sunday from 9 a. m. to 5 p. m.) Historical associations abound here. The Roger Williams House, which is still standing at the corner of North and Essex Streets, is noted for having been the building in which some of the early examinations of persons charged with making use of witchcraft were held. Gallows Hill, where executions took place, is an elevation in the western part of the city. The frame of the original first meeting-house, built in 1634, is still to be seen, in the rear of Plummer Hall. But, to the sentimental tourist, the associations clustering about the scenes of some of Hawthorne's romances are in Salem (as in Boston) more precious than any others, than even historical facts. Hawthorne was born in Union Street in 1804. The house is now occupied by two families, and is fast going to decay. It is a two-story wooden house, and was once painted brown. The house on Mall Street, where Hawthorne wrote "The Scarlet Letter," is also standing, and is somewhat more pretentious than the Union Street house. The Custom House desk of pine where he made his first rough draft of " The Scarlet Letter " is sacredly preserved in the reconstructed old First Church, before mentioned. Another building, the Ingersoll House, dating from 1662, is called "The House of the Seven Gables," although Hawthorne declared that he drew entirely upon his imagination for the site of his Puncheon mansion.

Sudbury. 26 miles from Boston. Longfellow has immortalized the old inn at Sudbury in his famous "Tales of a Wayside Inn," from which the following extract is taken. Of the personages introduced into these Tales the musician was the late Ole Bull — whose widow and daughter now reside in Cambridge — and the Sicilian was Luigi Monti.

"As ancient is this hostelry
As any in the land may be,
Built in the old colonial day
When men lived in a grander way
With ampler hospitality;
A kind of old Hobgoblin Hall
Now somewhat fallen to decay,
With weather stains upon the wall,
And stairways worn, and crazy doors,
And creaking and uneven floors,
And chimneys huge and tiled and tall."

Swampscott. 12 miles, on the Eastern Railway. The summer home of numerous well-known wealthy Bostonians. There are many elegant villas, and several fine hotels, among them being the Lincoln and Ocean Houses. The beaches are of good length, and the bathing, on account of the comparative warmth of the water, is very enjoyable.

Wellesley. 15 miles. Boston and Albany Railway. This is one of the most beautiful towns in the chain of park-like suburbs surrounding Boston. Here is located the great Wellesley College for young ladies. The celebrated grounds of William Emerson Baker known as Krino Park and Grotto, are visited by many thousands of people every summer, while near by is the Hunnewell Estate, with its noted Italian-terrace Garden.

Wenham, a pretty town, 22 miles from Boston, is noted for its Wenham Lake, from which, in years gone by, ice was cut by the Tudor Ice Company, of Boston, and sent to England. Ice is known in London, to-day, as " Wenham," taking its name from Wenham Lake. (Wenham is in Essex County, on the Eastern Division of the Boston and Maine Railway.)

PUBLIC PARKS.

A few years ago Boston began to realize that with the rapid increase in population there came the need of more open spaces in which the people might find rest and recreation, and that the time to lay out these public parks was before desirable territory for such grounds had been laid out into streets and covered with dwelling houses. Boston *sometimes* looks ahead a little, and in the matter of parks, she has recently taken steps in a true, progressive direction. The following is a list of old and new public parks and squares:

Arboretum Park, Jamaica Plain, W. Roxbury District. 164 acres. Reached by steam railway, Boston and Providence line to Forest Hills Station, or by street-cars, Jamaica Plain line.

Back Bay Park. On the "made land" of the Back Bay or New West End Territory. Avenues lead to it from West Chester Park Street and Beacon Street. It is constructed on a novel plan, combining effects of "wild gardens," groves of trees and shrubbery, water-basins, etc., diversified by carriage-drives and promenades. The Back Bay cars take one quite near.

Belmont Square. Bounded by Sumner, Webster, Seaver and Lamson Streets, East Boston. Area, 30,000 square feet.

Blackstone Square. Bounded by Shawmut Avenue, West Newton, Washington and West Brookline Streets. Area, 105,100 square feet.

Boston Common. Bounded by Tremont, Park, Beacon, Charles and Boylston Streets. Area, 48¼ acres.

Brighton Square. Between Rockland Street and Chestnut Hill Avenue, Brighton District. Area, 25,035 square feet.

Bromley Park. From Bickford Street to Albert Street. Area, 20,975 square feet.

Cedar Square. Cedar Street, Roxbury District. Area, 26,163 square feet.

Central Square. Between Meridian Street and Border Street, East Boston. Area, 32,310 square feet.

Chester Park. From Washington Street (No. 1750) to Harrison Avenue (No. 841), South End.

Chester Square. From Washington Street (No. 1747) to Tremont Street (No. 780), South End. Area, 74,000 square feet.

City Square. Near Main, Bow and Chelsea Streets, Charlestown District.

Commonwealth Avenue Parkway. From Arlington Street to West Chester Park Street. A beautiful promenade, with lawn, four rows of shade trees, a number of fine statues, etc. Area, 429,500 square feet.

Dorchester Square. Meeting House Hill, Dorchester District. Area, 56,200 square feet.

East Chester Park. From Harrison Avenue (856) to junction of Cottage and Boston Streets. Area, 9,300 square feet.

Eaton Square. Church and Bowdoin Streets, Dorchester District. Area, 13,280 square feet.

Fort Hill Square. Oliver and High Streets. A park upon the site of Fort Hill, removed some years since. Area, 29,480 square feet.

Fountain Square. From 15 Fountain Street, Roxbury District.

Franklin (West Roxbury) Park. A large territory in the West Roxbury District, which has been opened to the public in its natural state. Division walls have been removed, and the people are permitted to roam at will over its hills, plains and meadows, or through its woodlands. Naturally one of the most picturesque and beautiful tracts in New England, it must eventually become, when artistic features have supplemented its present wildness, one of the most charming great public parks of the world. The most elaborate plans for heightening the beauty of its original features have been prepared. It is visited by large numbers, especially on Sundays. It is estimated that on certain holidays and Sundays the number of visitors from all directions has reached 50,000. If better facilities for transportation were afforded even larger numbers would probably assemble. The Park already contains about one thousand acres, and it will probably be enlarged by the addition of several estates adjoining. The main entrance is from Blue Hill Avenue. (Take Franklin Park or Oakland Garden street-cars at Temple Place.)

Franklin Square. Bounded by Washington Street (Nos. 1534 to 1548), East Newton, James and East Brookline Streets, South End. Area, 105,205 square feet.

Independence Square. South Boston. Bounded by Broadway, Second, M and N Streets. Area, six and one-half acres.

Jackson Square. Chestnut Hill Avenue, Union and Winthrop Streets. Area, 4,300 square feet.

Jamaica Pond Park. The shore of Jamaica Pond, West Roxbury District. Area, 31,000 square feet.

Lewis Park. Highland Street and Highland Avenue. Area, 5,000 square feet.

Lincoln Square. Emerson, Fourth and M Streets, South Boston. Area, 9,510 square feet.

Linwood Park. Centre and Linwood Streets, Roxbury District. Area, 3,025 square feet.

Longwood Park. Park and Austin Streets, Roxbury District. Area, 21,000 square feet.

Louisburg Square. Between Pinckney and Mount Vernon Streets, West End. Embellished with statues of Aristides and Columbus.

Lowell Square. Cambridge and Lynde Streets. Area, 5,772 square feet.

Madison Square. Bounded by Sterling, Marble, Warwick and Westminster Streets. Area, 122,191 square feet.

Maverick Square. Sumner and Maverick Streets, East Boston. Area, 4,398 square feet.

Marine Park. City Point, South Boston. This is a unique public resort, comprising a number of acres fronting on the water. From the shore extends a wide pier, several hundred feet in length, affording a delightfully cool promenade on a hot day or evening. Seats are placed along the entire length of the pier. The marine view is a superb one. (Street-cars of either the Scollay sq. or Park sq. lines of the South Boston railway carry passengers directly to the Marine Park.)

Montgomery Square. Tremont, Clarendon and Montgomery Streets. South End. Area, 550 square feet.

Mount Bellevue Park. The summit of Mount Bellevue, West Roxbury District. Area, 27,772 square feet.

Mount Bowdoin Square. Top of Mount Bowdoin, Dorchester District. Area, 16,000 square feet.

Orchard Park. Orchard Park, Chadwick and Yeoman Streets. Area, 92,592 square feet.

Park Square. Columbus Avenue, Pleasant and Eliot Streets. Area, 2,867 square feet. Here is placed the Emancipation Group, a notable work of statuary.

Pemberton Square. Between Tremont and Somerset Streets. Area, 3,390 square feet.

Prescott Square. Prescott, Trenton and Eagle Streets, East Boston. Area, 12,284 square feet.

Public Garden. Bounded by Boylston, Charles, Beacon and Arlington Streets. Area, 24¼ acres. One of the most attractive and beautiful parks in the world.

Putnam Square. Putnam, White and Trenton Streets, East Boston. Area, 11,628 square feet.

Sullivan Square. Bounded by Main, Cambridge, Gardner and Sever Streets, Charlestown District. Area, 56,428 square feet.

Thomas Park. Telegraph Hill, South Boston. Area, 190,000 square feet.

Union Park. Between Tremont Street and Shawmut Avenue. Area, 16,050 square feet.

Washington Park. Bainbridge and Dale Streets, Roxbury District. Area, 396,125 square feet.

West Chester Park. Between Tremont Street and Columbus Avenue. Area, 10,150 square feet.

Winthrop Square. Winthrop, Common and Adams Streets, Charlestown District. Area, 38,450 square feet.

Worcester Square. Between Washington Street and Harrison Avenue. Area, 16,000 square feet.

GYMNASIUMS.

A Number of years ago a great impetus was given to gymnastic training in Boston by Dr. George B. Winship, "the strong man." Later, Dr. Dio Lewis did much to promote physical health, especially among young women. The city and suburbs are now well supplied with finely-appointed gymnasiums, as follows:

Boston Young Men's Christian Association Gymnasium. 174 Boylston Street.

Boston Young Men's Christian Union Gymnasium. 18 Boylston Street.

Boston Young Women's Christian Association Gymnasium. Corner of Berkeley and Appleton Streets.

Butler Gymnasium. 43 West Street.

Catholic Young Men's Gymnasium. Prospect Street, cor. Harvard, Cambridgeport. Splendidly equipped. 105 ft. long by 93 feet wide; 66 ft. high.

Hemenway Gymnasium. Harvard University, Cambridge. Said to be one of the best-equipped gymnasiums in the world.

Turn Hall Gymnasium. 29 Middlesex Street.

Wells Memorial Gymnasium. 987 Washington Street.

BEACHES AND SEASIDE RESORTS.

Broad in the sunshine stretched away,
With its capes and islands, the turquoise bay,
And over water and dusk of pines
Blue hills lifted their faint outlines.
—JOHN GREENLEAF WHITTIER.

Atlantic Hill. A noted eminence at Nantasket, upon which is situated the Atlantic House. (See *Nantasket*).

Beachmont. (See *Revere Beach*).

Black Rock. A Nantasket resort. Exceedingly picturesque.

Brant Rock. In Marshfield. A favorite resort.

City Point. South Boston. For the perspiring citizen or stranger who wishes to find a cool temperature within a short distance, a ride of about thirty minutes upon one of the open cars of either the Scollay Square or Park Square lines of the South Boston Horse Railway, will take him to City Point, where he can usually enjoy cool, ocean breezes to his heart's content. Now that the new Marine Park has been opened, with its broad pier extending several hundred feet into the waters of Dorchester Bay, sheltered from the sun and from rain for the distance of three hundred and fifty feet, and having a double row of seats its entire length, the number of people who make an excursion to this point is daily on the increase. On the first warm day after the pier was constructed (1886) a multitude of people visited this Park. The Park Commissioners have arranged for the preservation of perfect order. The invigorating salt-air breezes, the beautiful view of the vessels passing in and out of the harbor; of Fort Independence, Thompson Island, etc., and the pleasant ride to the Point, combine to form a very attractive excursion, for an outlay of ten cents.

Cohasset. This is one of the most beautiful and romantic spots along the whole coast. Here a large theatrical colony have summer homes. Lawrence Barrett has a fine residence. William H. Crane, Stuart Robson, Harry Meredith, George C. Boniface and others have pleasant homes here. (Cohasset is 20 miles from Boston, on the Old Colony Railway).

Cottage Park. (See *Winthrop*).

Crescent Beach. (See *Revere Beach*).

Crystal Bay, (See *Winthrop*).

Downer Landing. One of the most beautiful spots in Boston Harbor is

Downer. Partly sheltered from the strongest force of Old Ocean and the winds by projecting headlands and rocky points, it is much patronized by those who prefer placid basins to high-rolling breakers, and quiet, picturesque views to the more bold surroundings of some of the other resorts near the city. Here one may bathe in water that is more shallow and is less cold than at other beaches, and there are many unique features which bring visitors here who seldom go to the other seaside resorts. Here is the noted Melville Garden, with an area of twenty acres, within which are offered innumerable attractions — boating, fishing, bathing, dancing, bowling, shooting, and opportunities for playing billiards, ball, croquet, tennis, lacrosse, etc., while swings, flying horses, and other amusements please the young. There are bear-pits, and numerous other objects of interest. It is a great resort for picnic parties from all sections of New England. One of its features consists of an immense clambake pavilion — seating nearly a thousand people at one time—where mammoth heaps of clams cooked in the primitive manner of the Indians, and taught by them to the early settlers of Boston, namely, by baking them upon stones upon which a hot fire has been burning, placing over them seaweed to hold the heat. Ears of green corn are cooked in the same manner, and at the same time. These clambakes are greatly enjoyed by the rural population who swarm to Downer Landing on hot summer days, crowding the great harbor steamers to the limit permitted by law. Downer Landing has quite a large colony of summer residents from Boston and other cities. There is an excellent hotel, the Rose Standish House. That a certain degree of exclusiveness pervades the community may be gathered from the following, from the pen of Nora Perry: "Downer Landing is a retreat for the cottagers, chiefly; and, still and high, it looks down upon Nantasket's whirl and bustle with a little of the holier-than-thouativeness that comes so natural to the Bostonian. Ask these quiet dwellers, enthroned upon their height, if they visit Nantasket frequently, for a day's junketing, and see with what a superior air of pity for your ignorance you will be answered. You might as well ask them if they spent Fourth of July on Boston Common." (Steamers for Downer Landing leave India Wharf, 288 Atlantic Avenue, frequently during the day. Sundays included. Trains on the Old Colony Railway carry passengers to Hingham).

Glades. At the extreme end of Scituate. A most romantic and beautiful spot. Here are the summer homes of several prominent Bostonians, among them Hon. Oliver Ames, Frederic L. Ames, Hon. Robert Codman and others.

Green Hill. One of the Nantasket resorts. The summer home of the Hanlon Brothers, the famous pantomimists.

Grover Cliff. A locality in Winthrop.

Hingham. About three miles from Nantasket Beach is the old town of Hingham. This is a summer home of quite a number of Bostonians, who admire its streets, shaded by fine old trees, and its many charming drives. Here is a statue of John A. Andrew. In the South Hingham burial-ground is a renowned magnolia tree. (Hingham is 17 miles from Boston, on the Old Colony Railway.)

Hough's Neck (or Bayside Park) lies north of Germantown, Quincy. It is reached by a three-mile carriage road from Quincy on the Old Colony Railway. As a place for summer residence, owing to its comparatively isolated situation and the superb views in every direction, it is coming to be regarded as one of the most desirable in the vicinity of the city.

Hull. George S. Hillard compared Nantasket and Hull to the Lido of Venice; but it was hardly fair toward Hull, say travellers. At Hull is the Hotel Pemberton, an imposing structure of Queen Anne architecture, and with spacious piazzas, band-stand, etc. The views from the Pemberton are extremely beautiful, in whatever direction one may look. The pier of the steamboat line is near the hotel, as is also the station of the Nantasket Beach Railway. Many passengers going to Nantasket leave the steamer at Hull and proceed the rest of the way by rail, thus giving the trip a pleasing variety. (For Hull take steamers of Rowe's wharf,—340 Atlantic Avenue— seven times each way daily. See timetable in daily papers. Street-cars to Rowe's wharf from head of Franklin Street. Rail *all the way* from Boston to Hull on Old Colony and Nantasket Beach Railways).

Jerusalem Road. (See *Nantasket*).

Marshfield.
O the sea, the sea!
And Marshfield.
DANIEL WEBSTER.

Small wonder that the great statesman, amid the cares of public life at Washington or his office duties in Boston, sighed for a glimpse of the spot he held dearer than all, his seaside summer home at Marshfield. This is a very pleasant old town, and one will feel well repaid for a visit. Here was for many years the home of the late Adelaide Phillipps. (Marshfield is reached by trains on the Old Colony Railway. It is 31 miles from Boston.)

Nahant. Longfellow — who had a summer residence here — sang :

" Till my soul is full of longing
For the secret of the sea,
And the heart of the great ocean
Sends a thrilling pulse through me."

Lady Mary Wortley Montague wrote: "In returning through the harbor of Boston from Nahant we were full of admiration of its scenery; the many lovely islands with which it is beautifully studded, and the superb view of Boston itself, so nobly surmounted by its crown-like State House, enchanted us." Nahant was the summer home of Agassiz and Prescott, as well as of Longfellow. At Nahant are some most attractive localities. For one who likes to see the breaking waves dash high, there is no place near the city more picturesque nor beautiful. (One can go direct by steamboat from India Wharf — 288 Atlantic av. — or by rail to Lynn, by Eastern or Revere Beach Railways, thence to Nahant by coach.)

Nantasket Beach. Peter Peregrine wrote: "The Nantasket Beach is the most beautiful one I ever saw. It sweeps round in a majestic curve, which, if it were continued so as to complete the circle, would of itself embrace a small sea. There was a gentle breeze upon the water, and the sluggish waves rolled inward with an languid movement, and broke, with a low murmur of music, in long lines of foam against the opposing sands. The surface of the sea was — in every direction — thickly dotted with sails, the air was of a delicious temperature, and altogether it was a scene to detain one for hours." His pen-picture of this delightful resort will find instant appreciation in the minds of all who have ever sojourned at this celebrated beach, although since it was written the surroundings upon the shore have vastly changed. Palatial hotels have been built, avenues have been laid out, and the former deserted rocky headlands are fast assuming the appearance of a summer city by the sea. For those of New England — and New York State also furnishes its quota — who really desire "a day at the beach," Nantasket offers the desired attractions. Here is a wide, hard, smooth beach, almost as even as a floor, seven miles in length, and sweeping in most graceful lines, with facilities for driving, walking, bathing, etc., that no beach on the coast can surpass. Above all, the adjoining shore is not a flat, tame, uninteresting waste of land, but consists largely of lofty, rugged, rocky headlands, rising majestically from the sea, and surmounted with structures of various styles of architecture. Along the Jerusalem road are scenes of the greatest beauty and picturesqueness, the waters surging in among the rocks in great masses of foaming surf, and casting showers of sparkling spray into the air. In a few moments after arriving at the beach one can by taking a Jerusalem road coach find as much seclusion as may be desired. But to the hundreds of thousands of people who run down to Nantasket for a few hours, or a few days, during the summer, the bustle of the great hotels, the excitement of the promenades, the quickening pulse which stirs great throngs of humanity, the music of the bands, the dinner, the plunge into the high-rolling surf, the various games, etc., are more tempting than the retirement to more secluded spots. The beach ordinarily presents the appearance of a town on a grand holiday; flags are flying, music fills the air, crowds of people arrayed in fine clothes are promenading, merry laughter comes from various cafes where numerous parties are partaking of a genuine old-fashioned clam-bake or a "fish dinner;" there are aquariums, merry-go-rounds, miniature elevated-railways, skating-rinks, Punch-and-Judy shows; peddlers of whips, toy-balloons, peanuts, pop-corn, lemonade; dime museums of five-legged heifers, fat women, circus-acrobats, and altogether one gets the impression that a Fourth-of-July celebration has been transferred here from Boston Common. The great Hotel Nantasket, situated directly upon the beach, with its grand covered promenades, piazzas, band-stand, etc., is the central point where gather the bulk of day excursionists, most of whom scarcely leave the immediate vicinity until they take the steamer for the return trip to the city. At a short distance, upon an elevation giving a superb panoramic view of land and sea, is the noted Rockland House, a favorite summer home of representatives of Boston's fashionable circles. Rooms here are in such great demand that early application is necessary in order to secure them. Both of these grand hotels are under the efficient management of Russell & Sturgis, who have won the gratitude of thousands of patrons for the acceptable manner in which they have administered to the comfort and pleasure of all who have come within their care. These gentlemen deserve all the popularity they have gained, and that their success increases from year to year is but a deserved tribute. The rapid development of the resources of this great pleasure-resort during the past few years is largely due to the enterprise, foresight and progressiveness of these popular hosts. The Atlantic House is beautifully located upon a high bluff, and is abundantly patronized. Scores of other hotels, cafes, etc., have been built along the beach and upon the highlands, all of which seem to be prosperous. The editor of a New York newspaper writes thus of this resort: "Bostonians are justly proud of Nantasket Beach, where one can get cultured clams, intellectual chowder, refined lager, and very scientific pork and beans. It is far superior, however, to our monotonous sand-beach (Coney Island) in its picturesqueness of natural beauty, in the American character of the visitors, in the reasonableness of hotel charges, and the excellence of the service." This is a pretty plain statement of simple facts. (To reach Nantasket take steamers leaving Rowe's Wharf — 340 Atlantic Avenue — eight times, each way, daily. See time-table in daily papers. Fare, 25 cents each way. Street-cars for Rowe's Wharf leave head of Franklin Street, corner of Washington Street, every few minutes. Persons going to Hotel Pemberton or Oregon House, Hull, take the same steamers. Those who prefer to go to Nantasket by rail, will find frequent trains on the Old Colony Railway to Hingham, thence by Nantasket Beach Railway).

Oak Island. A resort on Revere Beach.

Ocean Spray. In the town of Winthrop is located this popular and rapidly-growing summer resort. The beach is a very good one for bathing. There are several excellent hotels, the Shirley, the Hotel St. Leonards, etc. Numerous well-known actors and actresses have summer homes here, among them J. B. Mason, N. C. Goodwin, jr., H. E. Dixey, George W. Wilson, Jacques Kruger, W. F. Owen, James Nolan, Geo. Fortescue, Mrs. Octavia Allen, Miss Eleanor Cary and others. (Ocean Spray is reached by Boston, Revere Beach & Lynn Railway — 340 Atlantic Avenue — changing at Winthrop Junction. Cars run late at night, giving one facilities for getting home after the theatre).

Pemberton. (See *Hull*).

Plymouth.
"The hill of hallowed brow
Where the Pilgrim sleepeth now."
Every visitor to Boston should, if possible, make a pilgrimage to Plymouth Rock. Here is a quaint and beautiful old town. It is said that at least twenty-five thousand persons visit Plymouth every summer. Here is the historic rock upon which the Pilgrims landed; Pilgrim Hall, in which are many memorials of the forefathers (including Governor Carver's chair, Miles Standish's sword, etc.); the Pilgrim National Monument, surmounted by a gigantic ideal statue of "Faith"; the old Burying Hill; numerous old houses, some of them built previous to 1680; and various other objects of interest. There is a fine hotel here, the Clifford. (Plymouth is reached by the Old Colony Railway. It is 37 miles from Boston. There are frequent steamboat excursions to this town during the summer.)

Point Allerton. Adjoining Hull. Named for Isaac Allerton (agent of the Massachusetts Bay Colony), who came over in the "Mayflower."

Point of Pines. (See *Revere Beach*).

Point Shirley. In the town of Winthrop. A very pleasant resort. Here is Taft's Hotel, the most famous sea-side game-dinner house in the United States. Every known variety of fish, bird, etc., in its season is pretty sure to be found here. The wonderful extent of its larder and the rare excellence of its cookery have carried the fame of Taft's almost everywhere. The marine views from Point Shirley are grand. (Take Boston, Revere Beach and Lynn Railway — 340 Atlantic Avenue — changing cars at Winthrop Junction.)

Revere Beach. One of the most famous resorts on the Atlantic coast is Revere (or Chelsea) Beach, which can be reached in twenty minutes from Boston. This beach was not largely visited by Bostonians until after the building of the Boston, Revere Beach and Lynn Narrow-gauge Railway (through the efforts of A. P. Blake), which runs directly along the edge of the beach, giving the passenger a most charming panorama all along the route. The shore has been rapidly and almost completely covered with hotels, cafes, bathing establishments, etc., so that it forms nearly a continuous street from Chelsea to Point of Pines. Winthrop, Beachmont and Crescent Beach are becoming thickly populated sections, and there have been many pretty cottages erected, some of the owners residing here throughout the year. Facilities for enjoying fishing, boating, bathing, dancing, band concerts, etc., are numerous, and almost innumerable throngs — especially on Sundays and holidays — crowd all means of transit to this beach. Among the special attractions here are the Italian restaurants, where one can find such cooking of macaroni, spaghetti or vermicelli as would tempt the palate of the most fastidious epicure; many places where may be had a regular fish (or "shore") dinner, with all the "fixins," for the moderate sum of half a dollar; while here and there may be found establishments dear to the heart of many a hungry Yankee where baked beans are dispensed; to say nothing of the numerous houses where genuine clam-bakes are provided, smoking hot from the heated stones and seaweed, with all the accompaniments of green corn, melted butter and watermelons, concluding with the ubiquitous pie, selected from an indescribable variety. Here, also, may be had fish or clam chowder, in its perfection. Proceeding to the farther end of the beach we arrive at the celebrated resort, the Point of Pines, the fame of which has reached the greater portion of the country, judging from the sections from which come many of the guests of the great Hotel Pines, one of the largest and most elegant summer hotels in the United States. Here is also the Goodwood, another noted hotel; and numerous cafes. The extensive grounds are laid out in the most beautiful forms of modern landscape gardening, with lawns, flowers, etc., and, at nightfall, when the numerous arches of globes are illuminated, and the electric lights are displayed, the scene is one of great beauty and brilliancy. Concerts of band music are provided, and there are numerous other great attractions. The scene on the grand piazzas of the Hotel Pines during a band concert on almost any afternoon is an animated and most attractive one. Through the able management of Charles H. Thayer the Point of Pines has become one of the great popular summer resorts of the country. (Trains for Revere Beach leave the station of the B., R. B. & L. R. R. — 340 Atlantic av.— generally on every even hour of the day. Horse cars from head of Franklin st. run to the Railway station. Horse cars run to Revere Beach from Cornhill.)

Sagamore Hill. At Nantasket is the famous Sagamore Hill, where once the Indians dwelt, and held their councils. The wigwam of a sachem was here, and the savage court was held where now the picnickers spread their dinner-cloth.

Scituate.
"How dear to my heart are the scenes of
 my childhood,
When fond recollection presents them
 to view;
The orchard, the meadow, the deep-tangled wildwood,
And every loved spot that my infancy
 knew."

Thus sang Samuel Woodworth in his familiar poem, "The Old Oaken Bucket," the scene of which, in this old town, is visited by many. (Scituate is on the Old Colony Railway, 26 miles from Boston.)

Skull Head. A locality at Nantasket. So called from the fact that many human bones have here been found from time to time, together with tomahawks, arrowheads, etc., indicating that here the Indians fought their enemies, the Tarratines.

Strawberry Hill. Between Hull and Nantasket lies Strawberry Hill, a popular resort. Here is the Sea Foam House. Numerous private residences have been erected here. It may be reached by leaving the steamer at Pemberton and taking the train on the Nantasket Beach Railway.

Sunny Side. It is here that the celebrated Vokes Family make their summer home while in America. (See *Winthrop*).

Swampscott. One of the most fashionable resorts of wealthy Bostonians. Here are a number of excellent hotels. Swampscott is said to be "the coolest place on the entire North Shore." (On the Eastern Railway, 12 miles from Boston).

Winthrop. This beautiful peninsula, having less than one thousand acres in area, has more than eight miles of beach. It has several pretty and thriving settlements; Ocean Spray, Point Shirley, Sunnyside, Great Head, Cottage Park and Crystal Bay. Here Garibaldi sojourned for some time, in 1853; and Agassiz was no stranger to Winthrop's great natural beauties. To give some idea of the advance of the price of real estate here, it may be stated that in 1875 land on the present site of Ocean Spray was valued at but $35 an acre. (To reach Winthrop take Boston, Revere Beach and Lynn Railway, at 340 Atlantic Avenue).

BOSTON HARBOR.

The waters of the rebel bay
Have kept their tea-leaf savor;
Our old North-Enders in their spray
Still taste a Hyson flavor.
    OLIVER WENDELL HOLMES.

There is certainly no greater pleasure to the weary citizen on a hot afternoon than that afforded by a sail down the harbor of Boston, renowned the world over for its beauty, the number and size of its islands, its majestic fortresses, its bold headlands and magnificent views. Those who take excursions on sluggish, muddy rivers, through a tame, flat, uninteresting region, cannot realize the grandeur and beauty, the inspiriting, invigorating recreation that comes from a real visit to Old Neptune. Poets, authors and artists have combined to sound the praises of the beauties of Boston Harbor, but the half has not been sung nor told. Howells, the famous novelist, writes of it thus: "A light breeze ruffled the surface of the bay, and the innumerable little sail-boats that dotted it took the sun and wind upon their wings, which they dipped almost into the sparkle of the water, and flew lightly hither and thither like gulls that loved the brine too well to rise wholly from it. Larger ships, farther or nearer, puffed or shrank their sails as they came or went on the errands of commerce, but always moved as if bent upon some dreamy affair of pleasure; the steamboats that shot vehemently across their tranquil courses seemed only gayer and vivider visions, but not more substantial. Yonder a black sea-going steamer passed out between the far-off islands, and at last left in the sky above those reveries of fortification, a whiff of sombre smoke, dark and unreal as a memory of battle. . . . The steamships of many coast-lines gloom, with their black, capacious hulks, among the lighter sailing-craft, and among the white, green-shuttered passenger-boats; . . . and then, growing up from all, rises the mellow-tinted, brick-built city, roof, and spire, and dome, a fair and noble sight, indeed, and one not surpassed for a certain cleanly beauty by any that I know." Another eminent author, Charles Dudley Warner, writes: " What a beautiful harbor it is—everybody says—with its irregularly indented shores and its islands ! The day is simply delicious when we get away from the unozoned air of the land. The sky is cloudless, and the water sparkles like the top of a glass of champagne."

FORTS IN THE HARBOR.

Fort Independence. About two and one-half miles from the city (and only nine hundred yards from City Point, South Boston) stands majestic Fort Independence, of stone, erected on the site of Castle William. It is a fortress worthy of the name. Each of its five sides is guarded by bastions and flank defences, with howitzers of large size, in casemates, and on the barbettes are fifteen-inch Rodman guns. It has spacious quarters for garrison, storehouses, bakeries, rooms for ordnance, etc. Here, on Castle Island, has been a harbor defence for more than two hundred and fifty years, being the oldest military post held regularly for purposes of defence in the United States. The history of this great fort is an interesting one.

Fort Warren. On Georges Island, about six miles from the city, is Fort Warren, the great fortress which has been called "the key of Boston Harbor." The first fortifications here were raised in 1778. The present fort, the construction of which was begun in 1833 and finished in 1850, was built upon plans modelled upon those of the best fortresses of Europe. In 1861 the Webster Regiment encamped here. During the Civil War, after the "Merrimac" had begun its raids, the Government at Washington (hearing that a gentleman named Davis, in the South, had threatened, at Atlanta, to send several cruisers, among them the "Alabama," into Boston Harbor, to bombard the city of Phillips, Sumner and Garrison, "the hot-bed of anti-slavery") commanded Governor John A. Andrew to close up the entrance of the harbor by sinking there the hulks of vessels. This was not done, although other equally effective plans for defending the city were arranged. It was in the spring of 1861, at Fort Warren, that "Glory, glory, hallelujah!"—

"John Brown's body lies a mouldering in
        the grave,
His soul is marching on!"

was composed and first sung. The glee club of the Second Battalion light infantry were the first to sing it. The music was slightly varied from an old hymn-tune. The Twelfth Massachusetts Regiment, marching through Boston, combined their thousand voices in a grand chorus, and the army-song was then for the first time heard in the streets of any city. They afterwards sang it in New York and Baltimore, and regiment after regiment took it up until it swept through the entire army. It has well been called "the Marseillaise of the Rebellion." At this famous fortress, during the Civil War, were imprisoned hundreds of disloyal officers and civilians. Gen. Burnside alone sent eight hundred confederates here. Among the prisoners at the "Boston Bastille," as it was termed, were Alexander H. Stephens, "Vice-President of the Confederate States," who was a guest for five months; Major General Edward Johnson, Generals Gordon, Marmaduke, Jackson, Smith (T. B.), Trimble, Johnson, Hunton, Kershaw, Barton, Corse, Simms; Mason and Slidell, the Confederate agents; Harry Gilmour, Commodore Tucker, the officers and crews of the privateers, "Atlanta" and "Tacony," and numerous others. (A United States Steamboat makes several trips, each way, every day, between Central Wharf and Fort Warren).

Fort Winthrop. Governor's Island. In 1696 batteries were erected here. The construction of the present fortress was begun previous to the Civil War. The United States Government has here built enormous military defences, at an immense outlay. Underneath the apparently innocent tufted mounds are constructed vast subterranean arched passages, massive batteries, etc., while the citadel, a gigantic, earth-covered granite stronghold, shows merely its top above the mounds. This is really the strongest fortification in the harbor, probably, although presenting the least indications to that effect.

ISLANDS IN THE HARBOR.

As there are more than fifty islands in Boston Harbor, we have not the space to describe them, but will mention some of the larger and best known. Long Island is about five miles from the city. Here are earthworks for defence, a lighthouse, the light of which can be seen fifteen miles out. There are here colonies of Portuguese fishermen. Castle Island, upon which is Fort Independence; Governor's Island, with its Fort Winthrop; Georges Island, where is located Fort Warren; Thompson's Island, Spectacle Island, Lovell's Island, Gallop's Island, Deer Island, where Boston's House of Reformation, the House of Industry and the Almshouse are located; Ward's Island, belonging to Harvard University; Little Brewster, on which is Boston Light; Great Brewster, where Bug Light is situated; Lovell's Island, Calf Island, Green Island, Moon Island, Rainsford Island, Peddock Island, Apple Island, Snake Island, etc.

HARBOR EXCURSION STEAMBOATS.

Boston and Hingham Steamboat Company. Rowe's Wharf, 340 Atlantic Avenue. Among the steamboats of the line are the noted "Rose Standish," "Nantasket," "Twilight," "William Harrison," etc. Street-cars for Rowe's Wharf leave head of Franklin Street.

Boston and Nahant. India Wharf) 288 Atlantic Avenue. The steamer, "Julia," a fine boat, has been placed upon this line.

Empire State. Battery Wharf, 379 Commercial Street. This famous great steamboat makes daily excursions in the harbor during the summer season. The "Empire State" is an enormous three-decked steamer, of 1,700 tons, 320 feet in length and 80 feet beam, with grand saloons, promenade decks, dining rooms, etc. The Empire State makes trips to the North Shore, Isles of Shoals, Provincetown, the Fishing-Grounds, etc. E. W. McGlenen is the business manager. Street cars for Battery Wharf on East Boston or Chelsea Ferry lines.

Hingham, Hull and Downer Landing Steamboat Company. India Wharf, 288 Atlantic Avenue. Among the fine steamboats of this Company are the renowned "Governor Andrew," and "General Lincoln." Street cars for India Wharf leave head of Franklin Street.

Longer Excursions may be made by taking the steamboat "City of Gloucester" for Gloucester, (daily, Sundays excepted) from Central Wharf, 244 Atlantic Avenue, from June 1 to October 1, at 2 p. m.; steamboat "Longfellow" for Provincetown, from Battery Wharf, 379 Commercial Street, on Tuesdays, Thursdays and Saturdays, at 9 a. m. Street-cars for Central Wharf leave head of Franklin Street; for Battery Wharf take East Boston or Chelsea Ferry lines.

NANTASKET BEACH RAILWAY.

This railway runs from near the steamboat pier at Hull to Hingham. It passes Cushing Hill, Stony Beach, Point Allerton, Strawberry Hill and Nantasket. The line is nine miles in length. The fare is ten cents. The views from the car-windows are beautiful, and the air is generally cool and refreshing.

BOSTON OF TO-DAY.

"A map of busy life—
Its fluctuations and its vast concerns."
—COWPER.

(This department of the Cyclopedia of Boston has been arranged upon the plan of Charles Dickens' Dictionaries of London and Paris, the accuracy and value of which the writer of this work has practically tested during his visits to those cities).

Abattoir. (See *Brighton Abattoir*).

Academy of Arts and Sciences, American. (1780), 10B Beacon Street. One of the oldest and most noted societies in existence for the promotion of scientific knowledge.

Acme Club. (See *Dining Clubs*).

Adams House. (1883). 553 Washington Street. This renowned hotel stands on the site of the former Adams House, but greatly surpasses it in size, magnificence and luxurious furnishings. Here once stood the old Lamb Tavern, a famous hostelry of provincial days, from which several stage lines started. In 1767, in the month of July, the Boston and Providence Stage line was established, with the Lamb Tavern as the Boston terminus. This tavern was of wood, two stories in height,with a swing-sign, upon which was painted a white lamb. The present Adams House is seven stories high in front and eight stories in the rear. The front is of white marble, with polished red granite pillars and trimmings. It has three entrances from Washington Street. Its grand, lofty hall is brilliantly illuminated at night with incandescent electric lights. The cafe, for ladies and gentlemen, is ninety feet in length and nineteen feet high, and is decorated in the most elegant style. There are about 300 rooms for guests, the prices for which range from $1 per day upwards. The hotel is kept on the European plan. George G. Hall (formerly of Hall & Whipple) is the Proprietor.

Aiding Discharged Convicts. (1846). The Massachusetts Society for aiding discharged convicts is doing a noble work. There is every reason to believe that were it not for this kindly helping hand extended to those who find it difficult to obtain employment after coming out of prison, crime would be largely increased. Charles Sumner was one of the founders of the Society. Office at 35 Avon Street.

Allandale Spring. A noted resort in Jamaica Plain, West Roxbury District.

Almshouses. The Directors of Public Institutions have four almshouses under their control. Office 30 Pemberton Square. These almshouses are as follows: Rainsford Island, (Boston Harbor), for male paupers; Deer Island, (Boston Harbor), for women and children; Austin Farm, (West Roxbury District), for aged women; Charlestown Neck, for residents of the Charlestown District.

Amateur Dramatic Societies. In Boston and vicinity there are quite a number of societies of young persons aspiring to Thespian honors, among the most prominent being the "Footlight Club," of Brookline. Charlestown District has an Amateur Opera Club, the members of which possess an unusual amount of ability.

Amateur Photography is one of the most popular occupations for many ladies and gentlemen, whose leisure hours are thus,employed. Outfits may be obtained of the various dealers in photograph apparatus.

Ambulance Service. The ambulance system of Boston is arranged in the most comprehensive and perfect manner. Under the control of two great hospitals—the Massachusetts and City—the former looking after the sections of the city north of Berkeley and Dover Streets, and the latter covering the territory south of that line. Applications may be made at the nearest police station.

AME—ARC

American Board of Commissioners for Foreign Missions. (1810). 7 Beacon Street.

American House. (1835). 56 Hanover Street. This is one of the oldest, largest and most popular hotels of Boston. The present great building covers the sites of the old and renowned Merchants' Hotel, Hanover House, and also that once occupied by the residence of General Joseph Warren. The grand, spacious hall of the hotel is very attractive, and presents a busy scene when thronged by merchants from the West and South who make their home at the American while in Boston. Here, in the evening, after dinner, before attending any of the various theatres and other places of amusement, there is the appearance of a vast exchange, where representatives of every section of the country assemble to compare notes as to the condition of business in their respective cities. The American is kept on the good, old-fashioned American plan; its table is noted for being lavishly supplied with every substantial article of food as well as with every delicacy that its experienced *chef* can devise; its rooms are large, airy and provided with most luxurious furnishings; and everything that can in the least conduce to the comfort or convenience of its numerous guests is provided. It was the first hotel to furnish a passenger-elevator for the use of patrons. The American holds a foremost position among the great first-class hotels of the United States, and will continue so to do while the enterprising, liberal and experienced proprietors who now manage it shall control its fortunes. Henry B. Rice & Co. conduct the hotel.

American Peace Society. (1828). 7 Beacon Street.

Amusements. The places of amusement in Boston are numerous, and one's taste must indeed be difficult to please if the many entertainments provided do not offer something attractive. The reader will find in the departments of this work devoted to *Places of Amusement, Museums and Exhibitions, Summer Gardens*, etc., full particulars of the amusements furnished in what the majority of managers term, in the parlance of their profession, "the best show town in the country."

Ancient and Honorable Artillery. (1638). Armory at Faneuil Hall. This is the oldest military company in the United States. Its annual parade takes place on the first Monday in June, when the company listens to a sermon, has a grand dinner at Faneuil Hall, thence proceeding to the Common, where the Governor of the State delivers their commissions to the newly-elected officers.

Animals, Society for the Prevention of Cruelty to. 19 Milk Street.

Annexations. The following are the names of the territories annexed to Boston, with the dates, population, valuation, etc., at the time of annexation:

Year.	District.	Popul'n.	Valu'n.
1804..South Boston.			
1867..Roxbury		4,030	$26,551,700
1869..Dorchester		20,030	20,315,700
1873..Charlestown		32,040	35,289,682
1873..Brighton		5,978	14,548,531
1873..W. Roxbury		10,361	22,148,600

Apartment Houses. Family Hotels or French Flats were first introduced into America in 1859. The first apartment hotel to be constructed in the United States was the Hotel Pelham, at the corner of Tremont and Boylston Streets, in Boston. (See complete list of *Apartment Hotels*.)

Architecture. Boston is the finest city, architecturally, considered as a whole, in the United States. Washington has grand public buildings, other cities have handsome structures; but the general diffusion of good architectural models in Boston gives a better average of strength and beauty as prevailing characteristics than can be found elsewhere in the country. Whether one visits the rebuilt "burnt district," where miles of magnificent and substantial business structures have been erected, or the famous Back Bay residential quarter, where hundreds of the most palatial dwellings of Boston's "merchant princes" have been constructed, the fairminded will admit that there is no city in America that can in this respect equal the "Modern Athens." Among the structures which excite the surprise and admiration of visitors from foreign shores are the Museum of Fine Arts Building, Trinity Church, the New Old South Church, State Street Block, the Brattle Church (with its Bartholdi basreliefs) and many others. Good examples of the Greek school are St. Paul's Church, the Custom House, Quincy Market, Court House. Of the Italian Renaissance school are the Boston Athenæum and Boston Museum, while the French Renaissance has notable examples in the City Hall, the Post-Office, Horticultural Hall, etc. Of the Modern Gothic type, the Museum of Fine Arts and the Boston and Providence Railway Station are conspicuous. The Cathedral of the Holy Cross is a grand example of the Mediæval Gothic style.

Archway Bookstore. De Wolfe, Fiske & Co. 365 Washington Street. A very popular bookstore.

Area of Boston. The present area of the city is 23,661 acres, or 36.7 square miles, this being thirty times as large as its original area.

Armstrong Transfer Company. The introduction of this convenient and care-saving arrangement, in 1882, was a great boon to travellers. The system is a model one. Its safety, promptness, and efficiency combine to make it one of the greatest helps to those who wish to have their baggage properly looked after. The general office of the company, at 111 Arch Street, is connected by telephone and private wires with the various railway stations, hotels, etc. Any one wishing the services of the company has simply to give an order, and carriages and baggage-wagons are at once sent to any residence, hotel or business office in the city, for the conveyance of passengers or luggage to any railway station or steamboat pier. Passengers on inward bound railway trains or steamers can also check their baggage for delivery in any section of the city. The system is coming to be generally adopted by all travellers as it should be. Edward A. Taft is general manager; Fred S. Leonard, superintendent.

Art. Boston is a great art-centre. Its notable Museum of Fine Arts, a magnificently-equipped collection, comparing well with those of Europe, and having the largest and finest exhibition of casts in the country; its many other galleries; its Normal School of Art; Cowles Art School, School of Sculpture, John Lowell School of Design, Society of Decorative Art, Art Clubs, etc., and its numerous resident artists, with their classes, combine to give the city an artistic atmosphere of genuine value, instead of the superficial, meretricious, and speculative aspect so conspicuous in some sections of our country. Boston works in Art—as in Literature and Music—quietly, unobtrusively, steadily and progressively, without sensationalism or ostentation, in this respect emulating the example of the art-centres of the Old World, where culture is deep, wide-spread and lasting. (See *Colleges and Schools, Exhibitions, Art Galleries, Artists, Art Clubs, etc*).

Associated Press. In 1849 a number of daily and weekly newspapers combined to obtain telegraphic news, and to divide the expense between them. No new papers are admitted to the privileges of the association.

Athletics. There are a great many gentlemen in and around Boston who are deeply interested in Athletics. There are numerous organizations for promoting physical health, among them the Boston Athletic Club, the Irish Athletic Club, the Cribb Club, etc. (See *Recreation Clubs*).

Back Bay. This is the ugly name that has fastened itself upon the most aristocratic quarter of the city, although the section is now called "New West End" by many. This district is bounded by Charles River, Arlington Street, the Boston & Providence Railway and West Chester Park Street. The territory is what is known as "made land," having been reclaimed from the water of the original bay by being filled in with gravel. Among the most expensive and beautiful structures in this quarter are the Museum of Fine Arts, the Boston Art-Club House, Trinity Church, the New Old South Church, the First Spiritual Temple, the Arlington Street Church, the First Baptist Society Church, the Young Men's Christian Association Building, the Central Church, Notre Dame Academy, the great Mechanics' Exhibition Building, the Natural History Society Building, Institute of Technology Building, Children's Hospital, Chauncy-Hall School, Prince School, Hollis Church, Harvard Medical School, Massachusetts Bicycle Club House, the Hotels Agassiz, Berkeley, Bristol, Brunswick, Cluny, Copley, Guildford, Hamilton, Harold, Huntington, Kempton, Victoria, Vendome, Westland, etc. (This district is reached by the Clarendon and Vendome lines of Back Bay cars, also by the Huntington Avenue and Dartmouth Street lines).

Base Ball. (See *Recreation Clubs*).

Baths. The city is well provided with bathing establishments. Turkish, Russian, Roman, Electric, and Sulphur baths are to be had at 17 Beacon Street. The Turkish bath was established here by Dr. Dio Lewis, some years since, on an extensive plan. At 132 Tremont Street baths of various kinds are furnished. (See *Free Baths*).

Battle Flags. (See *Exhibition of Battle Flags*).

Beautifying Railway Station Grounds. Nearly all of the Railway lines running out of Boston endeavor to make the grounds of their suburban stations as attractive as possible. The Old Colony Railway Company in the spring of 1886 had 50,000 shrubs and plants set out along its line.

Bicycling. Boston is the great bicycling centre of the country. It has the largest clubs, the finest club-houses, the best streets and roads for cycling, in the world, outside of England, and the most general interest in the subject of any city in America. Visitors are amazed at the size and importance of cycling organizations here, and delighted with the roads. The Boston bicyclists sing—with Will Carleton—:

"Good-morning, fellow-wheelmen—here's a warm, fraternal hand,
As, with a rush of victory, we sweep across the land!
If some may be dissatisfied to see the way we ride,
We only wish their majesties could travel by our side!
For we are pure philanthropists, Unqualified philanthropists,
And would not have this happiness to any one denied.
We claim a great utility that daily must increase;
We claim from inactivity a sensible release;
A constant mental, physical and moral help we feel
That bids us turn enthusiasts, and cry, 'God bless the wheel!'"

The several bicycle clubs of Boston are described at length in the department of this work devoted to clubs. Many students and professional gentlemen take exercise on the bicycle or tricycle, while the tricycle is also beginning to be largely used by ladies.

Boating is a very popular recreation with Bostonians. There are various boat clubs who make Charles River their scene of exercise. (See *Clubs*).

Boffin's Bower. One of the noblest charities of Boston is known as Boffin's Bower. It is located at 1031 Washington Street. Founded by Miss Jennie Collins, in 1870, it has afforded assistance to hundreds of working girls, who have been furnished with meals, lodging, clothing, etc. Employment has been secured for many; good counsel — legal and otherwise — furnished; a reading room provided, and many other excellent features have been in operation. Free dinners for working girls are furnished during the winter. Donations are always acceptable.

Books. Book-publishers and booksellers are very numerous in Boston, as would be natural in a great literary centre. The only purely literary magazine in America, the Atlantic Monthly, is published here. Among the great publishers of books in the city are Houghton, Mifflin & Co., Ticknor & Co., D. Lothrop & Co., Roberts Brothers, Lee & Shepard, Little, Brown & Co. and Cupples, Upham & Co. (See *Old Corner Bookstore*.) There are a large number of booksellers who do not publish, and numerous antiquarian bookstores. (See *Old Book Stores*.)

Boston Beacon. A paper issued every Saturday morning from 295 Washington Street. It is filled to the brim with bright, interesting items relating to society, books, art, music, drama, etc. It contains cartoons satirizing local affairs. Cyrus A. Page is the publisher.

Boston Budget. This paper, issued on Sunday morning, is one of the brightest and most readable of the weeklies. It was established by M. M. Ballou, in 1878. It is now published by John D. Dwyer. John W. Ryan is the editor and dramatic critic. Mr. Ryan is one of our most experienced and ablest journalists, and has made the Budget a success. The special features of the paper are contributions by Ben: Perley Poore, entertaining paragraphs and much choice miscellany.

Boston Cab Company. (1885). The establishment of the Boston Cab Company has worked a complete revolution in the public carriage service of the city, and the hearty support its projectors have received augurs well for its continuance and still further development. In place of the dingy vehicles so frequently to be seen, the shabby harnesses, and the overworked horses, this Company supplies handsome new carriages, comprising coaches, broughams, landaus, victorias, coupes, etc., made expressly for this service, with fine horses and equipments; capable and polite drivers (wearing dark green coats and silk hats, and, in rainy weather, white rubber coats and hat covers); and with carriages brilliantly lighted at night, the latter being a great desideratum with persons who are quite naturally afraid of accidents happening in the dark, now that so much reckless driving of herdics, etc., is permitted. For shopping, making calls, pleasure-rides, theatre and party service, the Boston Cab Company furnishes conveyances that are as fine as a gentleman's private carriage, at very moderate prices. For carrying passengers from one railway station to another the rate is only 25 cents for each passenger, without baggage. There is no charge for hand luggage. The general offices of the Boston Cab Company are at 111 Arch Street. Edward A. Taft is President; Fred. S. Leonard, Superintendent.

Bostonian Society. An organization incorporated in 1881, for the purpose of promoting the study of the history of Boston and the preservation of its antiquities. Its rooms are in the Old State House.

Boston Memorial Association. The avowed objects of this society are "the ornamentation of the city of Boston, the care of its memorials, the preservation and improvement of its public grounds, and the erection of works of art within the limits of the city." Organized in 1880.

Brighton Abattoir. (1873). Brighton District. This Abattoir — modelled upon those of Paris — is a place much visited by those interested. A number of large buildings are devoted to the work of slaughtering, and so extensive and well-arranged are the plans of the Association that a thousand sheep and over three hundred cattle may easily be slaughtered every day. There are about fifty acres of land bordering on Charles River, controlled by the company, and the tracks of the Boston and Albany Railway and the Fitchburg Railway (Watertown branch) run directly to the doors of the Abattoir. (To reach the Brighton District take street cars from Bowdoin Square or Park Square, or steam cars on the Boston and Albany Railway).

Carney Hospital. (1635). Old Harbor Street, South Boston. Founded by a donation of $14,000 by the late Andrew Carney. It is conducted by the Sisters of Charity. It is an unsectarian institution, patients of all religious beliefs being received.

Cathedral of the Holy Cross. Washington Street, corner of Malden Street. This is a magnificent structure, occupying over an acre of land; the length of the building is 364 feet; width, at the transept, 170 feet, width of nave and aisles, 90 feet; height to ridgepole, 120 feet. The interior is beautifully and artistically finished.

Charity Bureau. Chardon Street.

Children, Society for the Prevention of Cruelty to. 1 Pemberton Square.

Chop Houses. Strangers in Boston, Englishmen especially, are at once impressed with the English aspect of the city and the people, and one of their first desires is to find a chop-house, "One of those snug, quiet little affairs where one can get a nice mutton chop cooked in the real English style, you know, such as one finds at the Criterion, the Gaiety, the Holborn, the Horse-Shoe, the Gatti, and Spiers & Pond's restaurants in London." In addition to the great hotels kept in the European style — such as Young's, Parkers, the Adams, etc., where the cooking of chops, steaks and meats of all kinds is excellent — there are a number of cosy restaurants where the serving of chops in true English style is made a specialty. Among those which have made the greatest fame as chop-houses are Park's (Bosworth St.); the Coolidge Café (Bowdoin Square), where patrons can see the chops cooked on the silver grill; Maine's (Hayward Place); Clark's, 543 Washington Street; Barrows', 37 Court Street, and several other places. Tennyson has immortalized the chop-house on Fleet Street, London, called "The Cock." If music be the food of love, chops may have been the source of inspiration of some of the Laureate's later poems.

Coasting. There are numerous hills in the suburbs where this sport is largely indulged in while the snow covers the ground. At times there is sufficient snow upon the Common to furnish good coasting-ground, and then there are some lively scenes. Bridges are often erected over the principal walks temporarily monopolized by the coasters. Numerous accidents, several of them fatal, have happened here to spectators as well as to the participants in this dangerous amusement. A line of double-runners, packed with men and boys, going down one of the long inclines of the Common at almost lightning speed is an enlivening scene, which is generally witnessed by throngs of people. (See *Tobogganing*.)

Costly Houses. Among the numerous expensive private residences in Boston are the dwellings at 353 Commonwealth Avenue (assessed for $225,000) and 306 Dartmouth Street (assessed for $210,000).

Daily Advertiser. (1812). 246 Washington Street. This is the oldest of the daily newspapers of Boston, having been established in 1812. (On the site of its former office on Court Street, corner of Franklin Avenue, once stood the printing office of Benjamin Franklin's brother James, where Benjamin himself learned his trade, in 1721. Franklin wrote the following lines as a warning to visitors to printing offices:

"All ye who come this curious art to see,
To handle anything must careful be;
Lest by a slight touch, ere you are aware,
You may do mischief which you can't
   repair.
Lo! this advice we give to every stranger:
Look on, and welcome, but to touch
   there's danger!")

The *Advertiser* contained in its first number the announcement that the commercial feature would be predominant, although politics would not be ignored. The paper has been styled "the Respectable Daily," a compliment it has always merited. William E. Barrett is its present able editor. Its dramatic critic is Henry A. Clapp, whose criticisms are characterized by a refinement, daintiness and poetical felicity of expression which add largely to the force of the analytical and discriminating treatment given them. Howard M. Ticknor is the musical critic, and his criticisms are written in the methods of the true musician and scholar. The art, literary and other reviews are of a high standard. The *Advertiser* is an excellent newspaper.

Distances. The length of the city, from its southerly to its northerly limits, is 11 miles. The width of the city from east to west, including the Brighton District, is 9 miles; the breadth of the business section, from Charles River to the Harbor, is 1½ miles. Distances from the Old State House, (at the corner of Washington and State Streets), to certain points, are given as follows: To Asylum Street, 1 mile; Canton Street, 1½; Camden Street, 2; Cedar Street, 3; Egleston Square, 3½; Green Street, (Jamaica Plain, West Roxbury District) 4; Forest Hills, 5; Roslindale, 6; Clarendon Hills, 7; Dedham line, 9.

Drama. (See *Places of Amusement*).

Drives. The roads about Boston are superb for driving. One can go in almost any direction and find charming, picturesque views. The Milldam road leads to Longwood, Brookline and Chestnut Hill, the favorite suburbs for drives. Other roads, through Jamaica Plain, Dorchester, etc., are also very attractive.

Electric Lights, now so common, were first introduced in 1880, in Scollay Square.

European-Plan Hotels. The hotels kept on the European plan, of providing meals and lodgings separately, now so numerous in this country, were unknown here until 1855. In that year the Parker House, of Boston, was opened, and it was the first hotel in the United States to be kept on the European plan.

Executions. All executions are now privately conducted within the enclosure of Charles Street Jail, near the foot of Cambridge Street.

Faneuil Hall. Whittier wrote (1844):

"Men!—if manhood still ye claim,
 If the Northern pulse can thrill,
Roused by wrong or stung by shame.
 Freely, strongly still,—
Let the sounds of traffic die:
 Shut the mill-gate,—leave the stall,—
Fling the axe and hammer by,—
 Throng to Faneuil Hall!
    *   *   *   *
Up, and tread beneath your feet
 Every cord by party spun:
Let your hearts together beat
 As the heart of one.
Banks and tariffs, stocks and trade,
 Let them rise or let them fall:
Freedom asks your common aid,—
 Up, to Faneuil Hall!"

The old Cradle of Liberty is still rocked whenever there is any question of great public interest at issue. Here, where freedom was nurtured; where, during the Rebellion, the people assembled to make counsel together, and to listen to burning words of eloquence from the statesmen who quickened the love of every true American for "one flag and an undivided country," are still to be seen Pilgrims from every State and every land, who seem to feel that it is a privilege to stand within this historic old landmark which connects the past with the present.

Foot Ball. There are several Foot Ball Teams in Boston and vicinity, among them being the Institute of Technology Team; the Harvard Team, Cambridge; the Roxbury Latin School Team, Boston Highlands. The Rugby game was introduced in 1876. Interest in this exhilarating game increases with every season.

Free Band Concerts. During the summer months concerts of band music are given upon the Common and other public grounds, on Sunday afternoons and on week-day evenings. Full particulars as to dates, time of beginning, programs, etc., are to be found in the daily newspapers.

Free Country Week. Under the management of the Young Men's Christian Union, 18 Boylston Street, about 3,000 poor children of Boston are sent into pleasant New England country towns for a week's vacation. In 1855 a Vermont farmer took three of these poor city children into his family for a week. The farmer and his wife became interested in the children, visited their poverty-stricken home in Boston, and have since invited not only all the children but the poor mother to be their guests for the "Country Week."

Free Day Excursions. The City Missionary Society, 19 Congregational House, (1 Somerset Street) provides free horse-car tickets, harbor-steamboat tickets and day excursions to the poor. In 1880, a gentleman sent $20 to this Society to give free open-horse-car rides to the poor during that summer. 200 persons were thus enabled to enjoy a ride into the suburbs. In 1885, 23,530 street-car rides were given to the poor, 3,509 harbor-steamboat tickets were distributed, and 4,690 enjoyed a day's vacation in the country.

Free Dispensaries. There are several Dispensaries for free medical treatment for those without means to consult other physicians. Among them are the Boston Dispensary, Bennet st., cor. Ash st.; Boston Homeopathic Dispensary, East Concord st.; Dispensary, Charity Building, Chardon st.; Dispensary, 14 Burroughs pl.; Charlestown Free Dispensary, 27 Harvard sq., Charlestown.

Free Excursions for Poor Children are arranged to take place during the summer vacation of the schools. There are eight or ten of these excursions to Lake Walden, Concord, about a thousand boys and girls being taken at a time. The charity is in the hands of a committee, who distribute the tickets by having them given out by the police to the poor children in their respective precincts. This noble charity is sustained by private contributions. Messrs. Peters & Parkinson, 35 Congress Street, are the treasurers.

Free Flowers and Fruit. The Boston Flower and Fruit Mission, established in 1869, was the first charity of this description to be organized anywhere. Miss Helen Tinkham, while walking across Boston Common in the year named, carrying a bouquet, was asked by so large a number of children for "just one flower, please!" that she was inspired with the idea that a Flower Mission should be organized. It was done, and the beautiful charity has grown to be a most extensive one. Flowers, plants, slips, fruit and vegetables sent to 33 Pleasant Street on Monday or Thursday between 8 a. m. and 12 m. (May to October), will be distributed to the ill or infirm poor, to hospitals, dispensaries, missions, diet-kitchens, work-rooms, school-rooms of the poorer districts, etc. Many a sad heart has been lightened by a gift of beautiful flowers, and many a couch of suffering made to seem less painful.

Free Lectures. Under the auspices of the Lowell Institute, courses of Free Lectures by some of the most eminent men of America and Europe are delivered during the winter at Huntington Hall, Technology Building, 191 Boylston Street.

Free Lodgings. Homeless wanderers may find lodgings at Charity Building, Chardon Street. It is expected, however, that able-bodied applicants will render a return for the accommodation by performing a certain amount of such light labor as may be given them, principally as a discouragement to vagrancy.

Freemasonry. (See *Orders and Secret Societies.*)

Free Musical Instruction. The Beneficent Society of the New England Conservatory of Music, 27 East Newton Street, Franklin Square, was organized in 1885 for the purpose of assisting young women and men without means in obtaining a musical education; furnishing, also, financial help, as well as aiding them to secure remunerative positions.

Free Natural History Exhibition. At Natural History Society Building, West Berkeley Street, between Boylston and Newbury Streets, on Wednesday and Saturday afternoons.

Free Rides. The Young Men's Christian Union, 18 Boylston Street, applies funds entrusted to its care for the purpose of defraying the expense of rides for invalids and poor persons into the suburbs.

Free Sunday Art Exhibition. The great collection at the Boston Museum of Fine Arts is open to all every Sunday afternoon. St. James Avenue, Copley Square.

Free Sunday Baths. The great floating, swimming-baths of Boston—(17 in number, 7 for women and girls, and 10 for men and boys) are open to all every Sunday during the summer months, from 6 to 9 a. m. (See *Free Baths* for location).

Free Sunday Natural History Exhibition. The famous Agassiz Museum of Comparative Zoology is open to all, on Sundays, from 1 to 5 p. m. Cars from Park Square or Bowdoin Square.

Free Sunday Reading Room. The reading-room of the Boston Public Library is open to all on Sunday, day and evening. 46 Boylston Street.

Free Vacations. The Community of the Holy Name, 24 Cortes Street, receives women and children for a ten days' vacation at their Summer Home at Weymouth. Applications are to be made to the Sister Superior.

Free Vaccination. At Charity Building, Chardon Street, all persons unable to pay for being vaccinated may receive this medical service free of cost. It is expected that every person will take this precautionary measure at least once in every seven years.

Frog Pond. This is the name of the small sheet of water on Boston Common.

Full Dress at the Opera or Theatres of Boston is not *de rigueur*, although quite generally worn by occupants of the boxes and orchestra stalls, as far as the gentlemen are concerned. Ladies do not wear full dress, as a rule, and it is almost the universal custom to see ladies in walking costume escorted by gentlemen in full evening dress. The effect impressed upon one is striking if not particularly pleasing.

Globe, Daily and Sunday. 238 Washington Street. Established in 1872, the first number being published on the morning of March 4 of that year. Maturin M. Ballou was its first editor. He was succeeded by Clarence S. Wason, who was followed by Edmund H. Hudson. It was not, however, until Col. Charles H. Taylor, who, after Mr. Ballou had retired from the general management of the new paper, took charge of affairs that it became successful. From an independent daily the *Globe* has become a Democratic paper of the most pronounced type. The present editor is James W. Clarke, one of the brightest journalists in the country, formerly of the *Traveller*, and previously of the *Sunday Times*, which acquired great prominence during his connection with it for its weekly caricatures of the Moody and Sankey revival meetings then being held in the Tabernacle. The *Globe* has now reached a very large circulation, with both its daily and Sunday editions. Its features include the publication of continued stories, people's column, pieces of music, and special articles upon local topics of interest. The musical and dramatic department, in charge of Charles W. Dyer, is one of the most attractive columns devoted to those subjects in any journal in the country, and is in great demand far and near.

Harbor. In another department of this work is to be found an allusion to the unique and picturesquely beautiful harbor, with its bluffs and rocky headlands, and its more than half a hundred green islands, the wonder and admiration of all visitors; the theme of many an apostrophe by famous poets, and frequent description by eminent authors; the scene in summer of "processions of floating palaces," as an English writer terms the great fleet of the harbor boats, filled with happy excursionists from the interior of Massachusetts, from New Hampshire, Vermont and Northern New York State; the huge ocean line steamers; the various boats running to home ports, etc. Among the steamboats making Boston their port are the "Gallia"— the greyhound of the sea — "Pavonia," "Scythia," "Cephalonia," "Catalonia," "Bothnia" and other great steamboats of the Cunard line between Boston and Liverpool; the fleets of the Allan, Warren, Leyland and Anchor lines running from Boston to Liverpool; the Furness line to London; the Wilson line to Hull, England; the Diamond Mail line for Hayti; the "Katahdin," "Penobscot," "Iowa," "Cambridge," "Tremont," "John Brooks," "State of Maine," "Cumberland," "Carroll," "Worcester," "Milanese," "Dimmock," "General Whitney," "Glaucus," "Saxon," "Dominion," "Alpha," "Ulunda," "Damara," "British Queen," "Assyria," "Caledonia," "Durham City," "Roman," "Spartan," "Boston City," "Chatham," "D. H. Miller," "Berkshire," "City of Macon," "Gate City," "City of Gloucester," "Longfellow," "Empire State," "Julia," "Rose Standish," "Twilight," "Nantasket," "William Harrison," "Governor Andrew," "General Lincoln," "Norseman," "Palestine," and numerous others, about one hundred in number — some of them being among the largest, finest and fastest ocean steamships ever constructed. Here may also be seen a vast fleet of yachts, among them the "Puritan," of world-wide celebrity, and others scarcely less renowned. Commercially, Boston ranks second only to New York, owing largely to the advantages its harbor offers to vessels of all kinds. An official report to the United States Government by Prof. Henry Mitchell on Boston Harbor as late as 1882, says: "Its great merit lies in a happy conjunction of many favorable elements; the facility and safety of its approaches; the ample width and depth of its entrances; and, above all, the shelter of its roadsteads. Perhaps *there is no harbor in the world where the inlets of the ocean are better adjusted to the amplitude of the interior basins*, or whose excellent holding-grounds are so easy of access and yet so land-locked. Her interior water-space is large, but it is divided by chains of islands into basins which offer sufficient room for the heaviest ships to ride freely at anchor." This statement, from one of the best known and most competent authorities (of the United States Advisory Council), has had great weight in calling attention to the vast natural advantages of the Harbor. With another extract from a report of the experienced captain of the English steamship, "Sorrento," we close the evidence of the attractiveness of Boston Harbor. He says: "During all my experience as an officer and commander of steamships in the Atlantic trade, *I have never before loaded at such magnificent docks*. The great depth of the water at low tides, and the spacious sheds and elevators, render the most complete facilities for the loading and discharging of large steamships." (See *Map of Boston Harbor* given in this work.)

Harbor Lights. Among the great lighthouses on the Atlantic coast are the famous Boston Light, at the entrance of the harbor, on Little Brewster Island, a revolving white light, which may be seen 18 miles at sea; Minot Light, on Minot Ledge, Cohasset Rocks; Bug Light, Long Island Light, on Long Island, etc. (See *Minot Light*).

Harvard Botanic Garden. Cambridge. Ernest Ingersoll in the *Century*, (June, 1886), writes: "Those horsecars which leave Bowdoin Square, Boston, every half hour for Mount Auburn, by the way of Garden Street, Cambridge, take the visitor nearest to the Botanic Garden of Harvard University and the residence of the venerable botanist, Dr. Asa Gray. Past Harvard Sq., and the Washington Elm, you leave the car at the arsenal and walk up Garden Street, following the track which the British soldiers took in 1775 when they started for Lexington and Concord." The Botanic Garden covers eight acres. It originated in 1805. Mr. Ingersoll says: "Passing out of the herbarium into the library, the hungry botanist will find it hard to go farther. No collection of books in this country approaches it. . . . How easy it must be to study botany in Cambridge! All day long and every day one may freely bring here treasures of his woodland search and find their names, not by picking them to pieces and laboriously searching among the dry technicalities of a dusty volume, but by comparison with their living brethren." The Botanic Garden is open freely to all, every week-day.

Harvard Musical College.
Cambridge. A department of Harvard University. This great classical Music School has the highest standard possible, the most exacting examinations, and thorough instruction. It is under the direction of John K. Paine, who is recognized throughout the musical capitals of Europe as America's greatest composer, and most eminent native musician. Mr. Paine, with the true simplicity and modesty so characteristic of real genius, is quietly but effectively moulding a national standard of music, and impressing upon the youth who come under his masterly method a love for what is really good and true in music, as well as stimulating them to attempt to give correct expression to such musical instincts and ideas as nature has bestowed upon them.

Healthfulness of the Back Bay.
According to the testimony of so eminent an authority as Edward H. Clarke, M. D., the quarter of Boston known as the Back Bay is a healthful place of residence. He testified that among his patients there he had not had a single case of typhoid fever. Oliver Wendell Holmes, M. D., gives similar evidence. Dr. Holmes, having written to Dr. Charles F. Folsom, then Secretary of the State Board of Health, with regard to this matter, received the following reply: "As to the Back Bay land, there is no evidence of any conditions unfavorable to health which can amount to proof. There is so much space and sunshine that, on the whole, the mortality is *the lowest in the city,*— perhaps largely due to the character of the population."

Hebrews.
Boston has about 10,000 Hebrews among its population.

Herald, Daily and Sunday.
(1846). 255 Washington Street. This great popular newspaper began its publications August 31, 1846, with an evening edition, being then but a small sheet, with four five-column pages, and sold for one cent a copy. William O. Eaton was its first editor. It began as an independent newspaper, and has always been conducted as such. Its original design was to be neutral in politics and religion, and it became "pledged to no religious sect or political party, always ready to rebuke both spiritual and political wickedness in high places, and call the servants of the public to an account whenever they abuse the trust committed to their care." Edwin C. Bailey became sole proprietor in 1856. In 1869, several members of the staff of the paper, comprising Royal M. Pulsifer, Edwin B. Haskell, Justin Andrews, Charles H. Andrews, and George G. Bailey bought out E. C. Bailey's interest in the *Herald*. Of this company George C. Bailey retired in 1871, and Justin Andrews in 1873, leaving Messrs. R. M. Pulsifer, E. B. Haskell, and Charles H. Andrews proprietors of the paper, and the same gentlemen constitute the firm to-day. In 1878 the present *Herald Building* was occupied. It is said to be the most finely-equipped newspaper office in the world, by those competent to judge. It covers a ground area of 6,200 square feet. It has six stories and a basement. The presses are of sufficient capacity to run off about 90,000 papers an hour. The managing editor is John H. Holmes, whose ability and experience particularly fit him for the duties of this responsible position. The dramatic editor is E. A. Perry, and the musical department is in charge of Frederick P. Bacon, both of whom make their columns exceedingly interesting. In the New York *Tribune* of April 25, 1886, is a reference to the *Boston Herald*, which may be appropriately quoted here. It is as follows: "A. M. Gibson, the newspaper writer, with whom I was talking about Boston yesterday, having just returned from there, said to me: 'It requires a pretty big stretch of imagination and a personal visit to Boston for a New Yorker to understand what a city there is over there. I confess that I was amazed when a friend took his map and with a string showed me that within a radius of eighteen miles of Faneuil Hall there are 900,000 inhabitants. I would scarcely have believed it. You can get some idea of the size of the city from the growth of the newspaper requirements. *The Boston Herald* has sixty reporters on its city staff. I doubt if there is a newspaper in New York that has more. They are all paid a salary, the lowest weekly stipend being $20.'" The circulation of the *Herald* is now as follows: Daily, 108,304; Sunday, 84,872.

Home Journal.
403 Washington Street. Samuel T. Cobb & Co., editors

and proprietors; W. Wallace Waugh, manager. Published every Saturday morning. The *Home Journal* is a bright, cleanly, family paper, bearing every evidence of thrift, as it deserves. Its special features are its chronicle of society movements, its able editorials, its literary, musical and dramatic departments and newsy hotel gossip. Charles M. Capen is the musical critic, and wields an able and caustic pen. Among the most interesting contributions recently have been Luther L. Holden's notes of travel. Altogether, the *Home Journal* furnishes as attractive a table of contents as the most cultured reader can desire.

Horseback Riding. Equestrianism is becoming more popular every year, especially among young ladies. A visit to any of the numerous excellent Riding Schools will convince any one interested of the truth of this statement. Lovers of this healthful exercise may also often be found in goodly numbers on the many beautiful avenues beyond the Milldam. The city, in laying out its various parks and avenues, has thus far utterly ignored the claims of equestrians. There are, however, several very pleasant and picturesque bridle-paths laid out through the fields and woods of Brookline and Longwood, on private grounds, and the public avenues of those beautiful suburban districts are admirably fitted for horseback riding. Leaving the dust of Beacon Street, one can branch off into shaded, retired roads and enjoy this exercise to the best advantage. Jamaica Plain,— in the vicinity of Jamaica Pond, —the Chestnut Hill Reservoir Park, and other suburbs are popular with equestrians.

Horse-Car Excursions. Among the pleasant excursions to be made at trifling cost by the open horse-cars are the following, (the fare being five cents, or not more than one cent a mile for all the long routes except to Milton, which is a ten-cent fare): Take a car with the sign Dorchester upon it as it turns from Temple Place up Tremont Street, beside the Common. The distance is nearly five miles, and the views after passing Grove Hall are beautiful. Take any car marked Oakland Garden, or West Roxbury Park, at Temple Place, corner Tremont Street, and the ride will be found extremely enjoyable. At the terminus of this line one can enjoy the natural beauties of the great West Roxbury (Franklin) Park, or visit Oakland Garden, with its theatre, cafés, promenades, etc. A pleasant ride is that to Milton (about six miles) through beautiful suburbs, and past fine old estates, cars for which route leave the corner of Washington and Bedford Streets every half hour. Other charming rides may be enjoyed by taking a Brookline horse-car near the Tremont House on Tremont Street; Forest Hills, from Tremont House; Jamaica Plain, from Tremont House; South Boston, to City Point, from Scollay Square or Park Square. Other long rides are those to Cambridge, Mount Auburn, Revere Beach, Lynn, Somerville, Chelsea, Arlington, etc. (The places mentioned in this list will be found described more fully under their respective names).

Hospitals. The three principal hospitals of the city are the Massachusetts, the City and the Carney Hospitals. A complete list will be found in another department.

Hospital Newspaper Society. This association provides newspapers and other reading-matter for the inmates of hospitals, homes, asylums and prisons. Boxes for the reception of such matter may be found at the various railway stations, or it may be sent to 113 Revere Street.

Hotel Elevators for guests were first introduced in Boston at the American House.

Hub of the Universe. Oliver Wendell Holmes, in his "Autocrat of the Breakfast Table," was the first to call Boston State House the Hub of the Solar System. The quotation is literally as follows: "Boston State House is the hub of the solar system. You couldn't pry that out of a Boston man if you had the tire of all creation straightened out for a crowbar!" Somehow or other the original expression has been changed to the "Hub of the Universe" and it sticks to Boston almost as firmly as its proper name.

Ice Skating. Skating on ice may be enjoyed in "zero weather" on the great Jamaica Pond, (Jamaica Plain, West Roxbury District); Fresh Pond, (Cambridge); and to a limited extent on the Public Garden Pond and the Frog Pond on the Common, the latter resorts being reserved for children. When the ice is in good condition at Jamaica Pond — the best place to go for this sport — the street-cars of the Jamaica Plain line (starting from Tremont House) carry a signal to that effect in the form of a skate placed above the front end of each car. (See *Boston Ice-Skating Club*).

Italian Colony. There are in Boston nearly 10,000 Italians, mostly living at the North End.

Journal, Daily. 264 Washington Street. Published morning and evening, with semi-weekly and weekly issues. It was established about half a century ago. It was formerly called *The Mercantile*

Journal. In 1841, John S. Sleeper, James A. Dix, and Henry Rogers were the proprietors, Capt. Sleeper being editor. As "Hawser Martingale" he had written some very popular "Tales of the Sea." James A. Dix was the next editor, and was followed by Stephen N. Stockwell. Col. Rogers did much to establish the *Journal* upon a secure footing, and succeeded in amassing a large fortune, being come time before his death the principal proprietor. Mr. Stockwell was a man of rare ability. Col. W. W. Clapp is the present editor, general manager and treasurer, his staff including the following: C. F. W. Archer, John W. Ayres, B. Leighton Beal, W. E. Bryant, (night editor), H. R. Chamberlain, George H. Dearborn, Frank Foxcroft, W. W. Hill, W. F. Hutchins, Arthur T. Lovell, Winthrop L. Marvin, Stephen O'Meara, (news editor), Henry O'Meara, (editor weekly, dramatic writer), A. C. Parker, Geo. H. Pratt, W. E. Robinson, J. H. Russell, W. H. Sanger, Z. A. Smith, C. B. Seagrave, Miss Grace W. Soper, Fred D. Stimpson, J. P. Sheehan, A. A. Wilder. Col. Clapp is a journalist of great and versatile natural gifts, schooled by long experience, and has won for the *Journal* a reputation of which he may well be proud. It is an excellent type of a thoroughly New England newspaper for the family.

Lacrosse. This game is rapidly becoming very popular here. It was first played prominently in this city as one of the Fourth of July sports on Boston Common, where it drew many thousands of spectators. The games were played between an Indian Club from Canada and the Boston Club. It is now recognized as one of the leading games, combining, as it does, the best features of the other games. Of the Boston Independent Lacrosse Club, James A. McGee is President and P. J. McLaughlin is Captain. The Cambridge Lacrosse Club has for President Charles C. Abbott, and for Captain Henry B. Hook. The Somerville Lacrosse Club's President is W. H. Cummings; Captain, F. C. Ross.

Lady Journalists. Among the ladies engaged upon the Boston press are the following: Mrs. A. M. B. Ellis ("Max Eliot"), *Herald;* Sallie Joy White, *Advertiser;* Susie Vogl, *Woman's Journal;* Lillian Whiting, *Traveller;* Miss Hatch, *Globe;* Miss Soper, *Journal;* Miss Aldrich, *Home Journal;* Mrs. Jenkins ("Jay"), *Herald;* Mrs. Washburn, *Globe,* Lucy Stone, *Woman's Journal.*

Latitude of Boston. The latitude of the city is 42° 21' 27.6" North.

Law and Order League. As strangely as it may appear, notwithstanding every public official is popularly supposed to have taken an oath to aid in the enforcement of the laws, a society has been formed having for its object the careful looking-after of the "servants of the people" to see that certain laws are thoroughly and impartially executed. The ramifications of this organization extend through all sections of the city, and its influence is strongly felt. L. Edwin Dudley is the Secretary of the League.

Longitude of Boston. The longitude of the city is 5° 59' 18.' East, from Washington, D. C., and 71° 3' 30' West, from Greenwich, England.

Minot Light, on Minot Ledge, Boston Harbor, is a gigantic lighthouse, which is viewed with great interest by all who pass it. The first lighthouse erected here, of iron, was destroyed in a great storm, two men being drowned. The present granite structure was built in 1858-60. Longfellow wrote of it as follows:

"The rocky ledge runs far into the sea,
  And on its outer point — some miles
    away —
The lighthouse lifts its massive masonry;
  A pillar of fire by night, of cloud by
    day."

Morgues. Places of sad interest to numerous visitors are the Morgues, of which there are two, one on North Grove Street and the other on Harrison Avenue, (City Hospital Grounds). They are the receptacles for the bodies of those found dead in streets, harbor, river or elsewhere. There are generally a number of bodies awaiting identification.

Mount Auburn Cemetery. The first burial-place to be laid out in the United States as a "garden cemetery" was that of Mount Auburn, Cambridge, in 1831, and although the plan has been imitated in other sections of the country Mount Auburn is still the loveliest spot for the interment of the dead, and the most celebrated cemetery in the land. Various causes combine to bring about this result. Its great area, its natural beauties, the age of its trees, the original and perfect designs of its gardening, taken in connection with the famous persons whose dust lies there, render it a place of sad interest to the thousands of people who visit it during every summer. It is evident that the memory of the dead is still kept green, as fresh flowers are placed upon many of the graves day after day. Here are buried Henry Wadsworth Longfellow, Charles Sumner, Charlotte Cushman, Erminia Rudersdorff, Louis Agassiz, Edward Everett, Anson Burlingame, Nathaniel Bowditch, William Ellery Channing, John Murray, Hosea Ballou, and numerous other men and women eminent in life, and closely identified with the name and fame of Boston.

At the time of the consecration of this cemetery, Charles Sprague wrote the following lines:

"We raise no shout, no trumpet sound,
No banner to the breeze we spread;
Children of clay! bend humbly round:—
We plant a city to the dead."

Longfellow's lot is numbered 580, Indian Ridge. The snow was softly falling on Sunday, March 26, 1882, when he was laid to rest, reminding one who was present of the illustrious poet's own lines at the time of the burial of Richard Henry Dana:

"We laid him in the sleep that comes to all
And left him to his rest and his renown.
The snow was falling, as if Heaven dropped down
White flowers of paradise to strew his pall:—
The dead around him seemed to wake and call
His name, as worthy of so white a crown."

When Charlotte Cushman visited Mount Auburn in 1874 for the purpose of selecting a lot which should be her final resting-place, she was shown several enclosures surrounded by costly and imposing monuments. She remarked: "These are all grand and beautiful, but haven't you a lot commanding an unobstructed view of the great city?" She was informed that there were a few lots for sale near the tower. While she and the official were on the way to the place designated, the graves of some of her once warmest friends were passed, and at each she paused for a moment and related some pleasant memories connected with their lives. Palm avenue, at the eastern side of the grounds, was reached, and, standing upon a little eminence, Miss Cushman exclaimed: "This is a delightful spot; see, yonder lies dear old Boston!" The lot is numbered 4,236. There are notable works of art throughout the cemetery, among them Milmore's "Sphinx," the Bowditch Statue, the Ballou monument, and others, while in the Chapel are statues of John Winthrop, John Adams, James Otis and Joseph Story. An interesting feature is the Ossili Memorial, erected in memory of Margaret Fuller Ossili, the famous writer and reformer, who was lost at sea, 1850. (Mount Auburn is reached by the Cambridge line of street-cars, from Bowdoin Square).

Music. Boston is generally conceded to be the musical centre of the United States, especially by disinterested musicians from abroad. Its great Handel and Haydn Society, the foremost oratorio organization in the country; its superb Symphony Orchestra, rivalling the best orchestras of Europe, conducted by Herr Wilhelm Gericke, acknowledged to be one of the leading musical directors of the world—; its noted singing clubs—the Boylston, Apollo, Cecilia, etc.—; its Euterpe Club for promoting the highest class of chamber music; its Conservatories and Music Schools, the most extensive in the country; its large number of resident musicians of national — and several of world-wide — fame, together with the high standard of musical taste pervading the entire community (which is due in some degree to the excellent system of teaching music in the public schools), are important factors in imparting to the city a musical atmosphere rivalling that of the capitals of the Old World. Within a few years a great and gratifying change has taken place in our musical affairs. For a long period there was no attempt made to develop or to encourage native artists or composers. On the contrary, everything was done to convince young Americans that they had no right to think for themselves in musical matters. They were made to feel that being living Americans instead of dead Germans there was no hope for them. English, French and Italian music, they were told, was no music at all. There had never been any such thing as American music, and never could be. It was downright nonsense to imagine for a moment that there would ever exist an American who could sing or play, but should such a phenomenal being happen to be born, he must perforce, sing and play only German music. It is not very creditable to our city that John Knowles Paine, the foremost of American composers, was not given a hearing by the Harvard Musical Association until after he had won recognition in Berlin. But now, happily, all is changed. The shackles that so long bore heavily upon our native youth are broken. To Calixa Lavallee may be given a considerable degree of credit for having assisted to emancipate us from the snobbery and toadyism that has so long prevailed among program-makers, who have seemed to recoil with horror from any work the name of which is in the English language. It is singular that it should have been necessary for a foreign musician to come among us to help stir our national and local pride, and to stimulate the growth and development of music of home production. But now that the great tide has turned; now that an overwhelming reaction has set in, what may we not expect from our own musicians? As an evidence of what has already been accomplished, we quote the following, from one of the ablest musical papers published, Freund's *Music and Drama*, New York: "A great many artists are settling in Boston, mostly young Americans, who have studied in Europe and have come home with their acquired stock of knowledge to spread the culture of music here. Boston is becoming the cradle of American musicians of prominence. From Boston there may one day arise the future American Beethoven."

Musical Students.
Boston swarms with students of music, who come from every State in the Union to take lessons at the various conservatories, music schools, etc., and of private teachers.

New York Correspondents
of Boston papers include the following. Of the *Traveller:* Mrs. John Sherwood (" M. E. W. S." and "Aglaia"); *Transcript:* Edgar W. Montgomery (" E. W. M."); *Herald:* Leander Richardson, Townsend Percy, and Clinton Stuart (" Walsingham"); *Globe:* George Alfred Townsend ("Gath"), and Joseph Howard, Jr., (" Howard"); *Commonwealth:* Hilary Bell; *Gazette:* Jeannette Gilder (" Brunswick ").

Observatories.
The Observatory at Harvard University and that at Blue Hill, Milton, have many visitors.

Offices
of Harvard University in Boston are: the office of the President and Fellows is at 70 Water st.; Treasurer, 70 Water st.; Dean of the Harvard Medical Faculty at Harvard Medical School, Boylston st., corner Exeter; Dean of Harvard Dental Faculty, Hotel Bristol, Boylston st.; Secretary of Harvard Veterinary Faculty, 50 Village st.

Old Corner Bookstore.
Probably the most noted bookstore in this country is the Old Corner Bookstore, at the corner of Washington and School Streets, where Oliver Wendell Holmes, James Russell Lowell, John Greenleaf Whittier, William Dean Howells, Julia Ward Howe, George Makepeace Towle, John Boyle O'Reilly, George Parsons Lathrop and other authors may often be met, as in former times Henry Wadsworth Longfellow, Ralph Waldo Emerson, Charles Dickens, Nathaniel Hawthorne, and many other celebrities gathered there. The building was erected in 1712. The firms of Booksellers who have occupied this famous corner, have been Carter & Hendee, Allen & Ticknor, Wm. D. Ticknor & Co., Ticknor & Fields, E. P. Dutton & Co., A. Williams & Co. The business is now conducted by Messrs. Cupples, Upham & Co., a firm of gentlemen who by ability and enterprise fully sustain the prestige of the far-famed house.

Old Bookstores.
The lover of old and rare books will find abundant means for gratifying his tastes in the noted antiquarian bookstores of Boston. Cornhill is the centre of this large business. At No. 60 on this street is Bird's Old Book Shop, where seekers after "first editions" and scarce historical and dramatic works make their haunt. Another well-known antiquarian bookstore is that of Burnham. 2 Milk Street, under the Old South Meeting House.

Old Buildings.
At either end of the short thoroughfare of School Street may be found old buildings of great historical interest. On the end cornering on Tremont Street is the famous old King's Chapel (1749), while at the end joining Washington Street is the building now known as the Old Corner Bookstore (1712). (On the latter site once stood the residence of the troublesome Anne Hutchinson.) A little above this building, on the corner of Milk Street, stands the Old South Meeting House (1729). Nearly opposite (where is now the St. Joachim store) stand the walls of the old Province House (1689). Returning past the Old Corner Bookstore and passing down Washington Street to the corner of State Street, we come to the Old State House (1748). Thence, proceeding through Washington Street and, turning to the right, we are at Faneuil Hall (1742). Returning to Washington Street and keeping on until Hanover Street is reached, Salem Street is but a few steps to the left. Taking our walk through Salem Street, passing on the way several old houses, at the farther end we come to the memorable Old North Church (1723), from the tower of which the lanterns were displayed as a signal to Paul Revere that the British troops were to move on Lexington. From here it is but a short walk to North Square, where stands the house in which Paul Revere lived.

Old North End.
The stranger will find a most interesting ramble by walking from the head of Hanover Street down through Salem and Charter Streets. On Salem Street is the famous old North Church where the lanterns were hung out. (See *Historical Tablets.*) On Charter Street is the old Copp's Hill Burial Ground, of great historic interest, and the old Phipp's house.

Palatial Back Bay Hotels.
In the aristocratic quarter of the city known as the Back Bay or New West End there are three Hotels which for size, magnificence and sumptuousness of furnishing equal any public houses in the world and eclipse most of those in the United States. Strangers are simply amazed at the splendor of these great Hotels, foreigners looking upon them with equal surprise and pleasure as evidences of the rapid development of the resources of "the new country, where everything is done on such a vast and magnificent scale," and as a proof of the advanced taste, culture and refinement of the great and rapidly growing metropolis of New England. It is but a few years since the territory upon which stand these superb Hotels was a waste of water and marsh, while to-day the surroundings are such as no capital in the world can surpass in grandeur of architecture, broad avenues and squares, and

all the accessories that indicate the opulence and luxury of the "merchant princes" of the second commercial city of the United States. Now that it is becoming the fashion for the English nobility and gentry who visit the United States to take steamers direct for Boston, it is but natural that the hotels arranged for the accommodation of this class of travel, as well as for the Americans who make a stay of a few weeks in Boston *en route* to the White Mountains or the hundreds of fashionable seaside resorts in the vicinity, should prepare for their reception in the styles corresponding with that of the grandest hotels in the world. This the proprietors of the Brunswick, the Vendome and the Victoria are qualified to do, from the abundant resources at their command. The Hotel Brunswick was opened in 1874. It is located on Boylston Street, corner of Clarendon Street, near Copley Square, and but a few steps from the Museum of Fine Arts, Trinity Church, New Old South, and other noted structures. The Brunswick covers over half an acre of land, is six stories high, and its exterior, of brick with sandstone trimmings, presents a grand appearance. The building originally cost about one million of dollars. It is considered to be perfectly fireproof. The Brunswick is famed throughout the country for the elegance, taste and luxuriousness with which its rooms are furnished. It has nearly 400 rooms. Every suite is furnished with a bath-room. The famous Whittier banquet, given here in 1877, to commemorate the poet's 70th birthday, is remembered as one of Boston's great literary gatherings. The Hotel Vendome is situated upon what Harper's *Weekly* has justly termed "the most magnificent avenue in America." Commonwealth Avenue is two hundred and fifty feet wide, from house to house, with a wide parkway running its entire length, and lined on either side with some of the most palatial residences in the world. The Vendome has a frontage on the avenue of 240 feet, and on Dartmouth Street of 125 feet, is eight stories high, its fronts, of white marble, presenting a most imposing appearance. Its grand banquet hall, 110 feet long, seats 350 persons. There are five other great dining-rooms. It has several parlors of large size. The Vendome was built at an expense of more than a million dollars. During the summer of 1886 the hotel was closed to the public for the purpose of refitting, the furniture, carpets, etc., being disposed of; and although the house has from the time of its opening been noted for the beauty and richness of its furnishings, the splendor of its new appointments far eclipses all former grandeur, and it is, today, probably the most expensively furnished public house in America, everything from the basement to the roof being entirely new and of the most modern and beautiful description. The Victoria is the newest of these great hotels, having been constructed in 1885-6. It is located on Dartmouth Street (just across the street from the Vendome), and is one of the most attractive edifices on the Back Bay, which is famed the world over for its superb and varied styles of architecture. The Victoria is of brick, seven stories high, and has been constructed expressly to give full scope to the plans of its proprietors for a model hotel on the European plan. Every well-established good feature of hotels designed upon this system has been retained, while all modern inventions and improvements, that can add to the comfort or luxury of its appointments, have been adopted. Of these palatial Back Bay Hotels, the Brunswick and Vendome are kept upon the American plan, and the Victoria on the European system. The proprietors of these three great Hotels are Amos Barnes and John W. Dunklee, whose experience, judgment and taste abundantly qualify them for the prominent and successful position they hold among the hotel proprietors of the country. (These Hotels may be reached by public carriages to be found at all of the railway stations and steamboat piers; by Vendome and Clarendon lines of Back Bay cars, etc. Passengers arriving on Boston & Albany Railway will save time and trouble by alighting at the Huntington Avenue station, which is within a few steps of any one of these three Hotels).

Parker House. (1855). School Street, corner of Tremont Street. Established by the late Harvey D. Parker. It was the first hotel in the United States to be opened on the European plan of furnishing meals and lodgings separately. Parker's occupies a unique position among the great hotels of the world, offering accommodations to the travelling public that are to be found in but few hotels. Its central location, its vast size, its excellent table, its elegantly-furnished rooms and sleeping apartments, its elevators, and various other equipments are of the highest degree of comfort and luxury combined. Parker's is a great rallying-point on election nights, and other occasions when important news is expected. Many clubs dine here. The proprietors, Joseph H. Beckman and Edward O. Punchard, are young gentlemen who have displayed tact, judgment, enterprise, and liberality in management. The rates for rooms range from $1.00 upward; suites $8.00 upward. There are 325 rooms, single and *en suite*. Of the office staff, J. Albert Butler is cashier; Frank W. Gilman, book-keeper; Sebastian Sommer, asst.; Louis P. Roberts, James A. Fitzsimmons, room-clerks; Frederick W. Draper, night-clerk.

Paris Correspondents of Boston papers are Edward King (*Journal*) and J. Henry Hayuie (*Herald*).

Patent Office Reports. At Bates Hall, Public Library, 46 Boylston Street, may be seen complete files of the United States Patent Office Reports.

Petty Provincialisms. The good, patient and long-suffering Bostonian still encourages the hope that the period is not far remote when the burning of a small, disused barn in the West Roxbury District will not cause half a million of people to be disturbed in their avocations during the day, nor aroused from their slumber at night, by the clang of alarm bells; when the police will keep the narrow sidewalks of Washington Street free from groups of persons who stand there for hours obstructing the passage of pedestrians; when all cab-drivers will be compelled to carry lighted side-lamps, as many now do voluntarily; when there will be a sufficient number of police stationed upon the Common and Public Garden to make those grounds as safe to cross at night as they are during the day; when the various street-railway lines will be required to run box cars alternately with the open ones, for the benefit of elderly and delicate persons; when street-cars will not be kept waiting for a passenger who is walking leisurely toward the car, a block away; when the platforms of street-cars on the inside—next to the other track —will be closed by gates, thus avoiding danger and delay; when bridges for foot passengers will be erected at all grade crossings of steam-railways, by order of the railway commissioners, thus reducing the number of fatal accidents at such crossings; when managers of theatres and other places of amusement will give the exact location of their houses in their advertisements, as well as the time for beginning and closing the performances; when ladies and gentlemen from the country will not insist upon walking four or five abreast, and clasping each other's hands, on Washington Street sidewalks; when building contractors will not occupy more than half of the street and all of the sidewalk while erecting new buildings; when those who throw orange peel and banana rind upon the sidewalk will be arrested, as they are in New York and other cities; when Devonshire Street will be permanently paved; when pedestrians will keep to the right of the sidewalk; when no one will be permitted to litter the streets and sidewalks with circulars and other rubbish; and when carts collecting ashes and garbage will do so early in the morning or late at night, particularly on the principal streets.

Pilot. (1838). 607 Washington Street. The first Roman-Catholic newspaper to be established in Boston,—having been founded by the well-known bookseller, Patrick Donahoe, the *Pilot* has become the leading and most influential Catholic paper in the United States, having a very large circulation throughout the country. It is edited by John Boyle O'Reilly, one of America's foremost young poets, whose fame is daily extending. He gives the *Pilot* a high literary tone, as would be expected from a gentleman of his rare scholarly tastes and genuine literary instincts. The *Pilot* is read and enjoyed by those of every religious belief. Its news is carefully and thoroughly gathered, and is reliable. Mr. O'Reilly has done much to encourage poets and writers, and his kindness will ever be cherished by them with gratitude.

Plays. All plays that are published may be had of Lee & Shepard, 10 Milk Street.

Polls. The number of Polls in 1885 was 112,140.

Population of Boston. The population of the city in 1780 was 25,000, in 1822, 49,291; in 1880, 362,535; in 1886, 401,987.

Post, Daily. (1831). 17 Milk Street. This Democratic, commercial newspaper —published every morning,—is issued from the Post Building, erected on the site of the house where Boston's great philosopher, patriot, and printer, Benjamin Franklin, was born. Colonel Charles G. Green was the founder of the *Post*, issuing its first number November 9, 1831. Charles G. Green, at the beginning of the publication of the *Post*, gave it the characteristics it has since retained in a great degree. Frederick E. Goodrich, George F. Emery, and Robert G. Fitch have, during recent years, successively been its editors, each conducting it with ability. Among those who have contributed to the *Post*, editorially and otherwise, have been Richard Frothingham, George Makepeace Towle, B. P. Shillaber ("Mrs. Partington"), George F. Babbitt, and Charles H. Hoyt. In 1886, Edwin F. Bacon, a gentleman qualified in the highest degree by scholarship, the most perfect journalistic training and long experience, assumed editorial charge of the *Post*, which was never brighter, more readable or newsy than at present. He is assisted by a large and efficient staff.

Promenade Concerts. Promenade—or as they are sometimes called "walk-about" or "smoking" concerts— are very popular in Boston. At the Oriental Garden, Shawmut Avenue; Boston Music Hall Garden, Winter Street; Summer Bazaar Garden, Mechanic Hall, Huntington Avenue; and at Oakland Garden, Blue Hill Avenue, these concerts are given during the summer evenings.

Public Pier. (1886). City Point, South Boston. A broad pier extending several hundred feet into Dorchester Bay. A very popular resort in summer.

Quincy House. Brattle Street. This is one of the largest and most popular hotels in the city. The present enterprising proprietors, J W. Johnson & Co., leave nothing undone that can minister to the wants of their numerous guests. Many clubs dine here.

Rapid Railway Trains. Although the United States is considerably behind England in the matter of fast railway trains there is an attempt now being made upon some of the lines running out of Boston to equal the fastest trains in the world, if not to surpass them. The "Flying Dude" train on the Old Colony Railway runs every day except Sunday between Boston and Woods Holl, a distance of 72 miles in 1 hour, 40 minutes. The train leaves Boston at 3.10 p. m. The "Flying Yankee" train also makes quick time.

Rate of Taxation. The rate of taxation in 1885 was $12.80 on $1,000.

Recognition of Boston Schools. The people of America have generally conceded the palm of superiority in public-school methods of education to Boston, whose schools are not only the best but the oldest in the country, the Boston Latin School having been established in 1635 (five years after the settlement of the city, and three years previous to the founding of Harvard University). The following is an extract from the report made by Rev. James Fraser, the English commissioner sent by Her Majesty, Queen Victoria, to investigate the Common School system of the United States, said report being presented to both houses of Parliament: "Taking it for all in all, and as accomplishing the end at which it professes to aim, the English High School of Boston struck me as *the model school of the United States.* I wish we had a hundred such in England." This was not a hasty estimate, but a decision arrived at after the most searching examination of the school-methods employed in the public schools of the principal cities of the United States, lasting for nearly a year. This report, from so competent, unprejudiced and intelligent a judge as Bishop Fraser, is a most valuable endorsement of Boston's school system.

Record, Daily. A bright little one-cent evening paper issued from the *Advertiser* office.

Recovery of Lost Goods. (1886). Lost and Found Bureau. 61 Bromfield Street. A novel departure from the old methods of finding or restoring lost articles has been made by the establishment, in a central quarter, of an office for this express purpose. Through the medium of this Bureau articles are restored to their owners without going to the trouble or expense of advertising. Any person finding an article is earnestly requested to leave information here concerning it. Any one who has lost any article may, by promptly reporting the loss here, be very likely to be placed in the way of recovering it.

Residences. Boston had 44,196 dwellings in 1886.

Revere House. (1847). Bowdoin Square. This is one of the most noted hotels of the city. It was named for Paul Revere. It occupies the site of the former residence of Kirk Boott, senior. It was once managed by Paran Stevens, one of the most notable of American landlords. Among eminent personages who have made the Revere their home while in Boston have been the Prince of Wales, the Grand Duke Alexis, the Emperor Dom Pedro, King Kalakaua; Presidents Filmore, Pierce, Johnson, and Grant; Generals Sherman, and Sheridan; Parepa-Rosa, Therese Tietjens, Adelina Patti, Christine Nilsson, and numerous others. The Revere is now conducted by J. F. Merrow & Co., who by their enterprise and liberal management amply maintain the old-time prestige of the house. The hotel can accommodate 250 guests.

Rich Men of the City. The following are among those who pay taxes on valuations of more than a quarter of a million of dollars:

Estate.	Tax Valuation.
Moses Williams	$3,300,900
J. M. Sears	3,244,400
Quincy A. Shaw	1,394,000
J. L. Gardner	1,316,300
Jas. L. Little	1,138.800
A. Wentworth	1,088,900
Isab'l P. Hunnewell	909,200
Harvey D. Parker	807,400
Wm. Sheafe	771,900
Sidney Bartlett	731,300
Moses H. Dow	714,800
Benj. P. Cheney	700,000
H. H. Hunnewell	690,200
T. Wigglesworth	686,400
Nelson Curtis	653,700
F. L. Ames	653,700
N. Curtis	653,700
Geo. C. Richardson	639,900
G. F. Burkhardt	621,000
Wm. F. Weld	622,000
Chas. Whitney	617,500
F. R. Sears	615,600
Otis Norcross	597,700
F. B. Hayes	593,500
John A. Lowell	567,000
Jacob Sleeper	544,200
Wm. P. Mason	526,100

RIV—SAF 253

Henry Lee	526,000
J. H. White	518,000
J. C. Haynes	515,100
C. F. Adams	514,600
Geo. C. Shattuck	510,000
Henry L. Pierce	506,200
Chas. Blake	492,500
J. J. Williams	479,100
J. B. Moors	477,500
Abigail Armstrong	473,600
D. W. Williams	471,000
Abbott Lawrence	462,500
G. Gardiner	448,500
Thos. E. Proctor	444,000
Wm. Gray	435,700
F. Brooks	424,000
M. H. Simpson	421,000
James S. Stone	416,000
J. French	412,400
James H. Beal	406,300
B. G. Boardman	406,300
Franklin King	389,200
R. T. Paine, Jr	380,000
C. A. Browne	378,700
P. W. Chandler	376,900
A. A. Marcus	367,300
Wm. H. Hill	364,700
C. W. Galloupe	362,100
F. H. Bradlee	360,700
T. L. Smith	358,200
C. A. Baldwin	355,700
C. A. Richards	355,500
D. F. Flagg	350,000
H. B. Rogers	333,700
P. T. Homer	329,700
J. Foster	326,600
L. R. Cutter	324,000
J. T. Eldridge	323,700
Moses Kimball	313,000
C. A. Johnson	307,500
J. C. Phillips	307,000
J. Deshon	306,950
J. D. Bates	306,500
E. V. Ashton	306,400
John Goldthwait	305,600
Cora L. Shaw	305,400
W. D. Pickman	302,000
D. Kennedy	294,400
S. Brooks	292,900
A. A. Burrage	282,300
Charles Roberts	282,100
J. Collamore	281,700
R. B. Brigham	281,400
Samuel B. Pierce	274,200
A. H. Allen	265,400
Eben D. Jordan	262,500
J. B. Thomas	261,000
Isaac Pratt, Jr	259,500
N. H. Bradlee	258,800
Leopold Morse	258,300
Leonard Ware	256,500
Wm. Sohier	255,200
E. L. Browne	254,200
Owen Nawn	253,000
George Higginson	252,000

Rivers. The Charles and Mystic Rivers furnish fine facilities for boating. (See *Boat Clubs*). Longfellow has immortalized the former beautiful stream in his celebrated Poem: "To the River Charles," from which we excerpt the following stanza:
"Thou hast taught me, Silent River!
Many a lesson, deep and long;
Thou hast been a generous giver;
I can give thee but a song!"

Roller-Skating. This form of amusement originated in Paris in 1819. It was the result of a theatrical expedient. According to Herr Hock, the stage manager, all who enjoy roller-skating are indebted for their sport to the famous composer, Meyerbeer. When his opera, " The Prophet," was produced in Paris, it was almost decided at one time to cut out the skating-scene in the third act, as the manager saw no way of converting the stage into a sheet of ice. At this crisis an ingenious stage hand came forward and suggested that ordinary skates might be placed upon wheels. The Opera House in Paris was therefore the first roller-skating rink in the world. The sport is not now as popular as formerly in Boston, although there are several rinks devoted to it during the amusement season. Among them are the following: Winslow's Boston Rink, rear 62 St. James Avenue, Back Bay; Olympian Rink, Mechanics Building, Huntington Avenue, Back Bay; Highland Rink, 754 Shawmut Avenue, Roxbury District; Columbia Rink, 1194 Washington st.; Argyle Rink, 888 Washington st.; Paris Rink, Paris st., E. B.; Phenix Rink, Webster st., E. B.; Alhambra Rink, City Point, S. B. Several of these Rinks are used for other purposes, music-gardens, etc., during the summer.

Rooms. A very pleasant method of living in Boston is to engage a furnished room by the week, and take one's meals at any of the numerous good restaurants. This is an economical way of living, besides the freedom it gives for lunching or dining whenever and wherever one chooses. Rooms to be let for lodgings are advertised in the *Transcript* and other daily papers.

Roses, Rhododendrons, etc. Boston roses, rhododendrons, chrysanthemums, lilies, smilax and other products of the floral kingdom are so celebrated all over the country that the merest reference to them is all that is necessary. Boston supplies New York with an enormous number of roses, especially, which seem to reach greater beauty and perfection in the suburbs of this city than elsewhere in this part of the country.

Safe Deposit Vaults. Housebreaking has decreased considerably since Public Safe Deposit Vaults have been established, as many wealthy citizens now keep valuables in these strong fire-proof and constantly-guarded repositories. (The vaults are connected with the police stations by electric signals.) The principal establishments are the

Security Safe Deposit Company, Equitable Building, Milk Street, corner of Devonshire Street; Union Safe Deposit Vaults, 40 State Street; Boston Safe Deposit and Trust Company, 87 Milk Street. (See *Storage Warehouse*.)

Sailors' Snug Harbor. (1852).

Quincy, (Germantown Village.) Ephraim Doane, Superintendent. A charitable institution. Conditions for admission: The applicant must have sailed for five years under the United States flag; must not be an habitual drunkard; and must not have any contagious disease. About forty sailors are in the home at present. Library of about 200 volumes. Managed by a Board of Directors in Boston. Open to visitors at all times. (Take Old Colony Railway to Quincy station, then public carriage to the Home.)

Saturday Evening Gazette.

(1813). 2 Bromfield Street. Established by William W. Clapp. As a Saturday paper, the *Gazette* took the initiative in issuing Sunday editions, eventually discontinuing the Saturday edition, and concentrating all its forces upon the Sunday paper. The *Gazette* has become almost a necessity to the cultivated classes of Boston and its environs. The editors since its founder's time have been Col. W. W. Clapp, (now manager of the *Daily Journal*), George B. Woods, Warren L. Brigham, and Colonel Henry G. Parker, its present editor and proprietor. Its contributors have included many noted writers, among them, B. P. Shillaber, ("Mrs. Partington"), George H. Monroe, ("Templeton"), and others. The principal features of the *Gazette*, which Col. Parker has developed into one of the most successful newspaper properties in the United States, are its able and incisive editorials; its resume of society events of the week; the dramatic and musical criticisms of Benjamin E. Woolf, (who has won celebrity as a dramatist and composer and as a critic of great analytical power and masterly diction); the weekly sermon of Rev. James Freeman Clarke; a sparkling New York letter written by Miss Jeannette Gilder, ("Brunswick"); together with able literary and art departments. M. P. Curran, the accomplished journalist, has for some time been connected with Col. Parker's corps of writers. The *Gazette* occupies a peculiar and enviable position among Boston's favorite papers.

Shaw Kindergarten Schools.

A philanthropic Boston lady — Mrs. Pauline A. Shaw — has established thirty or more free Kindergarten Schools in various sections of the city, defraying the entire expense herself. These Schools enlist the services of fifty teachers. Many poor children receive her bounty.

Smoking Restaurants. In

some of the hotels conducted on the European system there are rooms assigned for the use of those gentlemen who wish to light a cigar or cigarette at table. Such smoking restaurants are to be found at Young's, Parker's and other hotels, and are known also as "coffee-rooms," etc.

Soldiers' Home. (1882). Chelsea.

"For what he was and all he dared,
Remember him to-day!"

is the motto adopted by the noble founders of the Soldiers' Home in Massachusetts — Gen. Horace Binney Sargent, Gov. Alexander H. Rice, Gov. Wm. Gaston, Gen. Charles Devens, Capt. J. G. B. Adams, and others — opened on Powder Horn Hill, Chelsea, July 25, 1882. The Home accommodates 111 soldiers, and it now contains that complement. Conditions for admission: The applicant must be a resident of the State of Massachusetts; must have served in the Rebellion; must be unable to earn his living; and must not be in receipt of a pension. The sum of $65,000 was raised for this grand institution at a Fair held in Mechanics' Hall, Boston. Library, 2,500 vols. Here is a most interesting Museum of War Relics. Superintendent of the Soldiers' Home, James A. Cunningham. Open to visitors on every day except Sunday. (Take Washington Avenue, Chelsea, horse-car to the foot of Powder Horn Hill, and a flight of 148 steps conducts to the Home). Possibly it may be interesting to quote here a table given by Francis W. Palfrey in the "Memorial History of Boston," relative to the representation of Massachusetts in the Rebellion. He says, "In consulting it, it must be remembered that the 32d, 33d and 35th regiments of infantry did not go to the front till after the 1st of July, 1862, when the fighting of the Peninsula campaign, so called, was ended; that the 54th and 55th regiments of infantry were not organized till 1863, nor the 56th till 1864. . . . The 19th, though brigaded with the 20th, was absent from several engagements in which the 20th took part in the first year of the war, and engaged at least once when the 20th was not:—

Organization. Tot. Killed. Died. Deserted.
1st Regt......1981.. 93.... 88......155
2d Regt......2767..116....156......275
9th Regt......1922..153....195......241
11th Regt......2423.. 85....147......328
12th Regt......1758..128....126......191
13th Regt......1584.. 71.... 75......171
19th Regt......2469..104....169......174
20th Regt......3230..192....192......229
24th Regt......2116.. 63....147......112
28th Regt......2504..161....203......288
32d Regt......2969.. 79....198......163
33d Regt......1412.. 69....107...... 79
35th Regt......1665.. 91....134...... 40
54th Regt.col'd.1574.. 54....154...... 40
55th Regt.col'd.1295.. 52....132...... 27
56th Regt......1319.. 69....134......129

(See *Exhibition of Battle-Flags*).

South Boston Canoe Club.
Canoeing is becoming very popular, especially with ladies. It is easier than rowing, and affords the best of exercise, developing the muscles of the shoulders and chest. John Boyle O'Reilly is an ardent lover of this pastime, and has done much to make known its pleasures. The South Boston Canoe Club is at the foot of K Street. Joseph Frizzell is the Commodore of the Club.

Suburban Old Houses.
In the immediate vicinity of Boston the antiquarian will find numerous houses the age and history of which will prove interesting. Among these are the Cradock House at Medford (1634); the Deane Winthrop House (about 1649) at Revere; Yeamans House (1680) Revere; Floyd Mansion (1670) Revere; and others.

Summer Homes of Theatrical People.
Among the colonies of professional people who have summer homes near Boston are the following: Agnes Booth-Schoeffel, Mrs. D. P. Bowers, John Gilbert, Joseph Proctor, John B. Schoeffel, at Manchester-by-the-sea. Octavia Allen, Eleanor Cary, Eliza Weathersby, J. B. Mason, W. F. Owen, Nat. C. Goodwin, Jr., Harry E. Dixey, George W. Wilson, James Nolan, Jacques Kruger, George Fortescue, at Ocean Spray, Winthrop. Lawrence Barrett, William H. Crane, Stuart Robson, Harry Meredith, at Cohasset. Stella Boniface, George C. Boniface, George C. Boniface, Jr., Lizzie May Ulmer, George H. Ulmer, Charles H. Bradshaw, H. A. Weaver, at North Scituate. Marie Wainwright, Louis James, at Nahant. Sara Jewett, James E Murdoch, at Pigeon Cove. Hanlon Brothers, Green Hill, Nantasket. W. H. Fessenden, Myron W. Whitney. Alonzo Stoddard, George Frothingham, Spaulding Family, at Long Pond, Plymouth. Hutchinson Family, Lynn. George W. Howard, Caroline Howard, Cambridge. Mathilde Phillipps, Marshfield. Hattie Richardson, Chelsea. Katherine Corcoran, James A. Herne, Ashmont District. Charles H. Clarke, John W. Hague, at South Boston. Jean Davenport Lander, Lynn. Fred Stinson, Andover; Ida Mulle, Winthrop; Frank J. Pilling, Winthrop; Annie Clarke, Needham. (Edwin Booth, William Warren, Louis Aldrich, Charles Barron, Mrs. Thomas Barry, and many other professionals, have homes in Boston.)

Summer Population of the City.
There is a summer population in Boston (says the *Traveller*) of a very distinctive and interesting character. Boston, as the gateway to the mountains and the sea, has thereby all the transient guests who are passing through to summer resorts,— the wealthy and aristocratic visitors who, while in the city, sojourn at the fashionable Back Bay hotel, the Brunswick; and another distinctive class, composed of students, teachers, and other professional people, who come to Boston for a summer's work as the Mecca of learning and of good library facilities. There is a large army of those interesting summer guests who come to Boston to combine vacation, sight-seeing, and literary, or scientific, work. The magnificent privileges offered by the Public Library, the Athenæum (by the courtesy of Mr. Cutter), and by the Harvard College library, attract a most valuable and interesting social element to Boston. Students find that a summer may be passed here in comparative inexpensiveness. It is by no means necessary to board at a fashionable hotel in order to enjoy Boston, nor to doom one's self to the philistine horrors of a boarding-house. The furnished rooms to let supply a method of living that may be as exclusive and independent as one pleases, and as economical as his necessities indicate. The Bostonians, too, who stay at home in the summer find the city by no means deserted. The streets are thronged; the open horse cars jingle merrily along; the evening entertainments of light opera and comedy are well attended; and moonlight sails down the bay or morning excursions to Nahant and Nantasket offer their enchantments. It is out of the question that a seaport city so far north as Boston can ever be very warm, and the days are for the most part comfortable in temperature and filled with delightful interests.

Sunday Courier.
(1824). 309 Washington Street. It was founded as a daily paper by Joseph T. Buckingham, the first number having been issued March 1, 1824. Mr. Buckingham retired from the *Courier* June 24, 1848. Samuel Kettell was its next editor, and at his death Isaac W. Frye assumed the duties of the position. Afterward, George Lunt, the eminent author and poet, became the editor. Joseph B. Morse followed him. With the close of the year 1866, the daily edition was discontinued, and a company was formed to issue a Sunday edition, as at present published. The editors have been Warren L. Brigham, George Parsons Lathrop and Arlo Bates, who now conducts it with a high degree of literary and journalistic skill. The *Courier* is noted as having been the medium for a large number of eminent writers. Among its original contributions have been James Russell Lowell's notable "Biglow Papers," while such distinguished writers as Daniel Webster, Rufus Choate, Robert C. Winthrop, Edward Everett, William H. Prescott, George Ticknor and T. W. Parsons have frequently contributed to its columns in past years. For some time previous to the publication of the *Courier* as a Sunday paper Joseph B. Travers was associated with its management, and is now its

publisher and principal proprietor. He has succeeded in sustaining the high standard early established for the *Courier*. Louis C. Elson is the musical critic. Francis Chase writes the enjoyable dramatic *feuilleton*, following the late Joseph B. Bradford in that capacity.

Tax-payers. The number of Polls in 1885 was 112,140.

Tennis. Boston is the only large city in the country possessing a Tennis Court. It is located on Buckingham Street, near Dartmouth Street, and is in charge of Thomas Pettitt, the celebrated court-tennis champion of the world. This court was built in 1875.

Times, Sunday. 20 Hawley Street. One of the brightest and most readable weeklies of the city, is the *Times*, an old established newspaper, issued on Sunday morning. Among its former editors have been Robert C. Dunham, J. W. Clarke, H. Irving Dillenback and others. Mr. Dunham was for some years its publisher, issuing a daily edition. Mr. Clarke's period was signalized by the publication of a series of articles upon the Moody and Sankey revival which attracted wide attention. The *Times* is now published by D. S. Knowlton, who is also its editor. Special features of the *Sunday Times* are its interesting editorials on current events, society matters, literary columns, news notes, dramatic and musical departments. Its musical news and criticisms are extremely complete and well written.

Time. When it is 12 o'clock, noon, in Boston, it is 44 14 past four o'clock p. m., at Greenwich (England) observatory, and 36 minutes past eleven o'clock, p. m. at Washington, D. C.

Transcript, Daily. (1830). 324 Washington Street. The oldest evening paper in New England. The *Transcript* is the only really literary newspaper in America. It is conducted with a view to gratifying the tastes of the cultured people of Boston and suburbs, and that mission is successfully and admirably fulfilled. Nothing finds a place in the columns of the *Transcript* that cannot be read aloud in the drawing-room. The movements of prize-fighters and others of that class are as utterly ignored as if they did not exist. The *Transcript*, however, gives all the real news, its facilities in that regard being extensive, and the very latest telegraphic dispatches are always to be found in its various editions. Among the editors of the paper during its existence have been Lynde M. Walter, Cornelia M. Walter, Epes Sargent, Daniel N. Haskell, William A. Hovey, and Edward H. Clement, the present able editor, who assumed the duties of the position in 1881. Mr. Clement's literary taste and unerring journalistic instincts well fit him for the duties of editor of a newspaper of elevated tone. Eminent contributors have regularly enriched the columns of the *Transcript* — among them E. P. Whipple, Starr King, E. H. Chapin, and others — and the paper is to-day a favorite medium for celebrated writers. The musical department, in charge of William F. Apthorp, a musician, critic, and scholar of rare attainments, is widely read. The dramatic column, conducted by Francis H. Jenks, is no less interesting. The art, literary, and other departments are attractive features of this model evening newspaper.

Traveller, Daily. (1845). 31 State Street. Roland Worthington & Co. This popular evening paper was established April 1, 1845, being the first evening newspaper issued at two cents a copy. For quite a period, so Puritanical were the ideas of its first publishers, Messrs. Upton, Ladd & Co., that they absolutely refused to publish advertisements of theatres. Col. Worthington, to-day its chief proprietor and manager, early identified with its interests, was instrumental in bringing the *Traveller* to the front as a newspaper, and it has for years been recognized as a cleanly, bright evening paper for the family. The bulletins now so generally to be seen in front of newspaper offices were introduced at the *Traveller* office. The Saturday edition is made especially attractive owing to its excellent literary features, original stories and poems being presented, and as it is a double sheet it furnishes a very large amount of extremely readable matter. The special features of the *Traveller* are a Review of the Week, a Mail-Box department, etc. The dramatic and musical columns are especially inviting, while the literary tone of the paper is high. The letters of Mrs. John Sherwood (M. E. W. S.) attract universal attention. The staff of the *Traveller* is as follows: Reuben Crooke, managing editor; William F. Whitcher, leading editorial writer; Stephen O. Sherman, city editor; Edward J. French, telegraph editor; Charles P. Bond, financial editor; Arthur Colburn, dramatic editor; Fred T. Fuller, Legislative reporter; Lillian Whiting, literary and art critic; Duncan McLean, shipping editor; Benjamin A. Appleton, City Hall reporter; Thomas F. Anderson, special writer.

Trees. Every stranger in Boston desires to have pointed out the celebrated Gink-go Tree (Ginkgo Biloba of Eastern Asia). Oliver Wendell Holmes has made it known throughout the land by an allusion to it in "The Autocrat of the Breakfast Table." Thousands of people go every year to see this tree, citizens and strangers alike being interested in its peculiar history, growth, and foliage. The tree is on the Beacon Street Mall of the Common, nearly opposite the Joy Street entrance. It is on the corner of this Mall and the walk the farthest to the left from Joy Street. It is plainly labelled, and can therefore easily be found. This tree was transplanted to this spot from the garden of Gardiner Green, formerly on Pemberton Sq. (1835). Other rare trees on the Common — in addition to the grand old American Elm (*Ulmus Americana*) the English Elm (*Ulmus Campestris*) and the Dutch Elm (*Ulmus Montana*) are the Tulip Tree (*Liriodendron Tulipifera*); Red Oak (*Quercus Rubra*); Basswood (*Tilia Americana*); European Ash (*Fraxinus Excelsior*); Linden (*Tilia Parvifolia*); Sugar Maple (*Acer Saccharinum*); Sycamore Maple (*Psuedo Platanus*); European Ash (*Fraxinus Excelsior*); Norway Maple (*Acer Dasycarpum*), etc. On the Public Garden may be found the Sophora (*Sophora Japonica*); English Hawthorn (*Crataegus Oxyacantha*); Negundo (*Negundo Aceroides*); Kentucky Coffee Tree (*Gymnocladus Canadensis*); Tamarix (*Tamarix Gallica*); Weeping Dutch Elm (*Ulmus Montana*), — (a most remarkable Tree), in addition to fine Weeping Willows, Horse Chestnuts, Beeches, Silver Poplars, Maples, Tulip Trees, etc. (See *Arnold Arborctum* and *Harvard Botanic Garden*).

Tremont House. (1829). Tremont Street, corner of Beacon Street. The Tremont is one of the oldest of the present hotels of Boston. It is conducted on the American plan. Its table is noted for its excellence, and its rooms are furnished with great elegance. A tone of perfect comfort characterizes the entire establishment, and one cannot find a more desirable temporary or permanent hotel residence in the city. The house is especially liked by English tourists, who find about it many points of resemblance to London hotels of the first class. Charles Dickens wrote of it: "It has more galleries, colonnades, piazzas and passages than I can remember or the reader would believe." Silas Gurney is the proprietor. He has greatly modernized and improved the hotel since he assumed control of it. The Tremont is one of the great and prosperous hotels of the land. It is kept on the American plan.

Tuileries Balcony. The iron balcony in front of the third story window (on Hereford Street) of the new residence of Hon. John F. Andrew (son of the "War-Governor" John Albion Andrew) at the corner of Commonwealth Avenue and Hereford Street, was brought from the Tuileries, Paris, France.

United States Hotel. (1826). Beach Street, between Kingston and Lincoln Streets. This house covers nearly two acres of ground, and has about 500 rooms. Numerous families residing in the country, or in the smaller cities, make their winter home at the United States Hotel. Its proximity to several of the principal railway stations makes it attractive to large numbers of travellers. It has a good patronage from members of the theatrical profession. It is kept on the American plan. Hon. Tilly Haynes, the present proprietor, manages it very successfully.

United States Marine Hospital. (Northern Atlantic District, port of Boston). (1800). Chelsea. Under reasonable conditions strangers are permitted to visit the hospital and grounds.

United States Navy Yard. Charlestown District. Entrance at the junction of Wapping and Water Streets. A most interesting place to visit. There are seventy buildings, of iron, stone, brick and wood. It has an area of eighty-seven and a half acres. On the land side is a wall of granite twelve feet high, built in 1825-26. The steam-engineering building has a chimney 240 feet high (higher than Bunker Hill Monument, which is two hundred and twenty feet). There is a Naval Museum and Library, etc. The following-named comprise the Executive Board: Commodore, L. A. Kimberly; Captain of Yard, Joseph Fyffe; Pay Director, Gilbert E. Thornton; Paymaster, John F. Tarbell; Surgeon, George F. Winslow; Chaplain, Albert L. Royce; Admiral's Secretary, J. W. Hudson. Construction Department: Naval Constructor, George R. Boush; Engineer's Department: Chief Engineer, D. B. Macombe; Equipment Department, Commander, Albert Kautz; Yard and Docks Department: Civil Engineer, Frank O. Maxson; Navigation Department: Commander, Mortimer L. Johnson; Marine Barracks: Commanding Lieutenant, Col. J. L. Browne; Naval Rendezvous on board Receiving Ship "Wabash," Captain, Francis M. Bunce. (Chelsea and Lynn & Boston street-cars, from Cornhill, pass the gate.)

Valuation of Boston. Valuation in 1823, $44,806,800; in 1885, $685,404,600, being an increase in 62 years of $640,507,800! Nothing more positive could be adduced to demonstrate the gigantic strides Boston is taking in wealth and position among foremost cities.

Valuation of Leading Hotels. There are eighty-eight public Hotels in Boston, and one hundred and seventy-eight family Hotels, or apartment houses. The following is a list of these Hotels which have an assessed valuation of a quarter of a million dollars and upwards: Parker House, $665,000; Hotel Vendome, $625,000; Young's Hotel, $620,000; Adams

House, $515,000; Tremont House, $476,000; Hotel Brunswick, $475,000; United States Hotel, $337,000; Hotel Oxford, $317,000; American House, $310,000; Hotel Berkeley, $300,000; Hotel Boylston, $292,000; Commonwealth Hotel, $280,000; Hotel Pelham, $274,000; Quincy House, $250,000.

Visitors to Faneuil Hall. In 1885 there were about 10,000 visitors to Faneuil Hall.

Walks. The favorite route for pedestrians taking their "constitutional" is from the corner of Tremont and Park Streets across the Common and Public Garden, through Commonwealth Avenue Parkway to West Chester Park Street, then turning to the right to Beacon Street, then to the left over the Milldam, through Longwood to Brookline. If a still longer walk is desired one can keep on to Chestnut Hill. If already fatigued, street-cars, at Coolidge Corner, run into the city every few minutes. There are many other pleasant walks in West Roxbury, Jamaica Plain, Dorchester and Milton, and, in fact, the suburbs of Boston furnish pleasant and picturesque walks in almost every direction.

Weekly Commonwealth. 25 Bromfield Street. This popular weekly, long identified with the late Hon. Charles W. Slack, its editor and publisher for a quarter of a century, and issued as an organ for the discussion of anti-slavery questions, woman's rights, moral reforms, transcendentalism, art, literature, music, drama, etc., at the death of its eminent proprietor and editor (1885) was sold to D. N. Thayer & Co. Mr. Thayer retiring in 1886, the paper is now issued by the Commonwealth Publishing Company, the general features of the paper being retained. In addition a society department has been opened and several other changes made. The sermons of Rev. J. Kay Applebee, of the Parker Memorial Church, are still continued. Musical, dramatic, art, literary and social gossip —local and suburban—make the *Commonwealth* very attractive to many readers.

What Gives Boston its Commercial Rank. The amount of business transacted at the Boston Clearing House is second to that of New York only among the great cities of the country. The exchanges of the Boston House amounted during 1885 to the following: $3,515,700,000. The Philadelphia House during the same period had the following amount: $2,812,500,000. Chicago: $2,525,600,000. The amount at Paris was $813,200,000. Boston therefore surpassed Paris to the extent of $2,702,500,000; exceeded those of Chicago $990,100,000; and went ahead of Philadelphia to the sum of $703,200,000. Such figures as these demonstrate Boston's business importance, and give her the proud position of the second commercial city of the United States.

Winter Population. The population of Boston is largely augmented during the Fall, Winter and Spring months—or "the season"—by the coming into town of numerous wealthy families residing in other cities in the State, including Worcester, Springfield, Salem, Lynn, Lowell, Lawrence and other places, who take suites in the various elegant apartment houses now so rapidly multiplying in all the fashionable sections of Boston, or locate in the "swell" hotels like the Vendome, Brunswick, Oxford, Adams, Parker, Young's, etc. The Tremont, Revere, Commonwealth, American, United States and Quincy Houses also receive their full quota of such parties. By this means the varied great social, dramatic, musical, literary and educational advantages of a residence in the New England metropolis are gained in a great degree, and a beneficial change is experienced by those who flit to their summer homes throughout the Commonwealth when the flowers of May announce the approach of the "heated term."

Women's Industrial and Educational Union. (1877). 74 Boylston Street. For co-operation among women. Founded by Dr. Harriet Clisby. Here is a reading-room, an educational department, and an industrial department, where articles made by women are for sale. The Union welcomes all women to its rooms. The influence of this great institution is powerful and far-reaching.

Wool. Boston has the largest wool trade of any city in America. The houses engaged in it centre chiefly about Federal Street, Mathews Street and vicinity. Among the principal firms in this business are Hilton, Weston & Co., Denny, Rice & Co., Luce & Manning, Brown, Steese & Clarke, Williams & Coburn, Dewey, Gould & Dike, Nichols, Dupee & Co., Hallowell & Coburn, and Chamberlin Bros. & Co.

Writers for Out-of-Town Papers. Boston correspondents of papers published in other cities include the following: Edwin M. Bacon, Springfield *Republican;* R. L. Bridgman, New York *Post* and Worcester *Spy;* Arlo Bates, Providence *Journal;* Arthur Colburn, New York *Music and Drama;* Fred Walton Bacon, New York *Graphic;* Josephine Jenkins, Albany *Journal;* E. H. Talbot, Chicago *Tribune;* Arthur Leach, New York *Dramatic Times;* E. B. Rankin, Baltimore *Sun;* Louis Maas, New York *Musical Courier;* B. P. Shillaber, ("Mrs. Partington"), Hartford *Post;* Louis C. Elson, New York *Keynote;*

George H. Monroe, ("Templeton"), Hartford *Courant;* H. S. Kempton, Minneapolis *Tribune,* Mrs. A. M. B. Ellis, ("Max Eliot"), various papers; Apphia Howard, Philadelphia *Press,* Frank Forbes, Hingham *Journal;* G. H. Dickinson, New York *Dramatic News,* J. T. Fynes, New York *Clipper,* C. F. Currier, New York *Mercury,* Earle Marble, New York *Mirror.*

Yachting. Those interested in yachting will enjoy a visit to South Boston where the great club-houses of the Boston Yacht Club and the South Boston Yacht Club are located. The bay is almost covered with the fleets, presenting a beautiful sight. The victory of the "Puritan" has given Boston the right to feel a pride in its vast yachting interests.

Young's Hotel. (1845). Court Avenue, Court Square and Court Street. Established by George Young in 1845, succeeding Taft's noted Coffee-House, Young's Hotel has become celebrated as a first-class hotel. It is kept on the European plan. The present proprietor, J. Reed Whipple, is one of the most enterprising young landlords in the country. The house has been enlarged from time to time until it has become one of the largest in the city. It is especially noted for the excellence of its *cuisine.* It has immense resources for furnishing dinners, its three main dining-halls, and its two long lunch-counters accommodating hundreds of persons simultaneously. The ladies' cafe is fitted up sumptuously, its decorations being most artistically harmonious and striking in style. The sleeping-rooms are elegantly furnished. Young's is a favorite hotel with clubs, numerous organizations dining there regularly. Rooms are to be had for $1 per day upward, according to location.

UNITED STATES SIGNAL SERVICE.

Signal Service. The following code of signals was adopted by the weather bureau May 1, 1886. The indications are expressed by a system of flags, raised upon the United States Government Building, Post-Office Square. Flags are hoisted at 7.30 a. m., daily, the weather forecasts indicated by them covering a period of twenty-four hours. Flags should be read from the top of the staff downward. The signals adopted for the approach of wind storms are of three kinds, viz:

1. The cautionary signal.
2. The direction signal.
3. The on-shore signal.

The cautionary day signal is a square red flag with a black square centre, and a red light at night. It is hoisted when a wind with a velocity of thirty-five miles per hour or over is expected within one hundred miles of the station where displayed. This velocity is considered dangerous to all classes of shipping.

The direction signal is a square flag composed of two horizontal stripes, one black and one white. It is never displayed except with the cautionary signal flag, and indicates from what quadrant the dangerous wind is expected. For this purpose the compass is divided into northeast, southeast, southwest and northwest quadrants. There is no night signal for the direction signal.

The on-shore signal is a square flag composed of four small squares, two white and two black, and is only displayed on lake stations. The direction signal will not be hoisted with the on-shore.

In addition to these signals the observers will be supplied by wire from Washington with information at intervals during the display.

The direction of the wind will be represented as follows: The black bar above the white flying over the cautionary signal indicates a gale blowing from the northeast. The white bar above the black flying over the cautionary indicates a southeast gale. The black bar above the white flying under the cautionary indicates a northwest gale, and the white bar above the black flying under the cautionary signal indicates a southwest gale.

BANKS AND BANKING.

Banks. The banking capital of Boston is enormous, this city ranking second to New York only in banking interests. Boston is the richest city of its size in the United States. At the close of the Revolutionary War, with a population of 19,000, this city had two banks, one of them being then ten years old, in addition to a branch of the United States Bank. The number of banks in Boston at the present time is 84 (17 of which are savings banks). Following are the names and locations of the banks, which have an aggregate capital of about sixty millions of dollars:

Atlantic Nat., 1828, Kilby st., cor. Doane.
Atlas Nat., 1833, 8 Sears Building.
Bank of Deposit, 84 Devonshire st.
Blackstone Nat., 132 Hanover st.
Blue Hill Nat., Washington st., Dorch.
Boston Nat., 1853, 95 Milk st.
Boylston Nat., 1845, 616 Washington st.
Broadway Nat., 1853, 150 Devonshire st.
Bunker Hill Nat., 1825, 21 City sq., Chas'n.
Central Nat., 1873, 121 Devonshire st.
Columbian Nat., 1822, 65 State st.
Continental Nat., 1860, 51 Summer st.
Eliot Nat., 1853, 95 Milk st.
Everett Nat., 1865, Milk st., cor. Congress.
Faneuil Hall Nat., 1851, 3 So. Market st.
First Nat., 1863, 17 State st.
First Ward Nat., 1864, 1 Winthrop bl., East Boston.
Fourth Nat., 1875, 34 Blackstone st.
Freeman's Nat., 1836, 111 Summer st.
Globe Nat., 1824, 49 State st.
Hamilton Nat., 1832, 60 Devonshire st.
Howard Nat., 1853, 19 Congress st.
Lincoln Nat., 1882, 150 Devonshire st.
Manufacturers' Nat., 1873, Summer st.
Market Nat., 1832, 86 State st.
Massachusetts Nat., 1784, 69 Congress st.
Maverick Nat., 1854, 59 Water st.
Mechanics' Nat., 1836, 115 Dorchester av.
Merchandise Nat., 1875, 70 Kilby st.
Merchants' Nat., 1831, 2 State st.
Metropolitan Nat., 1875, 4 Post-Office sq.
Monument Nat., 1854, Thompson sq., Ch'n.
Mount Vernon Nat., 1860, 43 Chauncy st.
Nat. Bank of Brighton, Chestnut Hill av.
Nat. Bank of Commerce, 1850, 9 Sears building.
Nat. Bank of North America, 1850, 106 Franklin st.
Nat. Bank of Commonwealth, 1871, Devonshire, cor. Water.
Nat. Bank of Redemption, 1858, 85 Devonshire st.
Nat. Bank of Republic, 1859, 95 Milk st.
Nat. City, 1822, 61 State st.
Nat. Eagle, 1822, 95 Milk st.
Nat. Exchange, 1847, 28 State st.
Nat. Hide & Leather, 1857, 70 Federal st.
Nat. Market Bank of Brighton, Brighton District.
Nat. Revere, 1859, 100 Franklin st.
Nat. Rockland, 1864, 2343 Washington st.
Nat. Security, 1867, 79 Court st.
Nat. Union, 1792, 40 State st.
Nat. Webster, 1853, Congress st., corner Milk.
New England Nat., 1813, 67 State st.
North Nat., 1825, 100 Franklin st.
Old Boston Nat., 1803, 48 State st.
People's Nat., 1832 114 Dudley st.
Second Nat., 1832, 199 Washington st.
Shawmut Nat., 1836, 60 Congress st.
Shoe & Leather Nat., 1836, 150 Devonshire st.
State Nat., 1811, 40 State st.
Suffolk Nat., 1818, 60 State st.
Third Nat., 1864, 8 Congress st.
Traders' Nat., 1831, 91 State st.
Tremont Nat., 1814, 8 Congress st.
Washington Nat., 1825, 47 State st.
(See *Savings Banks*).

Co-Operative Banks. Homestead, 987 Washington st.; Merchants, 28 State st.; Pioneer, 987 Washington st.; West Roxbury, Elson Building, J. P.; Workingmen's, 987 Washington st.

Loan and Trust Companies. American Loan and Trust Co., 55 Congress st.; Boston Loan Co., 275 Washington st.; Boston Safe Deposit and Trust Co., 87 Milk st.; Collateral Loan Co., 328 Washington st.; International Trust Co., 45 Milk st.; Massachusetts Loan and Trust Co., 18 P. O. sq.; New England Trust Co., 85 Devonshire st.

Savings Banks. Boston Five Cents, 38 School st.; Boston Penny, 1371 Washington st.; Brighton Five Cents, Washington st., Brighton District; Charlestown Five Cents, Thompson sq., Charlestown District; East Boston, 16 Maverick sq., E. B.; Eliot Five Cents, 114 Dudley st., Roxbury; Franklin, 20 Boylston st.; Home, 186 Tremont st. (Masonic Temple); Institution for Savings, 2343 Washington st., Roxbury District; North End, 57 Court st.; Provident Institution for Savings, 36 Temple pl.; South Boston, 368 W. Broadway, S. B.; Suffolk, 47 Tremont st.; Union Institution for Savings, 599 Washington st.; Warren Institution for Savings, 25 Main st., Charlestown District.

MUSICAL ORGANIZATIONS.

The following is as complete and accurate a list of the operatic and concert companies, quartets, bands, orchestras, etc., of Boston, as the writer has been enabled to obtain. This directory will be of great value to local managers throughout New England, Northern New York, Canada, and the British Provinces, as well as to committees on entertainments given by associations, lodges, posts, lyceums, fairs, festivals, etc., in Boston and elsewhere. Any of the organizations named can be addressed in care of Oliver Ditson & Co., 451 Washington Street, Boston; or to any of the *Entertainment Bureaus* in Boston, a complete list of which is given in this work, or to the artists themselves. (In writing please mention the Cyclopedia of Boston).

Abercrombie Ballad Company, (1885). Charles Abercrombie, Director, 181 Tremont st.

Acme Juvenile Orchestra.

Adamowski-Hood Concert Company. Mollie Castleberg, soprano; Timothie d'Adamowski, violinist; Edward K. Hood, reader; May E. Reilly, pianist.

Allen's Orchestra. Charles N. Allen, director.

Alpine Male Quartet. (1885). C. H. Harbor, 1st tenor; I. P. Horton, 2d tenor; E. H. Hall, baritone; F. W. Howes, basso. E. H. Hall, manager, 19 West st.

Anacreon Club.

Arelamena Ladies' Quartet. Susie E. H. Munroe, 1st soprano; Susie A. Martin, 2d soprano; Gertrude L. Cooke, 1st contralto; Lucie J. Martin, 2d contralto. Mrs. S. A. Martin, manager, 83 Pearl st., Chelsea.

Ariel Quartet. Nellie E. Fox, 1st soprano; Ida Holt, 2d soprano; Fannie E. Holt, 1st alto; Mabel Mumler, 2d alto.

Arlington Quartet. Lizzie Webb Cary, Gertrude Edmands, Geo. W. Want, H. L. Cornell.

Ashman's Battalion Band, 7 Salem st.

Baldwin's Boston Cadet Orchestra. J. Thomas Baldwin, conductor. 1st violins, Vincent Akeroyd, Percy Hayden, Richard Kurth, Placido Fiumara; 2d violins, W. W. Sturtevant, E. T. Damon; viola, Geo. H. Rowell; 'cello, Harry Upham; double bass, Otto Lorenz, Henry G. Weston; piccolo and flute, August Damm, F. H. Eaton; oboe, A. L. de Ribas; bassoon, Louis Post; petite clarinet, Lorenzo White; clarinets, George Carney, Horatio T. Noyes; solo cornet, Thomas W. Henry; 1st cornet, J. Morley Flockton; 2d cornet, Charles C. Ward; French horn: Louis Werner, Fred. Grant; 1st trombone, Alfred Rigg; 2d trombone, Leroy Kenfield; bass trombone, Alfred J. Goddard; bass and snare drum, Stephen Newman; tympani, Henry D. Simpson; cymbals, E. E. Parker; tuba, Julius Gross. 63 Court st.

Barrow's Orchestra........34 Brattle st.

Beacon Concert Company. Avis Gray Harriott, Viola J. Palmer, Bertram J. Harriott, Ernst Ruppell.

Beacon Quartet. Edith Estelle Torrey, Sopha C. Hall, Arthur F. Burnett. Franklin A. Shaw. F. A. Shaw, manager, 175 Tremont st.

Beacon Trio. Viola J. Palmer, Bertram J. Harriott, Ernst Ruppell.

Beethoven Club. Charles N. Allen, Theodore Hunan, Carl Meisel, Wulf Fries, William Rietzl, Johannes Bletterman.

Beethoven Quartet. C. N. Allen, T. Hunan, C. Meisel, W. Fries.

Behr's German Orchestra. C. Behr, Chestnut av., Jamaica Plain.

Bijou Theatre Orchestra. John J. Braham, conductor.

Boardman's Band...230 Washington st.

Boston Banjo Concert Company. Mme. Anna Howes-Hernandez, Melquiades-Hernandez, Wm. A. Cole, Edmund Foster, C. A. Campbell. Fairbanks & Cole, managers, 121 Court st.

Boston Brass Band. D. C. Hall, leader. 103 Court st.

Boston City Band. Chas. Lindall, agt. 186 Washington st.

Boston Ideal Concert Company. Marietta R. Sherman, Annie A. Park, Nellie C. Park, Francis L. Moses, E. H. Frye, Fred G. Stetson.

Boston Ideal Opera Company. (1879). Marie Stone-Macdonald, Zelie de Lussan, Agnes Huntington, Lizzie Burton-Morsell, Tom Karl, Herndon Morsell, Wm. H. Macdonald, Henry C. Barnabee, W. H. Clark, George Frothingham. Samuel S. Studley, musical director; Fred Williams, stage manager; W. H. Foster, manager. Tremont House, Boston.

Boston Mandolin Quartet. George Barker, G. L. Lansing, H. W. Harris, H. W. Pattee. 180 Washington st.

Boston Maritana Opera Company (1885). Etta Kileski, Gertrude Edmands, J. C. Bartlett, Lon F. Brine, H. L. Cornell, Myron Clark. Leon Keach, director, 451 Washington st.

Boston Museum Orchestra. George Purdy, director. S. C. Bennett, 1st violin; J. L. Blodgett, 2d violin; Reuben Tower, viola; Max Korth, 'cello; Augustus Ellis, bass; J. B. Van Santvoord, flute; W. H. Abdy, clarinet; E. N. Lafricain, 1st cornet; John Sheridan, 2d cornet or clarinet; W. W. Reid, trombone or euphonium; Wm. Braham, drums and xylophone.

Boston Oratorio Society. J. G. Lennon, director.

Boston Orchestra. P. C. Meyrelles, director.

Boston Orchestral Club. B. Listemann, director.
Boston Star Concert Company. (1886). Medora Henson-Emerson, Nella Brown-Pond, Walter Emerson, Chas. F. Dennee. Ozias W. Pond, manager, 36 Bromfield st.
Boston Swedish Quartet.
Boston Symphony Orchestra. Wilhelm Gericke, conductor. Chas. A. Ellis, manager. Music Hall.
Boston Theatre Orchestra. N. Lothian, conductor.
Brown's Brigade Band, 226 Washing. st.
Buffum's Orchestra........103 Court st.
Camilla Urso Concert Company. Camilla Urso, Alice May Estey, Louis Miller. F. Luer, manager, 451 Washington st.
Campanari String Quartet. Leandro Campanari, Julius Akeroyd, Daniel Kuntz, Ernst Jonas.
Carter Concert Company. Helen E. H. Carter, Marie Hester, S. Kronberg, May Shepard, Ernst Ruppell.
Carter's Band and Orchestra. T. M. Carter, leader, 179 Washington st.
Cheeney Comic Opera Company. J. W. Cheeney, 451 Washington st.
Clarendon Male Quartet.
Clark's Orchestra..........103 Court st.
Commonwealth Male Quartet. (1879). Frank Swift, Alphonso Demerritt, F. R. A. Pingree, M. A. Metcalf. 36 Bromfield st.
Corelli Opera Company. Blanche Corelli, Lillian Larose, Annie M. Libby, Ricardo Morosini, Frank J. Binkhourst, J. L. Slattery, W. J. Clark, T. Whyte.
Crittenden Concert Company.
Davis' Brass Band..........18 Arch st.
Dearing's Band............103 Court st.
De Seve Concert Company. Abbie F. Hervey, Abby Clarke, Samuel M. King, Edw. K. Hood, Mme. De Seve, Alfred De Seve.
Edmands' Band......161 Washington st.
Emerson-Pierce Concert Company. Mamie E. Hitch, Walter Emerson, Carl Pierce, J. Frank Donahoe.
English Ballad Concert Company. Mrs. H. F. Knowles, Alta Pease, J. C. Bartlett, A. D. Saxon, Annie Coffin, Frank J. Smith.
Euterpe Concert Company. Jenny Patrick-Walker, Mary F. How, Alfred Wilkie, S. Kronberg, Lillian Chandler, Emma Le B. Kettelle.
Euterpe Ladies' Quartet. (1886).
Germania Band. W. C. Nichols, agent; 516 Washington st.
Germania Quartet. E. M. Bagley, B. Bowron, E. Strasser, G. W. Stewart.
Gilbert Opera Company. Florence Bate, Helen Adelaide Russell, Harriette Ernst, Mabel H. George, James A. Gilbert, J. A. Osgood, John Ramsay, S. P. Cutter, F. W. Soule. Manager, James A. Gilbert, 42 Blue Hill av.
Globe Theatre Orchestra. John C. Mullaly, conductor.
Gott Lyceum Opera Company. Annie C. Hunt, Lola Bernard, W. R. Day, Eugene Ormand, George C. Gott. 451 Washington st.

Grand Army of the Republic Quartet.
Handel and Haydn Society. (1815). Carl Zerrahn, director.
Hand's Band..............103 Court st.
Harvard Glee Club.
Harvard Quartet. (1884). A. P. Briggs, E. Howard, W. B. Stewart, J. H. B. Easton.
Hawthorne Quartet. (1884). Theodore Chute, J. G. Osborne, W. C. Robbins, A. D. Huntoon.
Higgins' Band and Orchestra. Concert Hall, Bowdoin sq.
Higgins' Concert Co.
Hollis Street Theatre Orchestra. Geo. Loesch, conductor.
Hunter Concert Company. Creighton House.
Hutchinson Family. (1840). John W. Hutchinson, Mrs. Lillie P. Hutchinson, Master Jack Hutchinson. High Rock, Lynn.
Hobbs' Band...............88 Court st.
Howard Athenæum Orchestra.
Ideal Banjo Trio. Albert D. Grover, E. M. Paine, A. A. Babb. 7 Exchange pl.
Ideal Quartet. Mixed voices.
Ideal Troubadours.
Imperial Banjo Quartet. (1885). Melquiades Hernandez, William A. Cole, Edmund Foster, C. A. Campbell. Fairbanks & Cole, Managers, 121 Court st.
Jenniebelle Neal Concert Company. Jenniebelle Neal, Marie Marchington, Marion Osgood, Charles E. Lindall, Howard M. Dow.
Joyce's Band.............92 Sudbury st.
Kelley Concert Company, 6 Music Hall.
Kneisel String Quartet. Franz Kneisel, Emanuel Fiedler, Louis Svecenski, Fritz Giese.
Kraft's Orchestra..........88 Court st.
Ladies' Carol Club. Fannie Sprague, Fannie Billings, Minnie Starkweather, Maud Burdette. 451 Washington st.
Ladies' Schubert Quartet. (1885). Jessie Edna Ollivier, Jennie Whitcombe Worcester, Grace Cobb Crawford, Annie Louise Whitcomb.
Listemann Concert Company. Bernhard Listemann, Edward Heindl, Henry Heindl, Fritz Listemann, Alexander Heindl, Henry Greene.
Lotus Glee Club. George C. Devoll, Harry G. Snow, Charles L. Lewis, Clifton F. Davis. Harry G. Snow, manager. 2 Music Hall Building.
Mme. Fry's Boston Concert Company.
Marion Osgood's Lady Orchestra. Mechanics Hall.
Mendelssohn Concert Orchestra.
Mendelssohn Ladies' Quartet. Clara J. Marsh, Marie M. Foster, Elizabeth M. Roberts, Hattie Whiting. 181 Tremont st., room 30.
Mendelssohn Male Quartet.
Mendelssohn Quintet Club. Sam Franko, Max Klein, Thomas Ryan, Julius Akeroyd, Fritz Giese.
Nemo Quartet.
New England Conservatory Male Quartet.
Norton's Band.............103 Court st.

Novello Club.......... E. H. Bailey, Dir.
O Connor's Band........... 103 Court st.
Oratorio Quartet. Charles Abercrombie, 181 Tremont st.
Oriental Garden Orchestra. George Loesch, conductor.
Oxford Quartet. (1885). T. H. Norris, J. H. Ricketson, A. D. Saxon, W. J. McLaughlin.
Park Family Concert Company.
Park Theatre Orchestra. E. N. Catlin, conductor.
Philomela Ladies' Quartet. (1884). Louise N. Baldwin, Emma C. Wheeler, Sara A. Peakes, Annie L. Mitchell.
Pierce's War-Song Company. Music Hall.
Popular Concert Company. Charles Abercrombie, 181 Tremont st.
Primrose Quartet.
Purdy's Chorus............... 3 West st.
Redpath Boston Concert Company. (1880). H. Louise Warner, Edith Christie, Ella M. Chamberlin, John Francis Gilder, Francis G. Reynolds. Redpath Bureau, 36 Bromfield st.
Richardson's Band. J. Howard Richardson, 1 Bosworth st.
Ripley's Band. W. S. Ripley, 88 Court st.
Rivals Concert Company. Etta Kileski, Alfred de Seve, Walter Emerson, Edward K. Hood, Mme. Alfred de Seve.
Ross' Band................. 103 Court st.
Rulinstein Male Quartet.
Rugby Quartet. Henry S. Polsey, Clarence M. Collins, Edward E. Cutter, William B. Robinson.

Ruggles Quartet. Herbert O. Johnson, William P. Meek, Geo. H. Remele, Geo. R. Clark.
Savage's Band........... 26 Portland st.
Schumann Female Quartet. (1882). Etta May Hunt, Addie Louise Clapp, Lizzie M. Hopkins, Lena Hinckley.
Schumann Glee Club. Arthur B. Hitchcock, director.
Shawmut Band...... 173 Washington st.
Smith's Band............... 103 Court st.
Snow's Boston Opera Company. H. G. Snow, Music Hall.
Solace Quartet. (1885). Furnishes music for funerals, memorial services, etc. Miss T. Falkner, Maud Burdette, C. L. Sanders, Henry W. Noble. 451 Washington st.
Spaulding Bell-Ringers. Georgie Dean Spaulding, W. P. Spaulding, Dudley H. Prescott. Neponset.
Suffolk Band............... 103 Court st.
Sweet Family....... 541 Washington st.
Technology Glee Club.
Temple Musical Company. A. D. Grover, E. M. Paine, A. A. Babb, G. E. Damon, Harry Bower, F. A. Hamnett, H. G. Fuller. 7 Exchange pl.
Temple Quartet. W. R. Bateman, E. F. Webber, H. A. Cook, A. C. Ryder.
Walker Quintet.
Webb Quartet.
Weber Male Quartet. Thos. E. Johnson, G. A. Daggett, W. L. Vinal, George R. Titus.
Windsor Theatre Orchestra. T. C. Gray, director.
Wood's Band....... 33 Central sq., E. B.

ENTERTAINMENT BUREAUS.

Among the Boston managers and others furnishing entertainments — dramatic, musical and literary — to lyceums, posts, lodges, associations, fairs, festivals, etc., throughout New England, Northern New York State, Canada, the British Provinces and other sections are the following:

Bachert, Max............... Hotel Pelham
Bacon, Fred. Walton.......... 43 Eliot st.
Bickford Bureau.......... 18 Boylston st.
Blish, George W........... 78 Tremont st.
Burdett & North........... 20 Dock sq.
Chickering Bureau........ 152 Tremont st.
Hathaway, Geo. H. & Co. 36 Bromfield st.
Hub Bureau................. 89 Court st.
Johnson's Dramatic Bureau. 550 Wash. st.
Jones, George A. & Co....... 23 School st.

Kelley's Bureau............. 6 Music Hall
M'Glenen, E. W....... 262 Washington st.
New England Dramatic Agency.......... 767 Washington st.
New England Musical Bureau.......... 149 A Tremont st.
Noyes, Miss Abby..... 451 Washington st.
Pelham, Walter............. 3 Music Hall
Pierce, Elmore A........... 2 Music Hall
Purdy, George H............ 3 West st.
Redpath Bureau........... 36 Bromfield st.
Roberts Bureau............ 2 Music Hall
Ross, Louis H. & Co........ 3 West st.
Snow, H. G. & Co........... 2 Music Hall
Thayer, Charles H......... Parker House
Webber & Ingersoll Bureau.......... 603 Tremont st.
Williams Bureau...... 258 Washington st.

STEAMBOATS.

Among the steamboats which are departing from and arriving at Boston are the following:

"Acadia"..........................Naples
"Alpha".................. Yarmouth, N. S.
"Anglian"......................Baracoa
"Assyria" (Anchor)............Liverpool
"Austrian"......................Glasgow
"Bavarian"....................Liverpool
"Berbice"....................Cienfuegos
"Bergenseren".................. Baracoa
"Berkshire," Norfolk; Baltimore; Washington.
"Borderer"................... Liverpool
"Boston City" (Furness)........ London
"Bothnia" (Cunard)...........Liverpool
"Bracanalie"..................... London
"British Crown"..................London
"British Queen" (Anchor).....Liverpool
"Bulgarian"...................Liverpool
"Caledonia" (Anchor)......... Liverpool
"Cambridge"....................Bangor
"Canadian" (Allan).............Glasgow
"Carn Brea"....................Havana
"Carroll "...................Halifax, N. S.
"Catalonia" (Cunard)........ Liverpool
"Cephalonia" (Cunard).......Liverpool
"Chatham," Norfolk; Baltimore; Washington.
"City of Gloucester".........Gloucester
"City of Macon"............... Savannah
"City of Truro"............... Antwerp
"Cumberland"..St. John; Halifax, N. S.
"Damara"...................Halifax, N. S.
"De Ruyter"................ ....Antwerp
"D. H. Miller".....Norfolk; Baltimore; Washington.
"Dimock"......................New York
"Dominion"............ Yarmouth, N. S.
"Dorian"......................Valencia
"Durham City" (Furness).......London
"Empire State"..........Boston Harbor
"Galileo"........................Hull, Eng.
"Gallia" (Cunard)..............Liverpool
"Gallina"..................... Hamburg
"Gate City"....................Savannah
"General Lincoln"..
...............Hingham; Hull; Downer
"General Whitney"............New York
"Glaucus"......................New York
"Governor Andrew".....
............Hull; Downer; Hingham
"Harrogate"..................... Barrow
"Hermann"....................Antwerp
"Iowa".........................Liverpool
"Jan Breydel"..................Antwerp
"John Brooks"............Portland, Me.

"Joseph Ferans"............... Palermo
"Julia"........................Nahant
"Kansas" (Warren)............Liverpool
"Katahdin"....................... Bangor
"Linn O'Dee".................... Baracoa
"Longfellow".............. Provincetown
"Lorenzo D. Baker"........ Port Antonio
"Milanese "..................... London
"Nantasket"..
........Nantasket; Hull; Pemberton
"Norseman" (Warren)......... Liverpool
"Nymphaea".....................Sagua
"Otranto "................... Hull, Eng.
"Palestine " (Warren).......... Liverpool
"Pavonia" (Cunard)........... Liverpool
"P. de Coninck"................Antwerp
"Penobscot"......................Bangor
"Ponca"....................Mediterranean
"Prussian" (Allan)..............Glasgow
"Roman"...................Philadelphia
"Roman"...................... Liverpool
"Rose Standish"........Hull; Nantasket
"Samaria" (Cunard).......... Liverpool
"Saxon "....................Philadelphia
"Scandinavian" (Allan)........ Glasgow
"Scythia" (Cunard)............Liverpool
"Sidonian "..................... Naples
"Spartan" (B. & Phila.) .... Philadelphia
"Star of the East"..Bath; Augusta, Me.
"State of Maine".S. John; Halifax, N.S.
"Stockholm City" (Furness).....London
"Tremont"..................Portland, Me.
"Twilight"............. Hull; Nantasket
"Ulunda "................. Halifax, N. S.
"Venetian "..................Liverpool
"Virginian"..................Liverpool
"Waldensian" (Allan).......... Glasgow
"Wetherby"...................Hamburg
"Welhaven "................... Baracoa
"William Harrison"...........Nantasket
"Worcester"................Halifax, N. S.
"Yesso "....................... Palermo

The Cunard Steamers for Liverpool sail from Cunard Wharf, East Boston, every Thursday; Halifax, N. S., Nickerson's Wharf; Yarmouth, N. S., Lewis Wharf; Digby and Annapolis, N. S., Commercial Wharf, for Philadelphia, Long Wharf; for Portland, Me., India Wharf; for Gloucester, Central Wharf; for Provincetown, Battery Wharf; for Nahant, India Wharf, for Hull, Downer, and Hingham, India Wharf; for Pemberton, Hull, Strawberry Hill, and Nantasket Beach, Rowe's Wharf. (For locations of these wharves see *Wharves*).

VOICE CULTURE.

Abell, Edith. (See *Colleges and Schools*).

Adams, Charles R. (See *Colleges and Schools*).

Larry, Flora E. (See *Colleges and Schools*).

Davis, J. W. 169 Tremont Street. Mr. Davis is one of the most successful teachers of vocal music in the city. He has a large number of pupils, representing various sections of the country, where his reputation as an able and thorough teacher has already gone. His method is an admirable one, and is well calculated to develop the voice to the full extent of its natural resources.

De Angelis, E. M., Mme. 149A Tremont Street. Among the eminent vocal teachers who make Boston their home is Mme. E. M. De Angelis. She was born in Florence, Italy; studied with Lamperti, the elder, Garcia, Marchesi; has sung in opera, etc. She located in Boston about fifteen years ago. Some of her pupils have won high renown on the operatic stage. Among her recent remarkably promising pupils is Miss Mattie Colby, whose success cannot fail to reflect great credit upon her accomplished teacher.

Garrett, Mme. (See *Colleges and Schools*.)

Hall, Edna, Mme. 206 Dartmouth Street. Mme. Hall occupies an enviable position among the foremost vocal teachers in the country. If the true test of an instructor's success be to measure the results accomplished with her pupils, Mme. Hall has achieved a triumph. Pupils come to her from every quarter, drawn hither by the best advertisement possible — that of the advancement of her pupils, which has been so marked as to excite wonder in the minds of those who have been witnesses of the progress made. Mme. Hall teaches the over-tone method, which is the basis of her success.

Osgood, George L. 149 A Tremont Street. Mr. Osgood has had conferred upon him the rare honor of having been enrolled among the distinguished pupils of Lamperti, of whose excellent method Mr. Osgood is so conspicuously successful an exponent. He has done much toward moulding a correct musical taste in America. His ability has not only been demonstrated with his private pupils, but his masterly training of the Boylston Club, the most artistic vocal organization in the country, has been as eminently successful.

Pennell, A. E. 157 Tremont Street. Mr. Pennell received a thorough course of training in Italy and London, and has had an extended experience in oratorio and church choir service, fitting him as a teacher of ability, taste and finish. His pupils receive a certain style, indicative of genuine artistic culture, which is easily distinguishable. His services may be had for concert, oratorio, etc.

Van Buren, Jeannette. (See *Colleges and Schools*).

Wheeler, J. Harry, whose early instruction was received from Garcia, of London, and Lamperti, of Milan, has had upwards of twenty years of experience as a voice teacher, and is undeniably among the most successful. He is instructor in English and Italian singing at the New England Conservatory of Music, where he has taught for the past eleven years. He is the author of a valuable work on "Vocal Physiology and Singing," etc. Many of his pupils have become well-known as teachers, church and operatic artists.

Wheeler, Lyman W. 161 Tremont Street. Mr. Wheeler's success as a teacher of vocal music would be considered phenomenal did not one know that the results he obtains are simply the natural consequence of the legitimate means employed. Many of the pupils of this eminent teacher adorn the operatic and concert stage. The success of Miss Jennie Sargent abroad is a recent tribute to Mr. Wheeler's skill. He invites all interested to call upon him on Mondays and Thursdays, between 2 and 3 p. m., for free advice and information.

MUSICAL INTERESTS.

Band Music Arranged. Music for bands and orchestras is arranged by George Lowell Tracy, City Hotel, Chelsea.

Berry, H. W. 592 Washington Street. Mr. Berry is the sole general agent for the celebrated Kranich & Bach grand, square and upright Pianofortes, as well as for the Prescott Parlor Organs. The Kranich & Bach Pianofortes received the highest award of the United States Centennial Exhibition, 1876, for "strongest and pleasing tone and excellence of workmanship." Mr. Berry also deals largely in second-hand pianofortes.

Boston Piano Company. 18 Essex Street, near Washington Street. This Company, E. Wilson & Co., proprietors, are manufacturers of square and upright pianofortes. For the past thirty years, they have been engaged in the manufacture of pianoforte hardware, an important element in the making of these instruments. The new mahogany uprights made by this Company are attracting wide attention.

Boston Piano Stool Co. 576 Washington Street. E. H. Loomis is agent for Joshua Briggs' piano stools and ottomans, which have found so much favor with musicians. These stools are so thoroughly constructed, as well as ornamental, that they are being adopted by principals of conservatories, music schools, seminaries and colleges, as well as in private families.

Briggs, W. H. 576 Washington Street. As the real merits of the Calenberg & Vaupel Pianofortes become known to the public of Boston and New England their popularity increases. These superior instruments are rapidly coming to the front at first-class concerts, their quality of tone, combined with great brilliancy, rendering them extremely popular with artists as well as with audiences.

Chickering & Sons' Pianofortes. (1823). 152 Tremont Street. This famous Pianoforte house, the oldest in the United States, has, since its establishment sixth-three years ago, manufactured 72,500 instruments, which have sung or are still singing the praises of the admirable quality and volume of tone, the brilliancy, the elastic touch, the exquisite beauty and finish of the mechanical environment of "the soul of the instrument." The name of this firm upon a Pianoforte guarantees its excellence in every particular. In proposing the health of the founder of this great house, it was given: "Jonas Chickering! like his own pianos: Upright, Grand, Square."

Estey Organ and Piano Company. 159 Tremont Street. This famous musical instrument manufacturing company was founded in 1846, and since that time, during a period of forty years, its organs have been sent to almost every section of the globe. At Brattleborough, Vt., it has twelve finely-equipped factories, employing 600 hands. The Estey trade-mark is a guaranty of superior workmanship in every department of the organs or pianos manufactured by them. Beauty of tone, power, durability; in short, a combination of musical and mechanical elements forming a perfect instrument. The warerooms in Boston are elegantly furnished, and are located opposite the Common, in an exceedingly pleasant and accessible quarter.

Fairbanks & Cole. 121 Court Street. These renowned teachers of the banjo (owing to the fashionable "craze" over that instrument, which bids fair to become permanent) are as busy as it is possible to be with pupils. As their instruments are manufactured under their personal supervision, and as they use their own instruction books, pupils have especial advantages. Their rooms are among the most interesting places to visit in the city. Their latest innovation, "Walker's Wrist-Rest," is a new invention that has already met with the hearty approval of banjo-players. It is destined to come into general use everywhere.

Hallet & Davis Piano Manufacturing Company. 167 Tremont Street. The instruments of this firm have long been noted for purity and extent of tone, perfection of action, and especially for the durable quality of materials used and the excellence and finish of their workmanship. Their Patent Agraffe Bridge, used in the manufacture of all their pianofortes, relieves the great downward pressure of the strings upon the sounding board, and preserves the full, round tone of the instrument, holding it in tune, also, for a long period. Many eminent *virtuosi* use the Hallet & Davis Pianoforte at their concerts. The house has been awarded over sixty first prizes.

Ivers & Pond Pianoforte Company. 181 and 182 Tremont Street. Visitors to Boston from New England, the Western and Southern States, are attracted to the ware-rooms of Messrs. Ivers & Pond, whose Pianofortes are now so favorably known throughout the length and breadth of the country. Perfection of tone, singing quality and mechanical excellence are the strong points of these fine instruments. Mr. W. H. Ivers, of this noted firm, was for a quarter of a century connected with the old house of Chickering & Sons, an experience which has fitted him to superintend the perfect construction of a pianoforte. Over *eighty* of the Ivers & Pond Pianofortes have been purchased for the New England Conservatory of Music, and are now in daily use there.

Louis H. Ross & Co's Music Store. 3 West Street.

McPhail & Co's Pianofortes. 630 Washington Street, corner of Essex Street. Eminent musicians, including John K. Paine, Carl Zerrahn, Geo. Henschel, Carlyle Petersilea, W. H. Schultze, and many others, have given emphatic testimonials to the excellence of the Pianofortes manufactured by McPhail & Co. That all this praise is warranted, one can have no hesitation in affirming. Among the styles manufactured by this far-famed house is the Imperial Upright, which has a beautiful singing quality, a most ductile action, and a thoroughness of tone and finish of mechanical construction so noticeable in all the instruments coming from this establishment.

New England Organ Co. 1299 Washington Street. Organized in 1871, this Company rapidly came to the front, owing to the excellence of its instrument. These organs, exhibited at the Mass. Charitable Mechanics Exhibition of 1878 in competition with instruments of older and famous makers, received the award of a first gold medal. The organs manufactured by this Company, of which George T. McLaughlin is the proprietor, are distinguished for pure, even tone, volume, durability, and beauty. The warerooms are well worthy of a visit from strangers interested in the growing musical importance of the city.

New England Piano Company. 32 George Street, Roxbury. The manufactory of this company is an immense structure seven stories in height, the lot of land being 225 feet long and 150 feet wide. Here are located the warerooms and also the main office of the company, Thomas F. Scanlan, proprietor. Mr. Scanlan has long been identified with the musical instrument manufacturing interests of Boston, and his enterprise and ability are well demonstrated in the magnitude and excellence of the work now being accomplished under his direction. The New England Piano has already been approved by thousands of patrons for its many fine qualities, as well as for the reasonable price at which it is sold.

Normal Music Course. The attention of musical educators throughout the country is being attracted to the Normal Music Course,—by those eminent musicians and teachers, John W. Tufts and H. E. Holt,—a progressive series of music readers, charts, etc., which has already been adopted in the public schools of New York, Brooklyn and other large cities. For its simple, practical and easily-comprehended features this Course must eventually come into general use. It receives hearty endorsement from the most eminent instructors. Edgar O. Silver, 30 Franklin Street, is general agent.

Old and New Violins. One of the foremost makers and repairers of violins in this or any other country is L. O. Grover, of this city; who, although modestly and faithfully fulfilling the duties of his avocation at his home, 27 Union Park, is well known through the excellence of his work upon the "king of instruments" by the owners of some of the most valuable violins in the world, which have been entrusted to Mr. Grover's masterly hands for repairs. Violins are forwarded to him from every section of the country, and are returned in perfect condition. Mr. Grover's wonderful ability, taste, judgment and enthusiasm so delighted Ole Bull that the great violinist not only gave him his rare instruments to adjust, but imparted to him information of incalculable advantage relative to violin-making.

Cliver Ditson & Co., the largest music dealers in America, and probably in the world, are at 449 and 451 Washington Street. They publish the *Musical Record*, which contains vocal and instrumental music to the value of one dollar in every number, and which is sold for ten cents by all newsdealers in the country.

Smith American Organ and Piano Company. 531 Tremont Street. This distinguished house has for many years stood in the foremost rank of American musical instrument manufacturers, and has largely contributed to the fame of Boston as a great musical centre. Among the recent instruments introduced by this firm is the Connoisseur Organ, constructed on a new and original principle, which is attracting attention from musical people everywhere. The characteristics of the Smith American Organs are quality of tone, design, workmanship and ease of action. The famous Steck & Co's Pianofortes are sold by this company.

Tyler, E. W. 178 Tremont Street. The celebrated Wm. Knabe & Co. Pianofortes are becoming as popular here as they have for some time been in other large cities, owing to the excellence of the instruments combined with Mr. Tyler's earnest and well-directed efforts to bring their superior merits properly before the public. The Knabe ranks among the few really great pianofortes of the world. It has long been a favorite with numerous eminent solo pianists, who are charmed with its brilliancy, power and richness of tone. Only the best materials are used in the construction of these fine instruments, a full lirfe of which may be seen at Mr. Tyler's easily-accessible and elegant warerooms. He is also agent for the noted Christie Upright Pianofortes, as well as for the Clough & Warren Organs.

Vose & Sons' Pianofortes. (1851). 535 Washington Street. This house was originally established by James W. Vose, the present head of the firm, thirty-five years ago, since which time nineteen thousand instruments have been manufactured by the house, and are now in use throughout this country and abroad. For power, sweetness and purity of tone; for responsive touch, and for standing in tune, these Pianofortes have attracted and held the attention of the musical public of the country.

Woodward & Brown Pianofortes. (1843). 175 A Tremont Street. The firm name of Woodward & Brown are "household words" in many American homes where their excellent Pianofortes are in constant use. The thorough construction of these instruments, the artistic and finished mechanical workmanship, combined with purity of tone, brilliancy and volume, complete a pianoforte that is a delight to musicians and music-lovers.

ART AND LETTERS.

Berlitz School of Languages. 154 Tremont Street. (Branches in New York, Brooklyn, Philadelphia, Baltimore, Washington, Minneapolis and St. Paul). Instruction is given in French, German, Italian, Spanish, Latin, Greek, etc. This institution is recognized everywhere as one of the best of its kind. Its large number of professors of modern tongues are all most highly-educated native teachers. The system of instruction is the celebrated Berlitz method, thoroughly tested in America and Europe. Conversation is a specialty. The students belong to the best classes of society. Terms begin at any time. Tuition fee: one term, daily lessons, $18. Private lessons are given. Lectures are free to pupils; fifty cents to others. Summer schools are held at Plymouth, Mass., and at Long Branch, N. J.

Dial Artist. W. W. Sprague, 339 Washington Street, has acquired wide reputation for his artistic skill in painting clock dials, glass signs, etc. Mr. Sprague's terms are quite reasonable.

Frost & Adams. 37 Cornhill. One of the most noted houses in the United States, as importers and wholesale dealers in artists' materials, art-school supplies, mathematical instruments, decorative art goods, art hand-books, supplies for architects, engineers and draughtsmen. Albert Levy's blue-process paper—for which Frost & Adams are United States agents—Winsor and Newton's famous water and oil colors, canvas, panels, brushes, etc., together with a full stock of artists' easels, stationery, and every detail of a complete outfit. The goods sold by Frost & Adams are of the first-class, and are furnished at most reasonable prices. They regularly supply many of the great art schools of the country. Visitors are always sure to find a great deal to interest, in this establishment. Catalogues, containing valuable information, are furnished to any applicant.

Home Journal Staff. Samuel T. Cobb, editor; Miss Mildred A. Aldrich, dramatic editor; Chas. L. Capen, musical critic; Wm. H. Downes, art editor; W. Wallace Waugh, manager; Wm. H. Daggett, assistant manager; F. M. Tyler, advertising department.

Loring's Library. 9 Bromfield Street. One of the institutions of the city. Established 1859. A circulating library of 16,000 volumes. Terms: two cents a day for each book.

Lowell & Stark. 112 Tremont Street. This new and enterprising firm, importers and dealers in artists' materials, decorative art goods, oil and water color supplies, picture frames, etc., are reaping a generous share of patronage. They have made arrangements with dealing manufacturers and dealers in Paris, London, and elsewhere to supply them with first-class goods which they furnish at reasonable rates. Strangers interested in art will be welcomed by these gentlemen.

Portrait Photographs. Bushby & Macurdy, 521 Washington Street, established in 1864, are celebrated for their artistic lighting and posing, which costs no more than ordinary work made in other establishments. Pure crayon portraits, and work in oil and water colors are features with this highly-artistic firm.

Restoring Paintings. D. D. Sinclair, 5 Pemberton Square, restores oil paintings.

Roberts Lecture and Musical Agency. 2 Music Hall Building. This Bureau has long been noted for the large list of prominent artists furnished to committees, etc., the members of the famous Boston Ideal Opera Company having originally been among them. Elmore A. Pierce, the distinguished elocutionist, reader and teacher, is its present manager. Engagements for leading musical and literary artists are made here.

Williams & Everett. 79 Boylston Street. This famous Art Store, so long a feature of Washington Street, is now established as the New West End Art Gallery at 79 Boylston Street. Here may always be found one of the largest and choicest collections of paintings, engravings, etc., to be seen in the United States. Strangers may pass an hour here profitably and pleasantly in examining the beautiful works of art. Here are to be seen the latest Rogers Groups, of which this firm are the agents. (See *Art Galleries*).

BOSTON POLICE DEPARTMENT.

Police Commissioners. Headquarters, 7 Pemberton Square. Albert T. Whiting, (salary $4,500), William H. Lee, (salary $4,000), William M. Osborne, (salary 4,000); Chairman, Albert T. Whiting; Clerk, Franklin C. Irving, (salary, $2,500). Superintendent of Police, Cyrus Small; (salary $3,000). Deputy Superintendent, Joseph R. Burrell; (salary $2,300). Clerk, Thomas Ryan. Property Clerk, Geo. E. Savory. Chief Inspector, Orinton M. Hanscom. Inspectors, Thomas F. Gerraughty, George O. Richardson, Charles L. Skelton, Patrick A. Mahoney, William Burke, Charles Glidden, Andrew Houghton, Joseph Knox, William B. Watts, and Dennis A. Mountain. Assistant Inspector, George M. Robinson. Inspector of Carriage Licenses, Sergeant Joseph H. Warren. Inspector of Wagon Licenses, Timothy R. Page. Inspector of Intelligence Offices, Benj. D. Burley. Inspector of Pawnbrokers, Wm. H. McCausland. Inspector of Claims, Wm. H. Dyer. Asst. Med. Examiner, Geo. Munroe. Lieuts., W. C. F. Tracy, Owen T. Winn. Geo. A. Walker, and James P. J. Haney. Asst. Clerks, Franklin S. French, and Ignatius A. Kelly. Messenger, Ebenezer S. Crocker.

Police Stations.
First Precinct: No. 209 Hanover Street. Captain, Henry Dawson. Lieuts., Orison Little, Lawrence Cain.
Second Precinct: No. 21 Court sq. Captain, Romanzo H. Wilkins. Lieuts., John F. Gardiner, Thomas Weir.
Third Precinct: Joy Street. Captain, Timothy A. Hurley. Lieuts., William S. Kendall, Edward F. Gaskin.
Fourth Precinct: No. 56 La Grange Street. Captain, H. C. Hemmenway. Lieuts., James H. Lambert, Richard F. Irish.
Fifth Precinct: East Dedham Street. Captain, Martin L. White. Lieuts., Edward M. Johnson, Wilbur Laskey, jr.

Sixth Precinct: Broadway, South Boston. Captain, Benjamin P. Eldridge. Lieuts., Henry O. Goodwin, James M. Coulter.
Seventh Precinct: Paris Street, above Maverick sq., East Boston. Captain, Joseph H. Bates. Lieuts., Joseph B. Blanchard, George W. Adams.
Eighth Precinct: Commercial, corner Battery Street. Captain and Harbor Master, Geo. F. Goold. Lieuts., Byron F. Bragdon, Louis W. Swan. Engineer Police Boat, Stephen Henton.
Ninth Precinct: Dudley, corner Mt. Pleasant Avenue. Captain, Lyford W. Graves. Lieuts., Francis H. Briggs, Wm. C. Downing.
Tenth Precinct: Tremont, corner Pynchon Street. Captain, James W. Twombly. Lieuts., Chas. C. J. Spear, Daniel E. Curran.
Eleventh Precinct: Adams Street, Fields Corner. Captain, Horace M. Ford, Lieuts., George Emerson, Michael Merrick, jr.
Twelfth Precinct: Fourth Street, near K. Captain, Elijah H. Goodwin. Lieuts., Charles S. Hildreth, Thomas H. Brown.
Thirteenth Precinct: Seaverns Avenue, Jamaica Plain. Captain, Paul J. Vinal. Lieuts., Andrew J. Chase, Geo. E. Haines.
Fourteenth Precinct: Washington st., Brighton Centre. Captain, David W. Herrick. Lieuts., Gustavus A. Smith, W. H. Brown
Fifteenth Precinct: Harvard Street, City sq., Charlestown. Captain, Oliver Ayers. Lieuts., Benjamin Williams, Wm. H. Brown.
Sixteenth Precinct: Boylston Street (Back Bay).
Street Railway Service: Sergeant Chas. W. Boyer in charge.
The salary of Captains is $4.00 per day. Lieutenants, $3.50. Sergeants, $3.25. Patrolmen, 1st year, $2.50; 2d year, $2.75; 3d year, and each succeeding year, $3.00.

BOSTON.

The following are extracts from a poem read by Ralph Waldo Emerson in Faneuil Hall, Dec. 16, 1873, the centennial anniversary of the destruction of the tea in Boston Harbor:

The wild rose and the barberry thorn
 Hung out their summer pride
Where now on heated pavements worn
 The feet of millions stride.
Fair rose the planted hills behind
 The good town on the bay,
And where the Western hills declined
 The prairie stretched away.
What care though rival cities soar
 Along the stormy coast,
Penn's town, New York and Baltimore,
 If Boston knew the most!

* * * * * *

Bad news from George on the English throne:
"You are thriving well," said he
"Now by these presents be it known
You shall pay us a tax on tea;
'Tis very small, — no load at all,
 Honor enough that we send the call!"

"Not so," said Boston, "good, my lord,
 We pay your Governors here
Abundant for their bed and board,
 Six thousand pounds a year.
(Your Highness knows our homely word),
 Millions for self-government,
But for tribute never a cent."

The cargo came! and who could blame
 If *Indians* seized the tea,
And — chest by chest — let down the same
 Into the laughing sea?
For what avail the plough or sail,
 Or land or life if Freedom fail?

The townsmen braved the English King,
 Found friendship in the French,
And Honor joined the patriot ring
 Low on their wooden bench.

O bounteous seas that never fail!
 O day remembered yet!
O happy port that spied the sail
 Which waited Lafayette!
Pole-star of light in Europe's night,
 That never faltered from the right.
Kings shook with fear; old empires crave
 The secret force to find
Which fired the little State to save
 The rights of all mankind.

* * * * * *

The sea returning day by day
 Restores the world-wide mart;
So let each dweller on the Bay
 Fold Boston in his heart,
Till these echoes be choked with snows
 Or over the town blue ocean flows.

Let the blood of her hundred thousands
 Throb in each manly vein;
And the wit of all her wisest
 Make sunshine in her brain.
For you can teach the lightning speech,
 And round the globe your voices reach.

And each shall care for other,
 And each to each shall bend;
To the poor a noble brother,
 To the good an equal friend.

A blessing through the ages thus
 Shield all thy roofs and towers!
God with the fathers, so with us,
 Thou darling town of ours!

PUBLISHERS' ANNOUNCEMENTS.

Dexter Smith's Cyclopedia of Boston will be issued June 1 of every year, revised and improved.

Copies of this work may be had of all newsdealers and booksellers in the United States and Canada. Communications addressed to Charles M. Cashin, Young's Hotel, Boston, will meet with prompt attention. Henry F. Gillig & Co., American Exchange, 449 Strand, London, England, will supply any orders for this work.

MISCELLANEOUS.

Apothecaries. Joseph T. Brown & Co., No. 504 Washington Street, corner of Bedford, rank among the oldest in the business. This is the place to get reliable goods, every article being selected under careful management and the closest scrutiny. Basett's Celebrated Mucilage, manufactured by this firm, is excellent and of the best quality.

Boston Storage Warehouse. Corner of West Chester Park and Westland Avenue (near Huntington Avenue). Frederick W. Lincoln, General Manager. This new building, surrounded on all sides by streets, with partitions of thick brick walls, offers especially fine facilities for the storage of household furniture, carriages, sleighs, pianos, pictures, mirrors, works of art, etc. Every possible safeguard has been provided; and all desirous of storing goods of any kind will here find every accommodation and protection.

Cancer Specialist. Mrs. M. A. Andrews, Hotel Waquoit, 251 Columbus Avenue, one of the most skilful cancer physicians in the world, can be consulted at her office at all times. Her system of treatment is safe, sure and comparatively painless. The most dangerous cases have been cured by her treatment after being given up by hospital physicians. She has been fully endorsed by hundreds throughout the State; and the written testimony can be seen by calling at her office, or send for circular.

Cashin's Ticket and News Agency. Young's Hotel. Here may be obtained choice seats for all theatrical and operatic performances, concerts, etc. Orders are received for tickets by mail, telegraph and telephone. Tickets for the Boston Symphony Concerts may be secured in advance from Mr. Cashin, orders for which will be filled as received, early application being necessary. New York and Boston papers are regularly supplied from this agency.

Chauncy Hall School, (for further description of which see department of Colleges and Schools,) devotes special efforts to the fitting of pupils for the Massachusetts Institute of Technology, in which great success has attended their perfect system of instruction. It also includes a kindergarten.

Clark's Hotel, No. 577 and 579 Washington Street, Boston, is now open. It is newly fitted up with every modern improvement and business convenience. Contains 68 sleeping-rooms and eight private dining-rooms. This hotel is for gentlemen only, and is on the European plan.

Commonwealth Hotel, R. W. Carter & Co., proprietors, is a beautiful marble building, situated in the best part of the city, 1697 Washington Street. It has every convenience, and best adapted to meet the wants of those wishing a quiet, first-class home. For further particulars see advertisement.

Cunard Line. The first steamship of the Cunard Line to arrive at Boston was the "Brittania," which left Liverpool July 4, 1840. She was 14 days and 8 hours in making the passage. The Cunard steamships were run regularly to Boston from that time. (It was not until eight years after that the line began to run steamships to New York also.) The present fleet between Boston and Liverpool includes the famous "Gallia," the "Bothnia," "Catalonia," "Scythia," "Cephalonia," "Pavonia," etc. The popularity of the Boston line is increasing every year.

Fairbanks & Cole occupy a foremost position as manufacturers of and dealers in banjos, an instrument which is becoming so fashionable with young ladies at the present time. They also teach this popular instrument. The reputation of their establishment is rapidly extending throughout the country. The excellence of their banjos, which have repeatedly taken prizes at various exhibitions, is endorsed by leading musicians. Their system of instruction has proved so successful that their pupils are among the best performers on this instrument. They deserve their great and rapidly increasing popularity. They are located very centrally at 175 Tremont Street, opposite the Common, lines of street railways, from all sections of the city, passing the door.

Gold and Silver Wares. Palmer, Bachelder & Co., 146 Tremont Street, have a beautiful assortment in gold and silver watches, French clocks, bronzes, and objects of art. This firm rank among the oldest in the city for honest dealing and reliability cannot be excelled.

Home and Day School. Mrs. S. H. Hayes, No. 68 Chester Square. This school will enter upon its sixteenth year, Tuesday, October 4, 1887. The school-building has been occupied several years, and has proved thoroughly adapted to school purposes. It is situated on one of the most beautiful parks of the city, and heated by steam throughout. Great attention is given to the sanitary condition of the house, especially with regard to plumbing and ventilation. Rooms are provided for nine resident pupils, and ample and agreeable accommodations for a large number of day pupils. Send for circular and terms.

Home and Day School for Young Ladies. Miss H. E. Gilman, No. 44 Rutland Square. It is the aim of the school to secure to resident pupils the results of a consecutive, uninterrupted course of study, without the sacrifice of all the advantages of home life. To this end all of the arrangements of the house are made. The young ladies of the family are much in the society of their teachers, and particular attention is given to their general manners and deportment. The next school year will open September 28, 1887, and will close June 15, 1888. For terms, send for circular.

Home and Day School for Young Ladies. Miss Abby H. Johnson, 18 Newbury Street, Boston. The next school year will open September 28th, 1887, and will close June 14th, 1888. This school is situated in the best part of the city, and ranks among our best female schools. The common and higher English branches; the ancient and modern languages are carefully taught, and the most conscientious care is taken and extended to all pupils attending this school. For terms, etc., send for circular.

Hotel Nantasket. Nantasket Beach, Boston Harbor. No seaside hotel in the country eclipses this in attractiveness or popularity. It is a grand structure, admirably fitted for the accommodation of a large number of guests; its rooms are finely furnished; its table is celebrated for its excellence, and every appointment of the hotel is maintained at the high standard required by the best class of the public who are seeking rest and recreation. Among the principal attractions are concerts given every afternoon and evening by Reeves' Band; billiards, boating, fishing, bathing, driving, etc. Messrs Russell & Sturgis — also proprietors of the Rockland House — conduct the Hotel Nantasket. (See *Nantasket*.)

Hygienic Dress. Mrs. Olivia P. Flynt is the inventor and manufacturer of the perfect weather protector as well as of improved hygienic under-dress for women and children. Dress reform for ladies, according to one of the eminent men of the day, is one of the great questions of the time; and it is a well-established fact that Mrs. Flynt actually preceded the organization of the Dress Reform Committee by a year or more, as her first patent was granted in 1873. Mrs. Flynt was awarded medals conferring highest honors by the Centennial Exhibition, 1876, and by the Mass. Charitable Mechanics Exhibition, 1881. Ladies will find much to interest them at Mrs. Flynt's, 319 Columbus Avenue. She has published an extremely interesting and valuable "Manual."

Immigrants. The number of immigrants landed at Boston during the year ending June 30, 1885, was 25,600, making this city the second port of entry in the United States.

Mme. Elizabeth E. Garrett is one of America's foremost teachers of vocal music, and ranks well with the leading teachers of Europe. She makes a specialty of placing the voice, and teaches according to the method which she sometime since discovered, and which has proved so successful as to elicit the admiration of Patti, the greatest executant of the day, and other leading artists, and especially has it received the endorsement of Mme. Marchesi, the famous Paris teacher, who finds nothing to change in the method of Mme. Garrett, who teaches the natural or anatomical system. Her success with pupils is her best testimonial. Mme. Garrett's address is Hotel Lafayette, 200 Columbus Avenue.

New Method of Dentistry. One of the greatest boons to mankind was the introduction of the now celebrated Sheffield Tooth Crown system of replacing teeth. The eminent dental practitioner, Dr. W. A. Lyon, 157 Boylston Street, has succeeded in establishing this system in the favor of the most prominent citizens of Boston and New England, who have testified to the superiority of the method over their own signatures. Dr. Lyons discards entirely the cumbersome plates formerly in use, and succeeds in placing teeth in natural position, giving them all the beauty and service of those lost by accident or decay. Those interested should seek his advice, for which no charge is made, and read the descriptive pamphlet furnished free.

Park House. This noted English chop-house was established in 1842 by Thomas D. Park — father of W. D. Park, one of the present proprietors — on what is now a part of the site of the Post-Office Building. In 1848 it was removed to Morton Place, Milk Street, thence to Central Court. In 1874 it was opened in its present location. It is elegantly fitted up, and has the reputation among foreigners and travelled Americans of being the best chop-house on the genuine English plan in the United States.

Preparatory School for Girls. 76 Marlborough Street. Miss S. Alice Brown and Miss Amelia L. Owen, graduates of Smith College, and experienced teachers, will open October 3, 1887, a school for girls twelve years old and over. Board in private families will be found for pupils residing out of town, if desired. The special design of this school is to prepare girls for college or scientific schools,—see advertisement,—and for further particulars send for circular.

Private School for Boys. Miss Helen M. Greenwood, No. 5 Charles Street, formerly Miss M. A. Matthews. This school has been established 17 years, designed for boys 6 to 14 years of age, fitting them most thoroughly for the Latin School, and all the higher preparatory schools in the city. Great care is exercised in developing each pupil in the way best adapted to make the most of his special ability. For terms, send for circular.

Private School for Boys. Mrs. Hale, 18 Boylston Place, Boston. This school has been established several years. Its special object has been the preparation of pupils for the Massachusetts Institute of Technology; also, fits for Harvard College. Boys of twelve years of age, who possess a fair knowledge of arithmetic, geography, and English are qualified to enter this school. Graduates of grammar schools can be prepared for the Institute in three years, for college in four years. The school-year begins the third week in September, and closes the third week in June. For terms, send for circular.

United States Hotel. This large, centrally located and extremely popular hotel is on Beach Street, near several of the principal railway stations. Its landlord is Mr. Tilly Haynes, one of Boston's best-known and most public-spirited citizens. Its accessibility renders it particularly attractive to families who come to the city to do shopping, or to attend theatres, concerts, lectures, etc. It is especially desirable as a winter home for New England people, while it is a favorite house for tourists and merchants from other cities. It is decidedly homelike in all its characteristics. Its table is renowned throughout the country for variety and excellence.

Voice Culture. Mrs. Jennie L. Miller, formerly 87 Waltham Street. The pupils under Mrs. Miller's instruction make rapid progress by the use of the breathing and technical exercises given. They are thorough and to the point. The voices become round, full and rich in quality in a short time, with conscientious work on the part of the pup'; her specialties being first, breath control; second, a relaxed and open throat; third, to teach how and where to place the voice to make sure of pure tones; fourth, to develop equally its entire range. Her attention is principally given to beginners, both of the reading and singing voice. Her address, for the summer months, care Oliver Ditson & Co.

Watches and Diamonds. Louis J. Wyman, 6 Winter Street, has a large and rapidly increasing patronage. Mr. Wyman is well known among dealers and others as being an expert in the selection of fine stones. He has the finest assortment in this city.

INDEX TO READING MATTER.

Adams, Samuel	11-17-24	Caucus, First	12
"After Life's Fitful Fever"	43	Celebration, Old-Time	7
Agassiz, Louis	43	Cemeteries	166
Aldermen, Board of	5	Chapel, King's	18
Allandale Spring	237	Charter	12
Almanac, First	15	Chilton, Mary	19
Almshouses	166	Church, Christ	12
Ambulance Service	237	Churches	126
Amusement Data	42	City Government	5
Annexations	238	City Point	230
Arboretum, Arnold	73	Clerks, City	5
Architecture, Colonial	13	Clubs	216
Area of Boston	239	Coasting	241
Art and Letters	268	College, Boston	48
Art, Early	13	College, Tufts	85
Art Galleries	98	College, Wellesley	86
Artistic Works	18	Colleges and Schools	45
Artists	100	Common, Boston	9-228
Art, Old-Time	7	Conservatory, Boston	48
Art, Teachers of	77	Conservatory, New England	68
Assessors	5	Council, Common	5
Associations	130	Courts	159
Asylums	164	Costly Houses	241
Athenæum, Boston	98-203	Cotton, John	39
Athenæum, Howard	90	Cows on the Common	13
Athletics	239	Crockett, David	13
Back Bay	239	Cushman, Charlotte	52-76
Back Bay Directory	105	Custom House	215
Bank, First	15	Cyclorama	91
Banks	260	Dark Day	13
Base Ball	239	Dentistry, Improved	270
Baths	239	Dickens, Charles	13
Baths, Free	215	Directory, First	15
Battle-Flags, Exhibition of	16	Distances	242
Battles, First	15	Downer Landing	230
Beaches	231	Dramatic Art, Teachers of	77
Beacon, Centry Hill	8	Drives	242
Bernhardt, Sarah	42	Drunkenness	13
Blaxton, William	39	Early English, Boston	10
Boarding-Houses	212	Eavesdropping	14
Boating	240	Education, Colonial	14
Books	241	Electric Lights	40-242
Booth, Edwin	32	Elegance in 1766	10
Booth, Junius Brutus	41	Eliot, John	39
Boston College	48	Elocution, Teachers of	78
Boston Data	39	Emerson, Ralph Waldo	43
Bostonians in 1788	9	Endicott, John	39
Boston in a Sad Plight	9	Engines, Fire	12-141
Boston in 1687	7-10	Equestrianism	246
Boston in 1699	9	Everett, Edward	43
Boston in 1719	9	Exchanges	214
Boston of Today	237	Executions	242
Boston, Siege of	25	Exhibitions	92
Bowditch, Nathaniel	43	Express Offices	197
Branding	12	Faneuil, Peter	22
Bridges	163	Ferries	161
Buildings, Public	103	Finances, City	6
Bureaus, Entertainment	263	Fire Alarm	114
Burgoyne	12	Flower and Fruit Mission	243
Burying-Ground, First	15	Forrest, Edwin	35
Byles, Mather	18	Forts	236
Cabs and Hacks	122	Franklin, Benjamin	8
Catholicism, Early	13	Free Dispensaries	242

FRE—SEC

Free Excursions	242
Freemasons	139
Gage, General	16
Garden, Oakland	91
Garden, Public	94
Gardens, Summer	99
Gas, First	15
Gilmore, P. S	33-42
Government, City	5
Grand Army	140
Gymnasiums	230
Hair-Dressing in 1800	16
Hall, Faneuil	15
Hall, Horticultural	
Hall, Music	
Halls, Public	102
Hancock, John	17-39
Handbill, An Old	7
Harbor, Boston	10-235
Harvard University	16-63
Hawthorne, Nathaniel	43
Hebrews	245
Hibernians	138
Hill, Bunker	12
Hill, Centry	11
Holmes, Oliver Wendell	10
Homes, Charitable	164
Horse-Car Excursions	246
Hospitals	164
Hotels	155
House, Old Cradock	13
Houses, Apartment	156
Hub of the Universe	246
Hutchinson, Ann	17
Islands in Boston Harbor	236
Irving, Henry	43
Indians	13-17
Inns, Old	20
Jones, Margaret	19
Julien, M	17
Kindergartens	66-254
Lacrosse	247
Lady Journalists	247
Lafayette	18
Languages, Teachers of	78
Latitude of Boston	247
Lane, Pudding	13
Law against Wearing Lace	18
Law and Order League	247
Law Prohibiting Tobacco	19
Libraries	201
Library, Public	201
Lind, Jenny	42
Lions in Boston	19
Literature, Early	14
Longfellow, Henry Wadsworth	43
Longtitude of Boston	247
Macbeth, First Performance of	10
Manchester-by-the-Sea	225
Markets	215
Marriage in 1687	19
Massacre, Boston	10
Mather, Increase	17
Mayor of Boston	5
Messengers	5-152
Military Organizations	153
Military, First	15
Minot's Ledge	247
Miscellaneous	271
Money, Continental	13
Monument, Bunker Hill	12
Monuments	189
Morgues	247
Mount Auburn	247
Museum, Agassiz	94
Museum, Architectural	99
Museum, Barnum	94
Museum, Boston	88
Museum, Fine Art	92
Musical Interests	206
Musical Organizations	261
Music, Growth of	248
Music in Schools	19
Music, Teachers of	79
Names, Boston's Early	10
Nahant	232
Nantasket	232
Navy Yard	257
Newspapers	206
Ocean Spray	232
Odd Fellows	141
Old Boston	7
Omnibuses	125
Opera House, Dudley Street	91
Orders and Secret Societies	138
Parks, Public	228
Patti, Adelina	42
Peabody, George	43
Percy, Lord	19
Philippe, Louis	16
Phillips, Wendell	43
Phillipps, Adelaide	43
Phipps, William	39
Pianoforte, First	7
Pinafore, First time of	36
Pirates in Old Times	22
Placard, An Old	17
Places of Amusement	87
Play Bills, Eventful	31
Plays in 1714	23
Point of Pines	233
Police	269
Pollard, Ann	7
Population	211
Post-Office	187
Printing Press, First	15
Profanity, Law against	23
Quakers	23
Railway, First	15
Railway Stations	163
Reading Rooms	201
Real Estate Bargains	8
Recovery of Lost Goods	252
Registrar, City	6
Reservoir, Chestnut Hill	233
Residences, Number of	252
Revere Beach	233
Revere, Paul	22-249
Rich Men of Boston	252
Riot, Draft	40
Riot, Theatrical	26
Rising, Early	14
Roller-Skating	253
Rooms, Furnished	273
Roses, Perfection of	253
Rubinstein, Anton	42
Safe Deposit Vaults	253
Sailors' Snug Harbor	254
Saltonstall, Richard	39
Salvini, Tommaso	38
Scalps, Indian	17
Scots' Charitable Society	19
Seaside Resorts	231
Secret Societies	138

Seminary, Lasell	66	Tennis Court	256
Servants, Old-Time	25	Theatres	87
Settlers, Early	14-25	Theatre, Boston	87
Shopping-Guide	213	Theatre, Bijou	89
Signal Service	259	Theatre, Germania	91
Slave-Owners	25	Theatre, Globe	88
Smith, Captain John	30	Theatre, Hollis Street	89
Societies	130	Theatre, Park	89
Soldiers' Home	254	Theatre, Windsor	90
Standish, Miles	19	Thoreau, Henry D	43
Statues and Monuments	189	Trees, Names of	256
Steamboats	204	University, Boston	51
Stone, Boston	11	University, Harvard	16
Streets, List of	167	Valuation of Boston	257
Streets, Why Crooked	7	Warren, Joseph	17-44
Streets, Old Names of	20	Warren, William	33-37
Street Cars	124	Washington, George	27-29
Suburban Excursions	223	Water Board	6
Sumner, Charles	43	Water, Introduction of	27
Sunday Laws	23-24	Walks, Favorite	258
Swearing, Penalty for	25	Waterhouse, Benjamin	9
Swords, Historical	17	Webster, Daniel	43
Tablets, Historical	28	Williams, Roger	18
Talleyrand	26	Wharves	161
Taxation, Rate of	252	Winthrop, John	27-39
Tea Party, Boston	10-11-16	Witchcraft in Boston	12
Technology, Institute of	66	Women, Boston	7-12
Telegraph Offices	146	Women, Patriotic	22
Telephone Offices	149	Women, Spinning	25
Temperance, Early	7	Women's Rights	28
Temple, Tremont	91		

INDEX TO ADVERTISEMENTS.

Cowles Art School	Map	Alfred Hales' Private School	9
Frost & Adams	Map	Elizabeth E. Garrett	10
Commonwealth Hotel	Map	Flora E. Barry	10
Hotel Vendome	Map	Miss Johnson's Private School	11
Profile House	Map	Mrs. S. H. Hayes' Private School	11
Hotel Victoria	Map	Miss Greenwood's School	11
Hotel Ponemah	Map	Miss Brown's Private School	11
Hotel Brunswick	Map	Miss H. E. Gilman's Private School	12
Boston & Albany and Old Colony R. R. Stations, and U. S. Hotel	2d page cover	Berlitz School of Languages	12
		Mrs. J. Miller, Voice Culture	12
Vose & Sons, Pianos	3d page cover	Russ B. Walker	12
United States Hotel	4th page cover	L Edna Martin	13
Berkeley School	ii	Dr. Gannett's School	13
Charles R. Adams	ii	Miss Rachel Noah	13
Dr. W. A. Lyon	iv	Boston School of Languages	13
American House	1	Wellesley College	14
United States Hotel	1	Turkish Baths	15
Armstrong's Transfer Company	2	Fairbanks & Cole	15
Boston Cab Company	2	Boston Storage Warehouse	15
Shore Line to New York	3	Chauncy Hall School	16
Van Buren, Jeannette	4	George L. Osgood	16
Joseph T. Brown & Co.	4	New England Conservatory of Music	277
Boston School of Oratory	5	Williams & Everett	278
Tremont School of Music	5	W. W. Sprague	279
Bickford School of Elocution	6	Sargent's Steam Laundry	279
Adams House	7	Normal Music Course	279
Clark's Hotel	7	Mrs. O. P. Flynt	280
Louis F. Wyman	7	M. A. Andrews, Mrs. Dr.	281
Palmer, Bachelder & Co.	8	Hotel Nantasket	282
Chas. M. Cashin	8	Monroe Conservatory of Oratory	283
Leroy Z. Collins	9	New England Piano Co.	284

www.ingramcontent.com/pod-product-compliance
Lightning Source LLC
Chambersburg PA
CBHW032057220426
43664CB00008B/1038